ARCHITECTURES OF THE ROMAN WORLD

ARCHITECTURES OF THE ROMAN WORLD

MODELS, AGENCY, RECEPTION

Edited by

NICCOLÒ MUGNAI

OXBOW | books
Oxford & Philadelphia

Published in the United Kingdom in 2023 by
OXBOW BOOKS
The Old Music Hall, 106–108 Cowley Road, Oxford, OX4 1JE

and in the United States by
OXBOW BOOKS
1950 Lawrence Road, Havertown, PA 19083

Paperback Edition: ISBN 978-1-78925-994-0
Digital Edition: ISBN 978-1-78925-995-7 (epub)

A CIP record for this book is available from the British Library

Library of Congress Control Number: 2023943784

Printed in Malta by Melita Press
Typeset in India by DiTech Publishing Services

For a complete list of Oxbow titles, please contact:

UNITED KINGDOM
Oxbow Books
Telephone (0)1226 734350
Email: oxbow@oxbowbooks.com
www.oxbowbooks.com

UNITED STATES OF AMERICA
Oxbow Books
Telephone (610) 853-9131, Fax (610) 853-9146
Email: queries@casemateacademic.com
www.casemateacademic.com/oxbow

Oxbow Books is part of the Casemate Group

Front cover: Thugga, Tunisia: Roman forum and Capitolium (photo N. Mugnai).
Back cover: (top left): Olympia, Greece: *Caldarium* of the South Bath (photo P. Vitti); (bottom): Cyrene, Libya: Basilica and north portico of Caesareum (photo R. Burns, Manar al-Athar).

This publication has been supported by grants from the Leverhulme Trust, the Craven Committee (University of Oxford, Faculty of Classics), the Ancient World Research Cluster (Wolfson College), and the Samuel H. Kress Foundation administered by the Archaeological Institute of America.

Contents

Acknowledgements

This book developed out of an international workshop held at Wolfson College, University of Oxford, in November 2022. On that occasion, contributors were asked to submit a first draft of their chapters, which were discussed in a collegial, stimulating environment. That was the first step of a process that eventually led to the present volume. This successful outcome would have been impossible without the motivation of all the authors whose texts are collected here – I would like to thank every one of them for their hard work, patience, and dedication. I should also extend my gratitude to the readers of these chapters and to the various persons who provided invaluable support from the early stages of this project through to its conclusion, in particular Janet DeLaine, Dominik Maschek, Stefano Camporeale, Susan Walker, and Patrizio Pensabene. The book is related to my research on 'Building, Living, and Experiencing Urban Spaces in the Greco-Roman World' as part of a Leverhulme Trust Early Career Fellowship held at the Faculty of Classics, University of Oxford. I am grateful to the Leverhulme Trust and the University of Oxford for funding my work.

Organization of the workshop was made possible thanks to the generous support of the Leverhulme Trust, the Craven Committee (University of Oxford, Faculty of Classics), and the Ancient World Research Cluster (Wolfson College). The staff at Wolfson made sure everything would run smoothly during the event, and I wish to thank them for their professional service. From the start of this project to the last, busy days that preceded submission of the manuscript, I was assisted in my work by two doctoral students at Oxford, Maria Theodora Tzeli and Luca Ricci. Their passion for the study of ancient architecture has proved to be a driving force to further enhance my own enthusiasm.

Publication of this book, in particular inclusion of colour illustrations throughout, was supported through generous grants from the Leverhulme Trust, the Craven Committee, Wolfson's Ancient World Research Cluster, and the Samuel H. Kress Foundation administered by the Archaeological Institute of America. I would like to thank these sponsors for believing in the quality of this project and for providing the means to publish it in the best way possible. I should also acknowledge the painstaking work of Oxbow's editorial team, in particular Julie Gardiner, Eduard Cojocaru, and Jessica Hawxwell. Their efficient organization enabled publication of this book in a very timely fashion. Last but not least, my warmest thanks go to my family for all the support they have provided since the beginning of my venture in the (challenging) academic world. Without their presence at my side, I would not have accomplished much.

List of figures

List of abbreviations

Abbreviations for ancient authors and texts are from *The Oxford Classical Dictionary (Fourth Edition)*.

The following abbreviations are used for epigraphic and papyrological corpora:

AE = *L'Année Épigraphique (1888–).*

CIG = *Corpus Inscriptionum Graecarum (1828–1877).*

CIIP = *Corpus Inscriptionum Iudaeae/Palaestinae (2010–).*

CIL = *Corpus Inscriptionum Latinarum (1863–).*

DFH = Khanoussi, M. and Maurin, L. (eds) 2000. *Dougga, fragments d'histoire. Choix d'inscriptions latines éditées, traduites et commentées (Ier–IVe siècles)*. Bordeaux: Ausonius Éditions.

IG = *Inscriptiones Graecae (1873–).*

IGLS = *Inscriptions grecques et latines de la Syrie (1929–).*

ILS = *Inscriptiones Latinae Selectae (1892–1916).*

IMylasa = Blümel, W. 1987–88. *Die Inschriften von Mylasa*. Bonn: Rudolf Habelt.

IPT = Levi Della Vida, G. and Amadasi Guzzo, M.G. 1987. *Iscrizioni puniche della Tripolitania (1927–1967)*. Rome: 'L'Erma' di Bretschneider.

IRCyr2020 = *Inscriptions of Roman Cyrenaica (2020)*, by Reynolds, J.M., Roueché, C.M. and Bodard, G., available at: https://ircyr2020.inslib.kcl.ac.uk/en/.

IRT2021 = *Inscriptions of Roman Tripolitania (2021)*, by Reynolds, J.M., Roueché, C.M., Bodard, G., Barron, C. and others, available at: https://irt2021.inslib.kcl.ac.uk.

PDura = Welles, C.B., Fink, R.O. and Gilliam, J.F. (eds) 1959. *The Excavations at Dura-Europos Conducted by Yale University and the French Academy of Inscriptions and Letters. Final Report V, Part I: The Parchments and Papyri*. New Haven-London: Yale University Press.

RIB = *The Roman Inscriptions of Britain (1965–).*

RIL = Chabot, J.-B. 1940. *Recueil des inscriptions libyques*. Paris: Imprimérie Nationale.

TAM = *Tituli Asiae Minoris (1901–).*

1

Architectures of the Roman World: An introduction

Niccolò Mugnai

Roman architecture(s): Recent approaches and developments

The last decade or so has witnessed a renewed interest in the architecture of ancient Rome and of the territories that formed part of the Roman Empire, with the development of new approaches, methodologies, interpretative tools, and targeted research questions that have allowed to better appreciate the multi-faceted nature of the built environment in the Roman world. From design and construction processes, to the decoration of buildings and how these shaped private and public life, encompassing a range of architectural forms and their adoption, adaptation, and reinterpretation across geographical and cultural boundaries within and beyond the Empire, even the definition itself of 'Roman architecture' no longer seems sufficient to explain the different elements of the same phenomenon and the regional or local variations that occurred under Roman rule – it would be more appropriate to speak of 'Roman architectures', as some of the chapters in this volume will argue.

These are exciting times, and one can rejoice at the amount of published works on these subjects. This is not the place to review all these studies on specific regional contexts or individual sites or buildings, but it is worth highlighting some of the latest developments in this discipline, looking at how modern scholarship has engaged with it. While scholars from the Anglophone world were not actively involved in the production of manuals or handbooks of Roman architecture for quite a long time, this trend has now changed. Essays on the architecture, as well as the art, of the Roman world were collected in Ulrich and Quenemoen (2014) and Marconi (2015). The recent monograph by Yegül and Favro (2019) has provided a valuable tool for the study and teaching of the architecture and urbanism of the Roman world – an update and a complementary resource, but not a replacement, of Ward-Perkins' classic *Roman Imperial Architecture* (1981). In this context one can place the fully revised, second edition of Sear's *Roman Architecture* (2021). More recently still, DeLaine's book (2023), though not a handbook in the traditional sense, has offered a welcome insight into this topic by exploring the relationship between architecture and Roman society – an investigation that is not limited to the buildings' extant remains but also looks at ancient written sources and visual representations. Beyond the English-speaking world, it is worth pointing out that the magisterial, two-volume set of Gros' *L'architecture romaine* has now come to its third updated edition (2011; 2017).

Particular attention has been paid in recent years to the dynamics of construction processes, as exemplified by the proceedings of the five international conferences on '*Arqueología de la construcción*'. These have engaged with the organization of building projects in the Italian Peninsula and in the eastern and western provinces (Camporeale *et al.* 2008; 2010); the economics of construction works (Camporeale *et al.* 2012); quarrying and exploitation of natural resources (Bonetto *et al.* 2014); building materials, engineering, and infrastructure (DeLaine *et al.* 2016). The connection between the ancient economy and architecture has been recognized as fundamental to understand how societies in the Roman world implemented construction projects (see, for instance, the essays in Maschek and Trümper 2022). Movement of materials was a major part of these enterprises, and the (re)assessment of the regional and pan-Mediterranean trade of stone under the Roman Empire proposed by Russell (2013) has provided a wealth of new data and interpretations (on the transport and 'standardized' production of marble for Roman building projects, see also Pensabene 2013; Toma 2020). Drawing upon DeLaine's seminal study of the Baths of Caracalla (1997), a strand of international scholarship has further developed and refined the methodologies to estimate costs of ancient constructions and manpower required for these projects, considering a series of variables from quarrying and transport of materials to human factors (for recent case studies, see Courault and Márquez 2020; Barker *et al.* 2023).

Matters of building design and layout have been addressed in a range of studies, such as those collected in Favro *et al.* (2015), where the impact of the architecture of the Roman Empire on later architectures is also discussed. The ornamentation of private and public buildings has been the subject of dedicated studies, which would be impossible to list all here, but useful insights on current trajectories can be gathered from the essays in Haug and Lauritsen (2021) and Haug *et al.* (2022), where the materiality, aesthetics, semantics, as well as the pragmatics of decoration and construction are assessed. Scholars have often paid special attention to the architectural ornament of Roman buildings, and a wealth of studies is available on individual edifices, sites, and regions. Among the latest developments in this field, one should stress the attempts to move away from mere typological classifications of these materials to propose a more comprehensive assessment by looking at their production, function, display, reception, and understanding in ancient societies (see, for example, Lipps and Maschek 2014; Pensabene *et al.* 2017).

This is by no means an exhaustive list of recent works, but hopefully it will serve as an indication of where modern scholarship is heading. The variety of subjects that can be grouped under the umbrella term 'Roman architecture' (or 'Roman architectures') speaks of the multiplicity of approaches, methods, and interpretative tools one can apply to the study of the built environment across the Roman world and beyond. In this respect, it is indicative that the essays on the architecture of the Classical world collected in Borbonus and Dumser (2022) come under the definition of '*Bauforschung*' – a German term that is literally translated as 'Research on Buildings' but that actually encompasses many more meanings.

Scope and organization of the book

The conception of the present volume is much indebted to this renewed interest towards the architecture of the Roman world. At the same time, however, the intention is to offer a study and research tool that does not just repeat what one can find in other recent works on this subject. Being aware of the risk of producing 'yet another book on Roman architecture' when this project was first conceived, the identification of specific questions to address and a careful selection of methodological approaches are key elements around which the volume has taken shape. First there is the matter of the geographical framework under examination. It is inevitable that most manuals of Roman architecture start their narrative with Rome and Italy, after which a selection of the architectural features in the regions annexed into the Roman Empire are passed under review (see, for instance, Ward-Perkins 1981; Morachiello and Fontana 2009; Gros 2011; 2017; Yegül and Favro 2019; Sear 2021). In this volume attention is paid specifically to the 'Roman World' outside the Italian Peninsula over a timeframe spanning from the second century BCE to the third century CE, with reference to earlier and later periods where relevant. The aim is to highlight some of the multifaceted features of the architectures beyond the centre of Empire, their function and significance within the local cultures, and the relationship that was established between periphery and centre. As one will realize when looking at the chapters in this book, 'architecture' is intended in the broad sense of the term, encompassing the buildings' technological components as well as their ornamental, sculptural, and epigraphic apparatuses.

No claim is made to cover the entirety of the Roman world outside Italy, nor every aspect of Roman-era architecture attested across these regions. The case studies collected here reflect inevitably the expertise and interests of the respective contributors, but some priorities were identified at the start of the project. One of these was the necessity of not limiting the scope of the volume to well-known areas of the Mediterranean, but to include less studied or marginal regions, as shown by engagement with the architectural evidence of Sardinia, Judaea, and Mauretania Tingitana in some of these chapters. It was also felt important to pay attention to the architectural trends in the territories of northern and north-west Europe, which are often treated too sweepingly in manuals or collections of essays on Roman architecture (one notable exception is represented by the essays in Lipps 2017, but unfortunately these are not cited in international scholarship as frequently as they would deserve).

The volume attempts to deal with a well-defined theoretical framework, where old-fashioned views of 'Roman provincial architecture' are being replaced by more nuanced approaches that take into account the peculiarities and active role of local forms of architecture across the Roman Empire. With regard to Roman construction, it has been recognized that a unidirectional model of transmission from centre to periphery is no longer workable, as many of these technologies were developed in specific areas of the Empire and spread from there (the case of vaulting techniques is particularly illuminating: see Lancaster 2015). Of course, this is not to deny the importance of architectural and technological innovation in Rome and the Italian Peninsula, which did spread to the provinces via colonization, the Roman army, and other conduits, but it is becoming clear that this process involved a range of factors and more attention should be paid to how these innovations were adopted and adapted locally. A renewed approach to Roman architecture can benefit from recent works on the art of the Roman Empire, where the concept of 'Roman provincial art' has been subject to critical scrutiny, and a closer look at the interconnectivity and exchanges among cultures under Roman rule has been encouraged (see, for instance, Scott and Webster 2003; Alcock *et al.* 2016).

The controversial term 'Romanization' is not used in this volume because of the much-heated debate this has generated especially in archaeological scholarship, where the term's ambiguous, often misleading meaning has been pointed out (among the vast literature on the subject, see Mattingly 2011, 3–42 and Revell 2014, with further references to these critiques and the different responses). Architectural studies, even recent ones, have been less affected by this debate. In the introduction to their book, Yegül and Favro (2019, 1–3) attempt to explain the meaning they assign to this term but then have to give further clarification when this does occur; in the chapter on North Africa, for example, 'Romanization' is to be intended essentially as a synonym for 'urbanization' (Yegül and Favro 2019, 494–96), but this does not apply to other instances. One does wonder whether use of such an equivocal term brings any benefit to the discussion at all (for this reason the term is avoided in DeLaine 2023). This is even more problematic when the analysis focuses on the architecture of the regions beyond Italy. A recent collection of essays (Mazzilli 2020a) has offered a valuable contribution to this topic, including a well-thought, critical review of current theoretical issues and research developments on the archaeology, art, and architecture of the Roman provinces (Mazzilli 2020b). One may question, however, the dichotomy between 'local inertia' and 'Romanization' in the title of that collection. It seems that certain 'monolithic' paradigms fail to explain the complex, architectural and cultural processes that shaped the Roman world and the discourse between the central authority and the local realities.

Three interconnected themes are explored in this volume: models, agency, and reception. These are central to the study of ancient architecture as they allow to examine the occurrence of architectural forms in a given context in relation to the respective socio-political, economic, cultural, and technological backgrounds. The term 'architectural model' is frequently used in modern scholarship when the circulation of decorative features is investigated, with particular regard to architectural ornament, but this also applies to the design and layout of buildings as well as to the technologies that allowed their construction. This transmission could take place in different ways and through different media – not exclusively from the centre to the periphery. In addition to the movement of architects, stonemasons, and building materials, in some instances the spread of a certain 'model' could happen in less physical forms through circulation of ideas. Architecture is to be understood as the outcome of a process where the patrons, engineers, workforce, and ultimately users all played their part. Agency is therefore a key component and deserves particular attention, even if the extant architectural or archaeological evidence is not sufficient on its own to address this subject and needs to be supplemented by written sources (texts and inscriptions) when they are available. The matter of reception applies both to ancient and modern understandings of architecture. In the ancient world, a range of expected and unexpected responses to buildings might have occurred within the local communities. The visual impact of monuments contributed to shaping and altering cityscapes to varying degrees through time, and this was often part of a vibrant interplay between 'old' and 'new' architectural forms. How much of these architectural processes was understood by contemporaries, and how they might have perceived them, is not always easy to tell but should be taken into consideration in any assessment of the role of architecture in ancient societies.

While thought was initially given to subdividing the book into three sections, each engaging with one of the three themes under examination, the idea was soon discarded. This might have been a neat organization, but ultimately an artificial one that would have not corresponded to the contents of the essays collected here. Readers will realize that authors often engage with more than one theme in their contributions. This was the intention when the project was conceived, thus offering an accurate reflection of the dynamic discussion and exchange of ideas that have led to this publication. The structure of the book is informed by the type of evidence and the specific issues that are considered in the essays. Chapters 2 (Russell *et al.*), 3 (Lancaster), and 4 (Vitti) focus on building materials and technologies. Matters of design, layout, and execution of construction projects are discussed in Chapters 5 (Thomas), 6 (Maschek), 7 (Hufschmid), and 8 (Previato). The role of buildings within the respective cityscapes, their ornamentation, and visual messages are addressed in Chapters 9 (Peleg-Barkat), 10 (Mugnai), 11 (Siwicki), 12 (Stinson), and 13 (Gasparini). Further thoughts on these subjects and a general conclusion are provided in Chapter 14 (DeLaine).

I would like to conclude this introduction with an observation. Much emphasis is placed in present-day academia on the concept of 'interdisciplinarity' – this is (rightly) presented as the key to a successful career. This volume features essays written by archaeologists, architects, civil engineers, architectural historians, and ancient historians, each of them voicing their opinion on the subject based on the respective expertise and as part of an engaging, collective dialogue. This shows that the study of ancient architecture is interdisciplinary in itself and perhaps this discipline would merit more space in current university curricula. It is my hope that use of this volume will not be limited to specialists of the sector, but that undergraduate and graduate students from various fields, as well as more general readers, may find these chapters of some interest.

References

Alcock, S.E., Egri, M. and Frakes, J.F.D. (eds) 2016. *Beyond Boundaries. Connecting Visual Cultures in the Provinces of Ancient Rome*. Los Angeles: Getty Publications.

Barker, S.J., Courault, C., Domingo, J.Á. and Maschek, D. (eds) 2023. *From Concept to Monument: Time and Costs of Construction in the Ancient World. Papers in Honour of Janet DeLaine*. Oxford: Archaeopress.

Bonetto, J., Camporeale, S. and Pizzo, A. (eds) 2014. *Arqueología de la construcción IV. Las canteras en el mundo antiguo: sistemas de explotación y procesos productivos (Padova, 22–24 de noviembre de 2012)*. Madrid: Consejo Superior de Investigaciones Científicas.

Borbonus, D. and Dumser, E.A. (eds) 2022. *Building the Classical World: Bauforschung as a Contemporary Approach*. Oxford: Oxford University Press.

Camporeale, S., Dessales, H. and Pizzo, A. (eds) 2008. *Arqueología de la construcción I. Los procesos constructivos en el mundo romano: Italia y provincias occidentales (Mérida, Instituto de Arqueología, 25–26 de Octubre de 2007)*. Mérida: Consejo Superior de Investigaciones Científicas.

Camporeale, S., Dessales, H. and Pizzo, A. (eds) 2010. *Arqueología de la construcción II. Los procesos constructivos en el mundo romano: Italia y provincias orientales (Certosa di Pontignano, Siena, 13–15 de noviembre de 2008)*. Madrid: Consejo Superior de Investigaciones Científicas.

Camporeale, S., Dessales, H. and Pizzo, A. (eds) 2012. *Arqueología de la construcción III. Los procesos constructivos en el mundo romano: la economía de las obras (École normale supérieure, Paris, 10–11 de diciembre de 2009)*. Madrid: Consejo Superior de Investigaciones Científicas.

Courault, C. and Márquez, C. (eds) 2020. *Quantitative Studies and Production Cost of Roman Public Construction*. Cordoba: Editorial Universidad de Córdoba.

DeLaine, J. 1997. *The Baths of Caracalla: A Study in the Design, Construction, and Economics of Large-Scale Building Projects in Imperial Rome*. Portsmouth, RI: Journal of Roman Archaeology Supplementary Series.

DeLaine, J. 2023. *Roman Architecture*. Oxford: Oxford University Press.

DeLaine, J., Camporeale, S. and Pizzo, A. (eds) 2016. *Arqueología de la Construcción V – 5th International Workshop on the Archaeology of Roman Construction. Man-Made Materials, Engineering and Infrastructure (Oxford, April 11–12, 2015)*. Madrid: Consejo Superior de Investigaciones Científicas.

Favro, D.G., Yegül, F.K., Pinto, J.A. and Métraux, G.P.R. (eds) 2015. *Paradigm and Progeny: Roman Imperial Architecture and its Legacy. Proceedings of a Conference Held at the American Academy in Rome on 6–7 December, 2011 in Honor of William L. MacDonald*. Portsmouth, RI: Journal of Roman Archaeology Supplementary Series.

Gros, P. 2011. *L'architecture romaine du début du IIIe siècle av. J.-C. à la fin du Haut-Empire, 1: Les monuments publics (troisième édition mise à jour)*. Paris: Picard.

Gros, P. 2017. *L'architecture romaine du début du IIIe siècle av. J.-C. à la fin du Haut-Empire, 2: Maisons, palais, villas et tombeaux (troisième édition mise à jour)*. Paris: Picard.

Haug, A. and Lauritsen, M.T. (eds) 2021. *Principles of Decoration in the Roman World*. Berlin: De Gruyter.

Haug, A., Hielscher, A. and Lauritsen, M.T. (eds) 2022. *Materiality in Roman Art and Architecture: Aesthetics, Semantics and Function*. Berlin: De Gruyter.

Lancaster, L.C. 2015. *Innovative Vaulted Construction in the Architecture of the Roman Empire: 1st to 4th Centuries CE*. Cambridge: Cambridge University Press.

Lipps, J. (ed.) 2017. *Transfer und Transformation römischer Architektur in den Nordwestprovinzen. Kolloquium vom 6. – 7. November 2015 in Tübingen*. Rahden: Leidorf.

Lipps, J. and Maschek, D. (eds) 2014. *Antike Bauornamentik. Grenzen und Möglichkeiten ihrer Erforschung*. Wiesbaden: Reichert Verlag.

Marconi, C. (ed.) 2015. *The Oxford Handbook of Greek and Roman Art and Architecture*. Oxford: Oxford University Press.

Maschek, D. and Trümper, M. (eds) 2022. *Architecture and the Ancient Economy. Proceedings of a Conference Held at Berlin (26–28 September 2019)*. Rome: Quasar.

Mattingly, D.J. 2011. *Imperialism, Power, and Identity. Experiencing the Roman Empire*. Princeton: Princeton University Press.

Mazzilli, G. (ed.) 2020a. *In solo provinciali. Sull'architettura delle province, da Augusto ai Severi, tra inerzie locali e romanizzazione*. Rome: Quasar.

Mazzilli, G. 2020b. L'architettura 'in prouinciali solo' (Gai. Inst. II, 7): per un contributo alla definizione delle forme della Baupolitik provinciale in età imperiale. In Mazzilli, G. (ed.), *In solo provinciali. Sull'architettura delle province, da Augusto ai Severi, tra inerzie locali e romanizzazione*. Rome: Quasar, 3–18.

Morachiello, P. and Fontana, V. 2009. *L'architettura del mondo romano*. Rome-Bari: Laterza.

Pensabene, P. 2013. *I marmi nella Roma antica*. Rome: Carocci.

Pensabene, P., Milella, M. and Caprioli, F. (eds) 2017. *Decor: decorazione e architettura nel mondo romano. Atti del convegno internazionale (Roma, 21–24 maggio 2014)*. Rome: Quasar.

Revell, L. 2014. Romanization. In Ulrich, R.B. and Quenemoen, C.K. (eds), *A Companion to Roman Architecture*. Malden, MA: Wiley-Blackwell, 381–98.

Russell, B. 2013. *The Economics of the Roman Stone Trade*. Oxford: Oxford University Press.

Scott, S. and Webster, J. (eds) 2003. *Roman Imperialism and Provincial Art*. Cambridge: Cambridge University Press.

Sear, F.B. 2021. *Roman Architecture (Second Edition)*. Abingdon: Routledge.

Toma, N. 2020. *Marmor – Maße – Monumente. Vorfertigung, Standardisierung und Massenproduktion marmorner Bauteile in der römischen Kaiserzeit*. Wiesbaden: Harrassowitz Verlag.

Ulrich, R.B. and Quenemoen, C.K. (eds) 2014. *A Companion to Roman Architecture*. Malden, MA: Wiley-Blackwell.

Ward-Perkins, J.B. 1981. *Roman Imperial Architecture*. Harmondsworth: Penguin.

Yegül, F.K. and Favro, D.G. 2019. *Roman Architecture and Urbanism from the Origins to Late Antiquity*. Cambridge: Cambridge University Press.

2

...incorrupti imbribus, ventis, ignibus omnique caemento firmiores? Earthen building materials in the Roman West

Ben Russell, Christopher Beckett, Tanja Romankiewicz, J. Riley Snyder, and Rose Ferraby

In Book 35 of his *Naturalis Historia*, immediately after his discussion of pozzolana, Pliny the Elder dedicates a short section of his account to reminding his readers of the varied uses of earth in building. It is worth quoting in full, given its succinctness (*HN* 35.48):

> *Quid? Non in Africa Hispaniaque e terra parietes, quos appellant formaceos, quoniam in forma circumdatis II utrimque tabulis inferciuntur verius quam struuntur, aevis durant, incorrupti imbribus, ventis, ignibus omnique caemento firmiores? Spectat etiam nunc speculas Hannibalis Hispania terrenasque turres iugis montium inpositas. Hinc et caespitum natura castrorum vallis accommodata contraque fluminum impetus aggeribus. Inlini quidem crates parietum luto et lateribus crudis exstrui quis ignorat?*
>
> Are there not in Africa and Spain walls made of earth that are called framed, because they are made by packing earth in a frame enclosed between two boards, one on each side, and so are stuffed rather than built; and do they not last for ages, undamaged by rain, wind and fire, and stronger than any rubble stone? Spain still sees the watchtowers of Hannibal and towers of earth placed on the mountain ridges. From the same source is also obtained the substantial turf suitable for the fortifications of our camps and for embankments against the violent flooding of rivers. At all events, who does not know that partition walls can be made of hurdles coated with clay and built with mudbricks? (translation H. Rackham, with minor modifications by B. Russell)

In this short passage Pliny mentions four building materials that were staples of Roman construction but which have been substantially overlooked in architectural history: rammed earth, turf, daub, and mudbrick. Although Pliny specifically references Africa and Spain, the remains of structures built in these earthen materials have long been known from all across the Roman world, both at rural and urban sites, in modest and utilitarian structures, as well as elite residences.

Despite their widespread use, few analytical studies of the use of earthen building materials in the Roman world exist, especially compared to the range of work on other, more canonically *Roman* building materials, such as brick, concrete, and marble. This stands in marked contrast to recent work on the global histories of earthen materials, including their use in areas once part of the Roman Empire, such as the medieval Maghreb and Spain (Houben and Guillard 1994; Jaquin *et al.* 2008). While the great masterpieces of Roman architecture were not created in earthen materials, a very considerable portion of the population of the Roman world lived in buildings constructed in timber and earthen materials. Analysis of these materials, and the various techniques that made use of them, therefore, can provide key insights into the discrepant architectural realities of populations within the Roman world, and the development of vernacular traditions that often adapted pre-Roman practices and sometimes outlasted Roman rule. Geoarchaeological methods can shed particular light on themes of interest to anyone working on Roman architecture: the sourcing, processing, and use of materials; the adaptation and refinement of construction techniques; the dissemination and transferral of knowledge and skills (see Hufschimd, this volume).

This chapter focuses on two categories of earthen structures: walls in either rammed earth or cob that were built using timber formwork; and turf walls. While the former have received some attention in previous scholarship on Roman architecture, turf walls have largely been ignored from an architectural perspective. Drawing on new analysis from sites in the north-western provinces, and existing research on regions bordering the Mediterranean, this chapter considers how and where these materials were used, the distribution of know-how relating to them, and the evidence for experimentation with, and adaptation of, them.

...quos appellant formaceos: Building in rammed earth

The walls that so attracted Pliny's attention in Spain and Africa were made 'by packing earth in a frame enclosed between two boards, one on each side, and so are stuffed rather than built'. An earlier reference in the Latin tradition to walls that are probably of the same type is made by Varro, in his *De re rustica*, who describes field walls in both Spain and the area around Tarentum, in Apulia, as being made of earth and gravel/pebbles in forms – *ex terra et lapillis compositis in formis* (*Rust.* 1.14.4; on these sources, and later ones which add little, see de Chazelles 2016, 12–13). For both Varro and Pliny the defining feature of this method of construction was the use of formwork. In modern scholarship such walls are called 'mass' earth walls; they are not built up of individual elements in the way that mudbrick or turf walls were constructed from individual mudbricks and turf blocks. The ancient authors say little about the make-up of the earthen mix used for these walls other than Varro's observation that it is often gravelly. The fact that both authors connect this technique with Spain, as well as individually with Africa and Apulia, also implies that they regard it as a technique best suited to warm and relatively dry climates.

The building technique Varro and Pliny describe has plausibly been identified as what in English is typically called rammed earth or in French (and internationally) *pisé*.[1] This technique has a long history, especially in medieval and early modern North Africa, Europe, and China, and is still widely used around the world (Houben and Guillard 1994, 6–7); indeed it has recently received considerable attention from engineers and architects as a sustainable construction method for contemporary projects.[2]

The earth used in rammed earth requires minimal processing. Soil from the building site or nearby is excavated, broken up, large inclusions taken out and is then ready for use. Fibres are not added as standard, as excessive shrinkage on drying is not expected. The best soil type for optimizing the mechanical strength of rammed earth is one with a high sand content, up to around 75%, and a low silty-clay component, ideally not more than 25–30%, though different guides to the technique offer a range of suggested 'mixes' (Williams-Ellis *et al.* 1947, 45–47; Maniatidis and Walker 2003, 8–9; Rael 2009, 17). Once dug and prepared, the earth is packed between formwork and compacted in layers. Rammed earth acquires its mechanical strength through compaction densification as well as suction – a phenomenon wherein microscopic bodies of water, trapped between soil particles, act to hold those particles together (Hamard *et al.* 2016b). To achieve the highest density possible, the soil for rammed earth is placed between formwork at its 'optimum water content' for compaction, which can appear reasonably dry (damp) (Maniatidis and Walker 2003). This is different from the soil mix used for mudbrick production, for instance, which is packed into moulds in a wet state, since the mechanical strength of mudbricks is provided through drying shrinkage densification, internal suction, and, to varying but small degrees, mineral cementation (Jaquin *et al.* 2009; Hamard *et al.* 2016b).

From a technological perspective what is especially interesting about rammed earth is the use of formwork. Since it is the compaction – the ramming – that gives rammed earth its mechanical strength, the formwork that holds the soil in place is key; without this the soil cannot be constrained and compacted. The formwork used for rammed earth construction needs to resist the expansive forces but also be moveable. Different types of formwork have been documented around the world and are typically made of wood, though nowadays metal is often used (Houben and Guillard 1994, 204–9). A basic division can be drawn between fixed and mobile formwork. Fixed formwork consists of upright panels framing the line of the wall that can be attached to posts secured to the ground or the foundations of the wall (Fig. 2.1) (Houben and Guillard 1994, 204). If these posts are inside the panels then vertical 'ghosts' of them will be left in the wall (de Chazelles 1990, 106–7, fig. 15); if they are placed on the outside of the panels then the only remaining trace of them might be a line of postholes along the face of the wall. While such fixed formwork can be assembled and used relatively easily, it requires considerable quantities of panels and posts. For this reason, most rammed earth today and in the documented past uses mobile formwork (Fig. 2.2). In its most basic form this comprises a pair of

Fig. 2.1. A form of fixed formwork for rammed earth in use in early twentieth-century Britain (from Williams-Ellis 1920, 99).

Fig. 2.2. A rammed earth wall under construction using mobile formwork in northern Vietnam (photo A. Boc).

panels, or shutters, arranged upright parallel to each other to form the sides of a box to which ends – end stops or end boards – can be added as required. These shutters, which run parallel to the faces of the wall, are held together by horizontal ties, struts or battens, sometimes ropes, which run perpendicular to the faces of the wall and leave behind characteristic putlog holes; these can be filled in later but are often left behind whatever surface coating or render is added. In more elaborate versions of mobile formwork, different types of braces are incorporated to ensure that it does not lose its shape, while wedges and spacers can be employed to make sure it is correctly adjusted (Maniatidis and Walker 2003, 49). This type of formwork is constructed over the foundations or wall footing and the earth rammed inside of it. It is then moved along the line of the wall and once a full course, or 'lift', of layers has been completed, it can be moved upwards to start the next course.

The formwork used for rammed earth construction, especially the fixed variety, is comparable to that employed in certain types of concrete construction in the Roman world (on this point, see Russell and Fentress 2016, 140–41; de Chazelles 2016, 15). The major difference, however, is that rammed earth formwork, at least the mobile variety, can be disassembled and moved immediately after the earth within it is compacted, whereas formwork for concrete presumably had to remain in place until it had set, and in vaults it may have been required until the material had fully dried (Maniatidis and Walker 2003, 48). In comparison, since the earth that is rammed in rammed earth is not overly wet, it does not need to be left to dry: the strength it derives from compaction and friction between its particles is present immediately. Rammed earth formwork is also endlessly reusable, since it does not get wet and so should not warp. Fourteenth-century Spanish sources show that formwork was highly valued and was commonly rented for specific jobs from specialist builders (Hamilton 1936, 214; Glick 1976, 149–50).

Like other walls built in earthen methods, rammed earth walls have to be protected from the elements. They tend to be raised above the ground on stone or brick socles or footings to prevent damp or frost damage, covered by projecting roofing, and rendered or plastered (Beckett *et al.* 2020). The thickness of rammed earth walls vary, but Williams-Ellis *at al.* (1947, 17, 24–25, 40) suggest that exterior walls of a single storey building should be 0.35 m wide, those of a two storey building 0.45–0.6 m, while 0.23–0.3 m is sufficient for internal dividing walls. If properly constructed and protected the walls can be both dense and durable; indeed the towers that Pliny mentions in Spain were over 200 years old by the time he was writing.

Roman rammed earth

Identifying rammed earth walls in archaeological contexts is not straightforward. Collapsed or degraded rammed earth walls tend to 'melt' back into deposits resembling those from which their primary materials were originally sourced. In the absence of the walls themselves, stone or brick footings and remains of plaster or other render can be used as proxies, but they rarely indicate the construction method employed. Rammed earth walls do occasionally survive to a height sufficient to allow their construction method to be identified, however. Some of the finest examples of still-standing Roman rammed earth walls, some up to 1.48 m high, can be found in House 2b at Ampurias, north-east Spain (Fig. 2.3) (de Chazelles 1990, 101–9). This elite *domus* was first constructed in the late first century BCE and it makes use of rammed earth throughout (rammed earth is used in the neighbouring house and elsewhere at the site too; see de Chazelles 2016, 20–21). Most of these walls were constructed on low stone footings, or dwarf walls, typically 0.3–0.4 m high, sometimes up to 0.5 m; one thin interior wall was built on a base of tiles just two courses high (personal observations of authors on site). The

Fig. 2.3. House 2b, Ampurias (photo B. Russell).

Fig. 2.4. House 2b, Ampurias: Detail of rammed earth wall showing lifts (photo B. Russell).

majority varied in thickness, to judge from their footings, between 0.5 and 0.52 m, though some are only 0.35–0.45 m thick, with the narrowest dividing wall surviving at just 0.23 m. The layers in which the earth was compacted in the walls are discernible by eye in most cases and range in height between 0.04 and 0.14 m, with most between 0.1 and 0.14 m deep (Fig. 2.4). Claire-Anne de Chazelles (1990, 104, figs 7–8; 1997, 101–3; 2016, 21, fig. 14) was able to identify a pair of putlog holes in one of the walls of this house, indicating the use of mobile formwork and suggesting that the walls were constructed in lifts of 0.53–0.63 m in depth, though in some cases they could have been deeper. Macroscopically the material used in the walls can be identified as comprising a significant amount of red-orange sand, with much smaller quantities of silt and clay, as well as small stones, gravel and even fragments of ceramics, bone, charcoal and metalworking debris, usually 10–20 mm in diameter, sometimes 20–50 mm (de Chazelles 1990, 102; 1997, 100; confirmed by personal observations of authors). These macroscopic observations have been confirmed by microscopic analysis by Cécile Cammas (2018, 174, table 6). Micromorphology analysed the voids and fissures, distribution of coarse fraction within the groundmass and the inclusions, and demonstrated that the earthen mixes used for the walls had been coarsely mixed, were relatively dry when applied, and were very strongly and homogeneously compacted (Cammas 2018, 163, table 2; 174, table 6; 176, fig. 11a–d). Lateral grooves visible on the top of at least one wall in House 2b, as well as another wall in the area of the forum, show that mobile formwork was in use at Ampurias, though it is possible that fixed formwork was also sometimes employed (de Chazelles 1997, 101, 104–5, fig. 107). Considering what has already been said about the similarities between rammed earth methods and Roman use of coffering for concrete construction, it is worth noting that the Roman city walls of Ampurias have superstructures of concrete set within formwork on top of a stone base, an unusual form of construction for structures of this sort (de Chazelles 1997, 111, figs 121–22; 2016, 21, fig. 15). These date to the first century BCE and are only slightly earlier than the rammed earth walls discussed above.

Cammas has used micromorphology to identify the same diagnostic features of rammed earth construction in other Roman walls, at Mouriès in southern France and Rirha in Morocco (on Mouriès: Cammas 2018, 174, table 6; 176, fig. 11e–g). At Rirha, samples were taken from two walls of a second-century CE Roman *domus*; these were both constructed with masonry bases, c. 1 m high, and had rammed earth preserved to a height of 0.35 and 0.4 m on top of these. Micromorphology confirmed that these walls were composed of silty sand and sandy silt aggregates, with various anthropogenic inclusions such as ceramics and charcoal (but also pieces of earlier mudbricks and mortar) indicating they were sourced from close to the surface and probably near the building site (Cammas 2018, 171–73, fig. 9; on earth construction at the site more generally, Roux and Cammas 2016a). The arrangement of the aggregates and fissures visible indicated that the earth had been applied moderately moist – though not very wet – and vertically compacted, strongly though not as much as at Ampurias and Mouriès (Cammas 2018, 173, fig. 10). Importantly, careful cleaning of one of these walls at Rirha also identified a row of three putlog holes close to the base of the mass earth wall, which provide clear evidence for the use of mobile formwork (Cammas and Roux 2015; Roux and Cammas 2016b; de Chazelles 2016, 18–19, fig. 11).

Walls similar to those at Ampurias and Rirha, but identified as rammed earth only macroscopically, have been found at a range of sites in North Africa: Kerkouane (Fantar 1984, 309–14), Utica (Russell and Fentress 2016, 134–36), Thysdrus (Slim 1985, 38; de Chazelles 2016, 16, fig. 7), and Acholla in Tunisia (Slim 1985, 38; de Chazelles 2016, 16); Tajurah in Libya (Di Vita 1966, 15; de Chazelles 1997, 97; 2016, 16); Volubilis (Lenoir 1985; Russell and Fentress 2016, 136) and Thamusida in Morocco (Camporeale 2008, 85–86; Cavari 2008, 259–60; Akerraz *et al.* 2009, 162). Of these, the site to have produced the earliest convincing evidence of rammed earth, in this case constructed with fixed formwork, is Kerkouane. There, vertical grooves (0.04–0.06 m deep, 0.12 m wide) were found in the stone socles of the walls of a house at the corner of the Rue du Temple and Rue des Artisans, which were presumably for upright posts, to which a fixed formwork was attached (Fantar 1984, 313, pls. 11–12; de Chazelles 1990, 106, fig. 15; 1997, 95–96). This structure is dated to the third century BCE. The earth used for the superstructure contained rubble and degraded and broken-up mudbrick, which the excavator identified as reused from a previous building.

Aside from this early example at Kerkouane, the bulk of the walls that have been plausibly identified as rammed earth in North Africa date to the Roman period, the majority of these to between the first century BCE and second century CE. Like the structures already discussed at Ampurias and Rirha, the houses in which many of these walls are preserved are far from humble. At Acholla and Volubilis rammed earth walls have been found in high-end *domus*, the Maison de Neptune and Maison des Fauves respectively, where they were then faced in painted wall plaster (Lenoir 1985; Slim 1985, 38). At Tajurah, the walls in question come from the Villa of the Nereids (Di Vita 1966, 15). At Thysdrus, the Maison de Lucius Verus, one of the largest known in the city, has rammed earth walls (Slim 1985, 38). At Thamusida, the rammed earth walls described by Cavari (2008, 259–60) come from a first-century CE building of uncertain function but which had painted wall plaster and was obviously of relatively high status. At Utica, some of the finest rammed earth walls uncovered to date come from the first-century CE Maison du Grand Oecus, located just to the east of the city's forum. Here two-storey rammed earth walls, some with projecting piers in the same materials were found (Figs 2.5–6). These were internal walls, faced with painted wall plaster, which enclosed rooms with floors of *opus sectile* and supported mosaic floors on the second storey (Russell and Fentress 2016, 134–36, fig. 6). This was opulent domestic architecture – some of the finest in the city – for which rammed earth was considered a perfectly suitable material.

The micromorphology carried out on the Ampurias, Mouriès, and Rirha samples confirmed that all of these walls were built in rammed earth. But the same analyses also show that there were slight variations possible within the technique, notably when it comes to the make-up of the earth mix, its moistness, and the intensity of compaction (Cammas 2018, 173, fig. 10). Similar variation in the exact materials used in the walling has been noted at other sites. The Kerkouane walls contained degraded mudbrick, for instance. At Acholla, the walls of the Maison de Neptune comprised beach sand mixed with shells (Slim 1985, 38). At Utica, relatively few large inclusions were found in the walls of the Maison du Grand Oecus and analysis identified the presence of very abundant beach sand, which also contained fish bones. To this tally of variation we can add the use of different formwork types, fixed at Kerkouane (and perhaps also Thysdrus: de Chazelles 1997, 97–98), mobile at Rirha and Ampurias, and uncertain elsewhere. At each of these sites the builders

Fig. 2.5. Maison du Grand Oecus, Utica: Collapsed rammed earth walls and piers with mosaic from an upper floor (photo E. Fentress).

Fig. 2.6. Maison du Grand Oecus, Utica: Collapsed rammed earth wall with plaster facing (photo E. Fentress).

responsible for these walls were adapting a largely standard technique to their own conditions, making use of slightly different soil mixes, and combining them with different sorts of inclusions and quantities of water. What connects these walls is that they were made of largely dry earth, compacted in layers between formwork and on these grounds they can reasonably be labelled as rammed earth walls.

Evidence from around the western Mediterranean and even as far north as Britain, however, reveals that rammed earth was not the only form of earth construction to make use of formwork. Indeed if we are prepared to move away from later (mostly modern) categorizations of construction techniques, we can identify a spectrum of approaches to earth building in the Roman period that often yielded impressive results.

Variations on a theme: Shuttered cob

In her survey of the known rammed earth walls of Punic and (mostly) Roman North Africa, de Chazelles spends some time considering the walls of a particular house at Lambaesis, in Algeria. The structure in question, 'une grande domus somptueusement décorée de mosaïques et de peintures', like the houses at Thysdrus and Utica, is an elite residence (de Chazelles 2016, 17–18). At the site generally, earth was used as infill in *opus africanum* walls, in both the form of mudbricks but also mass earth. In this *domus* the mass earth wall made use of a coarse, heterogeneous earthen mix, which contained vegetal material and was seemingly applied in a relatively wet state in layers 0.2–0.5 m deep. It was not possible to demonstrate that the earth had been compacted. Based on this evidence, de Chazelles (2016, 17–18) is reluctant to identify this material as rammed earth specifically, preferring instead to label it simply 'terre coffrée'. The builders of this structure were using shuttering, therefore, but they appear to have been handling the soil they packed between this formwork differently from the builders at Rirha, Utica or elsewhere.

Sites across the western Mediterranean have produced evidence for earth walls, like those at Lambaesis, that were probably constructed with the aid of formwork but the technique of which, in the absence of micromorphology, remains uncertain. Various sites in Spain have produced early evidence for earth walls which could have been constructed in rammed earth or using a wetter mix of soil and fibres.[3] Similar walls are relatively common at sites across Italy from the fourth century BCE onwards and have often been identified macroscopically as rammed earth (for relevant references, see Russell and Fentress 2016, 137–39). Recently a stretch of such walling has even been identified in the Late Antique baths at Gerace in Sicily (Wilson 2020, 482–83). Further east, the walls of at least one house on Delos seem to have been constructed in earth packed between shuttering, perhaps rammed earth (Zarmakoupi 2015, 10–11; Russell and Fentress 2016, 139). And similar walls have been found in Cyrenaica (at Ptolemais, for example: Żelazowski *et al.* 2011, 26, fig. 20). In Gaul, first- and second-century CE structures with mass earth walls probably constructed with the assistance of shuttering have been identified macroscopically at Cravant, Bram, Cavaillon, and Orléans (Coulon and Joly 1985, 93–94; de Chazelles and Guyonnet 2007, 109). Even as far north as Britain, mass earth walls that seemingly made use of formwork have been identified in first- and second-century CE contexts at Verulamium, London, Colchester, Canterbury, the villas at Farningham and Lullingstone in Kent, and the military site of Castell Collen (for references and further details, see Russell and Fentress 2016, 139–40).

It has been argued that some of these walls, especially in Spain and Italy, were probably constructed in rammed earth (Russell and Fentress 2016, 139). However, to prove this definitively would require sampling and detailed micromorphology. At the same time, the walls of the Lambaesis *domus* and some of these other structures were certainly *not* built in rammed earth; the earthen mix employed seems to have contained vegetation or other fibres and to have been applied wet. In many of these cases, the technique employed was closer to that of cob, or *bauge* in French. Cob walls are constructed out of a mix of earth and fibres (typically straw) applied in clods in a plastic, that is reasonably wet, state.[4] The earth is packed in place by hand or treading and not compacted to the same degree as rammed earth; it acquires its mechanical strength (which is usually less than that of rammed earth) through drying shrinkage densification and suction (Jaquin *et al.* 2009; Hamard *et al.* 2016a). As cob contains more water than rammed earth, it shrinks to a greater extent when drying; the vegetal fibres contained within the mix act to reinforce the material against cracking when shrinking. Cob walls are usually built up on a base by hand, their faces patted back to ensure they are vertical and then trimmed when they are dry; they tend to be raised in lifts, one on top of the other, with each left to dry before the next is added (Hamard *et al.* 2016a, 112).

Formwork is not required in traditional cob construction because the earth is not compacted to the same degree as in rammed earth and is not applied dry. However, detailed geoarchaeological analysis at the important Iron Age site of Lattes in southern France has shown that a largely unappreciated tradition of shuttered cob or *bauge coffrée* certainly existed in antiquity. At Lattes, the key evidence comes from a fourth-century BCE wall that struck the excavators as particularly homogeneous: in other words, it seemed to lack the visible layers of earth seen in other cob walls at the site (Roux and Cammas 2007, 88; 2010). The wall flanked the east side of an open courtyard and was 0.78–0.9 m wide (Roux and Cammas 2007, 89–90). The silty earth mix also included occasional small stones (40–50 mm wide) and fragments of mudbrick (sometimes burnt), charcoal and wood. Three lifts could be noted in the wall, the two fully preserved ones 0.3–0.4 and 0.38–0.48 m deep respectively. Micromorphology confirmed that the earthen mix had been applied in a moist state. Vegetal remains and other inclusions were probably a result of extraction of earth on or close to the building site, and close to the surface, rather than deliberate additions. Crucially, evidence for compaction at the edge of the wall, in the form of oblique elongated voids revealing deformation of the earth, shows that this material was pressed against a formwork that was then removed (Cammas 2018, 170). The fact that this wall was among the densest and most homogeneous excavated at the site implies that this use of formwork brought with it real benefits: it enabled the earthen mix to be packed into place more forcefully and offered additional support as it dried, preventing slumping. Modern work on cob construction indicates that the use of shuttering enhances the builders' control of wall dimensions, results in neater faces, and allows the soil mix to be applied in a more plastic state than in normal cob walls, which improves its workability within the formwork.[5]

Until recently the wall from Lattes was the only example of shuttered cob to have been identified by geoarchaeological analysis. Recent study of a pair of Roman walls in London by the current team, however, shows that this technique continued and was probably used right the way through the Roman period in the north-western provinces. The full analysis of these walls, from a site at Moorgate, will be published elsewhere.[6] But what this reveals is that much more work needs to be done on earth construction in the Roman northern provinces to understand the spread of building techniques and related know-how. London provides some of the richest evidence anywhere in the Empire for the largely overlooked Roman tradition of earth (here called 'brickearth') construction.[7] But we also know of large numbers of buildings built using earth at, for example, Colchester (Crummy 1984, 20–24), Lyon (de Chazelles *et al.* 1985; Desbat 1985; Clément 2016), and a range of sites in Germany (Precht 1971, 53–62; 2002, 183, 189, 193–94; Kraus 1999, 19–20, 48), and Switzerland (Rentzel 2013a–b).

Building in turf

Whereas the materials used in cob walls were extracted, mixed, and then applied in handfuls, the turf (*caespites*) that Pliny described next in the passage with which this contribution opened, required considerably less processing. 'Turf', in a literal sense, is the upper layer of a vegetated ground surface and comprises the topsoil and subsoil held together by the root mat of the vegetation. In turf construction, the 'turf blocks' or 'turves' are simply cut sections of this vegetated surface (Fig. 2.7).[8]

Fig. 2.7. Turf blocks stacked grass-down, ready for use as part of a structural testing experiment (photo B. Russell).

Turf has a long history as a building material, especially in the North Atlantic region (notably Iceland and Scotland), but also in the marshy areas of the Netherlands, northern Germany, Scandinavia, and North America.[9] In the Roman period, as Pliny notes, turf was commonly used in infrastructure and, in particular, military projects. All of the other ancient writers who refer to turf construction, in fact, do so with regard to military contexts (see Livy 25.36.5; Suet. *Aug.* 24.2). The most detailed of these sources is Vegetius (*Mil.* 3.8), in his directions for the building of a camp:

> *...cum sublati caespites ordinantur et aggerem faciunt, supra quem valli, hoc est tribuli lignei, per ordinem digeruntur. Caespes autem circumciditur ferramentis, qui herbarum radicibus continet terram, fit altus semissem, latus pedem, longus pedum semis.*

> ...the raised turf blocks (*caespites*) are laid out in line, forming a rampart. Above it, *valli*, that is stakes or wooden spars, are ranged along its length. The turf is cut around with iron tools, retaining the earth in the grass roots, 0.5 ft. high, 1 ft. wide and 1.5 ft. long. (translation N.P. Milner)

Camp and fort rampart walls constructed fully or partially in turf have been identified across the northern provinces (Jones 1975, 78–81). This material was also used for one of the largest military construction projects in the Roman Empire, the Antonine Wall in Scotland, while much of the western end of Hadrian's Wall was also originally built in turf.[10] The Antonine Wall, in fact, is the only Roman structure that is specifically noted as having been built in turf by an ancient source: it is described in the *Historia Augusta* (*Ant. Pius* 5.4) as a '*murus caespiticius*' – a turf wall (though the complexity of the structure will be discussed more below).

Archaeologically, turf blocks can often be identified by their stripy appearance, with the stripes being the layers of vegetation, topsoil, and subsoil of the original surface from which the block was cut; in soil science these are referred to as the O, A, and B horizons respectively (on the micromorphology of turf, see Huisman and Milek 2017). The distinct appearance of turf blocks has led to their identification elsewhere than Britain, including further south: turf was used in the ramparts of the Flavian legionary fortress at Strasbourg in France (Kuhnle 2018, 147–58), for instance, as well as in the Julio-Claudian fort at León in Spain (Morillo and García 2009, 392–93). Although the phenomenon has received little attention in scholarship, it is likely that other structures, especially in the Roman north, made use of turf for the superstructures of walls (on a building in turf constructed against the south side of the Antonine Wall, see Romankiewicz *et al.* 2022).

In many ways turf is the most straightforward of all earthen materials to use in construction. It requires cutting, trimming, and placing, but no other processing. Nevertheless, the cutting method, the size of the blocks, the depth they were cut from, how they were arranged in place, and the way in which this material was combined with others – especially stone and timber – in the complete structure are all revealing of the decision-making of those responsible, their training and the spread of know-how. In what follows we highlight two sites at which close analysis of Roman turf structures has provided detailed insights into turf use.

Ramparts – and their builders – at Vindolanda

Due to its preservation conditions, the material culture from Vindolanda, and especially the famous writing tablets, provides remarkable insight into the lives of Roman soldiers on the frontier (A. Birley 2002; Bowman 2004; R. Birley 2009). Although the site is rarely examined in architectural studies, these same preservation conditions make Vindolanda a crucial site for reconstructing the often overlooked turf and timber building practices of the Roman army. Of the nine forts constructed at Vindolanda, one on top of the other, the first six were all built in turf, earth, and timber. These range in date from the Flavian to Antonine periods (Periods I–VI, with the last of these having two phases), while the later forts at the site were built in stone. Where these early ramparts have been exposed during excavation they are often in good condition, with individual turf blocks clearly visible and organic material still preserved (and identifiable).

In 2019, three stretches of superimposed rampart were uncovered, datable to the Flavian (I and III) and Antonine (VI) periods of occupation of the site. These were documented and then sampled for micromorphological analysis (Fig. 2.8). The results – both macroscopic and microscopic – were combined with observations made on site during

Fig. 2.8. Section showing three phases of rampart at Vindolanda, with individual turf blocks and other features outlined and the divisions between ramparts marked (photo T. Romankiewicz).

earlier campaigns of excavation to build up a picture of turf building developments at the site over time. A detailed explanation of the approaches taken to these three ramparts has been published elsewhere (Russell *et al.* 2021); here, we summarize some of the key findings.

The first noticeable variation between the ramparts of the different periods of fort at Vindolanda can be discerned at their base. The Period I and II ramparts are laid on timber corduroy rafts of alder, birch, and oak branches or logs, mostly 0.08–0.15 m in diameter, split longitudinally. These were laid perpendicular to the long axis of the rampart, though a line of branches was sometimes also laid parallel to this axis along the face and rear of the rampart (for this arrangement at Strasbourg, see Kuhnle 2018, 148–49). In Period VI the first-phase rampart was laid on a similar raft but this was then expanded outwards in a second phase, with this extension laid on a raft of oak planks, some certainly reused from other structures (Fig. 2.9) (A. Birley 2007, 18–20). The rafts were laid in an earth mix with off-cuts of turf packed between them. Excavations in 2018 of a stretch of the Period I raft identified fragments of tent leather in this layer as well (Russell *et al.* 2021). These rafts were presumably intended to provide a solid and level base at the commencement of construction. The builders of the Period III ramparts did not consider whatever benefits a raft offered were worth the investment in timber and labour, however – the turf blocks of this rampart were laid directly on the ground surface.

These rafts are not the only timber elements used in the Vindolanda ramparts. At semi-regular heights up the superstructure of the ramparts further courses of timbers were laid across their widths. These lacing courses generally used thinner branches than the rafts, with alder and silver birch favoured. Where sampling was possible – in the Period III and VI ramparts – it was noted that these branches were laid in a mix of sub-soil material, probably sourced on site, perhaps from the ditch in front of the rampart, since at least one sample contained anthropic inclusions in the form of rubified clay fragments. These lacing courses are inserted roughly every 0.3–0.5 m up the rampart and they have been confirmed for the Period I, III, and both Period VI ramparts, while the Period II rampart is nowhere preserved to a sufficient height to judge whether its builders used them. Again, these features are found at other forts in Britain and elsewhere, sometimes more closely spaced (0.2–0.3 m in London, for example), sometimes further apart (0.6–0.7 m in Strasbourg).[11] They were possibly laid to prevent sagging or deformation.

The presence of these rafts and lacing courses shows that turf construction was not simply a matter of stacking blocks. This can also be noted within the turf elements of the superstructure. On top of the raft (or ground surface, in the case of the Period III rampart), as well as between the lacing courses, the turf blocks were laid in more or less neat courses. However, to ensure these courses were broadly

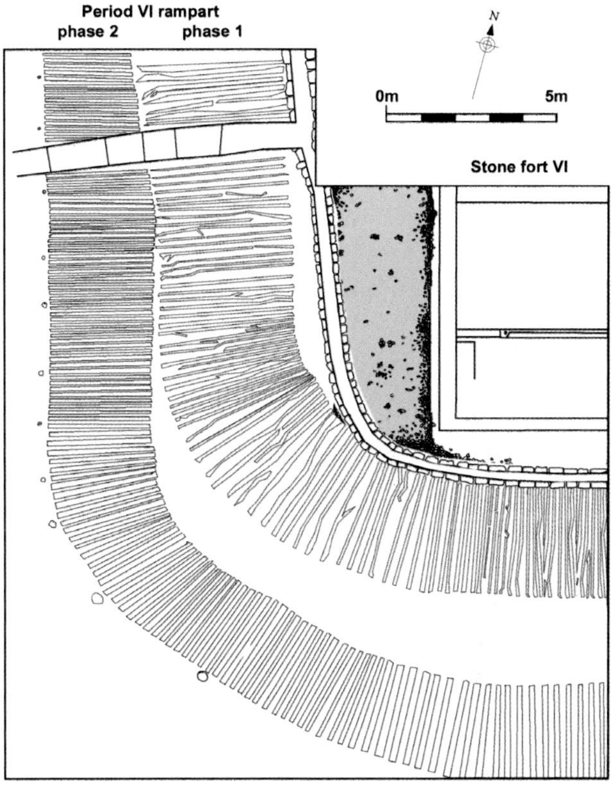

Fig. 2.9. Vindolanda: Plan of the Period VI rampart, phases 1 and 2, corduroy bases excavated in 2005–06 (© Vindolanda Trust).

level, a certain amount of trimming and adjustment had to take place, with off-cuts wedged in gaps between blocks and uneven areas levelled out with earth infill (Russell *et al.* 2021, 204–5). These efforts – and we can include the lacing courses here – were all intended to ensure the ramparts went up in regular stages and distributed the weight of the superstructure evenly. Without this attention the ramparts could easily have slumped or acquired irregular upper profiles that would have compromised their defensive efficacy. Turf was used in all the ramparts through their whole profile, except in the Period III ramparts, which seem to have been built with turf cheeks (or faces) and an earth core. This is another difference between this rampart and the others on the site.

Both macroscopic and microscopic analysis shows that the military builders at Vindolanda sourced turf from the area around the fort and placed the turf blocks in their ramparts grass-side down. Sometimes they even double-cut the turf, meaning that they managed to extract two blocks from one on top of the other, so deep was the root penetration; but even in these cases the blocks were inverted during construction. Across periods we can also see that blocks of broadly the same size were used, measuring on average 0.4 × 0.3 × 0.08 m. If we accept that these blocks have been compacted by the weight of the rampart and subsequent building and post-depositional factors, these dimensions are not dissimilar to those quoted by Vegetius (*Mil.* 3.8), which translate

Table 2.1. Details associated with the different periods of rampart.

Period	*Start date*	*Superstructure*	*Corduroy raft*	*Lacing course*	*Turf form*	*Unit*
I	c. 85 CE	Solid turf	Y	Y	Lozenge	*cohors I Tungrorum*
II	c. 90 CE	Solid turf	Y	?	?	*cohors I Tungrorum*
III	c. 100 CE	Turf cheeks and earth core	N	Y	Parallelogram	*cohors VIIII Batavorum*
VI (1)	140s–160s CE	Solid turf	Y	Y	Lozenge	*cohors II Nerviorum*
VI (2)		Solid turf	Y	Y	Parallelogram	?

as broadly 0.45 × 0.3 × 0.15 m. Blocks of this size would have weighed somewhere between 20 and 30 kg on average, a manageable weight for a soldier to lift and position, which perhaps explains their standard size across periods (Romankiewicz *et al.* 2022, 131). This standardization does not apply to the shape of the turf blocks, however. While the blocks used in the Period III and the second phase of the Period VI ramparts are parallelogram-shaped, with slightly angled ends, the Period I and first-phase Period VI blocks are lozenge-shaped. This morphological difference is most clear along the joint between the two phases of the Period VI rampart.

Careful comparison of these small details between ramparts reveals certain differences in practices within a generally fairly standard framework of how to build a turf and timber rampart (Table 2.1). We can see that the builders of the Period I and first-phase Period VI ramparts cut their turf blocks in a different way from the builders of the other ramparts; this may well result from the use of different tools (Russell *et al.* 2021, 34–35). The Period III builders, unlike all the others, decided not to put down a raft at the base of their rampart; and the second-phase Period VI rampart builders opted for oak timbers rather than alder or birch branches in their raft. Different units, in other words, took slightly different approaches to rampart building and might well even have had different equipment. The units stationed at the site were all auxiliaries and the unique documentary evidence from Vindolanda allows us to identify most of them. We know, therefore, that the *cohors I Tungrorum* built the Period I and II forts (as well as the Period IV fort, of which little survives); the *cohors VIIII Batavorum* the Period III fort; and the *cohors II Nerviorum* the first phase of the Period VI fort. The original troop mustering grounds for these units were in Gallia Belgica and Germania Inferior. While by the late first century and mid-second century CE few of the troops in these units would have come from these territories, the evidence from Vindolanda indicates that these units might still have had their own institutional practices and perhaps equipment – ways of doing things and kit – that caused the differences now discernible on the ground.

The apex of Roman turf construction: The Antonine Wall

The evidence from Vindolanda shows the potential complexities of Roman military structures in turf. Combining turf, the exact composition of which would have varied across terrains, timber, and other earthen mixes effectively and rapidly required a specific skillset and level of experience. However, since Roman military units on the march built camps on a daily basis, and every new unit arriving at a site like Vindolanda constructed their own new fort, the men responsible would soon have become experts in turf building. With every construction project new lessons would have been learned and it is arguably in the building of the Antonine Wall – probably the largest turf structure built in the Roman Empire, and perhaps anywhere (Fig. 2.10) – that we can see some of the results of these.

Archaeological investigations along the length of the Antonine Wall have largely confirmed the statement in the *Historia Augusta* that it was a turf wall, a *murus caespiticius*. Some variation in the composition of its superstructure has been proposed for parts of its eastern section: areas where the Wall seems to have had an earth core bound by turf cheeks

Fig. 2.10. The Antonine Wall rampart (right), its berm and ditch (centre), and upcast mound (left) just to the west of Roughcastle (photo B. Russell).

have been noted and others where 'clay' cheeks have been suggested.[12] However, the western and central sectors of the Wall seem to have been built entirely in turf, and it is also very likely that in the eastern sector it was the nature of the turf that was different rather than necessarily the mode of construction (on this point, see Keppie 1976, 77). A new section across the Wall at Laurieston, near Falkirk, excavated in 2020, certainly indicates this, though how representative it is remains uncertain. Based on this new work, and previous observations, certain insights into the relative sophistication of the structure compared to earlier turf ramparts can be noted.

Perhaps the most novel constructional feature of the Antonine Wall is its base. This is constructed in stone for the entire length of the monument and comprises two rows of dressed kerbstones between which is arranged a rubble raft (on the arrangement of the base, see Keppie 1974, 155–56; Breeze 2006, 71–72). Culverts, covered by large slabs, were built through this base at frequent intervals to ensure drainage from one side of the structure to the other, and it has also been argued that the porous base facilitated drainage of moisture from within the rampart itself (Fig. 2.11) (Romankiewicz *et al.* 2020, 126–27). At Laurieston it was noted that this base was itself laid into a bedding layer of mixed earth and turf off-cuts spread across the original ground surface, which had been stripped of its turf and levelled (Romankiewicz *et al.* 2022). On top of the stone base a levelling layer, again of mixed earth and turf off-cuts, was laid to even out any irregularities in the stone base. Comparable features have been noted elsewhere along the Wall (Romankiewicz *et al.* 2022, table 2), though not everywhere, and they imply that considerable efforts were put into providing a solid and level base that would also facilitate moisture management. All of this work required more investment of materials and labour than a typical fort rampart.

The Laurieston excavations also revealed that the builders of the Wall took particular efforts when it came to sourcing the turf used in the construction and arranging it in place. The Wall here comprised distinct cheeks (or faces) and a core (Fig. 2.12). Although the core was immediately identifiable as turf during excavation, and has a distinct multi-coloured appearance, the cheeks comprised a pale grey material that lacked any of the characteristically striped appearance of turf noted elsewhere – indeed, on first inspection, the cheek material appeared to be a series of clay blocks. Only following micromorphology was it possible to show that both cheeks and core were built in turf blocks, but that these came from different sources. The turf of the core seems to have been sourced on site and in the immediate vicinity of the Wall's corridor; they were cut from grassland on glacial till. The turf used in the cheeks, in contrast, developed on a clay and sand-rich soil, probably from a water meadow in an alluvial zone. This turf must have been brought from further afield, though the exact source cannot be pinpointed (Romankiewicz *et al.* 2022, 122–23, 128–30). Why the builders decided to use turf from two different sources is not clear but it is possible they found that the clay- and sand-rich variety was easier to cut and stack neatly than the siltier turf of the core. An alternative reason may be that the cheek

Fig. 2.11. Stone base of the Antonine Wall, with line of culvert marked, at New Kilpatrick (photo T. Romankiewicz).

Fig. 2.12. Excavations of the Antonine Wall at Laurieston: Excavation of the south cheek (top left), the kerb beneath the south cheek with the stone base beyond (top right), and the south cheek, to the right, and core, to the left, of the rampart in section (bottom) (photos B. Russell).

material was selected for moisture management. Depending on their relative hydraulic properties, the cheeks may have acted to wick moisture away from the core of the wall, thus maintaining its integrity, or could have accelerated evaporation, again supressing moisture levels overall. Further testing is required to understand the exact hydraulic role, if any, of the cheeks but, whatever the reasoning here, this pattern of sourcing shows the level of thought the builders were putting into their materials.

The builders of the Antonine Wall at Laurieston carried this care for constructional details through to the laying of the turf blocks. Unlike at Vindolanda, where the turf blocks appear to have been laid either parallel or perpendicular to the axis of the rampart, at Laurieston the blocks of the core were laid at an angle of approximately 45 degrees, with this orientation alternating course by course (Fig. 2.13). The blocks of the cheeks, on the other hand, were laid perpendicular to the long axis of the rampart, with their rear surfaces cut to receive the angled blocks of the core. This arrangement between core and cheeks shows these features were built up together, course by course, and so carefully keyed together. This arrangement avoids a sharp, straight juncture between cheeks and core, which could have been a potential weak point. This diagonal arrangement of turf blocks has not been described elsewhere in any detail but can be noted on at least one plan of an earlier trench across the Wall, opened just to the west of Laurieston (Bailey 1995, fig. 3). We have noted a comparable arrangement of turf blocks in the fort

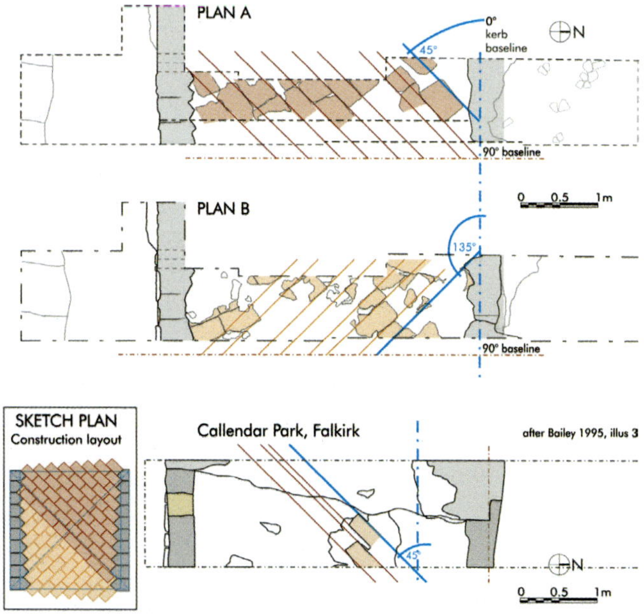

Fig. 2.13. Plans of two layers of turf blocks in the core of the rampart of the Antonine Wall at Laurieston (A and B), a comparison of the arrangement of the turf blocks at Callendar Park (after Bailey 1995, fig. 3), and a sketch plan showing the reconstructed construction layout (image T. Romankiewicz).

ramparts at High Rochester in Northumberland and there is apparently similar evidence from Carlisle.[13]

To date, no lacing courses have been identified at any point along the line of the Antonine Wall. It is possible that they were only used high in the structure and so have not survived, but it is more likely that they were not used at all, since timber was also not used in the base. At the same time, other features noted at Vindolanda and in other forts are not apparent here: the turf blocks were not all laid grass-down, but both grass-up and grass-down, potentially in an alternating pattern, though the section at Laurieston was not wide enough to confirm this; and double-cutting of turf did not take place – all of the blocks analysed have O horizons. What these constructional features suggest is that the builders of the Antonine Wall had learned from the roughly 100 years of experience that the Roman army had acquired of turf construction in Britain. Turf structures can survive for 20–50 years without major maintenance (Romankiewicz *et al.* 2020, 133–38). This was a structure built to last. In its stone base, the careful sourcing of materials in its superstructure, and their intricate arrangement we can see systematic planning and execution at work.

Conclusions

There were no ancient how-to-guides, no books of instructions, for building in earth (that we know of; it is possible that other military manuals, like Vegetius', contained more detail). Information about effective techniques was presumably disseminated by practitioners, either through migration or the movement of itinerant builders, and modified in response to local conditions (see Maschek, this volume). Certain techniques worked in certain locations, not others. Experimentation and adaptation within the broad parameters of particular techniques would have been incessant. In frontier zones, a major stimulus for these processes would have been the movement of military units, which were always heavily involved in construction and had their own ways of doing things. For these reasons we should be careful not to assume that the divisions between building techniques that are today applied by architects, engineers and other researchers would have meant much in antiquity (see also Siwicki, this volume, on the understanding of architecture in antiquity).

This is particularly clear in the case of the various Roman earth construction techniques employing formwork. While modern analyses tend to draw a clear line between rammed earth and cob, the evidence outlined above shows that in the ancient world the reality was more fluid. At certain sites builders were using dry, sandy and gravelly (sometimes shelly) mixes, which could then be intensely compacted. At other sites the earth they packed between their formwork was more clayey or silty, was used in a plastic state, and needed to be combined with fibres to stop it cracking when it dried. From a geotechnical perspective, these two techniques worked in quite different ways; the densification of the walls resulted from different mechanisms. From the perspective of an ancient builder, however, these two techniques would probably have been considered largely identical. They both involved the packing of earth mixes between formwork; they are both, from this application point of view, 'shuttered earth' and could also be described in the terms used by Pliny and Varro.

At these different sites we can see builders adapting accepted modes of construction for their own needs and according to what was available on site. These walls, therefore, are documents of on-site, ad hoc decision-making; and they reveal the importance of local savoir-faire in this process. Utica is an instructive example of this. Here it is striking that mudbrick is widely used in Punic (sometimes early Roman) structures, but that this is gradually replaced in construction by rammed earth from the first century BCE onwards (Russell and Fentress 2016, 135–36). We can assume this was due in part to the properties of the earth on site, which is indeed extremely sandy and low in clay. External support for this is provided by, of all people, Vitruvius, who tells us that the Utican magistrates demanded that mudbricks used in the city were dried for an extra-long period of time, presumably due to concerns over their quality.[14] If the local materials were poorly suited for mudbrick production they would also have been unsuitable for cob. In London, in contrast, the opposite was basically true. In the Moorgate walls, we can see builders who were probably quite familiar with mudbrick construction in the city, adapting the available materials to a shuttered mass earth walling technique. Across the city, in fact, we can identify a wide array of earth building techniques, sometimes within the same structure, which are perhaps reflective of the extremely cosmopolitan make-up of the city, especially in the first century CE, and the interaction between locals and immigrants (on this point, see Wallace 2016, 81–82).

Turf construction is no less varied and provides a picture of varied practices within an accepted broader framework. Perhaps more than with any other earthen materials, builders in turf were limited by the properties of their locally available materials: you cannot add anything to a turf block to make it either less clayey or less likely to crumble when dry. In the timber rafts and lacing courses, the levelling layers and patches at Vindolanda and elsewhere we can see the actions of different units responding to the material that was itself a reflection of the local landscape. In the form of the Antonine Wall, we can see how lessons learnt at sites like Vindolanda were put into practice and refined.

Occasionally the results of these on-site adaptation and experimentation processes can be baffling. The absence of a wooden raft beneath the turf of the Period III ramparts at Vindolanda is not easily explained, for example. Sometimes hybrid techniques emerge that cannot be easily understood: at the Villa Dar Buc Ammera, near Lepcis Magna, at least one wall of Flavian date has a hybrid technique combining rammed earth and concrete, for instance. The wall is divided between these materials longitudinally, with one face constructed in concrete for its entire height and the other in lifts of rammed earth between which are layers of concrete 0.08–0.1 m thick (Aurigemma 1962, 31; de Chazelles 1997, 97–98, fig. 102). The builders must have added these materials to the formwork at the same time and built them up in layers. This curious approach is a perfect illustration of the technical overlap between Roman rammed earth and concrete construction, but it appears not to have taken on elsewhere.

A final point is worth stressing. Although earth building materials have rarely been integrated into mainstream studies of Roman architectural history, the evidence for the distribution of these materials and their adaptation stands out more clearly in the Roman period than almost any other. In Britain, therefore, although turf construction is attested in the pre-Roman Iron Age and early medieval and later periods, we have nowhere near the wealth of archaeological evidence for turf use from these periods as we do from the Roman period. All of the largest original turf structures known from Europe date to the Roman period. And while later turf construction is associated with the North Atlantic, the turf walls from Léon (Julio-Claudian), from the newly discovered fort at Valkenburg (probably Julio-Claudian: the material from this site is being studied by the current authors), and Strasbourg (Flavian) predate many of the well-studied examples from Britain, which are largely Flavian and later. In the case of rammed earth, although much scholarship has focused on the origins of this technique, our best evidence for its use in antiquity comes from the Roman period. In North Africa, beyond Kerkouane, all of the rammed earth walls that have been studied to date come from Roman structures, often elite *domus* of the imperial period. In Spain and southern France a similar picture emerges. The earliest walls that de Chazelles is prepared to identify confidently as rammed earth in this region come from first-century BCE Roman houses at Ampurias. Shuttered earth construction broadly defined and using moveable formwork also only seems to have been introduced further north, in the Rhineland and then in Britain in the Roman period, from the first century CE onwards.

All of this hints at a degree of knowledge transfer and experimentation in the field of earth building in the Roman Empire that has yet to be fully appreciated. What detailed studies of structures built in even these apparently 'humble' materials reveal are the decisions made by their maker(s) and how these changed over space and time. Relatively few Roman earth structures have been intensively investigated using the techniques outlined above and those remaining constitute a largely untapped dataset that can fill important gaps in our understanding of everyday Roman architecture.

Acknowledgements

This work was supported by a Leverhulme Trust Research Project grant (RPG-2018-223). The analysis at Vindolanda was undertaken in collaboration with Andy Birley and the Vindolanda Trust; at Laurieston with Geoff Bailey, the Falkirk Local History Society, and the Edinburgh Archaeological Field Society.

Notes

1. In Spanish- and Portuguese-speaking countries this material is called *tapial* and *taipa* respectively, both derived from the Arab term *tabiya*. See Houben and Guillard 1994, 6–7; de Chazelles 2010, 312.
2. Maniatidis and Walker 2003; Jaquin *et al.* 2008; 2009; Beckett *et al.* 2020; Abhilash *et al.* 2021.
3. On the late third-century BCE evidence from the Iberian site at Calafell, see Belarte 2001, 33; Pou Vallès *et al.* 2001, 101; de Chazelles 2016, 19–20. More generally on the Spanish evidence, see de Chazelles 1990, 117; 2003; Russell and Fentress 2016, 137.
4. Houben and Guillard 1994; Keefe 2005; Watson and McCabe 2011; Hamard *et al.* 2016a.
5. Klein 2003, 125–28; Keefe 2005; Watson and McCabe 2011, 65.
6. The site in question is MOQ10 and excavated by MOLA; we are grateful to Louise Fowler for providing us with access to this material and collaborating with us on its analysis.
7. For an overview of the range of construction types identified in the city, see Perring and Roskams 1991, 71–84; Perring 2002, 92–95.
8. A note on terminology: in German 'turf blocks' are called *Grassoden*, *Rasensoden* or *Plaggen*, *Graszoden* or *Zoden* in Dutch; turf is distinct from peat, slabs of which are called (confusingly) *Torfsoden* in German and *Turfzoden* in Dutch. The French term for turf blocks is *mottes de gazon*; peat blocks are *mottes de tourbe*.
9. See, for instance, Uerkvitz 1997; Walker 2006; Sigurðardóttir 2008; Siegmüller 2010; Nicolay 2018; Stefánsson 2019; and on the 'soddies', turf-built houses, of Nebraska, see Welsch 1969.
10. On the Antonine Wall, Keppie 1974; Hanson and Maxwell 1983; Hodgson 2020; Romankiewicz *et al.* 2020; 2022; on the 'Turf Wall' of Hadrian, see Breeze 2019.
11. See, for example, Jones 1975, 89, pl. 5a; Frere and Wilkes 1989, 15–27; Dunwoodie *et al.* 2015, 45–47; Kuhnle 2018, 148–49, pls. 179–80, 182.
12. Macdonald 1925, 283–85; Steer 1961a, 94; 1961b, 322; Keppie 1976, 71–72, 77–78; Bailey 1995, 580.
13. Analysis of the High Rochester turf is forthcoming; for the Carlisle observation, which has not been published, we are grateful to William Hanson.
14. *De arch.* 2.3.2. Vitruvius says that at Utica mudbricks had to be left to dry for five years, while he recommends two years as the standard; these seem like very long times and it is possible that months rather than years are meant here.

References

Abhilash, H.N., Hamard, E., Beckett, C.T.S., Morel, J.-C., Varum, H., Silveira, D., Ioannou, I. and Illampas, R. 2021. Mechanical behaviour of earth building materials. In Fabbri, A., Morel, J.-C., Aubert, J.-E., Bui, Q.-B., Gallipoli, D. and Reddy, B.V.V. (eds), *Testing and Characterisation of Earth-based Building Materials and Elements: State-of-the-Art Report of the RILEM TC 274-TCE.* Cham: Springer International Publishing Switzerland, 127–80.

Akerraz, A., El Khayari, A. and Papi, E. 2009. L'habitat maurétano-punique de Sidi Ali ben Ahmed – Thamusida (Maroc). In Helas, S. and Marzoli, D. (eds), *Phönizisches und punisches Städtewesen*, Mainz: Philipp von Zabern, 147–70.

Aurigemma, S. 1962. *L'Italia in Africa. Le scoperte archeologiche (1911–1943). Tripolitania, vol. 1: i monumenti d'arte decorativa.* Rome: Istituto Poligrafico dello Stato.

Bailey, G.B. 1995. The Antonine frontier in Callendar Park, Falkirk: its form and structural sequence. *Proceedings of the Society of Antiquaries of Scotland* 125: 577–600.

Beckett, C.T.S., Jaquin, P.A. and Morel, J.-C. 2020. Weathering the storm: a framework to assess the resistance of earthen structures to water damage. *Construction and Building Materials* 242.10: https://doi.org/10.1016/j.conbuildmat.2020.118098.

Belarte, M.C. 2001. Les tècniques constructives al món ibèric. In Belarte, M.C., Pou, J.M., Sanmartí, J. and Santacana, J. (eds), *Tècniques constructives d'època ibèrica i experimentacio arquitectonica a la Mediterrània.* Barcelona: Universidad de Barcelona, 27–41.

Birley, A. 2002. *Garrison Life at Vindolanda: A Band of Brothers.* Charleston, SC: Tempus.

Birley, A. 2007. 2005–2006: Area A – the western defences of the stone forts. In Birley, A. and Blake, J. (eds), *Vindolanda Research Report. The Excavations of 2005–2006.* Bardon Mill: The Vindolanda Trust, 17–51.

Birley, R. 2009. *Vindolanda: A Roman Frontier Fort on Hadrian's Wall.* Chesterholme: Amberley Publishing.

Bowman, A.K. 2004. *Life and Letters on the Roman Frontier: Vindolanda and its People (Second Edition).* London: British Museum Press.

Breeze, D.J. 2006. *The Antonine Wall.* Edinburgh: John Donald.

Breeze, D.J. 2019. *Hadrian's Wall. A Study in Archaeological Exploration and Interpretation.* Oxford: Archaeopress.

Cammas, C. 2018. Micromorphology of earth buildings materials: toward the reconstruction of former technological processes (Protohistoric and Historic Periods). *Quaternary International* 483: 160–79.

Cammas, C. and Roux, J.-C. 2015. Étude des matériaux de construction en terre crue des sites antiques de Rirha (Maroc). *Archéopages* 42: 68–69.

Camporeale, S. 2008. Materiali e tecniche delle costruzioni. In Akerraz, A. and Papi, E. (eds), *Sidi Ali ben Ahmed – Thamusida, 1. I contesti.* Rome: Quasar, 62–178.

Cavari, F. 2008. I rivestimenti parietali. In Akerraz, A. and Papi, E. (eds), *Sidi Ali ben Ahmed – Thamusida, 1. I contesti*. Rome: Quasar, 249–63.

Clément, B. 2016. L'industrie de la brique crue dans la Colonia Lugdunum. Typologie, approvisionnement et organisation de la production. In DeLaine, J., Camporeale, S. and Pizzo, A. (eds), *Arqueología de la Construcción V – 5th International Workshop on the Archaeology of Roman Construction. Man-Made Materials, Engineering and Infrastructure (Oxford, April 11–12, 2015)*. Madrid: Consejo Superior de Investigaciones Científicas, 145–63.

Coulon, G. and Joly, D. 1985. Le centre. In Lasfargues, J. (ed.), *Architecture de terre et de bois. L'habitat privé des provinces occidentales du monde romain. Antécédents et prolongements: Protohistoire, Moyen Âge et quelques expériences contemporaines*. Paris: Éditions de la Maison des Sciences de l'Homme, 93–102.

Crummy, P. 1984. *Excavations at Lion Walk, Balkerne Lane and Middleborough, Colchester, Essex*. Colchester: Colchester Archaeological Trust.

de Chazelles, C.-A. 1990. Les constructions en terre crue d'Empúrias à l'époque romaine. *Cypsela* 8: 101–18.

de Chazelles, C.-A. 1997. *Les maisons en terre de la Gaule méridionale*. Montagnac: Éditions Mergoil.

de Chazelles, C.-A. 2010. Quelques pistes de recherches sur la construction en terre crue et l'emploi des terres cuites architecturales pendant l'Âge du Fer dans le bassin occidental de la Méditerranée. In Tréziny, H. (ed.), *Grecs et indigènes de la Catalogne à la Mer Noire*. Aix-en-Provence: Centre Camille Jullian, 309–18.

de Chazelles, C.-A. 2016. Recherches sur les origins de la construction en pisé en Occident. In Dellagi, M.M. (ed.), *Architecture en terre crue/Raw Earth Architecture*. Tunis: Académie Tunisienne des Sciences, des Lettres et des Arts, 9–44.

de Chazelles, C.-A. and Guyonnet, F. 2007. La construction en pisé du Languedoc-Roussilon et de la Provence, du Moyen-Âge à l'époque moderne (XIIIe–XIXe s.). In Guillard, H., de Chazelles, C.-A. and Klein, A. (eds), *Les constructions en terre massive: Pisé et bauge. Échanges transdisciplinaires sur les constructions en terre crue, 2*. Montpellier: Éditions de l'Espérou, 109–39.

de Chazelles, C.-A., Fiches, J.-L. and Poupet, P. 1985. La Gaule méridionale. In Lasfargues, J. (ed.), *Architecture de terre et de bois. L'habitat privé des provinces occidentales du monde romain. Antécédents et prolongements: Protohistoire, Moyen Âge et quelques expériences contemporaines*. Paris: Éditions de la Maison des Sciences de l'Homme, 61–71.

Desbat, A. 1985. La région de Lyon et de Vienne. In Lasfargues, J. (ed.), *Architecture de terre et de bois. L'habitat privé des provinces occidentales du monde romain. Antécédents et prolongements: Protohistoire, Moyen Âge et quelques expériences contemporaines*. Paris: Éditions de la Maison des Sciences de l'Homme, 75–83.

Di Vita, A. 1966. *La villa della 'gara delle Nereidi' presso Tagiura*. Tripoli: Directorate-General of Antiquities, Museums and Archives.

Dunwoodie, L., Harward, C. and Pitt, K. 2015. *An Early Roman Fort and Urban Development on Londinium's Eastern Hill. Excavations at Plantation Place, City of London, 1997–2003*. London: MOLA.

Fantar, M. 1984. *Kerkouane. Cité punique du Cap Bon (Tunisie)*. Tunis: Institut National d'Archéologie et d'Art.

Frere, S.S. and Wilkes, J.J. 1989. *Strageath. Excavations within the Roman Fort 1973–86*. London-Gloucester: Society for the Promotion of Roman Studies/Allan Sutton Publishing.

Glick, T.F. 1976. Cob walls revisited: the diffusion of tabby construction in the western Mediterranean world. In Hall, B. and West, D. (eds), *On Pre-Modern Technology and Science: Studies in Honor of Lynn White, Jr*. Malibu: Undena Publications, 147–59.

Hamard, E., Cazacliu, B., Razakamanantsoa, A. and Morel, J.-C. 2016a. Cob, a vernacular earth construction process in the context of modern sustainable buildings. *Building and Environment* 106: 103–19.

Hamard, E., Cammas, C., Fabbri, A., Razakamanantsoa, A., Cazacliu, B. and Morel, J.-C. 2016b. Historical rammed earth process description thanks to micromorphology. *International Journal of Architectural Heritage* 11.3: https://doi.org/10.1080/15583058.2016.1222462.

Hamilton, E.J. 1936. *Money, Prices, and Wages in Valencia, Aragón and Navarre, 1351–1500*. Cambridge, MA: Harvard University Press.

Hanson, W.S. and Maxwell, G. 1983. *Rome's North-West Frontier: The Antonine Wall*. Edinburgh: Edinburgh University Press.

Hodgson, N. 2020. Why was the Antonine Wall made of turf rather than stone? In Breeze, D.J. and Hanson, W.S. (eds), *The Antonine Wall: Papers in Honour of Professor Lawrence Keppie*. Oxford: Archaeopress, 300–12.

Houben, H. and Guillard, H. 1994. *Earth Construction: A Comprehensive Guide*. London: Intermediate Technology Publications.

Huisman, D.J. and Milek, K. 2017. Turf as construction material. In Nicosia, C. and Stoops, G. (eds), *Archaeological Soil and Sediment Micromorphology*. Oxford: Wiley-Blackwell, 113–19.

Jaquin, P.A., Augarde, C.E. and Gerrard, C.M. 2008. A chronological description of the spatial development of rammed earth techniques. *International Journal of Architectural Heritage* 2: 377–400.

Jaquin, P.A., Augarde, C.E., Gallipoli, D. and Toll, D.G. 2009. The strength of unstabilised rammed earth materials. *Géotechnique* 59.5: 487–90.

Jones, M.J. 1975. *Roman Fort-Defences to A.D. 117, with Special Reference to Britain*. Oxford: British Archaeological Reports.

Keefe, L. 2005. *Earth Building – Materials and Methods, Repair and Conservation*. Abingdon: Routledge.

Keppie, L.J.F. 1974. The building of the Antonine Wall: archaeological and epigraphic evidence. *Proceedings of the Society of Antiquaries of Scotland* 105: 151–65.

Keppie, L.J.F. 1976. Some rescue excavation on the line of the Antonine Wall, 1973–6. *Proceedings of the Society of Antiquaries of Scotland* 107: 61–80.

Klein, A. 2003. La construction en terre crue par couches continues, en Midi-Pyrénées, XVIe–XXe siècles. Contribution à l'identification des techniques. In de Chazelles, C-A. and Klein, A. (eds), *Échanges transdisciplinaires sur les constructions en terre crue. 1. Terre modelée, découpée ou coffrée. Matériaux et modes de mise en œuvre*. Montpellier: Éditions de l'Espérou, 417–37.

Kraus, K. 1999. *Die Befunde der Insula 39 in der Colonia Ulpia Traiana (Xanten)*. Oxford: Archaeopress.

Kuhnle, G. 2018. *Argentorate. Le camp de la VIIIe légion et la présence militaire romaine à Strasbourg, Volume 1*. Mainz: Römisch-Germanisches Zentralmuseum.

Lenoir, M. 1985. Le Maroc. In Lasfargues, J. (ed.), *Architecture de terre et de bois. L'habitat privé des provinces occidentales du monde romain. Antécédents et prolongements: Protohistoire, Moyen Âge et quelques expériences contemporaines*. Paris: Éditions de la Maison des Sciences de l'Homme, 47–59.

Macdonald, G. 1925. Further discoveries on the line of the Antonine Wall. *Proceedings of the Society of Antiquaries of Scotland* 59: 270–95.

Maniatidis, V. and Walker, P. 2003. *A Review of Rammed Earth Construction*. Bath: Natural Building Technology Group.

Morillo, Á. and García, V. 2009. The Roman camps at León (Spain): state of the research and new approaches. In Morillo, Á., Hanel, N. and Martín, E. (eds), *Limes XX. Estudios sobre la frontera romana / Roman Frontier Studies*. Madrid: Anejos de Gladius, 389–405.

Nicolay, J. 2018. *Huisplaatsen in De Onlanden. De Geschiedenis van een Drents Veenweidegebied*. Groningen: Barkhuis.

Perring, D. 2002. *The Roman House in Britain*. London-New York: Routledge.

Perring, D. and Roskams, S. 1991. *Early Development of Roman London West of the Walbrook*. London: Museum of London and the Council for British Archaeology.

Pou Vallès, J., Santacana Mestre, J., Morer de Llorens, J., Asencio Vilaro, D. and Sanmartí, J. 2001. El projecte d'interpretacio arquitectonica de la ciutadella iberica de Calafell (Baix Penedes). In Belarte, M.C., Pou, J.M., Sanmartí, J. and Santacana, J. (eds), *Tècniques constructives d'època ibèrica i experimentacio arquitectonica a la Mediterrània*. Barcelona: Universidad de Barcelona, 95–115.

Precht, G. 1971. Die Ausgrabungen um den Kölner Dom. Vorbericht über die Untersuchungen 1969/70 (1971). *Kölner Jahrbuch für Vor- und Frühgeschichte* 12: 52–64.

Precht, G. 2002. Konstruktion und Aufbau sogenannter römischer Streifenhäuser am Beispiel von Köln (CCAA) und Xanten (CUT). In Gogräfe, R. and Kell, K. (eds), *Haus und Siedlung in den römischen Nordwestprovinzen. Grabungsbefund, Architektur und Ausstattung*. Homburg-Saar: Ermer, 181–98.

Rael, R. 2009. *Earth Architecture*. New York: Princeton Architectural Press.

Rentzel, Ph. 2013a. Geoarchäologische Untersuchungen. In Deschler-Erb, E. and Richner, K. (eds), *Ausgrabungen am Basler Murus Gallicus 1990–1993 / Teil 1. Die spätkeltischen bis neuzeitlichen Befunde. Die römischen bis neuzeitlichen Funde*. Basel: Archäologische Bodenforschung des Kantons Basel-Stadt, 131–66.

Rentzel, Ph. 2013b. Mikromorphologische Untersuchungen zur Holzbautechnik der jüngsten HP. In Trumm, J. and Flück, M. (eds), *Am Südtor von Vindonissa. Die Steinbauten der Grabung Windisch-Spillmannwiese 2003–2006 (V.003.1) im Süden des Legionslagers*. Windisch: Kantonsarchäeologie Aargau, 65–70.

Romankiewicz, T., Milek, K., Beckett, C.T.S., Russell, B. and Snyder, J.R. 2020. New perspectives on the structure of the Antonine Wall. In Breeze, D.J. and Hanson, W.S. (eds), *The Antonine Wall: Papers in Honour of Professor Lawrence Keppie*. Oxford: Archaeopress, 121–41.

Romankiewicz, T., Russell, B., Bailey, G., Gardner, T., Snyder, J.R. and Beckett, C.T.S. 2022. 'Another wall of turf': geoarchaeological analysis of the Antonine Wall at 72 Grahamsdyke Street, Laurieston, Falkirk. *Proceedings of the Society of Antiquaries of Scotland* 151: 103–41.

Roux, J.-C. and Cammas, C. 2007. La bauge coffrée: appréhension d'un mode de construction inédit dans la ville protohistorique de Lattes, Hérault (duexième quart du IVe s. av. n. è.). In Guillard, H., de Chazelles, C.-A. and Klein, A. (eds), *Les constructions en terre massive: Pisé et bauge. Échanges transdisciplinaires sur les constructions en terre crue, 2*. Montpellier: Éditions de l'Espérou, 87–98.

Roux, J.-C. and Cammas, C. 2010. Les techniques constructives en bauge dans l'architecture protohistorique de Lattara, Lattes, Héault (milieu V^e^ – IVe s. av. n. è.). In Janin, T. (ed.), *Premières données sur le cinquième siècle avant notre ère dans la ville de Lattara*. Lattes: Association pour le Développement de l'Archéologie en Languedoc, 219–88.

Roux, J.-C. and Cammas, C. 2016a. L'architecture en terre crue. In Callegarin, L., Kbiri Alaoui, M., Ichkhakh, A. and Roux, J.-C. (eds), *Rirha: Site antique et médiéval du Maroc, II. Période maurétanienne (Ve siècle av. J.-C. – 40 ap. J.-C.)*. Madrid: Casa de Veláquez, 44–83.

Roux, J.-C. and Cammas, C., 2016b. Une architecture mixte. In Callegarin, L., Kbiri Alaoui, M., Ichkhakh, A. and Roux, J.-C. (eds), *Rirha: Site antique et médiéval du Maroc, II. Période maurétanienne (Ve siècle av. J.-C. – 40 ap. J.-C.)*. Madrid: Casa de Veláquez, 104–18.

Russell, B. and Fentress, E. 2016. Mud brick and pisé de terre between Punic and Roman North Africa. In DeLaine, J., Camporeale, S. and Pizzo, A. (eds), *Arqueología de la Construcción V – 5th International Workshop on the Archaeology of Roman Construction. Man-Made Materials, Engineering and Infrastructure (Oxford, April 11–12, 2015)*. Madrid: Consejo Superior de Investigaciones Científicas, 131–43.

Russell, B., Romankiewicz, T., Gardner, T., Birley, A., Snyder, J.R. and Beckett, C.T.S. 2021. Building with turf at Roman Vindolanda: multi-scalar analysis of earthen materials, construction techniques, and landscape context. *Archaeological Journal* 179.1: 169–210.

Siegmüller, A. 2010. *Die Ausgrabungen auf der frühmittelalterlichen Wurt Hessens in Wilhelmshaven. Siedlungs- und Wirtschaftsweise in der Marsch*. Rahden: Leidorf.

Sigurðardóttir, S. 2008. *Building with Turf (Translated by N.M. Brown)*. Skagafjörður: Skagafjörður Historical Museum.

Slim, H. 1985. La Tunisie. In Lasfargues, J. (ed.), *Architecture de terre et de bois. L'habitat privé des provinces occidentales du monde romain. Antécédents et prolongements: Protohistoire, Moyen Âge et quelques expériences contemporaines*. Paris: Éditions de la Maison des Sciences de l'Homme, 35–45.

Steer, K.A. 1961a. Excavations at Mumrills Roman fort, 1958–60. *Proceedings of the Society of Antiquaries of Scotland* 94: 86–132.

Steer, K.A. 1961b. Excavations on the Antonine Wall in Polmont Park and at Dean House in 1960. *Proceedings of the Society of Antiquaries of Scotland* 94: 322–24.

Stefánsson, H. 2019. *From Earth: Earth Architecture in Iceland*. Reykjavik: University of Iceland Press.

Uerkvitz, R. 1997. *Norddeutsche Wurten-Siedlungen im archäologischen Befund. Analyse und Interpretation aufgrund siedlungsgeographischer Modelle*. Frankfurt am Main: Peter Lang.

Walker, B. 2006. *Scottish Turf Construction*. Edinburgh: Historic Environment Scotland.

Wallace, L.M. 2016. *The Origins of Roman London*. Cambridge: Cambridge University Press.

Watson, L. and McCabe, K. 2011. The cob building technique. Past, present and future. *Informes de la Construcción* 63.523: 59–70.

Welsch, R.L. 1969. Sod construction on the Plains. *Pioneer America* 1.2: 13–17.

Williams-Ellis, C. 1920. *Cottage Building in Cob, Pisé, Chalk and Clay: A Renaissance (Second Edition Revised and Enlarged)*. London: Country Life Limited.

Williams-Ellis, C., Eastwick-Field, J. and Eastwick-Field, E. 1947. *Building in Cob, Pisé and Stabilized Earth (Revised Edition)*. London: Country Life Limited.

Wilson, R.J.A. 2020. The baths on the estate of the Philippiani at Gerace, Sicily. *American Journal of Archaeology* 124.3: 477–510.

Zarmakoupi, M. 2015. Les maisons des négociants italiens à Délos: structuration de l'espace domestique dans une société en mouvement. *Cahiers Mondes Anciens* 7: http://mondesanciens.revues.org/1588.

Żelazowski, J., Kowarska, Z., Lenarczyk, S., Lewartowski, K. and Yacoub, G. 2011. Polish archaeological research in Ptolemais (Libya) in 2010. A preliminary report. *Światowit* 9: 9–33.

3

Unusual terracotta tiles for the vaulting of Roman baths: An investigation into the exchange and diffusion of technical knowledge in the western Roman Empire

Lynne C. Lancaster

The builders in Rome are known for their use of vaulting to create vast covered spaces and intricate combinations of forms; the builders outside the imperial capital are less noted for their contributions to vaulted construction. Nevertheless, ingenious innovations also occurred far from the centre and spread in ways which provide a glimpse into some of the motivating factors behind the adoption of new types of construction. The two techniques examined in this paper – the armchair voussoir and the hollow voussoir (Fig. 3.1) – were never used in the capital itself and are limited largely to the western Roman Empire. They both are made of terracotta and were used almost exclusively in bath buildings, but they have distinctly different patterns of diffusion. Moreover, many of them bear stamps that provide some insight into their manufacture and dissemination which in turn sheds light on knowledge networks, cross-industry influence, and technology transfer in the western Empire.[1]

Armchair voussoirs

The armchair voussoir has a longer history than the hollow voussoir. Its earliest precursor occurs at Fregellae, Italy in a bath which originally dates to the second half of the third century BCE with a second phase in the second quarter of the second century BCE (Figs 3.2–3). Both phases had vaults made with ribs of flanged terracotta bars, some of

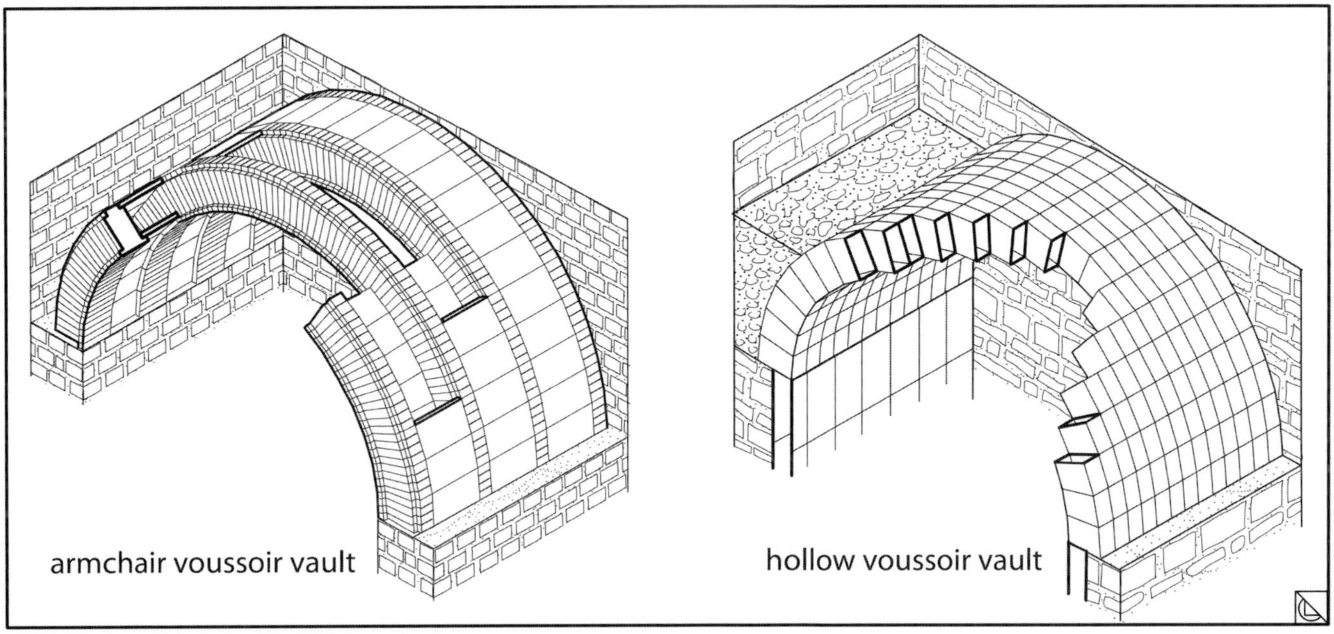

Fig. 3.1. The two vaulting systems discussed. A: Ribs of armchair voussoirs spanned by tiles. B: Hollow voussoirs (image L.C. Lancaster).

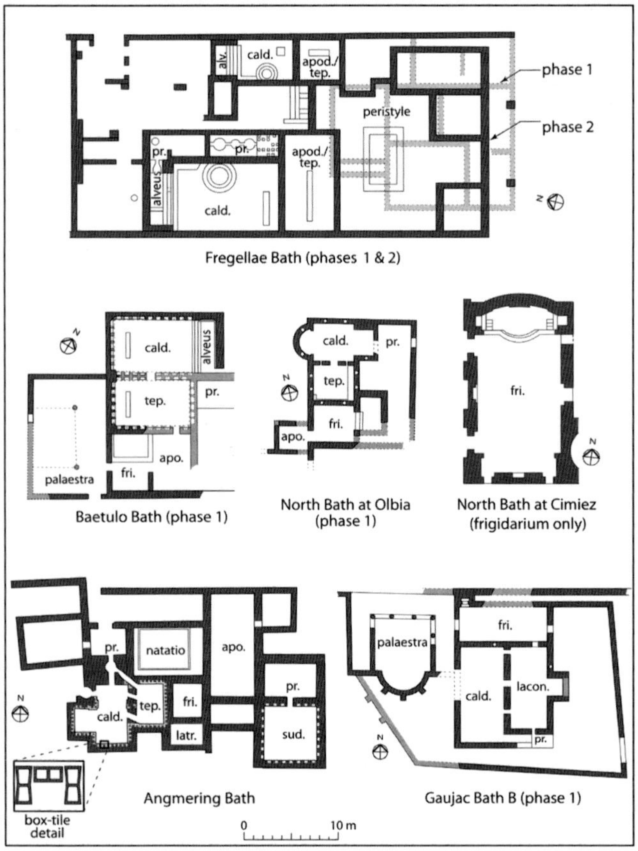

Fig. 3.2. Plans of bath buildings mentioned in the text (drawn to the same scale): Fregellae (based on Tsiolis 2006, fig. 3; 2013, fig. 2); Baetulo (based on Guitart Durán 1976, fig. 8a); Olbia (based on Bouet 2006, fig. 2); Cimiez (based on Benoit 1977, pl. 30); Angmering (based on Scott 1938, fig. 11); Gaujac (based on Bouet 2003, fig. 78; Charmasson 2003, fig. 6).

which were found built into the second-phase walls and must have belonged to the first phase. Nevertheless, most of the finds (not in their original fallen locations) relate to the second-century building. Curved tiles, which spanned between the ribs, were found among the pieces of terracotta bars. The excavator, V. Tsiolis, has published preliminary reports on the baths in which he notes that four different sized bars have been found. Some of the largest ones also have cuttings for lead connectors (Fig. 3.3), parts of which were still in place despite the post-destruction scavenging. The curvature of the largest bars indicates a span of around 6 m, which would correspond well with the men's *apodyterium/tepidarium* (Tsiolis 2001, 106, n. 88; 2006, 246; 2013, 90–93, 105, 111, n. 39).

The lead clamps would have been important for the stability of the structure – the 15 cm thickness of the ribs limits the distance each could span without clamps to resist tension. The theoretical minimum for the thickness of a semicircular arch (i.e., angle of embrasure of 180°) is the ratio of arch thickness (t) to free span (D) of 1:17.6 (Fig. 3.4). So, a 15 cm thick semicircular arch could only span 2.4 m without clamps. However, a flatter arch with

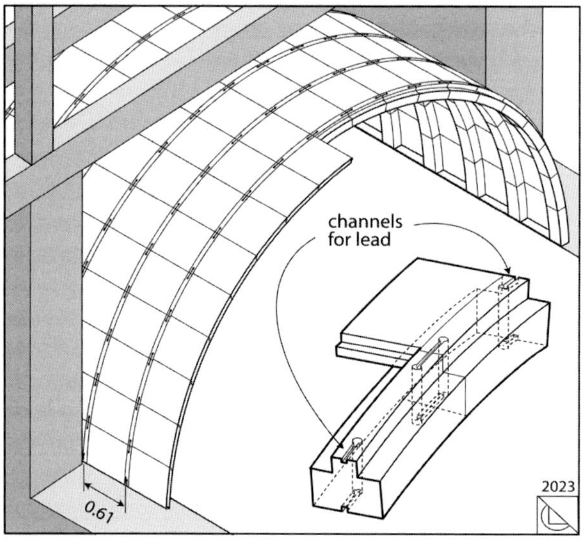

Fig. 3.3. Reconstruction of vault of armchair bars at the Republican baths at Fregellae (image L.C. Lancaster, based on Tsiolis 2001; 2006).

a lower angle of embrasure of 140° would theoretically be stable and remain in compression up to 7.1 m (these theoretical figures are derived from Ochsendorf 2006, 30, fig. 6). In reality, this span would be somewhat lower due to real-world circumstances. We do not know the angle of embrasure for the Fregellae vault, but for a 6 m span, the clamps would certainly have helped ensure stability if any tension developed in such thin arches.

The Fregellae bars are not singular. A similar type of armchair bar has been found in the excavation of a workshop at Massa, near Carrara (Fig. 3.5).[2] Each end of the Massa bar has the recessed groove on the top and bottom connected by a slightly oblique vertical channel. In addition, it has a vertical groove along each contact face. The material

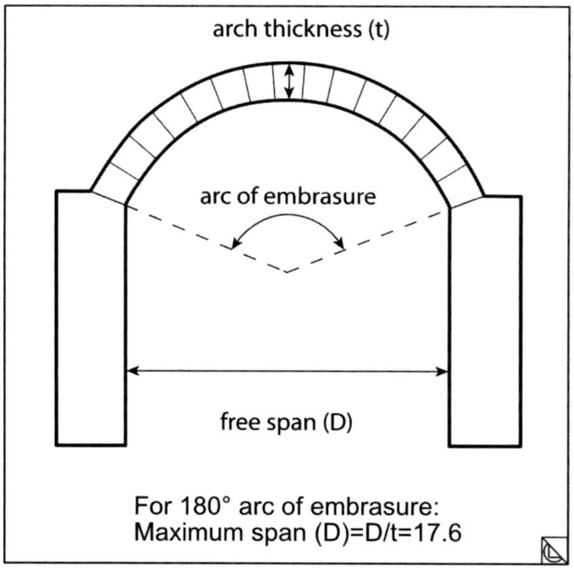

Fig. 3.4. Diagram giving formula for determining the maximum span of a semicircular arch of given thickness (image L.C. Lancaster).

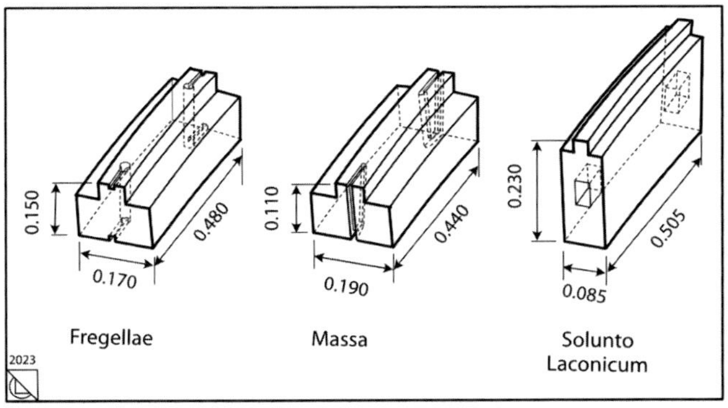

Fig. 3.5. Armchair bars (at the same scale) from Fregellae (based on Tsiolis 2001; 2006), Massa (based on Fabiani and Paribeni 2016, 83–84), and Solunto laconicum *(based on Sposito 2014, fig. 14).*

from the workshop can be dated to the late second–early first century BCE. At Solunto in Sicily, another example with grooves similar to the Fregellae bars has been found, but its original location is not known. Only the clamps at Fregellae are preserved, and their form is modelled on the lead clamps used to repair pottery, especially amphorae and dolia (Fig. 3.6).[3] Many such repairs occurred during the life use of the vessel well away from the workshop, but for very large vessels like dolia, which could develop cracks during the drying process, repairs were undertaken in the pottery workshop by cutting and drilling into leather hard clay and filling with lead after the firing (Cheung 2021, 180–81). So, those who made the bars could have also been familiar with this type of repair and shared their knowledge in the development of the new vaulting technique.

A fourth type of armchair bar, also from Solunto, is different from the others. A whole example has been found at the *laconicum* of the gymnasium (second century BCE) along with fragments of others, both at the *laconicum* and in the North Baths further down the hill.[4] It is taller (22 cm) and narrower (8.5 cm) than those at Fregellae and Massa and has a rectangular hole at either end for some sort of tenon connector (Fig. 3.5). The curvature of the whole bar is defined by a c. 7.3 m diameter circle (Fig. 3.7). The diameter of the *laconicum* itself is about 6.6 m; therefore, the bars could have covered it with an angle of embrasure of about 132°. The formula shown in Fig. 3.4 gives the theoretical maximum span of about 6.6 m. The tenons connecting the bars could have helped resist bending and provided an extra degree of stability. The thinner width of these bars would be appropriate for use in a dome because they all would have had to converge at some point towards the centre into a type of 'keystone', probably in the form of an oculus. At the top of the wall are a series of cuttings spaced about every 85 cm along the circumference (i.e., every 15°). The bearing plane has been gauged away so there is no way of knowing the original width of what were presumably slots for the roofing support. If they supported the armchair bars, the resulting dome would have been formed by 24 ribs, each pair supporting narrow flat tiles of stone or terracotta (Fig. 3.7). Some of the bars retain a partial coating of plaster along the bottom surface and the two sides up to the rebate for the bedding of a flat tile. Sposito (2014, 214–15, 217, fig. 14h) shows a drawing of the bar

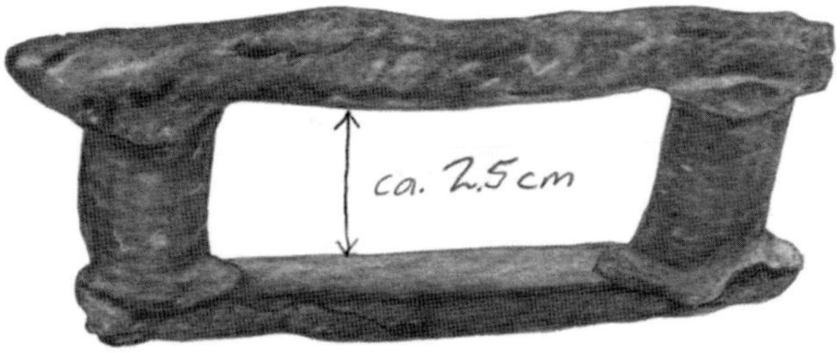

Fig. 3.6. Drawing of a lead clamp from a dolium repair at the oppidum of Entrement, second century BCE (image L.C. Lancaster).

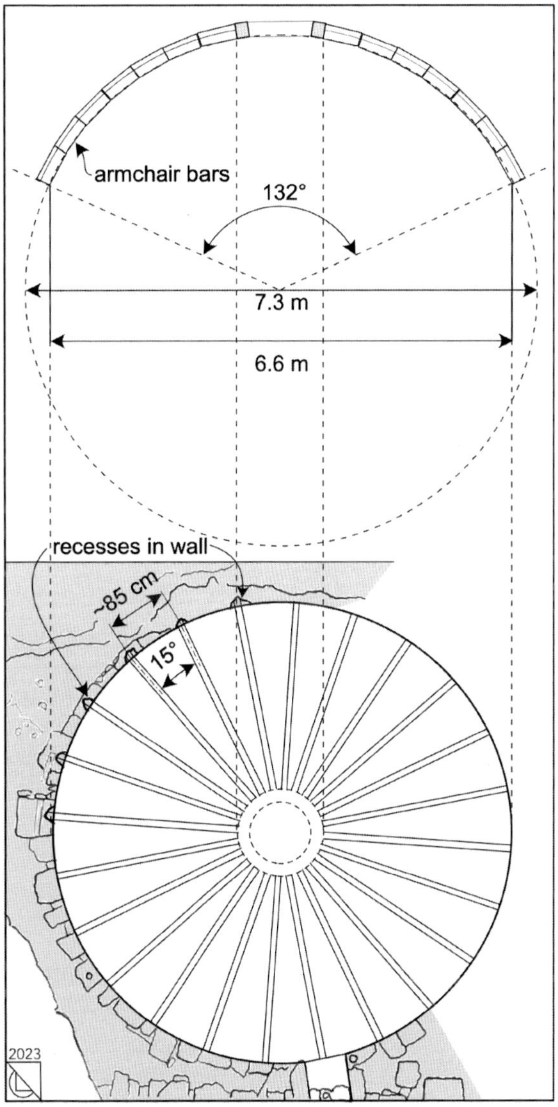

Fig. 3.7. Author's hypothetical reconstruction of a dome made of armchair bars at the laconicum *of the gymnasium at Solunto (image L.C. Lancaster, plan after Wiegand 1997, pl. 29).*

and notes the cuttings in the wall, but he proposes a flat timber roof and never refers to the armchair bars in his text. The *laconicum* is partially built into a hill and would have required some lighting and ventilation from above, as Vitruvius (*De arch.* 5.10.5) describes for *laconica*, so a flat roof is unlikely.[5] In any case, the narrow width and the height of these bars suggest that they were probably designed for this room, which is particularly enlightening given that a more typical armchair bar – wider (11.3 cm) with clamp channels – was also found elsewhere at Solunto. Thus, adaptation to fit different requirements can be seen in the different morphology of bars from the same site.

The vaults, or more appropriately 'ceilings', created by the armchair bars would not have required a full centring and thus had the advantage of reducing the number of centring frames and of eliminating the task of dismantling and moving a large wooden structure. Indeed, a full centring could not have been used because the builders had to have access from one side of a pair of ribs to lay the cover tiles between them, so the ribs had to be added one by one. Thus, the job could have been completed with one or two centring frames which could be removed and reused to support the subsequent rib(s).

Such fragile terracotta constructions were surely covered by a wooden roof structure. Indeed, they could have been constructed from below after the main roof was erected. In all the preliminary reports from Fregellae, the terracotta pieces are described as having the intrados coated with a layer of plaster and the extrados left bare (Tsiolis 2001, 106; 2006, 246), which implies that they were protected above. The design of the Fregellae bath with a roughly centred longitudinal wall and possibly two columns *in antis* on the front would support the reconstruction of a wooden gabled roof spanning the c. 21 m wide structure (Figs 3.2–3).[6]

Why would the builders at Fregellae have come up with such a complex terracotta ceiling system? The answer must lie in other innovative aspects of this bath, especially the heated communal immersion basin (*alveus*), a new feature which had only recently appeared in the Greek baths of Sicily and southern Italy (Trümper 2009, 151–52; 2019, 358–59). With the introduction of heated immersion basins came additional steam and moisture which could damage roof structures made of timber. That architects and builders were concerned with moisture damage in the heated rooms of baths is clear from Vitruvius' description of how to build a protective ceiling in a bath (*De arch.* 5.10.3):

> *Concamarationes vero si ex structura factae fuerint, erunt utiliores; sin autem contignationes fuerint, figlinum opus subiciatur. Sed hoc ita erit faciendum. Regulae ferreae aut arcus fiant, eaeque uncinis ferreis ad contignationem suspendantur quam creberrimis; eaeque regulae sive arcus ita disponantur, uti tegulae sine marginibus sedere in duabus invehique possint, et ita totae concamarationes in ferro nitentes sint perfectae. Earumque camararum superiora coagmenta ex argilla cum capillo subacta liniantur; inferior autem pars, quae ad pavimentum spectat, primum testa cum calce trullizetur, deinde opere albario sive tectorio poliatur. Eaeque camarae in caldariis si duplices factae fuerint, meliorem habebunt usum; non enim a vapore umor corrumpere poterit materiem contignationis, sed inter duas camaras vagabitur.* (Latin: Granger 1931)

> The vaulted ceilings (*concamarationes*) will certainly be more serviceable if they are made of concrete (*ex structura*). But if they are made of wooden beams, then suspend a ceiling of tiles underneath. But they are to be made in the following way: iron bars or arcs are to be made and hung from the timber beams on iron hooks set close together. The bars or arches should be placed so that tiles without raised edges can be set between two of them and be supported. In this way the whole ceiling can be finished so that it is supported on iron. And the joints on the upper surface of the ceiling should be filled with clay worked with hair; the lower surface, which faces the floor, should be covered with a roughcast of lime and crushed terracotta, and then finished with fine white stucco (*opus albarium*) or [painted?] plaster (*opus tectorium*). If these ceilings are made double in *caldaria*, they will be more effective, for the moisture from the vapor will not be able to damage the timber beams, but instead will be diffused between the two ceilings. (translation L.C. Lancaster)

Vitruvius does not say how to make the double ceiling, but he is clearly concerned with protecting the wood from rot. The same concern would apply to the ceiling of *laconica*, which he notes should be hemispherical to ensure that heat is distributed evenly and should have an oculus at the top (*De arch.* 5.10.5). This is important for understanding why the terracotta ceiling was developed. Both phases of the Fregellae bath were built before the advent of concrete vaulting in the second half of second century BCE, which Vitruvius, writing about a century later, recommends as preferable (*concamarationes… ex structura*). Therefore, the builders at Fregellae came up with the solution of the terracotta armchair bars to provide a moisture-proof ceiling. This was later substituted by the hanging terracotta ceiling described by Vitruvius in the passage above and eventually by the armchair voussoir system.

Another stage in the development of the rib system leading to the armchair voussoirs can be seen at a bath at Badalona, Spain (ancient Baetulo). The bath probably dates to the mid-first century BCE shortly after the foundation of the town (Guitart Durán and Padrós Martí 1990, 169–72). Its design was modelled on the fully developed Roman bath containing a *caldarium* with *alveus*, a *tepidarium*, a *frigidarium*, and an *apodyterium* (Fig. 3.2). In the *caldarium*, the excavators found the remains of vaulting ribs consisting of H-shaped terracotta tiles which had notches in the sides to form a groove to support tiles between each pair of ribs (Fig. 3.8). The H-shaped tiles were mould-made with the thickness at the bottom less than that at the top, so that they formed thin, wedge-shaped voussoirs; however, when put together the angle of their taper would have created a vault

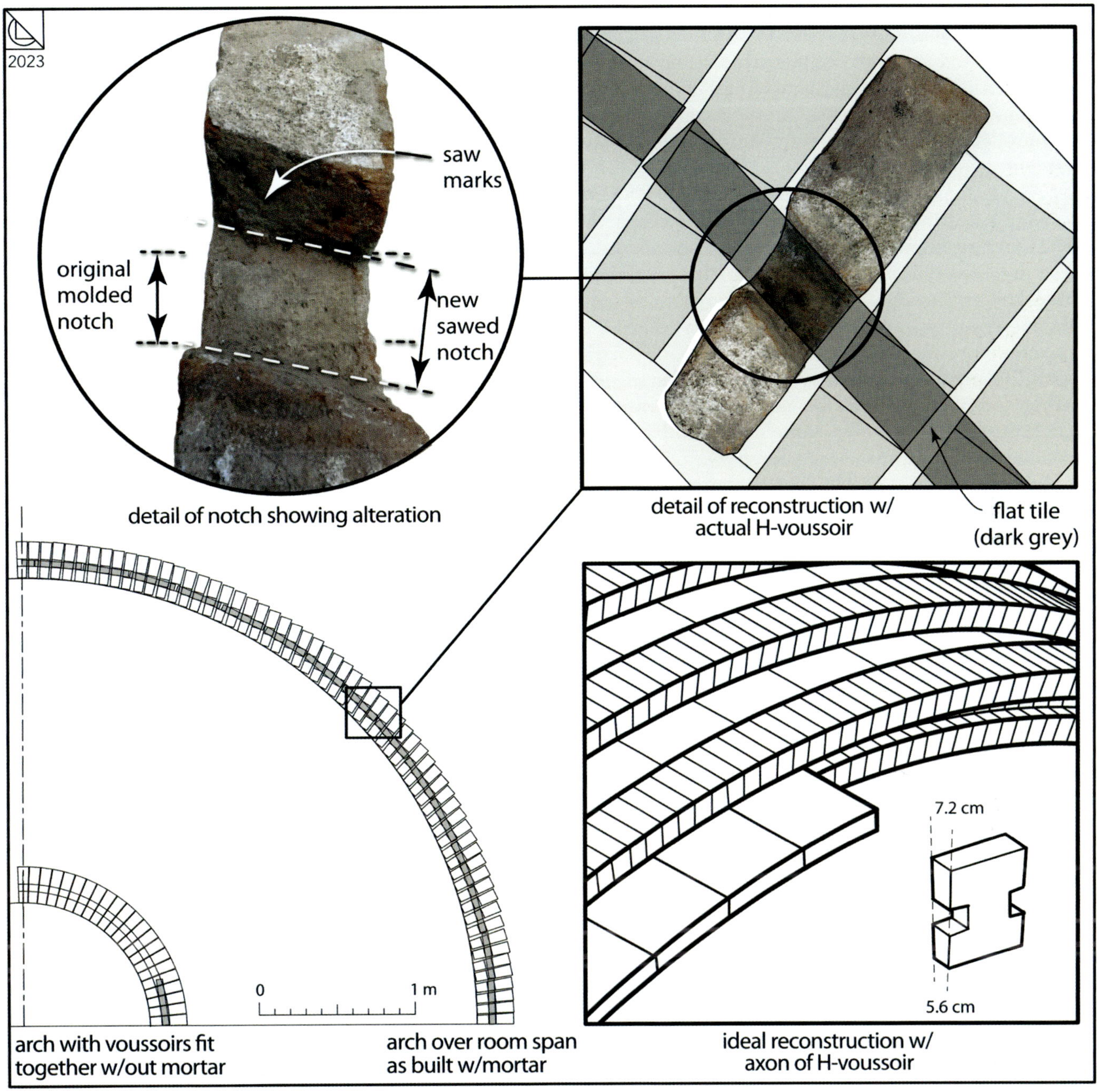

Fig. 3.8. Reconstruction of terracotta ceiling over caldarium *in the Baetulo baths (image L.C. Lancaster, based on Guitart Durán 1976, fig. 9). Note how the notches had to be enlarged to fit the flat cover tile.*

only about 1.5 m in span, which is much smaller than the span of the room they covered (c. 5.5 m). Consequently, when they were used to build the larger vault, the mortar joints moderated the angle. As the notches became progressively misaligned, they had to be recut, as demonstrated by the saw marks along the sides of the notches (Fig. 3.8). This is the earliest example known thus far of an attempt to use terracotta tiles rather than the terracotta bars to build ribs to support cover pieces, but the alterations imply that the technique was not yet perfected. The H-voussoirs were clearly formed in the terracotta workshop, but they then had to be modified on site as the problem became apparent during construction.

The true armchair voussoir eventually took two forms – one that supported a single layer of cover tiles and another that supported a double layer (as shown in Fig. 3.1). The earliest datable examples have been found outside of Florence at the Vingone workshop, active between 20 BCE and 20 CE

(Shepherd 2008, 188–200). The surviving fragments have flanges at the bottom, but no tops are preserved to indicate if a second layer of cover tiles was intended. The next datable examples are in two baths in southern Gaul from the first half of the first century CE, at Olbia and Gaujac (Fig. 3.2). The double-layer type occurs in the heated rooms of the North Baths at Olbia (Bouet 1999, 91, 113, fig. 54d). Both types were found in Bath B at Gaujac (Bouet 1999, 87, 91, figs 50d, 54c). Ultimately southern and western Gaul was the area of greatest proliferation (Fig. 3.9).

The purpose of the armchair voussoirs has often been assumed to be part of a heated vaulting system because the double-layer type created an air space in between, as recommended by Vitruvius. However, 21% of identifiable types (n=102) have supports for only one layer of tiles. Moreover, the double-layer type has been found in baths that had no wall heating and hence could not have been part of the heating system. This was the case at Olbia and at the North Baths at Cimiez (second or third century CE) (Fig. 3.2), where the voussoirs had both flanges and rebates. At Cimiez, they were used over the *tepidarium*, which had a hypocaust but no wall heating, and over the *frigidarium* (Bouet 1999, 93, fig. 55b) (Fig. 3.10). The armchair voussoir technique apparently developed from earlier attempts to provide a waterproof barrier for the wooden roof structure and not as a type of vault heating system (Lancaster 2015, 162–63). The double-layer type could have provided some additional protection for the roof timbers and acted as insulation. Some of the later double-layer armchair vaults could have been connected to the heating system (Lancaster 2015, 163–69) (see below), but we should not assume that this was the reason for the initial development of the technique, nor that all double-layered armchair vaults were necessarily heated.

Another purpose attributed to the armchair voussoir vaults was to reduce the lateral thrusts on the walls by lightening the vault. Structural analysis shows that if the walls are at least two Roman feet thick, the weight of the vault is not a concern until the span reaches about 5 m (Lancaster 2015, 182–83). Given the small spans (avg. 4.8 m), weight reduction was probably not a primary motive for using them. Nevertheless, there are two cases where the technique was surely used for structural reasons: the *frigidaria* of the North Baths at Cimiez (Figs 3.2, 3.10) and the nearby Port d'Orée baths at Fréjus, both of which had spans in the range of 9 m (for structural analysis, see Lancaster 2015, 187–89). Both baths date to the second or third century CE, so the structural use of the armchair voussoir technique was apparently a secondary development once it began to be employed in larger structures.

The armchair voussoirs spread further west into the Iberian Peninsula during the second half of the first century CE. Examples appear at the public baths at Labitolosa (Magallón and Sillières 2013, 269–72, 294–95), Arcaya (Loza Lengaran *et al.* 2014, 356–58, 423, 428), and Tongobriga (Tavares Dias 1997, 55, 133–34, 155–56, 174, 223–24). They have also been found in a first-century context at the Puente Grande villa (Torrecilla Aznar *et al.* 2002, 263, fig. 150), which is outside ancient Carteia where the public bath there may have also employed them (Lancaster 2015, 165–67). The initial use of the technique seems to have been mainly for small public baths (spans <5 m) during the rapid urbanization in Gaul and Iberia in the first century.

During the second century CE, the armchair vault system spread beyond the public baths in urban contexts to small baths within rural villas. As agricultural production of wine and olive oil increased, the landowners began to use their wealth to expand their *villae rusticae* with the addition of a more luxurious *pars urbana*, and a private bath was an inherent part of the upgrade (Tremoleda 2000, 184–85; Balmelle 2001, 98–101; Buffat 2011, 161). In fact, 46% of armchair voussoirs from identifiable contexts (n=120) come from villas, and more are likely from the unidentified contexts. Many villas had production facilities for the amphorae in which to export their goods, so terracotta production of architectural elements could easily be undertaken on an ad hoc basis. An example can be seen on the south coast of Narbonensis near Loupian where the workshop of Le Bourbou supplied both wine amphorae and terracotta tiles for the nearby villa of Prés-Bas, and armchair voussoirs have been found at both sites (Fig. 3.9) (Bouet 1999, 93, fig. 56c–e; Chabal *et al.* 2012).

Armchair voussoirs have also been linked to urban workshops. One of the most prolific producers of bath tiles in southern France was Clarianus, whose stamps appear on armchair voussoirs at three sites (Lyon, Roaix, and Vaison-la-romaine) and on other tiles distributed along the Rhone and Isère valleys (Bouet 1999, 183–86; Clément 2015, 161). Another urban producer of armchair voussoirs was Quietus, one of six known tile makers in a workshop at Llafranc, Spain (Fig. 3.9), who also supplied various bath and roof tiles to ancient Emporiae, 30 km to the north (Tremoleda 2000, 183, fig. 129; Barti *et al.* 2004, 128–30). The armchair voussoirs had the advantage of being easy to fabricate and could be adapted to a range of spans.

The map in Fig. 3.9 shows a broad distribution of armchair voussoirs in the western Empire, but most of the sites are located along coastal routes or along major rivers and their tributaries, which were primary arteries for transporting goods inland. Unsurprisingly, trade routes and knowledge networks often coincide. The highest concentration is in southern and western France. For the most part, the armchair voussoirs have not been found in northern and eastern France nor in Germany. Geographic connectivity could be one factor determining where the technique spread (or did not), but the large number of examples in villa baths in France and the Iberian Peninsula suggests that their popularity could have been related to the intensity of villa

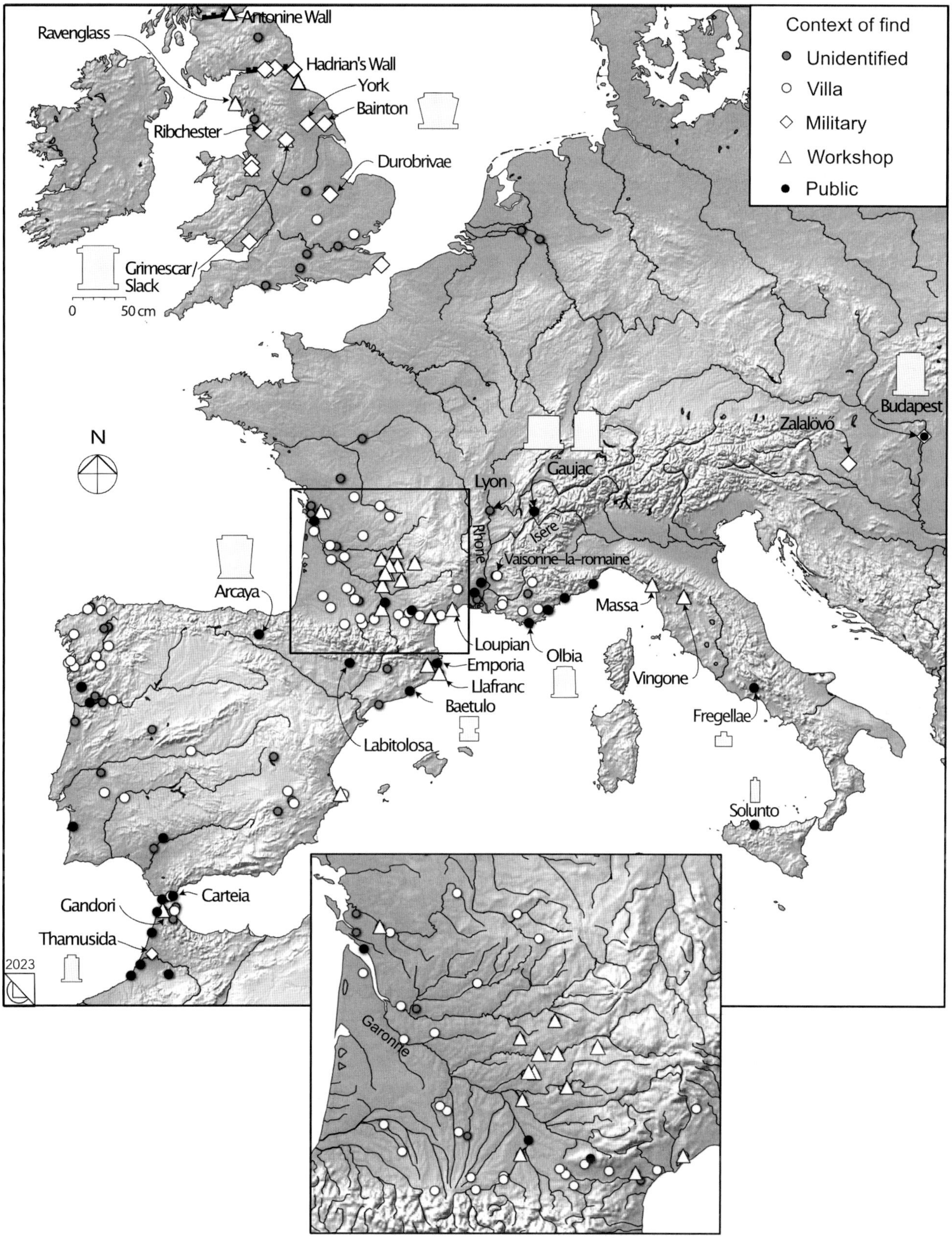

Fig. 3.9. Map showing distribution of armchair voussoirs. Voussoir forms shown at same scale. Inset shows Garonne valley detail (image L.C. Lancaster).

Fig. 3.10. North Baths at Cimiez (Nice), France. View of tepidarium *looking into* frigidarium *in background. Inset shows detail of armchair voussoirs remaining* in situ. *Slots for similar armchair voussoirs are visible in the* frigidarium *wall (photos L.C. Lancaster).*

culture via a kind of social network. Villas were venues for social interactions, and along with dining rooms, these small private baths provided luxurious spaces in which to entertain. Thus, word of mouth could have played a role in the uptake of the technique, especially along the Garonne valley where examples are numerous. However, a difficulty in tracing the diffusion and its mechanisms is that so many of the examples cannot be precisely dated.

The distribution of armchair voussoirs in Britain and Mauretania represents a different situation from France and provides more insight into production due to the greater use of tile stamps. In Britain, a majority of the armchair voussoirs occurs in military contexts (Fig. 3.9). At three sites – York, Bainton, and Durobrivae – the voussoirs bore the stamps of the *legio IX Hispana*, which was stationed at York from about 71 CE to sometime between 109–20 CE (Challands 1975, 21, fig. 9; Woodfield and Johnson 1989, 252). Auxiliary units also appear to have produced the armchair voussoirs. Unstamped examples were found at a workshop at Grimscar, in Yorkshire, along with roof tiles stamped by the *cohors IIII Breucorum*, a Pannonian auxiliary unit (Purdy and Manby 1973, 101–2, fig. 3), which had probably joined the *legio IX Hispana* for the 43 CE invasion (Spaul 2000, 322). During the first quarter of the second century, this workshop supplied the nearby fort at Slack. Examples of the same distinctive form of armchair voussoir have been found at both sites (Fig. 3.9). Other armchair voussoirs from the same period occur at a military kiln at Ravenglass (Woodfield and Johnson 1989, 252), at a small bath outside the fort at Ribchester (Bellhouse 1960, 9), and at four sites along Hadrian's Wall – Segedunum (Burnham 2002, 292), Cilurnum, Vindolanda, and Aesica (MacDonald 1931, 278–84).

In Britain, technological know-how could have come from Spain and southern Gaul, where the technique first proliferated. During the first century many of the provincial legionaries came from Roman colonies in Spain and Gaul (Birley 1980, 82–83). For example, we know of L. Duccius Rufinus of the *legio IX Hispana* who was from Vienne (*RIB* 673) and was buried at York. Middle ranking officers, especially centurions, were often involved in military building projects, such as those working on the construction of Hadrian's Wall, some of whom have the *gentilicia* of well-known colonial families from Spain and Gaul (Birley 1980, 77). In Pannonia, armchair voussoirs occur at the auxiliary camp at Zalalövő (Woodfield and Johnson 1989, 252) and at the second/third-century public baths at Budapest (Hampel 1890, 72, fig. 1.4), where fragments of tiles were found with the stamps of the *legio II Augusta* (Fig. 3.9). In the latter case, the military seems to have supplied material for a civilian project. Here too, movements of soldiers could explain the presence of armchair voussoirs so far from other concentrations. For example, we know of a veteran from the *ala I Pannoniorum Tampiana* (*CIL* XVI, 69) in Britain who earned his diploma in 122 CE and returned home to Brigetio where his diploma was found (Birley 1980, 93–94). Less easily traced are members of the extended military community, who could have come with their own technological knowledge acquired in their home territory.

The distribution of the armchair voussoirs in Mauretania Tingitana (modern Morocco) (Fig. 3.9) opens another window onto the relationship between tile production, urbanization, and the role of the state. The armchair voussoirs in Tingitana are largely associated with public baths from the second and third centuries CE (Camporeale 2015, 148–51), and they usually occur together with other types of specialized wall heating tiles which are only found in Tingitana and across the strait in Baetica (Fig. 3.11). Some of the armchair voussoirs in Tingitana bear imperial stamps: EX FIGVL CAES *ex figul(inis) Caes(aris)*; IMP AVG *Imp(eratoris) Aug(usti)*; ANTO AVG *Anto(nini) Aug(usti)* (Camporeale 2015, with bibliography). Those from a workshop at Gandori, outside of Tangiers, are particularly suggestive for the possible connection between military and imperial production. They were found together with roof tiles and wall bricks bearing the imperial stamp HADRI AVG *Hadri(ani) Aug(usti)* (the earliest of the datable imperial stamps) while others bore a military stamp, C∞ *c(ohors) ((milliaria))* (Ponsich 1970, 265–71), which probably refers to the *cohors II Syrorum milliaria equitata sagittaria civium Romanorum* (Spaul 2000, 419–20).[7] The same military stamp was found further south at Thamusida on a brick in a wall of the barracks (second half of first century CE). Archaeometric analysis indicates that the fabric is not local, which suggests that they were probably transported from the area around Tangiers. If the C∞ stamps found at Gandori also date to the first century, it could be that the

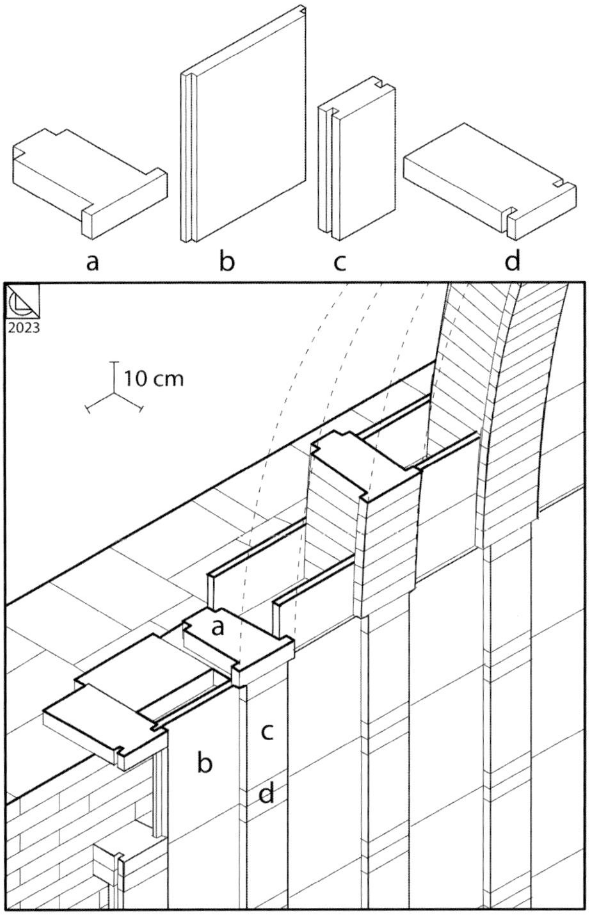

Fig. 3.11. Author's hypothetical reconstruction of wall heating system and armchair voussoirs used in Tingitana and Baetica (image L.C. Lancaster, based on Camporeale 2008, figs 4–5).

military workshop active in the first century became imperial property by the time of Hadrian (Camporeale 2015, 153). In Britain, tiles bearing both imperial stamps and military stamps have been found in the same workshop (but not on armchair voussoirs) at the fort at Carlisle and at the nearby military tilery at Scalesceugh (Warry 2010, 142). These examples thus raise questions regarding the relationship between military and imperial properties in supplying tiles.

Important to note is that armchair voussoirs and the special wall heating tiles (Fig. 3.11) that typically accompanied them (possibly for creating heated vaults) were not introduced into Tingitana by the military because, as we saw above, they had already been used during the first century across the Strait of Gibraltar around Carteia in the Puente Grande villa, a civilian context. Regardless of what entity was supplying the tiles for baths in Tingitana, the builders were using a local heating system that had been developed in southern Spain and remained used largely in the area known as the 'Circle of the Strait' (for other local building innovations, see contributions in this volume by Russell *et al.* and by Vitti).

Hollow voussoirs

The second vaulting technique is the use of hollow voussoirs, which have a much more restricted distribution, mainly in Britain with scattered examples in northern Gaul and Germany (Fig. 3.12). Armchair voussoirs and hollow voussoirs have sometimes been considered alternative methods of creating heated vaults, but as I hope to have shown, the armchair voussoir system developed from early attempts to protect wooden roof structures and probably retained that purpose throughout its life cycle, even if some of the vaults could have been heated. The hollow voussoir vault, to the contrary, was part of the heating system from its inception during the second half of the first century CE in southern Britain. The idea for heating vaults had already appeared in Italy as demonstrated by the *tegulae mammatae* that are still attached to the vault of the women's *caldarium* of the Stabian Baths at Pompeii (Schween 1936, 23; Jorio 1978–79, 179) (Fig. 3.13) and in the *caldarium* of the Suburban Baths at Herculaneum (Maiuri 1958, 150, 162–65). At the Stabian Baths, the vault heating was installed either in the Augustan renovation or in the repairs after the earthquake of 62 CE (M. Trümper, pers. comm.; for phase plan, see Trümper *et al.* 2022, 221, fig. 2). Given the narrow air space they created (c. 6 cm), the heating capacity of the baths was probably not greatly enhanced, but the system may have provided some insulation and reduced condensation. In contrast, the hollow voussoirs used together with box-tiles would have provided for more air circulation and greater efficiency as a result of convection (on convection in box-tiles: Yegül and Couch 2003).

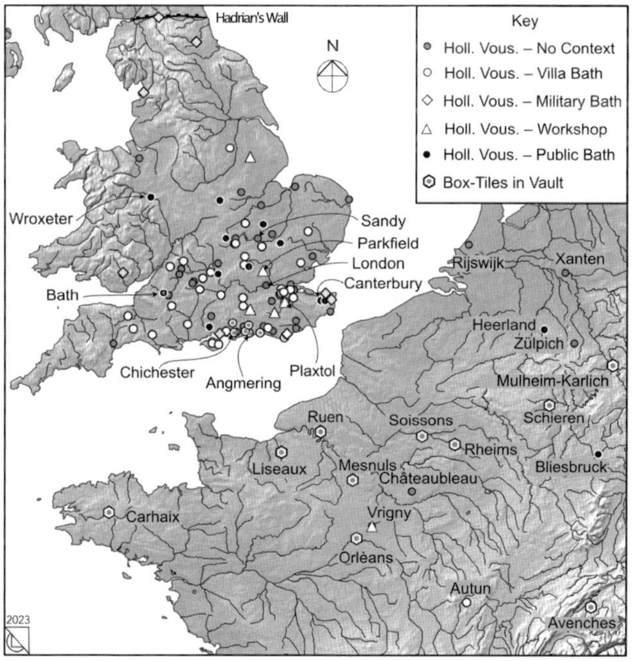

Fig. 3.12. Map showing distribution of hollow voussoirs and box-tile vaults (image L.C. Lancaster).

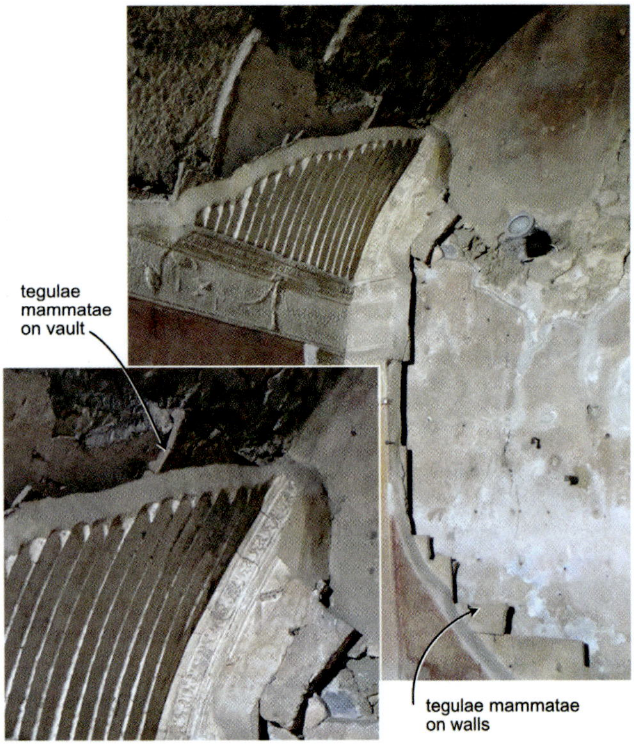

Fig. 3.13. Women's caldarium *of the Stabian Baths at Pompeii showing the* tegulae mammatae *on the walls and vault (photo L.C. Lancaster).*

The earliest type of hollow voussoir has been dubbed the 'Westhampnett' voussoir because examples were found reused in a church at Westhampnett, just outside of Chichester in West Sussex. It has a distinctive shape with semicircular cut-outs in the sides, which form circular vents when tiles are placed side by side (Fig. 3.14). This type of voussoir is noteworthy in that the workshop in which it was invented can be identified because of the use of a distinctive clay fabric (MOLS Fabric 3054) and the stamped patterns applied with a series of wooden roller dies (Betts *et al.* 1997, 19–20) (Fig. 3.15). The Westhampnett voussoir was made and used together with an unusual type of double flue box-tile (Fig. 3.14), which has the same type of semicircular cut-outs and bears the same stamped patterns as the voussoirs. The Westhampnett voussoir and other bath tiles bearing the same stamps have a regional distribution in Sussex in southern Britain (Fig. 3.12), although numerous examples have also been found in London albeit without context (Betts *et al.* 1997, 92–98); hence the products of this workshop have been dubbed the 'London-Sussex' group. The workshop was probably located in the environs of Chichester, where finds are densest, but the site has not been identified. The examples found with other datable finds indicate that this workshop was active during the Flavian period (Lancaster 2012, 424, with bibliography).[8]

Most of the Westhampnett voussoirs and the double flue box-tiles exist only as fragments in various museum collections, but at the villa at Angmering the tiles were found *in situ* which allows for a reasonable reconstruction (Fig. 3.14). The double flue box-tiles occurred in two variations: one rectangular and one hourglass shaped. Drawings and photographs show that the hourglass type was set perpendicular to the wall and embedded into it to form a type of dovetail joint, with the rectangular ones then set in between (Fig. 3.14 inset lower left). The wall was built up together with the box-tiles, which is unlike a typical bath where the wall was built first and the box-tiles attached with mortar and sometimes fixed with T-shaped nails. The box-tiles from this workshop are found predominantly in villas, including the luxurious residence at Fishbourne just outside Chichester. The workshop seems to have specialized in tiles for building baths, and the integration of the double flue box-tiles into the fabric of the structure implies that the workshop may have also had a hand in the design and construction of the baths (Betts *et al.* 1997, 52).

From the beginning, the use of this bath heating system in well-appointed villas suggests that its creation was part of the movement by the local wealthy elite to embellish their country residences as a means of expressing their *romanitas*. In the area around Chichester, the locals had already begun to adopt the trappings of Roman culture even before the invasion in 43 CE (Mattingly 2006, 76, 83, 387–89). We do not know the names of owners of the villas employing the new heating system, but studies of villa development in Sussex and elsewhere in southern Britain suggest a pattern of continuity with pre-existing roundhouses on many sites, which implies that there was generally no break in property control after the conquest (Taylor 2011, 182–83).

A few of the voussoirs have graffiti which provide some additional insight into the ethnicity of the tilemakers. Two, built into the Westhampnett church, bear CALVI and TFP, while three others with BIIL were found reused in a fourth-century CE bath at the Batten Hanger villa near Elsted (Lancaster 2015, fig. 100). R.S.O. Tomlin (2012, 421) has interpreted the first as the genitive of Calvus, a fairly typical Latin *cognomen*, and TFP as possibly indicating the *tria nomina* of *T(itus) F(lavius) P(---)*, a reading which would suggest a person who had recently received Roman citizenship under the Flavians (*RIB* II.5, 2491.126).[9] The BIIL graffito can be read as the prefix Bel-, which is typical of Celtic names, such as Bellicus and Belinatepus among others but not of Latin names (Tomlin 2012, 411). The only roller stamp (dies 31/59) to incorporate the name of a tile maker appears in the mid-second century on hollow voussoirs of Cabriabanus (a Celtic name) (Fig. 3.16), who was working in Kent. The die, crudely cut with some backwards letters and a misspelling, bears the Latin '*parietalem Cabriabanu(s) farbicavi* [*sic*!]' (the last word is a misspelling of *fabricavi*), which translates to 'I Cabriabanus made this wall tile' (Betts *et al.* 1997, 44). His Latin was not perfect, but he was clearly proud of his craft.

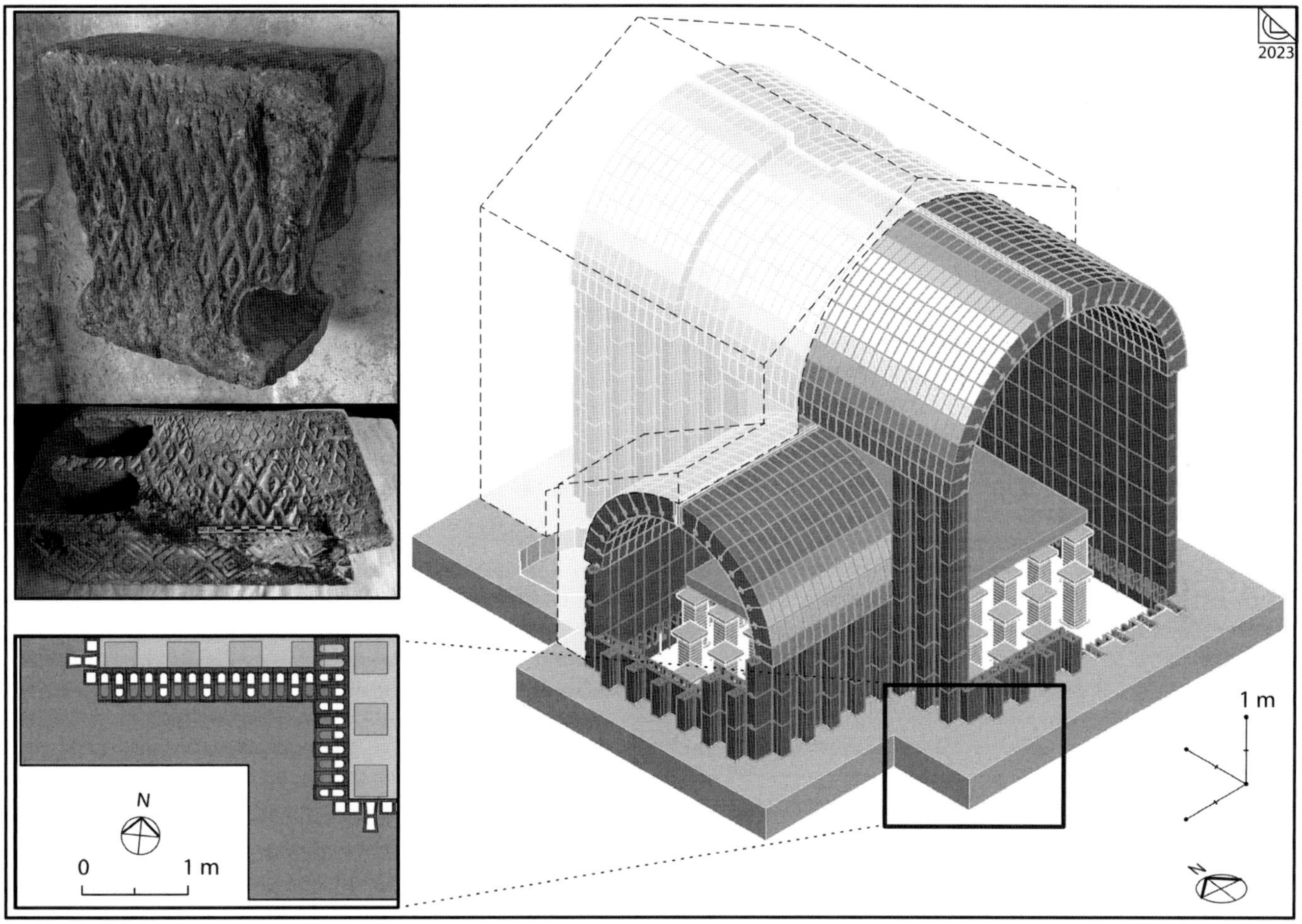

Fig. 3.14. Upper left: Westhampnett voussoir with die 21 and double flue box-tile from Angmering, with die 21 on the face and die 19 on the side (Barbican House, Lewes, accession #1953.16). Lower left: Detail drawing showing relationship between wall tiles and vault tiles. Right: Reconstruction of the caldarium *of the Angmering bath (image L.C. Lancaster, based on Scott 1938, figs 11–12).*

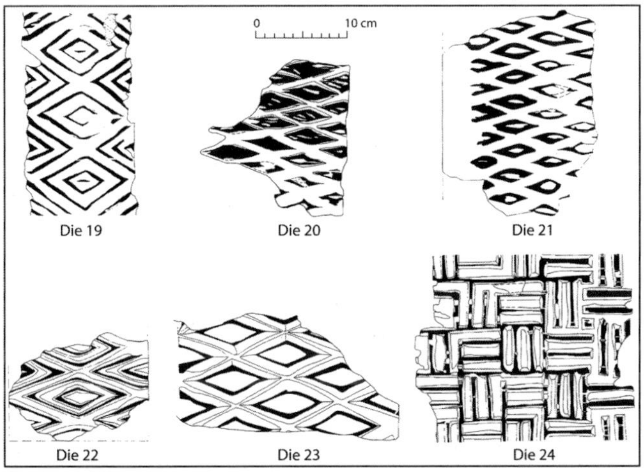

Fig. 3.15. Roller stamps used by 'London-Sussex' workshop (from Betts et al. *1994; die drawings courtesy of the Relief-Patterned Tile Research Group).*

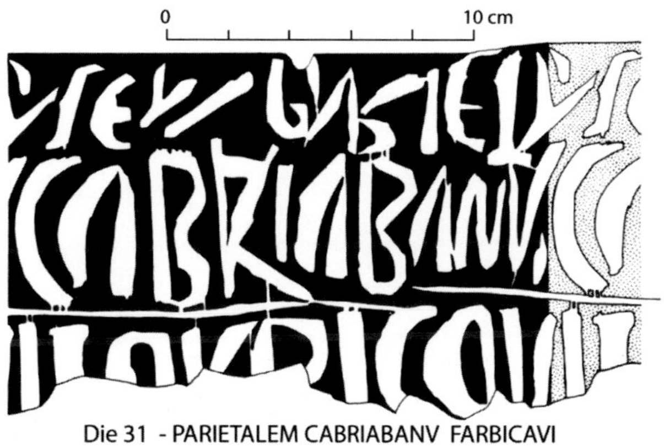

Fig. 3.16. Roller stamp die 31 of Cabriabanus (from Betts et al. *1994; die drawings courtesy of the Relief-Patterned Tile Research Group).*

The use of roller stamps to mark the tiles is another Gallic trait. This workshop is among the earliest to have used this stamping technique on tiles. The technique was based on the earlier use of roller stamps to prepare wattle-and-daub walls by providing a rough surface for a finish coat of plaster (Russell 1997, 47–50). Examples of patterned daub were found in the destruction levels of Boudica's revolt, which provides a *terminus ante quem* of 60/61 CE for the use of roller stamped daub in Britain, so it likely predates the roller stamped tiles.[10] The use of roller stamps on tiles appears to have been used for the same purpose. It occurs primarily on box-tiles and hollow voussoirs and was only applied to the sides that were to be covered with plaster. The advantage of roller stamping rather than combing, which is more common, is that the tiles could have been laid out side by side and rolled continuously rather than having to comb each individually. Some examples of box-tiles even display the joint where two passes of the roller met (Fig. 3.17).

The stamping method probably came from the Continent, where numerous examples of roller stamped daub are known, one of which, at Cologne, dates to the early to mid-first century CE (Thomas 1993, 277, fig. 115; see Lancaster 2015, 215, n. 3 for further examples). A different use of roller stamps appeared in Spain during the Flavian period. At Mérida (Barrientos Vera and Guiral Pelegrin 2007) and Cartagena Nova (Fernández Díaz 2007, 178–79, fig. 7), they were used to create decorative stucco reliefs. The designs consisted of repeating floral patterns combined with diamond patterns similar to those on the tiles in Britain. The idea for using roller stamps on clay walls, tiles, and stucco may have its roots in Gallic pottery workshops, where much smaller roller stamps were used to decorate pottery with marks forming diamond patterns. Examples date as far back as the first half of the first century BCE (Déchelette 1927, 991, fig. 679; Lancaster 2015, 150) (Fig. 3.18). The use of the roller stamps eventually came to Britain with the migration of construction workers across the English Channel once sites, especially London, underwent extensive building campaigns (Betts 1995, 222–25; Russell 1997, 50).

Fig. 3.17. Box-tile with die 71 in situ *at Billingsgate Bath, London (photo L.C. Lancaster). Note the vertical joint between the two passes of the roller in the centre of the tile.*

Hollow voussoirs spread throughout Britain during the second century, and a few continued to bear roller stamps, although the stamps were more often found on box-tiles; nevertheless, a study of fabric analysis together with the roller dies used on hollow voussoirs provides some insight into their production and distribution. The evidence suggests that there were some itinerant tile makers who specialized in box-tiles and hollow voussoirs. For example, die 32 (Fig. 3.19), which was only used on hollow voussoirs, is found on examples from Sandy and from Parkfield (50 km away) in different fabrics at each site, which implies that the person using it was travelling between sites with his die and using different clays in each place (Betts *et al.* 1997, 33). Other dies from Kent in southern Britain suggest that sharing kiln facilities was not uncommon. Hollow voussoirs of Cabriabanus (die 31/59, mentioned above) have been found at two villas in Plaxtol, one of which had an associated kiln (2.4 × 1.8 m) which produced tiles of the same fabric. Another example of die 31/59 was found 18 km away at a villa at Darenth, and another was found

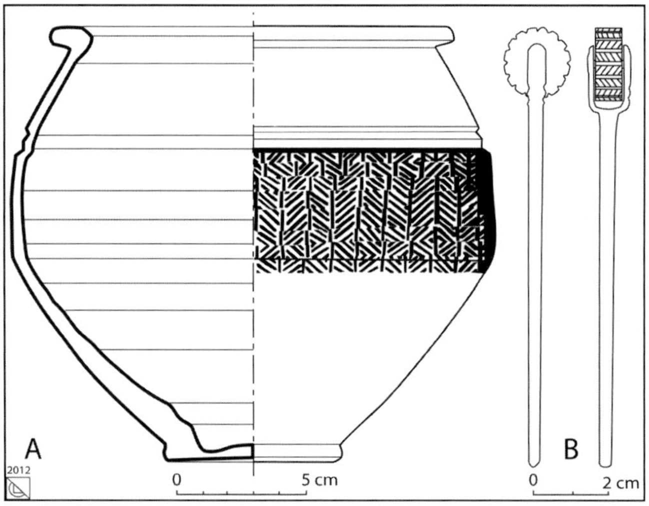

Fig. 3.18. A: Gallo-Belgic ware with roller-stamped decoration (40–110 CE) (after Santrot and Santrot 1979, pl. 55, no. 250c). B: Bronze roller die with handle (Rouen Museum, provenance unknown) (after Ferdière 1972, 133–34, no. 10).

Fig. 3.19. Roller stamp die 32 (from Betts et al. *1994; die drawings courtesy of the Relief-Patterned Tile Research Group).*

in London at Bishopsgate. Moreover, voussoir fragments in the same fabric but bearing a different roller stamp (die 73), also crudely cut, were found at other villas in Kent at Lullingstone and Chalk and again at Bishopsgate. These hollow voussoirs, which were made in the same fabric but each bearing a different stamp, suggest that two voussoir makers were using the same clay and kiln facilities. However, other box-tiles and hollow voussoirs from the same kiln were made in the same fabric but marked with a comb, which suggests that these two voussoir makers could have been sharing resources with other makers (Davies 2004, 175). Kiln sharing amongst different makers is also attested in pottery workshops in Gaul (Peacock 1982, 125–26) and North Africa (Mackensen 2009, 38). Kiln operation was a specialist task. Indeed, at terra sigillata workshops at La Graufesenque some of the graffiti found scratched into plates name *cassidani* or *flamines*, which refer to kiln masters in charge of the firing (Dannell 2002, 222). When a firing went bad it was a financial blow to potters and tilemakers alike, so having a skilled kiln operator was some insurance against disaster.

Unlike the armchair voussoirs in Britain, the hollow voussoirs only rarely appear in military contexts (Fig. 3.12). One explanation is that the hollow voussoirs had to be made to measure because the wedged shape of each voussoir was determined by the defining arc of each vault. In contrast, the armchair voussoirs were much thinner and could be used on vaults of varying sizes by modulating the mortar joint thickness (as seen at Badalona) (Fig. 3.8). The kit-like character of the armchair voussoirs was much better suited to the military mentality. The bespoke aspect of the hollow voussoirs may also explain why they were sometimes made by itinerant tile-makers – they required greater skill and patience to fabricate as well as some knowledge of the context in which they would be used. Over half of the hollow voussoirs in Britain with identifiable contexts (n=73) come from villas. As with the armchair voussoirs in Gaul they appear to have been part of the expansion of villa culture which followed urbanization.

The hollow voussoirs have also been found sporadically on the Continent, although more are coming to light as more material is documented and published. Those that are known so far occur mainly in northern and central Gaul and Germany (eight examples) (Fig. 3.12).[11] The distribution is notable for two reasons. First, these are the regions that were most directly connected culturally with Britain. Second, the examples occur in areas of northern Europe with a climate similar to Britain with high average humidity (>75%) and low average temperatures (<11°C) where a heated ceiling could be advantageous.

Whether the extrados of the hollow voussoir vaults was left bare or covered by a layer of mortar would have greatly affected their efficacy. Evidence is sparse, but it suggests that the extrados was covered by at least a layer of mortar and in some cases by a concrete fill above. The additional masonry would have acted as insulation to retain the heat, which could improve fuel efficiency and help to prevent excessive expansion and cracking of the vault (Lancaster 2012, 140–41). Any desire to reduce fuel was probably not due to lack of availability, as there was no dearth of wood in these areas. A more critical factor may have been the costs of acquiring and transporting the fuel to the site (DeLaine 2020, 90).

The hollow voussoirs are sometimes said to have been intended to lighten the vault, but most of the vaults are quite small (avg. 3.6 m). As noted earlier, the weight of a vault is not a structural concern until the span reaches about 5 m. The spans reconstructed from the remains of voussoirs reveal that most are under 5 m (Fig. 3.20). However, their presence in a few very large vaults (second/third century CE) – including those at Canterbury (9.5 m), Wroxeter (9.6 m), and Bath (13.6 m) (Lancaster 2015, 142–43, 184–87) – shows that they could be used for structural reasons, as with the armchair voussoirs used for the large vaults at Cimiez and Fréjus.

On the Continent, a parallel phenomenon to the hollow voussoirs is the use of box-tiles to construct vaults (Fig. 3.12).[12] These occur exclusively in bath ceilings. In at least two examples they were used to create cross vaults with the box-tiles being aligned along the diagonal groins – in Rouen over a cold pool (Barbet 2021, 21, fig. 18; Barbet and Lefèvre 2007, 430, fig. 3) and in Schiering, Luxembourg over a heated room (Biver *et al.* 2016, 58, fig. 13; 2020, 225). Like the double-layer armchair voussoirs, they may have provided some insulation value even if they were not heated. Dating is often ambiguous, but most seem to have been built in the second and third centuries. Their distribution in northern Europe coincides roughly with that of the hollow voussoirs, which suggests that the box-tiles may represent an easier-to-make, unheated version.

The use of the roller stamps on the earliest hollow voussoirs in Britain emphasizes its connection with Gaul as the builders, tile makers, and potters came into Britain after the Claudian invasion of 43 CE (Tyers 1996, 51–53). The spread of the hollow voussoirs (without the roller stamping) to the

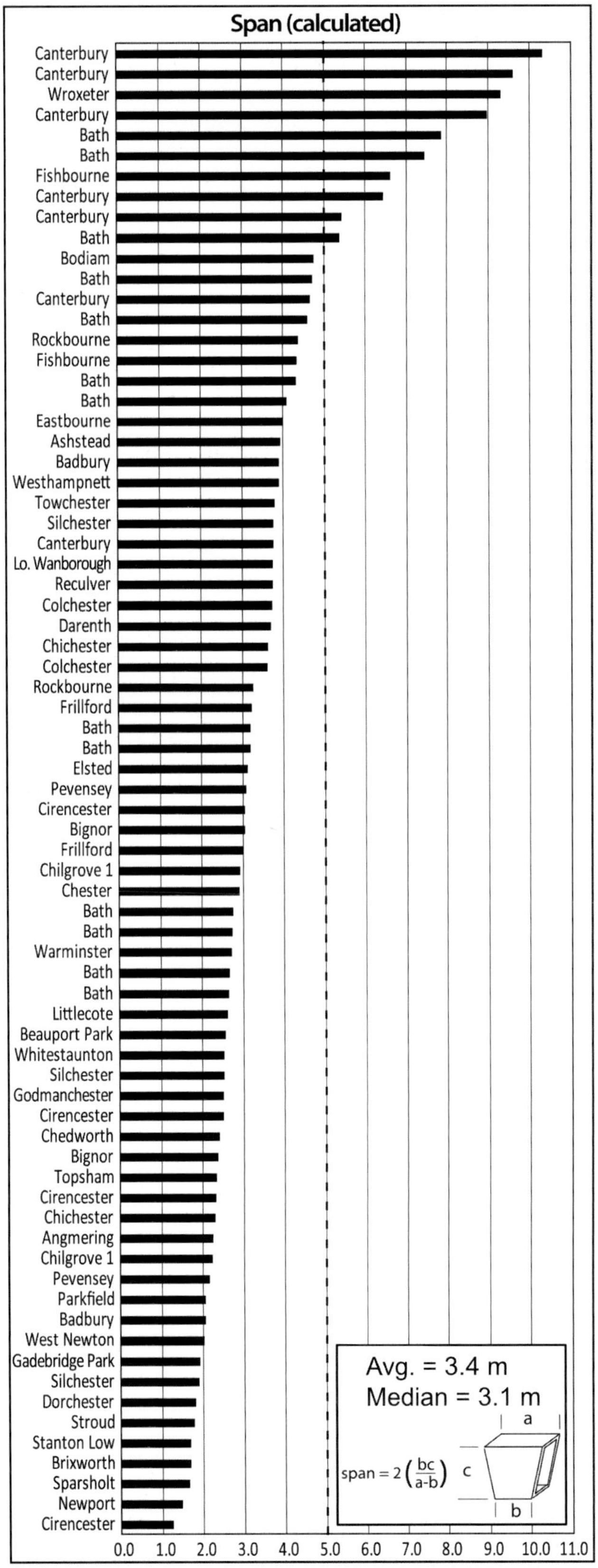

Fig. 3.20. Chart of vault spans calculated from extant hollow voussoirs in Britain using formula shown in inset (image L.C. Lancaster).

Continent could have been due to itinerant or immigrating tilemakers who travelled back across the Channel in the following centuries. This is also implied by the presence during the second half of the second century CE of the rare use of roller stamps outside of Britain (albeit on flat tiles) at 11 sites in a 30 km radius around Frankfurt, Germany (Baatz 1988; Lancaster 2015, 148).

Conclusions

Examining the use and distribution of these two vaulting techniques has highlighted the various catalysts behind their diffusion to different places. The armchair voussoir has a longer period of development, and its pattern of diffusion is more complex. The motivation for the initial development of the armchair bars from as early as the third century BCE (Fregellae) seems to have come from the need to create a waterproof ceiling to protect the wooden superstructure in the hot rooms of baths, an issue noted by Vitruvius (*De arch.* 5.10.3). The later versions using armchair voussoirs instead of the bars probably had a similar function, but the new method was much more flexible and could be used for rooms of different spans, so the tiles could be mass-produced and distributed, as shown by the armchair voussoirs of Clarianus and Quietus. The armchair voussoirs became particularly common in small villa baths, especially along the Garonne valley in France where workshops producing them have also been found (Fig. 3.9 inset). The earliest uses in Morocco and Spain tended to be in public baths during a period of intense urbanization. In Britain, the armchair voussoirs were used in both villas and in many military contexts. Once the idea spread, the technique became a kind of vault building kit that could be applied in a variety of situations. The centring necessary for building the individual ribs would have been much simpler to construct than that required for a heavy mortared rubble vault, and the curved form of the ceiling was ideal for channelling the condensation towards the sides of the room, a concern also mentioned by Vitruvius (*De arch.* 8.2.4). Ultimately it provided a quick and efficient method of constructing the ceilings in bath buildings.

The hollow voussoirs have a different story to tell. They are an invention of the second half of the first century CE. Current evidence suggests that they were first used in southern Britain and London. The roller stamped tiles from the bath at Angmering show that one workshop made the hollow tiles for both wall and vault, which together seem to have worked as a unified heating system. Later in the second century, some of the roller stamps on voussoirs suggest the presence of itinerant voussoir makers who travelled between sites and took part in communal firings with other makers.

The hollow voussoirs have a distribution concentrated in Britain, especially in villas, with examples also in Gallia and Germany. A factor in the limited distribution was no doubt the more time-consuming fabrication along with the necessity of designing the units for specific contexts. The hollow voussoirs were more suited to itinerant tile makers who could ply their trade near the construction site. The diffusion of the hollow voussoirs onto the Continent probably came from movement of the tile makers themselves, but given the lack of stamps on those from the Continent, such movements are difficult to trace. The use of box-tiles on the Continent to build small bath vaults may be a later offshoot of the hollow voussoirs.

Finally, we can see the significance of cross-industry knowledge exchange in architectural innovation. At Fregellae, the type of lead clamps used to join the armchair bars suggests that the craftsmen who made and/or repaired pottery could have had a role in developing the vault system. In Britain, the workshop using the London-Sussex group of roller tiles appears to have had an active role in developing the Westhampnett voussoir and the bath heating system of which it was a part. The tilemakers borrowed the idea of roller stamps from the builders who used them on daub, although the same die is never found on both media. In Spain, the roller stamps were used for decorative purposes to mould stucco during the Flavian period, which is also when they were being used on tiles in Britain. Ultimately, the use of roller stamps in architectural settings may have come from Gallic pottery workshops where small roller stamps had already been used for over a century to create similar diamond patterns as found on daub, stucco, and tiles. Thus, the analysis of these two techniques reveals the myriad of factors underlying the spread of technical knowledge within the western Empire and underscores the importance of looking at regional patterns and across craft disciplines.

Notes

1. This chapter has benefitted greatly from conversations with Benjamin Clément, Janet DeLaine, Francesca Diosono, Alain Ferdière, Norbert Hanel, Ian Haynes, Zoltán Havas, Martin Millet, E.J. Shepherd, R.S.O. Tomlin, Peter Warry, and Monica Trümper. For permission to examine tiles, I am grateful to Esther Gurri of the Badalona Museum and Emma O'Connor at Barbican House at Lewes.
2. Fabiani and Paribeni 2016, 82–83 suggest that iron clamps were used and fixed with lead, but any clamps would have been added at the site so there is no evidence for the nature of the clamps from the Massa workshop.
3. Details of the lead clamps from Fregellae have not been published and I have not examined them personally.
4. I thank Giovanni Polizzi for showing me the fragments of bars found in his excavation of the North Baths.
5. A similar sized circular *laconicum* at Akrai, Sicily also has a series of recesses around the wall, one of which still has a piece of terracotta lodged in it, but I was not able to examine its form; however, I know of no terracotta bars reported from the site.
6. The drawing in Figure 3.2 places the façade columns based on Tsiolis 2001, fig. 3; 2006, fig. 3, but Tsiolis 2013, fig. 2 shows one of the columns in a different location.
7. Roxan (1973, 847) suggests that the cohort was reduced to a quingenary unit after 122 CE to explain why it is no longer designated as '*milliaria*'.
8. Fulford and Machin (2021, 209) suggest the possibility of a slightly earlier date for their use.
9. I thank R.S.O. Tomlin for the suggested interpretation of TFP in our correspondence.
10. Fulford and Machin (2021) recently reported finding Nero-stamped tiles alongside roller stamped tiles in the waste from a kiln at Little London, which does not appear to have continued beyond the early Flavian period. They suggest that the earliest roller stamped tiles could have predated Boudica's revolt.
11. Lancaster 2015, fig. 87 showed a distribution map with only two examples (Xanten, Bliesbruck), but since then six more Continental examples have been published (Ferdière and Jaffrot 2015, 535–38, with bibliography).
12. For bibliography on these vaults constructed with box-tiles, see Barbet and Lefèvre 2007, 430–32; Biver *et al.* 2020, 225; Barbet 2021, 21.

References

Baatz, D. 1988. Verkleidungsziegel mit Rollstempelmustern aus Südhessen. *Saalburg Jahrbuch* 44: 65–83.

Balmelle, C. 2001. *Les demeures aristocratiques d'Aquitaine: Société et culture de l'antiquité tardive dans le sud-ouest de la Gaule*. Bordeaux: Ausonius Éditions.

Barbet, A. 2021. *Coupoles, voûtes et plafonds peints d'époque romaine: Ier–IVe siècle apr. J.-C.* Paris: Éditions Hermann.

Barbet, A. and Lefèvre, J.F. 2007. Peinture d'une piscine froide de Rouen. Station Métrobus, palais de justice. In Guiral Pelegrín, C. (ed.), *Circulación de temas y sistemas decorativos en la pintura mural antiqua. Actas del IX Congreso internacional de la Association internationale pour la peinture murale antique – AIPMA (Zaragoza, Calatayud, 21–25 septiembre 2004)*. Calatayud: Gobierno de Aragon, Departamento de Politica Territorial, Justicia e Interior; Universidad Nacional de Educacion a Distancia, 429–32.

Barrientos Vera, T. and Guiral Pelegrin, C. 2007. La decoración en relieve de Mérida: un taller del s. I d.C. In Guiral Pelegrín, C. (ed.), *Circulación de temas y sistemas decorativos en la pintura mural antiqua. Actas del IX Congreso internacional de la Association internationale pour la peinture murale antique – AIPMA (Zaragoza, Calatayud, 21–25 septiembre 2004)*. Calatayud: Gobierno de Aragon, Departamento de Politica Territorial, Justicia e Interior; Universidad Nacional de Educacion a Distancia, 165–72.

Barti, A., Plana, R. and Tremoleda, J. 2004. *Llafranc romà*. Palafrugell: Diputació de Girona.

Bellhouse, R.L. 1960. Excavations in Eskdale: the Muncaster Roman kilns. *Transactions of the Cumberland Westmoreland Antiquarian and Archaeological Society* n.s. 60: 1–12.

Benoit, F. 1977. *Cimiez, la ville antique*. Paris: De Boccard.

Betts, I.M. 1995. Procuratorial tile stamps from London. *Britannia* 26: 207–29.

Betts, I.M., Black, E.W. and Gower, J.L. (eds) 1997. *A Corpus of Relief-Patterned Tiles in Roman Britain*. Oxford: Oxbow Books.

Birley, A. 1980. *The People of Roman Britain*. Berkeley: University of California Press.

Biver, V., Stead, A.J. and Polfer, M. 2016. La villa gallo-romaine de Schieren (Luxembourg). *Archaeologia Luxemburgensis* 3: 42–62.

Biver, V., Groetembril, S., Lefèvre, J.F. and Lemoigne, L. 2020. Villa de Schieren (Grand-Duché de Luxembourg). Hercule, amours et compagnie. In Boislève, J. and Monier, F. (eds), *Peintures et stucs d'époque romaine: Études toichographologiques. Actes du 30e colloque de l'AFPMA (Arles, 24 et 25 novembre 2017)*. Bordeaux: Ausonius Éditions, 209–30.

Bouet, A. 1999. *Les matériaux de construction en terre cuite dans les thermes de la Gaule Narbonnaise*. Paris: De Boccard.

Bouet, A. 2003. *Les thermes privés et publics en Gaule Narbonnaise, Vol. 2*. Rome: École française de Rome.

Bouet, A. 2006. Chapitre II: Les thermes du nord. In Bats, M. (ed.), *Olbia de Provence (Hyères, Var) à l'époque romaine (Ier s. av. J.-C.–VIIe s. ap. J.-C.)*. Aix-en-Provence: Édisud, 65–68.

Buffat, L. 2011. *L'économie domaniale en Gaule Narbonnaise*. Lattes: Association pour le developpement de l'archéologie en Languedoc-Roussillon.

Burnham, B.C. 2002. Roman Britain in 2001. England: Hadrian's Wall. *Britannia* 33: 290–98.

Camporeale, S. 2008. La tipologia dei laterizi. In Akerraz, A. and Papi, E. (eds), *Sidi Ali ben Ahmed – Thamusida, 1. I contesti*. Rome: Quasar, 179–97.

Camporeale, S. 2015. I laterizi della Mauretania Tingitana. Materiali per una tipologia. In Bukowiecki, E., Volpe, R. and Wulf-Rheidt, U. (eds), *Il laterizio nei cantieri imperiali. Roma e il Mediterraneo. Atti del I workshop 'Laterizio' (Roma, 27–28 novembre 2014)*. Florence: All'Insegna del Giglio, 145–57.

Chabal, L., Figueiral, I., Pellecuer, C. and Bermond, I. 2012. Evidence of palaeogeographic constraints on woodlands on the shores of a coastal lagoon during antiquity. Charcoal analysis of the Prés-Bas Villa and Le Bourbou (Loupian, Hérault). In Badal, E., Carrión, Y., Macías, M. and Ntinou, M. (eds), *Wood and Charcoal. Evidence for Human and Natural History*. Valencia: Universitat de València, 115–24.

Challands, A. 1975. Two Roman stamped tiles from the Peterborough area. *Durobrivae* 3: 20–21.

Charmasson, J. 2003. Les thermes de l'oppidum de Gaujac (Gard). *Revue archéologique de Narbonnaise* 36: 133–76.

Cheung, C. 2021. Precious pots: making and repairing dolia. In Hochscheid, H. and Russell, B. (eds), *The Value of Making: Theory and Practice in Ancient Craft Production*. Turnhout: Brepols, 171–88.

Clément, B. 2015. Approvisionnement et organisation de la production de terre cuite architecturale en Gaule. L'exemple de la colonie de Lugdunum (Lyon). In Bukowiecki, E., Volpe, R. and Wulf-Rheidt, U. (eds), *Il laterizio nei cantieri imperiali. Roma e il Mediterraneo. Atti del I workshop 'Laterizio' (Roma, 27–28 novembre 2014)*. Florence: All'Insegna del Giglio, 158–67.

Dannell, G.B. 2002. Law and practice: further thoughts on the organization of the potteries at la Graufesenque. In Genin, M. and Vernhet, A. (eds), *Céramiques de la Graufesenque et autres productions d'époque romaine. Nouvelles recherches*. Montagnac: Éditions Mergoil, 211–42.

Davies, M. 2004. Cabriabanus. A Romano-British tile craftsman in Kent. *Archaeologia Cantiana* 124: 163–82.

Déchelette, J. 1927. *Manuel d'archéologie préhistorique, celtique et gallo-romaine. Tome 4: Second âge du fer ou époque de La Tène (deuxième édition)*. Paris: A. Picard.

DeLaine, J. 2020. Strategies and technologies of environmental manipulation in the Roman world: the thermal economy of baths. In Schliephake, C., Sojc, N. and Weber, G. (eds), *Nachhaltigkeit in der Antike: Diskurse, Praktiken, Perspektiven*. Stuttgart: Franz Steiner Verlag, 75–93.

Fabiani, F., and Paribeni, E. 2016. *Archeologia a Massa. Scavi all'ombra del Mercurio*. Rome: Edizioni Nuova Cultura.

Ferdière, A. 1972. Notes de céramologie de la Région Centre (supplément à la note n° 2 – molette de potier). *Revue archéologique du Centre de la France* 11.1–2: 132–37.

Ferdière, A. and Jaffrot, É. 2015. Tuiles en écaille et quelques autres types originaux de terres cuites architecturales de Gaule centrale et septentrionale. In Raux, S., Bertrand, I. and Feugère, M. (eds), *Actualité de la recherche sur les mobiliers non céramiques de l'Antiquité et du haut Moyen Âge. Actes de la table ronde européenne instrumentum (Lyon, Rhône, 18–20 octobre 2012)*. Montagnac: Éditions Mergoil, 517–52.

Fernández Díaz, A. 2007. Coexistencia de modas decorativas en la pintura mural del siglo I d.C. en el sureste peninsular. La presencia de un posible taller. In Guiral Pelegrín, C. (ed.), *Circulación de temas y sistemas decorativos en la pintura mural antiqua. Actas del IX Congreso internacional de la Association internationale pour la peinture murale antique – AIPMA (Zaragoza, Calatayud, 21–25 septiembre 2004)*. Calatayud: Gobierno de Aragon, Departamento de Politica Territorial, Justicia e Interior; Universidad Nacional de Educacion a Distancia, 173–83.

Fulford, M. and Machin, S. 2021. Building Britannia: pre-Flavian private and public construction across southern Britain. *Britannia* 52: 207–25.

Granger, F. 1931. *Vitruvius: On Architecture. Vol. I.* Cambridge, MA: Harvard University Press.

Guitart Durán, J. 1976. *Baetulo: topografía arqueológica, urbanismo e historia*. Badalona: Museo Municipal.

Guitart Durán, J. and Padrós Martí, P. 1990. Baetulo. Cronología y significación de sus monumentos. In Trillmich, W. and Zanker, P. (eds), *Stadtbild und Ideologie. Die Monumentalisierung hispanischer Städte zwischen Republik und Kaiserzeit. Kolloquium in Madrid vom 19. bis 23. Oktober 1987*. Munich: Verlag der Bayerischen Akademie der Wissenschaften, 165–75.

Hampel, J. 1890. A papföldi közfürdo. *Budapest Régiségei* 2: 51–74.

Jorio, A. 1978–79. Sistema di riscaldamento nelle antiche terme pompeiane. *Bullettino della Commissione Archeologica Comunale di Roma* 86: 167–89.

Lancaster, L.C. 2012. A new vaulting technique for early baths in Sussex: the anatomy of a Romano-British invention. *Journal of Roman Archaeology* 25: 419–40.

Lancaster, L.C. 2015. *Innovative Vaulted Construction in the Architecture of the Roman Empire: 1st to 4th Centuries CE*. Cambridge: Cambridge University Press.

Loza Lengaran, R., Loza Uriarte, M. and Niso Lorenzo, J. 2014. *Las termas romanas de Arcaya-Suestatium: memoria de las intervenciones arqueológicas en 'Otazibarra' (1976–1982)*. Vitoria-Gasteiz: Diputación Foral de Álava.

MacDonald, G. 1931. The bath-house at the fort of Chesters (Cilurnum). *Archaeologia Aeliana* (4th ser.) 8: 219–304.

Mackensen, M. 2009. Technology and organisation of ARS ware production-centres in Tunisia. In Humphrey, J. (ed.), *Studies on Roman Pottery of the Provinces of Africa Proconsularis and Byzacena (Tunisia): Hommage à Michel Bonifay*. Portsmouth, RI: Journal of Roman Archaeology Supplementary Series, 17–44.

Magallón, M.Á. and Sillières, P. 2013. *Labitolosa: la Puebla de Castro, province de Huesca, Espagne: Une cité romaine de l'Hispanie citérieure*. Bordeaux: Ausonius Éditions.

Maiuri, A. 1958. *Ercolano. I nuovi scavi (1927–1958)*. Rome: Istituto Poligrafico dello Stato, Libreria dello Stato.

Mattingly, D.J. 2006. *An Imperial Possession. Britain in the Roman Empire, 54 BC–AD 409*. London: Penguin.

Ochsendorf, J.A. 2006. The masonry arch on spreading supports. *Structural Engineer* 84.2: 29–36.

Peacock, D.P.S. 1982. *Pottery in the Roman World: An Ethnoarchaeological Approach*. London: Longman.

Ponsich, M. 1970. *Recherches archéologiques à Tanger et dans sa région*. Paris: Éditions du CNRS.

Purdy, J.G. and Manby, T.G. 1973. Excavations at the Roman tilery at Grimescar, Huddersfield. *Yorkshire Archaeological Journal* 45: 96–107.

Roxan, M. 1973. The auxilia of Mauretania Tingitana. *Latomus* 32: 838–52.

Russell, M. 1997. Relief-patterned daub. In Betts, I.M., Black, E.W. and Gower, J.L. (eds), *A Corpus of Relief-Patterned Tiles in Roman Britain*. Oxford: Oxbow Books, 47–50.

Santrot, M.-H. and Santrot, J. 1979. *Céramiques communes gallo-romaines d'Aquitaine*. Paris: Éditions du CNRS.

Schween, G. 1936. *Die Beheizungsanlage der Stabianer Thermen in Pompeji*. PhD Thesis, Technische Hochschule.

Scott, L. 1938. The Roman villa at Angmering. *Sussex Archaeological Collections* 79: 3–44.

Shepherd, E.J. 2008. Laterizi da copertura e da costruzione. In Shepherd, E.J., Capecchi, G., de Marinis, G., Mosca, F. and Patera, A. (eds), *Le fornaci del Vingone a Scandicci. Un impianto produttivo di età romana nella valle dell'Arno*. Florence: All'Insegna del Giglio, 165–200.

Spaul, J. 2000. *Cohors². The Evidence for and a Short History of the Auxiliary Infantry Units of the Imperial Roman Army*. Oxford: British Archaeological Reports.

Sposito, A. 2014. *Solunto: paesaggio, città, architettura*. Rome: 'L'Erma' di Bretschneider.

Tavares Dias, L. 1997. *Tongobriga*. Lisbon: Ministério da Cultura, Instituto Português do Património Arquitectónico.

Taylor, J. 2011. The idea of the villa: reassessing villa development in southeast Britain. In Roymans, N. and Derks, T. (eds), *Villa Landscapes in the Roman North*. Amsterdam: Amsterdam University Press, 179–94.

Thomas, R. 1993. *Römische Wandmalerei in Köln*. Mainz: Philipp von Zabern.

Tomlin, R.S.O. 2012. III. Inscriptions. *Britannia* 43: 395–421.

Tremoleda, J. 2000. *Industria y artesanado cerámico de época romana en el nordeste de Cataluña: época augústea y altoimperial*. Oxford: British Archaeological Reports.

Trümper, M. 2009. Complex public bath buildings of the Hellenistic period. A case study in regional differences. In Boussac, M.F., Fournet, T. and Redon, B. (eds), *Le bain collectif en Egypte: Balaneîa = Thermae = Hammâmât*. Cairo: Institut français d'archéologie orientale, 139–79.

Trümper, M. 2019. Development of bathing culture in Hellenistic Sicily. In Trümper, M., Adornato, G. and Lappi, T. (eds), *Cityscapes of Hellenistic Sicily. Proceedings of a Conference of the Excellence Cluster Topoi: The Formation and Transformation of Space and Knowledge in Ancient Civilizations (Berlin, 15–18 June 2017)*. Rome: Quasar, 349–93.

Trümper, M., Brunenberg, C., Esposito, D., Heide, T. and Zielke, K. 2022. The men's tepidarium of the Stabian Baths at Pompeii: quantification of its construction and remodeling processes. In Maschek, D. and Trümper, M. (eds), *Architecture and the Ancient Economy. Proceedings of a Conference Held at Berlin (26–28 September 2019)*. Rome: Quasar, 219–56.

Tsiolis, V. 2001. Las termas de Fregellae. Arquitectura, tecnología y cultura balnear en el Lacio durante los siglos III y II a.C. *Cuadernos de prehistoria y arqueología. Universidad autónoma de Madrid* 27: 85–114.

Tsiolis, V. 2006. Fregellae. Il complesso termale e le origini degli edifici balneari urbani nel mondo romano. In Torelli, M. and Osanna, M. (eds), *Sicilia ellenistica, consuetudo italica. Alle origini dell'architettura ellenistica d'Occidente (Spoleto, complesso monumentale di S. Nicolò, 5–7 novembre 2004)*. Rome: Edizioni dell'Ateneo, 243–55.

Tsiolis, V. 2013. The baths at Fregellae and the transition from balaneion to balneum. In Lucore, S.K. and Trümper, M. (eds), *Greek Baths and Bathing Culture. New Discoveries and Approaches*. Leuven: Peeters, 89–111.

Tyers, P.A. 1996. *Roman Pottery in Britain*. London: Batsford.

Warry, P. 2010. Legionary tile production in Britain. *Britannia* 41: 127–47.

Wiegand, A. 1997. *Das Theater von Solunt: ein besonderer Skenentyp des Späthellenismus auf Sizilien*. Mainz: Philipp von Zabern.

Woodfield, C. and Johnson, C. 1989. A Roman site at Stanton Low on the Great Ouse, Buckinghamshire. *Archaeological Journal* 146: 135–278.

Yegül, F.K. and Couch, T. 2003. Building a Roman bath for the cameras. *Journal of Roman Archaeology* 16: 153–77.

4

From dry to mortared construction: Building at Nikopolis and Olympia between the first century BCE and the first century CE

Paolo Vitti

Introduction

Greece experienced substantial changes during the Roman period that involved its cities, sanctuaries, and countryside. Scholarship has engaged with a wide range of research questions within the field of Roman-era architecture in Greece; however, building techniques have been constantly left aside, as it is evident when one looks at the proceedings of important conferences such as *What's New in Roman Greece?* (Di Napoli *et al.* 2018). In marked contrast to the numerous contributions on Classical- and Hellenistic-period construction (for instance, Martin 1965; Orlandos 1966; Coulton 1977), Roman-era construction in Greece has not attracted much interest, having been regarded as entirely subordinate to the development of building techniques in the Italian Peninsula. Studies like the one by Lugli (1957) have been used as the main reference for the analysis of buildings (see, for instance, the essay on brick-faced walls by Aupert 1990), thus failing to identify distinct and original regional approaches such as those that emerge from the study of vaulted construction (Vitti 2016).

A close look at the numerous remains of buildings, attempting in particular to understand which materials were selected and used, and how they were transformed and assembled, can become decisive in outlining a clearer perception of the dynamics that characterized the local building sector, clarifying aspects related to the dramatic change that Roman rule brought into the architecture of Greece. If it is true that Roman architecture was largely influenced by Hellenistic architecture, on the other hand, a decisive innovation was fostered in Roman times through new building techniques and the introduction of vaulted construction.

Decisive to the development of an original local building tradition in mortared construction in Greece was the use of brick, as opposed to stone. Beyond the specific case of vaults, a swift look at wall masonry construction reveals that builders were keen to explore original solutions, as in the case of the brick/stone reticulate facing used at Patras (see below). More broadly, how widespread (and identifiable) were regional building solutions, traditions, and practices in construction processes in Greece during the early imperial period? To attempt to answer this question, it is necessary to look first at the available materials that were employed for mortared masonry and, secondly, identify if there were any specific local traditions that influenced the building process. For this reason, the focus of this chapter is on the sites of Nikopolis (Epirus) and Olympia (Elis, western Peloponnese), which are located in two regions with specific geomorphological and environmental characteristics, and where several buildings dating to between the first century BCE and the end of the first century CE are attested.[1]

Early Roman Greece and the new boost of the building sector

Following the conquest of Corinth in 146 BCE, Greece fell into a period of crisis and disrepair connected to the effects of the Roman Civil Wars, in particular at the times of Sulla and Pompey. The collapse of the local economy as a consequence of Roman warfare did not give many opportunities for investment in building programmes (Marasco 1988). These harsh conditions can be detected in the disrepair of sanctuaries like the one of Asklepios at Epidaurus, which would not see any renovation until imperial times (Melfi 2007). It was only around the mid-first century BCE that a change started to take place with new policies that were meant to promote economic upturn. Indeed, the strategy that was focused on land investment, including the reassignment of land (Camia 2009), did not bring any tangible results until the Senate voted in favour of the establishment of new colonies. The investments made by wealthy Romans were mainly triggered by personal interests, while the new colonial foundations promoted by Caesar and Augustus – from Durres to Corinth, and from Dium to Philippi – mostly involved the redistribution of land (Alcock 1993; Rizakis 1996). Famous was the adversity of Atticus recorded in his correspondence with Cicero for setting a colony at Buthrotum, as this would have affected his estates in the region (Deniaux 1987; Eberle and Le Quéré 2017). The size of the new cities, particularly those founded or refounded by Augustus (Byllis, Patras, Nikopolis, Dium, Cassandrea, and Philippi), was unprecedented if compared to those that had been previously created under Caesar (Buthrotum, Photike, and Dyme), and encompassed large territories which would sustain their economy (Rizakis 1997). Land confiscation and expropriations occurred both on the west coast of Greece and in northern Greece, along the via Egnatia that connected Epirus to Thrace. The new administrative, cultural, and economic policy of Rome fostered the rebirth of Greece and promoted architectural programmes. The newly formed centres were characterized by civic and religious buildings that were influenced by architectural models from Rome and represented the colonists' civic identity – Corinth is a case in point with its numerous religious buildings around the main public area, together with two basilicas and *rostra* (Romano 2000).

In an earlier study (Vitti 2016), I have approached the impact of Roman construction in Greece with particular attention to vaulted construction. Although vaulting techniques were adopted here as early as the fourth century BCE, as shown by the examples of the Macedonian tombs or the stadium of Nemea,[2] the use of vaults after the Roman conquest departs from this earlier tradition. The introduction of mortared construction and the use of vaults in the elevation of buildings (i.e., not buried in the ground) reflect a change that occurred in the late first century BCE both in the construction industry and in the architecture of buildings. Interestingly, Roman vaulted construction was implemented in Greece in a different manner from other regions of the Empire or of Latium itself, namely because of the local preference for solid-brick vaults. This choice depended, among other things, on two main factors: the local tradition of fired-brick construction and the poor quality of mortar. In this chapter I comment on the first factor by introducing new evidence, based on the survey of edifices in the region of Elis. Regarding the quality of mortar, it seems evident that when a new building tradition was imported into a given region, there was a transition period during which the new technique had to be adapted to the materials that were available locally. Failures were frequent in the early phases of implementation of imported building techniques or use of new structural layouts. At the same time, variations from the original solutions were inevitable. Identifying how this knowledge transfer occurred is challenging, as the analysis should look at the earlier evidence dating to the transition period, which is frequently not as well preserved as the one that is subsequent to a long period of experimentation.

One of the driving factors for the implementation of new architectural programmes and the employment of new building techniques in Greece was represented by the arrival of new settlers in the colonies. Funerary architecture provides significant evidence for the changes that occurred at the end of the first century BCE. Particularly abundant is the epigraphic and archaeological evidence from the colony of Patras, the main port connecting Greece to Italy, where the material culture from its three necropolises reflects the mixed population of the city, mainly veterans and settlers, earlier inhabitants of Patras, and Achaeans that had moved to the city. The necropolises, in particular the North Necropolis, were shaped according to those in Rome, with rituals and tombs that were markedly Roman. As noticed by I. Dekoulakou (2009, 203), 'il rito di cremazione, *romanus mos*, come riporta Tacito, compare nella necropoli di Patrasso – almeno a giudicare dai dati di scavo – a partire dalla fondazione della colonia e dal concomitante insediamento di coloni e veterani romani'. Veterans from the two legions of Augustus were *de facto* responsible for importing new architectural models in the newly established colony, and their presence is recorded in a significant number of inscriptions (Rizakis 1998, 25–28, 49–52, 73).

Particularly meaningful is the example of the Mausoleum of Marcia Maxima (Fig. 4.1), whose Latin inscription on a tabula placed on the main façade reads '*Marciae Maximae / C. Laetili Clementis / uxori / Pavia fecit mater*' (Rizakis and Zoumbaki 2001, nos. 142, 162, 184). As suggested by the excavator, this funerary monument belonged to the family of a veteran of the first generation (Petropoulos 2007). The freestanding building, with vaulted burial chambers, was located in the countryside close to a villa and was built in mortared rubble faced with stone and brick. Since the construction was placed along the river Diakonari, the builders used materials that were sourced from it. A formal sense of dignity was reserved only to the façade, which was faced with an extremely accurate reticulate masonry framed by simple brick pilasters raising from a brick-moulded base. The two-toned decorative motif and the high quality of the brick masonry with thin mortar joints (similar, for example, to the Augustan phase of the Porta Leoni at Verona) suggest that the façade was left bare. The display of a reticulate facing along with a Latin inscription on the tabula clearly attested to the '*romanitas*' of the owner. Aside from the finely executed façade, the rest of the building shows an extremely poor masonry, made with a rough mortared rubble facing covered with painted plaster. A substantial difference from mortared rubble and reticulate facings found elsewhere, which was a distinctive solution adopted at Patras (as well as Olympia, see below), was the insertion of bricks and fragments of terracotta

Fig. 4.1. Patras, Mausoleum of Marcia Maxima: Façade with stone/ brick reticulate framed by brick masonry (photo P. Vitti).

among the stones to form a 'stone/brick reticulate'. It is likely that this particular solution depended on the poor bonding between the stones of the facing with the core of the wall, and because of the limited adhesive capacity of the mortar to bind the stones sourced from the river, which were cut and set with the smooth side facing the core of the wall. All in all, it is evident that the adoption of building techniques that were in use in the Italian Peninsula needed to be adapted to the local building industry and materials. Notably, the vaults of the mausoleum were built with bricks. With such poor mortar – characterized by a significant predominance of aggregates against lime – a concrete vault would not have been possible. The lack of suitable stone and the existence of a local tradition for brick construction (Vitti 2015) were driving factors for the widespread use of brick vaulting at Patras; this solution proved to be successful in a region where aggregates with pozzolanic properties were lacking (Vitti 2023).

Brick vaulting evolved in Greece during the first century CE to include an array of technical solutions which developed from the practical need to simplify the construction processes, to reduce costs, and to avoid time-consuming procedures such as the use of provisional timber supports (centring). More elaborate solutions were adopted in the articulated architectures of later buildings, including, beyond barrel vaults, sail vaults, cross vaults, and domical vaults. The unique geographical position of Greece, between East and West, resulted in the adoption of certain vaulting techniques that were unknown in Rome (Lancaster 2015; for other cases of regional variations in vaulting across the Roman world, see Lancaster in this volume) and were only scarcely adopted in Italy before the time of Justinian (Vitti 2013). Within this setting it is worth exploring how builders addressed wall construction. As a matter of fact, the abutments of the walls had to resist the thrust generated by the vaults; the soundness of the supporting masonry therefore became a priority. In the context of this chapter, I will explore the ways in which local materials and know-how were merged with building traditions that had developed in the Italian Peninsula, focusing on select examples from Nikopolis and Olympia.

1. Nikopolis in Epirus

Nikopolis was founded by Octavian in the aftermath of the battle of Actium, 31 BCE. In 27 BCE, the year of the first Actian Games, Nikopolis became part of Achaea, the new senatorial province with Corinth as its capital. This imperial foundation was formed through the synoecism of several settlements in the surrounding region, including Kassope, Ammotopos, Ambracia, and other centres from Akarnania and even Aetolia (Paus. 5.23.3; 7.18.8–9; 10.8.3–4; 10.38.4), with the evident purpose to populate the new city and provide its citizens with a vast territory (Purcell 1987; Zachos 2008). Prosperity was supported through privileges offered to the inhabitants. The displacement of the Actian Games from the sanctuary of Apollo Actius by the Ambracian Gulf to an area close to the altar that had been erected by Augusts to commemorate his victory was consistent with a policy that was meant to extend Roman influence on the religious realm; Nikopolis itself was located close to this new site of the Actian Games. A large Greek population lived here (Kirsten 1987; Zachos 2018; Hernandez forthcoming). Numerous edifices dating to this early building phase are preserved at this site. The discussion focuses here on the theatre of the *proasteion* and a small mausoleum, with the intent to examine two constructions of different size, function, patronage, and financial investment, in order to understand how mortared construction was executed.

1.1. The theatre at the proasteion

The theatre is located in the suburb north of the city (*proasteion*), at the foot of the hill where Augustus' Altar of Victory stood (Fig. 4.2). The theatre was part of a compound of monuments intended to commemorate the Actian Victory and to celebrate the Actian Games (Zachos 2012; 2018). The theatre, the stadium (Zachos 2016), and the altar all belong to the Augustan phase of the new settlement (Kontoyianni 2007; Zachos 2012, 170; 2018, 724–32). The two entertainment buildings shared similar structural and building solutions and were both enlarged at a later stage, but the early phases can be clearly distinguished from the later ones by looking at their building techniques. The first phase was characterized by the use of mortared stone for the walls and vaults, while brick was massively employed in the later phases, reflecting a change that impacted the local building industry throughout the first century CE.

The theatre was built against the slope of the hill, with a cavea that partially raised above the ground level and

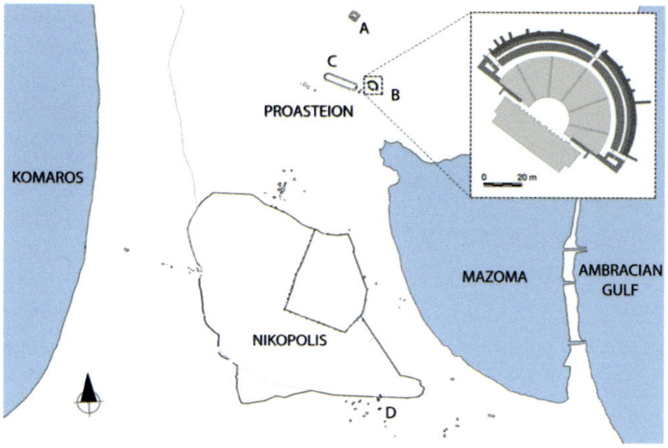

Fig. 4.2. Map of Nikopolis. A: Victory Monument of Actium; B: Theatre of the proasteion *(with detail of first-phase construction); C: Stadium; D: Mausoleum 6 (image P. Vitti).*

featured a thick circular wall. The lower part of the cavea was mainly laid on the ground, while the upper section was entirely built. The external retaining wall is 2.3 m thick and was buttressed with orthogonal walls of different length which were placed at irregular intervals. The two lateral ends of the curved wall feature a conspicuous ashlar masonry. Three openings served as *vomitoria* to the *praecintio* dividing the lower from the upper cavea. The observations that follow concern mainly the north-west outer sector of the theatre.[3] The main phase is defined by rubble masonry with three different types of facing and timber ties. The selection of materials and techniques reflects the rationale of builders to address the durability and structural stresses to which the different walls were subjected:

- Small-size rubble of beach rock (a sedimentary rock formed along the shoreline) was employed for the external facing of the curved wall and for the wall facing of corridors and rooms (Fig. 4.3). Reticulate masonry occurs exceptionally only on the façade of the central *vomitorium*. All the other wall facings that were not exposed to weathering and were probably left bare, were made with limestone. Given the thickness of the masonry (2.3 m), the poor bonding of the small stones employed for the facing did not compromise the solidity of the wall.
- Medium-size rubble of beach rock was used in the buttresses (Fig. 4.4) and the abutments of the vaults in the *vomitoria*. The stones have a roughly rectangular facing and are of very irregular size (some are only 4 cm high, others up to 15 cm). Larger stones were selected for the ends of the buttresses, but without forming cornerstones. Little care was paid to the bonding of the stones on the facing, which also emerges from the lack of headers.
- Ashlars were used in specific parts of the outer wall, with courses of variable height (Fig. 4.5). Bonding

Fig. 4.3. Nikopolis, theatre of the proasteion*: Graphic record of the west* vomitorium *with details of the facings of outer curved wall and buttresses (image P. Vitti).*

Fig. 4.4. Nikopolis, theatre of the proasteion*: Detail of the facing of the buttress (photo P. Vitti).*

Fig. 4.5. Nikopolis, theatre of the proasteion*: West corner of the building with mortared rubble masonry faced with ashlars (photo P. Vitti).*

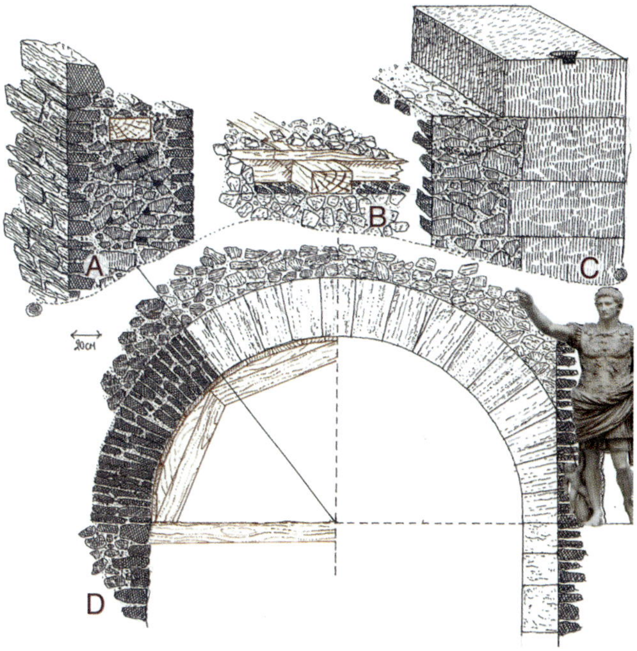

Fig. 4.6. Nikopolis, theatre of the proasteion*: Diagrams of masonry. A: Section of a buttress showing a timber beam; B: Axonometry showing two timber beams intersecting in the masonry of the outer curved wall; C: Axonometry of mortared rubble masonry faced with ashlars; D: Diagram of barrel vault of the* vomitorium *showing facing with stone voussoirs and core made with radially placed irregular stones (image P. Vitti).*

to the mortared rubble core was not always guaranteed. The stone heterogeneity (limestone, sandstone, conglomerate, *poros*) may attest to a possible reuse of materials from other buildings.[4]

The core of the walls was built with irregularly cut limestone and some river stones which were laid in abundant mortar. Sporadic bricks have been documented. The stones roughly correspond in size with those of the mortared rubble facing (c. 12–13 cm). The mortar's excellent adherence to the irregularly cut stones resulted in a sound structure, despite the poor bonding between facing and core of the walls. Several holes are visible on the outer curved wall (Fig. 4.6a). Because of their size (30 × 18–20 cm), they may not be interpreted as putlog holes for scaffolding. They are aligned in horizontal courses placed at irregular intervals and height (1.1–2.3 m) with timber imprints on the mortar. Other cavities with imprints were set parallel to the façade and intersected with those orthogonal to the wall as to create a grid (Fig. 4.6b). L. Leontaris (forthcoming) has documented timber ties of smaller sections and not forming a grid in other parts of the first-phase construction.

All the vaults of the first phase were made in stone and not brick, unlike contemporary structures in the Peloponnese. The three inclined vaults of the *vomitoria* were built with radially placed beach rock. It is worth noticing that the vault thickness (c. 44 cm) was achieved through the use of several irregularly cut stones of small size (Fig. 4.6d), whose length did not cover the whole thickness of the vault. As in brick vaults, the construction was not simultaneous with the superstructure, which was built after the completion of the vaults (thus not forming a single unit, unlike the construction of Roman concrete vaults). The timber formwork for the construction was composed of boards of 20 cm in width.

This quick overview of the theatre's north-western outer sector elucidates the 'Roman-style' character of the construction and its departure from the earlier dry masonry tradition. Stone ashlars, typically employed in the region for monumental buildings, were employed here only as facing of mortared rubble (Fig. 4.6c) and in selected sectors of the building that were exposed to particularly high stresses, as on the façade of the west *analemma*.[5] These ashlars were sourced from buildings in the abandoned sites of the region and reflect the way mortared construction enabled builders to reuse materials. It was indeed the confident and ubiquitous use of lime mortar that made possible to move away from local dry masonry traditions. The use of abundant lime mortar not only enhanced the possibility to recycle materials but reduced the labour needed to prepare these materials for construction.

Looking in more detail at how materials were processed and assembled, one can observe that mortared rubble was not formed with layered materials set in regular courses, as in best-practice dry rubble masonry construction, where irregular stones are laid in courses to form a single structure, from face to face of the wall. The use of mortar allowed a different type of construction by creating two facings first and then filling the space between them. This technique was quicker and resulted in what Vitruvius describes (with criticism) as a 'tripartite structure' (*De arch.* 2.8.7). Where the sections of the walls are visible, these show cavities resulting from pouring stone and mortar inside the facing and suggest that builders were not concerned about obtaining a higher density of the core by compacting mortared rubble. We can observe that the size of this stone rubble was too large to effectively tamp the nucleus (some imperial-period projects, especially in the Italian Peninsula, commonly employed a procedure where the size of the stone rubble decreased to the size of a fist, and the materials were disposed on regular layers in correspondence with each course of the facing). This Roman-period technique thus differed substantially from previous Greek techniques not only because it employed mortar, but also due to the fact that quality dry masonry in Classical and Hellenistic architecture featured stone laid in layers and carefully intertwined throughout the wall thickness. The introduction of mortared masonry during the late Republic had substantially altered the practice of dry masonry construction by establishing the practice of tripartite walls described by Vitruvius. The new technique was undoubtedly quicker, as stones were roughly reduced to the required size without the need to work them to increase the contact points between the faces as to transmit the stresses from one stone to the other. Mortar provided the medium for the transmission of stresses within the walls.

Calcareous stone used in the core of the walls of the Nikopolis theatre was extremely irregular and variable in size, enhancing both the use of chippings and adherence to mortar due to the rough surface. The builders' familiarity with the use of mortared rubble is reflected in the selection of materials and the types of facing in the different parts of the structure. Massive walls were in mortared rubble, as their facing only served to provide a formwork for the core and did not contribute to the wall's overall stability. Buttresses and the abutments of the vaults were faced with larger stones; their variable size towards the nucleus of the wall created a stronger bond that enhanced the stability of the structure. The character of building techniques adopted in the theatre can be better understood when the lack of brick vaults is considered. While brick vaults represented a typical feature of contemporary construction on the west coast of Peloponnese, at Augustan Nikopolis vaults were built with rough stones placed radially and had stone voussoirs as facing. Similar types of vaults can be found in late Republican buildings in Latium, such as the Sanctuary of Fortuna Primigenia and the basilica at Praeneste, the cryptoporticus of Piazza Tani at Tivoli, as well as examples at Alatri.[6]

What appears to be an eminently local solution at Nikopolis was the use of timber reinforcements in the walls. According to Leontaris (forthcoming), these reinforcements provided resistance to stresses during the hardening process of the mortar and prevented the creation of cracks due to unexpected movements of the soil. It is also likely that the grid formed by the timber beams was meant to avoid damage caused by seismic action, a natural hazard the region suffered from. Studies on more recent masonries reinforced with timber show that embedding timber into the masonry increases its compression strength (Vintzileou 2008). We can conclude that the timber elements placed at different levels and in different directions offered effective resistance to stresses generated by earthquakes. Since similar ties have been noted by Leontaris in other buildings of Nikopolis, we can assume that builders transferred the local expertise into building systems which were employed for the first time in the region.

1.2. Mausoleum 6 ('mausoleum with a triangular chamber')

To understand whether Roman building techniques were introduced only in major works such as the city walls (Zachos 2007) or the monumental constructions of the *proasteion*, it is worth analysing a small funerary building, Mausoleum 6 (Fig. 4.2d), located in the necropolis outside the south-east gate on the street leading to the port of Vathy, c. 70 m from the towers of the gate. Other funerary monuments belonging to prominent families have been found in close proximity. This mausoleum features a burial chamber that occupies a sector of an annular room, covered by a barrel vault and delimited by two radial walls, which is perceived as having a triangular plan (Fig. 4.7). The square podium of the building is 11 m wide and c. 2.7 m high,[7] and the drum above it is c. 8.2 m in diameter. Presence of an outer ashlar facing can only be inferred through the imprints it left on the mortared rubble masonry. In contrast, the corridor and the burial chamber are remarkably well preserved (Fig. 4.8). The corridor is still largely plastered (the plaster of the vault is uneven, highlighting its rough execution). The entrance is located on the back side of the podium (opposite the street). The limestone threshold is well preserved (Fig. 4.9c). The long corridor (5.2 m) fans out in two oblique walls ending against a curved wall. The chamber is covered by a barrel vault, with its impost resting on the curved wall and on the end arch of the corridor. Two rectangular niches (50 × 35 cm) can be seen on the oblique walls, while two circular niches (56 × 50 cm) flank a wider central niche (144 × 85 cm) on the curved wall. In one of the circular niches are the remains of a cavity, probably for an urn. A window is visible over the right-hand circular niche. Part of the vault has collapsed and most of the plaster is missing. A hole dug by looters in the middle of the chamber shows that the foundations of the building were c. 2 m high.

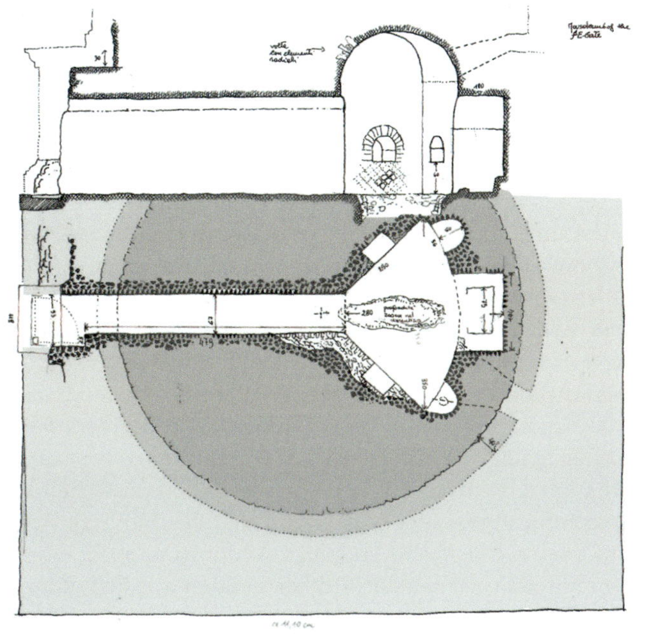

Fig. 4.7. Nikopolis, Mausoleum 6: Graphic record showing plan and section along the entrance corridor and the funerary chamber (image P. Vitti).

Fig. 4.8. Nikopolis, Mausoleum 6: View from the funerary chamber towards the entrance corridor (photo P. Vitti).

The mortared masonry on the outer side is composed of several types of stone, including beach rock, limestone, and *poros*. Stones were irregularly cut in small lumps laid randomly in abundant mortar in courses which seem to correspond to the height of the stone ashlars (30 cm?). The interior walls were faced in reticulate masonry (*tesserae* 8 × 8 cm) made with *poros* (Fig. 4.9). Large gaps in the masonry show the nucleus, which was made out mostly with *poros* stone roughly matching the size of the *tesserae*, together with some occasional larger stones. The rubble appears to be well compacted. The corners of the walls were made with rectangular blocks c. 5 cm high. The vaults were made with radially placed stones, roughly cut to form elongated stones which covered the entire vault thickness. This building technique is visible at the entrance end of the barrel vault (Fig. 4.10) and on a wide gap of the annular barrel vault of the burial chamber. The timber boards used for the centring have given a segmented profile to the barrel vault of the entrance corridor. The niches on the chamber walls were made with smaller stones, placed radially. The front arch was made with *poros* stones cut in voussoirs of irregular size.

The typology of the mausoleum and the building techniques are undoubtedly Roman. Its exceptionality is due to the fact that to date this is the only known example of

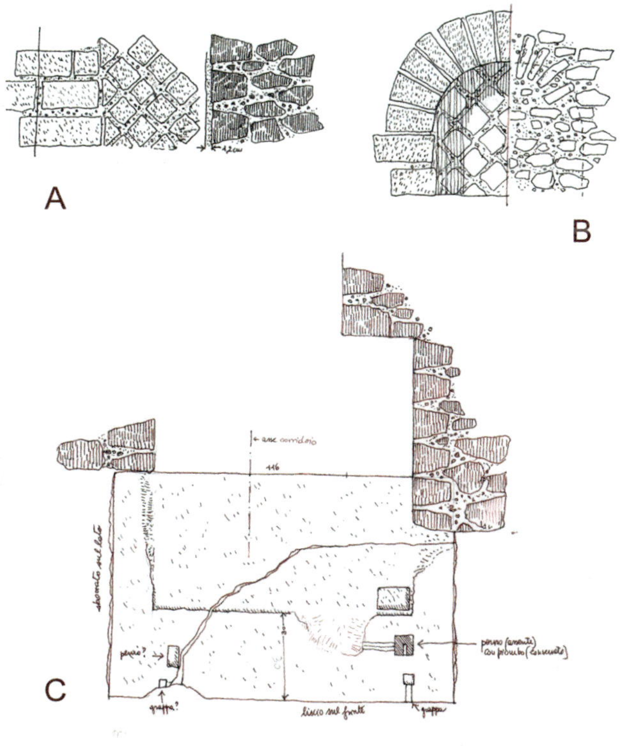

Fig. 4.9. Nikopolis, Mausoleum 6: Diagrams of the reticulate masonry (A), one of the side niches (B), and the entrance threshold (C) (image P. Vitti).

Fig. 4.10. Nikopolis, Mausoleum 6: View of entrance corridor from exterior. Note the radial disposition of stones forming the barrel vault and the horizontal layering of stones of the nucleus of the drum (photo P. Vitti).

a Roman *tumulus* mausoleum in Greece. In the absence of archaeological evidence, its dating to Augustan times or to the early first century CE can rely only on typological analogies (Flämig 2007, 37; Zachos and Karampa 2015). Another mausoleum located to the west of Mausoleum 6 has been dated to the second half of the first century CE (Leontaris forthcoming). This is a small rectangular edifice (4.5 × 6 m) with an entrance at the centre of one of the long sides, and three small niches for urns on the wall opposite the entrance. The mortared rubble walls had timber reinforcements. The chamber had a barrel vault made with radially placed stones. The presence of timber reinforcements and other details of the construction suggest this building should be associated with the early phase of building traditions at Nikopolis, before use of brick became widespread (in this building bricks were only used at the impost of the vault and in the niches). Although the rectangular mausoleum and Mausoleum 6 show some differences in the respective building techniques, they might both belong to this early phase within the first century CE.

Mausolea of similar *tumulus* type are found in Rome and Italy towards the end of the first century BCE (von Hesberg 1994, 113–14; Gros 2001, 422–23). Not all *tumuli* had a square podium and drum. However, the monumental size of some of them, often above 30 m in diameter (Eisner 1986), highlights the strong impact they had on the funerary landscape of the first-century BCE necropolises, and how this typology met the needs for ostentation of some powerful politicians, such as Munatius Plancus (Gros 2001, 430), the senator who oversaw the colonization of Buthrotum on behalf of Mark Antony (Cic. *Att.* 16.16). The mausoleum of M. Lucilius Paetus on the Via Salaria (diameter 35.6 m; height 4.25 m) is composed by a drum and an upper *tumulus*, with a corridor leading to a burial chamber where the urns were placed, as in the mausoleum of Nikopolis (Eisner 1986, 124–17, S4; Schwarz 2002, 196–97, M68, pl. 22.1–2). The 'Torrione' on the Via Praenestina is also similar (diameter 44 m). All these mausolea were built with mortared rubble and had a stone or marble facing. Smaller mausolea imitated the larger ones, such as those of the north-east side of the necropolis of Porta Nocera at Pompeii (D'Ambrosio and De Caro 1983), where ashlar masonry was imitated with plaster. The mausoleum of Nikopolis, with its mortared rubble structure and the exterior stone facing, was clearly inspired by models that had spread in the second half of the first century BCE and continued to be in use throughout the first century CE.

The lack of an inscription makes identification of the owner impossible. Flämig (2007, 147–48) does not exclude the possibility that this might have been a member of the Greek elite who had moved to the new city, and who chose to adopt such a particular type of funerary monument to showcase his '*romanitas*'. However, the well-executed reticulate, so similar to many facings made with the soft volcanic stone in Latium and Campania, and so different from the rougher mortared rubble facings employed in contemporary buildings at Nikopolis, might suggest the builders were familiar with these Italian examples, and if so, the patron could have involved foreign expertise on purpose. Beyond these conjectures, it is meaningful that this building bears witness to a transfer of architectural forms and techniques from abroad, in contrast to other buildings which show a more marked interaction with local building expertise.

2. Elis and Olympia

The second area of interest is the ancient city of Elis with the Sanctuary of Olympia.[8] The Elis region in the Peloponnese was characterized by its extremely fertile land, with water flowing from the mountain ridges of Arcadia, as also reported by Polybius (4.73.6–10). The local elite derived its wealth from farming activities, including horse breeding, cattle, and cultivation of flax, and played an important role in promoting the activities of the Sanctuary of Olympia. When Augustus founded the new colony of Patras in 14 BCE, Elis contributed to the growth and welfare of the colony. The geomorphology of most of the west coast of the Peloponnese is composed of Pliocene sediments rising from a plain made of gravel, sand, silt, and clay deposits. Together with the abundant timber, these materials influenced the building solutions adopted in this region. Particularly meaningful is the recurring – and not yet entirely explored – employment of fired bricks in the region of Elis. Albeit stone was the preferred building material, brick seems to have been intensively employed since the Hellenistic period in masonry construction, thus setting a precedent for its wide employment in the Roman imperial era. I will therefore examine some Hellenistic-period buildings at Elis and Olympia to investigate the local building tradition in brick construction and compare this to the use of brick in mortared construction.

2.1. Solid-brick masonry at Elis

Since the sixth century BCE Elis was responsible for organizing and managing the Olympic Games, which were held without interruption throughout antiquity. Despite the Peloponnese's general economic recession, it seems that in the first century BCE the local elite remained active, with a leading role in the Olympian Sanctuary (Lo Monaco 2004). In spite of the importance of the city, archaeological evidence is scarce and not many standing buildings survive, with a few exceptions – namely Roman buildings of the imperial period, such as the baths with the octagonal hall. All the Roman structures should be dated after the end of the first century CE. Several Hellenistic buildings, tombs, and kilns were discovered during excavations. Particularly meaningful to this study is the evidence of brick construction in Building DA. Located in the south-east agora, it is an excellent example of this tradition of construction in the region.

Building DA (Fig. 4.11) is identified in the archaeological reports as an ashlar construction using the 'typical large fired bricks of the region' (Andreou and Andreou 2012, 487). The late Hellenistic stone ashlar wall above the brick wall provides a *terminus ante quem* for the brick wall. The structure is formed by two walls meeting at a roughly right angle. The short side, 6.28 m long and oriented east–west, is characterized by stone ashlars placed at the west end of the wall, denoting either a passage or, more likely, the end of the wall. The opposite eastern end seems to have continued, but this portion of the structure was not excavated. The different width of the ashlars creates bonds with the brick wall. The long side has an opening (?) at the centre, and is 6.67 m long. Bricks measure 33 × 63 × 7 cm and are all placed as headers to form a 63 cm thick wall. The vertical joints fall at the centre of the bricks of the adjacent courses, forming a regular masonry. Bricks were set in a thin layer of clay, which might have served to distribute the weight in a homogeneous manner, thus compensating the minimal unevenness of their surface (the height of five-brick courses is 40–43 cm). The use of clay among fired bricks would suggest this masonry is not a *dry construction*. However, in this chapter, to distinguish this masonry from lime-mortared brick walls, I will use the term 'dry-brick walls'.

At the entrance of the site, in front of the Ephoreia, one finds a brick tomb reconstructed here after having been transferred from its original location. The tomb is made with similar bricks of 33 × 60–63 × 6 cm. In this case the wall thickness is given by the short side of the brick (33 cm). The rectangular form of the bricks thus made it possible to build walls with two different thicknesses, each determined by the respective side of the brick that was used. Thicker walls might have been made by setting several bricks on each course of a wall. Isodomic brick masonry is well documented in Greece, Epirus, and Magna Graecia – regions where the adoption of dry-brick construction is documented from the third century BCE onwards, as in the case of Apollonia (Döhner 2019). The thickness of fired bricks in Hellenistic and Roman architecture before the first century CE was consistent with that of mudbricks, with the difference that the Romans introduced lime mortar as a binder (Bonetto 2019). In dry masonry, it is likely that the greater thickness of bricks served to reduce the number of horizontal joints, thus making the structure stronger. In mortared masonry, the mortar joint was frequently of minimal thickness, as in some gates of the second half of the first century BCE, such as the Porta Palatina of Turin or the Porta Leoni in Verona.

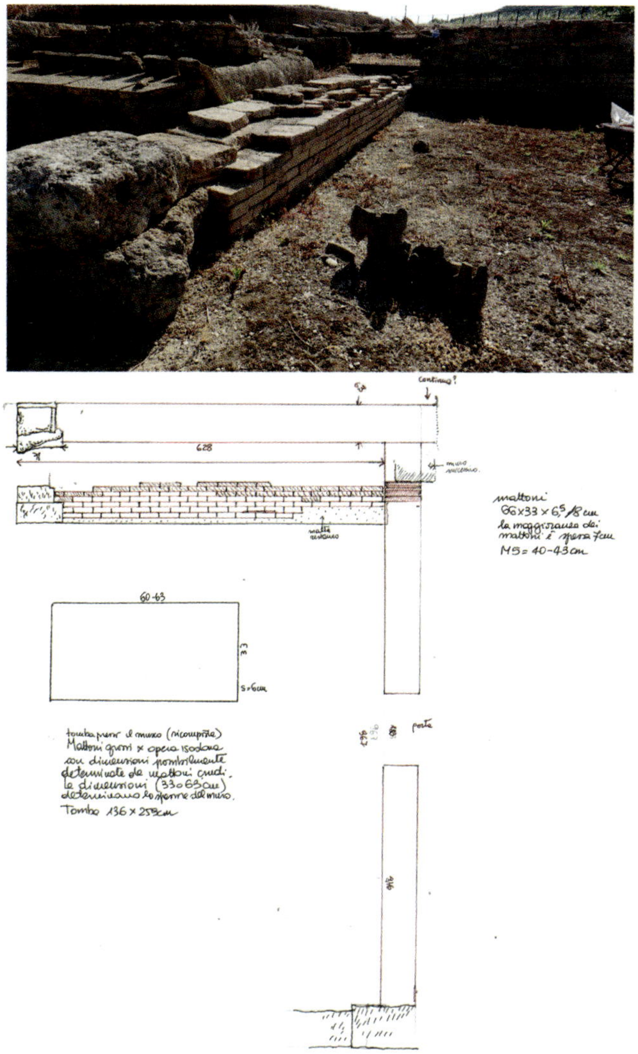

Fig. 4.11. Elis, Building DA: View and diagrams of the masonry (photo and image P. Vitti).

I have noted elsewhere (Vitti 2015) that bricks and broken tiles were used in the construction of walls and vaults in the neighbouring region of Patras. Here, brick vaulting might have been in use before the foundation of the colony. Conspicuous evidence of fired brick at Elis reinforces the hypothesis that when Roman builders started their activities in the region, they maintained the existing tradition of fired brick production while also developing mortared construction. Some aspects that fostered the use of fired bricks in Hellenistic times, such as their resistance to humidity, the possibility to shape and model fired clay for construction purposes, their modularity of construction, and the structural properties of bricks and of layered masonry (P. Vitti 2019), might also have played an important role in the choices made by Roman builders. However, as we will see, mortared masonry changed the way brick was used in wall masonry.

2.2. Solid-brick masonry at Olympia

Amongst the ancillary buildings that were needed to celebrate the festivals and religious festivities, Olympia had several bath complexes (Fig. 4.12). In the so-called 'Greek Bath' the use of fired brick is well documented during its first-century BCE phase (Kunze and Schleif 1944; Schleif 1944; Mallwitz 1958; Mallwitz 1972). The fifth-century BCE phase of this building included a large open-air pool and hip bathtubs in rooms I and II (Fig. 4.12a); at the end of the fourth century BCE, at the time when a *palaestra* was built to support the activity of the Games, a third room (III) was added to the west. The room had hip bathtubs on three sides. Later, in the early first century BCE, a room (IV) with hypocaust was added to the south.[9] The importance of this room stands in the extensive use of brick (Lo Monaco 2013; M. Vitti 2019).

The analysis of the first-century BCE brick masonry might help in defining the way builders approached construction in this period under Roman rule. A well-preserved brick wall stands in the area between rooms I, II, and III (Fig. 4.13), and this might date to the renovation of the early first century BCE. Bricks measure 34 × 65 cm, and are 7 cm thick (10 courses = 84 cm). They delimit a water tank waterproofed with lime-mortared broken bricks and terracotta bits (thickness 12 cm) and a 1.5 cm thick *signinum* layer. The fired-brick masonry was built carefully, as shown in the drawing in Fig. 4.14a. On the main wall the rectangular bricks were placed as stretchers to form the 34 cm thick wall. As in the example discussed for the city of Elis, bricks were laid with clay. The walls of the hypocaust in room IV were equally built with clay. They are thicker (Fig. 4.14b) and employ square bricks of 45 × 45 × 6–7 cm, which were used uncut or cut in two sizes of 30 × 45 or 15 × 45 cm, taking advantage of three parallel grooves (see M. Vitti 2019, fig. 4). The brick columns of the hypocaust (height 80 cm) were made with smaller and thinner square bricks (33 × 33 × 5.5 cm) spaced regularly. On the top of

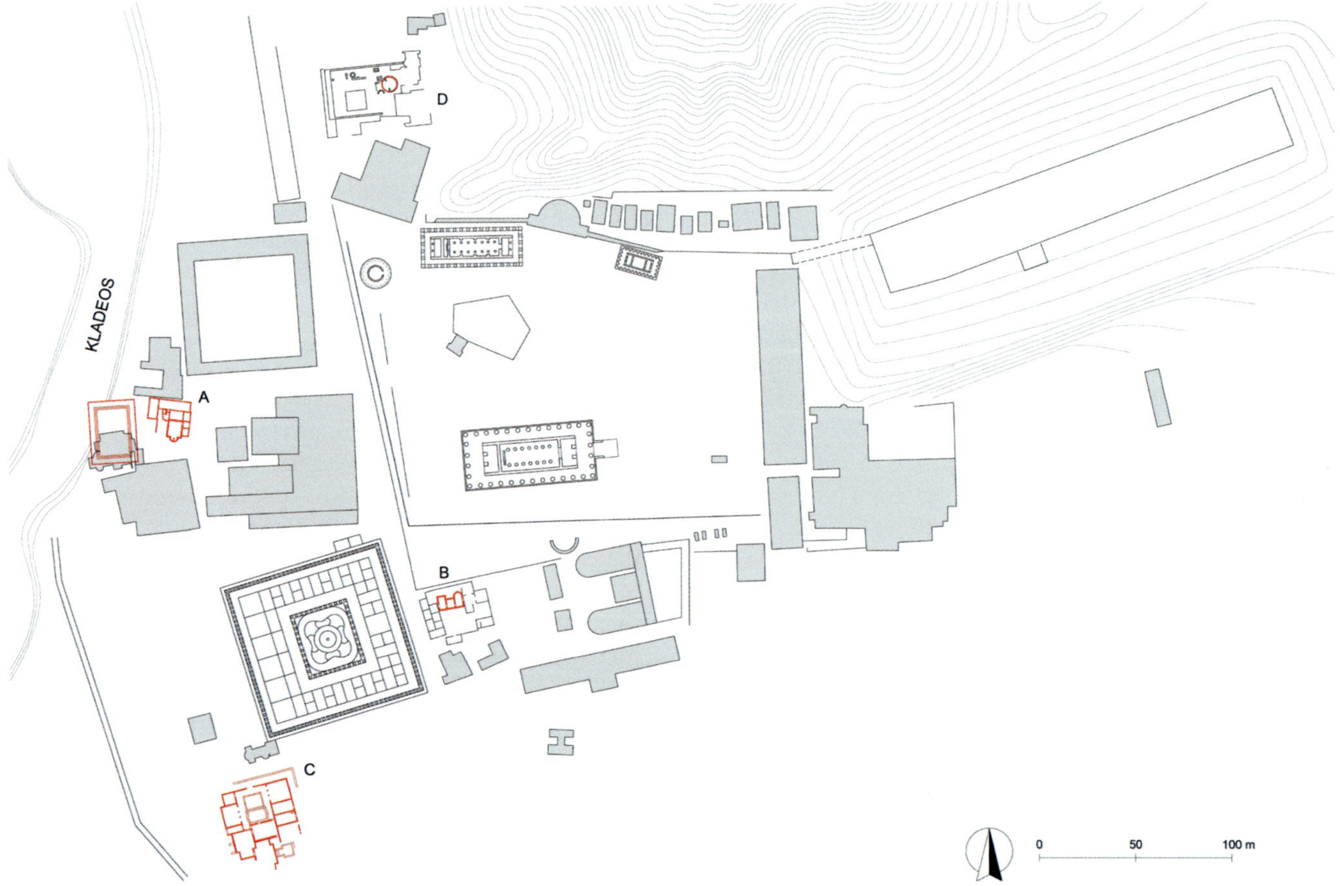

Fig. 4.12. Map of Olympia showing the bath buildings on the east side of the Altis. A: Greek Bath; B: South Bath; C: South-West Building; D: Bath building on the Kronos Hill (image P. Vitti).

each brick column is a larger brick similar in size to those of the wall. This brick supports a layer of reused roof pantiles. Thinner terracotta elements were used to level the height of the brick columns (Fig. 4.15). At the level of the hypocaust the perimeter wall was thicker (90 cm) with two square bricks determining the wall thickness. A recess towards the hypocaust reduced the elevation of the wall thickness to 67 cm; this was meant to provide a support for the pantiles upon which stood the floor. It is worth emphasizing that lime mortar was used for the floor and for waterproofing the interior wall. The floor was made of *opus signinum* with coarse aggregates (thickness 16 cm) and a brick floor with 2.7 cm thick rectangular *tesserae*. The waterproofing of the wall (thickness 20 cm) was made with mortared fragments of tiles and terracotta (similarly to the one used for the tank described above), which were laid on a layer of clay used to fill the gap between the pantiles and the wall (Fig. 4.16).

Based on the above, it appears that builders at Olympia in the first century BCE were still employing masonry construction without lime binders, while mortared construction was introduced only at a later stage. This is also confirmed by the evidence from the bath building that was added on the slope of the Kronos Hill, facing the stoa, during the first century BCE (Fig. 4.12d). This building displayed the typical Hellenistic bath facilities, with a 5.75 m large circular room (Sinn 2003) in which hip bathtubs were placed radially along the wall. However, construction of a suspended floor in room IV of the Greek Bath, according to the hypocaust system described by Vitruvius (*De arch*. 5.10), shows ties to the noteworthy early examples of the Stabian Baths at Pompeii and the baths at Fregellae (Yegül and Favro 2019, 65; Tsiolis 2013; Trümper *et al*. 2022; on Fregellae see also Lancaster, this volume), establishing a novelty at Olympia. This observation supports the hypothesis that the builders

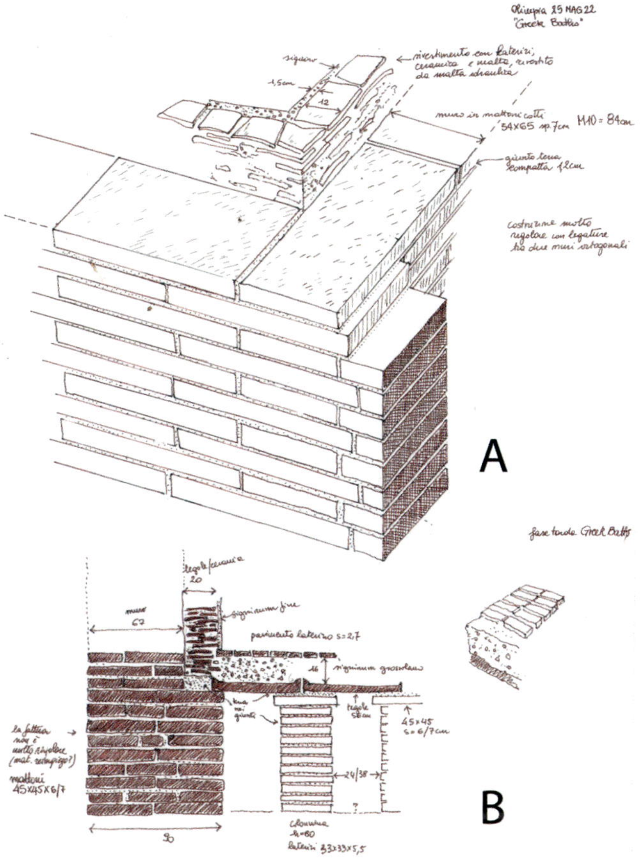

Fig. 4.14. Olympia, Greek Bath. A: Diagram of the solid-brick wall shown in Fig. 4.13; B: Section with detail of the wall and hypocaust in room IV (image P. Vitti).

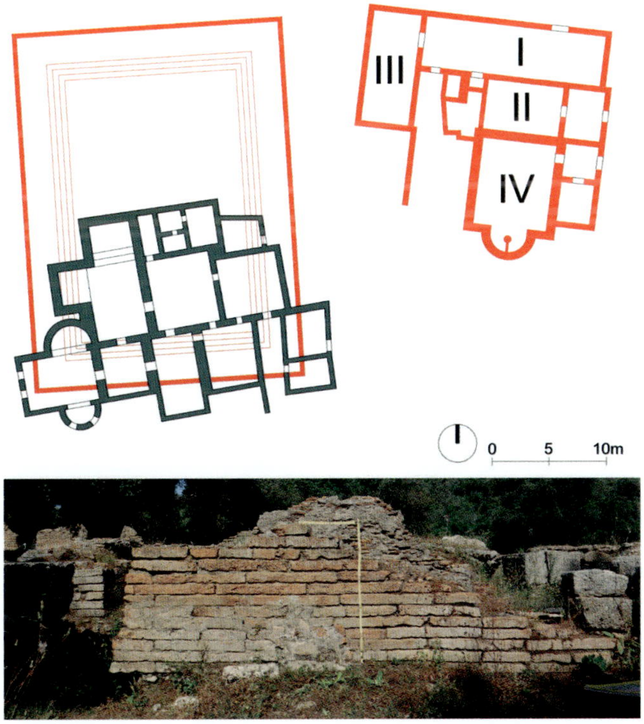

Fig. 4.13. Olympia, Greek Bath: Plan and view of solid-brick wall facing on the west side of room III (photo and image P. Vitti).

Fig. 4.15. Olympia, Greek Bath: View of the hypocaust in room IV (photo P. Vitti).

Fig. 4.16. Olympia, Greek Bath: View of the floor on suspensurae *in room IV, with solid-brick masonry wall visible on the left-hand side (photo P. Vitti).*

of the last building phase of the Greek Bath might have come from Italy. These builders followed a tradition of brick construction that already existed in this region, making a limited use of lime (as it has been noticed in the mausoleum of Marcia Maxima at Patras) only for those parts of the building that were directly exposed to humidity.

2.3. Early mortared masonry at Olympia

A change in building tradition at Olympia occurred with the large-scale introduction of mortared construction and the use of a stone/brick reticulate alternating with brick courses. Two buildings are considered here: the South Bath and the South-West Building.

2.3.1. The South Bath

Located south of the Altis, east of the Leonidaion, the South Bath (Figs 4.12b; 4.17) is composed of three wings around a central courtyard. The heated suite had three main rooms, built in a row: a *tepidarium* (with pool), a *laconicum*, and a *caldarium* (with pool). The structure is the result of several building phases and lacks in coherence, particularly when the position of the hot rooms north of the courtyard is considered. Excavations by Kunze (1944; 1958; 1961; 1962) would date the building to the third century CE; however, an earlier date is proposed for the *caldarium* and *laconicum* by I. Stamu and L. Leontaris (see Stamu 2021). This date does not rest on any archaeological evidence, but on the analysis of the entire complex and its building sequences. A dating to the first century CE is hereby considered probable. Additions and modifications to the original layout were made after the second-century CE modification of the wall of the Altis and the construction of the aqueduct by Herodes Atticus.

Our interest here is focused on the mortared masonry faced with stone/brick reticulate and brick courses. Particularly meaningful is the analysis of the *caldarium*, which is preserved up to the level of the vault. The west side of the *caldarium*, being a freestanding wall, had to withstand the thrust of the vault, and this might have provided a challenge to the builders. The wall is preserved to a remarkable height, and its foundations can be seen as well. The exterior was made of stone/brick reticulate alternating with brick facing, while the interior was faced entirely with bricks, probably as a consequence of its use as a hot room (Fig. 4.18). At the corners are stone ashlars of different size and height, which

Fig. 4.17. Olympia, South Bath: View of the north-west corner of the caldarium *(photo P. Vitti).*

Fig. 4.18. Olympia, South Bath: View of the interior of the caldarium *from south (photo P. Vitti).*

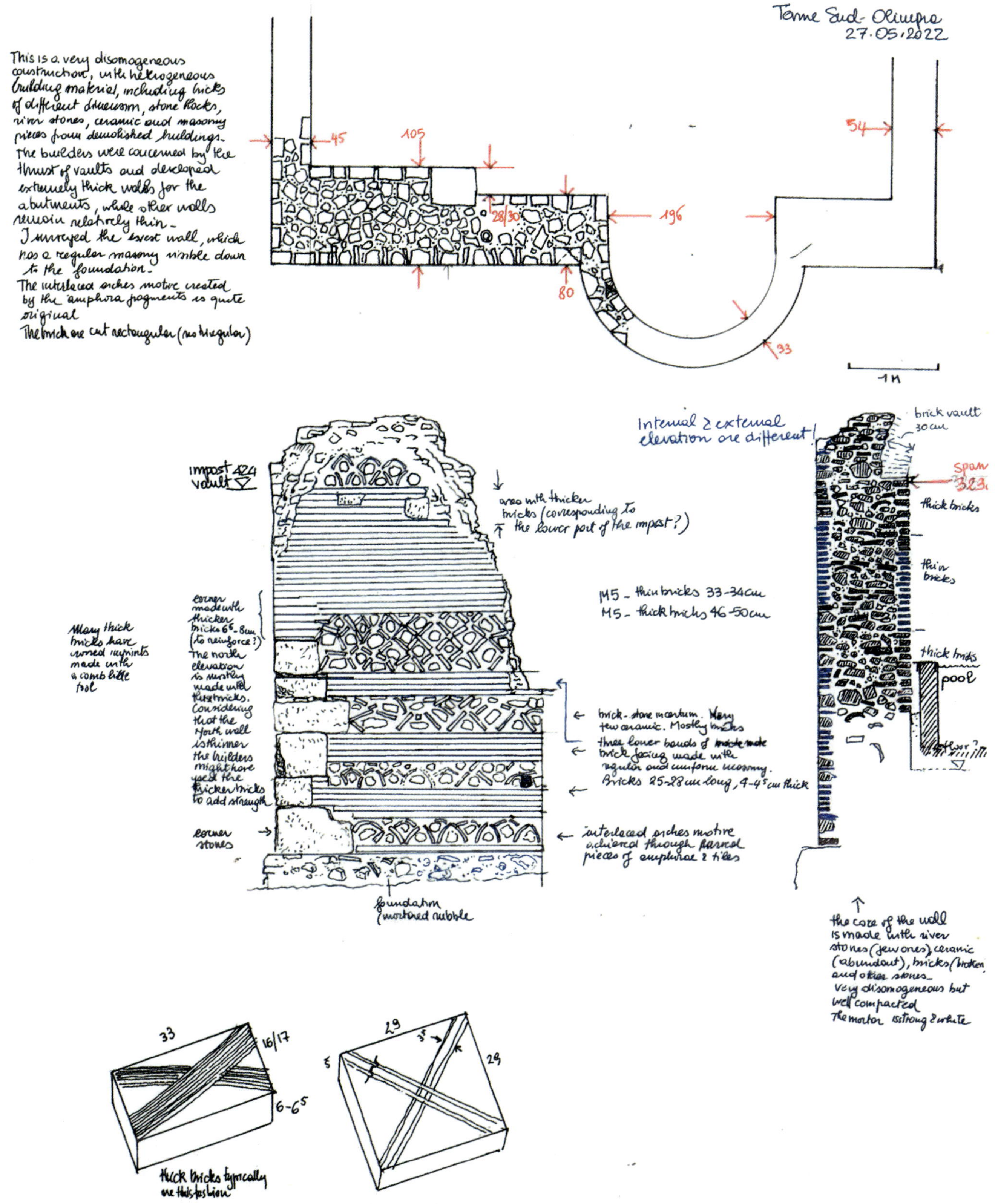

Fig. 4.19. Olympia, South Bath: Graphic record of the west wall of the caldarium (plan, outer elevation, and section) (image P. Vitti).

were meant to bond firmly the lower section of the wall. The stone/brick reticulate panels are irregular in height and technique. In the lowest panel, the stones are combined with bits of amphorae and tiles to form a rather unique motif of interlaced arches (the same motif appears also in the lunette of the north wall). In the upper panels, the bricks or straight tiles are laid more or less randomly. The upper half of the wall was made with a brick facing (Fig. 4.19). Bricks are square, with sides of 25–29 cm, and a thickness of 4–5 cm (five courses = 33–34 cm). Thicker bricks (6.6–8 cm) were used at the corner, just above the corner stones, and in the sector below the level of the impost of the vault. It is worth noticing that the interior wall also made use of thinner and thicker bricks, with thicker bricks used below the impost. The core of the wall was made with river stones, broken bricks, and other stones all set carefully in horizontal layers. This mixture of materials was well compacted. The vault was made with 30 × 30 cm bricks and a thick masonry to offer stability against the thrust (preserved up to the level of the haunches).

Sources of building materials were heterogeneous and resulted in a non-uniform execution. Builders took advantage of this wide array of materials: bricks of different size and thickness, stone blocks, river stones, ceramic, and recycled materials from demolished buildings. This variety attests to the versatility of mortared construction, but on the other hand, it must have challenged builders in achieving a sound masonry that was able to resist the thrust generated by the vault. The considerable thickness of the walls (80 cm in the hall and 105 cm in the rectangular apse with pool) compared to the span of the vault (3.23 m) shows that builders were well aware of the poor quality of the walls. In contrast, the walls at the two ends of the barrel vault that did not have to resist the thrust were remarkably thinner (north wall: 45 cm; south wall: 54 cm). The builders privileged the use of stone and brick for those parts of the wall that seemed to be structurally critical. Brick facing with its regular joints must have been perceived as more sound that the stone/brick reticulate. The rectangular shape increased bonding to the core of the wall, particularly with some bricks set as headers to create a deeper bonding with the mortared rubble. Particularly relevant to the understanding of the care behind the selection of materials and facing techniques is the fact that builders used different facings on the outer and inner sides of the wall. The selection of bricks of different size in selected part of the building shows a good understanding of Vitruvius' principles of tripartite masonry.

2.3.2. The South-West Building

This monumental complex (Fig. 4.12c), set on the south-west edge of the site south of the Leonidaion, was investigated in the 1990s (Sinn 1992, Sinn *et al.* 1993; 1994; 1995). It has two main building phases, both occurring within a short interval of time. The earlier phase (Fig. 4.20) has been dated to the mid-first century CE (Martin 2001). The walls were faced with brick (horizontal bands, corners, and facing of walls exposed to heat) and local calcareous stone (reticulate and relieving arches). Because of the minimal thickness of the joints and the neat stone cutting, the quality of this wall facing is unique in the context of walls with mixed stone and brick (Medri 2001). Single *poros* ashlars (i.e., not forming a continuous ashlar masonry, but embedded into the mortared masonry) were employed for the door jambs and the quoins (Fig. 4.21).

The expertise in construction can be observed in the wall to the east of room 11, which is shaped at a right angle (Fig. 4.22). Differently from other first-phase remains which were incorporated into the second-phase walls, this wall was demolished up to the level of the floors of the second phase. The wall was built on a stone foundation (width 80 cm) that protruded for c. 12 cm from the wall facing, in order to create a larger platform (Fig. 4.23). The north–south part of the wall is 59 cm thick, while the east–west part is 44 cm thick. Other walls in room 9 and 10 are 90 cm thick. Bricks were cut in triangular shapes, likely from *bessales*, and are 3.7 cm thick. The minimal height of the joints is reflected in the heigh of 10 courses (51.5 cm). The core of the wall was made with broken bricks and chunks of stones carefully laid in horizontal layers in abundant mortar. The roughly pyramidal *tesserae* of the reticulate wall are extremely long (14–20 cm); this was probably intended to

Fig. 4.20. Olympia, South-West Building: Plan showing first-phase structures in red (image P. Vitti).

Fig. 4.21. Olympia, South-West Building: View of the north-east corner of room 9. The dotted line shows the limit of the first-phase brick-faced walls. Ashlars used as quoins are highlighted in red (photo P. Vitti).

Fig. 4.22. Olympia, South-West Building: View of the stone and brick wall in room 11. The masonry above the reticulate facing belongs to the second phase (photo P. Vitti).

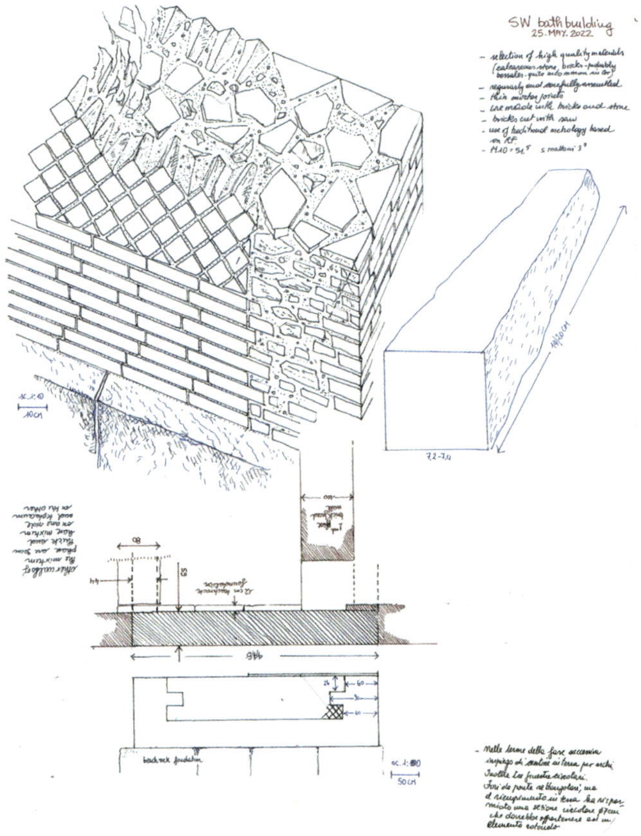

Fig. 4.23. Olympia, South-West Building: Graphic record of the first-phase walls of room 11 (image P. Vitti).

improve the cohesiveness of the masonry towards the core of the wall. The outer corner of the wall was made entirely with bricks; those at the edge were properly cut into a more rectangular shape to better bond the facing in the two directions of the wall. The brick and reticulate facings were made with the typical bonds, with the brick facing forming indentations into the reticulate: from a minimal width of 60 cm, the brick facing extends to 90 cm to better bond with the reticulate facing. The lower part of the wall was made with bricks, in order to have the reticulate portions framed into brick facings.

Unlike the mausoleum of Marcia Maxima at Patras described above, the mixed stone and brick masonry of the South-West Building at Olympia was not meant to be left bare. While both edifices can be ascribed to the same local building tradition, which can be traced in other constructions located between Patras and the region of Olympia, the high-quality execution and the exceptional use of bricks cut into triangular shapes might suggest a more direct involvement of builders connected with Rome. The lack of bands of bricks that do not go through all the thickness of the wall seems consistent with the lack of bonding courses in imperial constructions in Rome before the reign of Domitian. The use of stone ashlars in critical points of the masonry, as attested both in the South Bath and the South-West Building, appears consistently in Neronian-period structures such as the Domus Aurea. It might thus be suggested that the South-West Building was designed and executed by builders who were familiar with construction practices in Rome. At Olympia, like at Nikopolis, we therefore find buildings in which the local expertise played a major role, and others which were more influenced by contemporary building practices of the Italian Peninsula.

Conclusions

The buildings analysed in this chapter offer a significant, though limited, set of evidence of the ways in which builders in Roman-period Greece adopted lime-mortared construction in two different contexts. While the departure from earlier traditions of dry masonry or earth-mortared construction is evident, the ways builders approached mortared construction seems more nuanced, and it was certainly influenced by local materials, traditions, expertise, as well as patronage. The marked difference in the use of fired brick between the area of Nikopolis and the region of Patras seems to point in that direction. This heterogeneity of building solutions appears to have come to an end towards the end of the first century CE, when the use of brick facing was adopted on an increasing number of buildings, thus establishing a sort of technical *koine* in the use of building materials and construction techniques. Evidence is offered by monuments at Patras (Dekoulakou 2009), Olympia (for instance, the second phase of the South-West Building), and Nikopolis (such as the second phase of the theatre at the *proasteion*).

An important role in the dissemination of mortared construction at the end of the first century BCE must have been played by the local elites, who interacted with Roman settlers, including freedmen and *negotiatores*. As discussed by S. Zoumbaki (2008), during the first century CE Peloponnesian elites emulated the Roman upper classes to create connections with the central and local powers. It is possible that the assimilation of Roman architectural models also determined the need to adopt building techniques that were more suitable for vaulted construction than the local dry masonry. The most natural way to implement these architectural programmes was through the emulation of what had been already successfully experimented in the Italian Peninsula. The knowledge transfer from Roman builders to the Greek territory might have occurred in a variety of ways. Masonry such as that documented on the walls at Nikopolis, made with mortared rubble and faced with fired bricks (44 × 29 × 8 cm, or 29 × 29 × 8 cm), is very similar to that seen on contemporary fortifications in northern Italy (for example, Concordia Sagittaria, Turin, and Verona). One might argue that this masonry was directly inspired by those models and was brought to Greece by Roman builders. The 5 km brick-faced fortification of Nikopolis seems to be the result of a specific building programme that differs from all the other contemporary constructions in the city (such as the theatre, the stadium, or Mausoleum 6), where bricks are consistently missing.

The role of euergetism in the promotion of building programmes should be taken into consideration. In the case of Olympia, one would be tempted to explain the exceptional construction of the first phase of the South-West Building – which lacks the brick/stone reticulate typically in use in the region – with the involvement of external patronage and designers (if not workers). At Nikopolis, Mausoleum 6 recalls Italic features both in its design and execution, which would suggest a patronage strongly connected with, or influenced by, Rome. Literary sources show that the foundation of Nikopolis involved several euergetes, such as Herod the Great of Judaea (Joseph. *AJ* 16.146; on Herod's building programme see also Netzer 2018; Peleg-Barkat, this volume). However, it is difficult to understand how such high-rank sponsors could have influenced local building programmes, such as the stadium or the theatre. These two buildings are very similar in construction (Zachos 2016) and can be considered excellent case studies to assess the influence of local traditions on major projects at the end of the first century BCE. In this initial phase builders were not only concerned about the selection of local materials – with an articulated use of different types of stone and different building techniques – but also about the way buildings would have reacted to the thrust of the massive vaults that characterized the new architectures. The problem could not simply be addressed by increasing the thickness of the abutments – with all the problems related to the time needed for the hardening of lime mortars – but had also to take into account the possible effects of natural hazards such as earthquakes. The use of timber reinforcements inside the walls at Nikopolis is an evident testimony of the influence of the local expertise in the early phases of development of mortared construction in this seismic region. It is to be noted that the vaults in these early buildings at Nikopolis were mostly made with mortared stones placed radially, as seen also on Mausoleum 6. The similarities with mortared construction in Italy during the Late Republic – when major building programmes are documented in Latium and Campania (see, for instance, Cifarelli 2013) – attest to the presence of an experienced workmanship that was able to carefully select materials and techniques, as seen in the theatre. Whether these workers were local, as one may assume, or came from abroad, is hard to tell.

The application of mortared construction in the region of Patras and Elis differed from the one examined at Nikopolis. As pointed out in the discussion, the region had a longstanding tradition in fired-brick production, which might have determined the success of brick vaults. These vaults did not only provide structural soundness (even when employing poor types of mortar), but also made construction easier, since the reduced quantity of mortar in the joints allowed an immediate de-centring, which would have been impossible with the larger amount of mortar used in stone vaults. Contrary to the success of brick in vaulted construction, it appears that solid brick masonry was not adopted in the Peloponnese as no evidence of isodomic brick construction has been identified there so far. A possible explanation is the laborious execution of solid brick walls, if compared to the much quicker construction of walls made of tripartite mortared masonry.

The Mausoleum of Marcia Maxima at Patras is a significant example to understand how architectural models and mortared construction were adapted locally. The stone/brick reticulate used for the main façade (more irregular in other parts of the building) exemplifies how builders in this region adapted building techniques that were in use in Italy. The use of brick (or rather terracotta elements taken from roof tiles and containers such as amphorae) expressed the need to improve the bonding between the facing and the core of the wall, showing a capacity to interpret locally tripartite mortared masonry. It is worth emphasizing that the facing of walls was executed with significant irregularity within the same building, as in the stadium of Patras (dated to the reign of Domitian: Petropoulos and Pansini 2020). The evidence examined in this chapter offers additional data to our attempt to understand the use of this particular type of reticulate. The South Bath at Olympia shows that the contractor (and designer) was struggling to achieve the best quality possible with limited resources. The construction took advantage of bricks of different types, to a point that I suspect most of them were recycled from earlier buildings. The stone/brick reticulate attests to the same local tradition of the wall facings at Patras, including the brick bands that were not meant to create bonding courses. The use of stone ashlar quoins shows concerns about the need to reinforce those parts of the building which were more exposed to structural stresses. Similarly, numerous buildings in Rome employed different types of tufa and travertine for this same reason (Jackson *et al.* 2010). One wonders whether the South-West Building, which might have been constructed by builders from Italy, could have set a precedent for the adoption of stone ashlars at the corners of walls. In any case, the use of such stone ashlars seems to be a typical feature of these early buildings. A building located at Thelpousa, c. 40 km east of Olympia, offers a good example to understand the spread of local solutions across the region. The facing of this building is very similar to the one of the South Bath and includes, again, stones at the end of the walls and at the corners (Figs 4.24–25). Bricks used here are also square (c. one foot per side), with grooves on one side similar to the examples from Olympia. All of this shows a well-established local building tradition with a filtered transfer of building practices that had been developed in Italy.

More work on early first-century CE buildings in Greece will shed further light on the processes that I have attempted to outline here, and possibly this will confirm the role of local traditions and the adaptation patterns at a crucial moment when Roman-period construction techniques started developing through a marked change of earlier building practices. Building uncertainties and local solutions or compromises seem to come to an end with the end of the first century CE. The expansion of the brick production

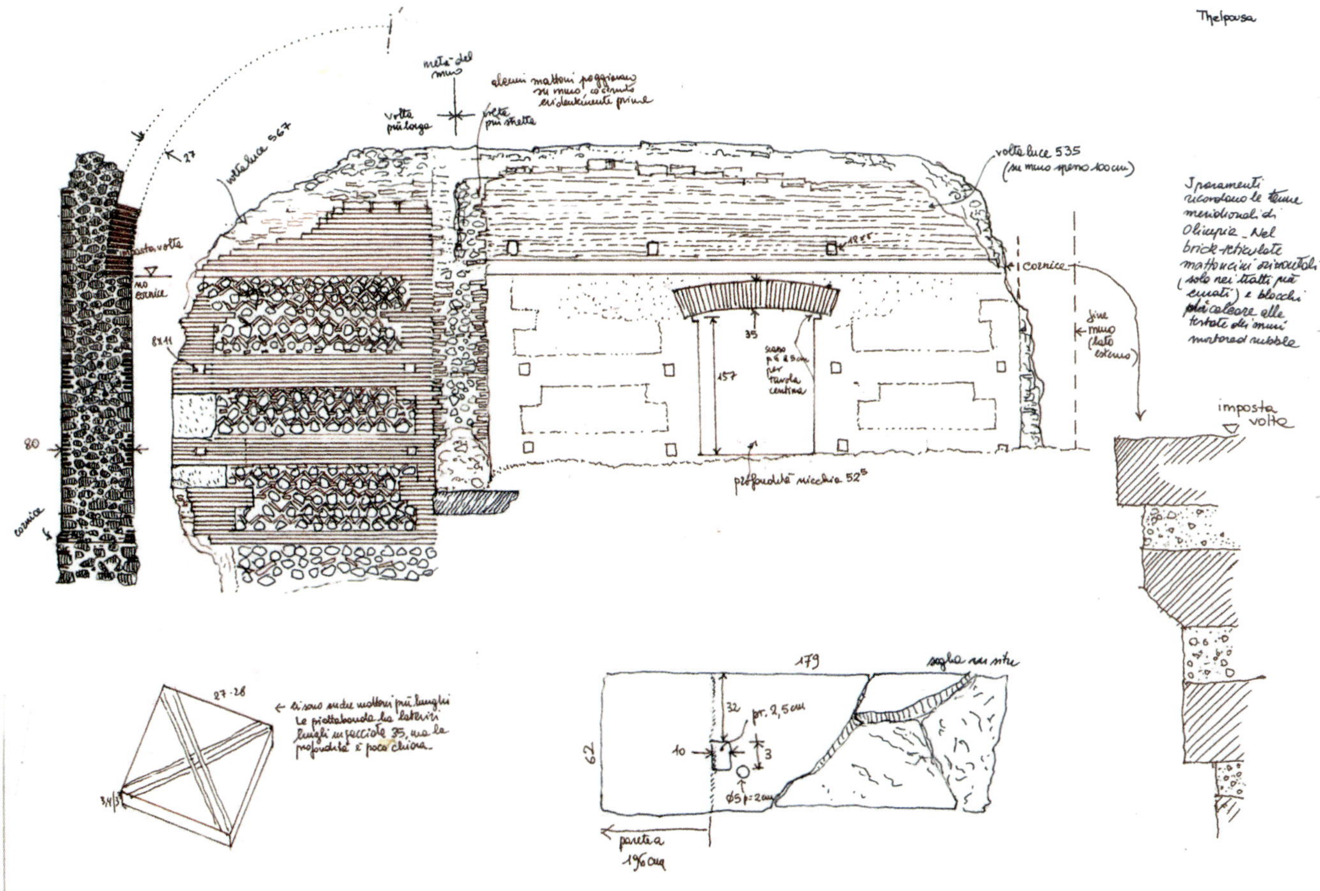

Fig. 4.24. Building at Thelpousa: Graphic record (image P. Vitti).

Fig. 4.25. Building at Thelpousa: View (photo P. Vitti).

industry – with the introduction of bricks that were not as thick as the Hellenistic ones – resulted in a large variety of bricks that were used both for new vaulting techniques and wall elevations. Brick bands were now employed all through the thickness of walls, similarly to the *bipedales* bonding courses found in Rome, which contributed substantially to the improvement of the structural behaviour of tripartite walls.

Notes

1. This research would not have been possible without the generous support of the School of Architecture of the University of Notre Dame and the permits granted by the Director of the Ephorate of Antiquities of Preveza, Dr Anthi Aggeli, and the Director of the Ephorate of Antiquities of Elis, Dr Erofili-Iris Kolia, as well as the Deutsches Archäologisches Institut (DAI) in Athens. Without the initiative of Niccolò Mugnai and Wolfson College (University of Oxford) this study would have never been conducted.
2. The discussion offered by M. Andronikos (1987) on the origin and chronology of barrel-vaulted construction is useful to address the exceptionality of vaulted structures in mainland Greece; according to him, the adoption of vaulted construction was consequent to the need to support the weight of the soil above the slab that covered the first monumental cist tombs (for instance, those at Katerini, second quarter of the fourth century BCE). See also Boyd 1978.
3. I wish to express my gratitude to Kostantinos Zachos, former director of the site, who has constantly supported my work since 2005. I am particularly grateful to Leonidas Leontaris for guiding me across the site on several occasions and for sharing with me his ongoing studies. His forthcoming article on the theatre's timber reinforcements has been instrumental for this chapter. I also thank Evvangelos Pavlidis for his support during my visits.
4. Since Nikopolis was created through a synoecism, it is likely that materials from abandoned buildings were transferred to the newly established city. When describing the walls of the stadium, K. Zachos (2016, 543–44) states that 'the walls (width: 1.50–1.55 m) are built of *opus vittatum* simplex, incorporating limestone blocks from earlier buildings into the corners. Large quantities of such spolia were built into other Augustan buildings at the site, including the victory monument, theater, and fortification wall gates. The impressive quantity of material used in the Augustan building program at Nicopolis was most probably transported from the nearby earlier settlement of Michalitsi'.
5. Π-shaped clamps were used for limestone ashlars and dovetail clams were used for *poros* ashlars: Zachos 2018, 726.
6. Blake and Van Deman 1947; Lugli 1957; Cifarelli 2013; Vitti 2020; Mogetta 2021.
7. The dimensions of the podium reported by C. Flämig (2007, 147: c. 9 m) differ from those indicated here. The width of c. 11 m is calculated from the centre of the tomb to the imprints of the blocks north of the entrance; the centre is calculated based on the curved wall of the triangular chamber.
8. My gratitude goes to Christos Liangkouras for his warm welcome at Olympia and for easing my visits at the site. Ioulia Stamu and Leonidas Leontaris have been very generous in sharing observations on the South Baths of Olympia as part of their studies conducted for the Ephorate of Antiquities.
9. An alternative date to the late first century BCE has been proposed by G. Ladstätter and reported by other scholars (Haseley 2006; Lo Monaco 2013) but remains undemonstrated.

References

Alcock, S.E. 1993. *Graecia capta. The Landscapes of Roman Greece*. Cambridge: Cambridge University Press.

Andreou, I. and Andreou, I. 2012. Αρχαία Ήλις. *Archaiologikon Deltion* 56–59: 484–96.

Andronikos, M. 1987. Some reflections on the Macedonian Tombs. *Annual of the British School at Athens* 82: 1–16.

Aupert, P. 1990. L'évolution des appareils en Grèce à l'époque impériale. *Bulletin de Correspondance Hellénique* 114: 593–637.

Blake, M.E. and Van Deman, E.B. 1947. *Ancient Roman Construction in Italy from the Prehistoric Period to Augustus*. Washington, DC: Carnegie Institution.

Bonetto, J. 2019. L'Italia settentrionale e le regioni contermini. In Bonetto, J., Bukowiecki, E. and Volpe, R. (eds), *Alle origini del laterizio romano: nascita e diffusione del mattone cotto nel Mediterraneo tra IV e I secolo a.C. Atti del secondo convegno internazionale 'Laterizio' (Padova, 26–28 aprile 2016)*. Rome: Quasar, 287–94.

Boyd, T.D. 1978. The arch and the vault in Greek architecture. *American Journal of Archaeology* 82.1: 83–100.

Camia, F. 2009. *Roma e le poleis. L'intervento di Roma nelle controversie territoriali tra le comunità greche di Grecia e d'Asia Minore nel secondo secolo a.C.: le testimonianze epigrafiche*. Athens: Scuola Archeologica Italiana di Atene.

Cifarelli, F.M. (ed.) 2013. *Tecniche costruttive del tardo ellenismo nel Lazio e in Campania. Atti del convegno (Segni, 3 dicembre 2011)*. Rome: Espera.

Coulton, J.J. 1977. *Ancient Greek Architects at Work: Problems of Structure and Design*. Ithaca, NY: Cornell University Press.

D'Ambrosio, A. and De Caro, S. 1983. *Un impegno per Pompei: fotopiano e documentazione della Necropoli di Porta Nocera*. Milan: Touring Club Italiano.

Dekoulakou, I. 2009. Monumenti delle necropoli di Patrasso durante il dominio romano. In Greco, E. (ed.), *Patrasso colonia di Augusto*.

Atti del Congresso internazionale (Patrasso, 23–24 marzo 2006). Athens: Scuola Archeologica Italiana di Atene, 163–210.

Deniaux, E. 1987. Atticus et l'Épire. In Cabanes, P. (ed.), *L'Illyrie méridionale et l'Épire dans l'antiquité. Actes du colloque international de Clermont-Ferrand, 22–25 octobre 1984*. Paris: De Boccard, 245–54.

Di Napoli, V., Camia, F., Evangelidis, V., Grigoropoulos, D., Rogers, D. and Vlizos, S. (eds) 2018. *What's New in Roman Greece? Recent Work on the Greek Mainland and the Islands in the Roman Period: Proceedings of a Conference Held in Athens, 8–10 October 2015*. Athens: National Hellenic Research Foundation.

Döhner, G.F.M. 2019. Examples of the early use of fired bricks in Apollonia (Albania). In Bonetto, J., Bukowiecki, E. and Volpe, R. (eds), *Alle origini del laterizio romano: nascita e diffusione del mattone cotto nel Mediterraneo tra IV e I secolo a.C. Atti del secondo convegno internazionale 'Laterizio' (Padova, 26–28 aprile 2016)*. Rome: Quasar, 67–76.

Eberle, L. and Le Quéré, E. 2017. Landed traders, trading agriculturalists? Land in the economy of the Italian diaspora in the Greek East. *Journal of Roman Studies* 107: 27–59.

Eisner, M. 1986. *Zur Typologie der Grabbauten im Suburbium Roms*. Mainz: Philipp von Zabern.

Flämig, C. 2007. *Grabarchitektur der römischen Kaiserzeit in Griechenland*. Rahden: Leidorf.

Gros, P. 2001. *L'architecture romaine du début du IIIe siècle av. J.-C. à la fin du Haut-Empire, 2: Maisons, palais, villas et tombeaux*. Paris: Picard.

Haseley, A. 2006. Masonry construction in Olympia, Greece, during the Roman imperial period. Mapping, classification and dating. In *Proceedings of the Second International Congress on Construction History (Queens' College, Cambridge University, 29/03–02/04/2006)*. Exeter: Short Run Press, 1517–40.

Hernandez, D.R. forthcoming. Epirus. In Burrell, B. (ed.), *A Companion to the Archaeology of the Roman Empire*. Hoboken, NJ: Wiley-Blackwell.

Jackson, M., Marra, F., Deocampo, D.M., Scheetz, B. and Vella, A. 2010. Analisi delle componenti geologiche delle murature del Foro di Cesare. *Scienze dell'Antichità* 16: 403–17.

Kirsten, E. 1987. The origins of the first inhabitants of Nicopolis. In Chrysos, E. (ed.), *Nicopolis I. Proceedings of the First International Symposium on Nicopolis (23–29 September 1984)*. Preveza: Municipality of Preveza, 91–98.

Kontoyianni, Th. 2007. Το θέατρο της Νικόπολης. In Zachos, K.L. (ed.), *Νικόπολις Β΄. Πρακτικά του Δεύτερου Διεθνούς Συμποσίου για τη Νικόπολη (11–15 Σεπτεμβρίου 2002)*. Preveza: Actia Nicopolis Foundation, 361–70.

Kunze, E. 1944. Die Ausgrabungen in den Jahren 1940 und 1941. *Bericht über die Ausgrabungen in Olympia* 4: 1–7.

Kunze, E. 1958. Die Ausgrabungen in den Wintern 1953/54 und 19454/55. *Bericht über die Ausgrabungen in Olympia* 6: 1–11.

Kunze, E. 1961. Die Ausgrabungen in den Frühjahren 1956 bis 1958. *Bericht über die Ausgrabungen in Olympia* 7: 1–11.

Kunze, E. 1962. Die Ausgrabungen in Olympia. *Archaiologikon Deltion* 16: 127–34.

Kunze, E. and Schleif, H. 1944. Die Badeanlage am Kladeos. *Bericht über die Ausgrabungen in Olympia* 4: 32–96.

Lancaster, L.C. 2015. *Innovative Vaulted Construction in the Architecture of the Roman Empire: 1st to 4th Centuries CE*. Cambridge: Cambridge University Press.

Leontaris, L. forthcoming. Timber reinforcements in concrete masonries of Nicopolis in Epirus, Greece. In Bonetto, J. and Previato, C. (eds), *Proceedings of the International Conference 'Terra, legno e materiali deperibili nell'architettura antica' (Padova, 3–5 giugno 2021)*. Padua: Università degli Studi di Padova.

Lo Monaco, A. 2004. L'élite elea ad Olimpia nel I sec. a.C. In Cébeillac-Gervasoni, M., Lemoine, L. and Reément, F. (eds), *Autocélébration des élites locales dans le monde romain: Contextes, images, textes (IIe s. av. J.-C. – IIIe s. ap. J.-C.)*. Clermont-Ferrand: Centre de Recherche sur les civilizations antiques, 287–305.

Lo Monaco, A. 2013. Fuori dall'Altis. Tende, bagni e propilei a Olimpia in età ellenistica. In Galli, M. (ed.), *Roman Power and Greek Sanctuaries. Forms of Interaction and Communication*. Athens: Scuola Archeologica Italiana di Atene, 125–42.

Lugli, G. 1957. *La tecnica edilizia romana con particolare riguardo a Roma e Lazio*. Rome: G. Bardi.

Mallwitz, A. 1958. Das Gebiet südlich der Bäder am Kladeos. *Bericht über die Ausgrabungen in Olympia* 6: 12–41.

Mallwitz, A. 1972. *Olympia und seine Bauten*. Munich: Prestel Verlag.

Marasco, G. 1988. *Economia, commerci e politica nel Mediterraneo fra il III* e *il II secolo a.C*. Florence: Università degli Studi di Firenze.

Martin, A. 2001. The South-West Building at Olympia. The ceramic and glass evidence for its dating. In Marc, J.-Y. and Moretti, J.-Ch. (eds), *Constructions publiques et programmes édilitaires en Grèce entre le IIe siècle av. J.-C. et le Ier siècle ap. J.-C. Actes du colloque organisé par l'École française d'Athènes et le CNRS (Athènes, 14–17 mai 1995)*. Athens: École française d'Athènes, 313–22.

Martin, R. 1965. *Manuel d'architecture grecque, volume 1: Matériaux et techniques*. Paris: Picard.

Medri, M. 2001. La diffusione dell'opera reticolata: considerazioni a partire dal caso di Olimpia. In Marc, J.-Y. and Moretti, J.-Ch. (eds), *Constructions publiques et programmes édilitaires en Grèce entre le IIe siècle av. J.-C. et le Ier siècle ap. J.-C. Actes du colloque organisé par l'École française d'Athènes et le CNRS (Athènes, 14–17 mai 1995)*. Athens: École française d'Athènes, 15–40.

Melfi, M. 2007. *I santuari di Asclepio in Grecia*. Rome: 'L'Erma' di Bretschneider.

Mogetta, M. 2021. *The Origins of Concrete Construction in Roman Architecture: Technology and Society in Republican Italy*. Cambridge: Cambridge University Press.

Netzer, E. 2018. *The Palaces of the Hasmoleans and Herod the Great (Reprinted and Expanded Edition)*. Jerusalem: Israel Exploration Society.

Orlandos, A.K. 1966. *Les matériaux de construction et la technique architecturale des anciens Grecs, I*. Paris: De Boccard.

Petropulos, M. and Pansini, A. 2020. The Roman stadium of Patras: excavations, analysis and reconstruction. *Annuario della Scuola Archeologica di Atene e delle Missioni Italiane in Oriente* 98: 382–416.

Purcell, N. 1987. The Nicopolitan synoecism and Roman urban policy. In Chrysos, E. (ed.), *Nicopolis I. Proceedings of the First International Symposium on Nicopolis (23–29 September 1984)*. Preveza: Municipality of Preveza, 72–90.

Rizakis, A.D. 1996. Les colonies romaines des côtes occidentales greques. Populations et territoires. *Dialogues d'Histoire Ancienne* 22.1: 255–324.

Rizakis, A.D. 1997. Roman colonies in the province of Achaia: territories, land and populations. In Alcock, S.E. (ed.), *The Early Roman Empire in the East*. Oxford: Oxbow Books, 15–36.

Rizakis, A.D. 1998. *Achaïe, II: La cité de Patras. Épigraphie et historie*. Paris: De Boccard.

Rizakis, A.D. and Zoumbaki, S. (eds) 2001. *Roman Peloponnese, I. Roman Personal Names in their Social Context (Achaia, Arcadia, Argolis, Corinthia and Eleia)*. Athens: National Hellenic Research Foundation.

Romano, D.G. 2000. A tale of two cities: Roman colonies at Corinth. In Fentress, E. (ed.), *Romanization and the City: Creation, Transformations and Failures. Proceedings of a Conference Held at the American Academy in Rome to Celebrate the 50th Anniversary of the Excavations at Cosa, 14–16 May 1998*. Portsmouth, RI: Journal of Roman Archaeology Supplementary Series, 83–104.

Schleif, H. 1944. Die Badeanlage am Kladeos. *Bericht über die Ausgrabungen in Olympia* 4: 32–104.

Schwarz, M. 2002. *Tumulat Italia tellus. Gestaltung, Chronologie und Bedeutung der römischen Rundgräber in Italien*. Rahden: Leidorf.

Sinn, U. 1992. Bericht über das Forschungsprojekt 'Olympia während der römischen Kaiserzeit', 1. Die Arbeiten von 1987–1992. *Nikephoros* 5: 75–84.

Sinn, U. 2003. Olympia: eine Spitzenstellung nicht nur im Sport. Eine neue entdeckte Badeanlage der hellenistischen Zeit. *Antike Welt* 34: 617–23.

Sinn, U., Ladstätter, G., Archer, M. and Völling, T. 1993. Bericht über das Forschungsprojekt 'Olympia während der römischen Kaiserzeit', 2. Die Arbeiten im Jahr 1993. *Nikephoros* 6: 153–58.

Sinn, U., Ladstätter, G., Archer, M. and Völling, T. 1994. Bericht über das Forschungsprojekt 'Olympia während der römischen Kaiserzeit', 3. Die Arbeiten im Jahr 1994. *Nikephoros* 7: 229–50.

Sinn, U., Ladstätter, G., Archer, M. and Völling, T. 1995. Bericht über das Forschungsprojekt 'Olympia während der römischen Kaiserzeit', 4. Die Arbeiten im Jahr 1995. *Nikephoros* 8: 161–82.

Stamu, I.L. 2021. *Unpublished Report: Αρχιτεκτονική Προμελέτη Στερέωσης και Αποκατάστασης Νοτίων Θερμών Αρχαίας Ολυμπίας, Υπουργείο Πολιτισμού και Αθλητισμού, Γενική Διεύθυνση Αρχαιοτήτων και Πολιτιστικής Κληρονομιάς, Διεύθυνση Προϊστορικών και Κλασικών Αρχαιοτήτων*. Athens.

Trümper, M., Brunenberg, C., Esposito, D., Heide,T. and Zielke, K. 2022. The men's tepidarium of the Stabian Baths at Pompeii: quantification of its construction and remodeling processes. In Maschek, D. and Trumper, M. (eds), *Architecture and the Ancient Economy. Proceedings of a Conference Held at Berlin (26–28 September 2019)*. Rome: Quasar, 219–56.

Tsiolis, V. 2013. The baths at Fregellae and the transition from balaneion to balneum. In Lucore, S.K. and Trümper, M. (eds), *Greek Baths and Bathing Culture. New Discoveries and Approaches*. Leuven: Peeters, 89–111.

Vintzileou, E. 2008. Effect of timber ties on the behavior of historic masonry. *Journal of Structural Engineering* 134.6: 961–72.

Vitti, M. 2019. Laterizi ellenistici in Grecia tra nuovi e vecchi dati. In Bonetto, J., Bukowiecki, E. and Volpe, R. (eds), *Alle origini del laterizio romano: nascita e diffusione del mattone cotto nel Mediterraneo tra IV e I secolo a.C. Atti del secondo convegno internazionale 'Laterizio' (Padova, 26–28 aprile 2016)*. Rome: Quasar, 35–52.

Vitti, P. 2013. Tradizione romana e tradizione bizantina nelle tecniche costruttive delle volte fra V e VI secolo: il caso delle mura aureliane. *Archeologia dell'Architettura* 18: 88–114.

Vitti, P. 2015. La costruzione nel Peloponneso romano: tradizione, sperimentazione e innovazione nell'uso del laterizio. *Archeologia dell'Architettura* 20: 190–205.

Vitti, P. 2016. *Building Roman Greece. Innovation in Vaulted Construction in the Peloponnese*. Rome: 'L'Erma' di Bretschneider.

Vitti, P. 2019. Fired bricks in Greece. In Bonetto, J., Bukowiecki, E. and Volpe, R. (eds), *Alle origini del laterizio romano: nascita e diffusione del mattone cotto nel Mediterraneo tra IV e I secolo a.C. Atti del secondo convegno internazionale 'Laterizio' (Padova, 26–28 aprile 2016)*. Rome: Quasar, 27–33.

Vitti, P. 2020. Innovazione e sperimentazione nella costruzione romana tra centro e periferia. In Aureli, G., Colonnese, F. and Cutarelli, S. (eds), *Intersezioni. Ricerche di storia, disegno e restauro dell'architettura*. Rome: Editoriale Artemide, 145–56.

Vitti, P. 2023. Lime and gypsum structural mortars in historic construction. In Nikita, E. and Rehen, T. (eds), *Encyclopedia of Archaeology, Second Edition*. Amsterdam: Elsevier, in press.

von Hesberg H. 1994. *Monumenta. I sepolcri romani e la loro architettura*. Milan: Longanesi.

Yegül, F.K. and Favro, D.E. 2019. *Roman Architecture and Urbanism from the Origins to Late Antiquity*. Cambridge: Cambridge University Press.

Zachos, K.L. 2007. Η οχύρωση και η πολεοδομική οργάνωση της ρωμαϊκής Νικόπολης: Νεώτερα στοιχεία και παρατηρήσεις. In Zachos, K.L. (ed.), *Νικόπολις Β΄. Πρακτικά του Δεύτερου Διεθνούς Συμποσίου για τη Νικόπολη (11–15 Σεπτεμβρίου 2002)*. Preveza: Actia Nicopolis Foundation, 273–98.

Zachos, K.L. (ed.) 2008. *Νικοπολη*. Athens: ΤΔΠΕΑΕ.

Zachos, K.L. 2012. Το Θέατρο της Νικόπολης. In Soueref, K.I. (ed.), *Αρχαία θέατρα της Ηπείρου*. Athens: Diazoma, 156–72.

Zachos, K.L. 2016. The stadium of Actian Nicopolis: observations on dating and architectural evolution. In Zambas, C., Lambrinoudakis, V., Simantoni-Bournia, E. and Ohnesorg, A. (eds), *ΑΡΧΙΤΕΚΤΩΝ. Τιμητικός Τόμος για τον Καθηγητή Μανόλη Κορρέ*. Athens: Melissa, 541–53.

Zachos, K.L. 2018. Recent investigations at the theater of Nicopolis: the Augustan building phase. In Lamboley, J.-L., Përzhita, L. and Skenderaj, A. (eds), *L'Illyrie méridionale et l'Épire dans l'Antiquité. VIe colloque international Musée National de Tirana (20–23 mai 2015)*. Paris: De Boccard, 721–34.

Zachos, K.L. and Karampa, M. 2015. *The Cemeteries of Nicopolis*. Athens: Ministry of Culture and Sports.

Zoumbaki, S.B. 2008. The composition of the Peloponnesian elites in the Roman period and the evolution of their resistance and approach to the Roman rulers. *Tekmeria* 9: 25–51.

5

Green shoots: Architectural transfer and sustainability in the architecture of the Roman provinces

Edmund Thomas

Old prejudices and new perspectives

Roman architecture is widely acknowledged as one of the most innovative architectural systems in world history. Architectural historians of different periods and public observers at large admire its ability to disperse architectural methods and technologies across wide areas and to take leading directions in invention within the Roman Empire. Technologically advanced structures like baths called for such a high level of expertise and ability to respond to eventualities that it is reasonable to assume that the combination of their technical needs and social importance made them 'a nexus of technology transfer in the Roman world' (Lancaster 2015, 193). The mobility of the military and their levels of specialism in technical fields have offered a ready explanation for the movement of architectural technologies.

As is widely acknowledged within the discipline, however, such assumptions raise questions of centralization and control (for instance, on the supply of decorative stones, see Russell 2013, 355–57). The prevailing view today is that questions of method and technique operated at a regional level, and innovations, as several of the chapters in this volume illustrate, were the result of local needs and adaptations to existing practice rather than centrally imposed systems (see, for example, contributions by Russell *et al.*, Lancaster, Vitti, Mugnai, and Stinson). In some cases, architectural advances in materials or techniques perhaps occurred outside Rome before their impact was visible in the metropolis itself.[1] This in turn raises the question of the motivations of local builders. If it is not possible to ascribe advances in technology simply to imperialism or political display, they may sometimes have arisen from concerns with resource or cost and with the durability of the building and its aesthetic contribution to the wider cityscape. This chapter starts to explore the evidence for sustainable practices in the architecture of the Roman provinces and their importance as a spur to architectural innovation.[2]

It is obvious, of course, that sustainability did not exist in the Greek or Roman world in the sense in which we understand the term today, namely as an ecological sensibility based on an awareness of climate change and the impact on this process of human interventions in the landscape. It is hard to find within surviving elite Greek and Roman literature any direct acknowledgement of the environmental costs of the consumption for energy of non-renewable resources. That does not mean, however, that there was no awareness in antiquity of the fragility of resource that is analogous to some extent to the modern concept of sustainability. The anxieties about durability in particular, a key demand among Roman provincial elites striving for monumental permanence, are also a critical theme of modern sustainability.[3] The selection of lasting materials has something in common with the priority of modern architects to seek enduring or renewable solutions. However, durability and sustainability are not, of course, the same. For instance, a widespread desire for permanence led to architectural practices in Italy and the Greek world such as the use of fired terracotta tiles to roof not only temples, regal houses, and other 'monumental' structures, but also ordinary domestic buildings, which could hardly be considered sustainable, when their introduction in the Archaic period involved an 'unprecedented use' of materials and energy resources (Lancaster and Ulrich 2014, 161). Moreover, attitudes to monumental building sometimes suggest the very opposite of sustainable design, namely a culture of prodigality and waste. Such perceptions find some reinforcement in the supposed impact of Roman architectural production and construction on the environment. One questionable past study paints an exaggerated picture of the implications of Greek and Roman interventions in the natural ecosystems of the Mediterranean by highlighting the environmental footprint of construction-related activities such as the quarrying and transportation of minerals, the manufacture of long timber for beams, and the abundant use of wood fuel to produce lime mortar, bricks, glass, and metallic architectural fittings, all of which created air pollution as well as high energy costs (Hughes 1994, 120–29). Another account describes the megalopolis of Rome in particular as 'the urban equivalent of a smouldering volcano' with myriad furnaces and open fires constantly burning wood fuel and especially the heating of its immense baths underpinned by procurement of combustible fuel on an unthinkable scale (Graham and Van Dam 2019, 330–31).

The changes to natural resources across the Mediterranean since Classical antiquity do not seem to reflect a society that privileged ecological conservation. In Italy, little remains of the coniferous forests once covering the Apennine slopes, from which timbers were hauled up to 50 km from the navigable course of the Tiber to form roofing trusses for Rome's basilicas or grand palatial spaces (Meiggs 1982, 327, 345). In Asia Minor, the cypresses of Lycia, and the vast forests of the Taurus mountains in Cilicia or the Amanus range in northern Syria that supplied Roman constructions so prodigiously may have suffered less than the cedar groves of Lebanon and Cyprus, which furnished costly buildings with their prized wood; but it is hard to gauge how diminished a fraction of their former states is their extent today and how far the exploitation of their natural resources has taken its toll (Meiggs 1982, 46, 87). Yet, as many have recognized, it is an exaggeration to attribute such lasting environmental damage to Roman ambitions, let alone to hold them responsible for the decline of the Roman Empire and the collapse of Classical antiquity more generally.[4]

The picture of Roman woodland management is more complicated. Most Roman cities mitigated the impact of forestry practices by relying on local sources of building timber and wood fuel. Deforestation around the Mediterranean coasts and uplands was irregular between the Bronze Age and the Middle Ages and not comparable to the changes in vegetation from the later medieval period and particularly from the nineteenth century as a result of considerable increases in population (Kull 2012, 233). In Asia Minor, a close environmental study of the vegetation of Sagalassos in the western Taurus mountains has indicated that the deforestation responsible for modern shortages of wood fuel and timber may not have begun until the twentieth century; in the Roman period, the coniferous forests on the slopes north of the city provided plentiful wood fuel, which, along with the availability of suitable clays, contributed to the establishment of a hub of industrial production outside the monumental centre (Vermoere *et al.* 2003, 169). The demands for timber and wood fuel of Rome itself and other large metropolitan centres such as Alexandria and, later, Constantinople were exceptional. It is too easy to assume from ancient accounts of Italian forests being 'used up' for Rome that this activity was wasteful and unrestrained without any thought for replanting.[5] The elites who controlled these resources knew of techniques for coppicing or tree-planting that helped to manage woodlands and make them more sustainable (Harris 2018, 227–28).

The difficulty, however, in seeking to render organized, even sustainable management practices into an ancient interest in sustainability is that the motives of the landowners and managers of such woodlands, which were often publicly defined resources leased out to private contractors, are not always clear. The emperor Hadrian sequestrated a vast area of Mount Lebanon supplying trees as imperial property, but we cannot know whether this was done to protect this resource from ecological depletion or simply to assert political and economic control.[6] One can only speculate about how interventions in the natural landscape were seen in antiquity. Contemporaries were certainly aware of the effects of human intervention. As Lucretius observed, 'men continuously compelled the forests to withdraw higher and higher into the mountains' (5.1370–71; all translations from Greek and Latin sources in this chapter are by the author). Yet this poetic conceit and philosophical observation is hardly an exact reflection of ancient forestry, and it would be anachronistic to take this image of 'the march of civilization' as an expression of 'green' concerns for the destruction of the landscape (Armstrong 2019, 297). It is unlikely that all ancient planners and patrons were as blind to this erosion of nature as their modern detractors have argued. The depiction of some individuals as ruthless *aedificatores* implies that not all were obsessed only with the constant competition for ever larger, more sumptuously decorated buildings. Nonetheless, among elite voices at any rate, the responses to large-scale construction ventures that might today provoke ecological protests lack articulation of environmental concerns.

The famous inscription of one such *aedificator* on the base of Trajan's Column provides an example. The antithesis of modern environmental activism, its boast about how much land was cleared, and how far the cityscape was transformed, to create space for Trajan's Forum, might perturb some modern readers as a sign of wanton disregard for the ecological impacts (*CIL* VI, 960 = *ILS* 294; Lepper and Frere 1988, 203–10). Yet the only surviving ancient reaction to its celebration of architectural achievement interprets the text as a rhetorical assertion without apparent awareness of that darker side (Dio Cass. 68.16.2). In the light of ancient moral criticism of obsessive building, it is not unthinkable that another, less elite ancient viewer of Trajan's projects would have read this inscription more negatively, or that an older observer who remembered the erosion of the Velia hill under Nero and the Flavians would have regarded the flattening of part of the Quirinal hill as no cause for celebration. It is perhaps arguable, however, that equity of land use, rather than outrage at environmental damage, motivated such responses, if they were articulated. Similarly, modern readers might feel disquiet at Aelius Aristides' remark (*Or.* 27) that the Temple of Hadrian at Cyzicus was now sufficient for sailors entering the Bosporus 'to take their bearings' from, instead of the peak of Proconnesus, reading this as another massive transformation of the natural landscape resulting from excessive quarrying activity, this time more gradual. Yet the orator's image springs from a laudatory comparison between buildings and landscape, rather than from any evident awareness of the human erosion of those mountain quarries, whose depletion was a rather later event with little visible impact on the horizon until the Middle Ages (Russell 2013, 224).

We may be on firmer ground with the practices exposed by archaeological evidence. Although these do not suggest a response to confrontation with impending climate change as experienced in modernity, escalating from the application of modern materials and technologies, they nonetheless reveal a concern with managing natural resources in order to sustain traditional ways of living. While the aim of durability in architecture is more equivocal, two other important elements of present-day ecologically focused practices appear as concerns shared by Roman builders. First, the demands for the ongoing maintenance and upkeep of civic facilities, and for the lasting provision of fuel for heating, which inscriptions often record as having been written into the funding of public buildings (especially baths), suggests an interest in making buildings sustainable (Fagan 1999, 163–64, 312–14, nos. 239–47). Although direct epigraphic evidence for such legally protected practices comes largely from the West, archaeological evidence helps to fill the gap for Asia Minor. For example, the history of the Hadrianic Baths at Aphrodisias in the third and fourth centuries CE, like that of many bath buildings in the western provinces, reveals a priority attached to conservation of heating and water resources in later antiquity that has attracted the label of 'sustainability' (McDavid 2019). Second, it is also possible to go beyond a desire on the part of ancient builders to maintain social practices for future generations and to see actual anxieties about resource, both in their uses of locally sourced materials and a desire for sustainability in ancient settlements generally, and in the written observations of elites on the availability of resources (for sustainability in ancient landscapes, see Citter 2015). If ancient literature does not indicate an understanding of sustainability in a form that climate activists might recognize today, the attitudes exposed sometimes betray comparable concerns. While few voiced an explicit awareness of environmental change like their modern counterparts, at least some of those who have left their thoughts in text reveal consciousness of the damage that construction might do to the natural environment. Horace's outcry (*Carm.* 3.1) at the builders who threw piles of *caementa* into the sea to create concrete piers has a similar moral air to anti-fracking activists' protests today against entrepreneurs who place profit before respect for landscape. At the beginning of Pliny's account (*HN* 36.1.1) of the exploitation of marble for sculpture and architecture, the prominent metaphor in his statement that 'all the materials we have mined (*tractavimus*) for this book might seem to have been created for humanity' presents an analogy between his own encyclopaedic history of this practice and the activity itself, which intimates the meddlesome nature of the quarrying of stone that he calls 'the principal insanity of human behaviour' (*praecipua morum insania*). Yet such hints in these voices of the presumptuousness or immorality of their contemporaries' use of natural resources are a long way from the modern conceit of a self-induced threat to a natural inheritance.

This chapter explores the relevance of these questions to Roman-era architectural practice in the provinces. In particular, it contends that present concerns with sustainability can illuminate the study of antiquity. Two recent works have started to reveal issues in ancient thought and practice comparable to modern ecological ideas. First, a conference in Stuttgart in 2008 qualified perceptions of abundance by highlighting ancient concerns with availability of natural resources (Olshausen and Sauer 2012). A second colloquium, at Augsburg in 2016, addressed the concept of sustainability (*Nachhaltigkeit*) directly (Schliephake *et al.* 2020). The editors argued that the anachronistic nature of the term was no reason to reject it altogether, but, rather, an encouragement to view it as a shorthand for forms of human interaction with the environment. One of the many spheres of human activity covered by the conference in which participants saw principles and concerns that resembled modern ones was the safeguarding of the supply of water to manage environmental resource (Locicero 2020). More importantly, another contribution considered how innovations in ancient architecture such as heating tubes and glazed windows were related to the motive of sustainability (DeLaine 2020). In surveying the practices in Roman-period construction, with particular reference to the eastern Mediterranean, the present chapter considers practices in the architecture of the Roman provinces more widely and argues that the aims of builders under the Roman Empire and in the twenty-first century may not be as far apart as generally considered, and that modern builders may even learn something from ancient practices.

Principles of 'green design' in the architecture of Roman Asia Minor

Many of the objectives for sustainable building today and in the future were also those of ancient builders. A recent manual for 'green design' in architecture signals as overriding priorities a building's environmental impact and the comfort and health of its occupants (Brophy and

Lewis 2011, 21). Awareness of environmental impact is not a new realization. As we saw in the previous section, ancient observers were also conscious of the impact of building on the natural environment. Parallels between the environmental crisis of the twenty-first century and the shortage of natural resources in Roman antiquity suggest that modern planners can learn from ancient solutions to these problems. For example, the management of water resources in the ancient Near East in response to scarcity offers lessons for today (Šulyová *et al.* 2021). This section considers how far builders in the Roman provinces, and in Asia Minor in particular, shared modern designers' priorities of comfort and health.

The comfort of users of architecture is measurable from four interconnected factors: first, thermal comfort, defined as 'a sense of well-being with respect to temperature'; second, visual comfort, achieved by the provision of light conditions that enable activities to be performed without undue strain or danger; third, air quality, the achievement of health and well-being through air flow in an occupied space that avoids noxious smells or an oppressive atmosphere; and, fourth, acoustic quality, the maximization of clear sound movements across a space and the reduction of discomfort caused by obtrusive internal or external noise (Brophy and Lewis 2011, 21–38). Such conditions within a building affect not only levels of comfort experienced by users, but also physical and mental health. Poor air quality, toxic materials, lack of daylight, and excessive noise can all have lasting consequences for well-being.

It is not hard to find confirmation from ancient authors that thermal comfort and well-being were also desirable effects of Roman architecture. This is most evident in writings about private Italian villa landscapes, for which the thoughts of some property owners survive, such as Pliny the Younger (*Ep.* 2.17.9; cf. 17) on his villa on the Laurentine shore southwest of Rome, showing that they valued the use of architectural technology both to achieve a 'healthy temperature' and to exploit and control the sun's natural warmth. A principle to which Pliny appeals, and one of the most commonly cited values in Romans' assessments of their built environment in general, is the concept of *amoenitas*. For rural areas, scholars recognize that this ideal involved a dialectical visual relationship between architecture and environment, intermeshed with elite ideals of pleasure (*voluptas*) and opulence (*luxuria*).[7] It also, however, encompassed feelings of physical environmental comfort, such as the presence of a cooling water supply: in this regard, deep wells and springs could compensate for the absence of dancing fountains (Plin. *Ep.* 2.17.25).

These sensibilities were not unique to those living in Italy. In the heat of summer and autumn, Herodes Atticus' Villa Cephisia outside Athens was enjoyed for 'the shade of its vast woodlands, its long, soft walkways, the cooling position of the house, the abundant, radiant, and brightly lit baths, and the attractiveness of the whole villa, everywhere singing with the sound of birds and bubbling waters' (Gell. *NA* 1.2.2). In an urban context too, water contributed to *amoenitas*, not only in the West, but also in eastern cities such as Antioch and Apamea (Vannesse 2011).[8] By the Augustan era, the cities of Asia Minor had a long-standing reputation for public *amoenitas* (Livy 39.1.3). The subsequent continuation of this tradition is evident in the well-studied abundance of fountains and other water features, which provided citizens and visitors with both healthy sustenance and visual appeal.[9] Few doubt that public fountains were an important status symbol for their communities (Wilson 1995; Piras 2000) and had socio-economic, socio-cultural, or socio-political importance as expressions of patronage and identity (Richard 2012; 2016), but the *amoenitas* of such structures was as important as their utility and health (Antico Gallina 2004). Aristides' fragmentary 'Panegyric on the Water at Pergamon' celebrates the addition of this vital urban resource through a new aqueduct, probably the 40 km long conduit from the Madradağ range to the north, with water 'most plentiful in quantity and most beautiful in beauty, as much as cities have been allocated' (*Or.* 53.3; Jones 1991, 112–15). Yet, although scholars recognize these demands as interconnected, and that a desire for economic profitability could sometimes compromise the ideal (Marzano 2010), they seldom consider their environmental implications. The provision of cooling water from public fountains, built into façades of baths from northern Gaul to Arabia, offered thermal comfort in warm climates (Bouet and Saragoza 2007).

The continued discharge of valued water resources may seem wasteful, but there are also signs that the construction of such displays did not always mean squandering resources.[10] The Peirene Fountain at Corinth is only the best-known example of how builders sought to preserve and restore existing hydraulic systems to offer inhabitants a healthy and sustainable way of life based on the constant flow of natural resources (Agusta-Boularot 2001, 228–29; Robinson 2011). At the sanctuary of Kapıkaya outside Pergamon, conduits cut into the rock and basins for water collection enabled regulation of the water from the natural spring filled by seasonal deluges (Nohlen and Radt 1978, 69–70; Weiss 2003, 269–70). In the city itself, the sanctuary of Isis at the 'Red Hall' included a complex system of water channels, basins, and cisterns, designed to capture and store natural water resources in order to maintain a regular flow for ritual purposes.[11] In their discussion of streetside fountains of Asia Minor in Late Antiquity, Ine Jacobs and Julian Richard (2012) have shown how planners prioritized maintenance of existing installations, but also devised new, more modest, and cost-effective structures to conserve water at a time when its supply was uncertain and subject to unpredictable political or social change.

Built structures could themselves be a source of thermal comfort and provide a healthier environment. Covered streetside porticoes, to western eyes the most distinctive feature of cities in Asia, were not only an imposing monumental feature, but also offered pedestrians protection from rain or, more significantly in Mediterranean climates, from scorching sunshine, by securing a regular current of cooler air (Byhet 2001–02). The colonnaded street was a major vehicle for ensuring such provisions on a large scale in the urban landscape, and its layout and orientation sometimes suggest a wish to respond to climatic needs.[12]

An analogy from Rome indicates how motives of public health contributed to the planning of such schemes. After the fire of 64 CE, the emperor Nero tried to apply the same model of broad open spaces to his 'new Rome', with rows of side streets (*vici*) 'measured out' (*dimensis*) rather than 'without distinction' as before, and 'broad spaces of avenues (*viae*), restricted heights of buildings, courtyards opened up, and porticoes added to protect the fronts of *insulae*'. These interventions, 'welcomed for their utility' and funded from the imperial fiscus, with incentives to individual property owners, 'brought a gloss to the new city' (Tac. *Ann.* 15.43.1–2). Some, however, believed that 'the old layout had been more conducive to health, because the narrow access routes and height of the buildings were not penetrated to the same extent by solar heat; but now the broad open space, exposed without any shade, burned in more oppressive temperatures' (Tac. *Ann.* 15.43.5). The appeal here to public health (*salubritas*) suggests that this criterion was also the rationale for Nero's changes. After a devastating fire, which had spread because of the close proximity of ramshackle, mostly wooden structures, prone to topple from insecure heights, these objections might have seemed counter-intuitive. More expansive open areas could be considered safer and more salubrious than incarcerating the city's inhabitants in a potentially confined environment, which, if not as overcrowded as traditionally imagined, was frequently polluted by insanitary hazards and smells of everyday domestic and industrial activities.[13]

It was not only temperature control, but airflow and quality that contributed to the inhabitants' comfort. Nero's other scheme after the fire was a canal through the insalubrious Pontine marshes south of Rome, which, although abortive and haughtily dismissed by Tacitus, was similarly aimed at public health and more sustainable subsistence (*Ann.* 15.42.1; Sallares 2002, 190). The impact of this 'putrid, nauseating' zone, as Tito Berti described it in 1884, remained lethal until the twentieth century, its seasonal, open marshes a source of malaria.[14] The later complaints of Pope Pius II Piccolomini on a visit to Mantua in 1459 give an idea of the problems of living in similar conurbations in the ancient Mediterranean: for all the magnificent architecture, 'dust in the summer and mud in the winter' compromised life there; 'the place was marshy and unhealthy; the heat was intense… very many were catching fever; nothing was to be heard except the frogs' (quoted by Nevola 2020, 33). The warm summer sunshine increased the stench and dangers of disease from decaying carcasses and other organic material, not only in Italy. Creating a healthy flow of air was a priority. At Patara, in the coastal marshland of Lycia, the velaria or canvas awnings installed in the theatre in the second century CE served to shade spectators from the sun's dangerous heat and helped to create a healthier atmosphere in the cavernous interior.[15]

The sun's rays were both a store of heat that needed modulation to achieve thermal comfort and a source of light for visual comfort. In the Classical period, Socrates, in Xenophon's *Memorabilia* (3.8.8–10), sees the open colonnade, or *pastas*, off the courtyard of a Greek house as the answer to combining those enduring but often conflicting criteria of design, beauty and utility:

> So, in south-facing houses, the sun casts light into *pastades* in winter, while in summer it provides shade for ourselves and for the structures. If it is fine like this, then, we should build the southward parts higher, so that the winter sun is not excluded, and the north-facing side lower so that cold winds do not penetrate them: in sum, a place where a man might retreat himself at all seasons and store his property most safely would naturally be the most pleasant and beautiful dwelling.

From the fourth century BCE houses at Priene adopted such 'passive design' to store solar energy (Figs 5.1–2) (Bainbridge and Haggard 2011, 53, fig. 2.18a–b). In the Hellenistic era the Rhodian peristyle described by Vitruvius developed this principle, and while its best surviving examples are at Pompeii – the Houses of the Dioscuri and the Golden Cupids – its name suggests its origin and perhaps more frequent adoption in the eastern Mediterranean, if not necessarily in Rhodes (*De arch.* 6.7.3; Winter 2006, 174). This device occurs not only in private houses, but also in public areas such as the courtyard between the Prytaneion and Bouleuterion on the north side of the Upper Agora at Ephesus including two altars or small temples, which has been interpreted as a temenos dedicated to Augustus and Artemis (see, most recently, Scherrer 1990, 98–101; 1995, 5). On the eastern side of the court, towards the Bouleuterion, a colonnade 87 cm taller than on the other sides, apparently of Hellenistic date and reused here in the Augustan period, exposes that side of the courtyard to the evening sun, while the lower colonnade on the northern side keeps out the prevailing southerly winds and the harsh heat of the sun (Figs 5.3–5).[16] The position is unrelated to the religious structures at the west end and seems designed for a more practical purpose, either to shelter human participants or to protect perishable items used in rituals. The use of this feature suggests either an interest in enhancing personal well-being or an inclination to look for what today would be called sustainable solutions.

The fourth contributor to comfort and well-being in architecture, acoustic quality, is more difficult to demonstrate as a priority of ancient architecture. Elite voices such as Martial

Fig. 5.1. Isometric reconstruction drawing of houses at Priene, showing sunlight on south-facing fronts (Bainbridge and Haggard 2011, used with permission from Chelsea Green Publishing).

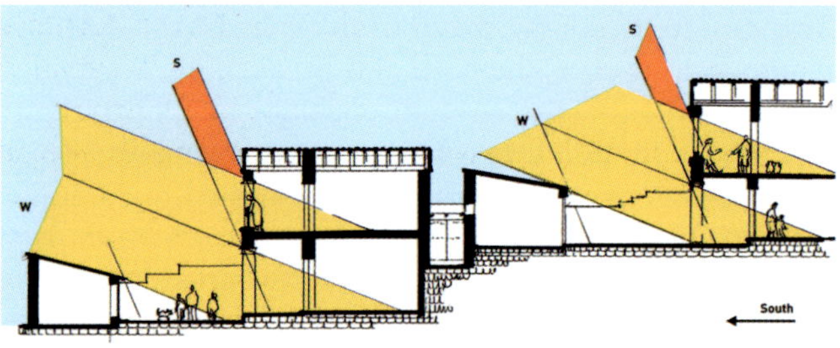

Fig. 5.2. Reconstructed section of the same houses at Priene, showing the admission of sunlight for residents (Bainbridge and Haggard 2011, used with permission from Chelsea Green Publishing).

and Seneca, however, demonstrate that this was perceived to be an issue of ancient living, providing abundant examples of obtrusive and undesirable internal or external noise in urban environments.[17] In the Augustan period, the jurist Labeo identified the raucous noise (*convicium*) of gatherings as an *iniuria* (*Dig.* 47.10.15). In Roman Gaul this may have been one reason for moving deafening industrial premises such as metalworking sites from well-to-do residential areas, where they are attested at Reims, to the peripheries of cities, as at Bordeaux, Autun, and Avenches (Goguey

Fig. 5.3. Ephesus, Upper Agora: Columns from a 'Rhodian peristyle' with higher east colonnade and lower north colonnade, re-erected at the north-east corner of the court identified as the Temenos of Augustus and Artemis (photo OeAI-OeAW).

2002, 268–70). However, the evidence for architectural adaptations of buildings to insulate them from such noise is scarce. There is, of course, extensive evidence for acoustic technologies since the Hellenistic period, using the science of harmonics to optimize sound quality for public performance, particularly known from Vitruvius; broken amphorae were possibly used as sounding vessels to enhance acoustics in the Odeion of Herodes Atticus in Athens and theatres at Aizanoi in Asia Minor, Hierapytna, Gortyn, and Lyktos in Crete, and Scythopolis in Arabia.[18] The focus of these installations on performance does not mean that ancient architects did not also take into account what we would call acoustic comfort. Some solutions enhanced acoustic quality by excluding obtrusive noise. Philostratus does not explain the choice of expensive cedar wood for the Odeion of Herodes Atticus, but its particular value is clear from the fact that the same patron risked a substantial financial penalty to fell trees in a sacred precinct (*V S* 2.1, 551; 2.5, 556). Modern users prize this material's capacity to create excellent sound precisely because of its ability to absorb sound and exclude unwanted background noise (Thomas 2017, 186–87, with

Fig. 5.4. Ephesus, Upper Agora: Detail of the re-erected columns at the north-east corner of the peristyle court (photo OeAI-OeAW).

Fig. 5.5. Ephesus, Upper Agora: View over rooms and re-erected colonnades off the court (photo M. Steskal, OeAI-OeAW).

further references; Madsen 2021, 430). Its effective provision of acoustic insulation also explains its use in Byzantine churches in Jerusalem (Shalev-Hurvitz 2015, 172). That was certainly a factor in its use to roof the stage of Herodes' Odeion and exclude the din from up to 5,000 spectators. Preserving the performers' utterances from being drowned out by such noise undoubtedly improved the audience's own acoustic comfort. The cost of this wood, however, limited its wider application. The absence of circumstantial knowledge about noise levels in and around ancient spaces makes it difficult to establish how much more widely architects in the Roman world aimed at acoustic comfort. This is one area of ancient architecture that needs more detailed investigation, perhaps with theoretical models of the passage of sound from social, religious, and commercial activities applied to archaeological examples.

The concern with thermal comfort is much clearer from both archaeological and literary evidence. For modern architects, this quality depends on achieving a balance between the heat produced by the body and the loss of heat to the surroundings. Such a balance depends on seven factors. Three – metabolism, clothing, and skin temperature – depend on natural determinants or individuals' cultural choices and are therefore not subject to social control or management. Metabolism is the sum of internal bodily chemical reactions that seek to maintain a stable body temperature; the production of metabolic energy, or heat, depends on physical activity. Clothing obstructs the exchange of heat between the surface of the skin and the atmosphere. Skin temperature is not constant like internal body temperature, but defined by a combination of metabolism, clothing, and room temperature. Exposed parts of the skin feel the impact of air temperature on the materials of the buildings around them. The buildings of the ancient Mediterranean were not intended for modern users in darker or heavier western clothing, but to provide light or heat to users wearing togas, chitons, himatia, tunics, and other light covering garments worn in the Roman East. As these fabrics kept the body warm in winter and cool in summer, architects too adjusted to these conditions.

If these three factors are conditions beyond architects' control, to which they must respond, the other four come from the surrounding environment and can be contained by good architectural design. These are air temperature, relative humidity, surface temperature of the elements in the room, and air speed. Architects can also take into account the part played by local conditions of specific sites. The sun streaming into buildings through windows, the flow of air within a room, and the body weight, subjective factors, and adaptation of the users all affect perceptions of thermal comfort, as is particularly clear from Pliny's assessment of his experience of his villa environments.[19] This is not, however, simply a reflection of how writers verbalized their experiences. Nor is it limited to rural or domestic architecture.[20] As we have seen, the architecture itself also reveals the desire to accommodate these factors. The next section will consider how far ancient architectural practices corresponded to the strategies promoted by modern advocates of green design.

Ancient strategies for sustainability

Modern architecture benefits from a range of innovative technologies and materials that help architects to fight climate change with renewable solutions. These solutions adopt both active and passive strategies. While active interventions may depend on the development of technologies not yet developed in antiquity, passive design strategies such as reducing demand for energy, water, and materials, or providing for energy needs to be met from renewable sources, were not just possible, but desirable. The Stuttgart conference revealed that many ancient societies experienced resource pressures not unfamiliar to modern cities, particularly from the third century CE, such as demands for water, metals, wood, and other materials. Yet, even if ancient writers in the second and third centuries sometimes refer to diminishing mineral reserves, most spoke of natural resources as if they were inexhaustible or would in time be replenished or replaced.[21] Strategies of passive design did not arise in the context of an ideological drive towards sustainability, as today, but their pervasive presence in ancient architecture in the provinces suggests that architects too shared some of the same sensibilities as their modern counterparts.

Open spaces, green spaces

The question of urban density highlighted by proponents of green design has much in common with the issues current in Rome after the fire of 64 CE. The different views taken on the form of the rebuilt city resemble the debates of modern planners about the ideal density of an urban layout. Efficient urban planning can reduce climate risks, and 'sustainable urban development patterns rely on the intensification and renewal of the existing fabric' (Brophy and Lewis 2011, 47). High-density building can mean lower energy consumption, less wasted space, and commercial benefits from concentrated populations, while lower densities can offer higher quality of life. The criticism of Nero's open, low-density layout by the grumbling senatorial coteries of Rome has some support from the modern view that confined layouts provide climate-responsive shading for cities in a warm climate (Brophy and Lewis 2011, 46). Half a century later, this debate is mirrored in Roman Bithynia. The arguments of Dio 'Chrysostom' Cocceianus for his new benefaction at Prusa were ecological as well as aesthetic: the stoa would give the city 'more space and open areas, shade in summer and shelter in winter' (Dio Chrys. *Or.* 47.13–15; Thomas 2007, 127). This claim is similar to modern arguments that reducing size or density improves microclimate. Similarly, in fifth-century CE Bordeaux (Burdigala), 'spacious' public areas brought its inhabitants a sense of well-being (Paulinus Pellaeus, *Eucharisticus* 44–47; Deschamps 2001–02, 451–52). Dio is not explicit about his opponents' arguments, but his focus on the positive impact of his stoa's height suggests that others had particularly criticized this aspect. One modern interpretation implies that the opposition stemmed from a conservative aesthetic reaction against an unfamiliar verticality, which Dio retorted was 'worthy of a great city' (Hanfmann 1975, 49). However, Dio's focus on the shade and shelter offered by his stoa seems to address also practical objections. For example, a plausible criticism might have been that the new building would block sunlight from neighbouring spaces. Similarly, modern planners complain that tall buildings 'have a more severe impact on the immediate external environment in terms of shade, wind turbulence and rain shadow' (Brophy and Lewis 2011, 47).

One of the principal modern strategies for sustainable urban planning is the provision of green space. In modern cities, theorists recognize that green spaces in built-up neighbourhoods can moderate local microclimate. Airflow and vegetation ensure that temperatures in urban parks can be 5–10° C lower than in densely built areas around them. As well as reducing pollution, they create zones for non-human animals and contribute to the social, physical, and psychological health of the human community (Brophy and Lewis 2011, 48–49). Many of these factors are relevant to ancient cities. Some have derided the extensive uncovered areas in the urban centre of Aphrodisias (Fig. 5.6) as a superfluity of 'conspicuously useless' public space aimed purely at 'pleasure and well-ordered leisure' (quotations from Smith 1996, 49). Such wide open spaces, however, could be interpreted as a means of regulating the solar environment to benefit the city population as a whole; planted with palm trees and adorned with an enormous, elongated marble pool, the Portico of Tiberius, later known as the 'Place of Palms' (Fig. 5.7), reflects principles of passive solar design, providing shade in summer heat and sunlight in winter, just as fountains used natural water sources to enhance public health.[22] These energizing open spaces and multi-functional areas for civic, recreational, or religious activities brought together transregional groups from a wide radius. They absorbed the sun's rays during the harsh winter months, while planted trees and colonnades provided protection against its heat in summer. The suggestion that the 'porticoes' of the Sebasteion (Fig. 5.8) 'had no practical function' overlooks their important social and environmental roles (Smith 1987, 95, followed by Burns 2017, 178). The absence of finds until Late Antiquity and of prepared floors in the sequence of rooms behind the side 'porticoes' cannot definitively show that these areas served no purpose. The colonnades kept their civic or commercial operations not only secure but sustainable, as their use up to the fifth century CE indicates. Within the open spaces, there was measured protection against scorching temperatures. Even in the early afternoon at the height of summer, the three-storeyed, 12 m high colonnade on the south side of the complex cast shadows at least 3 m long; before 10:30

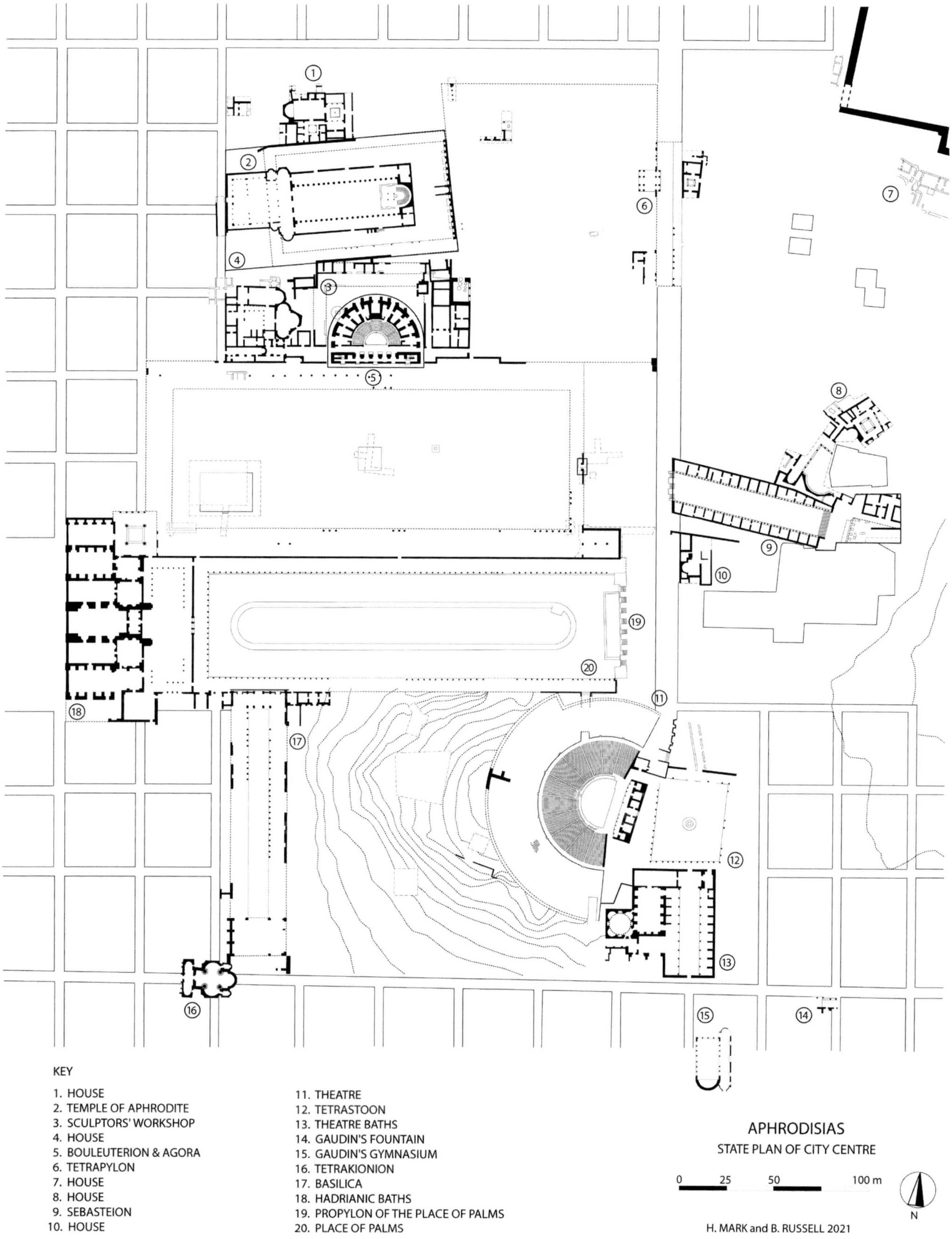

Fig. 5.6. Aphrodisias, state plan of the city centre (image H. Mark and B. Russell, courtesy of New York University Excavations at Aphrodisias).

Fig. 5.7. Aphrodisias, 'Place of the Palms' (photo B. Russell, courtesy of New York University Excavations at Aphrodisias).

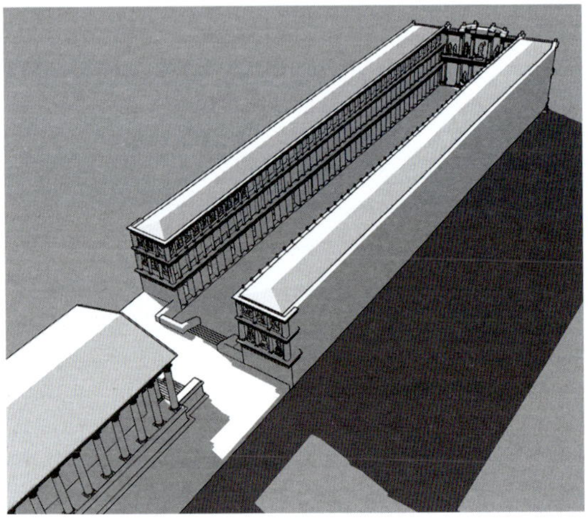

Fig. 5.8. Aphrodisias, Sebasteion: Reconstruction of shadows around 11:00 a.m. showing the shade provided by the high side structures (image P. Stinson).

in the morning or by 18:00 in the evening, they covered the whole court, 14 m wide.[23]

Responses to climate

A second strategy of modern urban design is to 'take account of prevailing winds in street layouts and orientations', with 'favourable solar orientations for streets and open spaces' in cooler climates, and exploiting the presence of shade in warmer ones (Brophy and Lewis 2011, 46). While the stone or brick materials of buildings form a heat store through their high thermal capacity, which contributes to high air temperatures, the presence of water has a cooling effect through evaporation, and vegetation provides shade and evapo-transpiration. Awareness of such factors, if not their scientific basis, is again best attested for private architecture in Roman Italy. However, Pliny's considerations regarding the cryptoporticus of his Laurentine villa apply also to urban planning (*Ep.* 2.17.16–19):

> Windows on both sides, in greater number towards the sea, individual ones facing the garden but fewer and in alternate bays. All are open when the day is windless and calm, and when it is turbulent on one side or the other, they open without injury where the winds rest... The cryptoporticus increases its heat from the reflection of the permeating sun, and as it contains the sun's heat so it checks and excludes the north-east wind, and there is as much cool behind as heat in front; it stops the south-west wind in the same way, and thus it checks and blocks winds from very different directions with its different sides. This pleasantness in winter is greater in summer, since before midday the *xystus* and after midday the nearest part of the *gestatio* and the garden are tempered by their own shadows, which fall on one side or the other, now shorter, now longer, as the day waxes or wanes. But the cryptoporticus itself lacks the sun most when it blazes most insistently on its roof. In addition, it receives gentle westerly winds through its open windows and diffuses them within the space, which never becomes oppressive with rancid, lingering air.

The cryptoporticus is a well-known example of structures designed to sustain regular commercial or social activities during hot summer months. It used to be thought of as a western feature, installed by architects from Rome; but, in addition to the example along the north side of the east–west street at Bosra in Arabia (Fig. 5.9), excavations at Aphrodisias have shown both private and public instances.[24] The terraces of the Temple of Domitian and Gymnasium of Vedius at Ephesus (Fig. 5.10–12) included similar subterranean structures (Yegül and Favro 2019, 610). The extreme microclimate of Roman Syria offers the clearest example of the attention of planners and architects in the eastern provinces to climatic considerations: two or three-storey houses in unusually resistant local stone; deep, uncolonnaded inner courtyards shaded from summer heat and winter winds alike; and flat terraced roofs for sleeping on hot summer nights (Yegül and Favro 2019, 787).

Fig. 5.9. Bosra, cryptoporticus, viewed below and behind the north portico of the colonnaded decumanus, *with openings at street level for light and ventilation (photo E.V. Thomas).*

Fig. 5.10. Ephesus, Gymnasium of Vedius: Site view of the terraced north front, with remains of the cryptoporticus to the right (photo M. Steskal, OeAI-OeAW).

Fig. 5.11. Ephesus, Gymnasium of Vedius: View of cryptoporticus from the east, showing remains of the excavated floor in the foreground (photo M. Steskal, OeAI-OeAW).

The modern strategy of laying out streets according to prevailing wind directions is familiar from Vitruvius' instruction not to orientate streets directly towards winds that may be detrimental with cold, warmth, or humidity. At Mytilene on Lesbos, he notes, the south wind causes sickness, the north-north-west wind provokes coughing, and the north wind is too cold for people to stay outside (*De arch.* 1.6.1–2). Galen later questioned this theory, observing that in a large theatre exposed to the sun few spectators caught fever, but it continued to be believed that fevers were carried in the atmosphere as seeds and actualized when entering suitable bodies (*De causis procatarticis*, 100–8; Nutton 1983, 4–7). Some archaeological examples hint at how planners in Roman Asia Minor may have laid out streets and buildings because of a conviction that winds carried infections. At Patara, where in the early nineteenth century it was still thought that the prevailing cold west wind spread malaria, the Roman baths and the 'basilica' with their long axes running east–west may have been

Fig. 5.12. Ephesus, Gymnasium of Vedius: View of cryptoporticus from the west, showing remains of the springing of vaults in the foreground (photo M. Steskal, OeAI-OeAW).

sited to prevent a disruptive and pestilential airflow across the building, although we now know that such fevers are spread by mosquitoes (Conder 1824, 230–32). Moreover, as modern theorists have observed from the siting of tall buildings, orienting a structure perpendicular to prevailing winds provides the least passive ventilation and so the most effective means to reduce wind loads, whereas aligning its shorter axis with prevailing winds would produce most wind ventilation (Günel and Ilgin 2014, 162). Rotation of the building's orientation to within 10 degrees of the wind direction, as in the plan of the Harbour Baths at Patara, achieves a reduction of 10–20% of the cross-wind building response, and thus secures the building better against wind loading, which is the second greatest danger to the stability of buildings after seismic events (Irwin *et al.* 2013, 35; Holmes and Bekele 2021, 1). Although this was not as serious a consideration as for modern high-rise structures, the prevalence of earthquakes in this region may have made architects more concerned with measures to support a building's stability (Heikell and Heikell 2018, 172). The city of Ephesus shelters from the direct impact of the prevailing winds blowing across the Gulf of Kuşadasi from the north and north-west by its layout transverse to their direction. The high west wall of the Harbour Baths at Patara acts as a windbreak to block the winds rushing off the ancient harbour from the heated rooms in winter. The larger expanse of the gymnasium of Verulanus, however, projects beyond the baths to allow cooling winds to fan into the open court in high summer.

Energy conservation

In terms of energy consumption, Roman architecture may seem particularly wasteful. Yet green design advises that 'energy efficiency at the urban scale is promoted by attention to land-use, density, transportation, water and waste –

and also by using the opportunity to support renewable energy sources cost-effectively at the urban scale' (Brophy and Lewis 2011, 50). The most important renewables are water, wind, and sun. The provision and storage of water is one of the best examples of Roman practices comparable to modern strategies of sustainability (Locicero 2017; 2020). Roman legislators recognized the importance of solar energy by laws that secured the right to solar heat and light, anticipating modern warnings against buildings that obstruct sunlight (*Dig.* 8.2.1–41, with Daube 1943). While ancient architecture lacked the modern technology for creating solar means of heating, Romans were aware of the potential of paned windows to distribute light efficiently within a building. Seneca, for example, notes that the most significant technological changes 'within our own memory' were 'the use of paned windows, which permit the transmission of clear light by means of transparent tile', and the introduction of piping within the walls of baths, 'through which the heat is circulated to heat evenly both the lowest and highest areas of the room'.[25] Faventinus and Palladius recommended that baths and winter reception rooms and dining-rooms be orientated to exploit the sun's heat.[26] To make the dining-room floor absorb the sun's heat in preparation for winter, Faventinus advised first to excavate the earth to a depth of two feet, pound it, and insert a rubble or brick floor, and then to gather cinders, trample them into a thick mass, and apply a six-inch layer of mixed sand, ash, and lime, whose surface, levelled with a square, looks like a black floor: 'the floor does not absorb cold in winter and will please the bare feet of your attendants with its warmth'.[27] The black surface absorbs heat from sunlight, and the rubble layer absorbs and stores the heat, which radiates into the room when the air becomes cooler than the rubble mass. Faventinus repeats this method of storing heat from Vitruvius (*De arch.* 7.4.4–5), who introduces it as a feature of rooms used in winter in the Greek world. Trees were not 'the only storable form of energy' available (as claimed by Graham and Van Dam 2019, 334).

Large openings allowed baths to enjoy the desirable benefits of natural lighting (highlighted as an ideal at Lucian, *Hippias* 7). Glass windows enabled architects to modulate the sun's heat. In the later second century CE, heated rooms of the Baths of Vedius at Ephesus and the Baths of Faustina at Miletus had arched windows, over 6 m wide, subdivided by wooden bars into rows of individual glass panes.[28] Large glazed windows probably also played an important role of heat retention along one side of the heated rooms of the Central and North Baths at Patara.[29] James Ring's reconsideration of Edwin Thatcher's earlier conclusion that the large south-facing windows of the Forum Baths at Ostia were unglazed shows how a form of double glazing could trap the exterior solar heat to retain the temperature of hot rooms in winter.[30] Ismini Miliaresis' recent theoretical analysis of the building speculates that single and double glazing could reduce the amount of fuel required to heat the baths with a loss of solar radiation in the rooms of only some 20% due to the opaqueness of the glass, and that this benefit was greatest in January, when the energy entering the rooms at midday, provided it was a cloudless day, was sufficient to offset the effects of ventilation from windows that were open.[31] Heat loss through doors was minimal (Miliaresis 2013, 260–63). She notes, however, that since the windows were not filled by single panes of glass but divided by wooden frames, imperfections in the sealing of joints between frames and glass would have reduced the efficiency of this process of heat retention.[32] The types of window glass listed in Diocletian's Price Edict (Barag 1987) and the range of tool marks on archaeological fragments (Allen 2002) give an idea of the complexity of glazing practice in the eastern provinces (for window glass in the Near East, see O'Hea 2007). Clearer types allowed views of the external landscape, while also controlling the sun's heat, as through the large arched openings of the exedra in the Large Baths at Tlos in Lycia and the windows of the Harbour Baths at Caunus (Önen 1993, 12; Yegül and Favro 2019, 690). Able to be opened or closed according to temperature and wind flow, windows offered an effective ecological means to retain or exclude heat and humidity. It was not only baths that took advantage. Recent excavations on the 'Tetrapylon Street' at Aphrodisias have revealed abundant window glass from the upper floors of the arcaded east colonnade.[33]

Renewable materials

As modern designers observe, the importance of glass for lighting and thermal performance outweighs the environmental impact from its manufacture (Brophy and Lewis 2011, 117). However, sustainable architecture needs to take account of the environmental impact of building materials. A proper assessment of this aspect should consider all three stages of a material's life cycle: its production and transportation to the site; its use and lifespan; and its eventual destination after the building's life (Brophy and Lewis 2011, 109). Of these, the production phase has the greatest environmental impact. The extraction of stone and metals, in particular, requires the mining of finite resources from the earth, and their further refinement potentially involves waste of a toxic nature. The sheer quantity of materials used in larger provincial building projects, especially those sponsored by the imperial government or intended to be visually exceptional, also raises the question of the environmental impact of their haulage. However, the energy needed to transport bulk materials is generally a function of distance travelled, mode of transport, and mass of material carried. This was considerably less in Classical antiquity than in the world of modern global freight, and the environmental impact of transportation was correspondingly less. The frequent use of locally sourced materials also reduced its impact. Even decorative stones employed in Asia Minor were often of local origin, and the costs of transporting other materials over longer distances were reduced by the use of water transport, which produces the least emissions of all forms of freight transportation (Whitelegg 1993).

Anatolia had a rich and variegated supply of building stone, ranging from tufa to marble and granite, and a long tradition of cut-stone construction before the Roman conquest, which continued to be the basis of monumental architecture in the Roman period (Yegül and Favro 2019, 603). The high thermal mass, strength, and durability of stone offer advantages in terms of sustainability, in addition to aesthetics. Although non-renewable, it was – and remains – abundant in most of the region. The quarrying process then as now was disruptive to the natural environment, but the use of reclaimed stone reduced that impact. The greatest environmental impact of stone is from its haulage. Here too the use of locally quarried materials and transportation by water from more distant quarries reduced the footprint. Local sources also gave architects and patrons the benefit of more regular reports from the quarry and even, as with Dio at Prusa, involvement in decisions there.[34] In one respect, ancient workshops were more sustainable than their modern equivalents. They did not have access to the cheaper synthetic substitutes for natural stone used today; these involve energy-intensive manufacture and a high environmental impact similar to modern concrete, which contains a high proportion of non-renewable sand and gravel, involves heavy carbon dioxide emissions from the production of cement, and is difficult to dispose of or reuse (Brophy and Lewis 2011, 115–16).

During the imperial period, architects in Asia Minor also started to make use of brick and tile, although less frequently than in the West. The fertile valleys and plains between the hills produce good clay for brick, both fired and unbaked. The clays used in architecture of the Roman provinces might strictly be considered non-renewable, but their gathering from local fields did limit environmental damage; and the ecological impact of burning fuel to bake clay in a kiln even at high temperatures was very limited: coppice wood or harvest waste used in Romano-British kilns was readily available and renewable, and in wood-poor regions such as North Africa, as in traditional pottery workshops in Egypt today, chaff and straw were accessible, low-cost substitutes which also suited seasonal production (Leitch 2019, 54–59; Martin 2019, 68). The energy cost of ancient bricks was substantial; a calculation of the embodied energy – the quantity of energy required to process and transport a material – of a typical wood-fired brick in modern Uganda as 4.26 MJ/kg (Olweny *et al.* 2017), even more than that in a typical modern brick, calculated as 3.00 MJ/kg, up to three times that of concrete (Hammond and Jones 2008, 94, with 93, table 2), makes it one of the most energy-intensive of bulk building materials. On the other hand, the use of reclaimed bricks, which was probably widespread though impossible to quantify precisely, economized on the energy costs of the firing process. Architects in Asia Minor also gave thought to the application of brick in their structures. Rather than applying it abundantly as a facing for mortared rubble, as in Rome, they took advantage of its solidity and insulation as a structural material, not across the whole wall, but in combination with stone (Yegül and Favro 2019, 609). Lime mortar has a lower embodied energy than brick (Hammond and Jones 2008, 93, table 2). The expense, however, of producing lime for mortared rubble in both early structures like the Baths of Capito at Miletus and later ones such as the Gymnasium in Sardis resulted in walls and vaults with too many rubble stones and too little mortar to give the structure cohesive strength (Yegül and Favro 2019, 608; DeLaine 2021; Lancaster 2021).

As with stone, the production of the bronze that provided the often overlooked but important fittings of Roman buildings such as door frames and architectural ornamentation was highly energy-intensive. These are rarer in the architectural evidence of the eastern provinces than in the West, although ornamental bronze appliqués survive from high-status buildings like the Traianeum at Pergamon.[35] Yet, although non-renewable in themselves, they too were subject to frequent re-use and recycling.

Among the most prolific building materials in Roman Asia Minor, as elsewhere in the Empire, was timber, above all for roofing and frames of doors and windows. Its harvesting had a less damaging effect on the environment than the production of non-organic materials. Light, strong, durable, and easy to work according to the traditional practices of Asia Minor, it has the potential to be a renewable resource, if subject to proper forestry practices. Timber production in the Roman world could hardly be expected to meet the extensive requirements that govern modern forestry.[36] Even today, with such regulations in place, the World Wildlife Foundation claims that the international timber trade is the main threat to the world's forests. The renewability of this material depends on the growth of new timber being in balance with or in excess of the rate of harvesting, something difficult to achieve in view of the centuries-long lifespan of trees like beech that were used in construction. Moreover, even if timber is a renewable resource, it is not a sustainable one without a constant balance between depletion and replacement (Hammond and Jones 2008, 96). In Anatolia, the abundance of forests providing wood for building, particularly in the coastal regions of the south and southwest and in the Pontic and Caucasus ranges to the north, compares favourably with the dearth of building timber in central Italy, which according to written sources was already acute by the Augustan period.[37]

Nonetheless, as we have seen, the supply of building timber across the Roman Empire was not as critical as previous scholars had supposed. Thanks to extensive and effective management of woodlands and a far-flung distribution network integrated at least within large regions such as Asia Minor, most cities could either maintain a constant provision of long timber for roof beams, scaffolding, and other construction needs from nearby areas or have continued access by water transport to timber from more distant sources. The problems of the demand for timber stemmed not only from supply sufficient to meet the exponential demand for heating and industrial production as well as construction, but also from transportation and storage. It is easy to forget, but hard to overestimate the problems in finding storage for such bulky materials on a large scale.[38] Not only lack of space prevented storage of timbers in bulk. The rainy winters and hot summers of the Mediterranean caused wood to rot.[39] In smaller communities across the Empire, these problems were more manageable. Provincial cities might have their own designated public woodlands to provide more sustainable sources both of timber for public buildings and wood for heating fuel, which minimized costs of storage and transportation (Harris 2018, 225). The *Commentum de controversiis*, a Late Antique text on land surveying, attests the existence of woodlands assigned to colonies or municipia 'to supply timber for repairs to public buildings'.[40] Examination of building timbers in Roman Britain suggests that they originated from local woodlands, from which military installations managed their own supplies (Rackham 2003; Graham and Van Dam 2019, 334). In the East, these aspects have not been the object of systematic study, but there are indications of similar efforts to secure local supplies. At Trebenna in eastern Lycia, half of the timber used by a private benefactor to construct the ekklesiasterion was from a 'public' source.[41] If strategic military factors largely determined the siting of Roman colonies in southern Asia Minor, the abundant natural resources of their heavily wooded surroundings, as at Antioch in Pisidia, offered an additional advantage.[42] At Dura-Europos, on the edge of the Syrian desert, the supply of wood fuel for bath buildings was so critical that it was under military control.[43]

Other organic materials that lack the environmental impact of the timber trade are the most renewable of all. Straw, gathered from the stems of wheat, oats, and barley left over from the grain harvest, is readily available and has very low environmental impact, as well as excellent insulating properties.[44] For cities on the fertile coastal plains of Asia Minor, this agricultural waste also had limited transportation costs. Earth, made up of different grades of pulverized stone from small pebbles to silt, bonded together with clay and water, and sometimes sand or straw, is likewise highly sustainable; its structural strength can be increased by adding lime, although the energy involved in its production has environmental implications.

Because of their degradable qualities, the presence of these materials in ancient architecture is hard to trace. However, more is becoming known about the use of earth in construction, for example in the north-west provinces (see Russell *et al.*, this volume). Early visual representations suggest that these building resources were traditional and long-standing. On the paintings in the recently discovered Lale Tepe tomb in Lydia, zigzag patterns with diagonal stripes appear to indicate thatched roofs (Stinson 2008, fig. 27). The use of organic materials continued into the Roman period. Vitruvius reports that inhabitants of the unforested plains of Phrygia, where building timber was in short supply, constructed houses from 'natural mounds (*tumulos*)', presumably of earth, which presented a pyramidal shape with logs fastened together at the apex, and covered them with reeds, brushwood, or marshland sedge. He notes how these 'methods of construction make winters very warm and summers very cool' (*De arch.* 2.1.5). This may refer to the Central Anatolian plateau, where building timber is scarce, and, because of its 'extremely effective weather protection', this form that is attested in tumulus burials may have been widespread in domestic architecture in Anatolia more generally (Summerer and von Kienlin 2016, 509). The construction of walls from adobe blocks of mudbrick or rammed earth with flat, earth roofs has endured from Çatalhöyük eight millennia ago to today (Bainbridge and Haggard 2011, 17–18). Modest houses in the region may have had flat roofs, covered with earth instead of tiles (Yegül and Favro 2019, 696). Blocks of earth compressed by hand to produce 'rammed earth' can produce walls no thicker than a wall in brick or concrete yet with equal hardness, strength, and durability and effective heat retention (Brophy and Lewis 2011, 114). Even today, perhaps a third of the world's population lives in houses of earth, and more in developing countries (Minke 2006). In modern Greece, earthen architecture based on precedents in Asia Minor is used as a sustainable alternative to high-energy modern materials (Mousourakis *et al.* 2020). An obstacle to using these low-impact materials today is that they are labour-intensive and require specialist skills, but in Anatolia such skills were acquired through long-rehearsed tradition.

Recycling and reuse

The final phase in the life cycle of materials includes their removal after a building's destruction or after they cease to be useful within it. An effective strategy of green design that avoids most energy and economic costs of production and transportation is either to reuse them in their existing form or to recycle them into a new form for incorporation into other buildings. In general, reuse is better than recycling, which is better than incineration or landfill.

The reuse of materials from demolished buildings used to be a widespread practice in architecture, but this is harder with modern materials such as reinforced concrete and with habituated wastage. Some practices in Roman architecture, by contrast, facilitated salvage of materials. For example, modern theorists suggest that, if materials cannot be reused on the same site, they should 'be easily disassembled rather than destructively demolished'; they advocate prioritizing materials that are valuable for recycling and using lime mortar to allow easier cleaning and reuse of bricks (Brophy and Lewis 2011, 111). Constructions in the Roman period made ample use of recyclable metal and lacked the ubiquitous modern plastics that are an obstacle to recycling, while the common use of lime mortar accelerated construction and expediated subsequent reuse of bricks, particularly from the later fourth century CE when the demand for new bricks was reduced.[45] Lime slaking pits at Limoges in Aquitania show how lime was preserved for later maintenance and repair (DeLaine 2021, 9). In addition, elements that could be removed whole, like ashlar blocks, columns, and capitals, were more valuable for reuse.

Modern theorists seeking to achieve a 'greener architecture' urge that it is more sustainable to refurbish and reuse existing buildings than to demolish and build anew (Brophy and Lewis 2011, 111). Refurbishment, they argue, not only involves consumption of fewer materials and less energy for demolition and transportation, but is also usually less labour-intensive than new build and has added cultural benefits in preserving buildings of the past or learning from their uses of materials and techniques that meet modern ideals of sustainability (Brophy and Lewis 2011, 20). In the Roman world, the frequent reuse of materials from older structures fits these circumstances. The study of reuse and recycling in antiquity is still in its infancy. A bias towards Late Antiquity in the evidence studied up to now has encouraged the belief that reuse of architectural ornament and other building materials occurred only in the fourth and fifth centuries, prompted by textual evidence from that period for legislation on reuse, and that recycling too belonged to periods of 'decline' or want (on this point see also Siwicki, this volume). It is common therefore to regard reuse as an example of thrift rather than as evidence for sustainable practices. That may, however, take too narrow a view of sustainability, defined only by the parameters of the present-day concept. In the recent excavations of the 'Tetrapylon Street' at Aphrodisias, the presence of newly carved architectural elements alongside reused ones suggests that the reuse may have been a conscious choice, rather than an economic necessity.[46] The reuse of older materials may have been a restrained response to the availability of natural resources comparable to practices advocated today. The number of documented examples from earlier periods when decline and thrift were less of an issue is growing and may only be the tip of the iceberg.[47] Archaeologists can generally identify such cases by the presence of visibly anomalous features in later constructions, whereas the probably more widespread reuse of less distinctive and less recognizable components such as bricks or unornamented stone blocks is harder to spot. A recent study of recycling of materials in several sectors of the economies of the Roman world suggests that it was more mainstream than previously considered and typical of periods of economic growth and stability as well as times of crisis (Duckworth and Wilson 2020, 6).

Innovation, sustainability, and architectural transfer

Walter Scheidel's recent monograph on the failure of the Roman Empire argues that the greatest advances in technology came in the Hellenistic East prior to Roman conquest, that the high imperial period saw only 'diffusion and incremental improvement', and that the gradual disappearance of Roman dominion and control of natural resources in the critical times of Late Antiquity again 'allowed a culture of innovation... to take hold' (Scheidel 2019, 503–5). This cannot completely apply to architectural techniques, materials, and styles, which developed considerably during the early Empire, in the provinces as well as in Rome. It is possible, however, that issues with resources provided the catalyst for such advances or shifts in architectural practice. Scholars no longer assume that architectural innovations necessarily originated in Rome. Smaller communities with more limited resources and networks also saw the introduction of new materials and techniques. For instance, mortared rubble construction emerged in the context of the decentralized needs and resources of Roman and Latin colonies such as Cosa and Luna (Mogetta 2021), although the scarcity of examples from Rome in this period prevents decisive confirmation that these innovations preceded similar developments there. Beyond the Italian Peninsula examples multiply. In Sicily in the third century BCE, and commonly in North Africa, interlocking tubes of terracotta arranged in closely spaced rows helped to construct vaults without costly wooden centring (Lancaster 2015, 99–128). In Roman Britain, builders later experimented with constructing barrel vaults fashioned from voussoirs of hollow fired brick (Lancaster 2008, 275; see also Lancaster, this volume).

In Asia Minor, architects and civic bodies or private individuals involved in the design or patronage of public buildings frequently had access to a wide repertoire of architectural knowledge that derived from Hellenistic practice and theory. There were two main drivers for further changes in design. The first was what is known as 'architectural transfer', the replication in provincial contexts of features familiar from Rome and Italy. This was often politically motivated; but, even if the results are clear enough because of their differences from earlier modes of building, it is difficult to ascertain and impossible to generalize the mechanisms that effected such transfers of method, style, or technology. The term is usually applied to architectural ornament, where even the direction of transfer – from metropolis to province or vice versa – is disputed.[48] This was no top-down process of dissemination of styles. Georg

Plattner (2004; 2017) explained such transfers first by positing the circulation of 'pattern books' with designs between different centres and then by imagining the shipment of actual blocks, from which artists copied directly. However, composite capitals in the Ionian cities were not replicas transplanted from a pattern book, but precise and locally devised and developed constructions that derived from the fusion of the Corinthian with an Italic conception of the Ionic, and, if some examples closely resembled examples in Rome, others were more creative local adaptations (see Stinson, this volume).[49]

This argument also applies to the transfer of architectural techniques. I have previously compared the use of mortared rubble for vaulted buildings in Asia Minor, first attested in the harbour buildings at Ephesus and more visibly in the Baths of Capito at Miletus, to 'translation' (Thomas 2013). The term is applicable because, in each case, both with ornament and with techniques, the replicated version is not an exact copy of the source, but modified by the input of traditions and materials at the destination. This avoids earlier characterizations of eastern versions of mortared rubble as inferior and inauthentic, lacking in pozzolana, rather than as reflections of divergent local practices, which added different kinds of aggregate to the slaked lime to produce the mortar (see Vitti 2021, and in this volume). At Kos (Livadiotti 2005, 183; Lancaster 2021, 9), Sagalassos (Degryse *et al.* 2002, 1459), and in Cilicia (Ward-Perkins 1981, 275; Dodge 1987, 107), builders exploited natural deposits of volcanic ash similar to Italian pozzolana to produce resilient lime mortars. Architects developed distinctive and sustainable equivalents, adapted to local resources and skills.[50]

Transfers of this nature responded also to the second impetus for architectural change, economic need, or, in its extreme form, crisis. The driver might be scarcity of materials or shortage of human resource with the appropriate skills. These two motivations of architectural transfer and economic need might often coincide. The use of terracotta in vaulting was both an adaptation of Roman precedent and a response to resource needs (Lancaster 2015, and in this volume). The demands of sustainable building also encouraged experimental use of *tubuli* to conserve heating in baths. The hypocaust is perhaps the most famous example of an architectural technology transferred from Rome to its provinces. Developed in Campania, it enabled Roman architects to heat the floors of bath buildings and then to insulate the walls by creating a cavity for the circulation of hot air. Four principal methods were used to create this cavity, which differed according to the type of equipment used: box flues (*tubuli*); 'lugged tiles' (*tegulae mammatae*); spacer tubes; and terracotta 'nails', or spacer pins (Lancaster 2015, fig. 18.8a–d). The last three of these were all in use in the Great Bath at Corinth (Biers 1985, 46). The use of lugged tiles and box flues is common throughout the Roman Empire; the use of spacer tubes is more unusual. The fourth method appears in the early Flavian baths at Cadyanda and Patara in the 'remote and, technologically speaking, apparently uninventive' region of Lycia, the latter as early as 68–69 CE (Farrington 1995, 101–3). The spacer pins provided a more robust system of heating than lugged tiles. Thus architectural technologies in heating and insulating baths developed away from the main centres in response to local environmental conditions.

Conclusion

The technological conditions of Roman Asia Minor differed considerably from those of modern architecture. Although the environmental footprint of settlement and commerce in the Roman provinces was heavy, this was not a period of impending ecological crisis like today. Urban development between the establishment of the province of Asia in 133 BCE and the end of the second century CE experienced and profited from favourable ecological and climatic conditions.[51] Nonetheless, builders faced similar issues to those experienced in architecture today: a concern with using resources efficiently; costs of transportation; high-energy costs in production. Textual evidence confirms that elites were aware of these problems and prioritized the same issues of health and thermal comfort in both public and private architecture. The methods used show similarities to strategies advocated by proponents of green design today in response to the present-day climate emergency. These methods arose in the context of ecological need. They may not have trumpeted the value of sustainability that rings out today, but many of the questions of modern strategists find answers in ancient solutions to environmental needs. They used local materials where possible, incorporated the reuse and recycling of materials as an integral part of architectural practice, and valued aspects such as durability and thermal comfort that are recognized today as the foundations of a sustainable architectural future.

It is impossible to consider here everything that bears on the theme of sustainability. The focus has been on new building, but it is worth adding that the architecture of Asia Minor was undoubtedly more sustainable because of the important and widespread practices of maintenance and restoration. Baths were their most frequent object, but other buildings too, including colonnaded streets, saw constantly refurbishments with both new and old materials. The ideological presentation of such restoration as substantially new work, to the credit of the patron, is misleading; it was usually a less transformative act and one of many successive works of updating necessary to the continued survival of these local communities and their adaptation to changing social and political circumstances.[52]

Notes

1. For example, the use of concrete, and vaulted gateways at Paestum, Pompeii, and in Etruria: Mogetta 2021.
2. For the relations between innovation and sustainability more widely, see Van der Leeuw 2012.
3. See Lane 2012 for sustainability in antiquity more generally; and, for the driver of durability in ancient architecture, see for instance Thomas 2007, 4; 2014, 70–71.
4. Such a view, as presented by Hughes 1994, is not generally accepted. See the trenchant criticisms by Scarborough 1994 and Franconi 2016.
5. See Harris 2018, 221, citing, for instance, Strabo 4.203 and 5.222.
6. Recorded by well over 200 inscriptions at the boundaries of this state woodland: see *IGLS* 8.3 and *AE* 2006, 1572–75 (cited by Harris 2018, 211).
7. Ghini and Palladino 2016; cf. Galliazzo 2003–04; Armirotti *et al.* 2009. For the visual sense of the term, cf. Plin. *Ep.* 2.17.12, citing the distant view of *villas amoenissimas* spread out along the coast.
8. In the West, for instance Lugdunum in Gaul: Chomer 2013; cf. the response by Rogers 2018, 20 to Schmölder-Veit 2009, 23–25, claiming that utility and health were factors in public water displays in the West, but *amoenitas* only for private ones.
9. See, most recently, Dorl-Klingenschmid 2001; Uğurlu 2009; Longfellow 2011; Quatember 2011.
10. For the water imprint of the nymphaeum at Aspendos, see Piras 2006.
11. Salditt-Trapmann 1970, 5–6; Deubner 1977, 236–37; Nohlen 1998, 91–95; Weiss 2003, 228–32.
12. Although his account generally emphasizes aesthetic and practical reasons for the phenomenon, Burns 2017, 315 briefly acknowledges the relevance of climatic factors ('sun, rain, sea breezes') in the layout of colonnaded streets.
13. The classic account of these hazards of Roman urban life by Scobie 1986 is partially challenged by Laurence 1997, who stresses the subjective aspect of Juvenal's Third Satire on which much of this image is based, and Lo Cascio 2006, 58, who regards Scobie's assumption of overcrowding as anachronistic and questions how confined ancient living conditions were. However, for efforts in Roman cities to combat continuous 'urban filth', see Dupré Raventos and Remolà 2000 and the texts presented by Hanoune 2002, including an inscription on the arch at Thigibba warning of divine anger at those who urinated there (*AE* 1949, 48) and a reference to 'putrid animal smells' in fifth-century CE Jerash (*CIG* 8655). Gogey 2002 also highlights the anti-social behaviour in Roman Gaul caused by pollution, smells, and industrial noise.
14. Quoted by Pratesi and Tassi 1977, 137–40; translation by Sallares 2002, 169–70.
15. For the inscription (*TAM* II.2, 409) recording the velarium installed at Patara, see Thomas 2007, 82, fig. 83.
16. For the excavation of this space, see Miltner 1959, 293–94 and Eichler 1961, 67–68; on the date of the peristyle, see Alzinger 1970, 1648–49; 1974, I, 55–57 and II, 33, fig. 62. For a brief description of this space, which, however, emphasizes its religious uses, see Friesen 2001, 99–101.
17. Sen. *Ep.* 51.5; 56.1; 83.7; Mart. 3.58; 12.47; in more detail, Goguey 2002, 264–68.
18. Vitr. *De arch.* 5.4–5. Sounding vessels: Thielscher 1953, 350–51. For the Odeion, see Pittakis 1858, 1707–14.
19. See esp. Plin. *Ep.* 2.17 and 5.6. For sunshine, the two windows of a cubiculum in Pliny's Laurentine villa 'admit the east and restrain the west', and one corner of the room 'traps and intensifies a very pure sun' (2.17.6–7); compare the windows of the heliocaminus (2.17.20). For air circulation: the dining room in the centre of his Tuscan property 'receives a very salubrious breeze from the valleys of the Apennines' (5.6.29); by contrast, the cryptoporticus of his Laurentine villa checks the stormy south-west wind in that region and breaks the force of other winds (2.17.17; cf. 2.17.4 for the storms).
20. For this kind of comfort in urban environments, see, more generally, Hanoune 2002.
21. Grassl 2012, 138, citing Strab. 5.2.6, C 224 and other references. For awareness of diminishing resources, see, for instance, Plut. *Mor.* 434a and Cyprian *Ad Demetr.* 3.
22. On the health-related and ecological benefits of green space, see Jennings *et al.* 2019, 7–24; and for the 'Place of Palms', see Wilson *et al.* 2016; Wilson and Russell forthcoming.
23. I would like to thank Phil Stinson for sharing information that will appear in his forthcoming book on the Sebasteion.
24. 'Western': Ward-Perkins 1973, 55–56. Bosra: Mogdad 1973. Aphrodisias, 'Cryptoporticus House': Erim 1990, 13; Smith 1996, 48–50; public, between the 'Nymphaeum' terrace and the decorated hall: Ratté and Smith 2004, 169.
25. Sen. *Ep.* 90.25, with DeLaine 2020, 80–84. As Humphrey *et al.* 1998, 23 note, this does not in itself imply the use of solar heating.
26. Faventinus, *De diversis fabricis architectonicae* 14, in Plommer 1973, 62–63. Cf. Palladius, *Opus Agriculturae* 1.40.
27. Faventinus, *De diversis fabricis architectonicae* 26, in Plommer 1973, 74–75. Cf. Palladius, *Opus Agriculturae* 1.9.
28. Baatz 1991, 10, fig. 4; Steskal and La Torre 2008, 44–47, pls. 206–7; DeLaine 2020, 81.
29. Farrington 1995, 10, 12, who, however, assumed that the windows were unglazed, following Thatcher 1956.
30. Ring 1996, reconsidering Thatcher 1956, 219–20. See the important reservations by DeLaine 2020, 84.
31. Miliaresis 2013, 263–64. Note the qualifications of DeLaine 2020, 84.
32. Miliaresis 2019, 42, and, in more detail, 2013, 264–71, with the qualifications of DeLaine 2020, 84.
33. Aphrodisias Excavations (2019) at http://aphrodisias.classics.ox.ac.uk/excnorthavenue.html.
34. Dio Chrys. *Or.* 40.7; cf. the advice for local magistrates of Plut. *Prae. ger. reip.* 811b-c; Thomas 2007, 84.
35. Rossignani 1969, 45–46. Another example is Conze 1913, 251, no. 3; and, without provenance, in the Istanbul Archaeological Museum: Rossignani 1969, 74, no. 24.
36. Brophy and Lewis 2011, 112. The international Forestry Stewardship Council (FSC) promotes sustainable forestry by enforcing a long list of principles to make timber a renewable resource: legal compliance; uncontested land tenure; respect of indigenous peoples' rights; maintenance of long-term well-being of forest workers and local communities; equitable use

of benefits from the forest; reduction of environmental impact of logging and maintenance of the ecological integrity of the forest; a continuously updated management plan; monitoring of the condition of the forest and the social and environmental impact of its management; maintenance of High Conservation Value Forests (HCVFs) of outstanding importance; and, finally, a guarantee that plantations contribute to promote the conservation of natural forests.

37. Meiggs 1982, 329. For instance, Diod. Sic. 14.42.4 appears to contrast the rich forests on the slopes of Mount Etna that Dionysius of Syracuse found 'full of valuable silver fir and pine *at that time*' with the increasing deforestation of his own day.
38. On the temporality and rapid turnover of bulk storage at Ostia and Portus in particular, see Van Oyen 2020, 155–57.
39. Vitr. *De arch.* 5.12.7 advises that shipsheds face northwards to avoid risk of rotting exposed to the hot southern sun. Sapwood was considered particularly prone to rot, while cedar from the Lebanon was particularly valued for its resistance: Ulrich 2007, 268; Plin. *HN* 16.76.197–98 and Vitr. *De arch.* 2.9.13 report that timber could be soaked in cedar oil to prevent decay.
40. Lachmann 1848–52, I, 114.3: *assignatae sunt silvae, de quibus ligna in reparationem publicorum munerum traherentur*; Campbell 2000, 66.
41. von Lanckoronski 1892, I, 224, no. 184; Onur 2005, 13–14, 164; cf. Nenninger 2001, 58–59.
42. Levick 1967, 42–55 overlooks these ecological considerations in emphasizing military motives for the siting of Roman colonies.
43. *PDura* 82: *missus lig[nator] balnei mil[es] I*; Nenninger 2001, 174.
44. Brophy and Lewis 2011, 113: 'standard sized straw bales have an insulation value of approximately 0.012 W/mK'.
45. DeLaine 2001, 244; Santangeli Valenzani 2007, 441; Machado 2019, 85; Vitti 2021, 4.
46. Jacobs 2022, 251. The excavation will be published as Jacobs, *Tetrapylon Street*. For reuse at Aphrodisias more generally, see also Ogus 2018; Wilson 2019, 199.
47. For examples in Rome and Corinth, see, respectively, Zink *et al.* 2020 and Frey 2015. For recycling of marble in the Pantheon, see Voigts 2020.
48. For example, Strong 1953, 138 argued for a Pergamene architect in Rome from the resemblance of ornament of three late Hadrianic buildings to motifs in the Traianeum at Pergamon, whereas Strocka 1988, comparing buildings at Ephesus, Miletus, and Side, argued that these features came to Asia Minor through craftsmen from Rome.
49. This goes beyond even Strong's suggestion (1960, 127) that the 'design reached Asia Minor during the Augustan period in a comparatively simple form which developed independently in the course of the first century'.
50. For earlier uses of lime mortar for rendering in Hellenistic Priene and mixtures of lime, sand, and volcanic ash to coat cisterns at Thera and in mainland Greece since the Archaic period, see Viaene *et al.* 1997, 405; for experiments with lime mortar in Attalid Pergamon, Waelkens 1987, 95, n. 7; and for mortared rubble as a replacement of Hellenistic earth and rubble fills, Waelkens 1989, 78.
51. Tan 2022 pushes back to the third century BCE the 'Roman Warm Period', usually placed between the end of the second and the end of the first centuries BCE and considered responsible for the stability of the high Empire.
52. For the lessons of comparisons between epigraphic and archaeological evidence for ancient restoration in the Roman provinces, see Thomas and Witschel 1992, with modifications suggested by Fagan 1996. See also Siwicki 2019, 39–81.

References

Agusta-Boularot, S. 2001. Fontaines et fontaines monumentales en Grèce de la conquête romaine à l'époque flavienne: permanence ou renouveau architectural? In Marc, J.-Y. and Moretti, J.-C. (eds), *Constructions publiques et programmes édilitaires en Grèce entre le IIe siècle av. J.-C. et le Ier siècle apr. J.-C. Actes du Colloque organisé par l'École française d'Athènes et le CNRS (Athènes, 14–17 mai 1995)*. Athens: École française d'Athènes, 167–236.

Allen, D. 2002. Roman window glass. In Aldhouse-Green, M. and Webster, P. (eds), *Artefacts and Archaeology: Aspects of the Celtic and Roman Worlds*. Cardiff: University of Wales Press, 102–11.

Alzinger, W. 1970. Ephesos B: Archäologischer Teil. In *Pauly-Wissowa Real-Encyclopädie, Supplement 12*. Stuttgart: J.B. Metzler, 1588–704.

Alzinger, W. 1974. *Augusteische Architektur in Ephesos (Two Volumes)*. Vienna: Österreichisches Archäologisches Institut in Wien.

Antico Gallina, M.V. 2004. *Acque per l'utilitas, per la salubritas, per l'amoenitas*. Milan: Edizioni ET.

Armirotti, A., Bertarione, S. and Framarin, P. 2009. Voluptas, luxuria et amoenitas in regione Consolata ad Aosta. Una villa da 'rivedere'. *Bollettino della Soprintendenza per i beni e attività culturali della Valle d'Aosta* 6: 66–71.

Armstrong, R. 2019. *Vergil's Green Thoughts: Plants, Human, and the Divine*. Oxford: Oxford University Press.

Baatz, D. 1991. Fensterglastypen, Glasfenster und Architektur. In Hoffmann, A., Schwandner, E.-L., Höpfner, W. and Baatz, D. (eds), *Bauplanung und Bautheorie der Antike*. Mainz: Philipp von Zabern, 4–13.

Bainbridge, D.A. and Haggard, K. 2011. *Passive Solar Architecture. Heating, Cooling, Ventilation, Daylighting, and More Using Natural Flows*. White River Junction, VT: Chelsea Green Publishing.

Barag, D. 1987. Recent important epigraphic discoveries related to the history of glassmaking in the Roman period. In *Annales du 10e Congrès de l'Association Internationale pour l'Histoire du Verre (Madrid-Segovie, 23–28 septembre 1985)*. Amsterdam: Association Internationale pour l'Histoire du Verre, 109–16.

Biers, J.C. 1985. *Corinth XVII. The Great Bath on the Lechaion Road*. Princeton: American School of Classical Studies at Athens.

Bouet, A. and Saragoza, F. 2007. Amoenitas urbium et évergétisme de l'eau. La fontaine monumentale des thermes de Cluny à Lutèce. *Revue Archéologique*: 3–64.

Brophy, V. and Lewis, J.O. 2011. *A Green Vitruvius: Principles and Practice of Sustainable Architectural Design (Second Edition)*. London: Routledge.

Burns, R. 2017. *Origins of the Colonnaded Streets in the Cities of the Roman East*. Oxford: Oxford University Press.

Byhet, T. 2001–02. Les portiques de rue dans les agglomérations de la Gaule romaine. Un élément de l'amoenitas urbium? *Caesarodunum* 35–36: 15–38.

Campbell, J.B. 2000. *The Writings of the Roman Land Surveyors: Introduction, Text, Translation and Commentary*. London: Society for the Promotion of Roman Studies.

Chomer, C. 2013. Salubritas et amoenitas, l'eau dans l'habitat de Lugdunum. In Ballut, C. and Fournier, P. (eds), *Au fil de l'eau. Ressources, risques et gestion du néolithique à nos jours*. Clermont-Ferrand: Maison des Sciences, 39–52.

Citter, C. 2015. Landscapes, settlements and sustainability. In Chavarría Arnau, A. and Reynolds, A. (eds), *Detecting and Understanding Historic Landscapes*. Mantua: SAP, Società archeologica s.r.l., 253–72.

Conder, J. 1824. *The Modern Traveller. Syria and Asia Minor, Vol. 1*. London: James Duncan.

Conze, A. 1913. *Altertümer von Pergamon, I.2: Stadt und Landschaft*. Berlin: De Gruyter.

Daube, D. 1943. Interference with light in Roman law. *Law Journal* 93: 180–90.

Degryse, P., Elsen, J. and Waelkens, M. 2002. Study of ancient mortars from Sagalassos (Turkey) in view of their conservation. *Cement and Concrete Research* 32.9: 1457–63.

DeLaine, J. 2001. Bricks and mortar. Exploring the economics of building techniques at Rome and Ostia. In Mattingly, D.J. and Salmon, J. (eds), *Economies beyond Agriculture in the Classical World*. London: Routledge, 230–68.

DeLaine, J. 2020. Strategies and technologies of environmental manipulation in the Roman world. The thermal economy of baths. In Schliephake, C., Sojc, N. and Weber, G. (eds), *Nachhaltigkeit in der Antike: Diskurse, Praktiken, Perspektiven*. Stuttgart: Franz Steiner Verlag, 75–93.

DeLaine, J. 2021. Production, transport and on-site organisation of Roman mortars and plasters. *Archaeological and Anthropological Sciences* 13.10: https://doi.org/10.1007/s12520-021-01401-5 (article 195).

Deschamps, L. 2001–02. L'amoenitas de la vie à Bordeaux dans la première moitié du Ve siècle d'après Paulin de Pella. *Caesarodunum* 35–36: 449–59.

Deubner, O. 1977. Das Heiligtum der alexandrinischen Gottheiten in Pergamon gennant 'Kizil Avli' ('Rote Halle'). *Istanbuler Mitteilungen* 27–28: 227–50.

Dodge, H. 1987. Brick construction in Roman Greece and Asia Minor. In Macready, S. and Thompson, F.H. (eds), *Roman Architecture in the Greek World*. London: Society of Antiquaries of London, 108–20.

Dorl-Klingenschmid, C. 2001. *Prunkbrunnen in kleinasiatischen Städten: Funktion im Kontext*. Munich: Verlag Dr. Friedrich Pfeil.

Duckworth, C.N. and Wilson, A.I. (eds) 2020. *Recycling and Reuse in the Roman Economy*. Oxford: Oxford University Press.

Dupré Raventos, X. and Remolà, J.-A. (eds) 2000. *Sordes Urbis. La eliminación de residuos en la ciudad romana. Actas de la reunión de Roma (15–16 de noviembre de 1996)*. Rome: 'L'Erma' di Bretschneider.

Eichler, F. 1961. Die österreichischen Ausgrabungen in Ephesos im Jahre 1960. *Anzeiger Wien* 98: 65–75.

Erim, K.T. 1990. Recent work at Aphrodisias 1986–1988. In Roueché, C. and Erim, K.T. (eds), *Aphrodisias Papers. Recent Work on Architecture and Sculpture*. Ann Arbor, MI: Journal of Roman Archaeology Supplementary Series, 9–36.

Fagan, G.G. 1996. The reliability of Roman rebuilding inscriptions. *Papers of the British School at Rome* 64: 81–93.

Fagan, G.G. 1999. *Bathing in Public in the Roman World*. Ann Arbor, MI: University of Michigan Press.

Farrington, A. 1995. *The Roman Baths of Lycia: An Architectural Study*. London: British Institute of Archaeology at Ankara.

Franconi, T.V. 2016. Ancient environmental problems. *Classical Review* 66: 493–95.

Frey, J.M. 2015. The Archaic colonnade at ancient Corinth: a case of early Roman spolia. *American Journal of Archaeology* 119.2: 147–75.

Friesen, S.J. 2001. *Imperial Cults and the Apocalypse of John: Reading Revelation in the Ruins*. Oxford: Oxford University Press.

Galliazzo, V. 2003–04. L'amoenitas del paesaggio romano nella Venetia. Un ambiguo rapporto tra natura e cultura. *Caesarodunum* 37–38: 41–62.

Ghini, G. and Palladino, A. 2016. Amoenitas loci. Il rapporto dialettico tra villa e paesaggio nel contesto del lago di Nemi. In Russo Tagliente, A., Ghini, G. and Mari, Z. (eds), *Lazio e Sabina, 11. Atti del convegno. Undicesimo incontro di studi sul Lazio e Sabina (Roma, 4–6 giugno 2014)*. Rome: Quasar, 63–74.

Goguey, D. 2002. Nuisances urbaines selon les auteurs latins. Confrontation avec les données de quelques villes gallo-romaines. In Bedon, R. (ed.), *Amoenitas Urbium. Les agréments de la vie urbaine en Gaule romaine et dans les régions voisines*. Limoges: Presses Universitaires de Limoges, 255–73.

Graham, B. and Van Dam, R. 2019. Modelling the supply of wood fuel in ancient Rome. In Izdebski, A. and Mulryan, M. (eds), *Environment and Society in the Long Late Antiquity*. Boston-Leiden: Brill, 330–41.

Grassl, H. 2012. Zum Problem der Nachhaltigkeit in der Ressourcenausbeutung im Altertum. In Olshausen, E. and Sauer, V. (eds), *Die Schätze der Erde. Natürliche Ressourcen in der antiken Welt. Stuttgarter Kolloquium zur Historischen Geographie des Altertums 10, 2008*. Stuttgart: Franz Steiner Verlag, 137–41.

Günel, M.H. and Ilgin, H.E. 2014. *Tall Buildings. Structural Systems and Aerodynamic Forms*. Abingdon: Routledge.

Hammond, G.P. and Jones, C.I. 2008. Embodied energy and carbon in construction materials – inventory of carbon and energy. *Energy – Proceedings of the Institute of Civil Engineers* 161.2: 87–98.

Hanfmann, G.M.A. 1975. *From Croesus to Constantine: The Cities of Western Asia Minor and their Arts in Greek and Roman Times*. Ann Arbor, MI: University of Michigan Press.

Hanoune, R. 2002. Amoenitas urbium? Quelques textes en réaction. In Bedon, R. (ed.), *Amoenitas Urbium. Les agréments de la vie urbaine en Gaule romaine et dans les régions voisines*. Limoges: Presses Universitaires de Limoges, 287–93.

Harris, W.V. 2018. The indispensable commodity: notes on the economy of wood in the Roman Mediterranean. In Wilson, A.I. and Bowman, A.K. (eds), *Trade, Commerce, and the State*. Oxford: Oxford University Press, 211–36.

Heikell, R. and Heikell, L. 2018. *Turkish Waters & Cyprus Pilot. A Yachtsman's Guide to the Mediterranean and Black Sea Coasts of Turkey with the Island of Cyprus*. St Ives, Cambridgeshire: Imray Laurie Norie & Wilson.

Holmes, J.D. and Bekele, S.A. 2021. *Wind Loading of Structures (Fourth Edition)*. Boca Raton, FL: CRC Press.

Hughes, J.D. 1994. *Pan's Travail: Environmental Problems of the Greeks and the Romans*. Baltimore: Johns Hopkins University Press.

Humphrey, J.W., Oleson, J.P. and Sherwood, A.N. 1998. *Greek and Roman Technology: A Sourcebook*. London: Routledge.

Irwin, P., Denoon, R. and Scott, D. 2013. *Wind Tunnel Testing of High-Rise Buildings. An Output of the CTBUH Wind Engineering Work Group*. Abingdon: Routledge.

Jacobs, I. 2022. Looking in two directions: urban (re)building in sixth-century Asia Minor. In Fowden, E.K., Çağaptay, S., Zychowicz-Coghill, E.P. and Blanke, L. (eds), *Cities as Palimpsests? Responses to Antiquity in Eastern Mediterranean Urbanism*. Oxford: Oxbow Books, 247–63.

Jacobs, I. and Richard, J. 2012. 'We surpass the beautiful waters of other cities by the abundance of ours': reconciling function and decoration in Late Antique fountains. *Journal of Late Antiquity* 5.1: 3–71.

Jennings, V., Browning, M.H.E.M. and Rigolon, A. 2019. *Urban Green Spaces. Public Health and Sustainability in the United States*. Cham: Springer.

Jones, C.P. 1991. Aelius Aristides, 'On the water in Pergamon'. *Archäologischer Anzeiger*: 111–17.

Kull, U. 2012. Pflanzliche Ressourcen im Mittelmeerrarum. In Olshausen, E. and Sauer, V. (eds), *Die Schätze der Erde. Natürliche Ressourcen in der antiken Welt. Stuttgarter Kolloquium zur Historischen Geographie des Altertums 10, 2008*. Stuttgart: Franz Steiner Verlag, 221–43.

Lachmann, K. (ed.) 1848–52. *Die Schriften der römischen Feldmesser. Vol. 1: Gromatici veteres ex recensione Caroli Lachmanni; diagrammata edidit S. Rvdorffvs. Vol. 2: Erläuterungen zu den Schriften der römischen Feldmesser von F. Blume, K. Lachmann, Th. Mommsen und A. Rudorff; indices von E. Bursian*. Berlin: G. Reimer.

Lancaster, L.C. 2008. Roman engineering and construction. In Oleson, J.P. (ed.), *The Oxford Handbook of Engineering and Technology in the Classical World*. Oxford: Oxford University Press, 256–84.

Lancaster, L.C. 2015. *Innovative Vaulted Construction in the Architecture of the Roman Empire: 1st to 4th Centuries CE*. Cambridge: Cambridge University Press.

Lancaster, L.C. 2021. Mortars and plasters – how mortars were made. The literary sources. *Archaeological and Anthropological Sciences* 13.10: https://doi.org/10.1007/s12520-021-01395-0 (article 192).

Lancaster, L.C. and Ulrich, R.B. 2014. Materials and techniques. In Quenemoen, C.K. and Ulrich, R.B. (eds), *A Companion to Roman Architecture*. Malden, MA: Wiley-Blackwell, 157–92.

Lane, M. 2012. *Eco-Republic. What the Ancients Can Teach Us about Ethics, Virtue, and Sustainable Living*. Princeton: Princeton University Press.

Laurence, R. 1997. Writing the Roman metropolis. In Parkins, H.M. (ed.), *Roman Urbanism: Beyond the Consumer City*. London: Routledge, 1–20.

Leitch, V. 2019. Fuelling Roman pottery kilns in Britain and North Africa: climatic, economic and traditional strategies. In Veal, R. and Leitch, V. (eds), *Fuel and Fire in the Ancient Roman World. Towards an Integrated Economic Understanding*. Cambridge: McDonald Institute for Archaeological Research, 53–61.

Lepper, F. and Frere, S. 1988. *Trajan's Column. A New Edition of the Cichorius Plates*. Gloucester: Alan Sutton.

Levick, B.M. 1967. *Roman Colonies in Southern Asia Minor*. Oxford: Clarendon Press.

Livadiotti, M. 2005. Note preliminari sulle tecniche costruttive di Coo in età ellenistica e romana. In Adembri, B. (ed.), *Aeimnestos. Miscellanea di studi per Mauro Cristofani, vol. I*. Florence: Centro Di, 178–87.

Lo Cascio, E. 2006. Did the population of imperial Rome reproduce itself? In Storey, G.R. (ed.), *Urbanism in the Preindustrial World: Cross-Cultural Approaches*. Tuscaloosa: University of Alabama Press, 52–68.

Locicero, M.A. 2017. Sustainable Romans? Exploring flexibility of the urban water cycle in Roman Ostia. In O'Sullivan, R., Marini, C. and Binnberg, J. (eds), *Archaeological Approaches to Breaking Boundaries: Interaction, Integration and Division. Proceedings of the Graduate Archaeology at Oxford Conferences 2015–2016*. Oxford: British Archaeological Reports, 117–25.

Locicero, M.A. 2020. Waters waters everywhere: sustainability and water supply strategies in the Roman harbour city of Ostia, Italy. In Schliephake, C., Sojc, N. and Weber, G. (eds), *Nachhaltigkeit in der Antike: Diskurse, Praktiken, Perspektiven*. Stuttgart: Franz Steiner Verlag, 57–74.

Longfellow, B. 2011. *Roman Imperialism and Civic Patronage: Form, Meaning, and Ideology in Monumental Fountain Complexes*. Cambridge: Cambridge University Press.

Machado, C. 2019. *Urban Space and Aristocratic Power in Late Antique Rome, AD 270–535*. Oxford: Oxford University Press.

Madsen, D.A. 2021. *Commercial Building Construction: Materials and Methods*. New York: McGraw Hill Education.

Martin, A. 2019. Kilns in a wood-poor environment: traditional workshops in the western delta of Egypt. In Veal, R. and Leitch, V. (eds), *Fuel and Fire in the Ancient Roman World. Towards an Integrated Economic Understanding*. Cambridge: McDonald Institute for Archaeological Research, 63–69.

Marzano, A. 2010. Le ville marittime dell'Italia romana tra amoenitas e fructus. *Amoenitas* 1: 21–33.

McDavid, A. 2019. Thermal sustainability: renovation of imperial thermae in Late Antiquity. *Architectural Histories* 7.1: 1–129.

Meiggs, R. 1982. *Trees and Timber in the Ancient Mediterranean World*. Oxford: Clarendon Press.

Miliaresis, I.A. 2013. *Heating and Fuel Consumption in the Terme del Foro at Ostia*. PhD Thesis, McIntire Department of Art, University of Virginia.

Miliaresis, I.A. 2019. Throwing money out of the window: fuel in the Forum Baths at Ostia. In Veal, R. and Leitch, V. (eds), *Fuel and Fire in the Ancient Roman World. Towards an Integrated Economic Understanding*. Cambridge: McDonald Institute for Archaeological Research, 39–50.

Miltner, F. 1959. XXII. Vorläufiger Bericht über die Ausgrabungen in Ephesos. *Jahreshefte der Österreichischen archäologischen Instituts in Wien, Beiblatt* 44: 243–314.

Minke, G. 2006. *Building with Earth: Design and Technology of a Sustainable Architecture*. Basel: Birkhauser.

Mogdad, S. 1973. Note préliminaire sur le cryptoportique de Bosra (Syrie). In *Les cryptoportiques dans l'architecture romaine. Actes du colloque de Rome (19–23 avril 1972)*. Rome: École française de Rome, 411–12.

Mogetta, M. 2021. *The Origins of Concrete Construction in Roman Architecture: Technology and Society in Republican Italy*. Cambridge: Cambridge University Press.

Mousourakis, A., Arakadaki, M., Kotsopoulos, S., Sinamidis, I., Mikrou, T., Frangedaki, E. and Lagaros, N.D. 2020. Earthen architecture in Greece: traditional techniques and revaluation. *Heritage* 3.4: 1237–68.

Nenninger, M. 2001. *Die Römer und der Wald: Untersuchungen zum Umgang mit einem Naturraum am Beispeil der römischen Nordwestprovinzen*. Stuttgart: Franz Steiner Verlag.

Nevola, F. 2020. *Street Life in Renaissance Italy*. New Haven-London: Yale University Press.

Nohlen, K. 1998. The 'Red Hall' (Kizil Avlu) in Pergamon. In Koester, H. (ed.), *Pergamon: Citadel of the Gods*. Harrisburg, PA: Trinity Press International, 77–110.

Nohlen, K. and Radt, W. 1978. *Kapıkaya: ein Felsheiligtum bei Pergamon*. Berlin: De Gruyter.

Nutton, V. 1983. The seeds of disease: an explanation of contagion and infection from the Greeks to the Renaissance. *Medical History* 27: 1–34.

O'Hea, M. 2007. Glass in late antiquity in the Near East. In Lavan, L., Zanini, E. and Sarantis, A. (eds), *Technology in Transition A.D. 300–650*. Boston-Leiden: Brill, 233–48.

Ogus, E. 2018. Urban transformations at Aphrodisias in Late Antiquity: destruction or intentional preservation? In Ng, D.Y. and Swetnam-Burland, M. (eds), *Reuse and Renovation in Roman Material Culture: Functions, Aesthetics, Interpretations*. Cambridge: Cambridge University Press, 160–85.

Olshausen, E. and Sauer, V. (eds) 2012. *Die Schätze der Erde. Natürliche Ressourcen in der antiken Welt. Stuttgarter Kolloquium zur Historischen Geographie des Altertums 10, 2008*. Stuttgart: Franz Steiner Verlag.

Olweny, M., Ndibwami, A. and Ahimbisibwe, A. 2017. Embodied energy of the common wood fired brick. In Schnabel, M.A. (ed.), *Back to the Future: The Next 50 Years. 51st International Conference of the Architectural Science Association (ANZAScA)*. Wellington, NZ: Architectural Science Association, 519–28.

Önen, U. 1993. *Lycia: Western Section of the Southern Coast of Turkey (Fourth Edition)*. Istanbul: NET Turistik Yayınlar.

Onur, F. 2005. Trebenna Tarihi [history of Trebenna]. III. Tarih. III.1. Roma dönemi and III. The history. III. 1. The Roman period. In Çevik, N., Varkivanç, B. and Akyürek, E. (eds), *Trebenna Tarihi, Arkeolojisi ve Doğasi – Its History, Archaeology and Natural Environment*. Antalya: Suna-İnan Kiraç Akdeniz Medeniyetleri Araştirma Enstitüsü, 7–20, 161–66.

Piras, S.A.G. 2000. Water luxury in Roman times: simply a matter of excellent planning and engineering or of politics and philanthropy? In Jansen, G.C.M. (ed.), *Cura Aquarum in Sicilia*. Leiden: Peeters, 247–53.

Piras, S.A.G. 2006. Façade nymphaea in Asia Minor: Aspendos, an example of massive urban water imprint. In Wiplinger, G. (ed.), *Cura Aquarum in Ephesus*. Leuven: Peeters, 397–400.

Pittakis, K. 1858. Περὶ Θεάτρου Ἡρώδου τοῦ Αττικοῦ. *Archaiologike Ephemeris*: 1707–14.

Plattner, G. 2004. Transfer von Architekturkonzepten und Ornamentformen zwischen Kleinasien und Rom in der Kaiserzeit. *Römische Historische Mitteilungen* 46: 17–35.

Plattner, G. 2017. New methods to understand tradition and transformation in Roman imperial architectural decoration. In Pensabene, P., Milella, M. and Caprioli, F. (eds), *Decor: decorazione e architettura nel mondo romano. Atti del convegno internazionale (Roma, 21–24 maggio 2014)*. Rome: Quasar, 79–86.

Plommer, H. 1973. *Vitruvius and Later Roman Building Manuals*. Cambridge: Cambridge University Press.

Pratesi, F. and Tassi, F. 1977. *Guida alla natura del Lazio e Abruzzo (seconda edizione)*. Milan: Mondadori.

Quatember, U. 2011. *Das Nymphaeum Traiani in Ephesos*. Vienna: Verlag der Österreichischen Akademie der Wissenschaften.

Rackham, O. 2003. *Ancient Woodland. Its History, Vegetation, and Uses in England (Second Edition)*. Colvend: Castlepoint Press.

Ratté, C. and Smith, R.R.R. 2004. Archaeological research at Aphrodisias in Caria, 1999–2001. *American Journal of Archaeology* 108.2: 145–86.

Richard, J. 2012. *Water for the City, Fountains for the People: Monumental Fountains in the Roman East. An Archaeological Study of Water Management*. Turnhout: Brepols.

Richard, J. 2016. Where do we go now? The archaeology of monumental fountains in the Roman and early Byzantine East. In Shilling, B. and Stephenson, P. (eds), *Fountains and Water Culture in Byzantium*. Cambridge: Cambridge University Press, 15–35.

Ring, J.W. 1996. Windows, baths, and solar energy in the Roman Empire. *American Journal of Archaeology* 100.4: 717–24.

Robinson, B.A. 2011. *Histories of Peirene: A Corinthian Fountain in Three Millennia*. Princeton: American School of Classical Studies at Athens.

Rogers, D.K. 2018. Water culture in Roman society. *Ancient History* 1.1: 1–118.

Rossignani, M.P. 1969. La decorazione architettonica in bronzo nel mondo romano. *Contributi dell'Istituto di Archeologia, Università Cattolica del Sacro Cuore, Milano* 2: 44–96.

Russell, B. 2013. *The Economics of the Roman Stone Trade*. Oxford: Oxford University Press.

Salditt-Trapmann, R. 1970. *Tempel der ägyptischen Götter in Griechenland und an der Westküste Kleinasiens*. Boston-Leiden: Brill.

Sallares, R. 2002. *Malaria and Rome. A History of Malaria in Ancient Italy*. Oxford: Oxford University Press.

Santangeli Valenzani, R. 2007. Public and private building activity in late antique Rome. In Lavan, L., Zanini, E. and Sarantis, A. (eds), *Technology in Transition A.D. 300–650*. Boston-Leiden: Brill, 435–49.

Scarborough, J. 1995. Review of J.D. Hughes, Pan's Travail: Environmental Problems of the Greeks and the Romans. *Classical Bulletin* 71: 29–32.

Scheidel, W. 2019. *Escape from Rome. The Failure of Empire and the Road to Prosperity*. Princeton: Princeton University Press.

Scherrer, P. 1990. Augustus, die Mission des Vedius Pollio und die Artemis Ephesia. *Jahreshefte des Österreichischen archäologischen Instituts in Wien* 60: 87–101.

Scherrer, P. 1995. The city of Ephesos from the Roman period to Late Antiquity. In Koester, H. (ed.), *Ephesos, Metropolis of Asia: An Interdisciplinary Approach to its Archaeology, Religion, and Culture*. Valley Forge, PA: Trinity Press International, 1–25.

Schliephake, C., Sojc, N. and Weber, G. (eds) 2020. *Nachhaltigkeit in der Antike: Diskurse, Praktiken, Perspektiven*. Stuttgart: Franz Steiner Verlag.

Schmölder-Veit, A. 2009. *Brunnen in den Städten des westlichen Römischen Reichs*. Wiesbaden: Reichert Verlag.

Scobie, A. 1986. Slums, sanitation, and mortality in the Roman world. *Klio* 68: 399–433.

Shaled-Hurvitz, V. 2015. *Holy Sites Encircled. The Early Byzantine Concentric Churches of Jerusalem*. Oxford: Oxford University Press.

Siwicki, C. 2019. *Architectural Restoration and Heritage in Imperial Rome*. Oxford: Oxford University Press.

Smith, R.R.R. 1987. The imperial reliefs from the Sebasteion at Aphrodisias. *Journal of Roman Studies* 77: 88–138.

Smith, R.R.R. 1996. Archaeological research at Aphrodisias, 1989–1991. In Roueché, C. and Smith, R.R.R. (eds), *Aphrodisias Papers 3. The Setting and Quarries, Mythological and other Sculptural Decoration, Architectural Development, Portico of Tiberius, and Tetrapylon*. Portsmouth, RI: Journal of Roman Archaeology Supplementary Series, 10–72.

Steskal, M. and La Torre, M. 2008. *Das Vediusgynasium in Ephesos: Archäologie und Baubefund*. Vienna: Verlag der Österreichischen Akademie der Wissenschaften.

Stinson, P. 2008. Lale Tepe. A late Lydian tumulus near Sardis II. Architecture and painting. In Cahill, N. (ed.), *Love for Lydia. A Sardis Anniversary Volume Presented to Crawford H. Greenewalt Jr*. Cambridge, MA: Harvard University Press, 25–47.

Strocka, V.M. 1988. Wechselwirkungen der stadtrömischen und kleinasiatischen Architektur unter Trajan und Hadrian. *Istanbuler Mitteilungen* 38: 291–307.

Strong, D.E. 1953. Late Hadrianic architectural ornament in Rome. *Papers of the British School at Rome* 21: 118–51.

Strong, D.E. 1960. Some early examples of the composite capital. *Journal of Roman Studies* 50: 119–28.

Šulyová, D., Vodák, J. and Kubina, M. 2021. Effective management of scarce water resources: from antiquity to today and into the future. *Water* 13.19: https://doi.org/10.3390/w13192734.

Summerer, L. and von Kienlin, A. 2016. Roofing the dead. Architectural allusions in Anatolian tumuli. In Henry, O. and Kelp, U. (eds), *Tumulus as Sema. Space, Politics, Culture and Religion in the First Millennium B.C. – Part I*. Berlin: De Gruyter, 501–12.

Tan, J. 2022. Climate change and Rome's changing Republic. In Balbo, M. and Santangelo, F. (eds), *A Community in Transition: Rome between Hannibal and the Gracchi*. Oxford: Oxford University Press, 21–54.

Thatcher, E.D. 1956. The open rooms of the Terme del Foro at Ostia. *Memoirs of the American Academy in Rome* 24: 169–264.

Thielscher, P. 1953. Die Schallgefässe des antiken Theaters. In Kirsch, H. (ed.), *Festschrift Frans Dornseiff*. Leipzig: VEB Bibliographisches Institut, 334–71.

Thomas, E.V. 2007. *Monumentality and the Roman Empire: Architecture in the Antonine Age*. Oxford: Oxford University Press.

Thomas, E.V. 2013. Translating Roman architecture into Greek regional identities. In Schubert, P., Ducrey, P. and Derron, P. (eds), *Les Grecs héritiers des Romains: Huit exposés suivis de discussions*. Geneva: Fondation Hardt, 147–91.

Thomas, E.V. 2014. The monumentality of text. In Osborne, J.F. (ed.), *Approaching Monumentality in Archaeology*. Albany: State University of New York Press, 56–82.

Thomas, E.V. 2017. Performance space. In Richter, D.S. and Johnson, W.A. (eds), *The Oxford Handbook of the Second Sophistic*. Oxford: Oxford University Press, 181–201.

Thomas, E.V. and Witschel, C.W. 1992. Constructing reconstruction: claim and reality of Roman rebuilding inscriptions from the Latin West. *Papers of the British School at Rome* 60: 135–77.

Uğurlu, N.B. 2009. *The Roman Nymphaea in the Cities of Asia Minor: Function in Context*. Saarbrücken: VDM Verlag.

Ulrich, R.B. 2007. *Roman Woodworking*. New Haven-London: Yale University Press.

Van der Leeuw, S. 2012. Invention, innovation and sustainability. Lessons from and for archaeology. In Giraud, J. and Gernez, G. (eds), *Aux marges de l'archéologie. Hommage à Serge Cleuziou*. Paris: De Boccard, 45–58.

Van Oyen, A. 2020. *The Socio-Economics of Roman Storage: Agriculture, Trade, and Family*. Cambridge: Cambridge University Press.

Vannesse, M. 2011. L'eau et l'amoenitas urbium. Étude du paysage urbain d'Antioche et d'Apamée. In Abadie-Reynal, C., Provost, S. and Vipard, P. (eds), *Les réseaux d'eau courante dans l'antiquité. Réparations, modifications, réutilisations, abandon, récupération. Actes du colloque international de Nancy (20–21 novembre 2009)*. Rennes: Presses universitaires de Rennes, 189–204.

Vermoere, M., Six, S., Poblome, J., Degryse, P., Paulissen, E., Waelkens, M. and Smets, E. 2003. Pollen sequences from the city of Sagalassos (Pisidia, southwest Turkey). *Anatolian Studies* 53: 161–73.

Viaene, W., Waelkens, M., Ottenburgs, R. and Callebaut, K. 1997. An archaeometric study of mortars used at Sagalassos. In Waelkens, M. and Poblome, J. (eds), *Sagalassos IV. Report on the Survey and Excavation Campaigns of 1994 and 1995*. Leuven: Leuven University Press, 405–21.

Vitti, P. 2021. Mortars and masonry – structural lime and gypsum mortars in Antiquity and Middle Ages. *Archaeological and Anthropological Sciences* 13.10: https://doi.org/10.1007/s12520-021-01408-y (article 164).

Voigts, C. 2020. Nachhaltigkeit oder Sparsamkeit? Verwendung oder Wiederverwendung von Marmorbauteilen im kaiserzeitlichen Rom. In Schliephake, C., Sojc, N. and Weber, G. (eds), *Nachhaltigkeit in der Antike: Diskurse, Praktiken, Perspektiven*. Stuttgart: Franz Steiner Verlag, 95–116.

von Lanckoronski, K. 1892. *Städte Pamphyliens und Pisidiens. Vol. II: Pisidien*. Vienna: F. Tempsky.

Waelkens, M. 1987. The adoption of Roman building techniques in the architecture of Asia Minor. In Macready, S. and Thompson, F.H. (eds), *Roman Architecture in the Greek World*. London: Society of Antiquaries of London, 94–105.

Waelkens, M. 1989. Hellenistic and Roman influence in the imperial architecture of Asia Minor. In Walker, S. and Cameron, A. (eds), *The Greek Renaissance in the Roman Empire. Papers from the Tenth British Museum Classical Colloquium*. London: Institute of Classical Studies, 77–88.

Ward-Perkins, J.B. 1973. The cryptoportico: a practical solution to certain problems of Roman urban design. In *Les cryptoportiques dans l'architecture romaine. Actes du colloque de Rome (19–23 avril 1972).* Rome: École française de Rome, 51–56.

Ward-Perkins, J.B. 1981 *Roman Imperial Architecture.* Harmondsworth: Penguin.

Weiss, C.F. 2003. *Living Fluidly: Uses and Meanings of Water in Asia Minor (Second Century BCE – Second Century CE).* PhD Thesis, Brown University.

Whitelegg, J. 1993. *Transport for a Sustainable Future: The Case for Europe.* London: Belhaven Press.

Wilson, A.I. 1995. Running water and social status in North Africa. In Horton, M. and Weidemann, T.E.J. (eds), *North Africa from Antiquity to Islam.* Bristol: Centre for Mediterranean Studies University of Bristol, 52–56.

Wilson, A.I. 2019. Aphrodisias in the long sixth century. In Jacobs, I. and Elton, H. (eds), *Asia Minor in the Long Sixth Century: Current Research and Future Directions.* Oxford: Oxbow Books, 197–221.

Wilson, A.I. and Russell, B. forthcoming. *Aphrodisias XV. The Place of Palms: An Urban Park at Aphrodisias.* Wiesbaden: Reichert Verlag.

Wilson, A.I., Russell, B. and Ward, A. 2016. Excavations in an urban park ('South Agora'), 2012. In Smith, R.R.R., Lenaghan, J., Sokolicek, A. and Welch, K. (eds), *Aphrodisias Papers 5. Excavation and Research at Aphrodisias, 2006–2012.* Portsmouth, RI: Journal of Roman Archaeology Supplementary Series, 77–90.

Winter, F.E. 2006. *Studies in Hellenistic Architecture.* Toronto: University of Toronto Press.

Yegül, F.K. and Favro, D.G. 2019. *Roman Architecture and Urbanism from the Origins to Late Antiquity.* Cambridge: Cambridge University Press.

Zink, S., Pflug, J. and Ceci, M. 2020. How a temple survives. Resilience and architectural design at Temple A of Largo Argentina in Rome. *Mitteilungen des Deutschen Archäologischen Instituts, Römische Abteilung* 126: 387–427.

6

Building cities on the Rhine and on the Danube: The socio-ecological diversity of Roman construction

Dominik Maschek

Introduction

Ambitious architectural projects were one of the hallmarks of the Roman Empire. In large parts of modern Europe, North Africa, and Western Asia, the remains of Roman buildings, such as amphitheatres, temples or city walls, are still a fundamental feature of contemporary urban and rural landscapes and of people's lived experience. From the first to the fourth century CE, Roman urbanism and construction, driven by imperial expansion, conquest, and consolidation, spread to large parts of central and north-western Europe.[1] Unsurprisingly, this widespread adoption of Roman architectural techniques and styles across the Empire has attracted a considerable amount of scholarly attention, mainly focused on matters of typology, political symbolism, and cultural significance.[2] Moreover, there have been intense debates in recent years about the drivers of Roman economic performance and the importance of urban centres, as well as the extraction and trade of building materials.[3] However, in most of these studies, architecture is merely taken as a proxy for something else, such as political power or economic growth. This does not take into account the crucial socio-economic role and processual nature of construction.[4] When considering the sheer effort it takes to erect monumental buildings, it becomes clear that such structures are not mere *symbols* of power or mere *political statements* or the *result* of economic growth, but the very process of construction is an important catalyst for socio-economic and political developments (Bernard 2018; 2021; Maschek 2022). Complex building projects require particular modes of organization which, rather than being simply projected upon them, very often emerge from the nature of specific tasks.

Although we can use methods such as architectural energetics to estimate the scale of these tasks in terms of time expended or calories consumed, the results only provide an order of magnitude for the total effort which went into a building.[5] They do *not*, however, lead to a straightforward explanation of why, underneath a veneer of typological uniformity, Roman architectural practice shows a significant degree of regional variation. Although the amount of time for a given task or the number of calories consumed are certainly as important as the training and knowledge of architects and craftspeople (Maschek 2016, 155–59), they were not the only factors influencing the planning and execution of Roman buildings.

Crucially, resources and building materials were not distributed equally across the Roman Empire. Extensive networks of supply and transportation were established in order to enable monumental construction. Different practices and trade were thus intimately interconnected, such as timber management for both construction and fuel, or ceramic production for tile and brick (see also Lancaster, this volume). This linked the construction sites with a wide landscape of quarries, woodlands, waterways, etc. Apart from being shaped by the rhythms and cycles of supply and demand of materials, Roman construction also eminently depended on immaterial resources, first and foremost technical and artisanal knowledge; this was the remit of particular social groups that could either be highly mobile, such as military engineers and *architecti*,[6] or rather sedentary and tied to particular urban centres, such as artisans' associations (*collegia*).[7]

Rather than simply being seen as manifestations of a unified architectural, and therefore cultural, practice, Roman construction sites need to be understood as veritable microcosms in which the task of building was tackled in the face of such remarkable social and ecological diversity. By looking at two case studies from the Rhine and Danube frontiers, this chapter highlights some key aspects of such microcosms, which may be useful for a shift in perspective towards a regional, but nonetheless comparative, approach in future studies on Roman architecture.

Monumental construction in Germania Inferior in the early second century CE: Xanten (*Colonia Ulpia Traiana*)

A new circuit of urban defences was amongst the first monumental building projects in the newly established *Colonia Ulpia Traiana* (Xanten) on the Lower Rhine (Germania Inferior), following its foundation in the late first or early second century CE. Complete with 22 towers, the wall was 3.4 km long and featured three large gates and a smaller gate at the town's river port (Fig. 6.1).[8] Whereas three sides of the wall circuit were built in greywacke with a core of concrete, the soft ground of the riverbank on the north-eastern side dictated two different modes of construction. With the clear intention to provide additional stability, its western stretch was founded on a grid of oak piles, topped by a densely packed rubble layer with clay and silt, a stratum of mortared rubble, and a compressed layer of clay and earth that supported a massive foundation of concrete (Fig. 6.2) (Kühlborn 1987, 479, fig. 3). The predominant building material in this sector was basalt from the Eifel region. In contrast, the eastern stretch of the north-eastern wall was built in greywacke. Here, the lowest layer of the foundations consisted of stacked stones which were set in clay, topped by another clay layer and the core of concrete.

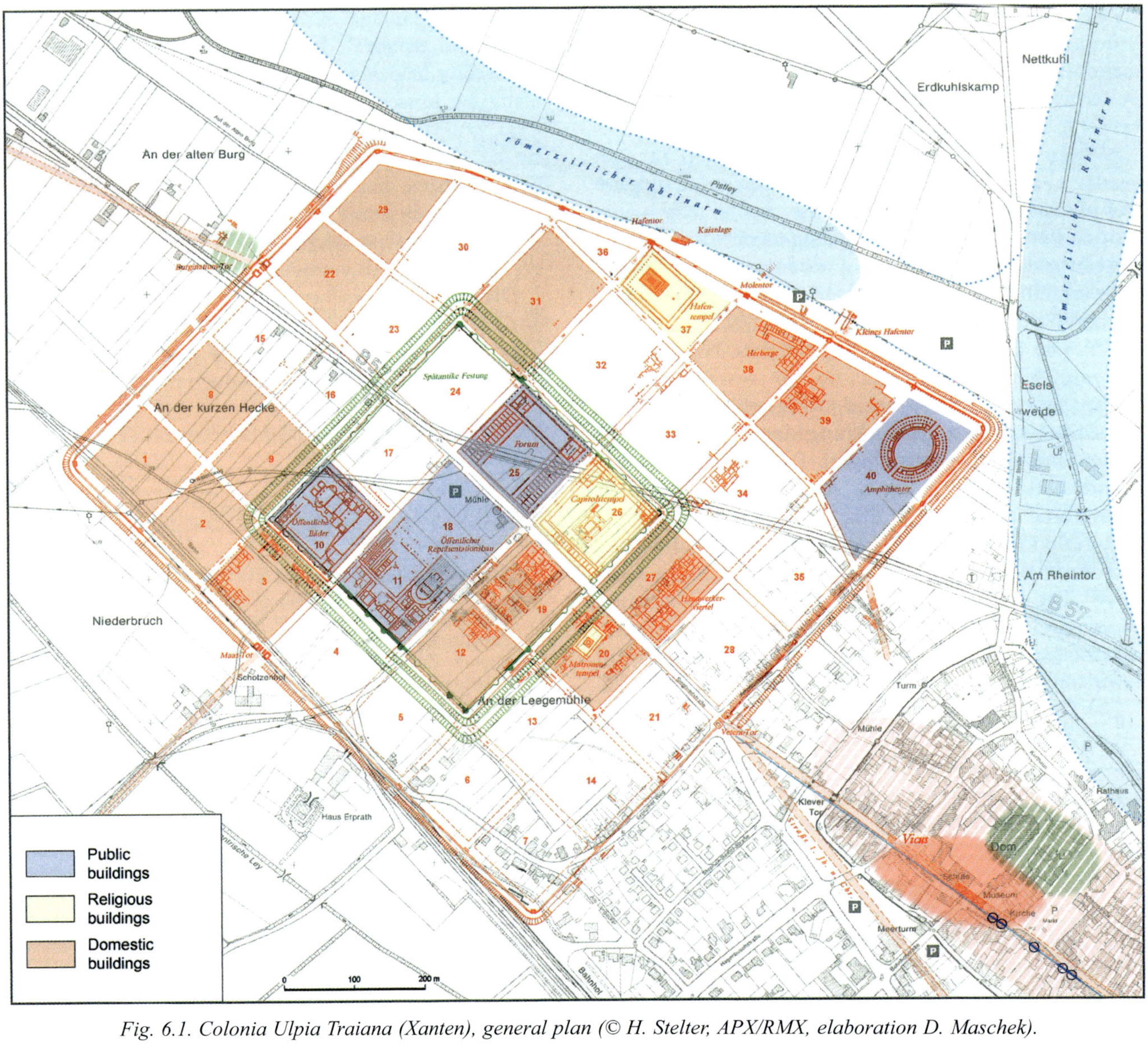

Fig. 6.1. Colonia Ulpia Traiana (Xanten), general plan (© H. Stelter, APX/RMX, elaboration D. Maschek).

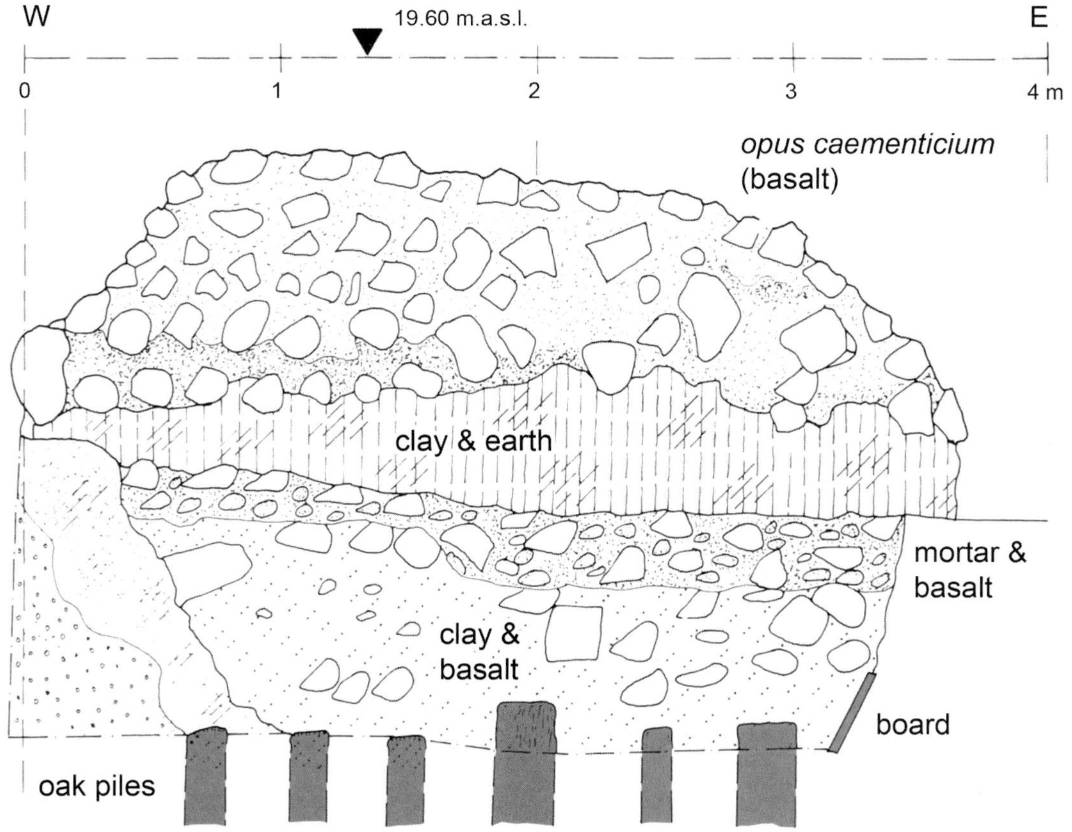

Fig. 6.2. Colonia Ulpia Traiana (Xanten), section through the north-eastern city wall (image D. Maschek, after Kühlborn 1987, 479, fig. 3).

The oak piles used on the north-eastern side of the wall were up to 1.8 m long, with a diameter of 0.15 to 0.35 m (Schießl 2021, 33, fig. 16). In the excavated areas, the density of piles was on average five per square metre. For each tower's foundations roughly 100 piles were used.[9] The wall was between 1.65 and 3.50 m wide, depending on the exact location, which, using the rounded average of 2.6 m without towers (values recorded in Schießl 2021, 30–39), equals a total of 2,444 m^2 of wall foundation and 12,220 oak piles, plus 700 piles for the seven towers. In total, this adds up to an impressive 12,920 oak piles of 1.8 m in length for the construction of the north-eastern side of the colony's city walls. In contrast, the foundations on the other three sides of the wall circuit did not feature oak piles and were exclusively built in greywacke. A layer of tufa debris was recorded in several excavations near the walls, which indicates the extensive processing of this material in the construction of the fortifications, either for the upper parts of the rubble core or for its more elaborate facing and the battlements (Precht and Rupprecht 1976, 350; Müller 2008, 281).

Based on dendrochronological samples from the extant oak piles, a *terminus post quem* for these building works has been established in the winter of 105/106 CE. Interestingly, timber did not come from the surroundings of Xanten, but from the middle Main region whence it was transported to the Lower Rhine (Schmidt 1987). Given this transport distance, it seems plausible to assume a chronological gap between the logs' winter felling date and their usage in the foundation works (Kühlborn 1987, 491). At the same time, the oak piles did not show any traces of drying before they were used in the construction, which means they had been kept reasonably fresh. Thus, the months from spring to autumn 106 CE can be established as the most probable period of construction for substantial stretches of the foundations along the north-eastern side of the city walls. Detailed observations on the different wall sectors show that their construction probably started simultaneously and would have been organized accordingly in multiple teams. A multi-phased, drawn-out construction process is therefore unlikely.[10]

Over the course of the second century CE, the structural and technological knowledge from building the urban defences was applied across the whole spectrum of monumental architecture at Xanten. Only one generation after the city walls, the 'Hafentempel' and its precinct were built in close proximity to the gate at the river port ('Kleines Hafentor'). The architectural structure and decoration of the 'Hafentempel' suggest a dedication between the Hadrianic period and the mid-second century CE.[11] Just as in the foundations of the Rhine-facing city walls, the builders of the temple podium (23 × 35 m) made ample use of wooden piles, presumably oak, with a length of up to 2.4 m. In this case, the piles were used as vertical supports to hold the formwork for the concrete. Imprints of the piles were preserved in the wall structure (Oenbrink 2021, 36–44, figs 22–24). On the podium's north-eastern side, a total of 87 piles has been recorded. This translates into 2.5 piles per metre, which allows us to reconstruct 58 piles each for the rear and front sides of the temple podium. Overall, 290 piles must have been used for this structure. There is no direct evidence for the existence of a full-blown pile grid, as in the case of the city walls or other monumental buildings in the colony, such as the Capitolium (*Insula* 26) (Stoll 1936, 187–88, table 36.1). However, in the light of the natural topography and the soft ground at the riverbank, the existence of such a grid below the temple podium is highly likely (Oenbrink 2021, 39).

Another monumental building project which made ample use of the particular techniques that had been implemented in the city walls was the forum (*Insula* 25). Although this complex had a long construction time, going back to the first century CE, the original design was substantially altered and enlarged at the end of Trajan's reign, or in the early years of Hadrian's, as indicated by brick stamps of the *legio VIII Augusta*.[12] A votive inscription for Antoninus Pius (*CIL* XIII, 8036) shows that the Rhine fleet stationed at Cologne was ordered to transport building stone for the forum of Xanten, which means that the construction was still underway in the year 160 CE. The process of building the forum therefore spanned at least one and a half generations, if not longer. Again, the foundations of the forum's basilica were supported by a grid of oak piles which were systematically placed and must have been part of the initial planning of the complex (Precht 2008, 344–45, fig. 206). As in the case of the city walls, the 'Hafentempel', and the Capitolium, the preserved parts of monumental masonry (such as the basilica's western foundations) were built in concrete and show imprints of the formwork, in particular wooden planks and upright posts (Precht 2008, 343, fig. 204).

Similar evidence has been gathered from excavations at the large public bath complex ('Große Thermen') in the western part of the town (Zieling 2003; 2008). This building featured massive concrete foundations and a number of heated rooms with thick mortar floors. The north-western and south-western walls of the *basilica thermarum* were founded on a grid of up to 3,000 oak piles from the Rhine-Main region. Interestingly, this technique was only used for two parts of the basilica's foundations and probably also for the foundations of the bathing rooms, which indicates a careful planning based on structural considerations. The trees from which the piles were cut had been felled around the year 125 CE (±5 years), and thus in the central period of Hadrian's reign.[13]

Monumental construction in Pannonia in the early third century CE: Carnuntum

Starting in the later Julio-Claudian period, a civilian town of substantial size developed next to the permanent legionary camp at Carnuntum. However, unlike in the previous case of Xanten, it was not before the late second–early third century CE that the urban area of the *Colonia Septimia Aurelia Antoniniana Carnuntum* was enclosed with city walls (Fig. 6.3).[14] Excavations on the southern outskirts of the town have shown that the erection of the urban fortifications went hand in hand with a thorough reconfiguration of the water supply and public infrastructure.[15] As established through recent archaeological investigations, the building techniques and materials of this wall circuit were homogeneous on all four sides of the urban perimeter. The wall's foundations were 0.6 m deep and 2.1 m strong. The foundations consisted of two rows of large, stacked stones which were set into the naturally occurring layers of gravel, sand, and clay. On top of these stones lay a solid mass of concrete that had been constructed in some sort of formwork. Above the foundations, the wall consisted of a lower section with a core made of small rubble in compact lime mortar; and an upper section with an almost mortarless core of packed earth, small rubble, and pebbles. Facing the defensive ditch, the concrete layer of the foundations was topped by a layer of large sandstone slabs. This layer constituted a plinth for a facing of sandstone orthostats and ashlars, integrated into the rubble core (Fig. 6.4).[16] By contrast, the facing on the opposite side of the wall was made of carefully cut, medium-sized stones laid in regular courses and bound by lime mortar.

The foundations and the outer face of the city walls significantly diverged from this technique due to the use of large stones, which were topped by a core of concrete and levelled by a layer of sand and limestone slabs. These slabs, alongside a certain percentage of the orthostats, showed clear signs of reuse and were partly marked with the number 'XIIII' which probably refers to the *legio XIV Gemina Martia Victrix*, Carnuntum's long-time garrison since the time of Trajan (see Kremer *et al.* 2021, 55–56, fig. 7). The shape and size of the reused architectural elements indicate that they were mostly sourced from funerary monuments.[17] This points to an organized process of dismantling older buildings and selecting and labelling stone for reuse, alongside the supply of large quantities of newly cut sandstone blocks from the Leitha quarries.[18] As at Xanten, an extensive layer of sandstone debris was recorded next to the walls, which shows that continuous stoneworking took place in the immediate vicinity (Fig. 6.5). The blocks were used for the wall's outer face and the battlements. Pieces of the same type and size

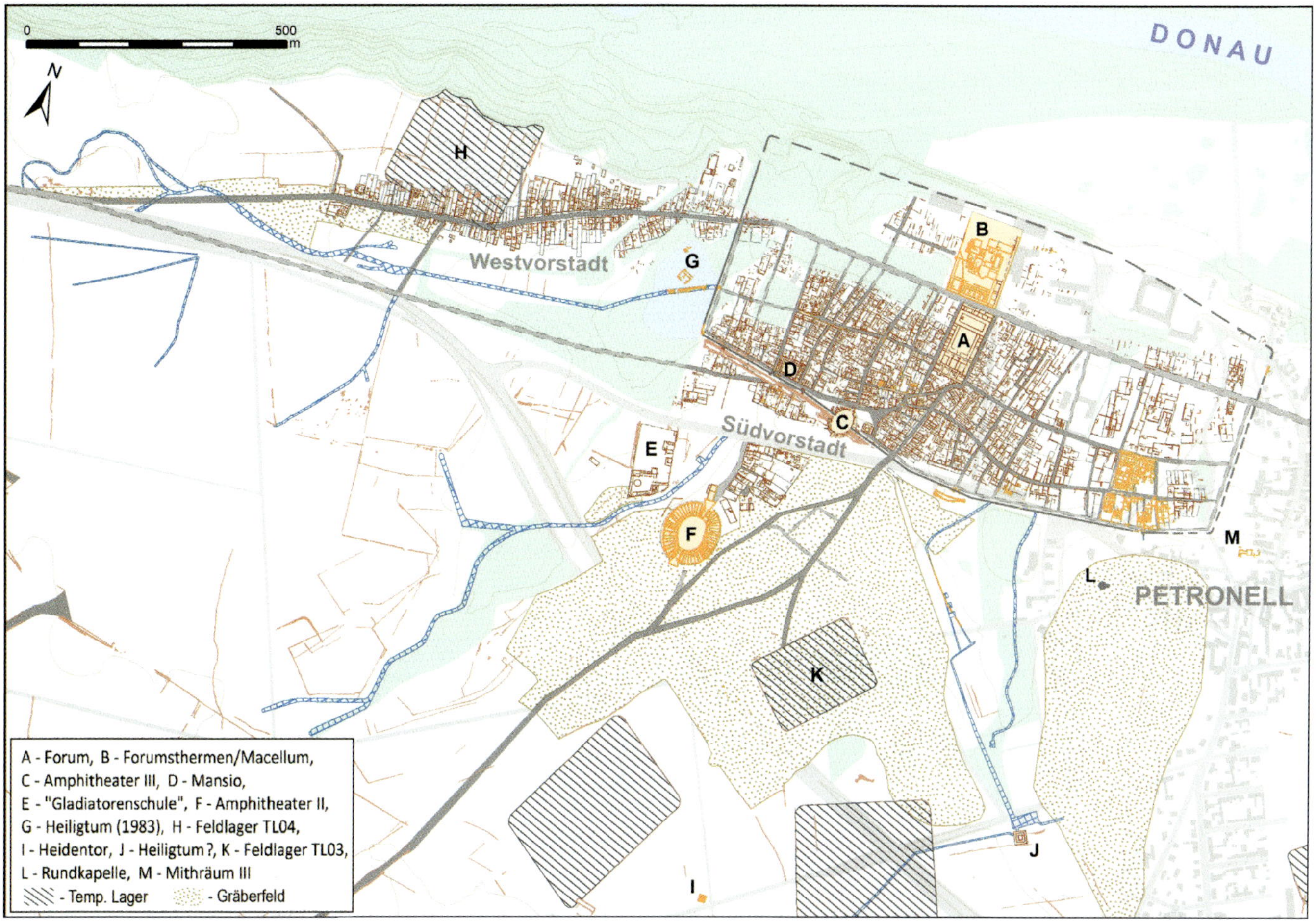

Fig. 6.3. Carnuntum, civilian town, general plan (© M. Wallner, Geosphere Austria).

were found in the nearby legionary camp and can be attributed to the Severan building phase of its fortifications (Ertel 1991, 183–92; Gugl *et al.* 2007, 58–64, 435–48).

One of the ashlars was marked with the acronym 'LIA', which was a common abbreviation for the *legio I Adiutrix* (Fig. 6.6).[19] This clearly proves the involvement of yet another of the three Upper Pannonian legions in the construction of the city walls. The *legio I Adiutrix* was stationed at Brigetio (Komárom) on the Danube, and until 214 CE it was under the command of the governor of Pannonia Superior.[20] It is likely that substantial forces of the legion were present at Carnuntum in 193 CE when Septimius Severus was proclaimed emperor by the Pannonian legions. A more regular presence, perhaps in the form of detachments (*vexillationes*), is attested by various funerary inscriptions of serving members and veterans of the legion who were buried

Fig. 6.4. Carnuntum, city walls: Foundations, plinth, and concrete core (photo D. Maschek).

Fig. 6.5. Carnuntum, layer of sandstone debris associated with the construction of the city walls (photo D. Maschek).

at Carnuntum in the second half of the second century CE.[21] As in the case of Mogontiacum (Mainz) in the mid-third century CE, it can perhaps be assumed that detachments of the *legio XIV Gemina* and *legio I Adiutrix* were commissioned to stay at Carnuntum and assist in building the city walls in the interest of the civilian population, while the bulk of the troops went off to fight in the civil war (Heising 2008, 157–65, 205–6).

Roughly at the same time as the urban fortifications and the underground water supply conduits, a monumental bath complex ('Palastruine') was erected in the town centre, just to the north of the forum (Öllerer 1998; Sedlmayer 2015). On this construction site, the reuse of materials played a much less prominent role than for the builders of the city walls. Overall, the mortar walls of the 'Palastruine' share the basic structural characteristics of domestic architecture, with a high standard of finishing.[22] However, the massive foundations of the bath building and the underground water infrastructure are more in line with the technological choices made for the foundations of the city walls, including traces of wooden formwork and much less regular, solidly mortared courses in the lower part of the baths' foundations (Sedlmayer 2015, 244, fig. 211). Indications of a mixed construction in ashlar blocks and mortared rubble are comparatively rare in the 'Palastruine', but they do occur, in

Fig. 6.6. Carnuntum, ashlar block with mason's mark of legio I Adiutrix *(photo D. Maschek; drawing M. Bru-Calderon).*

particular at the quoins reinforcing the corners of the main bathing suites (Sedlmayer 2015, 89–90, fig. 68). For most of the walls of the 'Palastruine', a construction layer of yellow sand, lime mortar, and earth was recorded (Sedlmayer 2015, 99, fig. 78a). This clearly points to the importance of mortar in constructing the core and the faces of the walls, perhaps also to the occasional working of particular small stones and quoins, but not, as in the case of the city walls, to the large-scale shaping of blocks by dedicated craftsmen who worked in considerably large areas.

Roman monumental construction on the Lower Rhine and on the Danube: Types of knowledge and socio-ecological diversity

These examples of monumental buildings from Xanten and Carnuntum provide useful cues for understanding the extent to which Roman construction projects were decisively shaped by factors such as knowledge, social organization, and environmental conditions. Through the analysis of commonalities and differences it becomes possible to gauge the impact of resource management and construction schedules on the development of regionally and chronologically diverse architectural practices.

In terms of knowledge, the urban fortifications and other buildings at both sites clearly reveal an overarching idiom which mainly manifests itself in principles of design and in the deployment of materials. As a matter of fact, structural considerations came first, as demonstrated by the usage of supporting oak piles and the interweaving of clay and stone layers in the foundations of the city walls at Xanten, or by the usage of large packed stones and deep concrete foundations at Carnuntum. Other features of such expert knowledge were the general design and the metrological framework chosen for the city walls at both Xanten and Carnuntum, as demonstrated by numerous comparable examples with similar dimensions from the Rhine and Danube provinces.[23] The knowledge behind these solutions can be sought in the education of engineers (*libratores*) and *architecti* who planned and oversaw the building projects, and which finds interesting antecedents in Rome, central, and northern Italy from the mid-Republican period to the first century CE.[24] Due to the close similarities with military fortifications, especially with respect to the size and spacing of towers, gates, and foundations, it has been argued that architects and builders with a military background played a crucial role in the construction of the Xanten walls (Geyer 1999, 123; Schießl 2021, 110–11). The high mobility of such specialists is indicated by inscriptions such as the famous monument of the water engineer Nonius Datus from the *legio III Augusta* at Lambaesis (see Cuomo 2011, 159–60), and by the letters of Pliny the Younger asking Trajan for an architect or *librator* who could help with substantial infrastructure works at Nicomedia (*Tra.* 10.41–42; cf. *Tra.* 10.61–62).

On the more granular level of detailed execution, the monumental buildings from Xanten and Carnuntum also reveal a strong adherence to what, in another context, I have proposed to call 'vernacular knowledge' or the knowledge of the craftspeople who made the buildings (Maschek 2022, 155–56). This type of practical knowledge is deeply embedded into local and regional conditions, such as the nature of raw materials and the typical rhythms of supply. It entails experimentation and the blending of different traditions, types of knowledge, and technical solutions. Both types of knowledge, expert and vernacular, are formed in a feedback loop between environmental factors, availability of resources, modes of transport, and human agency. Their implementation was contingent upon the 'chaîne opératoire', the schedule of the respective building projects, and the challenges they entailed (Fig. 6.7).

At both Xanten and Carnuntum, the first step was the detailed planning of the structures and required materials, followed by surveying and laying out the foundations. Then, the foundation trenches were dug and the continuous supply of building stones, lime, and wooden planks for the formwork needed to start. At Xanten, this was also the time when the supply of oak piles began. In the first year of construction those piles probably had to be drawn from stored stock, as the ideal cutting season for timber was between October and March.[25] The element of storage and availability of materials thus must also have played an important role in the initial planning process at both sites. This was of equal importance when it came to the subsequent construction of the walls from the foundations upwards. The structural stability of walls made of mortared rubble was highly sensible to changes in weather conditions and temperatures, and although ashlar blocks and other stone elements could be finished under the protection of shelters and roofs, their usage in mortared structures meant that they needed to be shaped in parallel with the rest of the building works. More complex supply chains and different climatic conditions thus acted as triggers for localized forms of knowledge, which led to the formation of technologically distinctive processes behind the creation of monumental architecture.

At Carnuntum, the planners and builders of the city walls were predominantly operating within an ecology of stone, lime, and water. Potential sources for the rubble used in the urban fortifications can be located at a distance of roughly 4 to 7 km from the building site, at the Hundsheim Mountains, whereas the large limestone blocks and a significant percentage of the limestone used for lime production were probably sourced at the Leitha Mountains, 30 km to the south of Carnuntum.[26] It is possible that the burning of limestone happened on site, as indicated by no fewer than

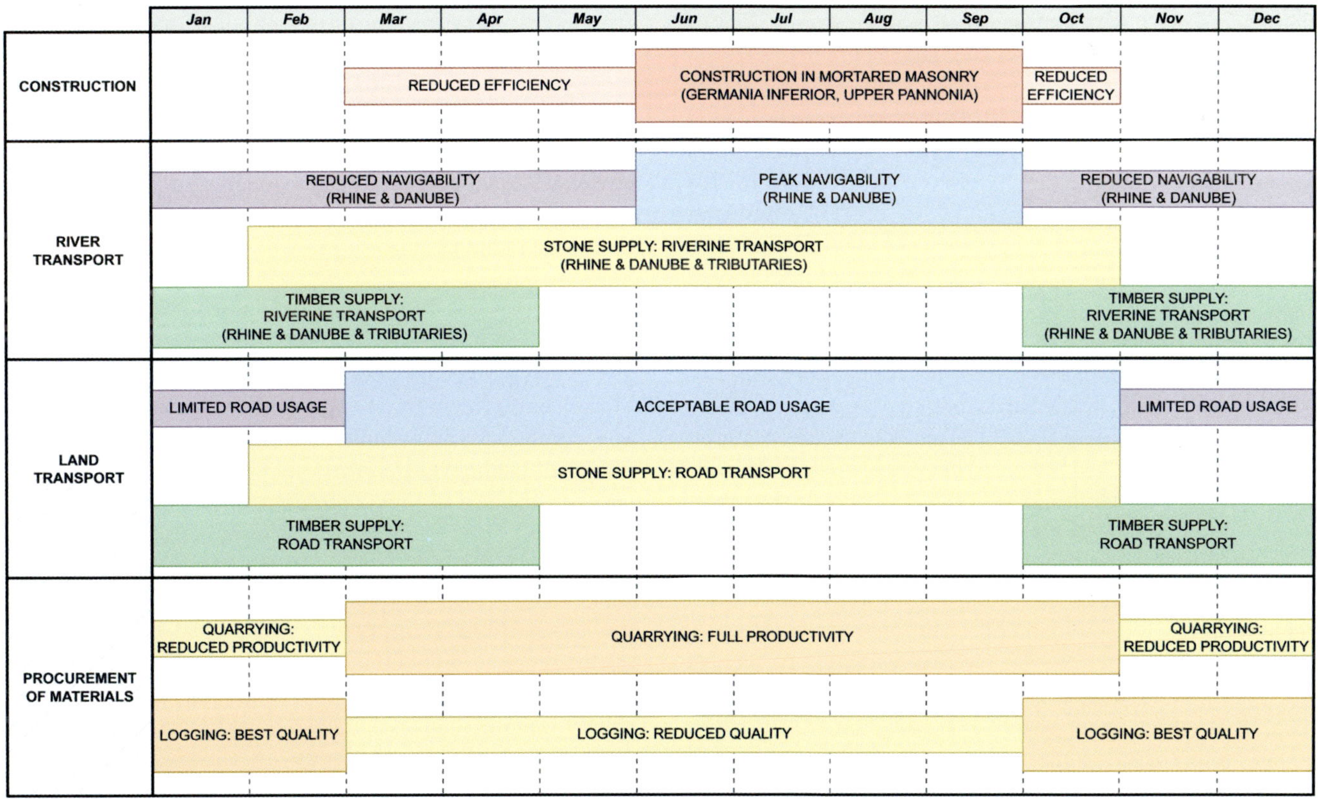

Fig. 6.7. 'Chaîne opératoire', logistics, and hypothetical schedule for monumental building projects at Xanten and Carnuntum, second to early third century CE (image D. Maschek).

Fig. 6.8. Carnuntum, potential lime kilns along the southern sector of the city walls (photo A. Konecny).

12 kilns that were clustered in a small area on the southern sector of the city walls (Fig. 6.8).[27] Lime slaking could draw upon an abundant reservoir of water, which had been made available through the creation of underground vaulted water supply lines when the city walls were under construction.[28]

The technical expertise applied in the walls' planning and construction relied on an integrated usage of mortared rubble and ashlar masonry, the latter with the usual metal clamps and pegs. Much effort went into the dismantling of older monuments, often from the suburban cemeteries, to source blocks for the plinth of the city walls. Masons' marks indicate that workers from two Pannonian legions played an important role in this process. The inner face of the city walls and the walls of the towers are much more in line with a different and more local type of vernacular builders' knowledge. They show a type of masonry that can be compared with a pre-existing tradition of building in mortared masonry, which had been established at Carnuntum from the first quarter of the second century CE onwards. The main evidence for this technique comes from domestic buildings, but also from the military barracks in the legionary fortress and the nearby auxiliary fort.[29] These walls usually featured foundations of packed rubble (limestone and sandstone), compressed with sand and pebbles, and topped by walls with a mortared rubble core and faces in regular, carefully pointed and finished courses. By contrast, the building process at the Great Baths ('Palastruine') relied heavily on deep concrete foundations and traditional styles of carefully finished mortar walls, whereas ashlars, cut stones, and the reuse of materials played a much less prominent role. In spite of some shared elements, the construction of the baths therefore had a different 'chaîne opératoire', different supply chains, and different logistics than the city walls, and it seems reasonable to assume that the project also drew upon a different workforce. Whilst the city walls were probably built by a mixed group of military units and civilian stonemasons, under the supervision of engineers and architects who had experience in devising military and urban defences, the technological choices implemented in the Great Baths point towards the involvement of urban craftspeople and *redemptores*.[30]

Although water was equally abundant at Xanten, the planners and builders of monumental structures at this site were operating in a substantially different environment than their fellow craftspeople at Carnuntum. First and foremost, there were no substantial local, or even regional, sources for building stone and for the production of lime. According to the most recent study, a total of 45,000 m^3 of stone material was needed for the colony's city walls (Schießl 2021, 108–10). Similar orders of magnitude have been estimated for the Severan-period urban fortifications of Sumelocenna and Bad Wimpfen (25,000 to 30,000 m^3), whilst the late Antonine wall circuit of Augusta Treverorum (Trier) may have required up to 200,000 m^3 of building stone (Gairhos 2008, 113; Heising 2008, 167–70). The tufa, basalt, and greywacke used for the city walls and in other buildings had to be shipped to Xanten over a distance of roughly 200 km from the quarries in the Eifel region (for example, at Mayen, Andernach, or Niedermendig), whilst substantial quantities of limestone came from even farther afield in Lorraine, 400 km from Xanten.[31]

Equally complex supply lines had to be put in place for the oak piles that were used in all of the monumental projects at Xanten discussed in this paper. According to dendrological analysis, timber came from the region along the Upper Rhine and the river Main. Based on the attested felling dates for the foundation piles of the city walls, we can envisage seasonal felling cycles which started in the winter of 105/106 CE with the procurement of huge amounts of timber and then continued, probably for a number of years, until the project was completed. Under such conditions, the provisioning and institutional curation of storage spaces along the main transport routes was of crucial importance, as the availability of stock very much dictated the rhythm of construction on the Lower Rhine. As the stratigraphy at Towers 2, 5 and 7 shows, the foundation trench and the pile grid for the wall foundations were laid out, excavated, and put in place in one continuous operation, followed by the separate pile grids for the foundations of the towers (Fig. 6.9) (Schießl 2021, 29–39, 50–52, 112).

Therefore, the continuous supply of suitable timber from the Upper Rhine/Main regions was crucial for the success of this first and pivotal building phase. Only then could the work on the concrete foundations start, for which the timber supply was still vital, as posts and planks were now needed in substantial numbers for the formwork. However, in contrast to the oak piles for the foundation grids, these posts and planks could at least partly be reused multiple times in different sections of the walls.[32] Similar practices are attested for the

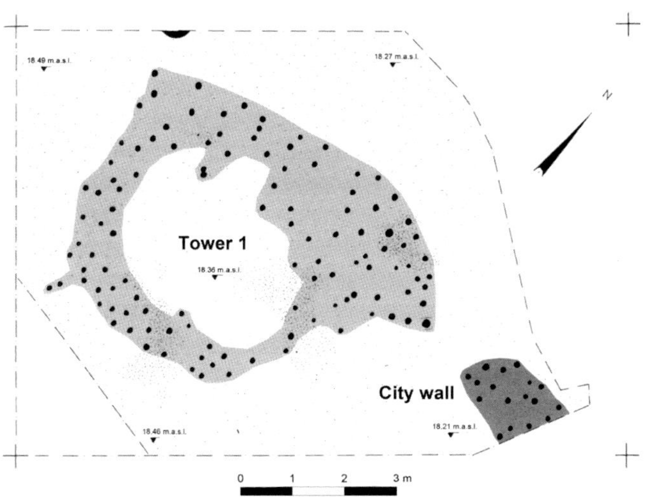

Fig. 6.9. Colonia Ulpia Traiana (Xanten), pile grid for Tower 1 and adjacent city walls (image D. Maschek, after Kühlborn 1987, 487, fig. 11).

other monumental buildings that were erected at Xanten over the course of the second century CE. Any disruption of the supply lines, for example due to seasonally changing conditions of overland or riverine transport, must have had a direct impact on the overall productivity of the construction site.[33]

Initially based on the expert knowledge of engineers and planners with a military background, several generations of builders at Xanten thus developed their own distinctive vernacular knowledge in an environment of extreme scarcity with respect to naturally available resources for stone architecture. This stands in pronounced contrast with Carnuntum, where a strong local tradition of building in mortared rubble had already emerged in the generations before the erection of the city walls and the Great Baths. As has become clear from the discussion above, the specific trajectories of such local building traditions and technological approaches were strongly shaped by socio-ecological conditions, rather than simply by the top-down implementation of 'Roman' knowledge by experts. *Libratores* and *architecti* undoubtedly provided an important input at crucial moments, for example in the planning process, but the completion of the buildings ultimately relied on vernacular knowledge and collective practices that were suited to the locally prevailing conditions. In other words, one could say that Roman architecture was the outcome of a process characterized by an overarching repository of technical knowledge and the local manifestations of socio-ecological diversity.

Conclusions and future perspectives

From the analysis of monumental buildings at Xanten and Carnuntum, it has become clear that Roman construction on the Rhine and Danube in the second and early third century CE was predicated upon a process of continuous behavioural adaptation. The availability of natural resources such as timber and building stone put planners and builders under locally specific conditions and constraints. This fostered particular systems of knowledge and modes of social and institutional organization and brought about a situation which has been described here as the 'socio-ecological diversity' of building.

In an important recent paper, Seth Bernard (2022, 52) has convincingly argued that the increasing population density which was triggered by high urbanization rates in the Roman period led to a fall in well-being, as evidenced by the analysis of human remains. On average, people from the most densely urbanized areas of the Roman Empire became shorter as they had to cope with malnutrition caused by increasing pressure on the food supply. The simple fact that monumental buildings could still be constructed on a massive scale by a population with poorer overall health is tentatively explained by Bernard with the dynamics of urbanization itself, as 'a higher Roman urbanization rate meant greater demand for builders, who required more daily calories for their work, while it also contributed to a lower equilibrium of smaller people with lower aggregate baseline maintenance costs'. Although this picture needs to be complemented by the regionally differentiated consideration of other environmental factors such as precipitation, climate, and topography, the link between urban development and demand for builders is convincing. It underlines the importance of not reducing the study of Roman architecture to an exercise in typology and design. Instead, a wider and regional perspective allows us to contrast and compare the processes and conditions of monumental building across the Roman world. The case studies from the Rhine and Danube provinces clearly demonstrate the degree to which monumental construction could trigger processes of social organization and the creation of knowledge and institutions, such as the co-operation between military and civilian builders.

Future studies will therefore need to look in more depth at the macro-scale of climate, precipitation, and mean temperatures across the Empire to further contextualize the socio-ecological diversity of Roman construction. Such climate data should be correlated with the usual times for harvesting in particular regions, in order to establish where the workforce, and in particular unskilled workers, might have come from. As in the case of Xanten, the logistics of Roman building projects were delicately balanced and hinged upon the best transport season. In the Mediterranean, based on the weather conditions, this would have probably been between March and October, although we need more fine-grained studies, ideally including data for monthly precipitation, to further substantiate this for other regions such as central and northern Europe.[34] Such data would also allow us to gauge other fundamental aspects of the socio-ecological diversity behind the creation of Roman architecture. For example, the availability of workers and the nature of the workforce might have varied considerably, depending on modes of land usage and agricultural production, as well as on the overall density of urbanization. Ultimately, different types of building materials and techniques (concrete, mortared rubble, ashlar without mortar, usage of timber in foundations) need to be mapped onto climate zones and zones of agricultural production, which will allow to recognize meaningful correlations and to explain phenomena such as the persistence of particular architectural types and styles in certain regions of the Empire.

This chapter has therefore proposed to conceptualize Roman architectural practice as part of a complex network of social and economic links between urban centres, their supply networks, and ecological factors (see also Hufschimd, this volume). As the preliminary analysis of socio-ecological diversity in two regions of the Empire has shown, such a perspective has the clear potential to change the conventional view of the Roman construction industry as a unified phenomenon, as it adds much-needed spatial and chronological nuance to what is sweepingly called 'Roman architecture'.

Notes

1. Ward-Perkins 1981; MacDonald 1982; Sear 1982; Gros 1996; 2001; von Hesberg 2005; Ulrich and Quenemoen 2014; Maschek 2017; Yegül and Favro 2019, 1–3; Mazzilli 2020.
2. See, for instance: Drerup 1966; Rakob 1967; Ward-Perkins 1981; MacDonald 1982; 1986; Gros 1996; 2001; 2006; Anderson 1997; Wilson Jones 2000; Thomas 2007; 2015; von Hesberg and Lipps 2010–11; Senseney 2011; Favro *et al.* 2015; Davies 2017; Pensabene *et al.* 2017.
3. For instance: Jackson and Marra 2006; Bowman and Wilson 2009; 2011; 2013; Hayward 2009; Hirt 2010; Russell 2013; 2017; Wilson 2014; Wilson and Flohr 2016; Flohr and Wilson 2017; Wilson and Bowman 2017; DeLaine 2018; Peveler 2018; O'Donnell 2020.
4. Exceptions: Skydsgaard 1983; Anderson 1997; DeLaine 1997; 2000a-b; 2001; 2003; 2006; 2017; 2018; Taylor 2007; Bernard 2013; 2016; 2018; Domingo 2013; Maschek 2020; Padilla Peralta 2020; Maschek and Trümper 2022.
5. On the methodology, see: DeLaine 2017; Brysbaert *et al.* 2018; Courault and Márquez 2020; Barker *et al.* 2022. For specific applications of architectural energetics to monumental buildings from the first century CE to Late Antiquity, see: DeLaine 1997; 2015; 2018; Barresi 2003; Camporeale *et al.* 2008; 2010; 2012; Domingo 2012; 2017; Bonetto *et al.* 2014; DeLaine *et al.* 2016; Maschek 2016; Barker *et al.* 2020; 2021; Intagliata *et al.* 2020; Courault 2022.
6. See, for example, Cuomo 2011. On different forms of knowledge in Roman architectural practice, see Maschek 2022.
7. Kolb 2008a–b; Hawkins 2016; Fabiano 2019.
8. Precht 1983; Kühlborn 1987; Geyer 1999, 117–21; Müller 2008; Schießl 2021.
9. Cf. Tower 7 on the wall's north-eastern corner: Kühlborn 1987, 487, fig. 11. For more evidence for the pile grids, see Kühlborn 1987, 478, fig. 2; 480, fig. 4; 485, fig. 10; Müller 2008, 282, fig. 164; Schießl 2021, 33–37, figs 13–21; 41, fig. 24; 45, fig. 28.
10. Oenbrink 2021, 187; Schießl 2021, 106–8. More cautious, albeit also opposed to the idea of more than one coherent building phase: Müller 2008, 283.
11. Precht 1983, 34; Kühlborn 1987, 491; Geyer 1999, 109, 134; Müller 2008, 283; Schalles 2008, 315; Oenbrink 2021, 189–91.
12. Precht 2008, 351–52; Schmidts 2018, 7–8, 94, 150, cat. B30a, table 44.1; Oenbrink 2021, 188. In total, the excavations of the forum have produced 107 stamped bricks, 75 of which were produced by military units.
13. Zieling 2008, 374–76, fig. 234. Oenbrink 2021, 188 dates the piles for the Great Baths to the period between c. 120 CE and 138 CE, which extends the date suggested by Zieling until the end of Hadrian's reign. Cf. Schmidts 2018, 96.
14. Maschek and Humer 2009a; Pacher 2009–11; Maschek 2012; Konecny 2013; Groh *et al.* 2014, 393–96.
15. Maschek 2008; 2010; Maschek and Humer 2008; 2009b; Maschek *et al.* 2010; 2011.
16. For this construction method, see also the later city walls of Gorsium (Ertel 1999, 7–8) and Mogontiacum (Mainz; Heising 2008, 2–5, fig. 3a).
17. Funerary monuments were also systematically dismantled for the construction of the mid-third-century CE city walls of Gorsium and Mogontiacum, albeit in a different historical context: Ertel 1999; Heising 2008, 91–94.
18. On the provenance of stone material at Carnuntum, see Kremer and Kitz 2016; Kremer *et al.* 2018; 2021.
19. Cf. the legion's quarry marks and masons' marks from Mainz: Büsing 1982, 22–23, 55–56, 96. On the abbreviations used by this legion on stamped bricks and tiles, see Brandl 1999, 45–47; Schmidts 2018, 6.
20. Kandler 1991, 237; Brandl 1999, 44–46. The close links between the three Upper Pannonian legions in the period before 214 CE is also attested by a joint votive inscription in honour of Caracalla, dedicated at Carnuntum: *CIL* III, 4452; 11093; Vorbeck 1980, no. 256.
21. Kandler 1991, 237; *CIL* III, 4462 = Vorbeck 1980, no. 2; *CIL* III, 4489 = Vorbeck 1980, no. 6; *CIL* III, 11221 = Vorbeck 1980, no. 3; *CIL* III, 11222 = Vorbeck 1980, no. 5; *CIL* III, 11240 = Vorbeck 1980, no. 1; *CIL* III, 14092 = Vorbeck 1980, no. 7; Weber 1976, 75 = Vorbeck 1980, no. 4.
22. Sedlmayer 2015, 85–93, 248–49. For the chemical and structural properties of the mortar used in the walls of the 'Palastruine', see Blümel and Horn 1963–64.
23. Cf. Wenzel 2000; Ortisi 2001; Gairhos 2008; Heising 2008.
24. For Roman recommendations on how to build upon soft ground, see the collected sources in Moraci 2017, 145–47. A detailed discussion of technical solutions for such foundation works in northern Italy is given by Previato 2016.
25. See Vitr. *De arch.* 2.9.1: 'timber should be cut from the very beginning of autumn to that time just before Favonius begins to blow' (translation I.D. Rowland). This, of course, pertains to a Mediterranean setting where the 'Favonian winds' began to blow in the spring: cf. Hor. *Carm.* 1.4.1; Plin. *HN* 2.122 (offering the date of 18 February). For the recommendation to fell trees in the winter, see also: Hes. *Op.* 412–14, 663; Theophr. *Hist. pl.* 3.5.3; 5.1.2; Cato *Agr.* 17.1; Cic. *Div.* 2.33; Colum. *Rust.* 11.2.11; Plin. *HN* 18.232; Palladius, *Opus Agriculturae* 2.22; 12.15.1; 13.2; *Geopontica* 3.1. 2; 15.3.

26. Kremer and Kitz 2016, 73–80; Kremer *et al.* 2018, 559–63; 2021, 48–51, 55–58.
27. Humer and Konecny 2009; Konecny 2012a. On lime production in the Roman world, see Dix 1982; Snyder 2020; DeLaine 2021.
28. Alternatively it has been suggested that the kilns could have served for the provisioning of the workforce: Konecny 2012b, 173–76; 2014, 272.
29. Examples in Kandler 1997; Stiglitz 1997; Cencic 2003; Humer *et al.* 2004; Baier *et al.* 2007; Gugl *et al.* 2007; Doneus *et al.* 2013; Groh *et al.* 2014; Sedlmayer 2015.
30. For the organization of the Roman building trade and its socio-economic dimensions, see Anderson 1997; Kolb 2008a-b; Bernard 2016; 2019; Gerding 2019.
31. Bockius 2000; Giljohann and Wenzel 2015, 19–22; Ruppiene 2015, 3–6, 232; Schaaff 2015, 195–211.
32. See Lancaster 2005, 28–30, 48–49; Coutelas and Hourcade 2016, 266–70.
33. On seasonal changes in the navigability of rivers, see Franconi 2016; 2023.
34. Cf. Bernard 2013; Scheidel 2014; Erdkamp 2016; Groenhuijzen 2022.

References

Anderson, J.C. 1997. *Roman Architecture and Society*. Baltimore: Johns Hopkins University Press.

Baier, C., Humer, F. and Konecny, A. 2007. Zivilstadt Carnuntum – Haus II: die Grabungen im römischen Stadtviertel des Archäologischen Parks Carnuntum in den Jahren 2003 bis 2005. *Carnuntum Jahrbuch*: 177–230.

Barker, S.J., Coombe, P. and Hayward, K. 2020. London's Roman defensive walls: logistics of transport and construction. In Courault, C. and Márquez, C. (eds), *Quantitative Studies and Production Cost of Roman Public Construction*. Cordoba: Editorial Universidad de Córdoba, 453–87.

Barker, S.J., Hayward, K. and Coombe, P. 2021. Londinium's Landward Wall: material acquisition, supply and construction. *Britannia* 52: 277–326.

Barker, S.J., Snyder, J.R. and Ward, C.A. 2022. Reflections on energetics studies and Roman architecture. In Maschek, D. and Trümper, M. (eds), *Architecture and the Ancient Economy. Proceedings of a Conference Held at Berlin (26–28 September 2019)*. Rome: Quasar, 59–110.

Barresi, P. 2003. *Province dell'Asia minore: costo dei marmi, architettura pubblica e committenza*. Rome: 'L'Erma' di Bretschneider.

Bernard, S.G. 2013. The transport of heavy loads in antiquity: lifting, moving, and building in ancient Rome. In Altekamp, S., Marcks-Jacobs, C. and Seiler, P. (eds), *Perspektiven der Spolienforschung 1: Spoliierung und Transposition*. Berlin: De Gruyter, 99–122.

Bernard, S.G. 2016. Workers in the Roman imperial building industry. In Verboven, K. and Laes, C. (eds), *Work, Labour, and Professions in the Roman World*. Boston-Leiden: Brill, 62–86.

Bernard, S.G. 2018. *Building Mid-Republican Rome: Labor, Architecture, and the Urban Economy*. Oxford: Oxford University Press.

Bernard, S.G. 2019. The economy of work. In Lytle, E. (ed.), *A Cultural History of Work in Antiquity*. London: Bloomsbury, 19–32.

Bernard, S.G. 2021. Tecniche edilizie e società nella Roma medio repubblicana. In D'Alessio, A., Serlorenzi, M., Smith, C.J. and Volpe, R. (eds), *Roma medio repubblicana: dalla conquista di Veio alla battaglia di Zama. Atti del convegno internazionale (Roma, 5–6–7 aprile 2017)*. Rome: Quasar, 299–313.

Bernard, S.G. 2022. Food, energy, and architectural production in the Roman world. In Maschek, D. and Trümper, M. (eds), *Architecture and the Ancient Economy. Proceedings of a Conference Held at Berlin (26–28 September 2019)*. Rome: Quasar, 35–57.

Blümel, O.W. and Horn, H. 1963–64. Der Aufbau des Mörtels der Palastruine. *Carnuntum Jahrbuch*: 92–98.

Bockius, R. (ed.) 2000. *Steinbruch und Bergwerk: Denkmäler der römischen Technikgeschichte zwischen Eifel und Rhein. Katalogbuch zu den Ausstellungen in den Museen von Mayen und Andernach*. Mainz: Verlag des Römisch-Germanischen Zentralmuseums.

Bonetto, J., Camporeale, S. and Pizzo, A. (eds) 2014. *Arqueología de la construcción IV. Las canteras en el mundo antiguo: sistemas de explotación y procesos productivos (Padova, 22–24 de noviembre de 2012)*. Madrid: Consejo Superior de Investigaciones Científicas.

Bowman, A.K. and Wilson, A.I. (eds) 2009. *Quantifying the Roman Economy: Methods and Problems*. Oxford: Oxford University Press.

Bowman, A.K. and Wilson, A.I. (eds) 2011. *Settlement, Urbanization, and Population*. Oxford: Oxford University Press.

Bowman, A.K. and Wilson, A.I. (eds) 2013. *The Roman Agricultural Economy: Organization, Investment, and Production*. Oxford: Oxford University Press.

Brandl, U. 1999. *Untersuchungen zu den Ziegelstempeln römischer Legionen in den nordwestlichen Provinzen des Imperium Romanum: Katalog der Sammlung Julius B. Fritzemeier*. Rahden: Leidorf.

Brysbaert, A., Klinkenberg, V., Gutiérrez Garcia, A. and Vikatou, I. (eds) 2018. *Constructing Monuments, Perceiving Monumentality and the Economics of Building: Theoretical and Methodological Approaches to the Built Environment*. Leiden: Sidestone Press.

Büsing, H.H. 1982. *Römische Militärarchitektur in Mainz*. Mainz: Philipp von Zabern.

Camporeale, S., Dessales, H. and Pizzo, A. (eds) 2008. *Arqueología de la construcción I. Los procesos constructivos en el mundo romano: Italia y provincias occidentales (Mérida, Instituto de Arqueología, 25–26 de Octubre de 2007)*. Mérida: Consejo Superior de Investigaciones Científicas.

Camporeale, S., Dessales, H. and Pizzo, A. (eds) 2010. *Arqueología de la construcción II. Los procesos constructivos en el mundo romano: Italia y provincias orientales (Certosa di Pontignano, Siena, 13–15 de noviembre de 2008)*. Madrid: Consejo Superior de Investigaciones Científicas.

Camporeale, S., Dessales, H. and Pizzo, A. (eds) 2012. *Arqueología de la construcción III. Los procesos constructivos en el mundo romano: la economía de las obras (École normale supérieure, Paris, 10–11 de diciembre de 2009)*. Madrid: Consejo Superior de Investigaciones Científicas.

Cencic, J. 2003. Römische Wohnbauten in Carnuntum. *Carnuntum Jahrbuch*: 9–116.
Courault, C. 2022. L'économie du remploi dans la construction des remparts tardifs en Occident. In Maschek, D. and Trümper, M. (eds), *Architecture and the Ancient Economy. Proceedings of a Conference Held at Berlin (26–28 September 2019)*. Rome: Quasar, 275–314.
Courault, C. and Márquez, C. (eds) 2020. *Quantitative Studies and Production Cost of Roman Public Construction*. Cordoba: Editorial Universidad de Córdoba.
Coutelas, A. and Hourcade, D. 2016. Les techniques et les étapes de la construction des salles de soutènement des thermes de Longeas (Chassenon, France). In DeLaine, J., Camporeale, S. and Pizzo, A. (eds), *Arqueología de la Construcción V – 5th International Workshop on the Archaeology of Roman Construction. Man-Made Materials, Engineering and Infrastructure (Oxford, April 11–12, 2015)*. Madrid: Consejo Superior de Investigaciones Científicas, 251–73.
Cuomo, S. 2011. A Roman engineer's tales. *Journal of Roman Studies* 101: 143–65.
Davies, P.J.E. 2017. *Architecture and Politics in Republican Rome*. Cambridge: Cambridge University Press.
DeLaine, J. 1997. *The Baths of Caracalla: A Study in the Design, Construction, and Economics of Large-Scale Building Projects in Imperial Rome*. Portsmouth, RI: Journal of Roman Archaeology Supplementary Series.
DeLaine, J. 2000a. Building the Eternal City: the construction industry of imperial Rome. In Coulston, J. and Dodge, H. (eds), *Ancient Rome: The Archaeology of the Eternal City*. Oxford: Oxbow Books, 119–41.
DeLaine, J. 2000b. Organising Roman building and space. *Journal of Roman Archaeology* 13: 486–92.
DeLaine, J. 2001. Bricks and mortar: exploring the economics of building techniques at Rome and Ostia. In Mattingly, D.J. and Salmon, J. (eds), *Economies beyond Agriculture in the Classical World*. London-New York: Routledge, 230–68.
DeLaine, J. 2003. The builders of Roman Ostia: organisation, status and society. In Huerta Fernández, S. (ed.), *Proceedings of the First International Congress on Construction History (Madrid, 20th–24th January 2003)*. Madrid: Instituto Juan de Herrera, Escuela Técnica Superior de Arquitectura, 723–32.
DeLaine, J. 2006. The cost of creation: technology at the service of construction. In Lo Cascio, E. (ed.), *Innovazione tecnica e progresso economico nel mondo romano. Atti degli incontri capresi di storia dell'economia antica (Capri, 13–16 aprile 2003)*. Bari: Edipuglia, 237–52.
DeLaine, J. 2015. The Pantheon builders: estimating manpower for construction. In Marder, T.A. and Wilson Jones, M. (eds), *The Pantheon from Antiquity to the Present*. Cambridge: Cambridge University Press, 160–92.
DeLaine, J. 2017. Quantifying manpower and the cost of construction in Roman building projects: research perspectives. *Archeologia dell'Architettura* 22: 13–19.
DeLaine, J. 2018. Economic choice in Roman construction: case studies from Ostia. In Brysbaert, A., Klinkenberg, V., Gutiérrez Garcia, A. and Vikatou, I. (eds), *Constructing Monuments, Perceiving Monumentality and the Economics of Building: Theoretical and Methodological Approaches to the Built Environment*. Leiden: Sidestone Press, 243–70.
DeLaine, J. 2021. Production, transport and on-site organisation of Roman mortars and plasters. *Archaeological and Anthropological Sciences* 13.10: https://doi.org/10.1007/s12520-021-01401-5 (article 195).
DeLaine, J., Camporeale, S. and Pizzo, A. (eds) 2016. *Arqueología de la Construcción V – 5th International Workshop on the Archaeology of Roman Construction. Man-Made Materials, Engineering and Infrastructure (Oxford, April 11–12, 2015)*. Madrid: Consejo Superior de Investigaciones Científicas.
Dix, B. 1982. The manufacture of lime and its uses in the western Roman provinces. *Oxford Journal of Archaeology* 1.3: 331–45.
Domingo, J.Á. 2012. Los costes de la arquitectura romana: el capitolio de Volúbilis (Mauretania Tingitana). *Archeologia Classica* 63: 381–418.
Domingo, J.Á. 2013. The differences in Roman construction costs: the workers' salary. *Boreas* 36: 119–43.
Domingo, J.Á. 2017. El coste del Arco de Caracalla en Theveste (Tébessa, Argelia): verificación empírica de una metodología de cálculo. *Archeologia dell'Architettura* 22: 35–53.
Doneus, M., Gugl, C. and Doneus, N. 2013. *Die Canabae von Carnuntum: eine Modellstudie der Erforschung römischer Lagervorstädte: von der Luftbildprospektion zur siedlungsarchäologischen Synthese*. Vienna: Verlag der Österreichischen Akademie der Wissenschaften.
Drerup, H. 1966. Architektur als Symbol: zur zeitgenössischen Bewertung der römischen Architektur. *Gymnasium* 73: 181–96.
Erdkamp, P. 2016. Seasonal labour and rural-urban migration in Roman Italy. In de Ligt, L. and Tacoma, L.E. (eds), *Migration and Mobility in the Early Roman Empire*. Boston-Leiden: Brill, 33–49.
Ertel, C. 1991. *Römische Architektur in Carnuntum*. Vienna: Verlag der Österreichischen Akademie der Wissenschaften.
Ertel, C. 1999. Spolien aus der westlichen Stadtmauer von Gorsium. *Alba Regia* 28: 5–51.
Fabiano, J. 2019. Builders and integrated associations in fourth-century CE Rome: a new interpretation of AE 1941, 68. *Journal of Late Antiquity* 12.1: 65–87.
Favro, D.G., Yegül, F.K., Pinto, J.A. and Métraux, G.P.R. (eds) 2015. *Paradigm and Progeny: Roman Imperial Architecture and its Legacy. Proceedings of a Conference Held at the American Academy in Rome on 6–7 December, 2011 in Honor of William L. MacDonald*. Portsmouth, RI: Journal of Roman Archaeology Supplementary Series.
Flohr, M. and Wilson, A.I. (eds) 2017. *The Economy of Pompeii*. Oxford: Oxford University Press.
Franconi, T. 2016. Climatic influences on riverine transport on the Roman Rhine. In Schäfer, C. (ed.), *Connecting the Ancient World: Mediterranean Shipping, Maritime Networks, and their Impact*. Rahden: Leidorf, 27–46.
Franconi, T. 2023. The environmental context of riverine trade in the Roman world. In Bentz, M. and Heinzelmann, M. (eds), *Sessions 4–5: Single Contribution*. Heidelberg: Propylaeum, 231–34.
Gairhos, S. 2008. *Stadtmauer und Tempelbezirk von Sumelocenna: die Ausgrabungen 1995–99 in Rottenburg am Neckar, Flur 'Am Burggraben'*. Stuttgart: Theiss.
Gerding, H. 2019. Public building and clientage: social and political aspects of Roman building industry. In Möller, D. (ed.), *Vetenskapssocieteten i Lund: Årsbok 2019*. Lund: Vetenskapssocieteten i Lund, 17–29.

Geyer, C. 1999. Das 'Kleine Hafentor' der Colonia Ulpia Traiana: ein Rekonstruktionsversuch. In *Xantener Berichte, 8: Grabung, Forschung, Präsentation*. Cologne: Rheinland Verlag, 61–171.

Giljohann, R. and Wenzel, S. 2015. Verwendung und Verbreitung von Lothringer Kalkstein zwischen Andernach und Mayen in römischer Zeit. *Berichte zur Archäologie in Rheinhessen und Umgebung* 8: 19–39.

Groenhuijzen, M.R. 2022. Evaluating hypotheses about local transport systems through spatial and network analysis: the Dutch part of the Lower Rhine limes and its hinterland. In Brughmans, T. and Wilson, A.I. (eds), *Simulating Roman Economies: Theories, Methods and Computational Models*. Oxford: Oxford University Press, 254–70.

Groh, S., Láng, O., Sedlmayer, H. and Zsidi, P. 2014. Neues zur Urbanistik der Zivilstädte von Aquincum-Budapest und Carnuntum-Petronell. *Acta Archaeologica Academiae Scientiarum Hungaricae* 65: 361–404.

Gros, P. 1996. *L'architecture romaine du début du IIIe siècle av. J.-C. à la fin du Haut-Empire, 1: Les monuments publics*. Paris: Picard.

Gros, P. 2001. *L'architecture romaine du début du IIIe siècle av. J.-C. à la fin du Haut-Empire, 2: Maisons, palais, villas et tombeaux*. Paris: Picard.

Gros, P. 2006. *Vitruve et la tradition des traités d'architecture: Fabrica et ratiocinatio*. Rome: École française de Rome.

Gugl, C., Kastler, R. and Doneus, M. 2007. *Legionslager Carnuntum: Ausgrabungen 1968–1977*. Vienna: Verlag der Österreichischen Akademie der Wissenschaften.

Hawkins, C. 2016. *Roman Artisans and the Urban Economy*. Cambridge: Cambridge University Press.

Hayward, K. 2009. *Roman Quarrying and Stone Supply on the Periphery – Southern England: A Geological Study of First-Century Funerary Monuments and Monumental Architecture*. Oxford: Archaeopress.

Heising, A. 2008. *Die römische Stadtmauer von Mogontiacum – Mainz: archäologische, historische und numismatische Aspekte zum 3. und 4. Jahrhundert n.Chr.* Bonn: Habelt.

Hirt, A.M. 2010. *Imperial Mines and Quarries in the Roman World: Organizational Aspects, 27 BC–AD 235*. Oxford: Oxford University Press.

Humer, F. and Konecny, A. 2009. KG Petronell, MG Petronell-Carnuntum, VB Bruck an der Leitha. *Fundberichte aus Österreich* 48: 424–26.

Humer, F., Konecny, A. and Maschek, D. 2004. Zivilstadt Carnuntum – Haus I: die Grabungen im römischen Stadtviertel des Archäologischen Parks Carnuntum in den Jahren 2001 und 2002. *Carnuntum Jahrbuch*: 89–178.

Intagliata, E., Barker, S.J. and Courault, C. (eds) 2020. *City Walls in Late Antiquity: An Empire-Wide Perspective. Proceedings of a Conference Held at the British School at Rome and the Swedish Institute of Classical Studies in Rome on 20–21 June 2018*. Oxford: Oxbow Books.

Jackson, M.D. and Marra, F. 2006. Roman stone masonry: volcanic foundations of the ancient city. *American Journal of Archaeology* 110.3: 403–36.

Kandler, M. 1991. Die Legio I Adiutrix und Carnuntum. In Maxfield, V.A. and Dobson, M. (eds), *Roman Frontier Studies 1989: Proceedings of the XVth International Congress of Roman Frontier Studies*. Exeter: University of Exeter Press, 237–41.

Kandler, M. (ed.) 1997. *Das Auxiliarkastell Carnuntum 2: Forschungen seit 1989*. Vienna: Österreichisches Archäologisches Institut in Wien.

Kolb, A. 2008a. Aspekte der Organisation im Bauhandwerk. *Zeitschrift für schweizerische Archäologie und Kunstgeschichte* 65: 23–26.

Kolb, A. 2008b. Das Bauhandwerk in den Städten der römischen Provinzen: Strukturen und Bedeutung. *Tyche* 23: 101–16.

Konecny, A. 2012a. Die südliche Peripherie der Zivilstadt von Carnuntum: neue Evidenz aus den Grabungen 2001–2009. In Reinholdt, C. and Wohlmayr, W. (eds), *Akten des 13. Österreichischen Archäologentages: klassische und frühägäische Archäologie (Paris-Lodron-Universität Salzburg vom 25. bis 27. Februar 2010)*. Vienna: Phoibos Verlag, 271–80.

Konecny, A. 2012b. Neues zur Wasserversorgung im alten Carnuntum: Evidenz aus den Grabungen in der Zivilstadt 2001–2011. *Carnuntum Jahrbuch*: 167–83.

Konecny, A. 2013. Neues aus der Zivilstadt Carnuntum: die Grabungen an der Stadtmauer im Fischteich von Schloss Petronell. *Acta Carnuntina* 3.1: 4–9.

Konecny, A. 2014. Die Wasserversorgung der Zivilstadt Carnuntum. In Trinkl, E. (ed.), *Akten des 14. Österreichischen Archäologentages am Institut für Archäologie der Universität Graz vom 19. bis 21. April 2012*. Vienna: Phoibos Verlag, 177–84.

Kremer, G. and Kitz, I. 2016. Steindenkmäler und Steingewinnung: neue interdisziplinäre Forschungen im Rahmen des CSIR Carnuntum. In Humer, F., Kremer, G., Pollhammer, E. and Pülz, A. (eds), *Akten des 3. Österreichischen Römersteintagung in Carnuntum, 2.-3. Oktober 2014, Hainburg a.d. Donau*. Vienna: Amt der NÖ Landesregierung, 71–85.

Kremer, G., Kitz, I., Moshammer, B., Heinrich, M. and Draganits, E. 2018. Stone monuments from Carnuntum and surrounding areas (Austria): petrological characterization and quarry location in a historical context. In Matetić Poljak, D. and Marasović, K. (eds), *ASMOSIA XI: Interdisciplinary Studies on Ancient Stone. Proceedings of the XI International Conference of ASMOSIA (Split, 18–22 May 2015)*. Split: Arts Academy, 557–65.

Kremer, G., Insulander, S., Draganits, E., Kronberger, M., Moshammer, B., Mosser, M. and Rohatsch, A. 2021. Stone supply for Carnuntum and Vindobona: provenance analysis in a historico-economical context. In van Limbergen, D. and Taelman, D. (eds), *The Exploitation of Raw Materials in the Roman World: A Closer Look at Producer-Resource Dynamics, Panel 4.4*. Heidelberg: Propylaeum, 47–62.

Kühlborn, J.-S. 1987. Einige Beobachtungen zum Bau der Stadtmauer der Colonia Ulpia Traiana. *Bonner Jahrbücher* 187: 475–94.

Lancaster, L.C. 2005. *Concrete Vaulted Construction in Imperial Rome: Innovations in Context*. Cambridge: Cambridge University Press.

MacDonald, W.L. 1982. *The Architecture of the Roman Empire, 1: An Introductory Study (Second Edition)*. New Haven-London: Yale University Press.

MacDonald, W.L. 1986. *The Architecture of the Roman Empire, 2: An Urban Appraisal*. New Haven-London: Yale University Press.

Maschek, D. 2008. Archäologie und Bauforschung im Bereich von 'Haus IV b–c' der Zivilstadt Carnuntum: neue Ergebnisse. *Archäologie Österreichs* 19.2: 29–30.

Maschek, D. 2010. Archäologie und Bauforschung im Bereich von 'Haus IV b–c' der Zivilstadt Carnuntum: Ergebnisse der Grabungskampagne 2009. *Archäologie Österreichs* 21.1: 29–31.

Maschek, D. 2012. 'Ad aeternitatem perfectus habeatur sine vitio murus' (Vitr. I 5): neue Befunde zur Lage und Datierung der Stadtmauer von Carnuntum. In Reinholdt, C. and Wohlmayr, W. (eds), *Akten des 13. Österreichischen Archäologentages: klassische und frühägäische Archäologie (Paris-Lodron-Universität Salzburg vom 25. bis 27. Februar 2010)*. Vienna: Phoibos Verlag, 289–96.

Maschek, D. 2016. The Marble Stoa at Hierapolis: materials, labour force and building costs. In Ismaelli, T. and Scardozzi, G. (eds), *Ancient Quarries and Building Sites in Asia Minor. Research on Hierapolis in Phrygia and Other Cities in South-Western Anatolia: Archaeology, Archaeometry, Conservation*. Bari: Edipuglia, 393–402.

Maschek, D. 2017. Transfer, Rezeption, Adaption: archäologische Erklärungsmodelle zur Verbreitung römischer Steinarchitektur zwischen Struktur und Prozess. In Lipps, J. (ed.), *Transfer und Transformation römischer Architektur in den Nordwestprovinzen. Kolloquium vom 6. – 7. November 2015 in Tübingen*. Rahden: Leidorf, 35–45.

Maschek, D. 2020. Assessing the economic impact of building projects in the Roman world: the case of late Republican Italy. In Courault, C. and Márquez, C. (eds), *Quantitative Studies and Production Cost of Roman Public Construction*. Cordoba: Editorial Universidad de Córdoba, 45–67.

Maschek, D. 2022. The meaning of building materials in late Republican architecture: moving from semantics to pragmatics. In Haug, A., Hielscher, A. and Lauritsen, M.T. (eds), *Materiality in Roman Art and Architecture: Aesthetics, Semantics and Function*. Berlin: De Gruyter, 151–62.

Maschek, D. and Humer, F. 2008. KG Petronell, MG Petronell–Carnuntum, VB Bruck an der Leitha. *Fundberichte aus Österreich* 47: 569–71.

Maschek, D. and Humer, F. 2009a. KG Petronell, MG Petronell–Carnuntum, VB Bruck an der Leitha. *Fundberichte aus Österreich* 48: 417–20.

Maschek, D. and Humer, F. 2009b. KG Petronell, MG Petronell–Carnuntum, VB Bruck an der Leitha. *Fundberichte aus Österreich* 48: 421–22.

Maschek, D. and Trümper, M. (eds) 2022. *Architecture and the Ancient Economy. Proceedings of a Conference Held at Berlin (26–28 September 2019)*. Rome: Quasar.

Maschek, D., Fuchs, D. and Weißmann, B. 2010. KG Petronell, MG Petronell–Carnuntum, VB Bruck an der Leitha. *Fundberichte aus Österreich* 49: 300–4.

Maschek, D., Fuchs, D. and Weißmann, B. 2011. Archäologie und Bauforschung im Bereich von 'Haus IV b–c' der Zivilstadt Carnuntum: neue Ergebnisse der Kampagne 2010. *Archäologie Österreichs* 22.1: 23–25.

Mazzilli, G. 2020. L'architettura 'in prouinciali solo' (Gai. Inst. II, 7): per un contributo alla definizione delle forme della Baupolitik provinciale in età imperiale. In Mazzilli, G. (ed.), *In solo provinciali. Sull'architettura delle province, da Augusto ai Severi, tra inerzie locali e romanizzazione*. Rome: Quasar, 3–18.

Moraci, A. 2017. Fondazioni 'indirette' su palificate di consolidamento nel Campo Marzio. *Ostraka* 26: 145–64.

Müller, M. 2008. Die Stadtmauer der CUT. In Müller, M., Schalles, H.-J. and Zieling, N. (eds), *Colonia Ulpia Traiana: Xanten und sein Umland in römischer Zeit*. Mainz: Philipp von Zabern, 277–90.

O'Donnell, K.E.A. 2020. *The Quarries of Hadrian's Wall: Materials and Logistics of a Large-scale Imperial Building Project*. PhD Thesis, University of Edinburgh.

Oenbrink, W. 2021. *Der Hafentempel auf Insula 37 der Colonia Ulpia Traiana, Xanten. Tempelbau und Temenos des coloniazeitlichen Heiligtums: Architektur, Baudekor, Skulptur*. Oppenheim am Rhein: Nünnerich-Asmus Verlag & Media.

Öllerer, C. 1998. Zum Forschungsstand der sogenannten Palastruine (Große Therme) von Carnuntum. *Carnuntum Jahrbuch*: 65–132.

Ortisi, S. 2001. *Die Stadtmauer der raetischen Provinzhauptstadt Aelia Augusta – Augsburg: die Ausgrabungen Lange Gasse 11, auf dem Kreuz 58, Heilig-Kreuz-Str. 26 und 4*. Augsburg: Wißner.

Pacher, M.W. 2009–11. Die Stadtmauer von Carnuntum in ihrem östlichen Verlauf. *Carnuntum Jahrbuch*: 173–78.

Padilla Peralta, D. 2020. *Divine Institutions: Religions and Community in the Middle Roman Republic*. Princeton: Princeton University Press.

Pensabene, P., Milella, M. and Caprioli, F. (eds) 2017. *Decor: decorazione e architettura nel mondo romano. Atti del convegno internazionale (Roma, 21–24 maggio 2014)*. Rome: Quasar.

Peveler, E. 2018. *The Supply of Building Materials to Construction Projects in Roman Oxfordshire: Logistics, Economics, and Social Significance*. DPhil Thesis, University of Oxford.

Precht, G. 1983. The town walls and defensive systems of Xanten-Colonia Ulpia Traiana. In Maloney, J. and Hobley, B. (eds), *Roman Urban Defences in the West: A Review of Current Research on Urban Defences in the Roman Empire with Special Reference to the Northern Provinces, Based on Papers Presented to the Conference on Roman Urban Defences Held at the Museum of London on 21–23 March 1980*. London: The Council for British Archaeology, 29–39.

Precht, G. 2008. Das Forum. In Müller, M., Schalles, H.-J. and Zieling, N. (eds), *Colonia Ulpia Traiana: Xanten und sein Umland in römischer Zeit*. Mainz: Philipp von Zabern, 341–53.

Precht, G. and Rupprecht, G. 1976. Xanten, Colonia Ulpia Traiana: Bericht über die Forschungen vom 1.4.1976 bis 28.2.1975. *Bonner Jahrbücher* 176: 337–56.

Previato, C. 2016. Costruire in terreni paludosi: sistemi di fondazione e bonifica in uso in età romana in Italia settentrionale fra tradizione e innovazione. In DeLaine, J., Camporeale, S. and Pizzo, A. (eds) 2016. *Arqueología de la Construcción V – 5th International Workshop on the Archaeology of Roman Construction. Man-Made Materials, Engineering and Infrastructure (Oxford, April 11–12, 2015)*. Madrid: Consejo Superior de Investigaciones Científicas, 209–30.

Rakob, F. 1967. Römische Architektur. In Kraus, T. (ed.), *Das römische Weltreich*. Berlin: Propyläen Verlag, 153–201.

Ruppiene, V. 2015. *Natursteinverkleidungen in den Bauten der Colonia Ulpia Traiana: gesteinskundliche Analysen, Herkunftsbestimmung und Rekonstruktion*. Darmstadt: Philipp von Zabern.

Russell, B. 2013. *The Economics of the Roman Stone Trade*. Oxford: Oxford University Press.

Russell, B. 2017. Stone use and the economy. In Wilson, A.I. and Bowman, A.K. (eds), *Trade, Commerce, and the State in the Roman World*. Oxford: Oxford University Press, 237–64.

Schaaff, H. 2015. *Antike Tuffbergwerke am Laacher See-Vulkan*. Mainz: Verlag des Römisch-Germanischen Zentralmuseums.

Schalles, H.-J. 2008. Der Hafentempel. In Müller, M., Schalles, H.-J. and Zieling, N. (eds), *Colonia Ulpia Traiana: Xanten und sein Umland in römischer Zeit*. Mainz: Philipp von Zabern, 310–18.

Scheidel, W. 2014. The shape of the Roman world: modelling imperial connectivity. *Journal of Roman Archaeology* 27: 7–32.

Schießl, J. 2021. *Die Stadtmauer der Colonia Ulpia Traiana, Xanten*. Oppenheim am Rhein: Nünnerich-Asmus Verlag & Media.

Schmidt, B. 1987. Ein dendrochronologischer Befund zum Bau der Stadtmauer der Colonia Ulpia Traiana. *Bonner Jahrbücher* 187: 495–503.

Schmidts, T. 2018. *Gestempelte Militärziegel außerhalb der Truppenstandorte: Untersuchungen zur Bautätigkeit der römischen Armee und zur Disposition ihres Baumaterials*. Wiesbaden: Harrassowitz Verlag.

Sear, F.B. 1982. *Roman Architecture*. London: Batsford.

Sedlmayer, H. 2015. *Große Thermen, Palästra, Macellum und Schola im Zentrum der Colonia Carnuntum*. Vienna: Österreichisches Archäologisches Institut.

Senseney, J.R. 2011. *The Art of Building in the Classical World: Vision, Craftsmanship, and Linear Perspective in Greek and Roman Architecture*. Cambridge: Cambridge University Press.

Skydsgaard, J.E. 1983. Public building and society in ancient Rome. In de Fine Licht, K. (ed.), *Città e architettura nella Roma imperiale. Atti del seminario del 27 ottobre 1981 nel 25° anniversario dell'Accademia di Danimarca*. Odense: Odense University Press, 223–27.

Snyder, J.R. 2020. From forest to trowel: the economics of mortar production in Late Antiquity. In Courault, C. and Márquez, C. (eds), *Quantitative Studies and Production Cost of Roman Public Construction*. Cordoba: Editorial Universidad de Córdoba, 471–503.

Stiglitz, H. (ed.) 1997. *Das Auxiliarkastell Carnuntum 1: Forschungen 1977–1988*. Vienna: Österreichisches Archäologisches Institut in Wien.

Stoll, H. 1936. Ergebnisse der Ausgrabung bei Xanten im Winter 1934/35. *Germania* 20.3: 184–88.

Taylor, R. 2007. *Roman Builders: A Study in Architectural Process*. Cambridge: Cambridge University Press.

Thomas, E.V. 2007. *Monumentality and the Roman Empire: Architecture in the Antonine Age*. Oxford: Oxford University Press.

Thomas, E.V. 2015. Roman architecture as art? In Borg, B. (ed.), *A Companion to Roman Art*. Chichester: Wiley-Blackwell, 344–64.

Ulrich, R.B. and Quenemoen, C.K. 2014. Introduction. In Ulrich, R.B. and Quenemoen, C.K. (eds), *A Companion to Roman Architecture*. Malden, MA: Wiley-Blackwell, 1–5.

von Hesberg, H. 2005. *Römische Baukunst*. Munich: C.H. Beck.

von Hesberg, H. and Lipps, J. 2010–11. L'architecture romaine, évolution d'un champ d'études depuis les années 1950. *Perspective: actualités de la recherche en Histoire de l'Art* 2: 215–39.

Vorbeck, E. 1980. *Militärinschriften aus Carnuntum (2. Auflage)*. Vienna: Amt der Nö. Landesregierung.

Ward-Perkins, J.B. 1981. *Roman Imperial Architecture*. Harmondsworth: Penguin.

Weber, E. 1976. Neue Inschriftenfunde aus Carnuntum. In Stiglitz, H. (ed.), *Neue Forschungen in Carnuntum mit Beiträgen zur Entwicklung pannonischer Städte und Villen*. Vienna: Österreichischer Bundesverlag für Unterricht, Wissenschaft und Kunst, 71–79.

Wenzel, C. 2000. *Die Stadtbefestigung von Nida-Heddernheim*. Frankfurt: Museum für Vor- und Frühgeschichte.

Wilson, A.I. 2014. Quantifying Roman economic performance by means of proxies: pitfalls and potential. In de Callataÿ, F. (ed.), *Quantifying the Graeco-Roman Economy and Beyond*. Bari: Edipuglia, 147–67.

Wilson, A.I. and Bowman, A.K. (eds) 2017. *Trade, Commerce, and the State in the Roman World*. Oxford: Oxford University Press.

Wilson, A.I. and Flohr, M. (eds) 2016. *Urban Craftsmen and Traders in the Roman World*. Oxford: Oxford University Press.

Wilson Jones, M. 2000. *Principles of Roman Architecture*. New Haven-London: Yale University Press.

Yegül, F.K. and Favro, D.G. 2019. *Roman Architecture and Urbanism from the Origins to Late Antiquity*. Cambridge: Cambridge University Press.

Zieling, N. 2003. *Die Grossen Thermen der Colonia Ulpia Traiana: die öffentlichen Badeanlage der römischen Stadt bei Xanten*. Cologne: Rheinland Verlag.

Zieling, N. 2008. Die Thermen. In Müller, M., Schalles, H.-J. and Zieling, N. (eds), *Colonia Ulpia Traiana: Xanten und sein Umland in römischer Zeit*. Mainz: Philipp von Zabern, 373–89.

7

Provincial-sized monumentality: The construction site of the Roman theatre of Augusta Raurica (Switzerland)

Thomas Hufschmid

Introduction

The Roman colony of Augusta Raurica is located about 10 km east of Basel (Switzerland) on the left bank of the Rhine. Skilfully exploiting the local topography, the ancient town developed on two naturally formed terraces. According to epigraphic evidence, the *colonia Paterna* (?) *Munatia* (?) *Felix* (?) *Apollinaris Augusta Emerita Raurica* was founded in 44 BCE by L. Munatius Plancus on the site of what might have been a small settlement probably dating back to the late Celtic period (Berger 2012, 17–20). The early Roman settlement corresponded to a small town with an obvious military presence during the Tiberian-Claudian period (Fig. 7.1, no. 2). The forum, first erected in the Augustan period, was entirely rebuilt in stone around the mid-first century CE (Berger 2012, 78) (Fig. 7.1, no. 1). The town's socio-political situation changed fundamentally after the events of 69 CE, which affected the Helvetic area and the later Germanic provinces. Of immediate significance was the Roman expansion into the area north of the Rhine that created a new geo-political order. In the Flavian period, Augusta Raurica started to experience an economic development that transformed the former border settlement into a flourishing trading centre where large-scale buildings of 'Mediterranean' design were erected in rapid succession (Berger 2012, 21–33).

The most significant, and certainly the most expensive, project was the construction of a monumental sanctuary on the hill of the so-called 'Schönbühl' (Figs 7.1, no. 3; 7.2a), dating to the time of Vespasian. For the erection of this complex, parts of a previous Gallo-Roman temple district were demolished and built over through insertion of a peripteral temple of Romano-Italic style set on a podium (Berger 2012, 134–37). To frame this complex, a 76.5 × 58.5 m double portico was built around it on an artificial terrace. A theatre of the so-called 'Gallo-Roman' type was built to the east of the complex (Hufschmid 2009a, 175–81; 2016, 183–89, figs 9–10, 16), connected to the Schönbühl sanctuary through a 20 m wide staircase. In its first phase of construction, this building was equipped with a circular arena and probably a one-storey stage building, thus serving

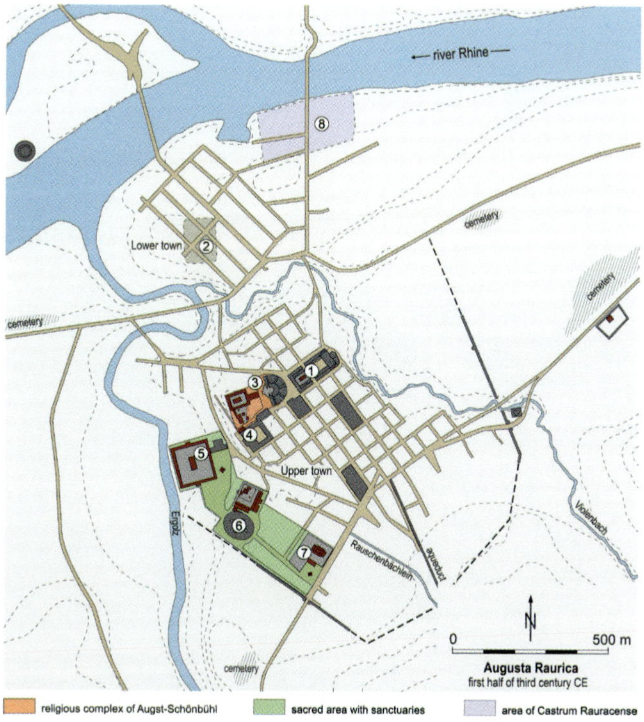

Fig. 7.1. Map of Augusta Raurica. 1: Tripartite forum; 2: Area of Tiberian-Claudian military camp; 3: Monumental complex of Schönbühl with temple and theatre; 4: 'Southern Forum'; 5: Sanctuary of Grienmatt; 6: Amphitheatre; 7: Sanctuary of Sichelen; 8: Area of later Castrum Rauracense (image Th. Hufschmid).

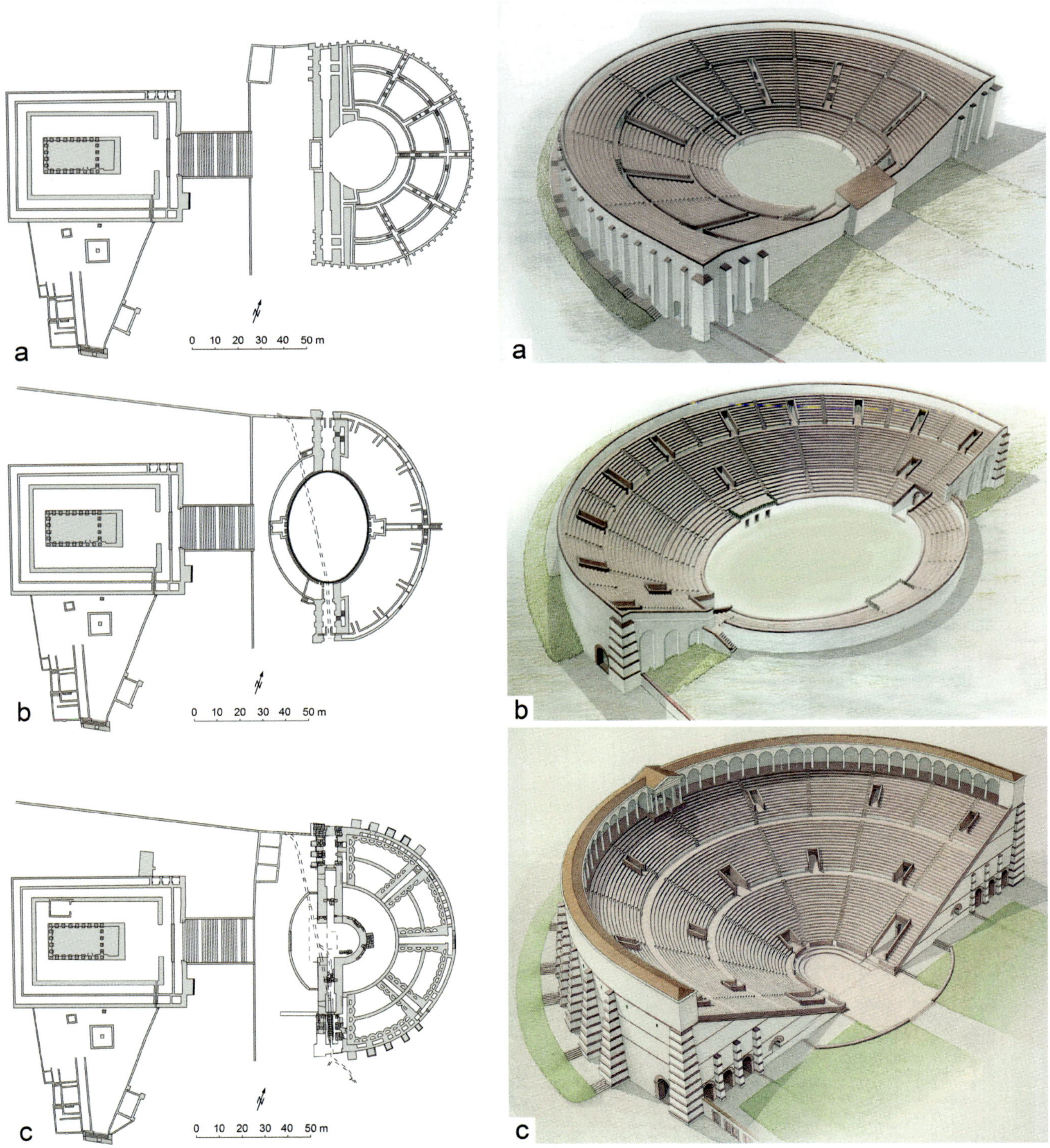

Fig. 7.2. Entertainment buildings of the Schönbühl complex, plans and isometric reconstructions. A: Theatre with circular arena and small stage building, c. 70–80 CE; B: 'Semi-amphitheatre' with reduced cavea on side facing the temple, c. 110 CE; C: Third theatre of 'Gallo-Roman' type with open stage facing the temple, c. 180 CE (images Th. Hufschmid and E.Ch. Weber).

a double function for both stage and arena performances. The theatre was an integral part of the sanctuary and of its cultic activities, rather than an independent place of entertainment. Inevitably, questions arise as to the interpretation of this monumental sanctuary. It was likely an imperial cult complex, perhaps sponsored by Vespasian himself and built with the support of the local military units, and it was therefore meant to serve as a victory monument and a tool of imperial propaganda of the Flavian dynasty (Hufschmid 2016, 182–87). Comparable religious complexes, which also featured the presence of a theatre, are known at Narbonne and Tarragona, dating to the Flavian period, and at Aventicum, dating to Trajan's reign (Hufschmid 2009a, 179–82, with further references).

At Augusta Raurica, the maximum expansion of the Roman Empire under Trajan coincided with the beginning of a period of economic prosperity that lasted over 150 years (Berger 2012, 23–24). Perhaps as a consequence of Trajan's victories in Dacia, an amphitheatre was built in the centre of the town around 110 CE, replacing the previous Flavian building (Fig. 7.2b). Due to the axial and visual relationship with the temple on the opposite side of the Schönbühl hill, this building with a 49 × 36 m arena took the shape of a 'semi-amphitheatre' (Hufschmid 2009a, 157–59; 2009b, 109–11). Towards the end of the second century CE, the population of the town (estimated at 10,000–15,000 inhabitants at this time) must have grown to such an extent that the 'semi-amphitheatre' with its rather modest capacity of c. 8,000 seats was no longer sufficient. It was therefore decided to build a new amphitheatre at a site on the southern edge of the town (Fig. 7.1, no. 6). The new building, with a capacity of around 13,000 seats, had a prominent façade facing the sanctuary in the Grienmatt area (Fig. 7.1, no. 5) and formed an integral part of the town's religious district in that sector.[1] A new stage theatre was built on the site of the demolished 'semi-amphitheatre' in the town centre (Fig. 7.2c). This building, dating from around 180 CE, had a capacity of 10,000–12,000 seats; unlike its predecessors, it had a monumental appearance that further emphasized the axial relationship with the temple opposite to it (Hufschmid 2009b, 110–14; Berger 2012, 89–104). A 3.35 × 2.65 m niche connected to the *prohedria* seems to have served as a place for the emperor's cult in the theatre, so that processions leading from the temple down the large flight of steps into the theatre would have ended there (Hufschmid 2016, 183–85). In the case of the theatre at Mérida, one such niche was identified thanks to epigraphic evidence as a *sacellum larum et imaginum* for members of the imperial household (Hufschmid 2016, 182–83, with references); other comparable examples are attested in Roman theatres from the northern provinces and across the Mediterranean.[2] In the light of recent research at the site, this latest theatre building is referred to as the 'third theatre of Augusta Raurica' (Fig. 7.3).

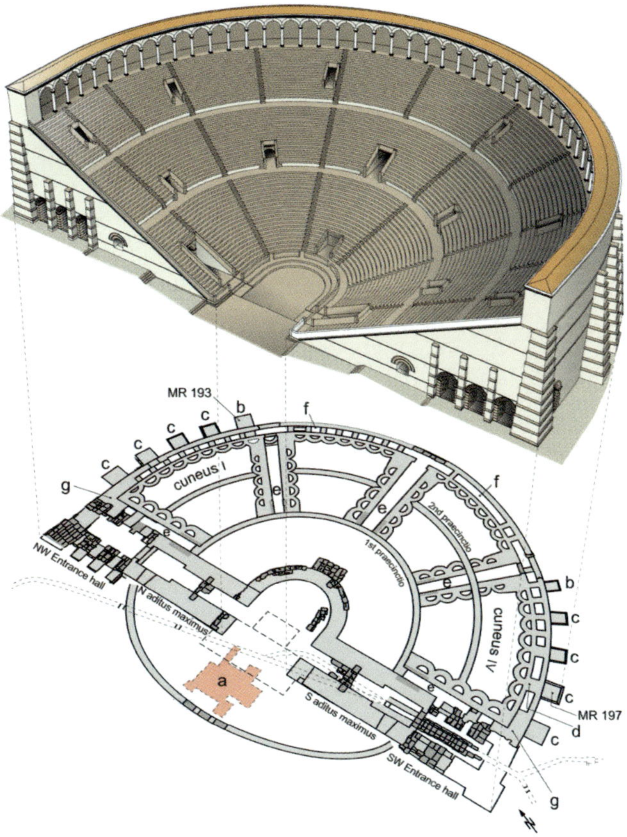

Fig. 7.3. Third theatre: Plan and isometric reconstruction, with indication of main features discussed in the text. A: Area of excavated building site; B–C: Buttresses added to original construction; D: Masonry connection on inner wall in the area of buttress MR 197; E: Vomitoria *of lower cavea; F: Double perimeter wall; G: Bricked up corner zones (image Th. Hufschmid).*

The building site of the third theatre of Augusta Raurica

As we have seen above, one rather spectacular element of the theatre's construction history is the sequence of three different superimposed entertainment buildings, which were erected in different periods. Not only is the sequence of these three buildings (one replacing the other) remarkable, but so is also the fact that their typology changed, thus showing a high level of multifunctionality (Hufschmid 2016, 177–80; Hufschmid and Späth 2016, 248–49, 256–58).

As part of a large-scale restauration project of the whole theatre site, which was carried out from 1991 to 2007, new excavations and a comprehensive technical and scientific study of the monument were undertaken. Besides the amount of new data provided by this ambitious programme, it was also possible to excavate the central part of the remarkably well-preserved building site of the third theatre, which was located in the western half of the arena of the former 'semi-amphitheatre' on an area of c. 75 m² (Figs 7.3a; 7.4).[3]

Fig. 7.4. View of excavated area of the theatre's building site, with mortar mixing places and sewer from phase H clearly visible (photo I. Horisberger-Matter).

The study of this complex archaeological stratigraphy (Fig. 7.5), which could be directly related to the building process of the monument, has not only provided a most interesting insight on how a Roman building site was organized and operated, but it has also helped to prove that during the construction period of the third theatre there was an interruption (hiatus) that lasted several years. Due to the lack of any written evidence, the reasons for this interruption are unknown, but it should be noted that this took place shortly after some major structural modifications to the building were implemented. Thus, one can consider that problems with the subsoil (most probably of hydrogeological nature) might have provoked statical concerns or even damage while the theatre was still under construction. The consequent measures, and the considerable financial impact on the project they entailed, had then to be adjusted before the work could continue (Aberson and Hufschmid 2012a, 258–60; 2012b, 20–23), just as we learn from Ulpian's *Digest* (1.16.7.1) and from Pliny the Younger's letters to the emperor Trajan, when the writer was governor in Bithynia and was confronted with the problem of unfinished buildings due to financial and technical issues (*Tra.* 10.38–39; see also Aberson and Hufschmid 2012a, 252–53; 2012b, 18–19). Due to the lack of analogous literary evidence from Augusta Raurica, the explanation for what we can see in the archaeological record must remain hypothetical. Unfortunately, the upper levels of the building site and the related stratigraphy were partially disturbed or even destroyed by post-Roman and early modern activities. Nevertheless, it was possible to work out a sequence of 16 main phases (some of which have up to four sub-phases) of building activities, which we could associate with the erection of the theatre. For the

Fig. 7.5. Section P83/3 of building site showing phases E–H, with example of polished slab used for micromorphological analyses (photo/image I. Horisberger-Matter and Th. Hufschmid).

purposes of this chapter, the overall 28 phases/sub-phases identified have been grouped into eight main phases (A–H) to provide a concise overview of the development of the construction site (see Figs 7.6; 7.8; 7.12–14; 7.16–17; 7.19).

Phase A: Installation of construction site and extensive sandstone work

Construction phase: establishment of the construction site and erection of the sandstone foundations for the theatre's entrance halls to the north and south (Fig. 7.6).

Due to the presence of the earlier 'semi-amphitheatre', it was necessary to level the area of the new construction site, which was set up in the zone of the former arena.[4] For this purpose, the demolition waste of the 'semi-amphitheatre' was used, from which all valuable building material such as small limestone blocks, large sandstone ashlars, and seating steps had previously been selected and made available for reuse. The remaining building debris consisted mainly of large pebbles, rubble stones and mortar, which had served as foundations for the cavea of the 'semi-amphitheatre'. On top of this thick demolition rubble layer, a humiferous loam sediment was selectively levelled out, which served as a base for the building site. This was presumably sediment that had accumulated during the excavation for the foundations of the third theatre and was disposed of immediately on the construction site without requiring much transport effort.

The earliest activity that can be detected on the site is characterized by widespread areas of rubble from coarse-grained sandstone, which were produced when large ashlars were cut to size.[5] This is undoubtedly waste from the dressing of the stone blocks for the foundations in the entrance areas to the north and south of the building, some of which weigh up to 2 tons. In these zones, the theatre had vaulted entrance halls supported by a system of arched walls, the construction of which rested on massive (over 4 m thick) ashlar foundations (Hufschmid 2009, 112–13, pl. 35). The processing of such large quantities of sandstone blocks also required a lot of

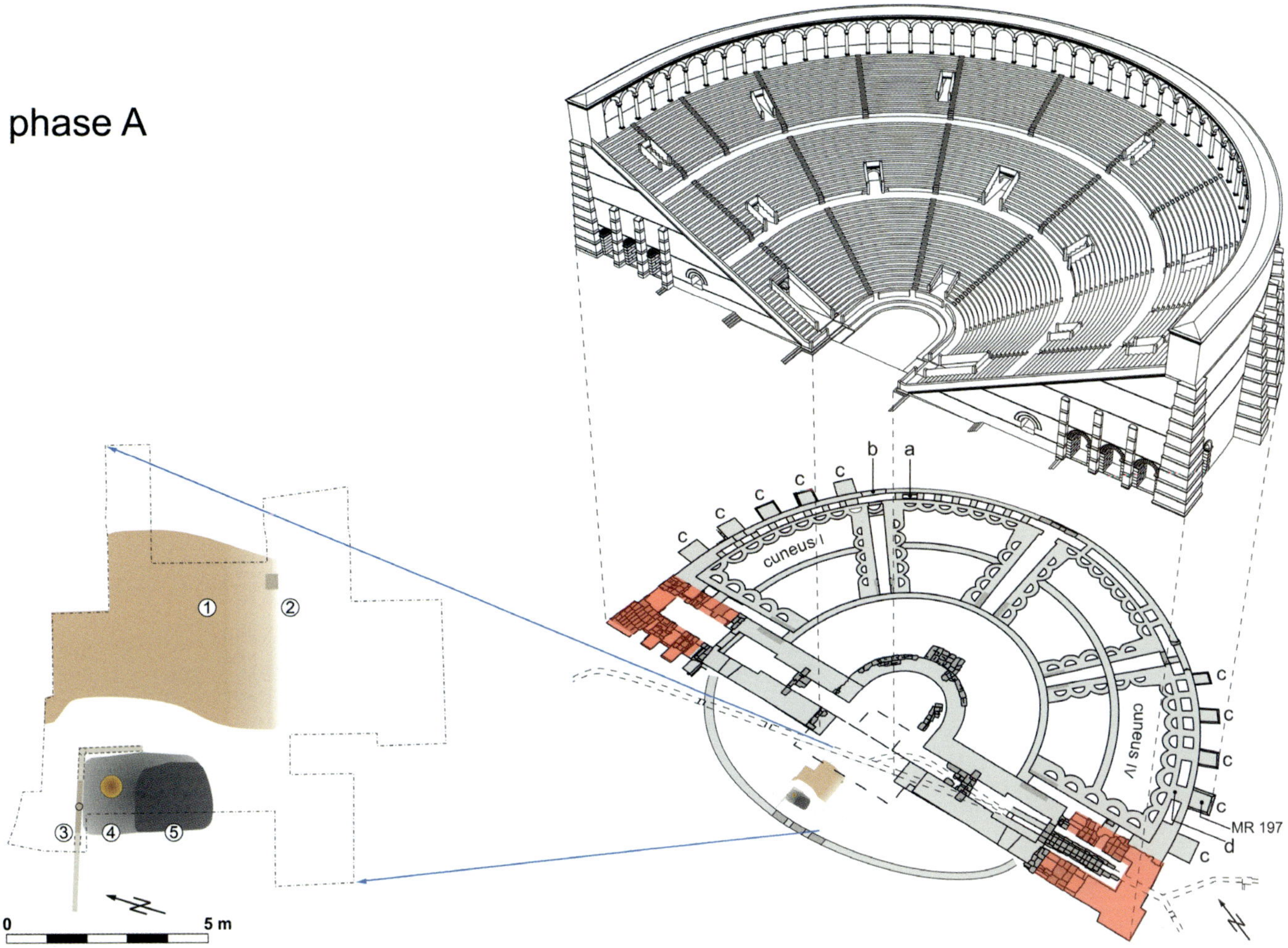

Fig. 7.6. Building site, phase A. 1: Sandstone rubble; 2: Foundation for ashlar?; 3: Posthole and trench for timber wall?; 4: Forge?; 5: Charcoal layer (image Th. Hufschmid).

tools that had to be sharpened or reforged regularly (see also DeLaine 1997, 132). This explains why, in connection with the sandstone rubble layers, a partially open (?) timber building was erected to the west, which housed the blacksmith's workshops.[6] In the layers of the destroyed forges from the different phases, fragments of so-called 'nozzle bricks' made of limestone (Fig. 7.7a) and clay (Fig. 7.7b) were found in considerable quantities. These elements were used to insert the bellows into the protective wall of the forge.[7]

Phase B: Tripartite division of the building site with large mortar mixing place, sandstone processing, and blacksmith's workshops

Construction phase: building of main entrance halls to the north and south, lower part of mortared masonry of the *aditus maximi*, and flank zones of *cunei* I and IV (Fig. 7.8).

In the zone where the sandstone blocks had been prepared in phase A, an extensive mortar mixing area was now created to produce light beige lime mortar. This mortar was used for the construction of large walls of *opus vittatum* masonry. Based on the construction sequence, these should correspond with the walls of the northern and southern *aditus maximi*, which were up to 4.2 m thick, as well as the lower parts of the double perimeter wall in *cunei* I and IV on the flanks (see Fig. 7.3 for location).

The mortar mixing place shows various layers of set lime mortar, at the bottom of which is an accumulation of partly slaked lime lumps (Figs 7.5; 7.9–10). This structure provides clues as to how the lime was brought to the site and slaked. It appears the so-called 'hot lime method' was used to prepare the mortar, in which the quicklime (crushed into small lumps), the gravel aggregate, and the sand were prepared in superimposed layers on the mixing site before water was poured over.[8] The insulating effect of the layers of gravel and sand aggregate above the lime greatly reduced the violent reaction that was created when slaking quicklime. The exothermic process of slaking lime reaches temperatures of up to 300° C; after mixing, a steaming mortar mass was produced that could be laid while it was still warm.[9] Larger

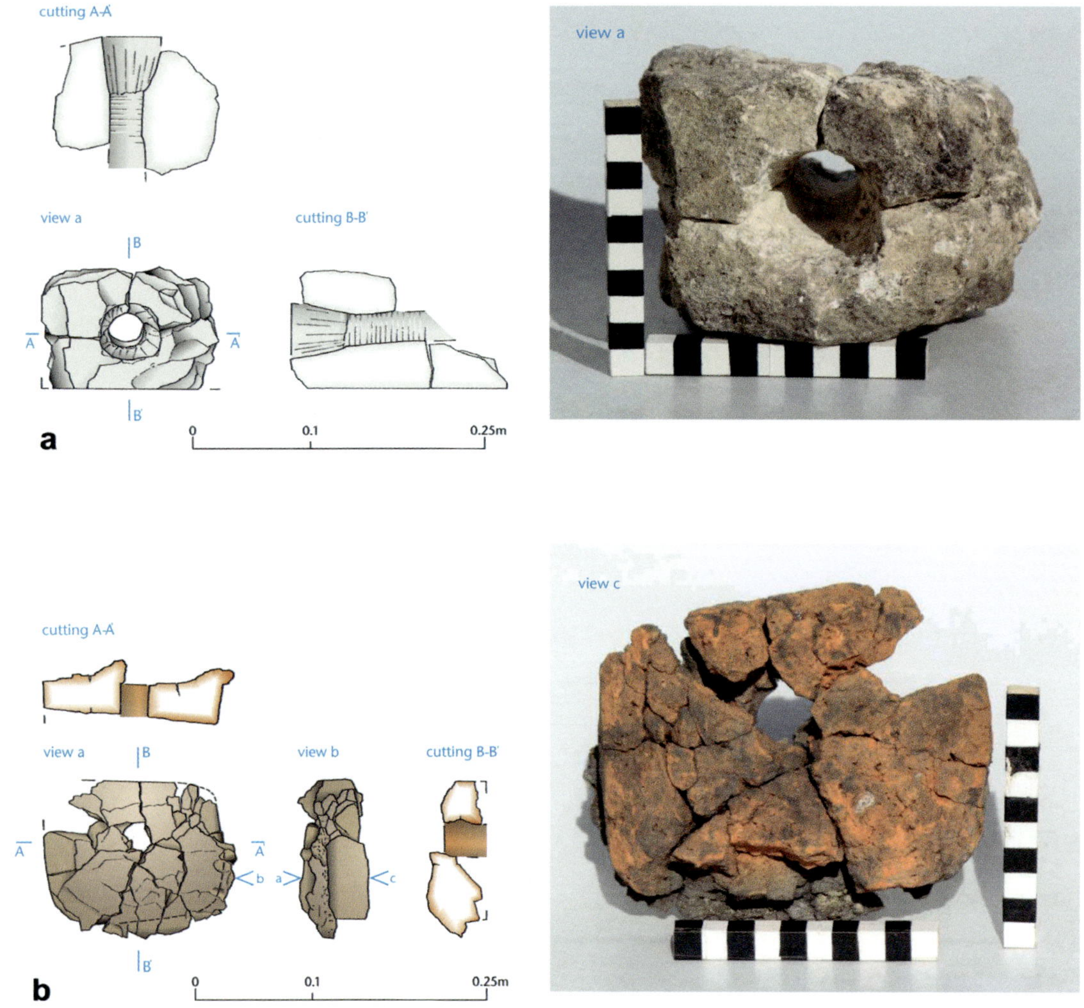

Fig. 7.7. Two examples of so-called 'nozzle bricks'. A: Element made of soft white limestone; B: Element made of clay with traces of glazing caused by heat (photos/images I. Horisberger-Matter).

pieces of lime that were not completely slaked or insufficiently burnt were separated out during mixing and remained on the mixing place at the lower edge of the mixed mortar batch. The advantage of this method was that the lime, which was needed in large quantities to produce mortar, did not have to be soaked beforehand whereas the transport (probably in baskets, wooden barrels, or amphorae) of the light quicklime to the construction site was much less laborious and costly.[10]

The stratigraphy within the mixing site shows that wooden boards had been laid at regular intervals and at right angles to each other on the mortar that had not yet set. The interpretation of these boards is not entirely clear, but we suspect they might have served as 'walkways' to prevent workers from burning their feet when moving around the fresh and caustic mortar. To the west of the mixing area was a zone of sand and limestone debris, as they generally occur during the preparation of small wall blocks for *opus vittatum* masonry (Fig. 7.11a).[11] Due to the large quantity required, however, the preparation of these blocks must have taken place elsewhere. Since we did not discover any more extensive traces of such stonemasonry activity within the construction site, it seems that, given the limited space available, most of the limestone blocks for the masonry were already prepared in the quarry and then delivered to the site in the appropriate shape and size. The limestone chips we discovered would not have been made while dressing the blocks, but while adjusting their size to the various courses, as is also usually the case in today's restoration works.[12]

In this phase, the building site was essentially divided into three zones from north to south. This division remained in place until the interruption of construction in phase E. The large mortar mixing area described above forms the centre of this sector of the construction site (Fig. 7.9).[13] However, it was slightly contained to the south, as an extensive zone for dressing sandstone was created there. As shown by the large quantity of work debris, one finds once more coarse-grained sandstone – the typical material that was used for the spot-loaded foundations and the massive, load-bearing pillars of the entrance halls. The sandstone processing, which took up a lot of

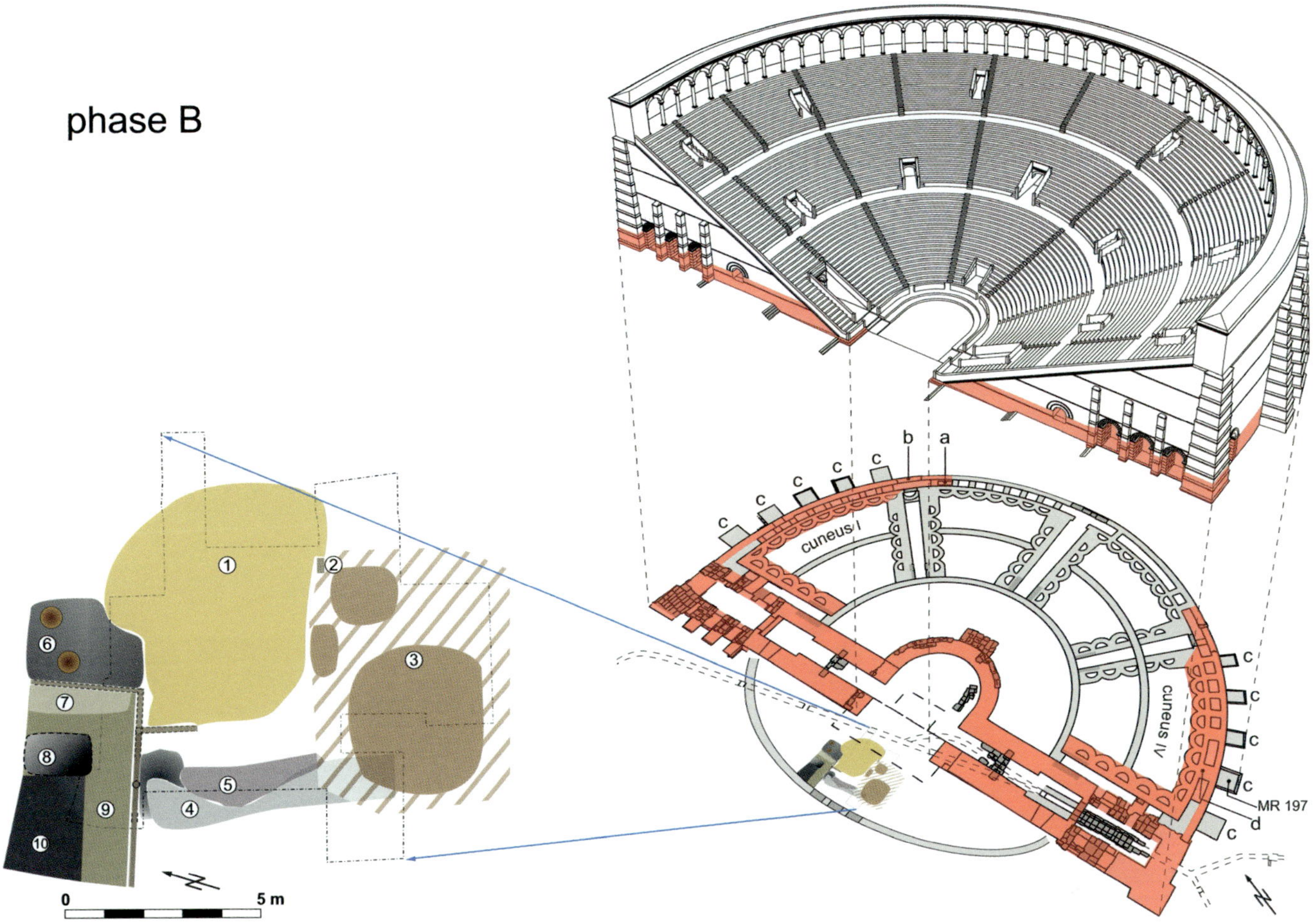

Fig. 7.8. Building site, phase B. 1: Mortar mixing platform; 2: Foundation for ashlar?; 3: Red sandstone chips from stone processing (entrance hall); 4: Area of limestone chips overlying earlier mixing site; 5: Dumping of sandstone waste; 6: Large layer of charcoal, probably connected to forges; 7: Mortar layer; 8: Ash pit and earlier charcoal layer; 9: Sandy-loamy surface with trampling; 10: Earlier charcoal layer (image Th. Hufschmid).

space, continued also in phases C–D, as indicated by the traces from an extensive sandstone construction there. As the wall structure of the theatre shows, there are only a few, very specific construction phases in which extensive quantities of large sandstone ashlars were needed. Apart from the foundations of the entrance halls, which had been built already in the earlier phase, these sandstone ashlars mainly belonged to the vaulted hall, which was provided with arched passageways (see reconstruction in Fig. 7.3), as well as the cavea. An installation of seating steps, however, is unlikely at such an early stage in the construction process, so we may assume that the extensive sandstone rubble that can be observed in phases B–D primarily relates to the construction of the entrance halls at the north and south corners of the building.

Fig. 7.9. Section P68 with overlay of different mortar mixing sites from phases B–C (photo I. Horisberger-Matter).

Although these halls were constructed in an ashlar technique from dry-joined sandstone blocks (Fig. 7.11b), the presence of an extensive mortar mixing area is nevertheless consistent with this phase, since the rear (eastern) parts of the halls were built in a mixed ashlar and mortared limestone masonry; moreover, the enclosing wall adjoining the halls to the east also consists of *opus vittatum* masonry. Since the theatre was built with its back to a slope to the east,

Fig. 7.10. Bottom: Traces of a forge (right) and accumulation of lime lumps at the bottom of a mortar mixing place. Top: Section with ash deposits from the forge and mortar mixing places at a higher level (photos I. Horisberger-Matter).

Fig. 7.11. Examples of stones used in the construction of the third theatre. A: Small masonry blocks, hard grey limestone; B: Keystone of arch from norther entrance hall, coarse-grained sandstone (photos I. Horisberger-Matter).

the parts of the building on the west side (*aditus maximi*, stage zone, and flank zones in *cunei* I and IV) were located at a lower level than those on the east side resting on the upper edge of the slope. The lower part of the cavea was thus completely leaning against the slope and only needed to be supported on the west side.

The forges to the north of the mixing place remained in operation. However, during phase B their number was reduced and instead a timber building was erected in the western half of the forge zone, of which individual posts and remains of the sill beam construction could be observed. Whether this building was completely or only partially provided with walls could not be deduced from the excavations. Neither could its exact use be determined, as it was only preserved in a sandy-loamy soil layer with clear traces of trampling on the surface and a pit containing charcoal sunk into it.[14]

Phase C: Mixing place for brick-aggregate mortar and storage of aggregates

Construction phase: change of construction concept – the planned staircases at the flanks are bricked up and large buttresses are erected along *cunei* I and IV (Fig. 7.12).

The organization of the construction site remained largely the same. However, the mixing place for the light beige lime mortar was continuously reduced in size to make room for different activities. The most important of these was the mixing of a reddish hydraulic brick-aggregate mortar (*opus signinum*) at the western edge of the central mortar mixing place.[15] In this context, a depot of crushed brick and brick dust was set up in the building directly adjacent to the north of the *signinum* mixing place; material was undoubtedly stored here as an aggregate for the mortar. At this stage at the latest, it must be assumed that the building was open on the south side and only had a closed wall to the north, facing the still-existing forges. The space to the south for dressing large sandstone ashlars continued to exist. In addition, a possible timber construction was erected at its eastern edge, but its traces were located mostly outside the excavated area. This might have been the base for a timber construction crane that served to lift the sandstone blocks prepared here.

A main feature of phase C is the production of hydraulic brick-aggregate mortar in large quantities.[16] This mortar is generally only found in the tufa vaults of the entrance corridors (*vomitoria*; see Fig. 7.3e), on the separately applied, red-painted joints of the wall surfaces, or in the renovations of wall facings that became necessary at later stages. In phase C, however, construction had not yet progressed to the point where these mixing places could be associated with any of the structures. It is therefore interesting to note that in the lower building zones, brick-aggregate mortar was also used in some selected locations. Without exception, these were parts where vertical construction was required to progress as quickly as possible, and therefore a mortar was needed whose initial strength was greater and setting time faster than

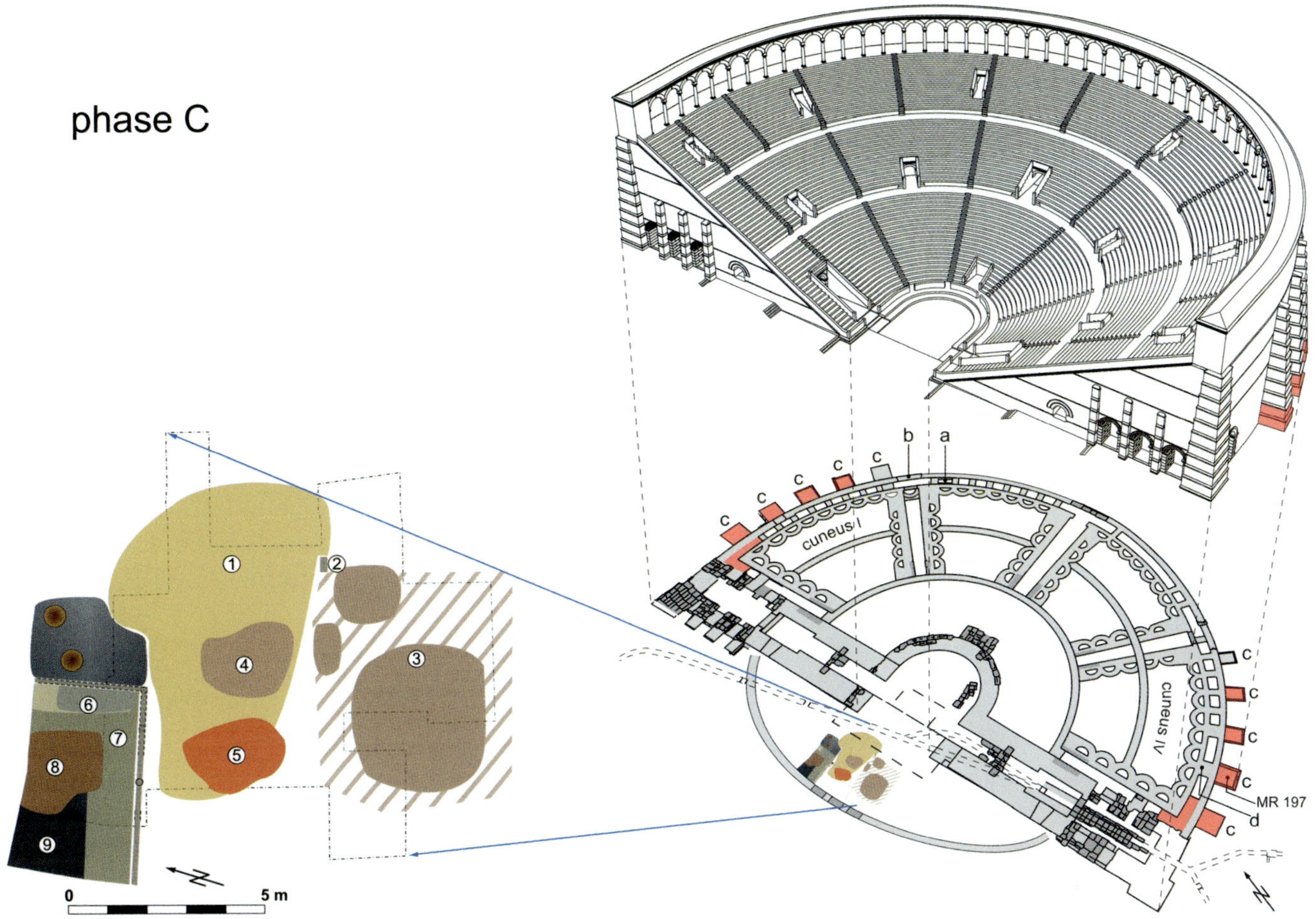

Fig. 7.12. Building site, phase C. 1: Mortar mixing platform with evidence of slaking activity; 2: Foundation for ashlar?; 3: Red sandstone chips from stone processing (entrance hall); 4: Sandstone waste; 5: Mixing platform for brick-aggregate mortar; 6: Gravel/sand depot; 7: Sandy-loamy surface with trampling, 8: Depot of crushed and powdered bricks; 9: Earlier charcoal layer (image Th. Hufschmid).

the ordinary air lime mortar. These are in fact areas where reinforcement measures were carried out on the structure during construction of the theatre (see further below). This involved the stonework of the corners directly east of the entrance halls and a total of 10 massive buttresses, which supported the flank zones in *cunei* I and IV (see Figs 7.3b–c; 7.21–23). In the case of the buttresses, our investigations proved that they were only inserted in a second moment into the outer enclosing wall and were merely attached to it in some places. However, this was only the case on the lower levels, while higher up they formed a solid bond and a solid wall structure with the double perimeter wall. The construction analysis clearly shows that the theatre was originally planned without buttresses and that construction of the perimeter walls had already begun (Fig. 7.23a). Apparently, however, structural problems arose soon after the start of construction and made it necessary to reinforce the corners and flanks of the building. The recognizable alternation of sections of the buttresses, which abut the perimeter wall on the lower level and are connected to it on the upper level, and which are divided by massive sandstone layers, shows how far the construction had already progressed at the time of these reinforcement measures (Figs 7.21–22). It can be seen that in *cunei* I and IV the construction had already reached an overall height of 4–5 m above the foundation level.

As mentioned, these reinforcement measures also extended to the wall corners at the transition from the entrance halls to the enclosure walls. Here the original plan was to build stairways leading from the halls to the *vomitoria* of the upper cavea passage (see Fig. 7.23). These staircases would have led eastwards from the entrance halls into a corridor that ran between the two perimeter walls (Figs 7.3; 7.23a) (Hufschmid 2023, fig. 16b). In order to reinforce the corners of the building, however, it was decided at the same time to wall up this corridor with solid limestone masonry (Figs 7.3; 7.23b) (Hufschmid 2023, fig. 16c). Hydraulic brick-aggregate mortar was also used for these walls, since a solid wall structure had to be built as quickly as possible over a height of several metres. These reinforcement measures, which were certainly costly, meant that the entire access to the theatre had to be adapted accordingly. From the halls, only the access stairs leading directly to the lower cavea passage were built, while the stairway accesses leading across the corners, which had been abandoned for structural reasons, could not be fully compensated for even by a change in construction.

Based on the construction heights ascertainable for phase C, the mixing places for brick-aggregate mortar can be clearly associated with the structural building adjustments described here. The sandstone waste in the adjoining zone to the south probably originated from the dressing of the ashlars for massive sandstone courses, which were applied to the buttresses at a regular interval of c. 1.5 m (Berger 2012, 98–99).

Phase D: Small mortar mixing place, dressing of small limestone and red sandstone blocks

Construction phase: sandstone arches and *opus vittatum* masonry of the entrance halls and of the *aditus maximi* (Fig. 7.13).

The mixing places for brick-aggregate mortar were abandoned and the large mixing place for light beige lime mortar was significantly reduced in size. Instead, a very thick layer of grey limestone debris was deposited in the zone of the former brick aggregate mixing place. In places, a layer of grey limestone rubble up to 30 cm thick testifies to the production or adaptation of large quantities of small blocks for the *opus vittatum* masonry. The production of building components (big ashlars and cornices) from coarse- and fine-grained red sandstone continued,[17] and the blacksmith's workshops in the northern part of the building also remained in place. In connection with these, there is also evidence of a timber structure erected over sill beams, perhaps a protective roof over the forges.[18] The building that served to store brick aggregate was also kept in place, although it is not possible to say exactly what it was used for.

The various deposits testify to building measures carried out with different construction methods and mixed wall courses in both ashlar and lime mortar techniques. The construction of the upper parts of the entrance halls and the adjoining *aditus maximi* with their characteristic, west-facing large and arched windows would fit well with this phase.

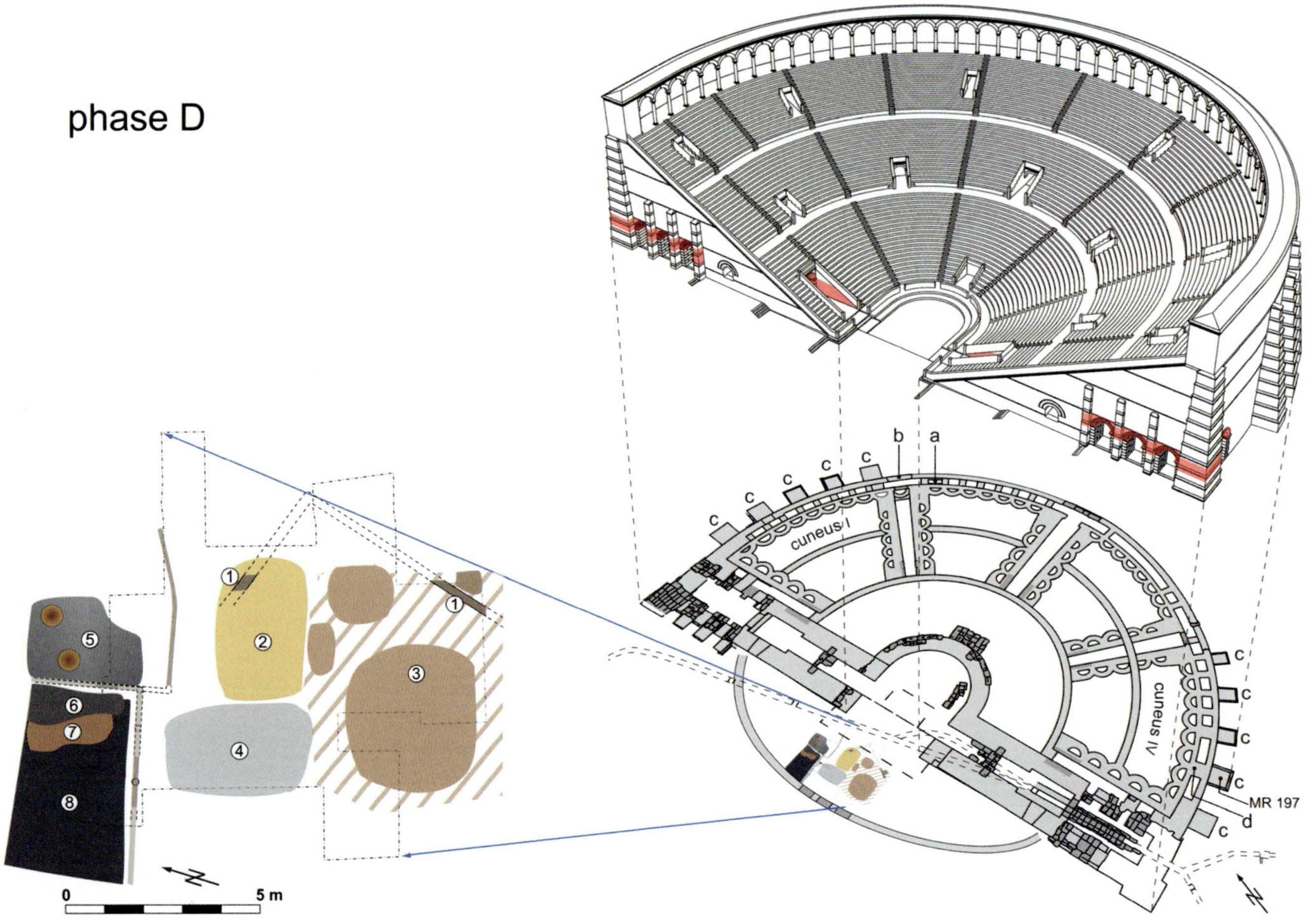

Fig. 7.13. Building site, phase D. 1: Wooden boards in the mortar of mixing area; 2: Mortar mixing area with white/grey lime mortar; 3: Red sandstone chips from stone processing (arches of entrance hall); 4: Layer of limestone chips from trimming blocks for opus vittatum*; 5: Large charcoal layer (area of probable forges); 6: Charcoal layer; 7: Depot of crushed and powdered bricks; 8: Loamy charcoal layer with trampling (image Th. Hufschmid).*

Phase E: Sandy-loamy deposits, weathered on the surface

Construction phase: interruption of construction activities for several years (Fig. 7.14).

This phase is characterized by a halt in construction activities. The mortar mixing places were no longer used, the blacksmith's workshops were abandoned, and the forges were destroyed and levelled. The building that served to store brick aggregates was demolished. Over the layers created by the construction activities, sandy-loamy sediments, in places also containing charcoal, were levelled out. As a result, the surface of these deposits remained exposed, showing signs of weathering and humification.[19]

It is evident that construction activities were interrupted over a period of several years, as confirmed by the micromorphological investigations and by various elements of the building infrastructure, such as the blacksmith's workshops that were even destroyed. Protective roofs and wooden structures crumbled or were deliberately demolished. The stratigraphy clearly points to an interruption of the works, which can also be seen in the signs of erosion on the theatre's structure (Fig. 7.15). We can only speculate about the reasons for this interruption, as no literary or epigraphic sources are available. Did financial or legal problems triggered by the reinforcement measures and the associated change in the theatre's design possibly lead to a temporary halt of the construction project?

Phase F: Resumption of work, dressing of components made of red sandstone

Construction phase: erection of the two easternmost buttresses along *cunei* I and IV (Fig. 7.16).

Phase F attests to the resumption of construction works after the interruption. The timber building to the north-west had been demolished in phase E, and only the lower part of its east wall remained; a depot with brick aggregate was built against this wall section.[20] On the sandy-loamy deposits, which mark the interruption of the building, a working place was set up for the finishing of sandstone components. Together with the brick aggregate, one wonders whether these activities could relate to the construction of the two easternmost buttresses, where this

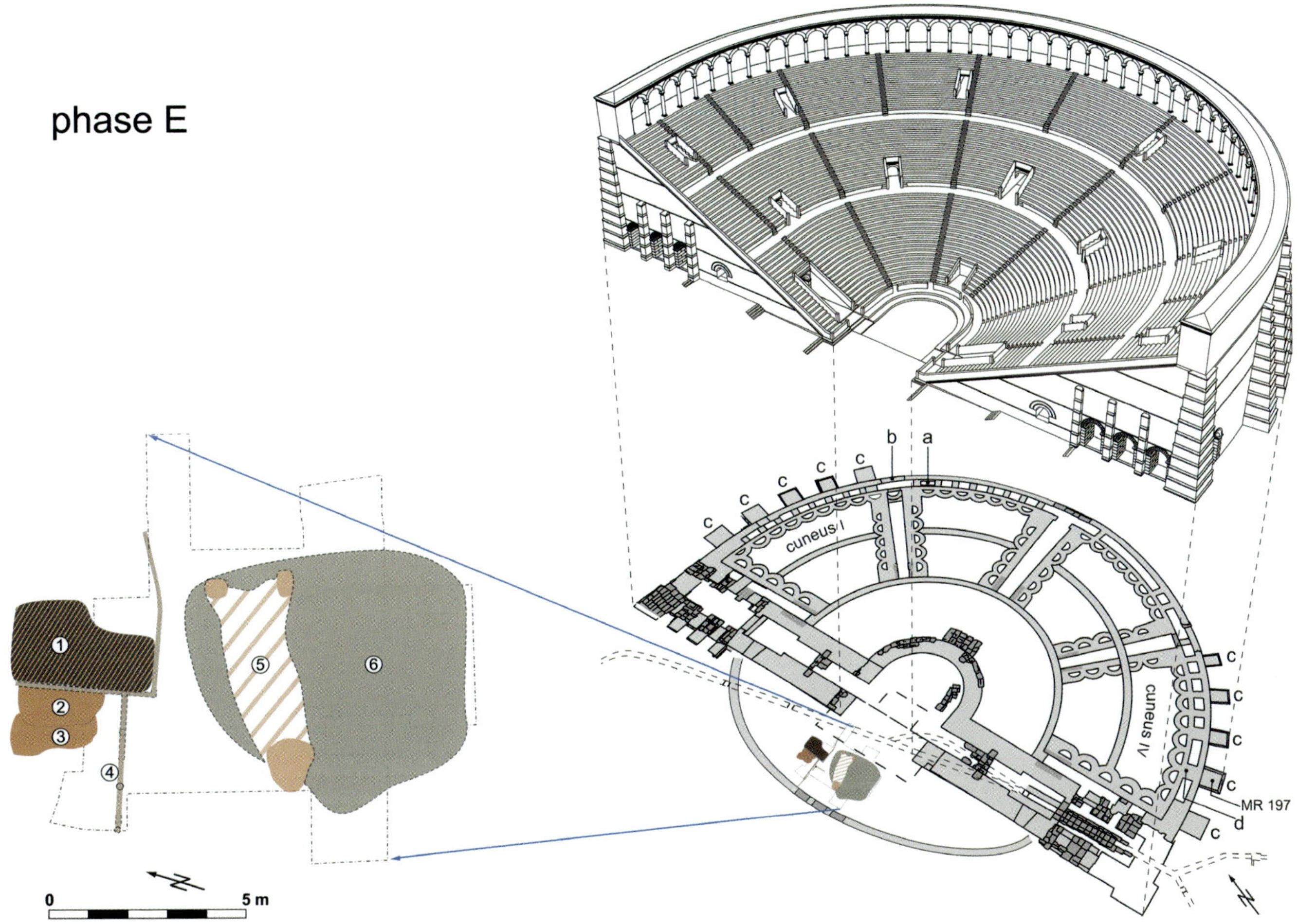

Fig. 7.14. Building site, phase E. 1: Destroyed forges; 2: Depot of crushed and powdered bricks, after hiatus; 3: Depot of crushed and powdered bricks, upper layer; 4: Abandonment of putative building; 5: Deposit of red sandstone waste; 6: Sandy-loamy layer (image Th. Hufschmid).

Fig. 7.15. Perimeter walls at the entrance to the north-east vomitorium, *with later built-over walls in the foundation area (photo I. Horisberger-Matter).*

kind of mortar was widely used. The brick aggregate depot (see Fig. 7.5) was presumably already laid out in view of the subsequent work in phase G, in which *opus signinum* was necessary for the construction of the tufa vaults to cover the *aditus maximi*. The zone with the destroyed blacksmith's workshops to the east of the brick aggregate depot remained unused in phase F.

Phase G: Large mortar mixing place, sawing of tufa voussoirs for the construction of vaults

Construction phase: preparation of the stone material to cover the *aditus maximi* with vaults of calcareous tufa and construction of the vaults in the western walls of the *aditus* (Fig. 7.17).

In this phase, an extensive mixing place for beige lime mortar was again set up in the centre of the building site (Fig. 7.18). It remained in operation for a long time, probably until the end of the construction of the theatre. The zone to the north-west, where the timber building stood before the interruption of the works, was levelled with sandy-loamy sediment over the brick aggregate deposits of the preceding phase F (see Fig. 7.5) and remained unused for some time, as shown by weathering traces on the surface revealed by

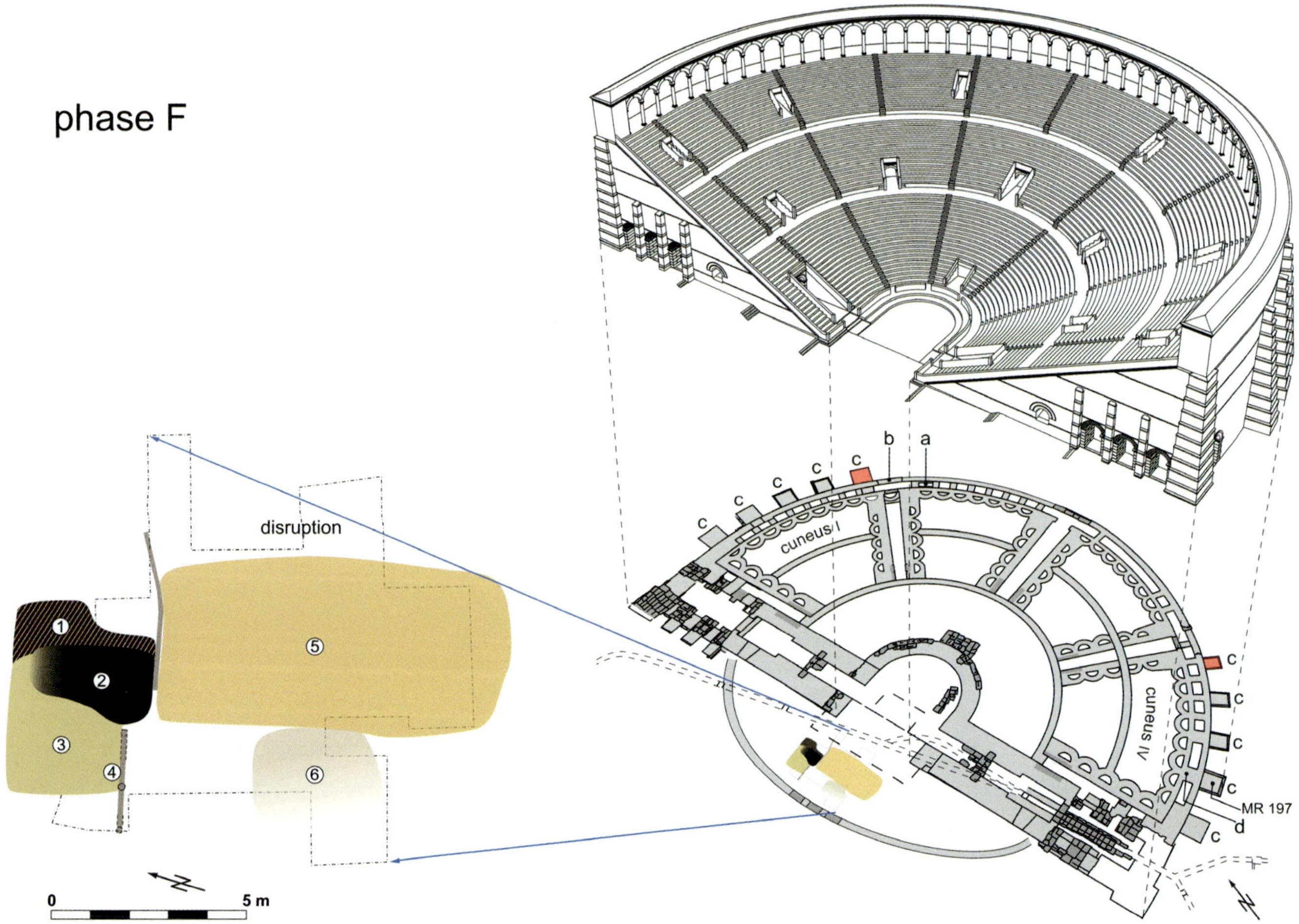

Fig. 7.16. Building site, phase F. 1: Destroyed forges; 2: Compact charcoal layer; 3: Sandy-loamy levelled layer with traces of weathering on surface; 4: Further deterioration of walls of earlier building; 5: Multi-phase, large mortar mixing area; 6: Large sand layer, 10–15 cm thick (image Th. Hufschmid).

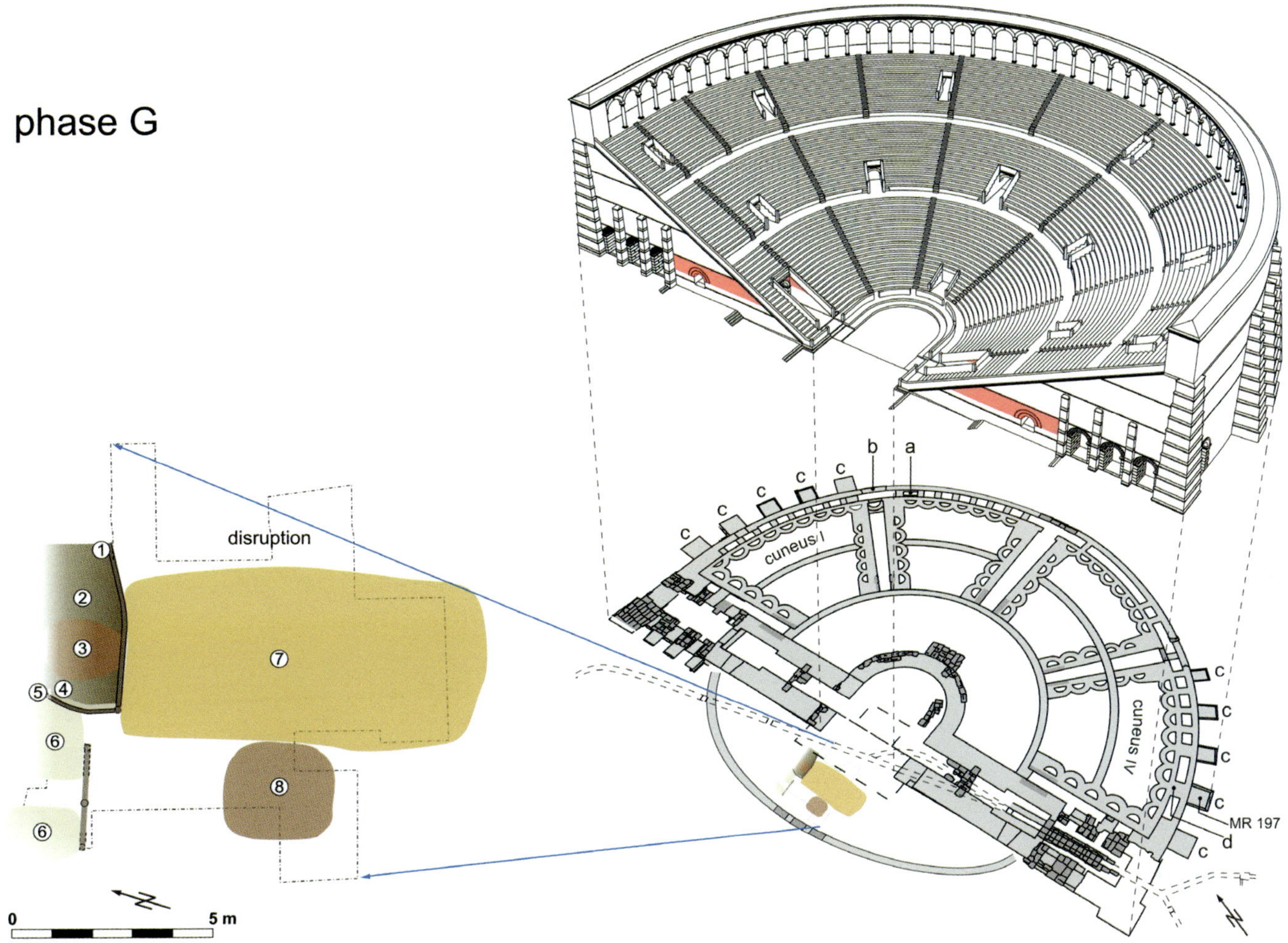

Fig. 7.17. Building site, phase G. 1: Timber wall; 2: Levelling; 3: Red sandstone and limestone waste; 4: Mortar for fixing base of timber wall; 5: Later timber wall; 6: Tufa waste; 7: Multi-phase, large mortar mixing area; 8: Red sandstone waste (image Th. Hufschmid).

micromorphological studies. To the west of the large mixing site, a deposit of sand was dumped from the very start, probably as an aggregate for mortar production. At a later stage, the waste from fine-grained sandstone was levelled out above it, probably from the production of the impost cornices at the base of the vaults of the entrance halls at the northern and southern corners.

Fig. 7.18. Mixing place for lime mortar (phases F–G) with a sewer subsequently dug into it (photo I. Horisberger-Matter).

At the site of the former timber building to the north-west, now demolished, a compact gravel area was laid out, serving as a ground for the future use of this space. Subsequently, the area to the north of the mortar mixing place was redesigned by creating a work zone in the eastern part, separated by timber posts, in which lime and sandstone blocks – possibly the voussoirs for the arches of the *aditus* – were dressed. In the gravel area, a workplace was set up for sawing wedge-shaped blocks (see Fig. 7.5),[21] which, combined with crushed brick mortar, served as voussoirs for the windows and vaulting of the *aditus*.

Phase H: Large mortar mixing place with wooden boards, small sewer, building with clay walls to the east, preparation of material for the construction of tufa vaults

Construction phase: building of the *opus vittatum* masonry of the outer wall and the *vomitoria*; vaulting of the *vomitoria* (Fig. 7.19).

The extensive mortar mixing area in the central sector was the focus of the construction site in phase H. Its size and thickness make it clear that extensive work of *opus vittatum* masonry bound with lime mortar took place at

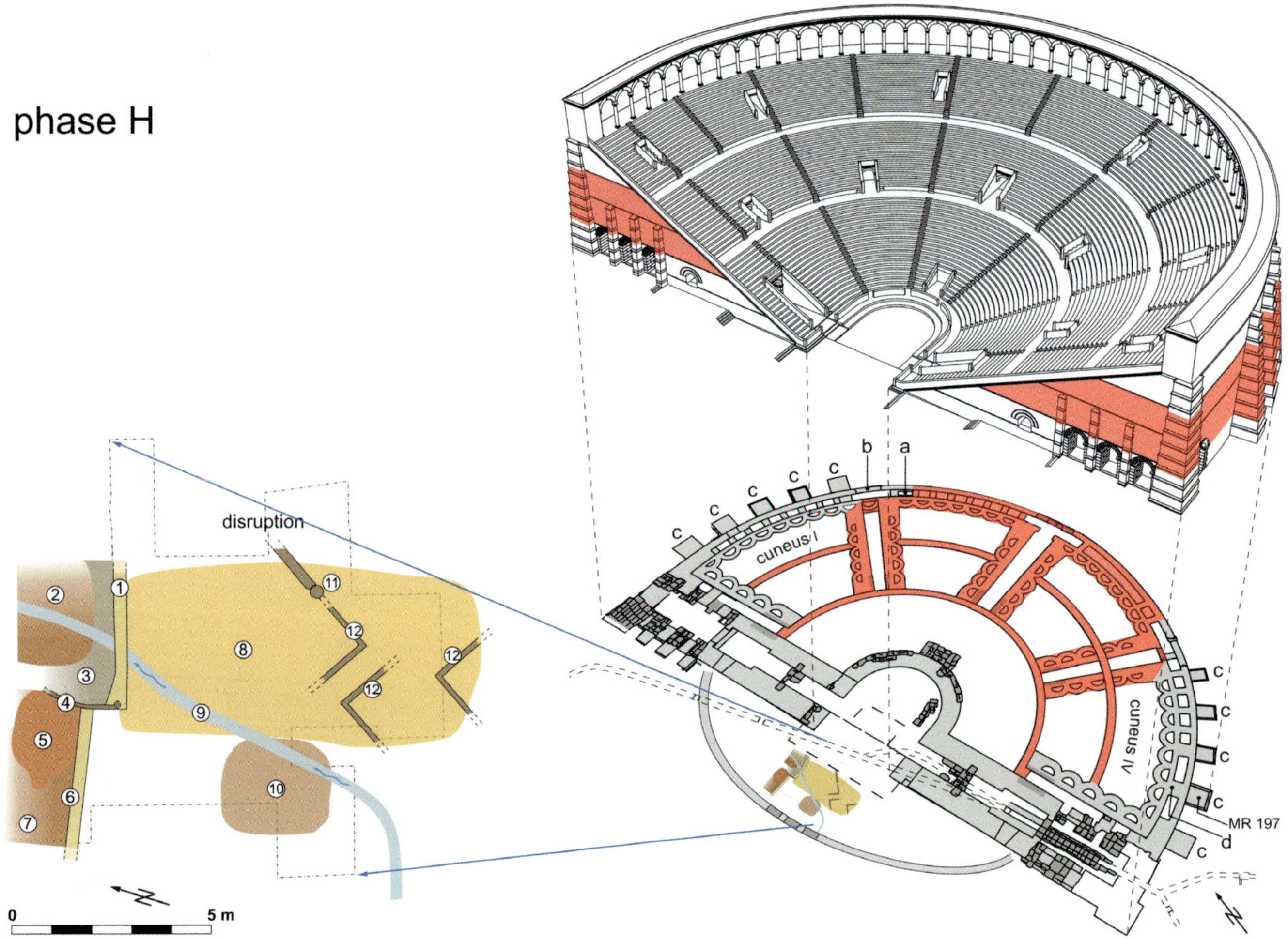

Fig. 7.19. Building site, phase H. 1: Clay wall; 2: Red fine-grained sandstone waste; 3: Levelling; 4: Later timber wall; 5: Brick aggregate depot; 6: Probable clay wall; 7: Levelled red sandstone waste; 8: Multi-phase, large mortar mixing area; 9: Sewer; 10: Layer with red sandstone waste; 11: Posthole in the mortar of mixing place; 12: Wooden boards in the mortar of mixing area (image Th. Hufschmid).

this stage. Based on the progress of the construction, we assume these wall sections must correspond with the lower levels of the perimeter walls and with the semi-circular '*praecinctio* walls' that supported the cavea corridors. A characteristic element of phase H is a small channel made of limestone, which crossed the building site diagonally from south-west to north-east (Figs 7.4; 7.18). The purpose of this channel, which due to its construction could not have served as a water supply (the open ground allows for part of the water to flow away), is not entirely clear. It may have served to drain the south-western zone of the building site. In the northern area, which had already been partially separated by a timber construction in the previous phase (Fig. 7.20), a separate activity zone was now created, presumably covered, and enclosed by either wooden or wattle-and-daub walls. In the western part of this area, sandstone was at first worked, while immediately to the east, but separated by a timber wall, a mortar mixing place for light beige lime mortar was created. With the sandstone

Fig. 7.20. Section P83 showing various building layers (brick aggregate depots, black ash layers from forges, and light beige deposits with tufa rubble are easily recognizable). On the right is a mortar strip with imprint of a thick wooden board, showing separation of areas (photo I. Horisberger-Matter).

worksite being transferred to the eastern room in a second stage, the covered zone was subsequently reused to create a new deposit for brick dust aggregate (see Fig. 7.5). This brick material is once more likely to be associated with the production of *opus signinum*, which was used to fix the tufa voussoirs of the window vaulting that were sawn to size in phase G.

In the last period of use of phase H, the small channel running through the site was abandoned and a row of wooden planks arranged at right angles to each other was again inserted in the mortar mixing place to facilitate walking. In addition, there is a posthole in the mixing place for a massive wooden post with a diameter of c. 32 cm, which belongs to a construction that cannot be identified more precisely – perhaps a building crane, or an installation for mortar mixing. Behind the clay wall of the shelter adjoining to the north, a workshop for sawing tufa was again set up above the sandstone rubble. In this case, it must have served for the voussoirs of the *vomitoria*, which were still unroofed, and were now eventually installed.[22] The evidence for the production of mortar containing crushed brick, as required for the construction of vaults from sawn tufa voussoirs, also suggests that the construction and vaulting of the *vomitoria* leading to the lower corridor of the seating area was carried out in this phase.

Unfortunately, the stratigraphy of the building site is only preserved up to phase H, because the upper layers were capped either by the ground levels of the theatre or by subsequent uses of the site in the early modern period (such as wine cultivation), as well as excavations during early archaeological work. We therefore do not have any deposits from the construction activities of the upper parts of the building – the seating tiers of the cavea made of sandstone ashlars and the portico of the *summa* cavea – which could have provided further information on the building process.

Observations on the theatre's static reinforcements and implementation of a modified design

Structural changes have been observed in several parts of the theatre, which show that adjustments and static reinforcement measures were made while the monument was still under construction. A selection of structural changes in three zones is presented here from a total of 10 investigated sectors, which can be regarded as representative of the various reinforcement measures and their consequences.[23]

Zone 1: Buttress MR 193 in cuneus *I (Fig. 7.21; for location see also Fig. 7.3)*

Remains of the preserved masonry of the outer perimeter wall of *cuneus* I prove that buttress MR 193, located to the north-west of the entrance to the north-east *vomitorium*, was added in a second moment to the perimeter wall. The buttress was only marginally connected to the outer

Fig. 7.21. Zone 1, static reinforcements. 1: Attached buttress MR 193; 2: Face of perimeter wall; 3: Breakout on wall face to insert the masonry of the buttress (photo I. Horisberger-Matter).

wall, at least on the lower level. It butted up against the masonry of the wall (with a clear joint), but the face of the perimeter wall was broken out at the points of attachment and the wall faces of buttress MR 193 were inserted with a 'pseudo-bond'. It can be assumed that at a higher level the buttress and the perimeter wall were bonded together. The archaeological analysis proves that at a certain moment, when the theatre was still under construction, the outer wall of the theatre along *cuneus* I was reinforced with massive buttresses measuring approx. 3.9 × 3.6 m at the base. This reinforcement indicates a change in the building design but does not necessarily presuppose an interruption of the construction. In theory buttress MR 193 could even have been added after the completion of the theatre; however, since buttress MR 189, belonging to the same series, was demonstrably added during the construction of the monument (as were the buttresses in *cuneus* IV, see below) (Aberson and Hufschmid 2012b, 21, fig. 5b), we can plausibly infer the same about MR 193.

Zone 2: Buttress MR 197 in cuneus *IV (Fig. 7.22; for location see also Fig. 7.3)*

In *cuneus* IV we find various building features which prove that the originally planned building was altered. As in *cuneus* I, the five large buttresses in *cuneus* IV were added at a later stage, but still during the construction of the theatre, after an adjustment to the design was necessary to implement a static reinforcement of the perimeter wall. The observations on buttress MR 197, which was probably completely dismantled in late Roman times, provide a clear picture of this change (see also Aberson and Hufschmid 2012a, 256–59, fig. 4; 2012b, 21, fig. 5a).

On the face of the inner perimeter wall, the remains of a prepared masonry joint are recognizable on the lower

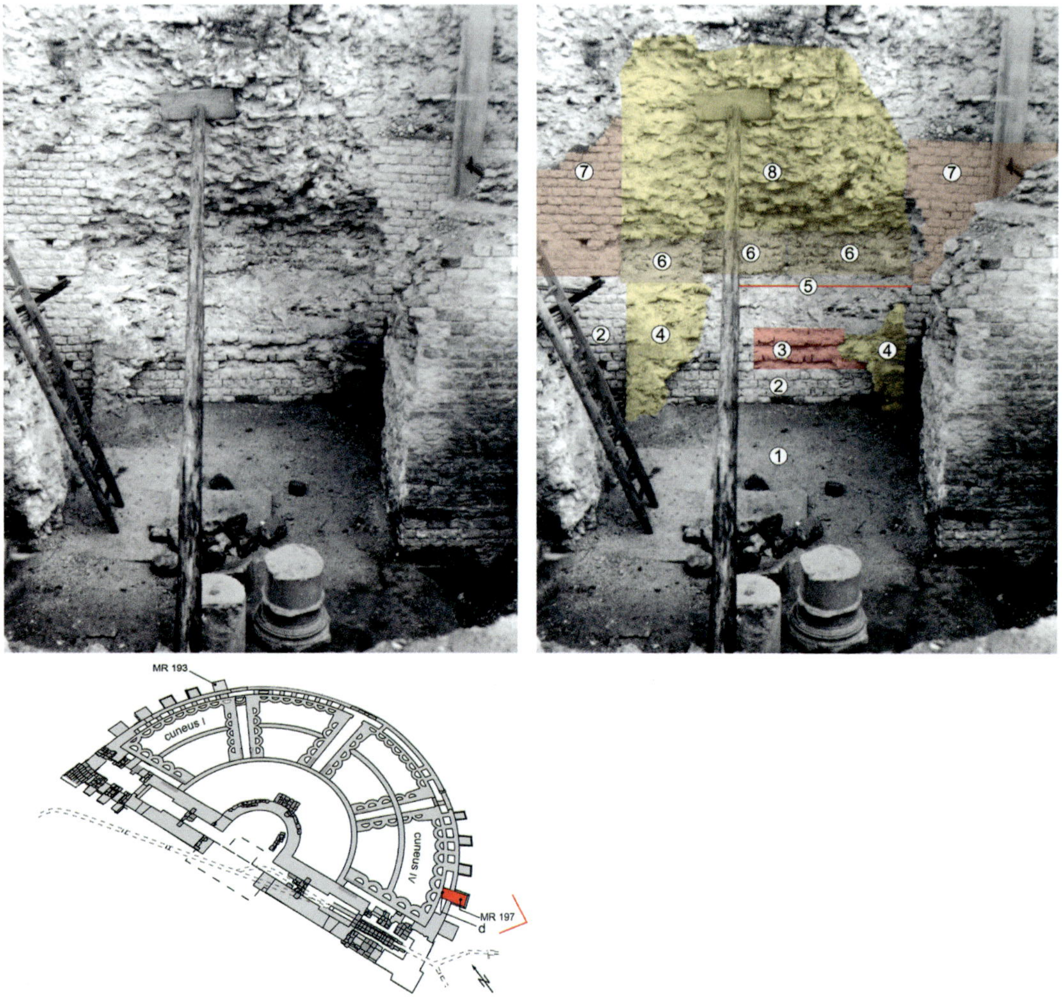

Fig. 7.22. Zone 2, static reinforcements. 1: Base of buttress MR 197; 2: Face of perimeter wall; 3: Prepared connection for insertion of transverse wall; 4: Buttress MR 197, probably demolished in late Roman times; 5: Approximate height of inner perimeter wall before change of construction design; 6: Imprints of red sandstone ashlars from buttress MR 197; 7: Upper level of inner perimeter wall bonded with buttress MR 197; 8: Shared masonry of inner perimeter wall and buttress MR 197 (photo/image Augusta Raurica Archive and Th. Hufschmid).

level. These blocks were intended to host a transverse wall at a later stage in the construction process, which would have served as a connection between the inner and outer perimeter walls. Such structures for bonding walls are found at regular intervals on both the inner and the outer walls, and, apart from exceptional cases, were used for clamping the transverse walls. In the case of buttress MR 197, however, the transverse wall was never executed. Instead, a massive buttress was added as a static reinforcement, which was attached to the face of the inner perimeter wall in the lower wall area and was built over the prepared contact zone for the transverse wall on the inner perimeter wall, joint with its core masonry. This method of construction can be observed up to the lower edge of one (presumably the second lowest) of the sandstone courses; and up to this height the inner perimeter wall must have already been built before construction of buttress MR 197 started. Above the course of sandstone ashlars, the imprints of which are clearly visible in the concrete core of the inner perimeter wall, this wall no longer has any face in the area of the buttress. Instead, there is a concrete core that connects the wall and the buttress and shows that the two elements were built at the same time. The fact that this was a genuine change to the original construction concept is proved by the interlocking brickwork.

It is difficult to say to what height the outer perimeter wall already existed at the time of the attachment of the buttress. The way in which the buttress broke through the wall (or was connected to it in a 'cross-shaped' manner) makes it clear that at the very least a breach was made into the perimeter wall to connect the buttress solidly to its structure.

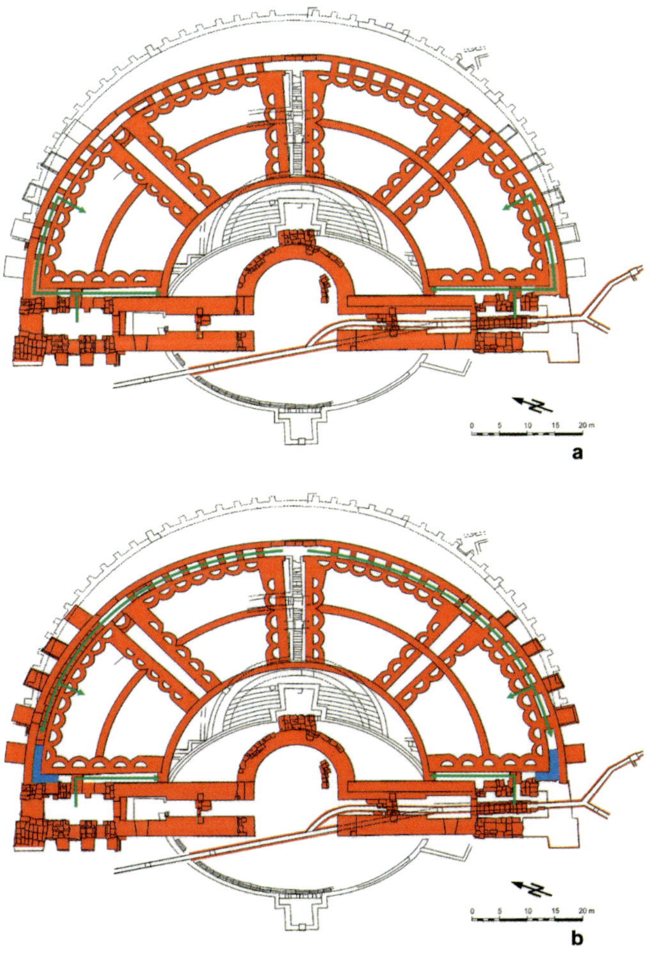

Fig. 7.23. Zone 3, static reinforcements. A: Originally planned perimeter without reinforcements in cunei *I and IV and intended access to* vomitoria *on third level. B: Executed solution with five buttresses in* cunei *I and IV and revised access to* vomitoria *on third level (image Th. Hufschmid).*

Zone 3: Bricking up of the corner corridors to the north and south (Fig. 7.23)

Together with the erection of the buttresses, the north-western and south-western corners of the wall were reinforced with masonry in the areas between the inner and outer perimeter walls. Originally, it had been planned to lead stairs from the entrance halls via the corners into a passage between the perimeter walls (traces of this initial layout are still visible in the remains of the halls), in order to open up the *vomitoria* on the third level (Fig. 7.23a) (Hufschmid 2023, fig. 16c). The bricking up of the corner corridors, mainly using brick-aggregate mortar, meant that the access system of the whole theatre had to be changed and adapted to the new design. As far as can be reconstructed, the affected *vomitoria* were ultimately accessed via the main entrance to the central passageway on the small axis; this means that from this entrance, five different *vomitoria* were served instead of only three as initially planned (Fig. 7.23b) (Hufschmid 2023, figs 16d, 17). This led to a deterioration of the access system, which, however, mainly affected the seats in the upper tiers that were reserved for the lower classes.

Conclusions

As the discussion above has shown, micromorphological investigations have proved to be an essential element for a better understanding of the complex stratigraphic remains of the theatre's building site. It was only thanks to the interdisciplinary co-operation between archaeologists, building experts, and geoarchaeologists that it was possible to achieve the results outlined here.[24] By consistently producing and evaluating section sequences cast in synthetic resin and analysing the thin sections obtained from them, certain features first became visible (see Fig. 7.5). This relates to information on the trampled surfaces, the deposition conditions of certain sediments, as well as the identification of erosion effects, which, together with observations on the building itself, support the hypothesis of a construction break (hiatus).[25] In addition, micromorphological analyses provided an essential contribution to the understanding of the mortar mixing places, the process for the preparation of lime mortar, and the evidence that quicklime was slaked on site and further used in the hot lime or dry slaking process (Fig. 7.9) (Affonso *et al.* 2022). This method of mortar production made construction easier and more efficient than using lime putty. As far as we know, the association between an ancient building and the stratified deposits associated to its construction is unique, and it is due to exceptional circumstances that these remains have been preserved at the theatre of Augusta Raurica. In this case, the building history of a Roman-period monument can be reconstructed not only from its architectural remains, but also from the deposits that were created during the construction process itself.

Observations from the stratigraphy of the building site at Augusta Raurica

The stratigraphic remains of the building site of the theatre at Augusta Raurica provide an in-depth insight into the dynamics of a major construction and make it possible to record building processes and the development of construction activities in detail. This shows that the working site was constantly adapting to the progress of the building work, and the various activity zones varied according to the respective needs. In the excavated portion of the building site, a clear tripartite division can be discerned for the main activities of stone working, mortar production, and forging (phase B). In the early phases of construction, the blacksmith's workshops were all located in the northern sector of the excavated area and were presumably moved to a different zone further to the north when work resumed after the interruption. Mortar mixing and workplaces for stone dressing, on the other hand, were primarily located in the southern half of the site. There they were usually placed next to each other, but could sometimes overlap, depending on the needs of the construction process. The early construction phases (A–F), which were mostly characterized by the working of large sandstone blocks for the corner foundations and the vaulted entrance halls, can be clearly distinguished from the later phases (G–H), during which the construction of mortared masonry and mixing of lime became the primary activities. It is interesting to note that in certain areas, very specific activities can be identified that only took place at certain stages. Directly north of the large mortar mixing areas, after the relocation of the blacksmith's workshops, a working place was set up where tufa blocks were cut into voussoirs for the vaulted passageways of the *vomitoria* (phase H).[26] Calcareous tufa was used exclusively in the construction of vaults of the theatre, and an adapted brick-aggregate mortar was employed for this purpose. Remains of the brick aggregate depots were found directly next to the tufa debris resulting from the voussoir production for the vaults (Fig. 7.5).

Storage areas for building stones could not be detected in the site stratigraphy, as these materials were probably entirely used in the construction and left no traces. This contrasts with the remains of 'waste' produced during these activities, such as charcoal deposits from forging activities, stone waste from the dressing of the sandstone and limestone blocks, or remains of mortar aggregates such as sand and pieces of bricks. Strictly speaking, these latter were not waste, but rather material deposits that were not completely exhausted in the construction. This interpretation shows that the amount of such materials (for example pieces of bricks) found in the stratigraphy should not be read as an indication of the quantities of mortar made with those aggregates, but it only provides information about the different types and qualities of mortar that were produced on the construction site.

It is also notable that the amount of recovered stone waste is rather modest in relation to the volume of the building. There is also considerably more sandstone waste than limestone chips, these latter normally occurring during the dressing of small blocks for the *opus vittatum* masonry. We can hypothesize that the small limestone blocks used for the mortared masonry (Fig. 7.11a) were brought to the building site in a ready-to-use state; these only needed to be slightly adjusted on site and there was no need for a large work site (see above, deposit of limestone chips in phase B). The situation was different with sandstone. Although this arrived on the work site shaped as large ashlars, these still had to be adjusted and reworked so that they could fit into the structure (Fig. 7.11b). Considerably more work was therefore required to dress the large sandstone ashlars, which is why this left more extensive layers of sandstone waste in the stratigraphy (see phases A–F). With regard to the small limestone blocks, much less work was needed, so not much waste was produced in relation to the quantity of stone that was used in the construction. On the other hand, the construction of the *opus vittatum* masonry required extensive mortar mixing areas, as the large volumes of mortar inevitably had to be prepared on site (Figs 7.9; 7.18). Due to the limited available space – the construction site was located in an area of the town that was densely built up at the end of the second century CE – much attention was paid to organizing the building site and the transport logistics of materials in the most efficient way possible.

Final remarks, issues, and further research

The link between the archaeological stratigraphy and the built parts of the theatre not only means that we can appreciate this monument as the result of a building process, but also that the stages of the construction process itself can be reconstructed. The same applies to the building materials, which can be assessed not only in terms of their use on the structure, but also through the required efforts and problems involved in their preparation and application. For such an important and versatile material as lime mortar, the identified mixing sites provide insights into issues of preparation, raw material delivery, and storage. Some questions can be raised: what was the effect of the processing and application of mortar on the overall quality of the building? And how did the types of raw materials, their supply, and preparation affect the construction process and the associated costs? It can be assumed that the production and use of mortar with the hot lime method resulted in more efficiency at lower costs, since lighter and drier lump lime could be delivered to the building site more easily than lime putty,[27] which would have required either to be transported in heavy barrels or put into large pits on site over a longer period. Due to the enormous amount of mortar that was needed for the construction of a monumental building such as the theatre of Augusta Raurica, only on-site processing of the lime and mixing of the mortar combined with its immediate use on the building seems to make sense from an operational standpoint.[28]

The study of the building site stratigraphy confirms what can be observed on the edifice itself: a high standard of construction technology existed for the erection of monumental buildings even in the northern provinces, along with an elaborate organization of construction sites and systems of supply. In this respect, the construction site of the third theatre at Augusta Raurica could compete with other large-scale building sites across the Roman Empire. It also appears that the architectural design of this building in its basic form and typology was imported from the Italian Peninsula/Mediterranean area. However, this did not remain unchanged but was adapted regionally, resulting in the development of new building types and regional expressions of Italic-Roman architecture (such as the so-called 'Gallo-Roman' theatre).[29] This process was influenced by local/regional, social and religious conditions, but also by the types of available building materials which had an impact on the adaptation of imported architectural models. How did this adjustment of construction methods and material requirements take place? An answer to this question is only possible through detailed technological studies and only if one acknowledges the fact that there was not one uniform 'Roman architecture' (and building technology), but rather, in view of the regional characteristics, a multitude of them (see also Maschek, this volume). A process of interaction between architecture (design), building materials (local/regional stone), and workmanship (building technology) can be identified, whereby the various components influenced each other.

In view of this regionality, however, one wonders whether what was identified at the building site of the theatre of Augusta Raurica may apply to other places. Building with mortar is a phenomenon that can be found across the Roman Empire. Can we therefore conclude that the method of working with mortar was similar everywhere and that the hot lime process was a common method, or was this technique limited to certain regions? We know that the lime and additives for hydraulic mortars varied from one region to another; in the Gallic and Germanic provinces, in the absence of pozzolana, trass and brick dust but also partly reactive rubble aggregates were added as hydraulic factors.[30] However, we do not know whether this adaption also changed the methods of producing and processing the mortar and thus the organization of the building site. We end up with the important question of which aspects of building logistics and processing of materials were generally valid for a Roman-period building site, and where instead local and regional peculiarities, mostly resulting from available materials and climate, began (see also contributions by Lancaster and by Vitti in this volume). For example, was a building site organized differently if construction could not take place all year round due to weather conditions? In any case, when carrying out a large public building project, the contracting authorities and funders would have played an important role, which is why imperial building projects are probably to be assessed differently from undertakings in the provinces in terms of their logistics and technologies.

Besides the technical and technological aspects discussed above, the construction site of the theatre at Augusta Raurica proves another important point: namely, that by adopting interdisciplinary methodologies and by exchanging knowledge among all those involved, it is possible to draw conclusions that reach beyond the technical aspects. An example for this is the interruption of works during construction of the theatre. To explain this, general considerations on Roman building practices are fundamental, beyond technical considerations or issues that might have been related to funding or administration. As shown by the massive buttresses that were added later during the construction (Figs 7.3a–b; 7.21–22) and by the bricking up of the staircases in the corner zones (Figs 7.3g; 7.23), unexpected complications with the ground around the building or the drainage system could arise despite solid architectural and construction knowledge, which had to be addressed in a way that was both technologically and financially viable. As expected, the result was the will to complete this building despite all the problems (Quatember 2022). But how to explain the interruption in the construction? Did the necessary reinforcement measures lead to considerable additional costs, which might have required political and even legal approval before the works could resume (Aberson and Hufschmid 2012a, 258–60; 2012b, 22–23)? Or was it even necessary to change the responsible administrative officer (*curator operis*)?[31] Even though we will probably never know the answer due to the lack of literary or epigraphic evidence, the insights we have gained can stimulate us to think further and provide an opportunity for broader historical considerations that go beyond the simple building process.

Notes

1. See Hufschmid 2009a, 57–155; 2009b, 114–16; Berger 2012, 113–30.
2. For example, at Aventicum, Salona, Amman, Elusa, Pergamon, and Hierapolis: see Ciancio Rossetto and Pisani Sartorio 1994–96, III.281; I.307; II.76; III.347; III.396; III.400; III.487.
3. Extensive, multi-phase stratigraphic sequences of ancient building sites are extremely rare. In most cases, only single stratigraphic deposits from the construction process have survived, which only rarely can be correlated with a specific construction phase of a building. For examples of roughly comparable stratigraphic sequences, see Serlorenzi 2010, 113–19; Volpe 2010, 89–91; Guyard *et al.* 2012, 232–37.
4. Trampling features on top of the truncated arena soil are direct evidence of the first building activities (Rentzel 2009, fig. 318). On the preparation and organization of a site before the start of construction, see also DeLaine 1997, 131.
5. The material is a coarse-grained, quarzitic sandstone that is weathering-resistant; during construction of the theatre, it was mainly used for foundation blocks, seating tiers, and statically exposed building elements like arches and doorways. It is a local material and the ancient quarries are located at a distance of 3–5 km on the other side of the Rhine (Rentzel 1998, 189–90; 2020, 170–71).
6. Forging facilities and associated buildings or protective roofs made of wood are regularly found in excavations of ancient building sites: for example, from the Capitolium of Brescia, late first century CE (Grassi 2014, 195, fig. 1; Dell'Acqua 2016, 277–80, fig. 2); from Caesarodunum/Tours, second half of the first – early second century CE (Loiseau 2012, 128); or from the sanctuary of Mars Mullo at Allones, early second century CE (Brouquier-Reddé and Gruel 2004, 322–25, figs 42–45).
7. Remains of forging equipment were found in phases A–D and F. Although well-known through iconographic sources, archaeological evidence of nozzle bricks is so far rather scarce (see Grassi 2014, 197; Dell'Acqua 2016, 277); these are mostly pieces of unbaked clay, while only a few examples made of limestone are known to date. For the design of a forge and the associated infrastructure, see Grassi 2014, 196, fig. 2.
8. The hot lime method for mortar production is known from various written sources of the Middle Ages and the Islamic era (see Marinowitz 2008, 80–81; Abdelsalam Hassan and Abdulrahman Al-Zahrani 2017, 36–38).
9. On the analysis of mortars from the theatre of Augusta Raurica, see Affonso *et al.* 2022. On the method of microscopic and micromorphological examination of ancient lime mortars, see for instance Wehby Murgatroyd 2016; Stoops *et al.* 2017.
10. Transport of quicklime in baskets is also considered by Janet DeLaine (1997, 113, table 7); for transport in half amphorae, see Giuliani 1990, 162, fig. 7.6.
11. At Augusta Raurica this masonry usually consists of small blocks (12–20 × 8–10 cm) of a hard silex-like limestone. Its origin is clearly local, with some quarries located even within the town periphery (Rentzel 1998, 188–90).
12. Antonio Dell'Acqua (2016, 278–79, fig. 3) mentions comparable deposits of stone chips, presumably also from the trimming of small blocks, at the building site of the Brescia Capitolium. There, due to the large quantity of cuttings, it is assumed that the debris originated from the production of the blocks on site. A workshop for trimming or fitting small pyramid-shaped building blocks of volcanic tufa on the building site itself was also found in the *horreum* of Monte Testaccio in Rome (Serlorenzi 2010, 116–17, figs 19–20).
13. A juxtaposition of different activity zones, in this case metal- and stoneworking, is also found on the building sites of the sanctuary of Mars Mullo at Allones (Brouquier-Reddé and Gruel 2004, 310–14, fig. 27) and of the Capitolium of Brescia (Dell'Acqua 2016, 277–80, figs 2–3).
14. The relocation and transformation of buildings on the construction site and the dislocation of forge facilities with subsequent use of the site for other purposes seem to be common phenomena in ancient construction sites (Brouquier-Reddé and Gruel 2004, 324). At Augusta Raurica, all forges were deliberately destroyed and then levelled, but never simply abandoned. This seems to have been a common procedure, as evidence from other sites shows (Grassi 2014, 196; Dell'Acqua 2016, 277, n. 24). For evidence of trampling features see also Rentzel *et al.* 2017.
15. The term *opus signinum* is used here following Ginouvès and Martin 1985, 51 (misunderstood by Giuliani 1990, 172). On the term and material, there designated by the modern Italian word *cocciopesto*, see Lancaster 2005, 58–59.
16. On the features and usage of hydraulic mortar, see Ginouvès and Martin 1985, 51; Giuliani 1990, 167–70; Coutelas *et al.* 2004; Lancaster 2005, 51–53.
17. On the different sandstone types and their origin, see Rentzel 1998, 189–90; 2020, 170–73.
18. Forges protected by timber structures are also known from other ancient building sites: see Brouquier-Reddé and Gruel 2004, 322–25, figs 42–45; Loiseau 2012, 126–27, fig. 10; Grassi 2014, 195–96.
19. Ph. Rentzel, report on the micromorphological investigations of the construction layers of the theatre.
20. As far as our investigations can tell, it seems that this brick aggregate was primarily obtained by crushing roof tiles and bricks (presumably waste from the local brick production).
21. White to light beige calcareous tufa was exclusively used for sawn wedge-shaped voussoir blocks for the vaulting of the *vomitoria* and the *aditus maximi*. This tufa is also a locally sourced stone from the banks of the Rhine, 2–5 km upriver (Rentzel 1998, 190).
22. On the *vomitoria* with their vaults of calcareous tufa, see Hufschmid 2002, 130–44.
23. For more evidence on this, see Aberson and Hufschmid 2012a, 254–59; 2012b, 20–22.
24. I would like to thank Philippe Rentzel and Maria-Thais Affonso from Integrative Prehistory and Archaeological Science at the University of Basel (IPAS) for their fruitful collaboration and for reviewing this manuscript.
25. On geoarchaeology and the methodology of micromorphology, see Goldberg and Macphail 2006.
26. On the architecture and building techniques of the *vomitoria*, see Hufschmid 2002.
27. For the example of quicklime that was stored for a renovation project in the Casa del Sacello Iliaco at Pompeii, as well

as further considerations on quicklime and slaked lime, see Lancaster 2005, 54, fig. 41. A similar finding is also known from the entrance area of the Casa del Moralista (Coarelli *et al.* 1993, 350).

28. This conclusion contradicts the remarks in DeLaine 1997, 132 ('the lime was probably slaked on site'), 189, where big lime slaking pits on the building site are proposed for the Baths of Caracalla in Rome.
29. See Hufschmid 2011; 2017, 178–90; Tardy 2011; Hufschmid and Späth 2016, 249–50, 257–58; Lipps 2017, 14–17.
30. Ginouvès and Martin 1985, 51; Giuliani 1990, 165, 167–74; Lamprecht 1996, 44–47, 59–87; Lancaster 2005, 54–57; Affonso *et al.* 2022.
31. On the administrative organization of building sites in Rome, see for example Lancaster 2005, 18–21.

References

Aberson, M. and Hufschmid, Th. 2012a. Bâtiments publics inachevés: crises et solutions. In Lamoine, L., Berrendonner, C. and Cébeillac-Gervasoni, M. (eds), *Gérer les territoires, les patrimoines et les crises. Le quotidien municipal II.* Clermont-Ferrand: Presses Universitaires Blaise-Pascal, 247–60.

Aberson, M. and Hufschmid, Th. 2012b. Unvollendete Bauwerke in römischer Zeit: unglückliche Umstände oder Inkompetenz? *Archäologie der Schweiz* 2012.4: 16–23.

Abdelsalam Hassan, S. and Abdulrahman Al-Zahrani, A. 2017. Slaking lime for restoration and conservation of historical buildings and materials, criticism of an Arabic historical manuscripts. *American Journal of Construction and Building Materials* 2.6: 33–39.

Affonso, M.Th., Hufschmid, Th. and Rentzel, Ph. 2022. Plasters of Augusta Raurica Roman theatre: a petrografic characterisation. In Bokan-Bosiljkov, V., Padovnik, A., Turk, T. and Štukovnik, P. (eds), *6th Historic Mortars Conference: 21st to 23th September 2022, Ljubljana, Slovenia. Conference Proceedings*. Ljubljana: Faculty of Civil and Geodetic Engineering, 215–33.

Berger, L. 2012. *Führer durch Augusta.* Basel: Schwabe.

Brouquier-Reddé, V. and Gruel, K. 2004. Le sanctuaire de Mars Mullo chez les Aulerques Cénomans (Allonnes, Sarthe) Ve s. av. J.-C. – IVe s. apr. J.-C. État des recherches actuelles. *Gallia* 61: 291–386.

Ciancio Rossetto, P. and Pisani Sartorio, G. (eds) 1994–96. *Teatri greci e romani. Alle origini del linguaggio rappresentato.* Torino: Seat.

Coarelli, F., La Rocca, E., de Vos Raaijmakers, M. and de Vos, A. 1993. *Pompeji. Archäologischer Führer*. Bergisch Gladbach: Lübbe.

Coutelas, A., Godard, G., Blanc, Ph. and Person, A. 2004. Les mortiers hydrauliques: synthèse bibliographique et premiers résultats sur des mortiers de Gaule romaine. *Revue d'Archéométrie* 28: 127–39.

Dell'Acqua, A. 2016. Tracce di cantiere dall'area del Capitolium di Brescia: evidenze archeologiche e materiali dai recenti scavi. In DeLaine, J., Camporeale, S. and Pizzo, A. (eds), *Arqueología de la Construcción V – 5th International Workshop on the Archaeology of Roman Construction. Man-Made Materials, Engineering and Infrastructure (Oxford, April 11–12, 2015).* Madrid: Consejo Superior de Investigaciones Científicas, 275–97.

DeLaine, J. 1997. *The Baths of Caracalla: A Study in the Design, Construction, and Economics of Large-Scale Building Projects in Imperial Rome*. Portsmouth, RI: Journal of Roman Archaeology Supplementary Series.

Ginouvès, R. and Martin, R. 1985. *Dictionnaire méthodique de l'architecture grecque et romaine, I. Matériaux, techniques de construction, techniques et formes du décor*. Paris: De Boccard.

Giuliani, C.F. 1990. *L'edilizia nell'antichità.* Rome: La Nuova Italia Scientifica.

Goldberg, P. and Macphail, R. 2006. *Practical and Theoretical Geoarchaeology*. Oxford: Wiley-Blackwell.

Grassi, E. 2014. L'officina di forgia. In Rossi, F. (ed.), *Un luogo per gli dei: l'area del Capitolium a Brescia*. Florence: All'Insegna del Giglio, 195–98.

Guyard, L., Bertaudière, S. and Cormier, S. 2012. Construction, démolition, récupération: réflexions autour du travail de la pierre sur le grand sanctuaire gallo-romain du Vieil-Evreux (Eure, France). In Camporeale, S., Dessales, H. and Pizzo, A. (eds), *Arqueología de la construcción III. Los procesos constructivos en el mundo romano: la economía de las obras (École normale supérieure, Paris, 10–11 de diciembre de 2009)*. Madrid: Consejo Superior de Investigaciones Científicas, 226–42.

Hufschmid, Th. 2002. Das Südost-Vomitorium des Theaters von Augst. Befunde zum antiken Gewölbebau. *Jahresberichte aus Augst und Kaiseraugst* 23: 127–45.

Hufschmid, Th. (with contributions by Rentzel, Ph., Frésard, N. and Fuchs, M.E.) 2009a. *Amphitheatrum in Provincia et Italia. Architektur und Nutzung römischer Amphitheater von Augusta Raurica bis Puteoli.* Augst: Römermuseum Augst.

Hufschmid, Th. 2009b. Theatres and amphitheatres in Augusta Raurica, Augst, Switzerland. In Wilmott, T. (ed.), *Roman Amphitheatres and Spectacula: A 21st-Century Perspective. Papers from an International Conference Held at Chester, 16th–18th February, 2007.* Oxford: Archaeopress, 105–17.

Hufschmid, Th. 2011. Aspects régionaux dans un monde impérial. Quelques réflexions sur l'architecture monumentale à Augusta Raurica et dans d'autres villes romaines de Suisse. In Reddé, M., Barral, Ph., Favory, F., Guillaumet, J.-P., Joly, M., Marc, J.-Y., Nouvel, P., Nuninger, L. and Petit, C. (eds), *Aspects de la romanisation dans l'Est de la Gaule.* Glux-en-Glenne: Bibracte, 203–13.

Hufschmid, Th. 2016. Drei Theater und ein Heiligtum: Aspekte von Kult und Ritus am Beispiel der römischen Theater von Augst. In Hufschmid, Th. (ed.), *Theaterbauten als Teil monumentaler Heiligtümer in den nordwestlichen Provinzen des Imperium Romanum: Architektur – Organisation – Nutzung. Internationales Kolloquium in Augusta Raurica, 18.–21. September 2013.* Augst: Römermuseum Augst, 175–92.

Hufschmid, Th. 2017. Provinzial statt provinziell. Architekturkonzepte und Baudekor in Aventicum/Avenches (CH), der Hauptstadt der Helvetier. In Lipps, J. (ed.), *Transfer und Transformation römischer Architektur in den Nordwestprovinzen. Kolloquium vom 6. – 7. November 2015 in Tübingen.* Rahden: Leidorf, 175–94.

Hufschmid, Th. 2023. Die Hauptzugänge zur Orchestra (aditus maximi) in den römischen Theatern der Schweiz. In Fellague, D. and Moretti, J.-C. (eds), *Entrez au théâtre! Journée d'étude sur les théâtres romains. Les couloirs d'entrée dans les théâtres romains (aditus maximi)*. Lyon: Maison de l'Orient et de la Méditerranée, in press.

Hufschmid, Th. and Späth, Th. 2016. Das Theater als Ort für Menschen und Götter – eine Synthese. Le théâtre, un lieu consacré aux hommes et aux dieux – synthèse. In Hufschmid, Th. (ed.), *Theaterbauten als Teil monumentaler Heiligtümer in den nordwestlichen Provinzen des Imperium Romanum: Architektur – Organisation – Nutzung. Internationales Kolloquium in Augusta Raurica, 18.–21. September 2013*. Augst: Römermuseum Augst, 245–60.

Lamprecht, H.-O. 1996. *Opus caementitium: Bautechnik der Römer*. Düsseldorf: Beton-Verlag.

Lancaster, L.C. 2005. *Concrete Vaulted Construction in Imperial Rome: Innovations in Context*. Cambridge: Cambridge University Press.

Lipps, J. 2017. Transfer und Transformation römischer Architektur in den Nordwestprovinzen. In Lipps, J. (ed.), *Transfer und Transformation römischer Architektur in den Nordwestprovinzen. Kolloquium vom 6. – 7. November 2015 in Tübingen*. Rahden: Leidorf, 13–31.

Loiseau, C. 2012. Les métaux dans les constructions publiques romaines: applications architecturales et structures de production (Ier – IIIe siècle ap. J.-C.). In Camporeale, S., Dessales, H. and Pizzo, A. (eds), *Arqueología de la construcción III. Los procesos constructivos en el mundo romano: la economía de las obras (École normale supérieure, Paris, 10–11 de diciembre de 2009)*. Madrid: Consejo Superior de Investigaciones Científicas, 117 29.

Marinowitz, C. 2008. Kalk- und Mörtelherstellung in historischen Bild- und Schriftquellen. Ein Aspekt für die Interpretation von Befunderhebung, wissenschaftlichen Untersuchungen sowie restauratorische Umsetzungen. In Grassegger, G., Patitz, G. and Wölbert, O. (eds), *Natursteinsanierung Stuttgart 2008: Neue Natursteinrestaurierungsergebnisse und messtechnische Erfassungen sowie Sanierungsbeispiele. Tagung am 14. März 2008 in Stuttgart*. Stuttgart: Fraunhofer, 71–87.

Quatember, U. 2022. Geldmangel und gebrochene Versprechen? Die Finanzierung öffentlicher Bauten und Phänomene der Unfertigkeit im kaiserzeitlichen Kleinasien. In Rumscheid, F. and Toma, N. (eds), *Unfertigkeit in antiker Architektur. Definition und Ursachen. Beiträge einer Sektion des Neunzehnten Internationalen Kongresses für Klassische Archäologie in Köln und Bonn am 23. Mai 2018*. Darmstadt: Wissenschaftliche Buchgesellschaft, 87–101.

Rentzel, Ph. 1998. Antike Steingewinnung im Hochrheintal. Eine Übersicht für die Gegend zwischen Basel und Rheinfelden. In *Mille Fiori. Festschrift für Ludwig Berger zu seinem 65. Geburtstag*. Augst: Römermuseum Augst, 185–91.

Rentzel, Ph. 2009. Der Arenaboden des Amphitheaters von Augst-Neun Türme. Geoarchäologische Untersuchungen. In Hufschmid, Th. (with contributions by Rentzel, Ph., Frésard, N. and Fuchs, M.E.), *Amphitheatrum in Provincia et Italia. Architektur und Nutzung römischer Amphitheater von Augusta Raurica bis Puteoli*. Augst: Römermuseum Augst, 569–77.

Rentzel, Ph. 2020. In Stein gemeisselt: Petrografie und Provenienz der Inschriftenträger von Augusta Raurica. *Jahresberichte aus Augst und Kaiseraugst* 41: 169–94.

Rentzel, Ph., Nicosia, C., Gebhardt, A., Brönnimann, D., Pümpin, C. and Ismail-Meyer, K. 2017. Trampling, poaching and the effect of traffic. In Nicosia, C. and Stoops, G. (eds), *Archaeological Soil and Sediment Micromorphology*. Chichester: Wiley-Blackwell, 281–98.

Serlorenzi, M. 2010. La costruzione di un complesso horreario a Testaccio. Primi indizi per delineare l'organizzazione del cantiere edilizio. In Camporeale, S., Dessales, H. and Pizzo, A. (eds), *Arqueología de la construcción II. Los procesos constructivos en el mundo romano: Italia y provincias orientales (Certosa di Pontignano, Siena, 13–15 de noviembre de 2008)*. Madrid: Consejo Superior de Investigaciones Científicas, 105–26.

Stoops, G., Canti, M. and Kapur, S. 2017. Calcareous mortars, plasters and floors. In Nicosia, C. and Stoops, G. (eds), *Archaeological Soil and Sediment Micromorphology*. Chichester: Wiley-Blackwell, 189–99.

Tardy, D. 2011. L'adoption des formes architecturales romaines. Une évolution complexe et progressive. In Reddé, M., Barral, Ph., Favory, F., Guillaumet, J.-P., Joly, M., Marc, J.-Y., Nouvel, P., Nuninger, L. and Petit, C. (eds), *Aspects de la romanisation dans l'Est de la Gaule*. Glux-en-Glenne: Bibracte, 319–23.

Volpe, R. 2010. Organizzazione e tempi di lavoro nel cantiere delle Terme di Traiano sul Colle Oppio. In Camporeale, S., Dessales, H. and Pizzo, A. (eds), *Arqueología de la construcción II. Los procesos constructivos en el mundo romano: Italia y provincias orientales (Certosa di Pontignano, Siena, 13–15 de noviembre de 2008)*. Madrid: Consejo Superior de Investigaciones Científicas, 81–91.

Wehby Murgatroyd, J. 2016. Lime mortar production in Ostia: material analysis of mortar from the Hadrianic period. In DeLaine, J., Camporeale, S. and Pizzo, A. (eds), *Arqueología de la Construcción V – 5th International Workshop on the Archaeology of Roman Construction. Man-Made Materials, Engineering and Infrastructure (Oxford, April 11–12, 2015)*. Madrid: Consejo Superior de Investigaciones Científicas, 45–55.

8

Building public baths outside Rome: The case study of Nora (Sardinia)

Caterina Previato

This chapter focuses on the logistics and economics of Roman construction sites, addressed through the analysis of the public baths of the town of Nora (Sardinia). Different buildings are examined and compared to define the organization and the management procedures applied in public architectural projects in a context located far from Rome. In particular, the building remains are used to reconstruct the dynamics of the supply of building materials, to define the technical knowledge applied in the projects, and to determine the cultural background of the workers involved in the construction process (on these subjects see also contributions by Vitti, Maschek, and Hufschmid in this volume). In this way it will be possible to analyse the relationship between the spread of Roman construction techniques across the Mediterranean and the persistence of local architectural traditions.[1]

Nora: A brief overview of the site

The town of Nora is located on a large peninsula along the southern coast of Sardinia, about 30 km west of Cagliari (Fig. 8.1). The first excavations at the site date back to the end of the nineteenth century, but most of the structures and buildings currently visible were unearthed in the 1950s.[2] The early settlement dates back to the Phoenician period (mid-eighth century BCE), when Nora was an important trade port (Bonetto 2009, 69–78; 2014; Bondì 2012, 82). After the conquest of Sardinia by the Carthaginians in the second half of the sixth century BCE, Nora developed into an urban centre and was provided with streets, four religious complexes, and several buildings with residential and commercial function.[3] In 227 BCE the town, as well as the whole island, became part of the Roman province of *Sardinia et Corsica*. The urban layout of Nora remained substantially unaltered until the Caesarian-Augustan age, when the town witnessed intensive building activities and was gradually equipped with typical Roman-style buildings and architectural complexes, including a forum and a theatre.[4] From the mid-second to third century CE, Nora experienced a further phase of urban development and renewal.[5] Several new buildings were constructed across the town, while some of the existing architectural complexes and private houses were restored. The streets were paved, and the sewer system renovated (Bonetto 2003, 29–31). At the same time, probably between the end of the second and the beginning of the third century CE, an aqueduct was built, the remains of which are still visible near the isthmus and the road leading to Nora.[6] The possibility of having running water enabled construction of several bath buildings, which are the focus of this chapter. They consist of four buildings situated in different urban sectors; three of them were built between the late second and early third century CE (Terme a Mare, Terme Centrali, Piccole Terme), and one probably slightly later (Terme di Levante).

The bath buildings of Nora

The Terme a Mare (Sea Baths)

The so-called 'Terme a Mare' are located in the western sector of the town, close to the sea. They are the largest baths known to date at Nora, extending for 57 m north–south and 41 m east–west. The building, already identified by Gennaro Pesce in the 1950s, was excavated in the 1970s by the Archaeological Superintendence of Cagliari.[7] This intervention made it possible to define the building plan and collect data on its chronology and construction process.

The building has a rectangular plan and faces north along street G–E, provided with a portico on this side (Fig. 8.2). A second portico is located on the eastern side. The western side, facing the sea, is less known as it is poorly preserved

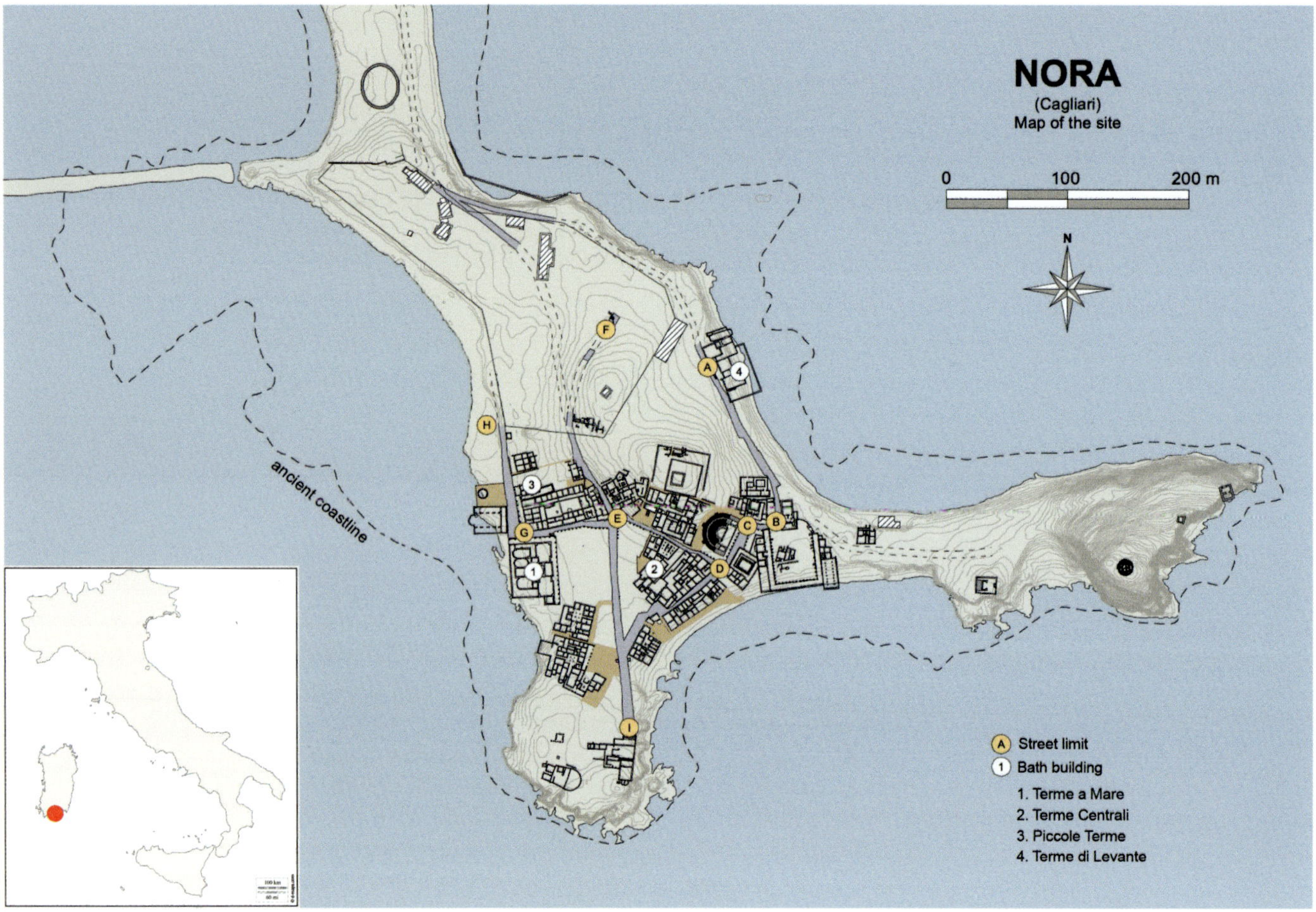

Fig. 8.1. Plan of the town of Nora with location of bath buildings discussed in this chapter (image C. Previato, after Bonetto et al. *2018).*

due to marine erosion. The main access to the building was on the north side: a staircase with three steps led from the street to the portico, and from there to the entrance hall (a). From the hall it was possible to access the *apodyterium* (b), paved with a mosaic, and the *frigidarium* (c), located in the centre of the building. The *frigidarium* has a square plan and was equipped with a niche on the eastern side and two symmetrical square pools on the northern and southern sides. Both the floor of the *frigidarium* and the pools had a marble revetment, of which only a few fragments are preserved. From the *frigidarium* it was possible to access the three heated rooms in the north-western sector of the building, all developing in east–west direction. The first room (g), rectangular in plan, was probably a *tepidarium*; the other two rooms, one with an ellipsoidal plan (f) and one with an apsidal rectangular plan (e), can be interpreted as a *sudatorium* and *caldarium*, respectively. From the *caldarium* (e), it was possible to return to the *frigidarium* through a small room (d), thus completing a ring path.

The baths had also a second entrance, which opened onto the eastern portico and led into a second hall (h), paved with a mosaic. From that room it was possible to access either the *frigidarium* (c) or a small room (i) and then a (heated) large rectangular apsidal room (l), which unfortunately has been almost entirely destroyed by the sea's erosive action.[8] The function of this room, variously interpreted as another *caldarium* for women or as a room for sunbathing, is unclear (Tronchetti 1985, 75). From the second hall (h) it was also

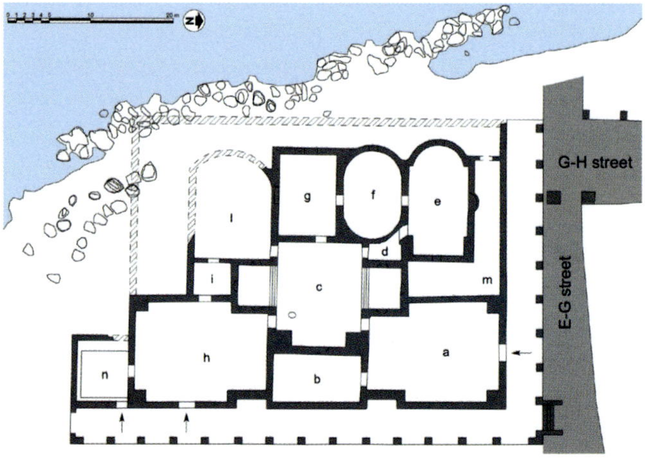

Fig. 8.2. Plan of the Terme a Mare (image C. Previato, after Bonetto et al. *2018).*

possible to access a latrine (n), equipped with a second entrance facing the eastern portico. The latrine seats, made of shaped sandstone blocks, are still visible on the room's east, south, and west sides. The heating of the hot rooms was provided by *praefurnia* located in the western sector of the building, which are no longer visible as they have been eroded by the sea and covered with earth, but the mouths of which are preserved along the rooms' perimeter walls. A service corridor (m) ran along the northern perimeter of the *caldarium*, then bending southwards. In this space was an additional *praefurnium*, which served to provide heating to a rectangular basin on the eastern side of the *caldarium*.

The water supply of the baths was probably provided by the aqueduct. On the basis of the discovery of collapsed masonry with hydraulic coating, it is believed that in the north-western sector of the building there were reservoirs connected to the aqueduct; these were located over the corridor (m) which supplied water to the pools by means of pipes placed inside the walls.[9] The reservoirs were probably accessible through a staircase, the remains of which were found near the *praefurnium* of the corridor. Wastewater flowed through a sewer underneath the floor, which was built with a concrete core and a revetment made of stone and tile and covered with 'cappuccina' tiles. The sewer passed under the hall (h) and the *frigidarium* (c), where it collected the pools' wastewater, and then headed towards the street, passing first through the latrine (n). A second sewer ran under the corridor (m).

The 1970s excavations made it possible to verify that the building was constructed in the Severan age (end of the second to early third century CE), as suggested by the chronology of the pottery recovered from the stratigraphic deposits under the floors.[10] The ground on which the baths were built was gently sloping from east to west, so after building the wall foundations, placed within small trenches excavated in the rock, it became necessary to create an

Fig. 8.3. Wall of the Terme a Mare, showing a concrete core and facing with bricks (photo C. Previato).

Fig. 8.4. Collapsed vault of the Terme a Mare (photo C. Previato).

artificial horizontal platform through a landfill and raise the floor level. A layer of pure lime was placed at the base, covered by a fill of soil about 1 m thick. Above that, a further layer of pure lime was laid and above it a 20 cm layer of yellowish clay was added, over which the floors were then laid. Subsequently, the walls were built above the foundations. These have a concrete core (*opus caementicium*) and a facing made of triangular-shaped bricks, with sides ranging from 20 to 26 cm and a thickness from 2.5 to 3.5 cm (Fig. 8.3).[11] The masonries were passed by courses of *sesquipedales* (45 × 45 cm) placed at regular intervals of 2.1 m, with the function of consolidating the wall section. A similar course of bricks was also placed at the base of the above-ground masonry. The core of the walls was composed of lime mortar and irregularly shaped sandstone elements arranged in horizontal courses. The same composition can be observed in the vaults of the rooms, which were found in a state of collapse and are still visible inside the building and in the area nearby (Fig. 8.4). They were shaped as cross vaults in the larger rooms and as barrel vaults in the smaller ones, and they incorporated brick ribs.

As for the floor plans, the heated rooms were characterized by the presence of hypocaust floors. The base floor, preserved in all the rooms, consisted of *bipedales* (60 × 60 cm), on which rested *pilae* about 80 cm high composed of square bricks with sides of 20–21 cm. Above that, an additional layer of bricks served as the base for the floor preparation levels. Hot air produced by the furnaces passed under the floors but also along the walls, where it flowed through gaps made with *tegulae mammatae* fixed to the wall by iron nails (Fig. 8.5).

The Terme Centrali (Central Baths)

The Terme Centrali are the second largest baths of Nora and are located in the town centre.[12] The building was brought to light by Gennaro Pesce in the last century and has been the

Fig. 8.5. The tegulae mammatae *used in the wall heating system of the Terme a Mare (photo C. Previato).*

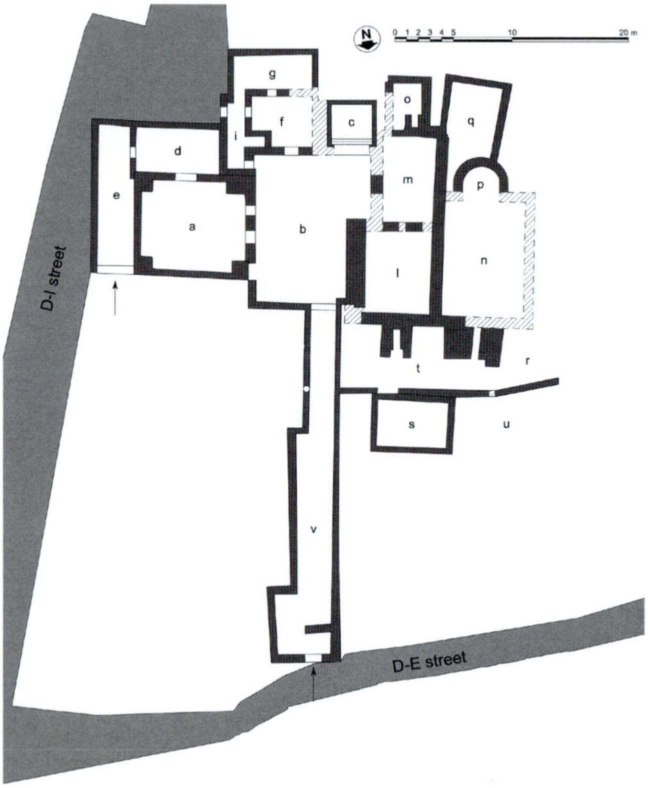

Fig. 8.6. Plan of the Terme Centrali (image C. Previato, after Bonetto et al. *2018).*

subject of stratigraphic excavations in recent years by the University of Milan.[13] According to the chronology provided by the excavation finds, the baths were built between the late second and early third century CE in an area previously occupied by private houses dating back to the first century CE (Marchesini and Ossorio 2007, 93; Frontori 2017a–b; 2018).

The baths were accessible from street D–I (Fig. 8.6). The whole plan of the building cannot be discerned with certainty as excavations are still in progress and the plan reading is made difficult by the overlapping of structures dating to different phases, but according to the layout the entrance hall can be identified in room (e). From here, passing through a hallway (d), it was possible to enter a large square room (a) paved with a mosaic and interpretable as an *apodyterium*. Room (a) gave access to the *frigidarium* (b) in the centre of the complex. This room, characterized by an L-shaped plan, was paved with a polychrome mosaic and was equipped with a central drain. The *frigidarium* featured a square pool on the southern side (c), accessible through some steps and decorated with a marble revetment. West of the pool there were three small service rooms (i, g, f), among which there was probably a latrine. From the *frigidarium*, proceeding westwards, it was possible to access a rectangular *tepidarium* (m) and from there a *sudatorium* (l) and finally a rectangular apsidal *caldarium* (n).[14] These rooms were heated through four *praefurnia* (o, q, t, r), two of which were used exclusively for the *caldarium*. The building was equipped with at least one elevated rectangular water tank, traces of which remain in the north-western sector of the complex (s). The cistern's water supply was probably provided by the aqueduct. In the late imperial period a second access was added on the northern side of the baths. At this stage a long north–south corridor (v) was built, paved with a mosaic. The corridor led from street D–E directly into the *frigidarium*.

As mentioned above, the bath building was built over earlier private edifices, which have been identified in several points underneath the floors of the baths' eastern compartments. Below the floor of the heated rooms, on the other hand, a platform made of squared sandstone blocks was found (Fig. 8.7). It is not clear whether it belonged to an earlier building or was instead intended as a foundation aimed at levelling the area and providing a solid surface for construction. In terms of construction techniques, the few surviving walls of the baths present a concrete core containing sandstone rubble of heterogeneous size and morphology and a facing made of sandstone blocks of around 10 cm in size, with the insertion of some courses of triangular-shaped bricks (Fig. 8.8). The foundations of the masonry were made

Fig. 8.7. Platform made of squared sandstone blocks under the floor of the heated rooms (photo C. Previato).

Fig. 8.8. Wall of the Terme Centrali with facing made of sandstone blocks and bricks (photo C. Previato).

Fig. 8.9. Praefurnium *with walls made of bricks (photo C. Previato).*

of irregular stones bonded by lime mortar, among which pebbles and fragments of andesite predominate. A larger use of brick can be observed in the perimeter walls of the *praefurnia* (Fig. 8.9). Square bricks were also used in the lower floors of the heated rooms, which were equipped with *suspensurae*.

The Piccole Terme (Small Baths)

The Piccole Terme are located in the western sector of the town, north of the Terme a Mare.[15] It is a modest-size building, rectangular in plan, which was partially excavated by Gennaro Pesce and in more recent years by the University of Genoa.[16]

The building was constructed between the late second and early third century CE in an area previously occupied by private dwellings (Fig. 8.10) (Giannattasio 2012). In its first building phase it consisted of a rectangular *frigidarium* (a) equipped with a marble *labrum* and paved with a polychrome mosaic with a drain in the centre, two heated rooms (b, c) possibly interpretable as *tepidaria*, and an apsidal *caldarium* (d) heated by a *praefurnium* located further east. The bathing path in this phase is not clear. According to the layout, access was from the west along street G–H. A rectangular hall (m) led to room (b) and from there the *frigidarium* (a) could probably be reached. Going back to room (b) and passing through room (c) it was then possible to reach the *caldarium* (d).[17] The modest size of the building at this early stage suggests it was probably a private bath, connected to the neighbouring houses.

At the beginning of the fourth century CE, the building was renovated and enlarged. The *frigidarium* was provided with a rectangular pool (h) (4.18 × 2.69 m) with walls featuring niches for statues and a marble facing. Further south, a new monumental access (i) opening onto street G–H was built. It consisted of some steps leading into a long corridor (g) that flowed into a large room (f) interpretable as an *apodyterium* given the presence, on the southern side, of a bench with triangular clothes lockers. The construction of these two rooms determined various modifications to the building's drainage

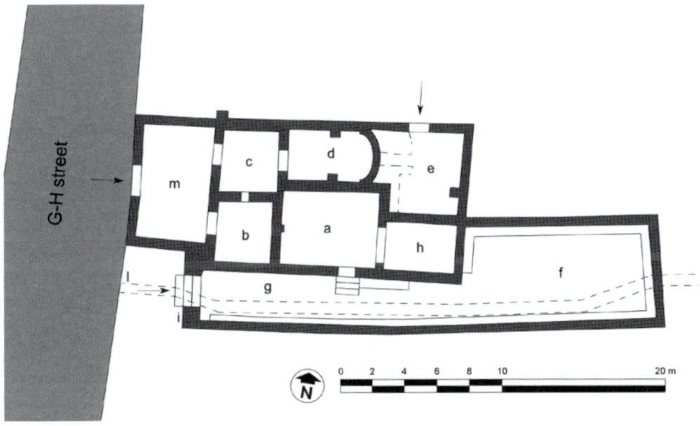

Fig. 8.10. Plan of the Piccole Terme (image C. Previato, after Bonetto et al. *2018).*

Fig. 8.11. The sewer under corridor (g) (photo C. Previato).

Fig. 8.12. Wall of the Piccole Terme with facing made of sandstone blocks and bricks (photo C. Previato).

system and involved construction of a new drain equipped with manholes that ran under the corridor and then flowed westwards into the sewer under street G–H (Fig. 8.11). Both the corridor (g) and the *apodyterium* (f) were paved with mosaics. Furthermore, the perimeter walls of room (e) were constructed. The larger size of the baths in this phase suggests the building had acquired a public function.

Both the first- and second-phase wall structures present a concrete core and a facing made of courses of roughly worked sandstone blocks alternating with two, three, or four courses of triangular-shaped bricks, and brick quoins at the corners (Fig. 8.12). The wall foundations were made of irregularly arranged andesite and rubble pebbles bound by earthen mortar. Between the foundation and the elevation a levelling course of 'pietra cantone' blocks was set. The only masonry structures characterized by a different

Fig. 8.13. Bricks of the pilae *in* tepidarium *(c) (photo C. Previato).*

technique are the perimeter walls of room (m), which are made of stones of various type and shape bound by lime mortar and arranged irregularly. As for the floor levels, the corridor (g), the *apodyterium* (h), and the *frigidarium* (a) were all paved with mosaics. Rooms (b) and (c) and the *caldarium* (d) had *suspensurae*, of which part of the *pilae* made of square bricks with a side of 21–23 cm and the base floors made of *sesquipedales* and *bipedales* remain (Fig. 8.13). Wall heating was provided by *tegulae mammatae*, some fragments of which were found during recent excavations (on the use of brick in these baths, see Giannattasio 2022).

The Terme di Levante (East Baths)

The fourth bath complex of Nora known to date is located in the town's eastern sector and was unearthed by Gennaro Pesce.[18] Regrettably, it has been heavily eroded by the sea in its eastern portion and its layout is only partially discernible (Fig. 8.14).

The building was accessed from the west along street A–B. The entrance hall consisted of a square room (a) of 9 × 9.5 m with a central pillar and paved with a mosaic. A doorway located on its eastern side provided access to a second large

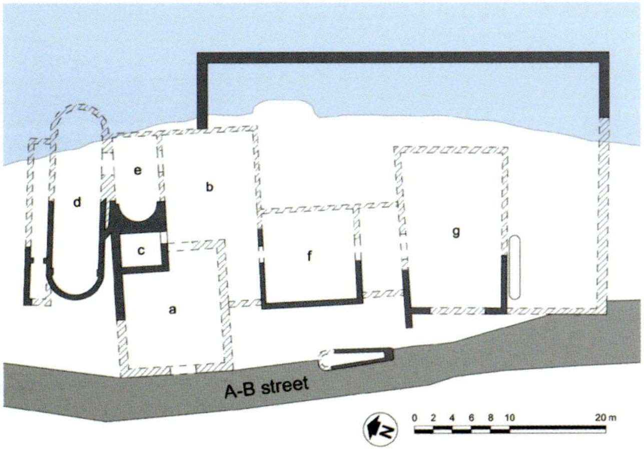

Fig. 8.14. Plan of the Terme di Levante (image C. Previato, after Bonetto et al. *2018).*

room, also paved with a mosaic, probably identifiable as a *frigidarium* (b). To the north, the *frigidarium* gave access to a small square room (c) and to two other rooms. The first room (e), preserved only in its western apse, can be interpreted as a *tepidarium* or *sudatorium*. Immediately to the north was the *caldarium* (d), a rectangular room also equipped with an apse on the western side. Both rooms were heated, as evidenced by the *suspensurae* still partially visible inside them. A furnace was placed just beyond the west apse of the *caldarium*. North and south there were two long, narrow service corridors. The articulation of the southern sector of the baths is more difficult to reconstruct. The *frigidarium* (b) was connected to a rectangular pool of 10 × 6 m covered with thick hydraulic plaster and interpretable as a *natatio* (f). To the south there were two rooms of unknown function; one of them (g) shows part of its mosaic floor. Further south there was a large cistern. The eastern limit of the baths, now obliterated by the sea, is probably to be recognized in a rectilinear north–south structure running parallel to the coast for 43.5 m and identified during an underwater archaeological survey.

According to Pesce, the rooms in the baths' northern sector rest on a foundation platform made of squared sandstone blocks, which was exposed as a result of the action of the sea on the eastern side of the building. Further south, the complex appears to be built on substructures, as evidenced by the presence of a rectangular vaulted room visible underneath room (g) (Fig. 8.15). The masonry structures of the building were constructed using different techniques. In the hall (a) and room (c) the walls are made of stone of various types and morphology, bound by lime mortar and irregularly arranged (Fig. 8.16). Conversely, the construction technique of the walls of the *caldarium* is more accurate, with a concrete core containing irregular fragments of sandstone, an outer facing made of a course of sandstone blocks alternated with one, two, or three courses of bricks, (Fig. 8.17), and an inner facing of triangular-shaped bricks. The outer facing of the northern wall of the *tepidarium* also features bricks

Fig. 8.15. The vaulted room under room (g) (photo C. Previato).

Fig. 8.16. Perimeter wall of room (b) made of irregular stones bounded with lime mortar (photo C. Previato).

(Fig. 8.18). The *suspensurae* system was adopted in the heated rooms. Only the base of these remains, as in the apse of the *tepidarium*, consisting of *sesquipedales* (45 × 45 cm) placed over a 20 cm thick layer of *cocciopesto* (Fig. 8.19). Nothing is known about the shape of the *pilae*, or about the wall heating system.

Fig. 8.17. The outer facing of the wall of the caldarium, *made of sandstone blocks and bricks (photo C. Previato).*

Fig. 8.18. The inner brick facing of the wall of the caldarium *(photo C. Previato).*

The Terme di Levante have not been excavated stratigraphically, so their date is not clear. According to the style of the mosaics currently visible they have been dated to the fourth century CE (Angiolillo 1981, 26–28), but existence of a previous building phase cannot be excluded.

The baths of Nora: Peculiarities and dynamics of the construction process

The analysis so far conducted highlights how the four baths differ in size, plan articulation, and evolution over time. Three of them show very irregular floor plans, probably due to the fact that they were built in already occupied urban areas, and they had to adapt to pre-existing structures and the available space. The Terme a Mare are the most regular building in terms of layout. This is perhaps related to the

Fig. 8.19. The base floor of the tepidarium *(photo C. Previato).*

absence of pre-existing structures on the construction site or, more likely, to the fact that construction of the baths resulted in a total obliteration of earlier structures, which was achieved through the laying of a significant fill of soil that resulted not only in a regularization of the floor level, but also in a considerable rise in elevation.

In terms of their plans, the buildings show various similarities. In all of them there are more or less large halls leading to the central sector of the building, represented by the *frigidarium*, which is always the largest room in the complex. The *frigidaria* of Nora present different plans, but inside them there is always at least one pool, which in all cases has a rectangular plan, a marble revetment, and is accessible through steps (Fig. 8.20). Moreover, niches for statues are included in the walls of the pools. In contrast, the *caldaria* seem to have more standardized morphologies: they always present a rectangular apsidal plan and are equipped with one or two *praefurnia* depending on their size. *Tepidaria* generally present a rectangular plan. The only exception is the *tepidarium* of the Terme di Levante, which appears to have an apsidal side; it should be noted, however, that this room is only partially known.

Fig. 8.20. Basin of the frigidarium *of the Terme a Mare (photo C. Previato).*

An examination of the construction process of the bath buildings reveals that particular attention was paid to the consolidation of the ground on which they were built. The best example is given by the Terme a Mare, at the base of which a 1 m thick fill of soil was placed, sandwiched between layers of pure lime. A major consolidation of the construction surface can also be recognized in the heated rooms of the Terme Centrali and of the Terme di Levante, which rest on a platform of squared sandstone blocks. It is unclear, however, whether this is a purpose-built foundation platform or a pre-existing structure reused as a foundation. This attention to the consolidation of the building surface makes us understand that, despite their current state of preservation, these buildings were meant to develop substantially in height.

With regard to building materials and techniques, strong similarities can be noted among the buildings examined. In all cases, the most common materials are sandstone and brick. The presence of sandstone is not particularly surprising, as it is a locally sourced material, which was in use at Nora since the Phoenician period and was quarried from various sites in the region around the town.[19] Apart from the large squared blocks in the foundation platforms, the sandstone elements in the wall facings are c. 10 cm in size and (more or less irregularly) parallelepiped-shaped. It is not clear whether these were newly made or reused elements, obtained from the cutting of blocks taken from earlier structures, although the substantial amount of material used in the construction would probably point to the first hypothesis. Of great interest is the extensive use of brick, a building material attested at Nora also in earlier buildings but which was only used in rather small quantities during those building phases.[20] Three types of bricks are attested in the bath buildings of Nora, with typically Roman dimensions: *bipedales* (60 × 60 cm), *sesquipedales* (45 × 45 cm), and *bessales* (20 × 20 cm) with thicknesses varying from 2.5 to 3.5 cm.[21] Unfortunately, no data are available to understand whether these were imported or locally produced materials since no stamps have been found on the bricks, nor have archaeometric analyses been conducted.[22] Again, given the quantities of the materials in place and considering that in the proximity of Nora there are clay basins suitable for brick manufacture, it seems that a local production is the preferable option. Alongside these materials is another stone of local origin, andesite, which is used exclusively in the foundations and in the form of elements of irregular size and shape.[23] In the bath buildings of Nora there are also some imported stone materials, used for both structural and decorative purposes. These are in particular the 'pietra cantone' found in the Piccole Terme (a stone quarried from the region around Cagliari); different types of marble from various Mediterranean quarries,[24] used in the form of slabs for wall and floor veneer; and volcanic pumices used in the binding mixtures of the buildings to improve their strength, probably coming from the Phlegraean Fields.[25]

If therefore we find a mix of local and imported materials, the masonry structures themselves appear to be built using non-local, typically Roman techniques. The walls in fact are all characterized by elevations with a core and facing structure, in which the core is made of concrete. In all the buildings examined, the *caementa* embedded in the lime mortar are sandstone fragments irregularly arranged. Again, an exception is given by the Terme a Mare, where the *caementa* are placed in horizontal courses both in the walls and in the vaults. As for the facings, two different techniques are attested. In the first case, the facings consist of horizontal courses of more or less regular sandstone elements of c. 10 cm in size alternating with courses of triangular-shaped bricks, with sides ranging between 21 and 27 cm. The number of brick courses as well as the height of the stone part and the rhythm with which the two materials alternate is highly variable from structure to structure. In some cases, brick quoins are present at the corners between structures built with this technique. This is the predominant technique in the Terme Centrali, the Piccole Terme, and the Terme di Levante. In contrast, in the Terme a Mare all the walls have a brick facing. The bricks are triangular in shape, and were obtained by cutting larger elements. In this case, through courses of *sesquipedales* were inserted into the masonry for the consolidation of the wall body. Brick facings are also attested in the other bath buildings, where they were used only in specific points, such as in the perimeters of the heated rooms and in *praefurnia*. Another typical Roman technique was used in all the buildings as hydraulic coating, that is *cocciopesto*.

As for the water supply to the baths, it is likely that this was provided by the aqueduct, whose construction seems to be contemporary with that of the baths.[26] The aqueduct had its source at Sa Guardia Mongiasa, located 1.5 km from Nora. In the extra-urban area, it was constructed on arches, the remains of which can be seen as far as the isthmus leading into the town. The aqueduct's urban section is not preserved, but it is assumed that inside the town, after supplying the Terme di Levante and the fountain on street A–B, it headed towards the town centre, reaching the putative *castellum aquae* on the southern slopes of the Tanit hill, of which only the basement remains, and the fountain below along street D–E. From there it probably proceeded both southwards, towards the Terme Centrali, and westwards, towards the Terme a Mare and the Piccole Terme. It has been hypothesized that in the western sector of the town the conduit ran above the portico of *insula* A and on the arch at the intersection of streets E–G and G–H (Tronchetti 1984, 45; Bejor 1994a, 855). Even if the main conduit has not been found, the fact that the aqueduct reached the western sector of Nora is demonstrated by the discovery of lead *fistulae* along street G–H (Pesce 1972, 83).

Final remarks

The analysis conducted on the bath buildings of Nora allows us to make some broader observations about the architects and workers involved in the construction process and the historical, social, economic, and cultural context in which the construction took place.

Firstly, it is clear that in these buildings only typically Roman construction methods were applied, such as the use of concrete in the wall cores and the vaults, and the stone and brick or only brick facing in the masonry structures. Considering the limited use, or the almost complete absence, of these techniques in earlier buildings such as the forum and the theatre (Ghiotto 2004, 185), and their use in other contemporary buildings such as the Roman Temple (Fig. 8.21),[27] it can be hypothesized that their spread was determined by the arrival at Nora between the end of the second and the third century CE of architects or builders who came from Rome or from central Italy, or who at any rate possessed non-local building expertise.[28] Even if there is no evidence for the identity and origin of those who were involved in the construction of the baths or other contemporary buildings, it can be supposed that these foreign experts acted as vectors for the dissemination and transmission of new technical knowledge to the local workforce (on similar processes see Vitti, this volume). Given the large number of buildings that were erected at Nora in the Severan age, it seems that the local builders became familiar with the new construction techniques rather quickly. However, looking at the different quality of execution of the structures, it can be observed that they did not always apply these techniques in the same way. In fact, if one compares the various baths, it can be noticed that there are clear differences both in the shape of the stone elements used in the wall facings, which can be more or less regular, and in the rhythm with which stone and brick were laid. Considering that the materials used in all the baths are the same, and therefore the different way in which sandstone blocks were worked was not due to the different workability of the stone, it can be assumed that in the town there were different groups of workers who were active at the same time, with different and more or less refined technical skills.

Fig. 8.21. Wall with facing of sandstone blocks and bricks in the Roman Temple (photo C. Previato).

With regard to raw materials, both traditional, locally sourced and easily supplied materials, such as sandstone and andesite, and new or imported materials, such as brick, Phlegraean pumice, and marble, were used. The presence and use of sandstone and andesite are not particularly surprising, given the ease of sourcing these materials, and only show that the architects were familiar with locally available resources and that the workers on the site were able to work these materials easily. In contrast, the extensive use of brick appears to be a highly innovative practice, given the limited use of this material in the town in earlier buildings.[29] Although we have no information on the possible production site of these materials, the substantial quantity of brick used in the baths of Nora points to a local production, as proposed by some scholars on the basis of the macroscopic analysis of the clay (for the Piccole Terme, see Giannattasio 2022, 37) and considering the availability of clay deposits around the town.[30] If so, it could be assumed that it was the construction of the bath buildings (and of other contemporary constructions with brick wall facings) that led to the development and/or growth of local manufacturing workshops engaged in the production of brick, thus having a significant impact on the local economy. However, this is currently only a hypothesis that needs to be confirmed in light of new data and research on brick production sites.

Equally noteworthy is the presence, in the binding mixtures, of pumices probably coming from the Phlegraean Fields. This shows, on the one hand, the knowledge of the architects who carried out the construction projects of the properties of these materials, which would provide solidity and durability to the structures, and on the other, the existence of trade relations with the Campanian area aimed at the supply of building materials. The presence of the same materials in other buildings of this period, such as the Roman Temple (Dilaria *et al.* 2023), confirms the spread at Nora in this phase of a shared technical knowledge that was applied at the same time in different construction sites. The use of marble for veneer, which was clearly determined by purely aesthetic purposes, attests both to the local contacts with various regions of the Mediterranean and to the wealth of the patrons.

All these elements confirm that in the period in which the baths were built, the town of Nora enjoyed a certain economic prosperity. At this stage, not only building materials and other goods arrived at Nora, but also technical knowledge that brought innovation to and modified the local building tradition, which in turn had an impact on Nora's society and economy. This building, economic, and cultural dynamism involved the entire town and found expression in the construction and restoration of numerous buildings and infrastructure: for instance, the paving of the streets, the renovation of the sewage system, and the construction of the aqueduct all date to this period.[31] This close link between the construction of the baths and the development of the town leads to questions about the patrons behind these projects. Unfortunately, nothing is known about the kind of financial initiative, public or private, that promoted these large-scale monumentalization works, nor is any evidence available on acts of euergetism at Nora that can be linked specifically to the construction of the bath. The fact that baths spread simultaneously at Nora as well as across Sardinia at this stage (Ghiotto 2004, 109–35) may lead to the hypothesis that this was due to a precise public (perhaps imperial?) activity to promote construction of this kind of buildings as bearers of a distinct social practice and as a symbol of *romanitas*. Indeed, it is not by chance that these interventions began at the time of Septimius Severus, who, having personally ascertained the modest level of urbanization of the local towns during his quaestorship of Sardinia twenty years before he became emperor (*Sev*. 2.4–5), might have contributed to some extent to their monumentalization (Ghiotto 2004, 203). Significant in this regard is the large number of inscriptions with dedications to third-century emperors, particularly to members of the Severan family, that have been found at Nora and in Sardinia.[32] At present, however, these remain hypotheses that may be confirmed in the future by new studies and research.

Notes

1. I would like to thank Niccolò Mugnai for the organization of the workshop and all the reviewers and in particular Janet DeLaine for her valuable comments and suggestions to improve the quality of my chapter.
2. On the history of excavations and research at Nora, see Mazzariol and Zara forthcoming. Since 1990, an archaeological mission involving the Universities of Padua, Milan, Cagliari, and Genoa has conducted excavations and research on the ancient town and its territory with the aim of reconstructing its history. The most up-to-date publication on Nora is a guidebook to the site published in 2018 which contains the main results of recent excavations (Bonetto *et al.* 2018).
3. Bartoloni *et al.* 1997, 67–97; Bonetto 2009, 182–84; 2021; Bondì 2012, 86–87.
4. Bejor 1994a, 845–58; 1994b, 109, 112; Bonetto 2002; Ghiotto 2004, 184–85; 2009, 323–26. On the forum, see Bonetto 2009. On the theatre, see Mistretta 1961; Pesce 1972, 60–68; Bonello Lai 1987; Bejor 1993; 2000; 2003; 2007; Amucano 1994; Melis and Columbu 2000; Bejor *et al.* 2003; Tosi 2003, 645–48; Ghiotto 2004, 77–81, 90–94; Columbu and Garau 2017; Previato 2020; Previato *et al.* 2022.
5. Bejor 1994a, 849–52; 1994b, 109–10; Ghiotto 2004, 185–86; Zara 2010–11; Fabiani 2013; Asolati *et al.* 2018, 99–146.
6. On the aqueduct, see Paoletti 1997; Ghiotto 2004, 146–48; Piu 2016; Cespa 2018, 16. The aqueduct was probably restored between 425 and 450 CE by Flaviolus, *praeses provinciae*, and Valerius Euhodius, *principalis ac primoris* of Nora: Ghiotto 2004, 148 with references.
7. Pesce 1972, 83–86; Angiolillo 1981, 32; Tronchetti 1985; 2001, 55–61; Ghiotto 2004, 115–16; Bonetto *et al.* 2018, 86–92.
8. According to C. Tronchetti (1985, 75), this room was not equipped with wall heating, but only with a heated floor.
9. Tronchetti 1985, 73. This solution is documented also in the baths of Convento Vecchio at Tharros, Sardinia.
10. Tronchetti 1985, 76–77. This chronology is also supported by the stylistic analysis of the mosaics of the *apodyterium* (b) and of the southern hall (h) (Rinaldi 2000–01, 115–16, nos. 64–65). The building was heavily restored in the first half of the fifth century CE and then destroyed by a fire (Tronchetti 1985, 77–79).
11. In some points, parallelepiped sandstone blocks were inserted into the brick facing. They are probably related to ancient restorations (Tronchetti 1985, 72).
12. Pesce 1972, 69–73; Angiolillo 1981, 10–15; Tronchetti 2001, 35–41; Canepa 2003; Ghiotto 2004, 116–17; Bonetto *et al.* 2018, 59–63; Frontori 2019.
13. On the recent excavations, see Iacovino and Mecozzi 2012; Iacovino 2013; Panero 2013; Frontori 2014; 2018; Albertoni and Frontori 2018; Frontori and Restelli 2018.
14. This interpretation of the bathing route and the function of rooms (a), (d), (e), (f), (g), (i), (l) differs in part from that proposed by other scholars (Frontori 2018), but it seems more likely given the layout and architectural features of the complex and in the light of comparisons with other bath complexes. I thank Janet DeLaine for her suggestions.
15. Pesce 1972, 81–82; Angiolillo 1981, 28–32; Tronchetti 2001, 52–53; Colavitti 2002; Ghiotto 2004, 117–18; Bonetto *et al.* 2018, 94–96.
16. On the recent excavations by the University of Genoa, see Giannattasio 2012; 2014; Giannattasio and Porro 2012; Albanese and Cosentino 2013.
17. Like for the Terme Centrali, this interpretation of the bathing route partially differs from previous proposals (Giannattasio 2012) on the basis of the building's layout and architectural features, and in the light of comparisons with other bath buildings. I thank Janet DeLaine for these suggestions.
18. On this building, see Pesce 1972, 107–9; Angiolillo 1981, 26–28; Tronchetti 2001, 20–22; Ghiotto 2004, 124–25; Bonetto *et al.* 2018, 22.
19. On the stone quarries of Nora and the use of sandstone, see Previato 2016, esp. 19–67.
20. The only building so far known in which brick is attested before the Severan age is the theatre: see Ghiotto 2004, 6–7; Previato 2020; Previato *et al.* 2022.
21. With regard to the Piccole Terme, it has been noted that the correspondence to the Roman metric standards is somewhat approximate, with deviations of a few centimetres: Giannattasio 2022, 37.
22. To date, a complete study of the bricks used in the buildings of Nora is still lacking. The only publications on this subject are fairly recent and concern the bricks from the Roman Temple (Piazza 2021) and the Piccole Terme (Gazzerro 2003; Giannattasio 2022).
23. On the quarries and use of andesite at Nora, see Previato 2016, 68–83.
24. The study of marbles from the baths of Nora is being carried out by Beatrice Marchet (University of Padua). So far, the types identified in the Terme a Mare are: greco scritto, bardiglio lunense, and cipollino; in the Terme Centrali: giallo antico; in the Piccole Terme: rosso antico, verde antico, giallo antico, greco scritto, portasanta, and fior di pesco.

25. The study of the mortars from Nora's bath buildings is currently in progress and the provenance of the pumices from the Phlegraean Fields must be confirmed through archaeometric analyses that are being carried out by Simone Dilaria, whom I thank for these preliminary observations. Phlegraean pumices were found in the Roman Temple, dated to the Severan age (Dilaria *et al.* 2023).
26. Paoletti 1997; Ghiotto 2004, 146–48; Piu 2016; Cespa 2018, 16.
27. The walls of the Roman Temple have a concrete core and a facing made of stone and brick (Dilaria *et al.* 2023). Also in the aqueduct are attested building techniques quite similar to those of the baths; the piers have a concrete core and a brick facing, while the arches have a stone and brick facing (Ghiotto 2004, 147).
28. The spread of typically Roman building techniques from the Severan age onwards is a phenomenon observable not only at Nora, but across all of Sardinia (see Ghiotto 2004, 20–22). This change in the construction methods primarily affected public architecture, while building techniques of Punic tradition remained in use in private edifices.
29. The only pre-Severan public building at Nora where brick is attested is the theatre. However, bricks were used here in limited quantities, as they are found only in the wall facings of the external niches and in some points of the stage building. It has been calculated that approximately 1,200 *bessales* were needed for the construction of the outer walls of the theatre (Previato 2020, 247).
30. On the geological and geomorphological features of the peninsula of Nora and the surrounding territory, see Di Gregorio *et al.* 2000; 2005–06; Melis and Columbu 2000, 106–7. See also the sketch drawing published in Columbu and Garau 2017, fig. 4.
31. The aqueduct is not dated stratigraphically, but its connection to the construction of the baths is evident, as also shown by the use of the same building materials and techniques: Ghiotto 2004, 146–48, n. 40.
32. Zucca 1994; 2005; Zara 2010–11, 155–73. Of particular interest is an inscription commemorating the restoration of the basilica at Nora by a *curator rei publicae*, that is, a commissioner appointed directly by the emperor: see Zucca 1994, 876–77, no. 43; Ghiotto 2009, 343–44.

References

Albanese, L. and Cosentino, V. 2013. Nora tardo-antica. Ricerche in corso nel quartiere nord-occidentale. *Lanx* 14: 107–22.

Albertoni, R. and Frontori, I. 2018. I vani di servizio delle Terme Centrali. *Quaderni Norensi* 7: 59–63.

Amucano, M.A. 1994. Il teatro romano di Nora: contributo per la rilettura architettonica e urbanistica. *Rivista di Topografia Antica* 4: 195–212.

Angiolillo, S. (ed.) 1981. *Mosaici antichi in Italia. Sardinia*. Rome: Istituto Poligrafico e Zecca dello Stato.

Asolati, M., Bonetto, J. and Zara, A. 2018. Un deposito rituale di antoniniani dal settore orientale dall'abitato di Nora (Sardegna). *Annali dell'Istituto Italiano di Numismatica* 64: 99–146.

Bartoloni, P., Bondì, S.F. and Moscati, S. 1997. *La penetrazione fenicia e punica in Sardegna. Trent'anni dopo*. Rome: Accademia nazionale dei Lincei.

Bejor, G. 1993. Nora II. Riconsiderazioni sul teatro. *Quaderni della Soprintendenza Archeologica per le Province di Cagliari e Oristano* 10: 129–39.

Bejor, G. 1994a. Romanizzazione ed evoluzione dello spazio urbano in una città punica: il caso di Nora. In Mastino, A. and Ruggeri, P. (eds), *L'Africa Romana. Atti del X convegno di studio (Oristano, 11–14 dicembre 1992)*. Sassari: Editrice Archivio Fotografico Sardo, 843–56.

Bejor, G. 1994b. Spazio pubblico e privato nella Sardegna romana: Nora. In *La ciudad en el mundo romano – La ciutat en el món romà. Actas del XIV Congreso internacional d'Arqueología Clásica – Actes del XIV Congrés internacional d'Arqueologia Clàssica (Tarragona, 5–11 septiembre/setembre 1993), 1. Ponencias*. Tarragona: Consejo Superior de Investigaciones Científicas, 109–13.

Bejor, G. 2000. L'area del teatro. In Tronchetti, C. (ed.), *Ricerche su Nora, I (anni 1990–1998)*. Cagliari: Grafiche Sainas, 177–82.

Bejor, G. 2003. Il teatro e l'isolato centrale. In *Nora 2003*. Pisa: Servizio editoriale universitario di Pisa, 71–80.

Bejor, G. 2007. Lo sviluppo della frontescena nei teatri dell'Africa romana: un possibile confronto per Nora? In *Teatri antichi nell'area del Mediterraneo: conservazione programmata e fruizione sostenibile. Atti del II convegno internazionale 'La materia e i segni della storia' (Siracusa, 13–17 ottobre 2004)*. Palermo: Centro regionale per la progettazione e il restauro, 81–89.

Bejor, G., Giraldi, P. and Valentini, O. 2003. Nora, lo scavo. Area E: campagna 2002. *Quaderni della Soprintendenza Archeologica per le Province di Cagliari e Oristano* 20: 88–124.

Bondì, S.F. 2012. Nora, da insediamento fenicio a città cartaginese. In Di Nocera, G.M., Micozzi, M., Pavolini, C. and Rovelli, A. (eds), *Archeologia e memoria storica. Atti delle giornate di studio (Viterbo, 25–26 marzo 2009)*. Viterbo: Università degli Studi della Tuscia, 81–94.

Bonello Lai, M. 1987. L'indagine demografica e gli edifici di spettacolo in Sardegna: l'anfiteatro di Cagliari ed il teatro di Nora. In Mastino, A. (ed.), *L'Africa Romana. Atti del IV convegno di studio (Sassari, 12–14 dicembre 1986)*. Sassari: Dipartimento di Storia, Università degli Studi di Sassari, 615–32.

Bonetto, J. 2002. Nora municipio romano. In Khanoussi, M., Ruggeri, P. and Vismara, C. (eds), *L'Africa Romana. Lo spazio marittimo del Mediterraneo occidentale: geografia storica ed economia. Atti del XIV convegno di studio (Sassari, 7–10 dicembre 2000)*. Rome: Carocci, 1201–20.

Bonetto, J. 2003. I sistemi infrastrutturali di Nora romana: la viabilità e il drenaggio delle acque. In Tronchetti, C. (ed.), *Ricerche su Nora, II (anni 1990–1998)*. Cagliari: Grafiche Sainas, 21–38.

Bonetto, J. 2009. L'insediamento di età fenicia, punica e romana repubblicana nell'area del foro. In Bonetto, J. (ed.), *Nora. Il foro romano. Storia di un'area urbana dall'età fenicia alla tarda antichità (1997–2006), I. Lo scavo*. Noventa padovana: Italgraf, 39–243.

Bonetto, J. 2014. Pula. Nora, teatro romano. In Manca di Mores, G. (ed.), *La Sardegna di Thomas Ashby. Paesaggi, archeologia, comunità. Fotografie 1906–1912*. Sassari: Carlo Delfino Editore, 300–1.

Bonetto, J. 2021. Nora nel V secolo: da emporio a colonia. In Botto, M., van Dommelen, P. and Roppa, A. (eds), *Il Mediterraneo*

Occidentale dalla fase fenicia all'egemonia cartaginese. Dinamiche insediative, forme rituali e cultura materiale nel V secolo a.C. Rome: Quasar, 91–106.

Bonetto, J., Bejor, G., Bondì, S.F., Giannattasio, B.M., Giuman, M. and Tronchetti, C. (eds) 2018. *Nora (Pula)*. Sassari: Carlo Delfino Editore.

Canepa, C. 2003. Nora: le Terme centrali. In Tronchetti, C. (ed.), *Ricerche su Nora, II (anni 1990–1998)*. Cagliari: Grafiche Sainas, 39–59.

Cespa, S. 2018. Urban water supply in Punic and Roman Sardinia. *WIREs Water* 5: https://doi.org/10.1002/wat2.1313.

Colavitti, A.M. 2002. Le Piccole terme di Nora: proposta di rilettura. In Khanoussi, M., Ruggeri, P. and Vismara, C. (eds), *L'Africa Romana. Lo spazio marittimo del Mediterraneo occidentale: geografia storica ed economia. Atti del XIV convegno di studio (Sassari, 7–10 dicembre 2000)*. Rome: Carocci, 1221–33.

Columbu, S. and Garau, A.M. 2017. Mineralogical, petrographic and chemical analysis of geomaterials used in the mortars of Roman Nora theatre (south Sardinia, Italy). *Italian Journal of Geoscience* 136.2: 238–62.

Dilaria, S., Previato, C., Bonetto, J., Secco, M., Zara, A., De Luca, R. and Miriello, D. 2023. Volcanic pozzolan from the Phlegraean Fields in the structural mortars of the Roman Temple of Nora (Sardinia). *Heritage* 6: 567–86.

Di Gregorio, F., Floris, C. and Matta, P. 2000. Lineamenti geologici e geomorfologici della penisola di Nora. In Tronchetti, C. (ed.), *Ricerche su Nora, I (anni 1990–1998)*. Cagliari: Grafiche Sainas, 9–18.

Di Gregorio, F., Floris, C., Matta, P. and Tronchetti, C. 2005–06. Ricerche geoarcheologiche sui centri fenicio-punici e poi romani della Sardegna centro-meridionale. Nora: nota 1. *Quaderni della Soprintendenza Archeologica per le Province di Cagliari e Oristano* 22: 47–85.

Fabiani, F. 2013. Nora: il secolo d'oro. In Graziadio, G., Guglielmino, R., Lenuzza, V. and Vitale, S. (eds), *Φιλική Συναυλία. Studies in Mediterranean Archaeology for Mario Benzi*. Oxford: Archaeopress, 407–14.

Frontori, I. 2014. Nora (Pula, Cagliari). Indagini archeologiche nel quartiere delle Terme Centrali, Area E (campagna di scavo 2013). *Journal of Fasti Online* 303: 1–11.

Frontori, I. 2017a. L'apodyterium delle Terme Centrali: campagna di scavo 2014. *Quaderni Norensi* 6: 75–80.

Frontori, I. 2017b. Il quartiere centrale: campagna di scavo 2015. *Quaderni Norensi* 6: 81–86.

Frontori, I. 2018. L'ingresso alle Terme Centrali. *Quaderni Norensi* 7: 53–58.

Frontori, I. 2019. Nora (Pula CA). Le Terme Centrali. In Medri, M. and Pizzo, A. (eds), *Le terme pubbliche nell'Italia romana (II secolo a.C. – fine IV d.C.): architettura, tecnologia e società. Atti del Seminario Internazionale di Studio (Roma, 4–5 ottobre 2018)*. Rome: Romatre Press, 259–65.

Frontori, I. and Restelli, L. 2018. Nuovi dati sul sistema di smaltimento delle acque nelle Terme centrali di Nora. In Buora, M. and Magnani, S. (eds), *I sistemi di smaltimento delle acque nel mondo antico. Atti del convegno (Aquileia, 6–8 aprile 2017)*. Trieste: Editreg, 767–74.

Gazzerro, L. 2003. Materiali edilizi (LAT). In Giannattasio, B.M. (ed.), *Nora Area C. Scavi 1996–1999*. Genova: Brigati, 271–73.

Ghiotto, A.R. 2004. *L'architettura romana nelle città della Sardegna*. Rome: Quasar.

Ghiotto, A.R. 2009. Il complesso monumentale del foro. In Bonetto, J. (ed.), *Nora. Il foro romano. Storia di un'area urbana dall'età fenicia alla tarda antichità (1997–2006), I. Lo scavo*. Noventa padovana: Italgraf, 247–373.

Giannattasio, B.M. 2012. Osservazioni preliminari sulle Piccole Terme. *Quaderni Norensi* 4: 69–75.

Giannattasio, B.M. 2014. Le Piccole Terme: conservazione e fruizione. *Quaderni Norensi* 5: 63–70.

Giannattasio, B.M. 2022. Nora, tipologia dei laterizi dalle Piccole Terme. *Quaderni Norensi* 9: 35–44.

Giannattasio, B.M. and Porro, C. 2012. Campagna di scavo 2010: le Piccole Terme. *Quaderni Norensi* 4: 19–39.

Iacovino, C. 2013. Il quartiere delle Terme Centrali: il deflusso delle acque. *Lanx* 14: 203–9.

Iacovino, C. and Mecozzi, P. 2012. Le Terme Centrali. Il sistema di smaltimento delle acque. *Quaderni Norensi* 4: 115–24.

Marchesini, B. and Ossorio, F. 2007. La XVI campagna di scavo. L'indagine archeologica dell'area di risulta tra il Peristilio Orientale e le Terme centrali (Amb. Cf). *Quaderni Norensi* 2: 90–97.

Mazzariol, A. and Zara, A. forthcoming. *Nora. La storia degli studi e delle ricerche. Viaggiatori, antichisti e archeologi a Nora tra la fine del XVI secolo e la metà del XX secolo*. Rome: Quasar.

Melis, S. and Columbu, S. 2000. Matériaux de construction d'époque romaine et relation avec les anciennes carrières: l'exemple du théâtre de Nora (Sardaigne SO – Italie). In Lorenz, J., Tardy, D. and Coulon, G. (eds), *La pierre dans la ville antique et médiévale. Analyses, méthodes et apports. Actes du colloque d'Argentomagus (Argenton-sur-Creuse, 30–31 mars 1998)*. Saint-Marcel: Musee d'Argentomagus – F.E.R.A.C., 103–17.

Mistretta, P. 1961. Il teatro romano di Nora. *Dioniso* 35.3–4: 28–37.

Panero, E. 2013. Il settore SE delle Terme Centrali: da quartiere residenziale a pars publica. *Lanx* 14: 180–93.

Paoletti, S. 1997. Nora V. Soluzioni tecniche dell'acquedotto romano di Nora. *Quaderni della Soprintendenza Archeologica per le Province di Cagliari e Oristano* 14: 159–64.

Pesce, G. 1972. *Nora: guida agli scavi*. Cagliari: Editrice sarda Fossataro.

Piazza, A. 2021. Il materiale laterizio. In Bonetto, J., Mantovani, V. and Zara, A. (eds), *Nora. Il Tempio romano 2008–2014, volume II.2. I materiali romani e gli altri reperti*. Rome: Quasar, 551–60.

Piu, F. 2016. L'acquedotto di Nora: studi e prospettive. In Angiolillo, S., Giuman, M., Carboni, R. and Cruccas, E. (eds), *Nora Antiqua. Atti del convegno di studi (Cagliari, Cittadella dei Musei, 3–4 ottobre 2014) (Scavi di Nora V)*. Perugia: Morlacchi Editore U.P., 191–95.

Previato, C. 2016. *Nora. Le cave di pietra della città antica (Scavi di Nora VI)*. Rome: Quasar.

Previato, C. 2020. Il teatro romano di Nora (Sardegna, Italia): logistica, forza-lavoro e tempistiche del processo costruttivo dell'edificio. In Courault, C. and Márquez, C. (eds), *Quantitative Studies and Production Cost of Roman Public Construction*. Cordoba: Editorial Universidad de Córdoba, 233–88.

Previato, C., Monego, M., Menin, A. and Achilli, V. 2022. A multi-scalar approach for the study of ancient architecture: structure for motion, laser scanning and direct survey of the Roman theatre of Nora (Cagliari, Sardinia). *Journal of*

Archaeological Science: Reports 43: https://doi.org/10.1016/j.jasrep.2022.103440.

Rinaldi, F. 2000–01. *Le pavimentazioni di Nora. Una revisione critica e cronologica.* Tesi di Specializzazione, Università degli Studi di Padova.

Tosi, G. 2003. *Gli edifici per spettacoli nell'Italia romana.* Rome: Quasar.

Tronchetti, C. 1984. Cagliari. In Anati, E. (ed.), *I Sardi. La Sardegna dal paleolitico all'età romana.* Milan: Jaca Book, 43–45.

Tronchetti, C. 1985. Le terme a mare. In *Nora. Recenti studi e scoperte.* Pula: Amministrazione comunale di Pula, 71–81.

Tronchetti, C. 2001. *Nora.* Sassari: Carlo Delfino Editore.

Zara, A. 2010–11. *Evoluzione urbana e nuovo assetto monumentale di Nora in età medioimperiale romana.* MA Thesis, Università degli Studi di Padova.

Zucca, R. 1994. Il decoro urbano delle civitates Sardiniae et Corsicae: il contributo delle fonti letterarie ed epigrafiche. In Mastino, A. and Ruggeri, P. (eds), *L'Africa Romana. Atti del X convegno di studio (Oristano, 11–14 dicembre 1992).* Sassari: Editrice Archivio Fotografico Sardo, 857–935.

Zucca, R. 2005. Iscrizioni inedite da Nora (Sardinia). *Epigraphica* 57: 536–44.

9

What have the Romans ever done for us? Early Roman Jerusalem as an urban centre between local tradition and Roman rule

Orit Peleg-Barkat

From King Herod's rule (37–4 BCE) until its destruction in the year 70 CE, the city of Jerusalem served as a major urban centre in Judaea, even when it ceased to serve as the capital of the province and came under direct Roman rule in 6 CE. King Herod, who ruled Judaea as a loyal client king, outshone his Hasmonean predecessors in embellishing the kingdom and its capital city with numerous monuments. His good relations with Augustus and his right-hand man, Marcus Agrippa, the peace and prosperity (*pax romana*) conveyed by Augustus, and Herod's own personal ambitions, led him to launch a staggering building programme that included the establishment or re-establishment of dozens of cities, towns, palaces, fortresses, and public buildings throughout Judaea, as well as beyond his realm.[1] In Jerusalem Herod built two palaces (*BJ* 1.401–2; 5.176–82, 238), several buildings for mass entertainment (*BJ* 2.44; *AJ* 15.268–76), fortifications, and many other structures. His greatest achievement, however, was the rebuilding of the Second Temple and the initiation of the expansion of the Temple Mount compound, which reshaped the entire eastern part of the city (*BJ* 1.401; *AJ* 15.380; Netzer 2006, 137–78).

Herod used his construction projects to promote his prestige as a Hellenistic-style king and to manifest his close connection to Augustus. Presenting oneself as a Hellenistic king, while at the same time displaying loyalty to Augustus and Rome, was not perceived as an inconsistency at the time and was practiced by other client kings, such as Antiochus I of Commagene or Juba II of Mauretania. Herod's constructions simultaneously declared his loyalty to his Roman patrons and publicized Roman support of his rule to his Judaean subjects. His affinity with and loyalty to Rome were expressed not just in direct ways, such as through the establishment of temples to the emperor's cult in Samaria/Sebaste (*BJ* 1.403; *AJ* 15.296–98; Reisner *et al.* 1924, 46–50, 170–80; Crowfoot *et al.* 1942, 123–35; Netzer 2006, 85–89), Caesarea Maritima (*BJ* 1.414; *AJ* 15.339; Kahn 1996; Netzer 2006, 103–6; Holum 2015), and Paneion (*BJ* 1.404–6; *AJ* 15.363–64),[2] or the naming of cities, buildings, or parts of buildings after the emperor or other members of the imperial family, but also in several indirect ways, by introducing specifically Roman types of buildings and Roman forms of decoration into his kingdom. For example, in many of his buildings, construction techniques that are explicitly Roman were utilized, the most prominent example being the use of reticulate masonry in Jerusalem, Jericho, and Paneion.[3] Use of genuine Roman materials is also well attested, such as pozzolana for hydraulic concrete used in the construction of the harbour of Caesarea Maritima (Hohfelder *et al.* 2007; Votruba 2007), or cinnabar – apparently originating from the imperial mercury mines in Spain – used as a red pigment for the wall decorations of his third palace in Jericho (Rozenberg 2008, 263–67).

In Jerusalem, he named his first palace north of the Temple Mount after Mark Antony (the 'Antonia Citadel': *BJ* 5.238), and the main wings in his second palace in the western part of the city after Augustus and Agrippa (*BJ* 1.402). He also added a basilical structure to the southern flank of the expanded Temple Mount compound, an act which resulted in a new design of the holy sanctuary subtly alluding to the newly erected Caesarea complexes in Alexandria and Cyrene (and possibly also Antioch), and thus transforming the expansion project of the Temple Mount into another homage to Augustus (Peleg-Barkat 2017, 101–4; 2021).

It has also been suggested by some scholars (for instance, Geiger 2009, 157–70) that the very idea of public building on a large scale in Herod's kingdom was influenced, to some extent at least, by the building programme of the *princeps* in Rome. Herod surely appreciated the economic consequences of such projects, and especially their benefits. In Flavius Josephus' (37–c. 100 CE) text we mostly hear complaints about taxes and exploitation, but one cannot ignore the notion that these projects were a healthy and beneficial way of reinvesting in the economy the gains from taxation, as they supplied livelihood for hundreds of people both in Rome and Jerusalem. Herod's construction projects in the cities of Judaea, and especially his rebuilding of the Temple in Jerusalem, determined a massive movement of the poor from rural areas to the city (Broshi 1987). Once the demand for labour diminished, these new residents of the city became an unemployed mass – hence the famous statement of Josephus, whether his figures are accurate or not,[4] concerning the 18,000 people that were out of work when the project eventually came to its end in 64 CE (*AJ* 20.219–22).

While Herod's contribution to the embellishment of the city and to the advent of Roman cultural influence on its art and architecture was never contested, less scholarly attention has been paid to the development of the city under direct Roman rule, after Archelaus' (Herod's son and successor) deposition from office in 6 CE. Nevertheless, archaeological work in recent decades in the Old City of Jerusalem has transformed the way we envision and understand Jerusalem in this formative period.[5] These excavations have revealed the long duration of the massive construction works that were related to the expansion of the Temple Mount compound and the creation of a new urban grid in the city's eastern sector. These construction projects indeed commenced under King Herod but were completed many years after his death. One of the major outcomes of these excavations is that, despite Josephus' harsh criticism of the Roman governors (prefects and later procurators: for instance, against Florus in *BJ* 2.277–558; *AJ* 18.25; 20.257), Jerusalem clearly enjoyed days of development and prosperity during the first century CE, at least until the reign of Agrippa I (41–44 CE). Indeed, once Judaea became a province, the collection of taxes became a point of tension among the Jews of the province, as taxes were now officially paid to the emperor for the glory of the Empire and not to the treasury of the king or ethnarch, who at least partly invested it back in public construction and other benefits for the local inhabitants. Still, the finds show, as is also attested through historical sources, that the Roman administration took part in the development of the city, taking care of its water supply (*AJ* 18.60) and infrastructure. The infamous prefect Pontius Pilate seems to have played a significant role in these constructions as shall be discussed below (Szanton *et al.* 2019, 162–63).

It is no wonder, therefore, that the early Roman period is considered as one of the major peaks in the history of Jerusalem. Tacitus calls Jerusalem a 'famous city' and estimates its population at hundreds of thousands of people (*Hist.* 5.2; 13), and according to Pliny the Elder it was by far the most famous city of the East (*HN* 5.15.1). Jerusalem was then a large city surrounded by a system of fortifications that included three walls (*BJ* 5.142–60). It had an elaborate water supply and drainage system, wide paved streets with adjacent shops, markets, monumental public buildings, palaces, and fortresses. The public buildings, the royal palaces and the residences of the upper class were decorated with Classical-style architectural decoration (see Peleg-Barkat and Ben-Haim 2017), frescoes (Rozenberg 2003), and mosaic floors (Talgam 2014, 15–19), and were furnished with tableware and other luxuries. In the extensive necropolis that surrounded the city were richly decorated tombs and tomb markers (Peleg-Barkat 2012), inside which the buried were placed in ossuaries and carved sarcophagi of various designs (Rahmani 1994; Foerster 1998). This prosperity is also apparent outside of Jerusalem, where growing numbers of rural estates and small towns show indications of individual wealth in the first century CE, such as large dwellings with elaborate decorations (mosaics, frescoes, etc.; Aviam 2011, 30) and monumental family tombs (Raviv and Zissu 2020), although of course on a smaller scale than in the main city.[6]

Still, upon entering the city, any visitor to Jerusalem could immediately recognize its distinctively exceptional character. It was very different from any other Hellenistic or Roman city they knew. Some of the differences lay in the daily practices of the inhabitants that related to Jewish purity laws, such as the many ritual baths installed in the basements of dwellings (Reich 2013) or the extensive use of chalkstone vessels that are immune to impurity (Magen 2002). While such habits might have escaped the attention of foreign visitors, there were two major aspects of the city that were clearly apparent in the public sphere and were unavoidably discernible by such visitors; firstly, nowhere to be seen were human or animal visual depictions, in accordance with the Second Commandment.[7] No statues adorned the streets and public buildings, and no figurative mosaics, wall paintings, reliefs or sculpture in the round decorated the houses of the elite.[8] Secondly, and not least apparent, was the fact that the city had but only one temple.

The Temple on Mount Moriah in the eastern part of the city was the single place of worship in Jerusalem and served as such for the entire Jewish community. Its singularity and centrality in the lives of the Jews evoked devotion that is reflected in many ways in the architecture and material culture of Jerusalem and Judaea. Funerary art, for example, bears several clear allusions to specific architectural features of the Temple Mount, attesting to the Temple-oriented identity of the deceased and their families (Peleg-Barkat 2017, 38–39). The fact that the Temple was the sole focal point of pilgrimage on the main three holidays also had a substantial impact on the network of roads leading to the city and that of the streets within the city itself. Special features of these roads and streets were added, which were meant to enhance the spiritual experience of the worshippers and maintain their purity upon arrival to the holy site, as shall be discussed below.

The sections that follow in this chapter examine Roman influence on the architecture of Jerusalem during King Herod's reign as well as under the Roman prefects. They also discuss the effects that the centrality and singularity of the Temple had on the planning, execution, and embellishment of buildings in the city. Several test cases stand at the focal point of the discussion. The Royal Portico, whose construction at the southern flank of the Temple Mount was initiated by Herod, is used to exemplify Herod's role in introducing Roman cultural influence into the city. The 'Stepped Street', namely the main thoroughfare that crossed the city from south to north and was paved during Pontius Pilate's governorship, is briefly discussed to illustrate the continued development of the city under direct Roman rule. To demonstrate the uniqueness of Jerusalem, as a Temple city and pilgrimage centre, the characteristics of this street, together with various unique features of the pilgrimage roads leading to the city, are examined. These characteristics show the ways in which the pilgrims' spiritual experience was deliberately enhanced through architectural features. Allusions to the Temple Mount architecture in early Roman funerary art and architecture, as well as in synagogue liturgical furniture, are also discussed as manifestations of the devotion of Jews in Jerusalem and Judaea to their Temple through the transformation of the Temple Mount's architectural features into a sort of Jewish emblem.

Herod's major contribution on the Temple Mount: The Royal Portico

In the eighteenth year of his reign (*AJ* 15.380),[9] King Herod began his most ambitious building project – the expansion of the Temple Mount compound and the rebuilding of the Temple. This enormous endeavour expressed Herod's status, but also served to accommodate multitudes of pilgrims contributing to the prosperity of the city. Since the location of the Temple and size were predetermined by tradition, the improvements he could have introduced were restricted to the use of more expensive materials and a greater height of the edifice (*AJ* 15.385–87). A much more demanding part of the project was the expansion of the Temple Mount beyond the natural topographical boundaries of the underlying hill (Mount Moriah), towards the Tyropoeon Valley in the west and the Kidron Valley in the south-east. The temenos was also expanded to the north, while only the eastern wall remained as it was due to the steep slope leading towards the Kidron Valley. In order to create a levelled surface for the Temple Mount platform (480 m long, 280 m wide), massive enclosure walls were built to support earthen fills.[10] It seems that the enormous efforts invested in extending the Hasmonean enclosure towards the south, despite the difficult topographic conditions, were mainly meant to create sufficient space for the construction of the most unique contribution to the renovated temenos – the Royal Portico (Netzer 2006, 165).

The *Stoa Basileios*, or Royal Portico, built on the southern flank of the Temple Mount, is an example of a new type of structure introduced into Judaea as part of King Herod's building programme (Figs 9.1–2). According to Josephus' description of this edifice (*AJ* 15.411–16),[11] it was long and narrow (one stade, namely c. 600 feet long, and 105 feet wide), and its façade was an open colonnade facing the courtyard of the Temple Mount compound similarly to stoas in Greek agorai. Nevertheless, its interior design – including a tall and wide central nave flanked by two narrower and shallower side aisles – is typical of Roman basilicas.[12] This combination of characteristics of a Greek stoa and a Roman basilica appears in other examples in the East, the market basilica of Ephesus dated to Augustan times being the earliest in this group (Fossel-Peschl 1982; Gros 2012, 17). In Judaea, no basilica structure nor similar complex porticoes are securely identified prior to Herod's ascension to power.[13] Recent excavations have shown that Herod might have built a basilica structure at Ashqelon on the coast (Bar-Nathan and Ganor 2021), and various clues suggest that he might have done so also at Samaria/Sebaste[14] and Herodium.[15] However, the only certain example remains the Royal Portico in Jerusalem. As such, it stands as the earliest example of a basilical structure in Judaea and anticipates later appearances of 'proper' basilicas in the region.

Although the architectural features of the Royal Portico are described in detail by Josephus, he fails to give any indication of the building's function. Nevertheless, due to its basilical layout, it has been suggested that the portico served purposes that are normally connected to the Roman civic basilica (perhaps more than any other type of structure, the basilica symbolized the Roman city and civic life, and was mostly used for commercial, judicial, political, and social functions). Still, as the Royal Portico was an integral part of the Temple compound, scholars normally link these functions with specific needs related to the ritual at the Temple. For example, it was proposed that the Royal Portico was the space in which Jesus scattered the money changers' coins and overturned their tables and those of dove sellers (see, for instance, Matt. 21.12; Dalman 1919, 271; Klausner 1930, 433). Mazar (1986, 71–72) suggested associating the Royal Portico with the *hanuyut* (shops) that were located along the boundaries of the Temple Mount. According to the Rabbinical sources (Bavli *Shabbat*, 15a), this was the location where the seat of the Sanhedrin was moved to around 30 CE. Another suggestion, proposed by Netzer (2006, 170), is that the Portico, being outside of the sacred *halachic* precinct, served as a place to offer hospitality to the King's distinguished, and many times non-Jewish, guests.

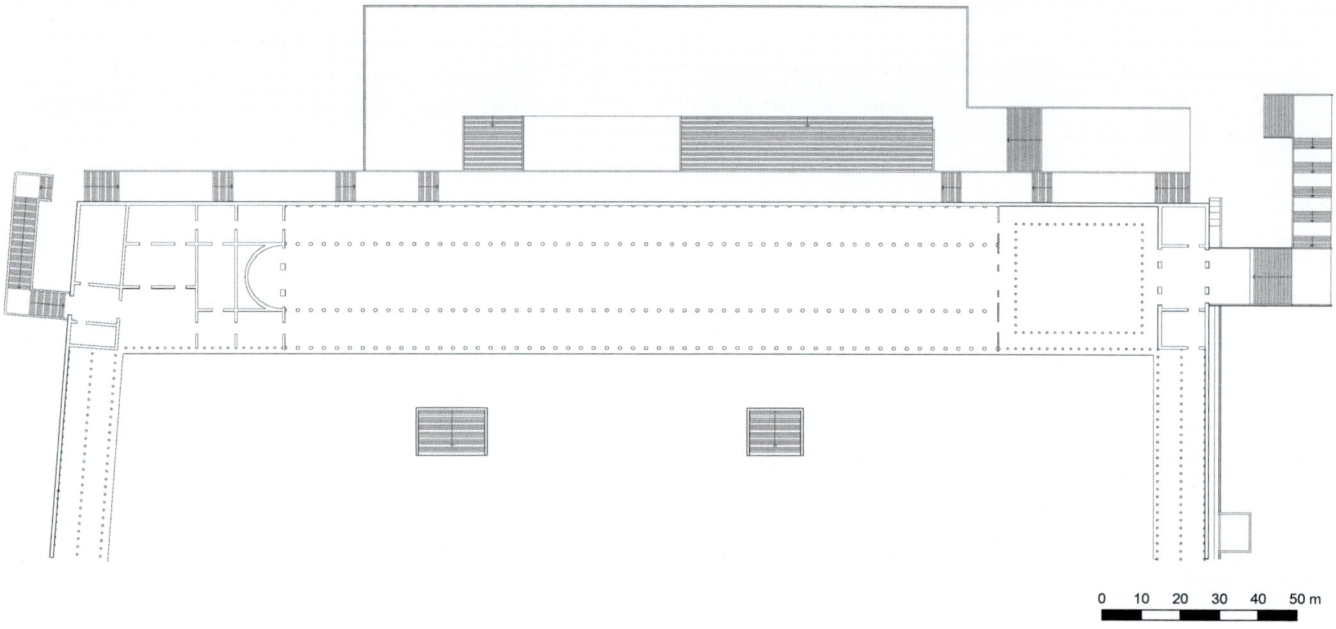

Fig. 9.1. Plan of the Royal Portico in Jerusalem (image D. Porotsky and M. Yagod).

Fig. 9.2. Reconstruction of the Royal Portico in Jerusalem, view from south-west (image S. Vinograd).

As to the motivation behind the addition of the Royal Portico to the renewed and expanded sanctuary, it was Foerster (1976, 980) who first suggested that the renovated Temple Mount compound with the Royal Portico's basilical structure on its southern flank derives from the architectural model of the 'Caesareum', which was well-known at the time of Herod and constituted a standard type of ritual and cultural centre, devoted mainly to the emperor's worship. According to literary sources and archaeological remains, the Caesareum complex consisted of a large temenos encircled with interior colonnades, a temple in the centre, and a basilica along one side (Mazar 1984, 145; 1986, 70; Ådna 1999, 36–50). The word 'Caesareum' (or καισάριον in Greek) was first used for the large compound in Alexandria (begun by Julius Caesar c. 48–47 BCE: Fishwick 1987, 62–72; McKenzie 2007, 177–78) by Strabo (17.1.9), who visited Alexandria in c. 25–20 BCE. Philo of Alexandria (first half of first century CE) describes it in more detail

(*Leg.* 22.150–51).[16] According to John Malalas (*Chronographia* 9.216), writing in the fifth century CE, Caesar erected a similar complex in Antioch, where he stayed for a short visit in 47 BCE. He built a basilica, which he named 'Kaisareion', in front of the temple of Mars of the *macellum* and set up there a bronze statue of Rome's Tyche (Sjökvist 1954, 86–94). Unfortunately, the complexes in Alexandria and Antioch have not survived. The plan of the Caesareum in Alexandria can be inferred from the plans of the temenoi of the Alexandrian Serapeum and Hermopolis Magna;[17] however, the earliest Caesareum to survive to date is the one at Cyrene. This complex, built in the second century BCE, originally served as the city's gymnasium and acquired the new name 'Caesareum' during the reign of Augustus. The compound at Cyrene includes a large courtyard surrounded by Doric porticoes and a (later) civic basilica on the north side (a small temple was also added in the middle of the courtyard in the Hadrianic period). The basilica has a central nave with two side aisles and a narrow narthex on the south-eastern end. At the other end of the building, there is a large apse with a screen wall and three openings (Smallwood 1952, 37–38; Ward-Perkins *et al.* 1958, 140, 168–81; Luni 1987; Trifogli 2014). It should be stressed, however, that the basilica is later than the Augustan compound and was added in a second phase, presumably in the Flavian period (Luni 1990, 101–20; on the architecture and date of this building see also Mugnai, this volume).[18]

The Royal Portico probably replaced a simpler portico from the Hasmonaean period that stood at the southern flank of the Hasmonaean compound. This readaptation of the portico into a basilica-like structure can be interpreted as a direct result of Roman influence, thus expressing a synthesis of Hellenistic architectural tradition with Roman aesthetic values.

Jerusalem under direct Roman rule: Continued building boom in the eastern part of the city

Until recently, despite clear hints in the New Testament and several passages in Josephus' writings (for instance, *BJ* 5.187; *AJ* 20.219; John 2.20), it was generally believed that King Herod lived to see the completion of not just the rebuilding of the Temple, but also the enlargement of the compound and the erection of the massive retaining walls.[19] Works that continued after his death were mostly referred to as pertaining to the surrounding porticoes, the streets and staircases leading to the Temple Mount and so forth. However, recent Israel Antiquities Authority excavations adjacent to the foundations of the southern part of the western enclosure wall of the Temple Mount have uncovered finds that, according to the excavators, suggest that the completion of the immense project of expanding the Temple Mount enclosure and building its retaining walls took place many years after Herod's death (Shukrun and Reich 2011; Shukrun 2012; Reich and Shukrun 2012). The excavation was carried out east of the drainage channel, which drained the Tyropoeon Valley underneath the main city thoroughfare and, in this section, ran parallel to the western enclosure wall of the Temple Mount. The excavators exposed several ritual baths, as well as other subterranean installations cut into the bedrock, all of which functioned as parts of basements of the houses that stood in this area prior to the expansion of the Temple Mount compound westwards. These houses were dismantled to make room for the new construction, and the rock-cut installations were filled in and sealed. Then several walls were built east of the drainage channel abutting the Western Wall. These walls supported fills that in turn served as the foundation for the paved street above. One of the installations discovered in this area was a *mikveh* (ritual bath) that was found filled and sealed below the foundations of the southern part of the Western Wall, right below Robinson's Arch. It probably originally belonged to the basement of a house that was dismantled once the works on the enlargement of the Temple Mount compound began. The fill of the *mikveh*, west of the Western Wall's foundation, contained eight coins that were all later than Herod's time. The latest of these coins were issued by the prefect Valerius Gratus under Tiberius and date to 17/18 CE. Other finds, including so-called Herodian lamps, attest to the *mikveh* being filled at least twenty years after Herod's death; therefore, the excavators suggest that the foundations of the Western Wall in this section were built even later (Shukrun 2012, 16–21).

The fact that it took so many years to complete Herod's massive enterprise is not surprising, taking into consideration the above-mentioned references in Josephus' writings and the New Testament that hint at a long duration of these renovations. This timeframe is also consistent with what is known about other large-scale projects in the eastern Roman Empire. For example, despite the fact that inscriptions date the Temple of Bel at Palmyra and the Temple of Jupiter Heliopolitanus at Baalbek respectively to 32 CE and to the second half of the first century CE, the planning of these structures and the carving of their architectural decoration are usually dated to a much earlier period in the late first century BCE and first half of the first century CE, respectively (see, for instance, Freyberger 1998, 69, 75). Other examples exist even in Rome, such as the Forum of Augustus, and Athens (Temple of Olympian Zeus). However, it should be noted that the excavations next to the foundations of the southern part of the western enclosure wall have not yet been fully published, and their implications for the date of other parts of the Herodian Temple Mount must still be assessed.

While the consequences of the *mikveh*'s excavations on the date of construction of the Western Wall's foundation are debated, it seems that recent archaeological excavations have proved beyond doubt that the street that ran along the Tyropoeon Valley should not be assigned to the time of Herod, but to the first century CE. The main thoroughfare of early Roman Jerusalem that connected the south-eastern gate and the Siloam Pool to the Temple Mount is remarkably well-preserved and was paved with enormous stone slabs (Fig. 9.3). The street itself (some 600 m long) is 7.5 m in width, but the presence of shops and other structures on both of its sides turns it into a much wider and dominant architectural feature within the city's urban layout. Underneath the street runs Jerusalem's '*cloaca maxima*', a massive partly built and partly hewn drainage channel that drains the Tyropoeon Valley and the buildings on both sides (Fig. 9.4). The paved street and channel have been known since the pioneering work of Ch. Warren (1884, 28–30). Later excavations (for instance, Mazar 1971, fig. 2; Reich and Billig 1999; Bahat 2013, 286–302) have recovered more data about the trajectory of the street and the details of its design, while its date has remained unclear with opinions ranging from the time of Herod to the time of Agrippa II (48 to 92 or 100 CE). Since 2013, the Israel Antiquity Authority has conducted excavations on a larger scale along the portion of the street from the Siloam Pool to the Temple Mount. These excavations have brought to light coins from sealed contexts under the street paving. In all the excavated areas, the latest coins from these fills date to the year 30/31 CE, namely from the time of Tiberius, thus in turn dating the street paving to the governorship of the fifth prefect of Judaea, Pontius Pilate (Szanton *et al.* 2019).[20] Especially significant is the lack of any coins from the time of Agrippa I, whose coins have been found in great numbers across the rest of the city.[21] The clear dating of the street paving to the days of Pontius Pilate matches both historical and archaeological evidence that attests to Pilate's investment in large-scale construction projects. Josephus recounts the incident in which Pilate spent money from the Temple's treasury to build an aqueduct (*BJ* 2.175). The text focuses on Pilate's cruelty, who had soldiers hidden among the crowd of Jews while addressing them, and when the Jews protested his actions, he gave the signal for his soldiers to randomly attack, beat, and kill people. However, Josephus and the Jewish petitioners in his recount fail to notice the positive side of his act, which was meant to fulfil the city's need for water supply. The famous inscription from Caesarea Maritima suggests that Pilate restored a monument in honour of the emperor Tiberius – a *Tiberieum* – in the capital of the province (*CIIP* II, 1277: identification of this building remains uncertain; see also Frova 1961; Alföldy 1999; Taylor 2006; Mugnai, this volume). The coins struck

Fig. 9.3. The Stepped Street leading from the Siloam Pool to the Temple Mount (photo A. Peretz, courtesy of Israel Antiquities Authority).

Fig. 9.4. The central drainage channel below the Stepped Street (photo Elef Millim Project, Wikipedia).

by Pilate with symbols that do not contain human figures in accordance with Jewish norms,[22] and the stability in the term of the high priest under his rule,[23] suggest on his behalf an aspiration for good relations with the Jewish population. He was certainly a dominant figure in the region and the excavators in Jerusalem suggested that he was the one who stood behind the construction of the street.[24]

Ascending by foot: Architecture designed to enhance the spiritual experience of pilgrims to the Temple in Jerusalem

Since movement is passing from one place to another, its nature is temporary, and it does not leave any record when completed. However, movement is acted out in a material setting and is directly affected by the physical shape of the surrounding environment and factors such as topography, weather, and vegetation. The use of specific architectural elements and spatial arrangements can influence, encourage, enable, or prevent patterns of movement.[25] The case of the pilgrims' movement towards Jerusalem as well as their movement within the city towards the Temple is especially telling.

The pilgrimage obligation in Judaism derives from the commandment to visit the Temple in Jerusalem 'three times a year' on the three festivals: 'on the Feast of Unleavened Bread, on the Feast of Weeks, and on the Feast of the Tabernacles' (*Deut.* 16.16). Historical sources from the early Roman period, such as the writings of Philo of Alexandria (*Spec.* 1.69), show that pilgrimage was practiced in this period by many of the Jews in Judaea and across the diaspora, who made their journey by land and sea (Magness 2022). Nevertheless, leaving one's home was not always possible and the long journey was hard and dangerous. Some Jews, therefore, managed to make the trip only once in their lifetime or none at all. The rabbinical sources (M. *Shekalim*, 1.1) state that to ease the pilgrims' journey – in preparation for the multitudes that were anticipated to flock into the city on Passover – the authorities of Jerusalem repaired the roads and water pools and marked the graves, as to prevent pilgrims from coming too near and becoming impure. Two recent studies have focused on two of these architectural aspects of pilgrimage to the city, namely the pilgrimage roads leading to the city and their special features, and the open water pools in the periphery of the city, whose existence and large number are unique.

A recent study (Tepper and Tepper 2013) has suggested identifying the specific routes taken by pilgrims to Jerusalem in the late Second Temple Period. This research focused on the distribution of ascents with steps cut into the bedrock (Fig. 9.5), showing that these ascents were more widespread than previously acknowledged and were most common in the Judaean mountains, but also existed in other parts of Judaea, the Galilee, and Negev. In all cases they were cut along roads leading to Jerusalem. In many cases the roads crossed close to natural fountains or other sources of water, while in other cases artificial water reservoirs were cut to fulfil the needs of the people on the road. Although these ascents are most difficult to date, their distribution, as well as the fact that ritual baths were found around some of them (not connected to any settlement or agricultural installation: Amit 1999), would prove their relation to the pilgrimage roads towards Jerusalem in late Second Temple Period, namely the early Roman period. Tepper and Tepper (2013, 26, fig. 6) rejected the previous notion that these ascents were an integral part of the imperial roads paved across the province mostly after the first and second Jewish Revolts (as argued, for instance, by Kloner 1996; Roll 2005), since many of the ascents are cut on secondary roads and are thus unlikely to have been paved by Roman soldiers. Also, such stepped ascents are not a common feature of Roman roads, which normally have a moderate slope and overcome topographic obstacles by using serpentine roads or bridges (von Hagen 1967; Radke 1971). Clearly, the steps were added not to make the ascent easier for road users, as sometimes the slope was moderate and did not necessitate the cutting of the steps. It seems that the cutting of the steps stemmed not from a physical need of the people walking along the road to Jerusalem but was done to fulfil a ceremonial or spiritual need (Tepper and Tepper 2013, 202–3).[26] The sets of steps scattered along the pilgrimage routes to Jerusalem reminded pilgrims of their destination and purpose. As is discussed below, such steps continued to shape the experience of pilgrims also after entering the city itself.

Once the city was in view, the pilgrims could notice the great number of open water pools, mostly on the outskirts or immediately beyond the city walls. David Gurevich (2017) dates nine of these pools to the late Hellenistic or early Roman periods, based on archaeological and historical evidence. Such a large number of open pools has no equivalent in any other cities across the Mediterranean and attests to the

Fig. 9.5. Stepped ascent along the road leading from Jericho to Jerusalem (photo Y. Tepper).

special measures adopted by the city administration to fulfil the needs of the thousands of pilgrims that flocked in the city during the holidays. While most of the pools served as water reservoirs with secondary functions (for instance, Tacitus says they were used in times of siege: *Hist.* 5.12.1), two of them – the Bethesda Pools north of the Temple Mount and the Siloam Pool in the south-eastern part of the city – served for mass ritual bathing, as attested by both the New Testament and the wide staircases leading down to their bottom. The latter one was especially important for two reasons; it was fed from the only natural spring in Jerusalem, the Gihon Fountain, and was adjacent to the main entrance to the city from the south-east. Indeed, entry into the city was possible from all sides but the topography of the city's surroundings, with the Kidron Valley to the east and Hinnom Valley to the south-west and south, naturally drew many of the worshippers to the main southern gate situated in the south-eastern part of the city by the Siloam Pool.[27] To the north of this pool a colonnaded promenade was unearthed, connecting the pool to the main thoroughfare that ran along the Tyropoeon Valley and connected the pool to the Temple Mount. Two main features mark the special character of the road. The first is the presence of many steps along it, making movement on carriages and wagons extremely uncomfortable. The second is the lack of sidewalks on both sides of the street. Only a narrow kerbstone separates the street pavement from the entrance to the shops and buildings on both sides (Szanton *et al.* 2019, 152). These two characteristics are uncommon in streets of major cities of the Roman period and attest to the fact that the street was mostly meant for pedestrians, so sidewalks were not a critical necessity. It was suggested by the excavators that the street was used during the holidays by pilgrims ascending to the Temple (Reich and Shukrun 2011; Szanton *et al.* 2019, 147). Ascension was an important element of the experience, as is attested by the rabbinical sources, which also recount the water libation ceremony on the Feast of Tabernacles that included a procession bearing water from the Siloam Pool to the Temple – a procession that most certainly passed through this street once it was paved (M *Parah* 3, 2).[28]

Pilgrims climbing up the stepped street finally reached their destination when they arrived at the Temple Mount's south-western corner (Fig. 9.6). Here, the layout of the street changed. The steps would disappear, and far more organized and monumentalized rows of shops and other structures appeared on both sides. This part of the street could easily host wheeled traffic and larger crowds of people flocking to the Temple from other parts of the city. To enable the continuation of movement in this crowded environment and to maintain the purity of the pilgrims, who were very close to reaching the Temple precinct, a brilliant and extraordinary solution was devised; instead of trying to squeeze walkways on the street level on both its sides, a sidewalk, which could be reached through a flight of steps, was laid on top of the row of shops that were built against the western and southern enclosure walls of the Temple Mount (Reich and Billig 1999, 33–40). The pilgrims who wished to reach the Temple would climb this flight of steps and walk a few meters above the hustling street level, which would elevate them from the profane crowd and let them one step closer on their ascension to the Temple (Fig. 9.7).

Going eastwards along the Southern Wall one would reach a plaza in front of some more steps leading to the southern

Fig. 9.6. A reconstruction of the Herodian Temple Mount looking north-east (image L. Ritmeyer).

Fig. 9.7. The steps leading to the walkway on top of the shops that abut the Temple Mount's Western Wall (photo courtesy of www.HolyLandPhotos.org).

Fig. 9.8. The steps at the foot of the Double Gate/Western Hulda Gate south of the Temple Mount (photo Wikimedia Commons).

Fig. 9.9. North-western dome of the Double Gate vestibule, looking south (photo O. Peleg-Barkat).

gates of the Temple compound (Netzer 2006, 174). The Double Gate or the Western Huldah Gate with its simple façade probably served as the main exit (Fig. 9.8), while the wider eastern Gate ('Triple Gate' or eastern 'Hulda Gate') with its adorned doorframe served as the main entrance (Peleg-Barkat 2017, 77, fig. 2.5).[29] The shallow domes inside the underground passageway behind the Double Gate are the only decorated architectural features of the Herodian Temple precinct that survive *in situ*, attesting to the grandeur of this building and the amount of funding that was invested in the construction (Fig. 9.9; Peleg-Barkat 2017, 121–68). Such monumental and exquisite decorations that many of the pilgrims arriving from small peripheral villages were not accustomed to, would have affected their experience and remained vivid in their memory after returning home. Jerusalem's residents, who knew the architecture of their sanctuary very well, must have also admired the quality and liveliness of these decorations. Indeed, we seem to find echoes of this admiration in their burial caves, sarcophagi, and ossuaries.

Allusions to the Temple precinct in funerary art and synagogue liturgical furniture

Several examples of allusions to the Temple and Temple Mount exist in the necropolis of Jerusalem, where the art decorating certain tombs imitated specific architectural features of the Herodian Temple Mount. Thus, for example, the façade of the so-called 'Umm el-Amad' tomb north-west of the city is decorated with carved ashlar blocks with drafted margins similar to the ones on the enclosure walls of the Temple Mount (Fig. 9.10).[30] There are several contemporary ossuaries decorated with carvings imitating courses of ashlars with drafted margins as well.[31] Two of Jerusalem's rock-cut Jewish tombs of the first century CE have shallow domes carved into their ceilings with decorations reminiscent of the domes of the Double Gate mentioned above. One such dome is carved into the ceiling of Chamber VI of the 'Grape-Clusters Tomb' in northern Jerusalem, and the second dome is carved into the ceiling of the main chamber in the 'Tomb of Annas, the High Priest' in Aceldama (Fig. 9.11; Ritmeyer and Ritmeyer 1994, 32–33). In the latter example, in the centre of the dome among acanthus calyces on the pendentives, there is a large radial rosette that creates a composition similar to that of the north-western dome inside the Double Gate passageway. There is little doubt that the artists who decorated these tombs were inspired by what they saw at the southern gate of the Temple Mount. It may be assumed that for people at the time, these imitations would have evoked the memory of the Temple Mount. They are therefore indications of the Temple-oriented identity of the tombs' owners.

A discovery in the town of Magdala near the Sea of Galilee, north of Tiberias, provides a striking example of how Jews used visual media in a conscious way in the period prior to the Temple's destruction. At this site,

Fig. 9.10. Eastern end of the façade of the so-called 'Umm el-Amad' tomb, Jerusalem (photo O. Peleg-Barkat).

Fig. 9.11. Large rosette carved into the ceiling of the 'Tomb of Annas', Aceldama, Jerusalem (photo L. Matassa).

Fig. 9.12. The Magdala Stone. A: General view showing one long side with an arcade and a circular object resembling a (Herodian?) oil lamp; B: Short side with the menorah flanked by two amphorae, and tabletop with a large rosette (photo Y. Yolovitch, courtesy of Israel Antiquities Authority).

a first-century CE synagogue decorated with mosaics and wall paintings was unearthed (Avshalom-Gorni and Najar 2013). On its floor a curious rectangular limestone block (the Magdala Stone) was found adorned on all sides with floral, architectonic, and other non-figurative motifs (Fig. 9.12). These motifs represent architectural features and objects that were clearly connected with the Temple in Jerusalem. The block was presumably used to place upon it the Torah scroll when the reading of the Torah in the synagogue was halted (Amit 2013, 174–75; Weiss 2021). A seven-branched menorah was carved on one of the short sides of the block, and this is the first representation of a menorah to be found in a late Second Temple-era synagogue. The amphorae that flank the menorah and what is perhaps the inner altar, within an architectural frame, resemble amphorae or vases that appear, albeit quite rarely, on contemporary ossuaries from Jerusalem.[32] On the other two sides of the block, inside an arcade, is what the excavators identified as a depiction of an oil lamp with a flame. The significance of oil lamps and their connection in Jewish eyes to Jerusalem is reflected in the 'Herodian, wheel-made knife-pared' lamp type, which was shown in a study by David Adan-Bayewitz *et al.* (2008, 37–85) to have had great significance for the Jewish inhabitants of Judaea. An analysis of the clay fabric has revealed that in Jewish sites the great majority of the Herodian-type lamps were brought from Jerusalem, while in pagan sites they were locally made. The context of these carved lamps and their proximity to the carved menorah attest to their symbolic significance, which was probably related to Jerusalem and the Temple.

Scholars have suggested relating the arcades and other architectural features depicted on the stone to the architecture of the Temple and its precinct.[33] The entire composition is therefore comparable with one of the most popular depictions on late Roman and Byzantine synagogue mosaics: an architectural façade flanked by a menorah, with each menorah in turn flanked by a shofar, the Four Species, and other Jewish motifs connected with the Temple. Scholars have linked this type of façade with that of the former Temple, the future Temple, or the Torah ark of the synagogue itself.[34] Thanks to the finds from Magdala, it can be suggested that the tradition of depicting the Temple inside the prayer hall of a synagogue probably began prior to the Temple's destruction, during the late Second Temple Period. It was a four- to six-day dangerous walk from Galilee to the Temple in Jerusalem, and not everyone could make this pilgrimage. However, feelings towards the Temple were strong and led the Galileans, at least those belonging to the community of Magdala, to carve a design of their own symbolic temple on this stone.

Conclusions

It is well agreed among scholars that by the later Second Temple Period Jews had developed a collective identity with a significant degree of cultural and religious commonality and a growing repertoire of historical memories. The linchpin of this commonality was the centrality and importance of the Jerusalem Temple. By the first century CE, we read of pilgrims flocking to the Temple from across the Roman Empire and contributing large sums of money to it as well. The power of the Temple lay in its singularity. Jerusalem had but one Temple, dedicated to the God of Israel, and the God of Israel had but one Temple, in Jerusalem. This intense focus and exclusivity generated much devotion among Jews towards their sacred site. Therefore, the Jews' expression of this devotion through visual media should come as no surprise. The fact that the inhabitants of Jerusalem themselves took active part in the completion of the expansion of the Temple compound initiated by Herod is now evident thanks to the results of recent excavations that date the completion of this expansion decades after Herod's death. The results also hint at the involvement of the Roman administration, especially under Pontius Pilate, in paving the main thoroughfare of the city leading towards the Temple and adding to the water supply of the city.

As much as Jerusalem was a thriving city in the first century CE, with monumental buildings adorned in Classical style, and Roman-style traffic routes, drainage systems, and waste collection mechanisms, its Jewish character was clear to everyone. No statues decorated the streets and monuments, and only one temple stood within its walls. Specific construction projects and adaptations of the city's architecture to the needs of the pilgrims were represented by the many open pools built on its outskirts, the special raised walkways in the vicinity to the Temple that were meant to assist the pilgrims in maintaining their purity, and the special stepped roads leading into the city and within the city itself that enhanced the pilgrims' sense of ceremonial festivity while making their way to the holy precinct.

Notes

1. For a thorough survey and discussion of Herod's construction projects see Netzer 2006. For an updated survey of Herod's palaces see Netzer 2018. For further discussions on Herod's building programme and the ideology it reflected, see Roller 1998; Lichtenberger 1999; Japp 2000; Richardson and Fisher 2018.
2. Three different identifications have been proposed for the location of this temple: see Netzer 2006, 218–22; Overman and Schowalter 2011; Berlin 2015.
3. Netzer 2006, 314–15. A small portion of a reticulate masonry wall is also preserved in Caesarea Maritima's promontory palace, but this is probably post-Herodian in date (Lichtenberger 2009, 50, n. 38).
4. One should note that the writing of Josephus is sometimes characterized by a tendency towards dramatization and exaggeration (Kasher and Witztum 2007, 7–8).
5. The excavations, whose results are briefly discussed here, are mostly salvage or development-led excavations, conducted by the Israel Antiquities Authority west and south of the Temple Mount. I refer here mainly to the excavations in the 'Western Wall Tunnels' (west of the Temple Mount), 'Davidson's Centre/ Temple Mount Archaeological Park' (south and south-west of the Temple Mount), and at the City of David. Most of these digs have not yet produced final excavation reports, but only preliminary accounts, in some cases available only in Hebrew. Despite political controversies (some of the excavations are funded by the right-wing 'Ir David Foundation' that aims to strengthen the Jewish connection to Jerusalem and to renew the Jewish community in the City of David, which is also part of the Arab neighbourhood of Silwan) and sometimes professional criticism (some of the excavations are conducted below ground, inside tunnels, instead of the normal practice of excavating from surface to bedrock) of several of the digs (see, for instance, Kletter 2019), many of these excavations have led to unexpected findings that change the way we understand Herodian Jerusalem and therefore cannot be overlooked.
6. Still, villages in general, and Judaean villages in particular, are often depicted as being more religiously and ethnically homogeneous than cities, which are seen as more diverse and economically stratified. Imported pottery is especially rare outside of Jerusalem, but apparently this was mainly due to Halachic reasons (see, for instance, Killebrew 2010, 195).
7. It should be stated that this negative approach towards figurative art reflects a sharp shift in Jewish habits during the Hasmonaean period and comes after almost a millennium during which the use of figural art was widespread, if not

dominant in Jewish society. Scholars have raised various explanations as to why this occurred under the Hasmonaeans. Some promoted Sadducean (Smith 1967, 60) or Pharisaic (Frey 1934, 274; Goodenough 1953–68, vol. 1: 132; vol. 4: 11) influence, while others treated it as a wider phenomenon reflecting either a reaction against Hellenization and foreign influences (Cohen 1954, 167), or as a traumatic reaction to the 167 BCE desecration of the Temple by Antiochus IV (Avigad 1976, 277–78). More recently, Levine (2005, 11–16) has argued that the reason for this change may lie in the particular importance of the role played by the Book of Deuteronomy in shaping Hasmonaean policy.

8. Exceptions are rare and prove the rule. Apart from two examples of frescoes from Jerusalem and Herodium that depict birds (Broshi 1976, 84–85, pl. 19; Corbo 1989, pl. 5) and a table decorated with a fish relief (Avigad 1983, fig. 185.4), the most significant example of figurative art in this period comes from the royal box of the small theatre on the slopes of Herodium, decorated with painted hanging pictures featuring various landscapes that include animals and humans (Rozenberg 2013, 179–89).
9. Although Herod was announced king of Judaea already in 40 BCE, it was only in 37 BCE that he gained control over Jerusalem and became king *de facto*. If we count his reign as beginning in 37 BCE, the eighteenth year of his reign was 19/20 BCE. However, according to *BJ* 1.401, Herod began building the Temple in the fifteenth year of his reign, that is, in 22/23 BCE. According to Schürer (1973, I: 369, n. 12), the earlier date probably refers to initial preparations and not to the construction itself.
10. The architecture of the Herodian Temple Mount compound and of the Temple itself has been discussed in many scholarly works by historians, archaeologists, engineers and others, from de Vogüé (1864) and Warren (1884) in the nineteenth century to Reidinger (2004) and Netzer (2006, 137–78) more recently. These scholars have proposed various reconstructions of the Temple Mount compound, as well as the Second Temple, based on the archaeological findings and descriptions in the writings of Josephus and the Mishnah. The dearth of remains and the contradictions among historical sources have led to various problems with each of these reconstructions.
11. Even though none of its masonry survives *in situ*, the elaborate description of the edifice by Flavius Josephus has allowed for many scholarly attempts at reconstructing the building's plan and elevation (see, for instance, the most recent ones in Gros 2005; Netzer 2006, 165–71; Cabaret 2018). In a previous study (Peleg-Barkat 2017; 2019), I have presented a new reconstruction proposal, which was based for the first time on architectural fragments found at the foot of the southern enclosure wall of the Temple Mount. These previously ignored pieces of columns, column bases, friezes, and cornices come in high probability from the Royal Portico, according to their findspot in the destruction debris, as well as their size and stylistic features.
12. The basilica appears in the archeological record later than the portico. Unlike the portico, the basilica is generally a closed structure, thus offering better protection against weather and noise from the street. These advantages were possible thanks to the development of clerestory windows and improvements in roof construction, allowing more light into the inner hall and avoiding the clutter thanks to the large number of columns. On the development of the portico, basilica, and connection between the two, see Ward-Perkins 1954, 69–71; Coulton 1976, 180–83.
13. It should be mentioned that Yotam Tepper (1999) suggested identification of a basilica in Seleucid Beth Yeraḥ/Philoteria, south-west of the Sea of Galilee. However, this is a rather small structure (~10 × 15 m) with eight crudely built internal supports replacing a Ptolemaic-period complex of eight small rooms, identified as shops, and no remains of a nearby agora have been identified.
14. Although the excavators dated the colonnades of the basilica and forum at Samaria/Sebaste to the end of the second century CE, they noted that the supporting walls of the forum were built much earlier, during the Herodian period. This led them to suggest that the forum and basilica had been already built under Herod; however, their exact layout is unclear (Crowfoot *et al.* 1942, 31–90; Segal 2017, 418–19). This early date is supported by large-scale Herodian architectural decorative elements that can be seen today on the site of the basilica (author's personal observation).
15. The 'Large Palace' at Lower Herodium is poorly preserved. Contrary to Ehud Netzer's proposal to identify the remains of the large rectangular complex south of the Course and Pool Complex as palatial quarters (Netzer 2006, 190, fig. 40), the current Herodium Expedition proposes to identify it as an elongated basilica (personal correspondence with Roi Porat). This identification is based on the plan of the massive foundation of this edifice.
16. According to Philo, several 'Caesarea' were known in his day, the most beautiful of which was the one in Alexandria, built by the harbour. It comprised a large compound surrounded with porticoes that held libraries, gardens, halls, open exedras, and courtyards. Inside the compound itself a temple was built in honour of Julius Caesar as the successor of the Ptolemaic rulers. Pliny the Elder mentions two large obelisks, the so-called 'Cleopatra's Needles', which were placed by the temple of Julius Caesar not far from the harbour (*HN* 36.14.69; Sjökvist 1954, 95–98; Ward-Perkins *et al.* 1958, 137; McKenzie 2007, 177).
17. The plan of the Caesareum complex in Alexandria probably originated in an earlier compound dedicated to Ptolemaic ruler cult. A somewhat similar sanctuary from the times of Ptolemy III Euergetes (246–221 BCE) was discovered in Hermopolis Magna (el-Ashmunein). It consists of an elongated rectangular temenos with interior Doric porticoes and the approach along the main axis to a mixed Doric-Corinthian temple at its centre (McKenzie 2007, 56–58, figs 74–78). Another complex, which might have set the example for the plan of the Caesareum and is actually the closest to the Herodian Temple Mount, though smaller in size, is the Serapeum of Alexandria, also built by Ptolemy III. The temenos of the Serapeum had simple colonnades around three sides and a stoa across the south side. Similarly to the Temple Mount, the entrances are not on the axis of the temple itself due to topographical reasons (McKenzie *et al.* 2004, 81–84, fig. 8).
18. It should be mentioned that the Herodian Temple Mount with its Royal Portico shares similar characteristics with a

group of urban compounds in the eastern Mediterranean with similar ground plans, which include a courtyard surrounded by porticoes with a rather narrow basilica structure running along one side (albeit with no temple in the centre). The state agora of Ephesus, which dates to the reign of Augustus, is the earliest in this group; other examples, such as the agorai of Cremna and Smyrna, date to the second century CE (Winter 2006, 51–64).

19. See, for example, Warszawaski and Peretz 1992 with a detailed estimation on the workforce needed to complete the works in just eight years, in accordance with Josephus (*AJ* 15.420) who states that Herod would 'busy himself' with the construction of the porticoes and outer courts, and these he finished building in eight years.
20. Traditionally, Pontius Pilate's governorship is dated to 26–37 CE; however, several scholars have suggested that both historical sources and numismatic evidence point to a much earlier date for the start of his term around 18 or 19 CE (see Schwartz 1992, 182–217; Lönnqvist 2014, 4–5).
21. In the 1990s, when excavating the paved street at the foot of the Western Wall below Robinson's Arch, several coins were discovered in a test pit underneath one of the street's paving stones; the latest of these coins could be dated to the year 29/30 CE. Still, the excavators (Reich and Billig 1999, 35) proposed that a repaving of the street took place under Agrippa II, as suggested by Josephus (*AJ* 20.219–22).
22. See, for instance, Lönnqvist 2014, who also suggests that archeometallurgical examination of Pilate's coins shows a reduction of the lead component in the metal alloy, and this should be connected to the need to use lead for the pipes of the aqueduct built at that time in Jerusalem. A recent study by Yechezkel *et al.* 2021 has dated construction of the Biar Shaft Tunnel (part of the Upper-Level Aqueduct of Jerusalem) to around the mid-first century CE, based on C^{14} dating of charcoal found in plaster samples from the tunnel. This timeframe is certainly consistent with the historical sources that link the construction of an aqueduct with Pontius Pilate.
23. During Pilate's office as prefect there was a single high priest that served in office, while his predecessor Valerius Gratus had replaced the men in this office four times (*AJ* 18.33–35).
24. Another surprising discovery that attests to municipal administration in first-century CE Jerusalem came from the southern part of the eastern slope of the City of David, where a massive landfill from early Roman times was excavated (Gadot 2022). This landfill was identified as the result of a most sophisticated garbage collection system, which could be dated through coins and fragments of pottery from the early first century CE to the time of the First Revolt. The landfill rose to a towering height, from the bottom of the valley to the walls of the city. Ancient examples of similar large-scale collection and long-term storage of garbage in a landfill are scarce, even though garbage disposal was always a chronic problem, especially in large cities. The alternating layers of garbage and soil suggest there was a deliberate attempt to systematically cover the garbage to prevent unpleasant smells and to deter scavengers. The excavators suggest that there was a mechanism in place to clear streets and houses, using perhaps donkeys to collect and throw away the garbage. This system might have developed out of a combination of Roman administration experience and a growing observance among Jews of religious purity norms.
25. In recent decades, a growing research interest to explore movement and the flow of people has developed in the social sciences; see, for instance, Tim Cresswell (2011) who promoted a New Mobilities Paradigm that aims to gain further insights into the social implications of movement and into the processes that enable, prevent, and shape mobilities.
26. Support to the claim that steps had a special sanctity in Jewish thought and beliefs can be found in many of the biblical references that attribute a certain importance or sanctity to stepped ascents, such as those leading to the altar in the Temple or to King Solomon's throne (Exod. 20.26; 1 Kings. 10.19–20).
27. The pool was discovered in 2004. Excavations showed that steps existed on at least three sides of the pool; there are three sets of five steps, two leading to a platform, before the bottom is reached, and it has been suggested that the steps were designed to accommodate various water levels. The pool is stone-lined, but underneath there is evidence of an earlier phase that was merely plastered and dated by coins to no earlier than the start of the first century BCE. The second phase, with its stone paving, was dated to the first half of the first century CE – another testimony to the hectic construction activities that took place in the city in this period (Reich and Shukron 2011, 245).
28. Another stepped element along the route of the street is an impressive pyramid-shaped staircase located in a place that is clearly visible from afar by passers-by making their way to the Temple (Szanton and Uziel 2015). The excavators suggested identifying the monument as a podium that attracted the public's attention when walking on the city's main street, but whose exact function remains an enigma due to the lack of parallels. One possible suggestion is to identify it according to later rabbinic sources as the 'Stone of Claims' that existed in Jerusalem in this period and functioned as a sort of lost-and-found desk (*Bava Metzia* 28.B).
29. This proposal matches the information provided by the Rabbinical sources, which explain that one of the southern gates functioned as entrance and the other as exit: 'whosoever it was that entered the Temple Mount came in on the right and went round and came out on the left' (M *Middoth* 2, 2).
30. The tomb known as the 'Umm el-Amad Cave' is a rock-cut tomb with a *distylos in antis* façade that was carved in the Wadi Ramot to the north of ancient Jerusalem (Avigad 1945, 75–82). Another example of such carvings comes from a site called Deir ed-Derb (Qarawat Bani Hassan) in western Samaria, 40 km south-west of Nablus. The walls of this tomb's entrance hall are all carved with 'imitation' courses of ashlars with drafted margins (Magen 2008, 149–53, fig. 23).
31. Rahmani 1994, nos. 34, 217, 353, 420, 455, 481, 668, 730. For a general discussion see Jacobson 2000, 135–54.
32. Rahmani (1994, 34, nos. 213, 325, 378, 399) claims that their depiction on the ossuaries originates from the amphorae that surmounted some of Jerusalem's tomb monuments, such as 'Herod's Family Tomb' and the 'Tomb of Absalom', which are similar to those on the contemporary tombs of Nabataean Petra. Amphorae also appear on Jewish coinage, for example on coins minted during the second and third years of the First

Revolt against the Romans and on coins struck during the Bar-Kokhba Revolt. Scholars suggested that the amphorae on these coins represent the vessels containing wine or oil used in the Temple service: see, for instance, Meshorer 2001, 121, 146–47.

33. Both Aviam (2013, 207–16) and Talgam (at a talk presented at the Hebrew University on 29 May 2014) suggested identifying the arcades on the long sides of the stone as the porticoes of the Temple precinct, and the other motifs as vessels used in the Temple ritual.
34. Such depictions exist, for example, on the mosaic floors of the synagogues at Hammat Tiberias, Beit Alpha, and Sepphoris. Some scholars believe that such scenes depict actual synagogue arks flanked by a menorah on either side (for instance, Sloane 1934, 1–12), while according to others, these depictions were linked to the Temple and its cult, and in artistic terms signify the messianic longing for the rebuilding of the land and the Temple (for instance, Revel-Neher 1986–87, 135–46).

References

Adan-Bayewitz, D., Asaro, F., Wieder, M. and Giauque, R.D. 2008. Preferential distribution of lamps from the Jerusalem area in the Late Second Temple Period (late first century B.C.E. – 70 C.E.). *Bulletin of the American Schools of Oriental Research* 350: 37–85.

Ådna, J. 1999. *Jerusalemer Tempel und Tempelmarkt im 1. Jahrhundert n. Chr.* Wiesbaden: Harrassowitz Verlag.

Alföldy, G. 1999. Pontius Pilatus und das Tiberieum von Caesarea Maritima. *Scripta Classica Israelica* 18: 85–198.

Amit, D. 1999. A Miqveh complex near Alon Shevut. *'Atiqot* 38: 75–84.

Amit, D. 2013. Between form and function: the evolution of the synagogue as an institution from the Second Temple Period through Late Roman and Byzantine periods as reflected in changes in architectural and interior designs. In Zissu, B. (ed.), *Jerusalem and Eretz-Israel* 8–9 *(Studies in Honour of Amos Kloner)*. Ramat-Gan: The Ingeborg Rennert Center for Jerusalem Studies, Bar Ilan University, 166–71.

Aviam, M. 2011. Socio-economic hierarchy and its economic foundations in first century Galilee: the evidence from Yodefat and Gamla. In Mor, M., Stern, P. and Pastor, J. (eds), *Flavius Josephus: Interpretation and History*. Boston-Leiden: Brill, 29–38.

Aviam, M. 2013. The decorated stone from the synagogue at Midgal: a holistic interpretation and a glimpse into the life of Galilean Jews at the time of Jesus. *Novum Testamentum* 55: 205–20.

Avigad, N. 1945. The Umm al-'Amad Cave. *Qedem* 2: 75–82. [Hebrew]

Avigad, N. 1976. *Beth She'arim: Report on the Excavations during 1953–1958. Catacombs 12–23*. Tel Aviv: Masada Press.

Avigad, N. 1983. *Discovering Jerusalem*. Nashville: Thomas Nelson.

Avshalom-Gorni, D. and Najar, A. 2013. Migdal. *Hadashot Arkheologiyot – ESI* 125: www.hadashot-esi.org.il/report_detail_eng.aspx?id=2304&mag_id=120.

Bahat, D. 2013. *The Jerusalem Western Wall Tunnel*. Jerusalem: Israel Exploration Society.

Bar-Nathan, R. and Ganor, S. 2021. The basilica of Ashkelon between Herod and the Severan dynasty. In Dell'Acqua, A. and Peleg-Barkat, O. (eds), *The Basilica in Roman Palestine. Adoption and Adaptation Processes, in Light of Comparanda in Italy and North Africa*. Rome: Quasar, 109–31.

Berlin, A.M. 2015. Herod, Augustus, and the Augusteum at the Paneion. *Eretz-Israel* 31: 1–11.

Broshi, M. 1976. Excavations on Mount Zion, 1971–1972. *Israel Exploration Journal* 26: 81–88.

Broshi, M. 1987. The role of the temple in the Herodian economy. *Journal of Jewish Studies* 38: 31–37.

Cabaret, D.M. 2018. La basilique royale du temple hérodien selon Flavius Josèphe et les dernières découvertes archéologiques. *Revue Biblique* 125: 57–89.

Cohen, B. 1954. Art in Jewish law. *Judaism* 3–2: 165–76.

Corbo, V.C. 1989. *Herodion: gli edifici della reggia-fortezza*. Jerusalem: Franciscan Printing Press.

Coulton, J.J. 1976. *The Architectural Development of the Greek Stoa*. Oxford: Clarendon Press.

Creswell, T. 2011. Mobilities I: catching up. *Progress in Human Geography* 35.4: 550–58.

Crowfoot, J.W., Kenyon, K.M. and Sukenik, E.L. 1942. *Samaria-Sebaste I: The Buildings at Samaria*. London: Palestine Exploration Fund.

Dalman, G.H. 1919. *Orte und Wege Jesu*. Gütersloh: Bertelsmann.

de Vogüé, C.J.M. 1864. *Le Temple de Jérusalem*: *Monographie du Haram ech-Cherif*. Paris: Noblet & Baudry.

Fishwick, D. 1987. The Caesareum at Alexandria again. *American Journal of Ancient History* 12: 62–72.

Foerster, G. 1976. Art and architecture in Palestine. In Safrai, S. and Stern, M. (eds), *The Jewish People in the First Century, 2: Historical Geography, Political History, Social, Cultural and Religious Life and Institutions*. Assen: Fortress Press, 971–1006.

Foerster, G. 1998. Sarcophagus production in Jerusalem from the beginning of the common era up to 70 C.E. In Koch, G. (ed.), *Akten des Symposiums '125 Jahre Sarkophag-Corpus' (Marburg, 4–7 Oktober 1995)*. Mainz: Philipp von Zabern, 295–310.

Fossel-Peschl, E.A. 1982. *Die Basilika am Staatsmarkt in Ephesos*. Graz: Selbstverlag.

Frey, J.-B. 1934. La question des images chez les Juifs à la lumière des récentes découvertes. *Biblica* 15: 265–300.

Freyberger, K.S. 1998. *Die frühkaiserzeitlichen Heiligtümer der Karawanenstationen im hellenisierten Osten – Zeugnisse eines kulturellen Konflikts im Spannungsfeld zweier politischer Formationen*. Mainz: Philipp von Zabern.

Frova, A. 1961. *L'iscrizione di Ponzio Pilato a Cesarea*. Milan: Istituto Lombardo di Scienze e Lettere.

Gadot, Y. 2022. *The Landfill of Early Roman Jerusalem: The 2013–2014 Excavations in Area D3*. Jerusalem: Ancient Jerusalem Publications.

Geiger, J. 2009. Rome and Jerusalem: public building and the economy. In Jacobson, D.M. and Kokkinos, N. (eds), *Herod and Augustus: Papers Presented at the IJS Conference, 21st–23rd June 2005*. Boston-Leiden: Brill, 157–70.

Goodenough, E.R. 1953–68. *Jewish Symbols in the Greco-Roman Period* (13 vols.). New York: Pantheon Books.

Gros, P. 2005. La basilique d'Hérode à Jérusalem. Une lecture de Antiquités Judaïques 15.413–417. In Mols, S. and

Moorman, E. (eds), *Omni pede stare. Saggi architettonici e circumvesuviani in memoriam Jos de Waele*. Naples: Electa, 177–82.

Gros, P. 2012. Basiliques civiles de Gréce at d'Asie Mineure. In Cavalier, L., Descat, R. and des Courtils, J. (eds), *Basiliques et agroas de Gréce et d'Asie Mineure*. Bordeaux: Ausonius Éditions, 13–23.

Gurevich, D. 2017. The water pools and the pilgrimage to Jerusalem in the Late Second Temple Period. *Palestine Exploration Quarterly* 149.2: 103–34.

Hohfelder, R.L., Brandon, C. and Oleson, J.P. 2007. Constructing the harbour of Caesarea Palaestina, Israel: new evidence from the ROMACONS field campaign of October 2005. *International Journal of Nautical Archaeology* 36.2: 409–15.

Holum, K.G. 2015. The Gods of Sebastos: King Herod's harbor temple at Caesarea Maritima. *Eretz-Israel* 31: 51–68.

Jacobson, D.M. 2000. Decorative drafted-margin masonry in Jerusalem and Hebron and its relations. *Levant* 32: 135–54.

Japp, S. 2000. *Die Baupolitik Herodes' des Grossen: die Bedeutung der Architektur für die Herrschaftslegitimation eines römischen Klientelkönigs*. Rahden: Leidorf.

Kahn, L.C. 1996. King Herod's Temple of Roma and Augustus at Caesarea Maritima. In Raban, A. and Holum, K.G. (eds), *Caesarea Maritima: A Retrospective after Two Millennia*. Boston-Leiden: Brill, 130–45.

Kasher, A. and Witztum, E. 2007. *King Herod: A Persecuted Persecutor – A Case Study in Psychohistory and Psychobiography*. Berlin: De Gruyter.

Killebrew, A.E. 2010. Village and countryside. In Hezser, C. (ed.), *The Oxford Handbook of Jewish Daily Life in Roman Palestine*. Oxford: Oxford University Press, 189–209.

Klausner, J. 1930. *Jesus von Nazareth: seine Zeit, sein Leben und seine Lehre*. Berlin: Suhrkamp Verlag.

Kletter, R. 2019. *Archaeology, Heritage and Ethics in the Western Wall Plaza, Jerusalem: Darkness at the End of the Tunnel*. London: Routledge.

Kloner, A. 1996. Stepped roads in Roman Palestine. *ARAM* 8: 111–37.

Levine, L.I. 2005. Figural art in ancient Judaism. *Ars Judaica* 1: 9–26.

Lichtenberger, A. 1999. *Die Baupolitik Herodes des Großen*. Wiesbaden: Harrassowitz Verlag.

Lichtenberger, A. 2009. Herod and Rome: was Romanization a goal of the building policy of Herod? In Jacobson, D.M. and Kokkinos, N. (eds), *Herod and Augustus: Papers Presented at the IJS Conference, 21st–23rd June 2005*. Boston-Leiden: Brill, 43–62.

Lönnqvist, K. 2014. The chronology and tenure of Pontius Pilate, new evidence for re-dating the period of office. Judaea and Rome in coins, 65 BCE–135 CE. *Spink Numismatic Circular* 120.4: 1–7.

Luni, M. 1987. Il ginnasio-cesareo nel quartiere monumentale dell'agorà. In Stucchi, S. (ed.), *Da Batto Aristotele a Ibn El-'As. Introduzione alla mostra*. Rome: 'L'Erma' di Bretschneider, 41–46.

Luni, M. 1990. Il ginnasio-Caesareum di Cirene nel contesto del rinnovamento urbanistico della media età ellenistica e della prima età imperiale. In *Giornata lincea sulla archeologia cirenaica (Roma, 3 novembre 1987)*. Rome: Accademia Nazionale dei Lincei, 87–120.

Magen, Y. 2002. *The Stone Vessel Industry in the Second Temple Period: Excavations at Hizma and the Jerusalem Temple Mount*. Jerusalem: Israel Exploration Society.

Magen, Y. 2008. Tombs ornamented in Jerusalem style in Samaria and the Hebron Hills. In Magen, Y. (ed.), *Judea and Samaria: Researches and Discoveries*. Jerusalem: Civil Administration of Judea and Samaria, 141–64.

Magness, J. 2022. Journey to Jerusalem: pilgrims and immigrants in the time of Herod. *Biblical Archaeology Review* 48.3: 42–49.

Mazar, B. 1971. The excavations in the Old City of Jerusalem near the Temple Mount: second preliminary report, 1969–1970 seasons. *Eretz-Israel* 10: 1–34. [Hebrew]

Mazar, B. 1984. The Royal Portico in the southern part of the Temple Mount. In Shanks, H. (ed.), *Recent Archaeology in the Land of Israel*. Washington: Biblical Archaeology Society, 141–47.

Mazar, B. 1986. The Royal Portico in the southern part of the Temple Mount. In Mazar, B. (ed.), *Excavations and Discoveries*. Jerusalem: Mosad Bialik, 65–72. [Hebrew]

McKenzie, J.S. 2007. *The Architecture of Alexandria and Egypt, c. 300 BC to AD 700*. New Haven-London: Yale University Press.

McKenzie, J., Gibson, S., Reyes, A.T. and Grimm, G. 2004. Reconstructing the Serapeum in Alexandria from the archaeological evidence. *Journal of Roman Studies* 94: 73–121.

Meshorer, Y. 2001. *A Treasury of Jewish Coins: From the Persian Period to Bar Kokhba*. Jerusalem: Yad Ben Zvi.

Netzer, E. 2006. *The Architecture of Herod, the Great Builder*. Tübingen: Mohr Siebeck.

Netzer, E. 2018. *The Palaces of the Hasmoneans and Herod the Great (Reprinted and Expanded Edition)*. Jerusalem: Yad Ben-Zvi.

Overman, J.A. and Schowalter, D.N. 2011. Preliminary conclusions. In Overman, J.A. and Schowalter, D.N. (eds), *The Roman Temple Complex at Horvat Omrit: An Interim Report*. Oxford: British Archaeological Reports, 101–4.

Peleg-Barkat, O. 2012. The relative chronology of tomb façades in early Roman Jerusalem and power displays by the élite. *Journal of Roman Archaeology* 25: 403–18.

Peleg-Barkat, O. 2017. *The Temple Mount Excavations in Jerusalem 1968–1978, Directed by Benjamin Maza. Final Reports, Vol. V: Herodian Architectural Decoration and King Herod's Royal Portico*. Jerusalem: Qedem.

Peleg-Barkat, O. 2019. Reimagining Herod's Royal Portico. *Biblical Archaeology Review* 45.4: 32–38, 88.

Peleg-Barkat, O. 2021. The Royal Portico on the Temple Mount: between historical text and archaeological finds. In Dell'Acqua, A. and Peleg-Barkat, O. (eds), *The Basilica in Roman Palestine. Adoption and Adaptation Processes, in Light of Comparanda in Italy and North Africa*. Rome: Quasar, 69–89.

Peleg-Barkat, O. and Ben-Haim, A. 2017. Monumental Ionic columns from Areas Q and H. In Geva, H. (ed.), *Jewish Quarter Excavations in the Old City of Jerusalem, Conducted by Nahman Avigad 1969–1982, VII: Areas Q and H, Final Report*. Jerusalem: Israel Exploration Society, 68–95.

Radke, G. 1971. *Viae Publicae Romanae*. Stuttgart: Alfred Druckenmuller.

Rahmani, L.Y. 1994. *A Catalogue of Jewish Ossuaries in the Collection of the State of Israel*. Jerusalem: The Israel Antiquities Authority.

Raviv, D. and Zissu, B. 2020. Tombs with decorated facades in the Judean countryside. *Zeitschrift des Deutschen Palästina-Vereins* 136: 152–75.

Reich, R. 2013. *Miqwa'ot (Jewish Ritual Baths) in the Second Temple, Mishnaic and Talmudic Periods*. Jerusalem: Yad Ben-Zvi and Israel Exploration Society. [Hebrew]

Reich, R. and Billig, Y. 1999. Excavations near the Temple Mount and Robinson's Arch, 1994–1996. *Qadmoniot* 117: 31–40. [Hebrew]

Reich, R. and Shukrun, E. 2011. The Pool of Siloam in Jerusalem of the Late Second Temple Period and its surroundings. In Galor, K. and Avni, G. (eds), *Unearthing Jerusalem*. Winona Lake: Eisenbrauns, 241–55.

Reich, R. and Shukrun, E. 2012. Excavations in Jerusalem beneath the Paved Street and in the Drainage Channel next to Robinson's Arch. *Qadmoniot* 142: 66–73. [Hebrew]

Reidinger, E.F. 2004. The Temple Mount platform in Jerusalem from Solomon to Herod – an archaeological re-examination. *Assaph* 9: 1–64.

Reisner, G.A., Fischer, C.S. and Lyon, D.G. 1924. *Harvard Excavations at Samaria 1908–1910*. Cambridge, MA: Harvard University Press.

Revel-Neher, E. 1986–87. L'alliance et la promesse: le symbolisme d'Eretz Israël dans l'iconographie juive du moyen âge. *Journal of Jewish Art* 12–13: 135–46.

Richardson, P. and Fisher, A.M. 2018. *Herod: King of the Jews and Friend of the Romans (Second Edition)*. London: Routledge.

Ritmeyer, L. and Ritmeyer, K. 1994. Potter's field or high priest's tomb? *Biblical Archaeology Review* 20.6: 22–35, 76–78.

Roll, I. 2005. Terrestrial transportation of the Roman army in the East: the case of Judaea/Palestina and its road network. In Visy, Z. (ed.), *Limes XIX: Proceedings of the XIXth International Congress of Roman Frontier Studies Held in Pécs, Hungary, September 2003*. Pécs: University of Pécs, 1166–70.

Roller, D.W. 1998. *The Building Program of Herod the Great*. Berkeley, LA: University of California Press.

Rozenberg, S. 2003. Wall painting fragments from Area A. In Geva, H. (ed.), *Jewish Quarter Excavations in the Old City of Jerusalem. Final Report, II: The Finds from Areas A, W and X-2*. Jerusalem: Israel Exploration Society, 302–28.

Rozenberg, S. 2008. Hellenistic and Roman wall paintings in the land of Israel and their parallels. In Rozenberg, S. (ed.), *Hasmonean and Herodian Palaces at Jericho. Final Reports of the 1973–1987 Excavations, Vol. IV: The Decoration of Herod's Third Palace at Jericho*. Jerusalem: Israel Exploration Society, 283–424.

Rozenberg, S. 2013. Interior decoration in Herod's palaces. In Rozenberg, S. and Mevorah, D. (eds), *Herod the Great: The King's Final Journey*. Jerusalem: The Israel Museum, 166–223.

Schürer, E. 1973. *The History of the Jewish People in the Age of Jesus Christ, 175 B.C. – C.E. 135 (Translated and Revised by G. Vermes, F. Millar and M. Goodman)* (3 vols.). Edinburgh: T&T Clark.

Schwartz, D.R. 1992. *Studies in the Jewish Background of Christianity*. Tübingen: Mohr Siebeck.

Segal, A. 2017. Samaria-Sebaste: portrait of a polis in the heart of Samaria. *Études et Travaux* 30: 409–30.

Shukrun, E. 2012. Did Herod build the foundations of the Western Wall? In Meiron, E. (ed.), *City of David. Studies of Ancient Jerusalem: The Thirteenth Annual Conference*. Jerusalem: Megalim, 13–27.

Shukrun, E. and Reich, R. 2011. Jerusalem, Robinson's Arch preliminary report. *Hadashot Arkheologiyot – ESI* 123: http://www.hadashot-esi.org.il/report_detail_eng.asp?id=1884&mag_id=118.

Sjökvist, E. 1954. Kaisareion: a study in architectural iconography. *Opuscula Romana* 1: 86–108.

Sloane, J.C. 1934. The Torah shrine in the Ashburnham Pentateuch. *Jewish Quarterly Review* 25: 1–12.

Smallwood, E.M. 1952. The Hadrianic inscription from the Caesareum at Cyrene. *Journal of Roman Studies* 42: 37–38.

Smith, M. 1967. Goodenough's 'Jewish symbols' in retrospect. *Journal of Biblical Literature* 86: 53–68.

Szanton, N. and Uziel, J. 2015. On the question of the stepped stone monument from the Second Temple Period in the City of David. In Meiron, E. (ed.), *City of David. Studies of Ancient Jerusalem, 10*. Jerusalem: Megalim, 19–39. [Hebrew]

Szanton, N., Hagbi, M., Uziel, J. and Ariel, D.T. 2019. Pontius Pilate in Jerusalem: the monumental street from the Siloam Pool to the Temple Mount. *Tel Aviv* 46.2: 147–66.

Talgam, R. 2014. *Mosaics of Faith: Floors of Pagans, Jews, Samaritans, Christians, and Muslims in the Holy Land*. Jerusalem: Yad Ben-Zvi.

Taylor, J.E. 2006. Pontius Pilate and the imperial cult in Roman Judaea. *New Testament Studies* 52: 555–82.

Tepper, Y. 1999. A basilica at Beth Yeraḥ? Beth Yeraḥ revisited. *Tel Aviv* 26.2: 271–82.

Tepper, Y. and Tepper, Y. 2013. *Road that Bears the People: Pilgrimage Roads to Jerusalem in the Second Temple Period*. Tel-Aviv: Hakibbutz Hameuchad. [Hebrew]

Trifogli, A. 2014. Dal ginnasio ellenistico al forum di Cirene. In Luni, M. (ed.), *Cirene 'Atene d'Africa', VII. Cirene greca e romana*. Rome: 'L'Erma' di Bretschneider, 183–97.

von Hagen, V.W. 1967. *Roman Roads*. London: Weidenfeld and Nicolson.

Votruba, G.F. 2007. Imported building materials of Sebastos harbour, Israel. *International Journal of Nautical Archaeology* 36.2: 325–35.

Ward-Perkins, J.B. 1954. Constantine and the origins of the Christian basilica. *Papers of the British School at Rome* 22: 69–90.

Ward-Perkins, J.B., Balance, M.H. and Reynolds, J.M. 1958. The Caesareum at Cyrene and the basilica at Cremna. *Papers of the British School at Rome* 26: 137–94.

Warren, C. 1884. *Plans, Elevations, Sections, etc. Showing the Results of the Excavations at Jerusalem, 1867–1870, Executed for the Committee of the Palestine Exploration Fund*. London: Palestine Exploration Society.

Warszawaski, A. and Peretz, A. 1992. Building the Temple Mount: organization and execution. *Cathedra* 66: 3–46. [Hebrew]

Weiss, Z. 2021. The 'Magdala Stone Table': its function and role in determining the liturgical furniture in the ancient synagogue. *Journal of Roman Archaeology* 34: 608–31.

Winter, F.E. 2006. *Studies in Hellenistic Architecture*. Toronto: University of Toronto Press.

Yechezkel, A., Negev, Y., Frumkin, A. and Leibner, U. 2021. The shaft tunnel of the Biar Aqueduct of Jerusalem: architecture, hydrology, and dating. *Geoarchaeology* 36: 897–924.

10

Building and reshaping public spaces in North Africa in the early imperial period: The examples of Thugga, Lepcis Magna, and Cyrene

Niccolò Mugnai

Under the Roman Empire, cities across the Greco-Roman world underwent phases of architectural and urban development that defined or reshaped their built environment. This phenomenon was related to the socio-political events that characterized the cities' history, being linked to the cultural background of the respective communities and their engagement with the ever-expanding power of Rome. This chapter looks at how public spaces witnessed new construction activities and the reshaping of pre-existing buildings in three North African cities: Thugga (Africa Proconsularis, Tunisia), Lepcis Magna (Tripolitania, West Libya), and Cyrene (Cyrenaica, East Libya). The timeframe encompasses mainly the first century CE, from Augustus to the Flavians, although earlier phases are considered where relevant. The choice of these case-studies was driven by their different historical, cultural, and artistic traditions, to investigate how the growth of their civic districts was influenced by a range of architectural trends and how these were adopted, adapted, and experienced by the local societies.

Thugga is a hinterland site that was part of the kingdom of Numidia until it was annexed as the Roman province of Africa Nova in 46 BCE (known as Africa Proconsularis from Augustus onwards). Under Roman administration, the population of this city was grouped into two juridical entities, a *civitas* of local inhabitants and a *pagus* of Roman settlers, which were kept in place until the creation of the municipium under Septimius Severus (Poinssot 1983, 9–13). Lepcis Magna was founded as a Phoenician/Punic emporium on the coast of Tripolitania around the seventh–sixth century BCE. With the creation of Africa Proconsularis, Lepcis kept its status as a *civitas libera et foederata* until its promotion to municipium under the Flavians and to colony under Trajan (Kenrick 2009, 90–91). Cyrene was a Greek foundation dating to the seventh century BCE; its history and urban features were deeply influenced by contacts with the Greek homeland. This first phase was followed by Ptolemaic rule and eventually Roman government with the creation of the province of Crete and Cyrene in 74 BCE (Kenrick 2013, 1–6, 148–49; the city is referred to as a *civitas* in the local epigraphy).

By engaging with the architectural evidence from these three sites, no claim is made to identify a single pattern that applies to the entirety of North Africa, or even to the regions where these cities were located. It is important, however, to assess how the built environment of these contexts evolved throughout the period under consideration. The aim of the chapter is to assess the responses to the broader historical and political developments that took place under Roman rule, connecting them, when possible, to the shape and appearance of monuments that people used on a daily basis. Along with the analysis of the buildings' architectural features, attention is paid to the display of inscriptions and sculptural ornament, and how these could be employed to convey messages to viewers.

Thugga: From a Numidian plaza to Roman civic centre

The Roman civic centre of Thugga developed on a terrace of the hill that was occupied by earlier constructions dating to the mid-second century BCE. This predecessor of the Roman forum is commonly referred to as a Numidian plaza or agora (see Khanoussi 2003, 140–43; Saint-Amans 2004, 44–49). The continuous use of this space in the imperial period determined a series of transformations to its layout and architectural components, the most conspicuous of which were the construction of a portico surrounding the plaza under Antoninus Pius (*DFH* 29) and the dedication of the

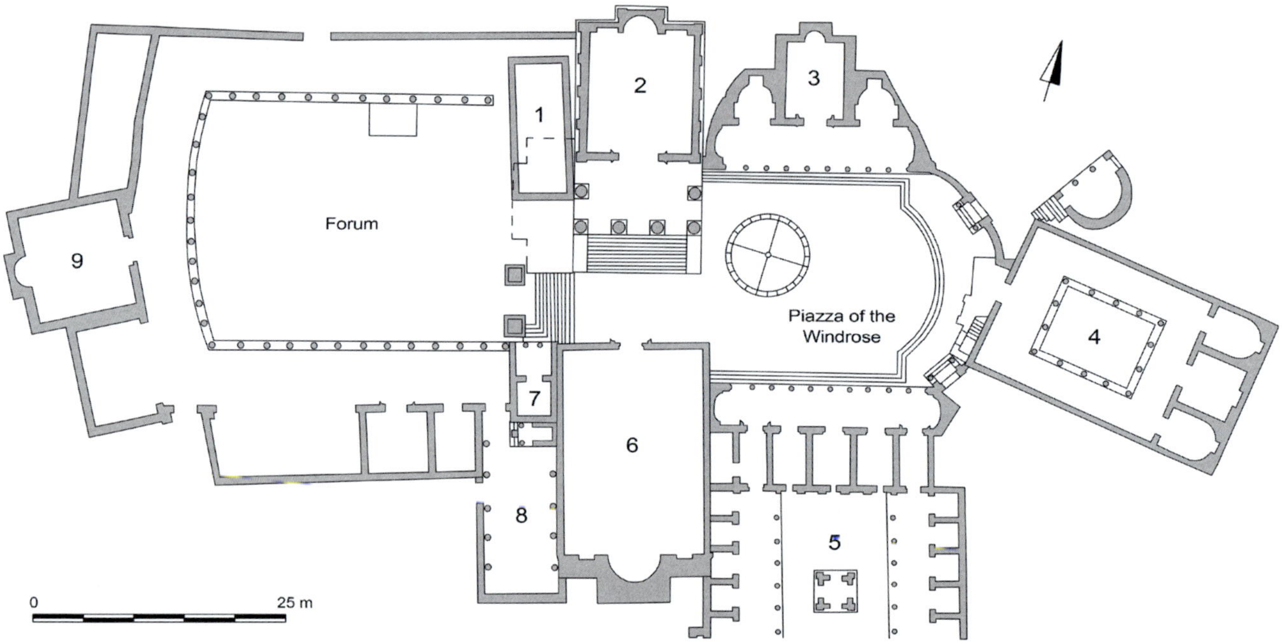

Fig. 10.1. Thugga: Plan of forum area and annexed spaces. 1: Numidian Monument; 2: Capitolium; 3: Temple of Mercury; 4: Sanctuary of Fortuna; 5: Market; 6: Apsidal edifice; 7: Temple with sacellum; 8: 'Colonnaded Hall'; 9: Curia (image N. Mugnai, after Aounallah and Golvin 2016, 258, fig. 14; Ardeleanu 2021, pl. 20b).

Capitolium to Marcus Aurelius and Lucius Verus in 166–69 CE (*DFH* 31). Further changes were caused by the erection of a fortress enclosing the area of the forum during the Byzantine reconquest of North Africa (Poinssot 1983, 40–41). These building activities obliterated most of the Numidian and early imperial phases, leaving only scant architectural traces behind (Figs 10.1–2). On the other hand, Thugga's rich epigraphic dossier includes a significant number of inscriptions that provide information about constructions and patronage in these earlier periods (Khanoussi 1997; Bullo 2002, 122–28; Saint-Amans 2004, 59–78). In recent years, attempts have been made to connect the monuments cited in these texts to the extant remains. An architectural survey was carried out as part of a French-Tunisian project, which investigated the evolution of the forum and annexed spaces from the Numidian to the Byzantine era (Aounallah and Golvin 2016, 29–389). Subsequently, a reassessment and new insights into the Numidian and early imperial phases were presented by S. Ardeleanu (2021, 223–42). Both studies have the merit of shedding new light into these stages of Thugga's urban, social, and political history. The aim here is to review some of their arguments and offer additional, or alternative, suggestions as appropriate.

Fig. 10.2. Thugga: View of forum area from north-west (photo N. Mugnai).

The evidence from the Numidian period deserves attention because of the impact it had on the later Roman forum. Various elements of architectural decoration were discovered around this area, some of which were scattered on the ground, while others were recycled in later constructions, especially in the Byzantine fortress. These elements include Aeolic, Ionic, and other types of capitals, as well as blocks of Egyptian gorge (cavetto) cornices, all of which were common features of Numidian-era architecture (Aounallah and Golvin 2016, 32–46, figs 14–47; see also Rakob 1979; Quinn 2013). The French-Tunisian team identified the remains of wall foundations underneath the apsidal edifice facing the Capitolium on the south side of the forum and perhaps on the piazza's western end (Aounallah and Golvin 2016, 64–71, figs 74–85), but while they were keen to interpret these as evidence of Numidian sacred buildings, the scarcity of data recommends caution.[1] In contrast, the ruins of a structure next to the west side of the podium of the Capitolium had already been interpreted as a Numidian-period edifice (Fig. 10.3). The opening of sondages along its foundations during a German-Tunisian excavation programme confirmed a date in the second half of the second century BCE (Hiesel and Strocka 2002, 73–74, pl. 7a–b). The architectural remains consist of a rectangular podium (14.6 × 6.35 m) with a moulded plinth at the bottom and two courses of ashlar blocks on top. This edifice is known as the Monument or Temple of Massinissa on the basis of a bilingual Punic-Libyan inscription (*RIL* 2) that is generally associated with it, which records the dedication of a sacred building in honour of the deceased king Massinissa by the citizens of Thugga during the tenth year of Micipsa's reign, c. 139–37 BCE.[2] While this proposed identification is plausible, the inscription was not recovered in this spot but further to the east by the Temple of Mercury in the Piazza of the Windrose (indeed the location of the Temple of Massinissa was initially sought to the north of that building). The text is engraved on a block measuring 33 cm in height and 25 cm in depth, while the two preserved ashlar courses above the moulding of the podium are 53 and 50 cm high respectively (a putative third course is 48 cm in height) and c. 60 cm deep, so the relationship between the inscription and the masonry may not be so straightforward. Furthermore, other Libyan texts were found around the agora/forum, bearing the names of individuals and perhaps references to building activities (*RIL* 3–4, 6–7; Ghaki 1997). It seems likely to hypothesize the presence of Numidian-period structures, some of which were presumably of public and sacred character, and whose existence may be corroborated at least in part by the finds of the French-Tunisian team and those from other sondages excavated by the German-Tunisian project (Hiesel and Strocka 2002, 74). Given the existence of multiple, albeit fragmentary, remains and inscribed texts, an unequivocal attribution of *RIL* 2 to the edifice to the west of the Capitolium should be taken with caution, and it may be preferable to refer to this building simply as a 'Numidian Monument'.

Fig. 10.3. Thugga: Remains of podium of Numidian Monument, view from north-west (photo N. Mugnai).

The elevation of this structure remains conjectural. The French-Tunisian team reconstructed an open peristyle with Ionic columns above the podium (Aounallah and Golvin 2016, 56–58, figs 60–62), which would recall the so-called 'Victory Monument' of Micipsa at Simitthus and the monument of Kbor Klib (see Rakob 1979, 120–32, figs 30–48; 1994, 8–28, figs 5–34, pls. 5–36; Ferchiou 1991); the main façade of the building would therefore be the one on its long side looking to the west (Fig. 10.4a). In contrast, Ardeleanu identified this as a temple proper, perhaps distyle *in antis*; the main façade would be the short one looking to the south towards the Oued Khalled valley (Ardeleanu 2021, 227–28, although no graphic reconstruction is provided).[3] Some of the architectural elements found in this zone may be associated with this monument, in particular Ionic column capitals, Aeolic pillar capitals, and Egyptian gorge cornices. One problem with the hypothesis of the French-Tunisian team is the number of columns for which there is insufficient evidence. At the same time, Ardeleanu's proposal of a long and narrow temple may equally raise some questions; this terrace featured a wide open space in the Numidian phase, so it is not clear why the front of this important building was so awkwardly reduced in width, especially if the purpose was to emphasize its visibility towards and from the valley underneath. On balance, a reconstruction as a closed podium with a wide façade looking west may be preferable, which would also be supported by the comparable size of this monument with the one at Simitthus (12.15 × 5.65 m: Rakob 1994, 5–8, figs 3–6).[4] As to the layout of the upper part of the podium and the storey above it, the architectural evidence is scant. However, if a connection between the two buildings at Simitthus and Thugga is accepted, one might reconsider whether two figured capitals with sphynxes among volutes and acanthus leaves could have belonged to the Numidian Monument (Ferchiou 1989, 202–5, no. VIII.I.2, pl. 54a–b; Aounallah and Golvin 2016, 40–41, figs 39–40). These were found around the agora/forum, but their association with this building is usually discarded on the basis of their proposed chronology in the first half of the first century BCE (Ferchiou 1989, 204–5; Saint-Amans 2004, 46; Ardeleanu 2021, 227). This argument rests solely on stylistic observations, such as the simplification of the carving that would make them later in date than the examples from the monument of Simitthus.[5] However, more attention should be paid to the types of stones employed – yellow marble at Simitthus, local limestone at Thugga – and to the artisans' skills, which may point to a different carving quality rather than a different date (Fig. 10.5). Their size is also comparable, both being c. 50 cm in height (an approximation of the Punic or other cubit), which would fit with the ashlar blocks of the podium at Thugga. While their decorative motifs might have been sourced in part from Hellenistic traditions of South Italy (see Rakob 1979; Coarelli and Thébert 1988), they were an eclectic type of ornament that became a distinctive feature of

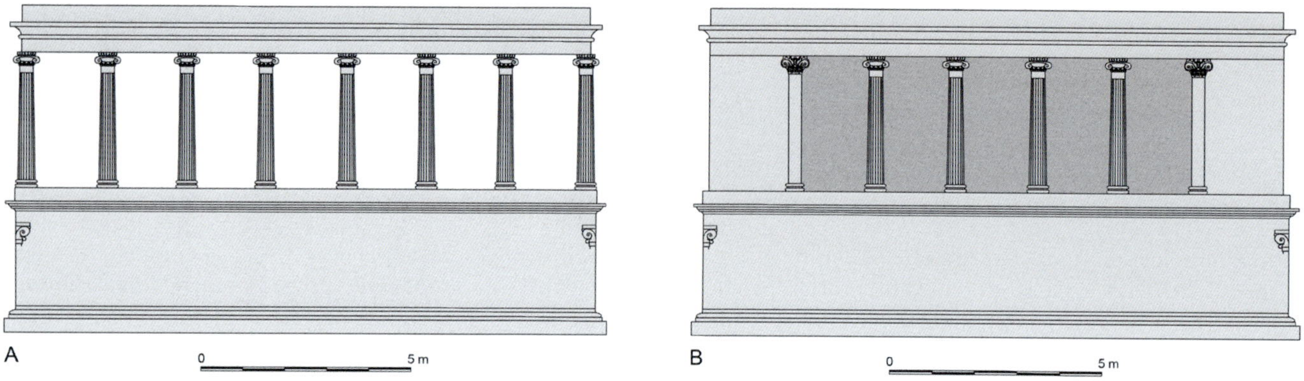

Fig. 10.4. Thugga: Numidian Monument, restored elevation of west side. A: Reconstruction with open peristyle according to Aounallah and Golvin 2016; B: An alternative hypothesis with upper storey enclosed on three sides and including figured capitals (images N. Mugnai, after Aounallah and Golvin 2016, 57, fig. 62).

the Numidian-period architectural language (Quinn 2013). These styles were frequently associated with prominent monuments, so contemporary viewers would have become rapidly accustomed to them (Fig. 10.4b).

The fate of this Numidian Monument in the imperial period is of relevance to Thugga's historical and political developments. The city was divided into two juridically distinct communities: a *civitas* of indigenous inhabitants, to which a *pagus* of Roman settlers from Carthage was added during Augustus' or Tiberius' reign (Aounallah 2010, 65–67, 123–30; Beschaouch 2011, with references). From this moment on, a Roman forum started taking shape in the area previously occupied by the Numidian agora, reaching the apex of its monumentality by the late Antonine period. It is generally thought that the Numidian Monument was destroyed and built over, and some have used this as an example of aggressive Roman behaviour to impose a 'coercive urbanism' (Fentress 2021, 167–68). The southern part of the monument is now concealed under a tripartite tribune, but this structure (probably *rostra*) was not erected until the early third century CE (*CIL* VIII, 26593). The French-Tunisian team proposed to identify the remains of an early imperial arch in the spot that was later occupied by this tribune, which caused destruction of most of the Numidian Monument and reconfiguration of its northern end as a small Roman temple (Aounallah and Golvin 2016, 100–13, figs 38–58). However, the lack of evidence for this arch and temple as well as some issues with the proposed phasing were flagged up by Ardeleanu (2021, 234 and n. 2219), and his remarks seem well-grounded. The Antonine portico in the forum did not obliterate the Numidian Monument and the same applies to the Capitolium, the podium of which has roughly the same alignment of this earlier structure and only overlaps with a small portion of its south-east corner. Furthermore, the original moulding at the south-west corner of the Numidian Monument is still visible *in situ* underneath the Severan tribune; had the southern portion of the building been razed in the early imperial era, this decoration should have been destroyed or recycled in the putative Roman temple, but that was not the case. These considerations suggest the monument was in all probability left in place in the forum, where it was gradually surrounded by other constructions that defined the shape of the Roman civic centre.

Fig. 10.5. Figured capitals with acanthus leaves and sphynxes. A: Simitthus, 'Victory Monument' (photo N. Mugnai); B: Thugga, forum area (Rakob 1994, pl. 40a).

The prolonged presence of this building in the plaza would have had a marked visual and ideological impact.

By connecting the Numidian Monument with the cult of Massinissa, Ardeleanu (2021, 233–36) argued for a link between the cult of the Roman emperors and that of the Numidian dynast, which would have survived until at least the late second century CE. As pointed out above, we cannot prove an association of this edifice with Massinissa, so this argument must remain a suggestive hypothesis. It is unquestionable that the distinctive architecture and decoration of the monument – whichever reconstruction of its elevation one prefers – made it stand out among the other edifices, which displayed a canonical repertoire of imperial-style architectural ornament (this was the case with the Corinthian order of the Antonine portico, the Capitolium, and the buildings in the Piazza of the Windrose attached to the forum's east side). Such visual discrepancies are not unheard of in the context of urban and architectural developments of cities under the Roman Empire, and their occurrence at Thugga is even less surprising given the particular status of the city and its subdivision into a *civitas* and *pagus*. A physical, as well as a juridical and religious separation between the two communities in the early imperial era was often advocated in past scholarship (for instance: Poinssot 1919, 171–76), but recent research has largely revised this theory (see Khanoussi 1994; 2003; Saint-Amans 2004, 108–10). A less rigid demarcation of religious practices can be glimpsed from an altar set up by a member of the *civitas*, Iulius Venustus son of Thinoba, in honour of the deified Augustus and of the emperor Claudius in 48 CE under the supervision of a patron of the *pagus*, C. Artorius Bassus (*DFH* 46; Christol 1991, 624–27; Saint-Amans 2004, 299–300, no. 25), which proves the imperial cult was diffused among both communities by the mid-first century CE.[6] The altar might have been displayed somewhere in the forum and it is significant, as recently observed, that the inscribed text is framed by a decoration featuring columns with Aeolic capitals, which might have reminded viewers of the ornamentation of the Numidian Monument as well as other local buildings such as the Monument of Atban (Ardeleanu 2021, 235–36, fig. 102). The continuity of pre-Roman decorative traditions under the Roman Empire occurred frequently in North Africa (see Pensabene 2016; Mugnai 2022, 252–53, 275). At Thugga, again, the shape of the architrave-frieze of the Temple of Caelestis, dedicated c. 222–35 CE, clearly recalls an Egyptian gorge cornice (Golvin and Khanoussi 2005, 108–13, figs 29–37). This reminiscence of Numidian-era decorative styles may have been understood only by a minority of viewers at that stage, but their occurrence on a major urban sanctuary attests to the role these traditions still played within the local artistic and cultural background.

The Julio-Claudian period was characterized by intensive building activities in the forum, as shown by various dedicatory inscriptions and (few) architectural remains.[7] These provided the plaza with a layout that was maintained essentially unaltered until the subsequent transformations of the Antonine era, as no evidence of significant building interventions is (yet) known for the Flavian period. Most constructions were dedicated by magistrates from Carthage (*duumviri*, *patroni pagi*), and were paid for and executed by members of the *pagus Thuggensis*. The earliest extant dedication to an anonymous deity dates to 32–36 CE; this probably refers to a temple (the location is unknown) that was financed by C. Pomponius Restitutus and dedicated by L. Iulius Crassus (*DFH* 68; see also the revised date in Saint-Amans 2004, 374–75, no. 117). Earlier readings attempted to restore the letters IOM at the beginning of this text, suggesting dedication of a temple to Jupiter Capitolinus (see *CIL* VIII, 26475; Khanoussi 1997, 118), but later revisions have ruled out this possibility. A well-known, and much discussed, inscription provides information about building activities carried out under Tiberius, 36–37 CE, all of which were dedicated by the *duumvir* L. Manlius Bucco and financed by the *patronus pagi* L. Postumius Chius.[8] The text is engraved on a monolithic entablature (width 3.97 m, height 0.48 m), which was recycled on the outer face of the Byzantine fortress' south wall (Fig. 10.6). The dedication records the paving of the forum and of the area in front of the *templum Caesaris*, and the erection of an *ara Augusti*, an *aedes Saturni*, and an arch. It is generally believed the inscription was placed above the arch mentioned in the text, which would have marked the entrance to the forum from the south, but this remains speculative. The assumption is based on the current location of the entablature, which is thought to correspond to the zone of the original setting, but stone artefacts, even bulky ones, could be moved around considerably when they were recycled.[9]

The identification of the buildings cited in this text has puzzled scholars for a long time and attempts have been made to link epigraphic and archaeological data. Attention has focused on the forum proper, but perhaps one should not exclude the area of the Piazza of the Windrose, which was monumentalized under Commodus (*DFH* 34; *CIL* VIII, 26483–84, 26486, 26530, 26533) and it is uncertain what it looked like in the early imperial era. It is also possible that construction of the Capitolium could have obliterated a previous building, leaving no trace of its existence.[10] From the text it is evident that the *templum Caesaris* and the unpaved forum already existed when the inscription was set up. The temple is generally understood to be dedicated to the living emperor Tiberius.[11] It may correspond to the building that was restored around the mid-first century CE by M. Licinius Tyrannus, a freedman of M. Licinius Rufus (a *flamen perpetuus Augusti* from Carthage), while the original temple had been erected by Rufus' grandmother, Viria Rustica (*DFH* 25). This supposed cult of Tiberius at Thugga is unique in the context of the Roman imperial cult and has been explained either as a form of private worship (Rives 1995, 107–10; Ardeleanu 2021, 229, n. 2188), or

Fig. 10.6. Thugga: Byzantine fortress, recycled inscription of L. Postumius Chius, DFH *23 (photo N. Mugnai).*

as an exceptional municipal homage to this emperor for the establishment of the *pagus* (Beschaouch 2011, 1809).[12] This might be the case, but uncertainties remain around the subject of cult. Augustus as *Caesar* can probably be excluded, given that an *ara Augusti*, and not an *ara Caesaris*, is mentioned in this same text and the absence of the title of *divus* (*ara divi Augusti*) does not seem sufficient to suggest any other interpretation. Perhaps the possibility of a temple dedicated to Julius Caesar should not be ruled out altogether. The nomenclature is peculiar; one would rather expect a reference to a *templum divi* or *templum divi Iulii*, but Caesar played a key role in the creation of Africa Nova through annexation of the former kingdom of Numidia, and therefore such a public homage at Thugga might be justifiable.[13] In conclusion, a straightforward association of this temple with Tiberius should be taken with caution, and other hypotheses may be equally valid.

The French-Tunisian team proposed to identify the *templum Caesaris* with the square hall (12.5 × 12.1 m) behind the Antonine portico on the west side of the forum (Aounallah and Golvin 2016, 76–89, figs 1–20). This edifice was initially proposed as a candidate for the *aedes Saturni* cited in the same Tiberian inscription (Poinssot 1919, 177), but its layout and the presence of square holes on the paving slabs, seemingly meant to support wooden benches, suggested instead identification as a curia (Balty 1991, 97–99, fig. 65; Saint-Amans 2004, 74). A sondage was excavated in 2007 in front of the building, which revealed a series of structures that the French-Tunisian team interpreted as the remains of the original pronaos. This was supposedly destroyed in the Antonine period during construction of the portico and conversion of this putative temple into a curia (Aounallah and Golvin 2016, 156–58, fig. 28), but this is problematic. The wall in the north sector of the sondage, interpreted as part of the staircase, is not aligned with any of the other walls of the building, thus casting serious doubts on the existence of a pronaos. Furthermore, the attempted reconstruction of the façade of this Tiberian (or earlier) edifice includes a Corinthian capital of much later date; this is a typical example of the Romano-Carthaginian style diffused in North Africa from the second century CE onwards (see Pensabene 1986, 364–67, figs 25–33; Mugnai 2022, 251–52), which can be compared, for instance, with the Corinthian capitals of the Antonine portico in the forum of Thugga. On the basis of these remarks, identification of the building as a curia is preferable, although its date remains an open question.[14]

A different location in the forum for the *templum Caesaris* was argued for by Ardeleanu (2021, 229–35, figs 98–101), who proposed to recognize it with the small rectangular edifice (c. 7.8 × 4.6 m) on the southern side of the plaza, opposite the short flank of the Numidian Monument. Most of this building is now concealed by the Byzantine fortress and its front was affected by the redevelopments of the forum in the Antonine era, but it can be reasonably restored as a distyle temple *in antis* (Fig. 10.7). The French-Tunisian team had suggested a pre-Roman date for it, followed by modifications in the Julio-Claudian period perhaps to host the cult of Saturn (Aounallah and Golvin 2016, 59–64, figs 63–73; 98–100, figs 35–37). Ardeleanu's arguments against a pre-Roman date are convincing: in particular, ashlar masonry without mortar was used in Numidia at least until the late first century CE, and the same applies to the two Attic bases with identical tori and without plinth that probably decorated the façade of the temple. The Tuscan capital currently placed above one

Fig. 10.7. Thugga: Remains of early imperial temple within Byzantine fortress, view from north-east (photo N. Mugnai).

of these bases did not belong to the columns of the temple, given its smaller size. The façade was likely Ionic – this being the favoured order in Africa Proconsularis until the second century CE, with a broad range of local variations (Ferchiou 1989, 170–72, 490–94; see also the case study of Lepcis Magna below). Ardeleanu argued for an ideological link between the front of this building and the one of the Numidian Monument, intended as a Temple of Massinissa, since the two buildings would have faced each other according to his interpretation. This reconstruction may have some problems, but regardless of the shape and orientation of the façade of the Numidian Monument, it is undeniable that its proximity to this temple created a strong visual connection that must have caught the viewers' attention.

With regard to the rear side of the temple, a small aedicula/sacellum (4.4 × 2.5 m) was added to its southern wall with an east–west alignment (Aounallah and Golvin 2016, 126–29, figs 65–68). It features an enclosure preceded by a pronaos – on which one now finds two Attic column bases with identical tori, this time with a plinth – and three steps on the front with an altar in the middle (this was added at a later stage) (Fig. 10.8). This structure was built after the temple, but probably still within the Julio-Claudian era. Considering its connection to the temple, one may wonder whether this small monument could be interpreted as the *ara Augusti* cited after the *templum Caesaris* in Postumius Chius' list of buildings. This remains a hypothesis; an alternative location of the *ara* in the middle of the apsidal building opposite the Capitolium, as proposed by the French-Tunisian team (Aounallah and Golvin 2016, 90–94, figs 21–25), is possible but it does not rest on any solid evidence given the poor state of the remains. The matter of Chius' *aedes Saturni* is equally problematic. A Temple of Saturn exists on the plateau to the north of the theatre, which replaced an open-air sanctuary of Baal; it was erected by the *civitas* of Thugga in the late first century CE and was probably restored in the Antonine period (Saint-Amans 2004, 348–53, nos. 85–86). An earlier temple in the forum, however, must be assigned to the *pagus*. The identifications advanced so far are conjectural. If one excludes the building to the west (curia) and the temple to the south (*templum Caesaris*?), this leaves the apsidal building or some other phantom edifice that may have disappeared under the Capitolium or in the Piazza of the Windrose. On the other hand, if Chius' activity was to be interpreted as a rededication of a pre-existing building, rather than construction of a new one, could this be the Numidian Monument? The Monument of Micipsa at Simitthus might have been rededicated to Saturn, but this did not happen until the Severan era. While the monument itself was not altered, apart from the addition of Latin inscriptions, a complex with lateral porticoes was built around it that deeply transformed the layout and perception of the building (Rakob 1994, 36–37, figs 13–14). None of this can be identified around the Numidian Monument at Thugga in the Julio-Claudian era, so a rededication at that stage should probably be excluded.

Further building activities in the forum in the first century CE are known through inscriptions. Fragments of a *tabula ansata* were recovered in various spots, recording construction of a stepped arch (*arcus et gradus*) under Caligula, which was rededicated to Claudius in 43 CE (*DFH* 24). The dedication was made by L. Iulius Crassus and the monument

Fig. 10.8. Thugga: Sacellum at the back of early imperial temple, view from south-west (photo N. Mugnai).

financed by C. Caesetius Perpetuus, both of which were *patroni pagi*. The location of the arch is unknown, but the French-Tunisian team suggested this may have marked the junction between the forum's eastern side and the area of the later Piazza of the Windrose (Aounallah and Golvin 2016, 124–25; see also Mazzilli 2016, 281). There is no architectural evidence to support this hypothesis, but the mention of steps in front of the arch would be consistent with the different levels of the two areas. If one accepts this proposal, the erection of this monument would have created a formal connection between the forum and the space to its east, where other public buildings were erected under Claudius. A fragmented entablature (*DFH* 26) bears the dedication of a Temple of Venus and Concordia by the *flaminica* Licinia Prisca, wife of that Licinius Tyrannus who restored the *templum Caesaris* in the same years. Some have argued this Julio-Claudian temple should be located to the east of the Piazza of the Windrose, where the Sanctuary of Fortuna, Venus Concordia, and Mercury was built under Hadrian (*DFH* 136) and was rededicated only to Fortuna by Severus Alexander (Saint-Amans 2004, 155–58, 315–19, nos. 47–49; Ardeleanu 2021, 237–38 is more cautious about this proposal). Familial ties and involvement in public euergetism in this area are further shown by the market's dedication by M. Licinius Rufus, patron of M. Licinius Tyrannus, in 54 CE (*DFH* 69). This building on the south side of the Piazza of the Windrose, adjacent to the apsidal building opposite the Capitolium, was refurbished and expanded under Commodus, but part of the original paving was exposed during excavations (De Ruyt 1983, 212–18, figs 82–84; Aounallah and Golvin 2016, 128–32, figs 69–72).

As part of his arguments on the role of the imperial cult in the forum, Ardeleanu (2021, 239–42, fig. 103) proposed a different hypothesis for the location of the arch of Caligula/Claudius, which might have been placed at the southern end of the so-called 'Colonnaded Hall' behind the temple with sacellum (the putative *templum Caesaris*) (Fig. 10.9). This suggestion is as conjectural as the one advanced by the French-Tunisian team due to the lack of any physical evidence; this area was involved in (re)building activities at later stages that concealed most of the original phases, and many of the architectural elements here are not *in situ*. However, regardless of the position of the arch, Ardeleanu's reinterpretation of this hall as a structure that gave access to the forum from the south deserves attention. This platform of c. 24 × 8 m features a row of columns in front of the inner walls on both long sides. The argument that this might have been unroofed due to the span of c. 7 m between the two rows should probably be rejected, as construction of a roof supported by timber trusses would have been doable – this being a sensible choice to provide shade considering the local climate.[15] Ardeleanu's identification of this platform as an open-air processional thoroughfare with lateral colonnades – a small-scale version of a monument such as the

Fig. 10.9. Thugga: 'Colonnaded Hall' behind early imperial temple, view from south-west (photo N. Mugnai).

Sebasteion of Aphrodisias – should probably be revised. The temple's decentred position also raises some questions about its relationship with this structure, which remains difficult to pin down. Having said that, one cannot exclude that one of the entrances to the forum could have been located on the south side of this structure. If so, this hall would have served to lead visitors to an area of the plaza where the Numidian Monument was to be seen in a dominant position, engaging in an architectural and ideological 'dialogue' with the other Roman-period edifices around it.

Lepcis Magna: Creating an architectural façade for civic and religious life

The forum of Lepcis Magna, known as the Old Forum (*forum vetus*), is located in a key area of the site corresponding to the core of the previous Punic emporium, as shown by archaeological materials and remains of structures of the seventh–sixth century BCE that were excavated on the eastern side of the Roman plaza (Howard Carter 1965; De Miro and Polito 2005, 121–27). Unlike Thugga, where a monumental development of the civic centre had already started in pre-Roman times, this process does not appear to have taken place at Lepcis Magna before the Augustan era (Ward-Perkins 1982, 29–32; see Di Vita 1968; 1982 for different considerations on the city's early urban expansion). At that time the forum started acquiring its shape as a trapezoidal square (c. 55 × 55.4 m) surrounded by sacred and civic buildings, a layout that was maintained unaltered even during later adaptations and changes (Figs 10.10–11). Despite construction of a second forum under the Severans (*forum novum severianum*), the Old Forum did not lose its central religious and civic role but kept functioning alongside the new one.[16] Architectural surveys of the main forum buildings have allowed a good understanding of their features and modifications through time.[17] The importance of the Old Forum from a broader historical and socio-cultural perspective has been discussed by various scholars (for instance Musso 2008; Quinn 2010; Kreikenbom 2011), while a recent study has looked at the visual experience of these monuments from the Augustan to the Antonine period and at the relationship between the forum and other sectors of the city (Mugnai 2021). The socio-political use of the local architecture and its discourse with imperial Rome is of particular relevance, especially during the early stages of development of this space in the first century CE. Attention here focuses on the characteristics of the buildings that were added to the plaza, the adoption and adaptation of certain architectural and decorative motifs, and the agendas of the individuals who were involved in Lepcis Magna's urban embellishment.

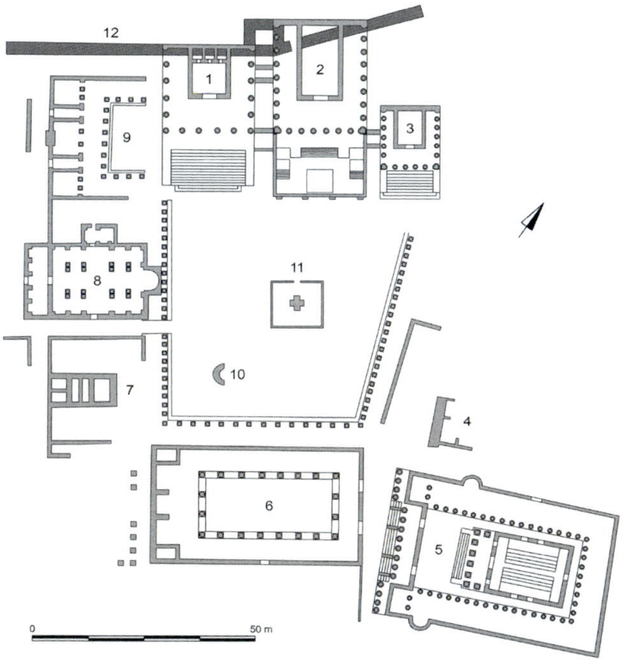

Fig. 10.10. Lepcis Magna: Plan of the Old Forum. 1: Temple A; 2: Temple B; 3: Temple C; 4: Phoenician-Punic building; 5: Curia; 6: Basilica; 7: Temple of Magna Mater; 8: Temple/church; 9: Antonine temple; 10: Severan exedra; 11: Baptistery; 12: Byzantine wall (image N. Mugnai, after Kenrick 2009, 110, fig. 44; Livadiotti and Rocco 2018, pl. 1).

The main monumental façade of the Old Forum was the one on the north-west side, where three temples were erected over around 30 years. These edifices, named here Temples A–C from west to east, can be regarded as examples of the Romano-Italic type, being set above a raised podium with an emphasis on their frontal side. Despite the different construction phases, the temples were meant to be seen as a single unity once they were all completed, which is

Fig. 10.11. Lepcis Magna: View of the Old Forum from south-east with Temples A–C in the background (photo M. Kenawi, Manar al-Athar).

confirmed by the use of stone arches to support platforms that connected their podia together (although of later date, this layout recalls the three temples in the forum of Sufetula). Temple A is the earliest in date; architectural stratigraphy and other details suggest it was built around the end of the first century BCE or at the start of the first century CE (Masturzo 2003, 723–28; 2005, 66–77).[18] The remains of its elevation are poorly preserved, but the temple can be restored as a rectangular building of c. 21 × 35 m, with a peripteral *sine postico* layout, featuring Ionic columns and a Doric entablature. Most of its architectural decoration is made of sandstone; this material started going out of use with the exploitation of the limestone of Ras el-Hammam, which became the main building stone in the city throughout the first and second centuries CE. This temple is traditionally associated with the cult of Shadrapa (Liber Pater/Bacchus), one of the two *dii patrii* of Lepcis Magna together with Milk'Ashtart (Hercules). Inscriptions from the forum may support this identification (*IPT* 31; *IRT2021* 274–75, 289, 295, 583; Marmouri 2017), although some scholars have proposed alternative possibilities, such as a Capitolium (Masturzo 2005, 129–31; Musso 2008, 182–89)[19] or a temple dedicated to the joint cult of Shadrapa/Liber Pater and Milk'Ashtart/Hercules (Quinn 2010, 58).

The second building to be added to the forum's north-west side was Temple C, the smallest of this series of sacred edifices (13.3 × 21.8 m: Ricciardi 2005) (Fig. 10.12). The date of its dedication is secure thanks to the inscription by the proconsul Cn. Calpurnius Piso, 4–5 CE (*IRT2021* 520), which forms part of the paving on the front of the temple. It has long been acknowledged that this two-line text was formerly meant to develop on a single line (Di Vita-Evrard 1990), and it has been recently suggested that its original setting might have been on the entablature of Temple C rather than on the paving (Mugnai 2021, 104).[20] Although most of the literature refers to this building as the Temple of Milk'Ashtart/Hercules, this attribution is purely speculative in the absence of any epigraphic or other evidence. The temple's architectural features exemplify the principal patterns recognizable at Lepcis Magna in this period. Despite the layout as a Romano-Italic temple, the Ionic order of the peristasis displays Lepcitanian characteristics, such as the capitals' exuberant ornamentation and their proportions that diverge from the canonical Ionic design. These motifs are attested on various public monuments across the city, creating a well-defined architectural language (Ricciardi 2005, 340, 353–61, figs 3.25–31, 3.43–50; Mahler 2006, 159–61, nos. 117–32 IK, pls. 29–32).[21] At the corners of the temple façade, there are heart-shaped pillars inspired by architectural solutions from the Hellenistic-Alexandrian world, which became a common component of Lepcis' architecture – it is possible this cultural encounter occurred via Cyrenaica (Caputo 1966–67, 33–34; Rocco 2010, 30–34; see also the case study of Cyrene below). The agency of a proconsul in

Fig. 10.12. Lepcis Magna: Temple C, view from south-west (photo R. Burns, Manar al-Athar).

the dedication of this building is significant in the context of the relationships between the Roman State and Lepcis Magna, a *civitas libera et immunis*. It is notable that the presence of Rome was remarked through the choice of a Romano-Italic temple layout and the occurrence of a Latin inscription that showcased Calpurnius Piso's name. At the same time, distinctive elements of Lepcitanian tradition on the temple's elevation might have engaged with the local audience more directly, since these had become a familiar and easily recognizable feature of the city's built environment.

The same considerations apply to Temple B, which was built under Tiberius and dedicated c. 23–29 CE (Livadiotti and Rocco 2005, 230–31; Musso 2008, 176–79). The neo-Punic text on the door lintel of the cella (*IPT* 22; regrettably, the identity of the dedicant is not preserved)[22] and the recovery of colossal marble heads of the goddess Roma and Augustus are a clear indication of the cult that was worshipped in it.[23] It is plausible that a Latin inscription complemented the neo-Punic dedication, and the discovery of a fragment of a *tabula ansata* that would fit with the entablature of the porch supports this hypothesis (Livadiotti and Rocco 2005, 213, figs 2.47–48; Rocco 2016, 67–69, fig. 8; see also Wilson 2012, 282–84). The temple (c. 21 × 39 m) is provided with a tribunal on the front of the podium, which was decorated with limestone ship prows that recalled the layout of *templa rostrata* (Livadiotti and Rocco 2005, 193–200, figs 2.30–32; Rocco 2010, 22–23, figs 2–3). References to metropolitan monuments such as the Temple of Divus Julius and the Temple of Venus Genetrix are all too evident. The adoption of this symbology to convey messages of imperial rule was further strengthened by the presence of groups of sculptures, which are mentioned in the text of the neo-Punic inscription and are attested through numerous finds from this area. An inscribed pedestal on the tribunal supported a quadriga of Drusus and Germanicus (*IRT2021* 334; Trillmich 2014; Rocco 2016, 69–76, figs 10–14), while the front of the cella and the porch of

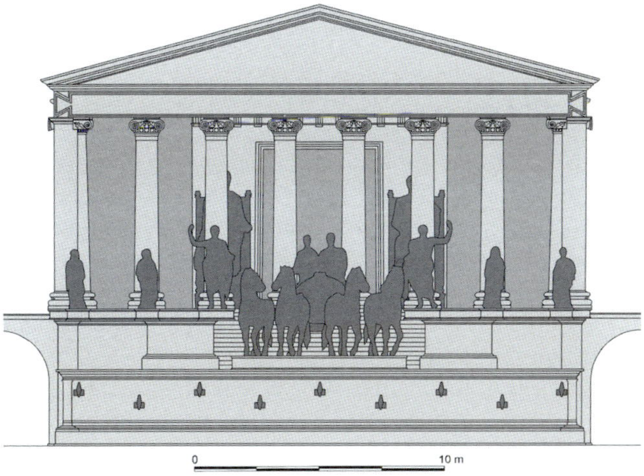

Fig. 10.13. Lepcis Magna: Temple of Roma and Augustus, reconstruction of façade with proposed setting of statuary groups (image N. Mugnai, after Rocco 2016, 75, fig. 14).

the temple were crowded with statues of members of the Julio-Claudian dynasty: Livia, Tiberius, Agrippina the Elder, Antonia Minor, Livilla, Vipsania Agrippina, and perhaps a second group of Drusus and Germanicus (Aurigemma 1940, 49–79, figs 29–56; Rose 1997, 182–84, pls. 220–29; Boschung 2002, 8–9, nos. 1.3–10, pls. 3–7; Livadiotti and Rocco 2005, 231–35, figs 2.63–65) (Fig. 10.13).[24] The iconography of these statues adheres to the imperial-style trends established in Rome, and they must have been executed by trained sculptors who were familiar with the current fashion.

The Ionic order of the temple's peristasis has nothing to do with metropolitan styles, while it displays marked local characteristics like the decoration of the other two temples. At the corners of the façade one finds again heart-shaped pillars of Alexandrian-Cyrenaican influence. The vegetal ornamentation of the Ionic capitals takes the form of oblique palmettes (Livadiotti and Rocco 2005, 276–79, fig. 2.99; Mahler 2006, 157–58, nos. 98–106 IK, pls. 26–27), a motif that has been much discussed in the literature. Some scholars have interpreted it as a derivation from the Italic-Ionic style that was popular in Sicily and South Italy especially in the second and first centuries BCE (Ward-Perkins 1968, 105–7; 1970, 14–15; Masturzo 2005, 99; Ricciardi 2005, 360; Bigi 2006, 2359–61; Mahler 2006, 58),[25] while others have regarded it as a Hellenistic tradition of the south-eastern Mediterranean (Livadiotti and Rocco 2005, 210–11; Rocco 2010, 26). The issue with some of these interpretations lies in their rigidity, which seeks a direct influence from one model or the other, while the shape of these capitals was ultimately a Lepcitanian creation. That said, the peculiar form and the position of the palmettes do recall the Sicilian and South Italian types (Fig. 10.14), not being attested with these same characteristics on any other Hellenistic examples. The artisans from Lepcis Magna must have been inspired by those forms, at least to some extent (perhaps indirectly?), and adapted them to the local context. This choice was made under the supervision of the architect in charge of the construction – less plausibly by the patron. It is important that this type of decoration was applied to a temple that was so loaded with Roman imperial ideology: in its final shape, the building successfully blended local and external influences together, becoming part of Lepcis' architectural language (Mugnai 2021, 107).[26] Visually, this resulted familiar (and appropriate) to passers-by, occasional viewers, and those who gathered daily in the forum, even though most of them would have been unaware of the iconographic and ideological influences that led to its creation.

Given the abundance of archaeological evidence, these temples are always considered when discussing the architectural and socio-political role of the Old Forum, but they should not be looked at in isolation from the other components of the plaza, as they were all meant to be part of complementary building projects. The main problem lies in the poor preservation of the other edifices, which prevents us from achieving a complete picture of the area. In particular, the layout of the forum' eastern side in this period is barely known. Some structures are preserved above the

Fig. 10.14. Ionic capitals with lateral palmettes. A: Lepcis Magna, Temple of Roma and Augustus (photo BSR Archive, wplib 49-XIII-30); B: Sicily, Monte Iato, Peristyle House 1 (photo N. Mugnai); C: Pompeii, forum basilica (photo N. Mugnai).

remains of the seventh–sixth century BCE, although these are limited to the foundation levels. It has been argued that this space might have been occupied by a portico around the first century BCE, while a rectangular hall would have been added in front of it in the first century CE, directly facing the plaza (Masturzo 2003, 720–21; 2016, 561–63, figs 1, 3–4). The proposed interpretation of these remains as a court sanctuary is only a hypothesis, but if the general chronology is confirmed, this would be compatible with the main development of this public area during the Augustan and Julio-Claudian phases. At the same time, recent stratigraphic excavations underneath the church that was built on the west side of the forum at the intersection with the *cardo maximus* have exposed remains of a large wall that belonged to a previous, monumental edifice (Kreikenbom and Mahler 2010, 42–47, figs 14–17; Mahler 2012, 50, fig. 2). Due to the limited extent of the sondage, nothing more can be said about the function of this building, although it must have been either of civic or sacred character, while archaeometric analyses have confirmed construction took place in the first half of the first century CE. Despite the patchy nature of these remains, it is evident that the east and west sides of the forum were supposed to have a monumental appearance, perhaps being both provided with sacred edifices to create a visual and functional link with the three temples on the north-west side. The forum was completed to the south by a civic basilica (c. 47.5 × 27.5 m), referred to as the *basilica vetus* in a later Constantinian inscription (*IRT2021* 467). It was built at some point after the reign of Augustus and before the mid-first century CE (Ward-Perkins 1949, 401; De Miro and Polito 2005, 127), but like the buildings on the east and west sides, it is poorly preserved and the shape of its elevation is conjectural. The remains show that while the long side of the basilica faced the plaza, the main two entrances were on the short east side, opening onto a narrow square outside the south-east corner of the forum.

A more formal interconnectivity among the forum buildings was obtained through the paving of the piazza and construction of porticoes on the east, west, and south sides under Claudius. At least part of the limestone paving visible today belongs to this phase, while the extant porticoes with Carystian green marble columns date to a refurbishment of the second half of the second century CE; the aspect of the original porticoes is unknown, although they probably featured either Ionic or Tuscan limestone columns. Epigraphic evidence attests to these building activities and their patronage. Four bilingual, Latin and neo-Punic stelae were set up on the front of the tribunal of the Temple of Roma and Augustus (*IRT2021* 338; *IPT* 26a–b) (Fig. 10.15). The text, identical on all of them, records the edification of *columnas cum superficie et forum de sua pecunia* by Caius, son of Anno. The dedication was made by the proconsul M. Pompeius Silvanus and his legate Q. Cassius Gratus in 53–54 CE; the inscription also specifies these works were carried out by Balitho Commodus, son of Anno Macer. Although the Latin text was longer and more prominent than the neo-Punic (Wilson 2012, 287–89), the repetition of both scripts on four stelae and their position spanning the entire width of the tribunal made sure this message was successfully conveyed in both languages to those standing in front of them (despite the larger characters, the Latin text, like the neo-Punic, was readable only when one was in close proximity to the inscriptions, and not from afar: Mugnai 2021, 108–9). This public display of the names of the builder and funder was consistent with the practice of euergetism at Lepcis in this period, and visibility and accessibility of these texts were a fundamental part of the process. These works must have required significant funding and workforce, as suggested by a second fragmented (Latin) inscription that was recovered around Temple C. This belonged to an honorary base set up by the Lepcitanians for C. Phelyssam, son of Macer and grandson of C. Anno, *ob columnas et superficiem et forum stratum honoris caussa* (*IRT2021* 615). The partially preserved name of Balitho Commodus at the bottom of this text would indicate a date similar to that of the four bilingual stelae, showing this

Fig. 10.15. Lepcis Magna: Bilingual Latin and neo-Punic stele in front of Temple of Roma and Augustus, IRT2021 *338 (photo R. Burns, Manar al-Athar).*

enterprise was achieved through the involvement of more than one wealthy individual, each of them perhaps being responsible for a specific sector of the plaza.

The Augustan and Julio-Claudian era provided the Old Forum with the main monumental components to be expected in a Roman-style civic centre, although their reception occurred in a way that paid careful attention to the dialogue between local peculiarities and Rome-driven tendencies, similarly to some of the patterns identified at Thugga. The forum of Lepcis, however, was also subject to a significant phase of construction activities under the Flavians, for which epigraphic and archaeological evidence survives. These activities were not limited to the forum but involved other sectors of the city as well, particularly the harbour. The principal explanation is to be found in the promotion of Lepcis from *civitas libera et immunis* to Roman municipium in 73–74 CE (Di Vita-Evrard 1984), which initiated a period of new architectural development that culminated with the dedication of the imposing Flavian Temple on the harbour's west quay in 93–94 CE.[27] This process determined a gradual, but irretrievable, assimilation of further elements of Roman imperial style that shaped the layout of Lepcis' architecture. The most evident acquisition was the occurrence of the Corinthian order: examples of limestone capitals datable to this period, such as those from the market (refurbishment of the north *tholos*) and from the Flavian Temple, clearly attest to the adoption of metropolitan motifs by the local ateliers (Bianchi 2005, 210–14, figs 23–28; Mahler 2006, 24–25, 147, nos. 1–4 KK, pl. 1).[28] Like in the previous phases, however, the introduction of new architectural and decorative trends did not involve a *tabula rasa* of local styles, and it frequently occurred that different traditions overlapped.

In terms of new constructions, a sacred building was added to the west side of the forum. This was located in the spot between the basilica's north-west corner and to the south of the Roman edifice underneath the church; it was separated from the latter through the final stretch of the *cardo maximus* that led into the plaza. This new building featured a rectangular enclosure (21.4 × 25.5 m), inside which a small temple on a podium (7.5 × 10.2 m) was positioned abutting the back wall. The remains are poorly preserved and the building awaits full publication, but its basic architectural features have been discussed in preliminary reports (Montali 2016a–b). The typology of the mouldings on the podium and the use of Ras el-Hammam limestone are consistent with a chronology in the latter half of the first century CE (Montali 2016a, 90–94, figs 6–7; 2016b, 307–12, figs 7–16). The temple was accessed via a frontal staircase, while its elevation is difficult to restore: it could have been either a small tetrastyle building, a temple *in antis*, or an *oikos*. The enclosure had three entrances on the east side opening onto the plaza, although the visibility of its front was not immediately evident to passers-by, as it was in part concealed behind the forum portico. Despite the uncertainties about the elevation and other details, the connection of the building with the cult of Magna Mater is plausible thanks to a dedicatory inscription that has been attributed to it (*IRT2021* 300). The Latin text, engraved on blocks belonging to an entablature, records the dedication of a *templum Matris Magnae* to the emperor Vespasian in 73 CE by the proconsul Q. Manlius Ancharius Tarquitius Saturninus and his legate Volumnius Memor Felix. The funds for this construction and its ornamentation (200,000 sesterces) were provided by a local notable, Iddibibal [---] son of Balsillec, grandson of Annobal and great grandson of Asmun; the last part of the text mentions a second name, Passienus Maris [---], but the gap at the end prevents us from understanding his involvement in this enterprise. With the temple of Magna Mater, the religious façade of the forum's west side was reinforced, for it is possible that also the edifice under the church might have served a sacred function. This process saw its conclusion with the addition of a sanctuary within a porticoed court on the north end, which was dedicated by Calpurnia Honesta to Antoninus Pius in 152–53 CE and probably hosted the cult of an Augustan deity (see *IRT2021* 370; Mugnai 2021, 110–12, with references).

Finally, the architectural façade of civic life in the forum was boosted in the Flavian period through edification of a monumental curia outside the plaza's south-east corner. A recent study has provided valuable data to reconstruct the layout, chronology, and developments of this building (Livadiotti and Rocco 2018). A date of construction under the Flavians is confirmed by archaeological finds recovered from a sondage; it has also been hypothesized that a dedication to Vespasian of 77–78 CE by the proconsul C. Paccius Africanus through his legate and *patronus municipi* Cn. Domitius Ponticus (*IRT2021* 342) might have been displayed here (Livadiotti and Rocco 2018, 143–47, 378–79).[29] The curia proper took the form of a Romano-Italic, hexastyle temple on a podium (Fig. 10.16), placed within a rectangular enclosure (c. 35 × 55 m) with porticoes on three sides. Almost nothing survives of the curia's elevation in this phase (the façade was renovated with Corinthian marble columns in the Antonine era). The front of the enclosure, however, was decorated with large Corinthian limestone columns, which emphasized the prominence of this building in front of everyone's eyes. In contrast, the inner porticoes featured Ionic columns that attest to the continuous popularity of this order at Lepcis, having become one of its distinctive components and a marker of the local architectural taste (Livadiotti and Rocco 2018, 84–112, figs 57–97). The east–west orientation of this complex created a direct link with the basilica on the opposite side, thus strengthening the civic role of the two buildings in the context of the newly promoted municipium. Importantly, the curia was placed on the road leading from the forum to the harbour

Fig. 10.16. Lepcis Magna: Podium of the curia, view from west (photo R. Burns, Manar al-Athar).

and, therefore, to the Flavian Temple. When this latter monument was completed at the end of the first century CE, the memory of the Flavian dynasty would have been fixed within Lepcis' community through this cluster of buildings around this area.

Cyrene: Public spaces between continuities and new ideologies

In Roman times, daily public duties at Cyrene were performed in two monumental areas: the agora and the Caesareum/forum, located respectively at the western and eastern edges of the city's central quarter. These areas constituted the core of public life; an appraisal of the use, development, architectural and ideological impact of the respective buildings is presented here. Religious activities were also performed in other sectors of the city, especially in the Sanctuary of Apollo on the Myrtousa, but these fall beyond the scope of this chapter and are not included in the discussion.

The agora

The heart of the city's civic and religious life, Cyrene's agora witnessed a long continuity of use with its earliest phases dating back to the foundation of the Greek colony in the seventh century BCE. By the end of the second century BCE, this space had already acquired the more prominent monumental features that would define its shape even in later periods (Bonacasa and Ensoli 2000, 59–73; Kenrick 2013, 168–80). The agora is divided into two sectors: a lower terrace, corresponding to the public plaza proper; and an upper terrace with edifices lining up on the *skyrota* (the so-called 'Street of Battos') (Figs 10.17–18). The buildings of the agora were excavated by Italian teams and most of the results published in a series of volumes.[30] A recent study has looked at the development of this space from its origins to the late Roman era, highlighting the connections between the agora's evolving layout and the socio-political events that characterized the life of Cyrene and Cyrenaica (Scott 2013, 14–44).[31] This is a valuable approach that has enhanced our understanding of this area, although its focus is more on the topography of the agora than the architecture, and on the earlier phases, with particular attention to the tensions between the monarchic and democratic governments (sixth to fourth centuries BCE) and to the period of Ptolemaic rule (c. 323 to 96 BCE). At first glance, the timeframe spanning from the early Augustan era to the end of the first century CE would appear of lesser importance, which is due to the agora's monumentalization being already well-advanced by then. Later (re)building activities, in particular those that took place after the destructions caused by the Jewish Revolt of 115–16 CE, had a notable impact on earlier public complexes at Cyrene. Hadrianic interventions are identifiable across the whole city, perhaps in the context of the emperor's establishment of the Panhellenion; the introduction of imperial-style features, such as the use of the Corinthian order, enriched and in part reshaped the repertoire of Cyrene's architecture (Pensabene and Gasparini 2017; see also Gasparini, this volume).[32] While the early imperial period has left fewer traces of building activities in the agora, one can recognize an active involvement of individuals in the visual development of the plaza (in agreement with, and on behalf of, the Roman State), which is even more evident when the extant epigraphic and sculptural evidence is taken into account.

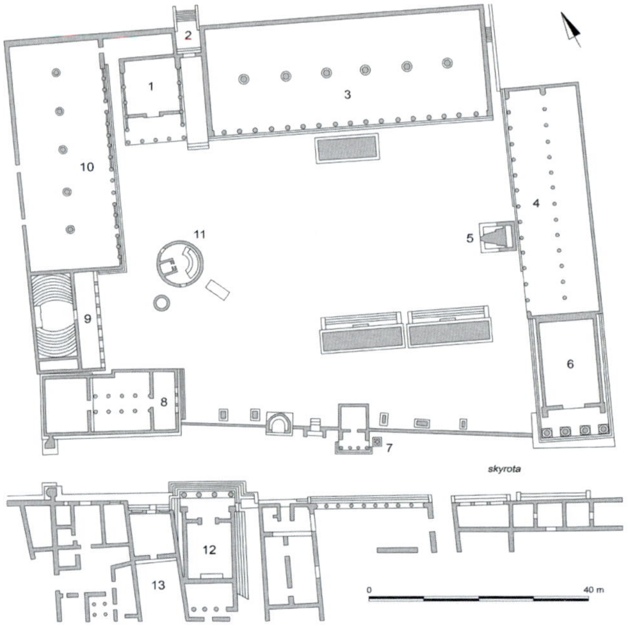

Fig. 10.17. Cyrene: Plan of the agora. 1: Augusteum; 2: Propylon; 3: North Stoa; 4: East Stoa; 5: Naval Monument; 6: Temple of Asklepios; 7: Honorific column; 8: Temple of Apollo Archegetes; 9: Assembly building; 10: West Stoa; 11: Temple of Demeter and Kore; 12: Temple of Zeus; 13: Nomophylakeion *(image N. Mugnai, after Bonacasa and Ensoli 2000, 77).*

Fig. 10.18. Cyrene: View of agora from east (photo J. Chick, Manar al-Athar).

The north side of the agora received particular attention in the Augustan and Julio-Claudian period (Fig. 10.19). The architectural layout of pre-existing buildings was affected only to some degree, but such interventions were well-defined in scope. The most evident changes occurred to the pedimental structure originally built in the second half of the second century BCE to cover a sacred well at the north-west corner of the agora. This building was slightly expanded on the rear side and the intercolumniations on the two long sides were blocked off through insertion of screen walls (Stucchi 1965, 207–10, figs 125–28; 1967, 70–71; 1975, 196, fig. 185). The architrave on the front was provided with a Latin inscription recording the new dedication – probably by the proconsul Q. Lucanius Proculus between the end of the first century BCE and the start of the new era – and a second text was added underneath during a later restoration perhaps under Tiberius (*IRCyr2020* C.104) (Fig. 10.20). At this stage the well inside the building was obliterated and the structure acquired the new function of Augusteum; dedications were set up in honour of Apollo Augustus, Diana, and other Augustan goddesses or female members of the imperial family (*IRCyr2020* C.106–9; Callot 1999, 159–60, 310–11). It has also been suggested that a portrait of Agrippina Minor, recovered in the area of the Sanctuary of Apollo, might have been moved there in antiquity from its original setting in the Augusteum (Walker 1994, 183, n. 19).[33] The architecture of this edifice is significant, as it shows a blending of Doric and Ionic features already in its second-century BCE phase: the columns have Doric capitals, unfluted shafts (the visible flutes were added in the Augustan phase), and Attic bases at the bottom; the entablature is also of a mixed Doric-Ionic type (Stucchi 1965, 192–203, figs 114–21). This contamination of Doric architecture with Ionic elements is attested on a limited number of buildings in Asia Minor and the Italian Peninsula from the late Hellenistic period onwards.[34] At Cyrene, however, it was a recurring feature that characterized the layout of various buildings at different stages: for instance, Doric columns with bases occurred in the agora's West Stoa as early as the third century BCE (Stucchi 1975, 118–19, fig. 99; Bacchielli 1981, 113–16, 125–26, figs 82–83; Bonacasa and Ensoli 2000, 67–68), and identical columns were replicated in the East Stoa when this was erected around the second century CE (Stucchi 1965, 280–84, figs 183–85).[35] This consideration alone should suffice to discourage use of labels such as 'conservatism' when looking at the continuity of Doric-style architecture at Cyrene across the Hellenistic and imperial eras. In contrast, this was part of a fluid architectural language that defined the visual experience of buildings and was perceived as an appropriate form of *decor* in line with the city's socio-cultural background.

As a further marker of Augustan power claims within the agora, the North Stoa was provided with a new Greek inscription on its entablature, recording the (re)dedication of the building to Zeus Soter, Roma, and Augustus (*IRCyr2020* C.114). The architecture of the stoa was not altered: Doric columns (of a more canonical version than those of the Augusteum) lined up on the front, while Ionic columns were placed in the interior, all of them dating to the major phase of the building's development in the early second century BCE (Stucchi 1965, 147–77, figs 84–99). The use of a Greek text for the Augustan rededication was a clever choice to find a right balance with the Latin inscription of the Augusteum, thus managing to address different audiences. These two buildings created a seamless unity along the north side of the agora, which was further reinforced through a series of building activities that took place in the late Augustan period. A Latin text inscribed on a block of the stoa's west anta mentions a

Fig. 10.19. Cyrene: North side of agora with extant remains of Augusteum (left) and North Stoa (right), view from south (photo R. Burns, Manar al-Athar).

restoration of this *porticus Augusta* (a rather evocative name) probably by the proconsul C. Clodius Vestalis (*IRCyr2020* C.113). This same person is believed to have built a propylon, in the form of a plain arch, on the staircase between the Augusteum and the North Stoa to monumentalize the access to the agora from the north (Stucchi 1965, 228–35, figs 145–49; 1975, 214–15, fig. 204). A fragmentary Latin inscription with the name of the proconsul was probably placed above

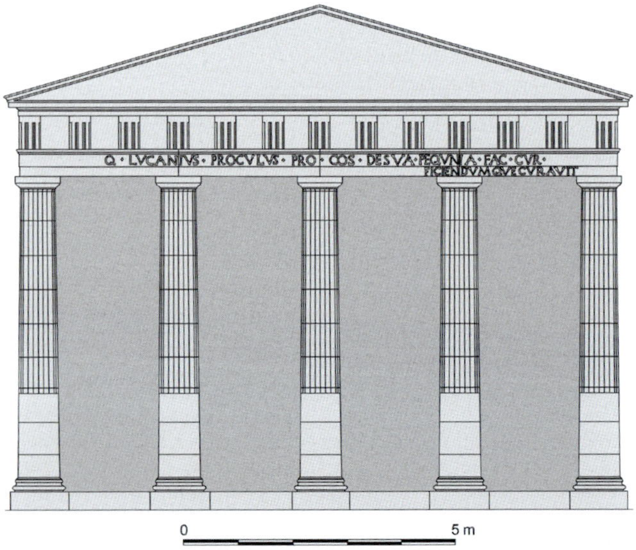

Fig. 10.20. Cyrene: Reconstructed façade of Augusteum with Latin inscription of Q. Lucanius Proculus, IRCyr2020 *C.104 (image N. Mugnai, after Stucchi 1965, 215, fig. 132).*

the archway; a second text was inscribed on a block inside the corridor of the propylon, recording the proconsul's dedication *per veteranos Augusti* (*IRCyr2020* C.116–17). The simplicity of the propylon's architecture recalls the shape of the so-called 'Arch of Tiberius' on the *cardo maximus* at Lepcis Magna, which was erected to celebrate the proconsul C. Rubellius Blandus and his enterprise to pave the city streets in 35–36 CE (*IRT2021* 330–31). It has been argued that the plainness of the Lepcitanian arch was meant to visually emphasize the importance of the text and the identity of the dedicant, and similar remarks apply to the propylon at Cyrene (see Mugnai 2021, 93, fig. 13). The agency of Clodius Vestalis in this sector of the agora is further attested through a fourth inscription bearing his name, this time in Greek, which has been associated with a monument – perhaps the pedestal of an equestrian statue – erected in his honour (*IRCyr2020* C.115; Stucchi 1975, 215). This code switch between Latin and Greek was consistent with the dedications of the Augusteum and North Stoa, thus broadening the respective target audiences. The prominence of Vestalis around this cluster of monuments aimed to showcase his importance within Cyrene's community, along with the unequivocal affirmation of imperial power that became strongly connected with these buildings from this moment on.[36]

Augustus' direct and indirect engagement was not limited to the northern sector of the plaza, however. The pre-existing assembly building on the west side, placed between the Temple of Apollo Archegetes and the West Stoa, was refurbished at this stage through insertion of new seating

Fig. 10.21. Cyrene: Buildings lining on west side of agora, view from east (photo M. Kenawi, Manar al-Athar).

Fig. 10.22. Cyrene: East side of agora with Naval Monument, view from south (photo M. Kenawi, Manar al-Athar).

(Stucchi 1975, 203). Very little is known of the building's elevation, but its importance in the context of Augustan socio-political interventions is demonstrated by the presence of a stele in front of it, bearing a Greek inscription that recorded six edicts of Augustus (the first four edicts date to 7–6 BCE, the last two to 4 BCE: see *IRCyr2020* C.101, with references). These texts provided a series of juridical regulations about the relationship between local and Roman citizens in the province. Apart from the intrinsic relevance of these edicts to the life of Cyrene's community, their setting was also carefully chosen: the proximity to the Temple of Apollo Archegetes (one of the oldest sanctuaries in the agora, originally dating to the last quarter of the seventh century BCE: Purcaro 2001, 25–36) was no coincidence, and one should also note the presence of the circular Sanctuary of Demeter and Kore immediately to the north-east. It would not be surprising if this same area had hosted other honorary and votive dedications that were discovered in the agora.[37] It is also important to consider the visual axis between the assembly building and the opposite east side of the agora, where the imposing Naval Monument stood (Figs 10.21–22). This consisted of a female statue (plausibly a Nike) standing on top of a ship prow, which has been dated on stylistic grounds to the mid-third century BCE and associated with the dynastic union of Berenice II and Ptolemy III that linked together Cyrenaica and Egypt (Ermeti 1981, 127–34; Bonacasa and Ensoli 2000, 88). Egyptianizing elements, themes of victory, and the presence of a well-recognizable *rostrum* were symbols that could be all too easily re-exploited by Augustan politics in the aftermath of Actium.[38]

One last example of Augustan interest towards the agora may be offered by an honorific column that was erected by the wall marking the border between the lower and upper terraces, placed directly on the *skyrota*. The column has a fluted shaft with a tier of acanthus leaves at the bottom and rests on a tall pedestal; it is crowned by a (fragmentary) Corinthianizing figured capital, on top of which a statue would have stood. The date is not firmly established: it was initially attributed to the Hellenistic period (Stucchi 1975, 142), but afterwards a date between the end of the first century BCE and the first century CE was proposed and is now generally accepted (Stucchi and Bacchielli 1983, 63–71, figs 40–45). The style of the acanthus does recall Hellenistic-Alexandrian examples of the second and first centuries BCE, but it has been established that these decorative traditions persisted in Cyrenaica throughout the first century CE (Pensabene and Gasparini 2017, 664–70, figs 12–25). The two extant figures carved on the capital may reproduce Demeter and Nike, and such images, along with the acanthus to be linked to Apollo, would fit nicely with mainstream Augustan art (Di Filippo Balestrazzi 1996). The use of a Corinthian(izing) order was extraneous to Cyrene's architecture at this stage, so its appearance on an honorific column would have served to further emphasize its visual impact on passers-by along the *skyrota*. Whoever the dedicant was, the erection of this column can be understood within the series of dedications and rededications that shaped the layout of the agora under Augustus.

Little evidence survives of later Julio-Claudian and subsequent building/rebuilding activities, and it is possible that the agora did not undergo any major changes before the traumatic events of the Jewish Revolt. A fragmented block recovered behind the north wall of the Augusteum bears traces of an inscription set up by a *praefectus cohortis*, perhaps in honour of a son of the imperial house (*IRCyr2020* C.111). A much-damaged text was inscribed on a column on the façade of the Augusteum, possibly suggesting some restoration of the building (*IRCyr2020* C.105). At the outer south-east corner of the plaza, on the *skyrota*, evidence of a (sacred?) edifice was found underneath the second-century CE Temple of Asklepios. Only part of the foundations of this earlier building could be identified, while the shape of its elevation remains unknown; the associated finds would suggest a date around the mid-first century CE (Stucchi 1965, 235–37). More tangible evidence comes from the agora's upper terrace: three blocks of an architrave with a partly erased dedication of Domitian were found in the *nomophylakeion*, the city archive (*IRCyr2020* C.92). This may either refer to a restoration of the pre-existing structure or to a newly built portico, but the position of the building behind the Temple of Zeus would have prevented most viewers from noticing any changes to its layout.

The Caesareum

In the Roman period, public life at Cyrene was not limited to the agora but also thrived in the area occupied by a large rectangular enclosure (approx. 52 × 81 m) known as the Caesareum, located in the eastern sector of the city along the *skyrota* (Fig. 10.23). This *quadriporticus* was originally built in the second century BCE as the city's public gymnasium – an edifice of particular importance given the role of this institution in the Greek world, including Cyrenaica (Luni 1976).[39] It acquired the new name of Caesareum around the turn of the era, thus showing a close association with imperial agency, which became even more obvious through its change of function to become a forum. The building was kept in use for public purposes until the late third century CE, when it was eventually occupied by private dwellings.[40] The overall layout of the second century BCE was maintained afterwards: the inner open space was surrounded by a Doric portico and access to the complex was granted via two large propyla on the east and south sides. This type of Doric architecture appears to be more traditional if compared to that of some monuments in the agora, as it displayed sober features on both the outer and inner sides of the edifice (Ward-Perkins *et al.* 1958, 140–49). A connection between this building and the agora, however, was intended since the

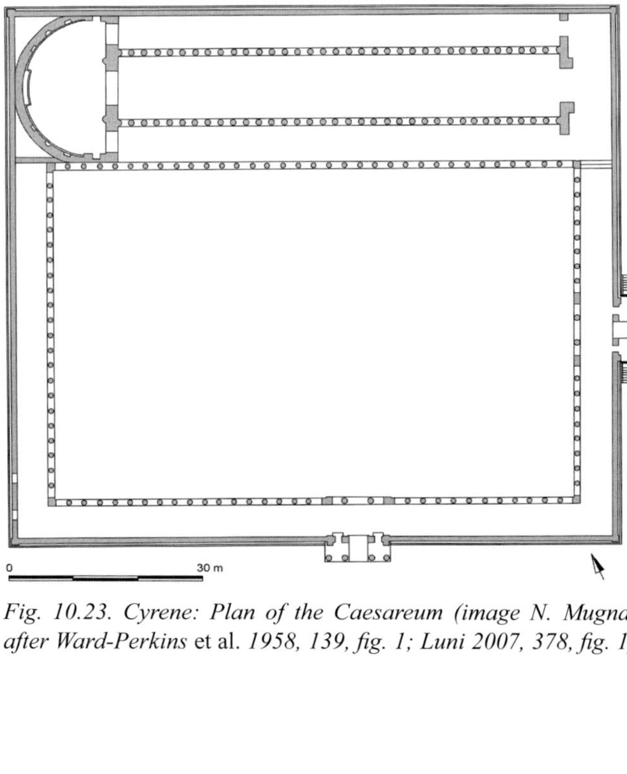

Fig. 10.23. Cyrene: Plan of the Caesareum (image N. Mugnai, after Ward-Perkins et al. *1958, 139, fig. 1; Luni 2007, 378, fig. 1).*

Fig. 10.24. Cyrene: Enclosure of Caesareum and first stretch of the Stoa of Hermes and Herakles, view from south-west (photo R. Burns, Manar al-Athar).

moment of its construction and was achieved through the so-called 'Stoa of Hermes and Herakles' – a monumental and unique structure, stretching for some 123 m on the *skyrota* from the gymnasium's south-west corner towards the agora (Stucchi 1967, 102–10, figs 78–88; Luni 2002) (Fig. 10.24). Lavishly decorated with Telamon-type statues of Hermes and Herakles facing the street, it was initially used as a *xystos* (running track), but when the gymnasium was converted into a forum, this structure became a covered portico through erection of a Doric-style colonnade along the internal axis (the columns had Doric capitals, plain shafts, and bases at the bottom: Luni 2002, 137–41, figs 35–40). This connection between the agora and the gymnasium/Caesareum via the Stoa/portico created a visual, as well as ideological, link that passers-by would have not ignored.

Like in the agora, inscriptions played an important role in the reconfiguration of spaces and uses under the building's new course as a Caesareum-forum (see especially Ward-Perkins *et al.* 1958, 158–64; Gasperini 1971; Luni 1992). A fragmentary Greek text set up on behalf of Rome (for the deified Caesar?) is dated to the Augustan period and might be the earliest attestation of 'Roman' engagement with this edifice (*IRCyr2020* C.2). However, if the text was part of the entablature on the uppermost course of the outer south wall, where it was repositioned during the pre-war restorations, this would have probably affected its legibility and casual viewers may have failed to grasp its significance in full. In contrast, the inscriptions that were added on the entablatures of the two propyla would have stood out more prominently. It should be noted straightaway that these were all written in Latin. The architrave on the outer face of the South Propylon bears a text recording a restoration by M. Sufenas Proculus (*IRCyr2020* C.9) (Fig. 10.25), a wealthy citizen who was also responsible for rebuilding the Strategeion in the Sanctuary of Apollo (*IRCyr2020* C.225–26) and for setting up a dedication to Tiberius in the agora (*IRCyr2020* C.118; see also Żelazowski 2014–15, 252–56). The latter inscriptions are dated to 4–14 CE, so it seems likely that his activity in the Caesareum took place at around the same time. It has been argued that the lower unfluted portions of the propylon's column shafts were remade during Proculus' restoration, who intended to update the architecture of the complex to more current canons of the period (Luni 1992, 130–32, fig. 4). This, however, remains speculative, as Cyrene's architecture already shows a degree of deviation from 'orthodox' principles in earlier periods, and this continued throughout the course of its history (see above). Further restorations to the building occurred in the post-Augustan era (mid-first century CE?), as shown by a fragmentary inscription probably recording the name of C. Rubellius Blandus, who is known for his governorship of Crete and Cyrene (*IRCyr2020* C.4). There is some controversy as to the setting of this text: it was restored on the left-hand side of the entablature of the East Propylon's inner face, but some have claimed it might have come from the inner side of the South Propylon instead (Gasperini 1971, 7–9; Luni 1992, 132–35). Finally, the central parts of the entablatures on both faces of the East Propylon carry inscriptions recording a further restoration of the *porticus Caesarei* by a legate, [---] Pacilaeus, perhaps in the later first century CE (*IRCyr2020* C.3–4; Gasperini 1971, 9–10;

Fig. 10.25. Cyrene: Caesareum, South Propylon with Latin inscription of M. Sufenas Proculus, IRCyr2020 *C.9 (photo M. Kenawi, Manar al-Athar).*

Luni 1992, 140–43). Regardless of the extent and nature of these three interventions, which are not easy to determine, the respective promoters aimed to showcase their agency along with imperial ideology. The choice of conspicuous spots in the newly repurposed Caesareum and the use of Latin were means to address a target audience that might have been receptive to these themes.

The most significant architectural (and political) change to this complex took place with the insertion of a civic basilica on the north side (69.4 × 21.6 m). This new edifice, provided with a central nave and two lateral aisles, reused the colonnade of the pre-existing Doric portico on its façade, while it obliterated a series of rooms behind it that must have served to the use of this area as a gymnasium (Fig. 10.26). The basilica suffered major damage during the Jewish Revolt and was rebuilt under Hadrian, so most of its extant remains, including a newly designed exedra on its short west side, belong to this reconstruction (Luni 1990, 101–20; 2007; Luni and Cellini 1999). The date of the first basilica is uncertain. It is generally attributed to the Flavian period, but no firm archaeological data have been published yet in support of this assumption (Luni 1990, 101; 2007, 388; Luni and Cellini 1999, 30). It appears this argument rests mainly on the discovery of two statues – one of them (perhaps a priestess) is convincingly dated to the Flavian era on stylistic grounds – which were recycled along with other materials underneath the floor of the later Hadrianic basilica (Rosenbaum 1960, 46, no. 22, pl. 18.1–2; Luni 1990, 106, fig. 11; 2007, 388). The presence of these statues, however, only confirms that honorific dedications were set up in the building under the Flavians but cannot prove the basilica was erected at that time. It is worth looking back at J. Reynolds' comments on a fragmentary text from this edifice, which is partly preserved under a later Hadrianic inscription (*IRCyr2020* C.20; Ward-Perkins *et al.* 1958, 161). On these fragments one can read the word [---] *sili*[---], to be restored as [*ba*]*sili*[*cam*], and some erased letters that seem to be attributable to the imperial titles of Nero, forming part of the basilica's dedicatory inscription.[41]

Fig. 10.26. Cyrene: Interior of the basilica and north portico of Caesareum, view from north-east (photo R. Burns, Manar al-Athar).

If this reading is correct, the construction of the building should be associated with this emperor, who was popular in Cyrenaica and is known for having granted citizenship to local elite families, like his predecessor Claudius.

Julio-Claudian involvement in public life at Cyrene may be further attested through dedication of statues of the imperial family. An interesting discovery was made in 1989 during excavation of a trench in the south-east zone of Cyrene to bring electricity to the Caesareum (Walker 1994). A set of statues was recovered during these works, which had been probably removed from their setting to be burnt in a lime kiln. One group is composed of a female statue and a male one, to be identified respectively with Valeria Messalina and perhaps Claudius (Walker 1994, 167–72, figs 1–9). The second group comprises three figures that may represent Germanicus, Antonia Minor, and Drusus (Walker 1994, 172–76, figs 10–18). These sculptures were meant for public display and a provenance from the Caesareum may be plausible. Their most striking characteristic is the presence of Cyrenean portrait features, such as almond-shaped eyes and full lips, pointing to the work of local ateliers (Walker 1994, 181–82). The choice of such marked facial features, which were extraneous to Roman imperial-style portraiture (in sharp contrast with the statues from the Temple of Roma and Augustus at Lepcis Magna), helped to create a stronger connection between these figures and the local audience.

Concluding remarks: Architectural, urban, and visual development

The analysis of public spaces in these three North African cities shows interesting points of similarity, despite the different historical, socio-political, and urban processes that defined each of them. The role of private euergetism and the activity of provincial governors in funding and dedicating public buildings stand out. The significance of this phenomenon can be extended to the whole region of Africa Proconsularis, where this was the norm for the construction of civic and religious edifices throughout the first century CE (Jouffroy 1986, 197–99; Bullo 2002, 223–48). While public municipal funding became widespread from the Antonine period onwards, this did not replace altogether the involvement of wealthy individuals. Epigraphic and architectural data are available at Lepcis Magna that show the continuity of private interventions in this period (see Mugnai 2021, 112; *IRT2021* 363, 370, 1086–87). Similarly, the further development of Thugga's civic district under the Antonines is significant to highlight the importance of local elite families in funding new constructions (Aounallah and Golvin 2016, 141–217; *DFH* 7, 27–29, 31–32), and private donors were largely in charge of the rebuilding programme across the city of Cyrene after the traumatic events of the Jewish Revolt (Spawforth and Walker 1986, 96–101; Walker 2002).

These forms of private euergetism suited the agendas of those who promoted them, allowing them to showcase their role within the community. At the same time, this took place under the watchful eye of the Roman State, and there is no doubt these building/rebuilding activities served to reinforce imperial agency, more or less directly, in these provincial urban settings. The constructions carried out by Postumius Chius in the forum of Thugga under Tiberius show the connection between the institution of the *pagus* of Roman settlers and the city's monumental development. The recurring presence of names of proconsuls on major monuments at Cyrene also attests to the intention to remark Rome's engagement: Lucanius Proculus on the Augusteum, Clodius Vestalis on the North Stoa and annexed buildings, and Rubellius Blandus on one of the propyla of the Caesareum (in addition to the wealthy citizen Sufenas Proculus mentioned on the same building). The paving of the Old Forum of Lepcis Magna and the erection of porticoes under Claudius can be assigned to at least two private sponsors, Caius son of Hanno and C. Phelyssam, but this enterprise must have been supervised and approved by the local municipality on behalf of the central power. Inscriptions were an essential component of these buildings to convey ideological messages, and their presence was therefore a requirement and a symbol of appropriateness, whether viewers were able to read them or not. Regrettably, we do not know the extent of (Latin, Greek, and neo-Punic) literacy among the local populations. However, the use of large epigraphic texts and their conspicuous position on monuments might still have served as a visual trigger, and at the very least they would have caught one's attention when passing by or standing in front of them.

The physical shape of buildings was subject to a range of factors, but it is important to observe that construction activities in these three cities in the early imperial era aimed to achieve a balance between local elements and Rome-driven influences. The preservation of the Numidian Monument in the forum of Thugga is a case in point: its prominent position created a dynamic dialogue with the other edifices around it, whose construction should be assigned to members of the *pagus*. Once again, this shows that the two communities of *pagus* and *civitas* were interconnected and used the same public spaces, which invites to rule out once and for all old-fashioned views that argued for a physical, social, and religious separation between these two juridical entities. The sacred buildings erected in Lepcis Magna's forum blended together a variety of architectural and decorative motifs. While their plan and layout recalled the Romano-Italic temple design and the use of imperial-style statuary was meant to establish a connection with current metropolitan trends, their architectural ornament was deeply influenced by local traditions that survived through time, and these constituted the essential repertoire of the locally available stonemasons. The transmission of design principles or building styles from the centre of Empire was not directly connected to the movement of people, given that only a small number of families from the Italian Peninsula are attested at Lepcis

Magna (Birley 1988; Mugnai 2021, 112, with references). Finally, Cyrene offers ample evidence for the continuity of local architectural forms, most of which were a hybrid solution that combined together elements of the Doric and Ionic orders – a fashion that started early on and continued without interruption into the later imperial era. These traditional architectures, however, acquired a new function as bearers of imperial messages through rededications (see, for example, the Augusteum, the North Stoa, and the gymnasium/Caesareum) and the addition of newly built complexes such as the basilica in the Caesareum/forum. Unlike the statues at Lepcis Magna, imperial portrait statuary that was displayed in public contexts at Cyrene maintained strong local features, which, along with the visual layout of monuments, was an effective tool to create an amalgamation between the background of the city's inhabitants and the new social and political reality of the period.

Notes

1. As pointed out by Ardeleanu (2021, 228, n. 2175), it is regrettable that no pottery or other finds recovered from these and other sondages were discussed in Aounallah and Golvin 2016, thus often leaving questions about the chronology of architectural remains open.
2. Bullo 2002, 120–22; Khanoussi 2003, 140–42; Aounallah and Golvin 2016, 48–50; Ardeleanu 2021, 224–25; more cautious remarks in Saint-Amans 2004, 46.
3. Ardeleanu (2021, 225) interprets some inner blocks perpendicular to the wall of the podium as a foundation for the cella wall. However, due to the poor state of preservation, it is difficult to understand whether these fitted with the original masonry or belonged to later phases along with other blocks currently scattered inside the monument.
4. The Kbor Klib monument is much larger (c. 45.4 × 8.9 m) and should probably be discarded as a direct parallel for the structure at Thugga.
5. It has also been argued that these capitals might be a first- or second-century CE production that revived Hellenistic styles (Pensabene 2016, 241–42), but again this proposal rests on mere stylistic considerations.
6. An active engagement of members of the *civitas* in honouring Roman emperors is further attested through a series of dedications of the Flavian period, at least some of which might have been set up in the forum: *DFH* 3 (a double dedication to Vespasian and Domitian, 71–79 CE); *AE* 1997, 1650; *CIL* VIII, 26520; Ardeleanu 2021, 236–37.
7. Bullo 2002, 122–28; Saint-Amans 2004, 60–78; Aounallah and Golvin 2016, 75–140; Ardeleanu 2021, 229–42. Information on statuary from the forum is very limited, and no systematic record exists of the sculptures held in the local storehouse: Aounallah and Golvin 2016, 132, nn. 122–23. The recently published catalogue of portraits in the Bardo Museum (Baratte *et al.* 2022) does not include any statues from the forum of Thugga.
8. See *DFH* 23; Bullo 2002, 122–25; Saint-Amans 2004, 60–76, 300–1, no. 26; Beschaouch 2011, 1806–9; Aounallah and Golvin 2016, 113–17; Ardeleanu 2021, 229–35.
9. A good example is represented by the church on the west side of the Old Forum at Lepcis Magna, where cornice blocks were recycled from the Arch of Trajan, which lies some 360 m away from the forum: see Mahler 2006, 108, 235–37, nos. 826–52 KG, pls. 106–13.
10. Aounallah and Golvin (2016, 121–24) reconstruct the plan of a distyle temple *in antis* under the Capitolium and associate it with the inscription *DFH* 68, but this is not supported by any extant evidence (Ardeleanu 2021, 238, n. 2257).
11. Saint-Amans 2004, 73; Beschaouch 2011, 1808–9; Aounallah and Golvin 2016, 114–15; Ardeleanu 2021, 229.
12. Tiberius allowed erection of a temple to himself, Livia, and the Senate at Smyrna in 23 CE, but he rejected the request from an embassy of Baetica to build a temple to himself and Livia in 25 CE (Fishwick 2002, 111–12; 230). An inscription from Caesarea Maritima records restoration of a *Tiberieum* under Pontius Pilate, but the name is unconventional and this building probably had nothing to do with the imperial cult (*CIIP* II, 1277; see also Peleg-Barkat, this volume).
13. I would like to thank John Wilkes for these considerations. The hypothesis of a temple of Julius Caesar is rejected by Saint-Amans 2004, 73, n. 95 and Beschaouch 2011, 1808; Bullo 2002, 124, n. 397 leaves the question open.
14. The presence of a square apse, identified by the French-Tunisian team on the rear wall of the building and partly hidden by the Byzantine fortress (Aounallah and Golvin 2016, 85, figs 14, 18), would not be incompatible with a curia.
15. I would like to thank Janet DeLaine for her helpful observations on this point.
16. This process of duplication of public plazas in North Africa, known as 'Polyzentrismus', is examined by Kleinwächter 2001 (including Lepcis Magna) and Scheding 2019 (central area of Africa Proconsularis).
17. Masturzo 2003, 707–33; 2005; Livadiotti and Rocco 2005; 2018; Ricciardi 2005; Rocco 2010; 2016; Kenrick 2009, 109–13 for a good summary.
18. Di Vita (1968; 1982, 553–58) had proposed an earlier date around the start of the first century BCE, but the more recent study of this temple by Masturzo (2005) ruled out this hypothesis.
19. This suggestion is difficult to accept because of the early chronology of the temple: see the issues raised in Di Vita 2005; Quinn 2010, 57; Quinn and Wilson 2013, 153–55; Mugnai 2021, 104.
20. A different hypothesis attributes the inscription *IRT2021* 625, also bearing the name of the proconsul, to the entablature of the temple (Di Vita-Evrard 1990, 317–18; Ricciardi 2005, 367), but this is problematic because the inscription was not found anywhere near the forum area.
21. The features of Lepcis Magna's early imperial architectural ornament are examined in detail by Bianchi 2005, 191–210, figs 1–22; Bigi 2006; Mahler 2006; Rocco 2010; Mazzilli 2016, 182–91, figs 182–98.
22. The neo-Punic text states that the dedication of the temple was made under the two *sufetes* B'LYTN, son of Anno G. Saturninus, and BDMLQRT, son of BDMLQRT Tapapi [---] RYQL. The family of the Tapapii is well known for its euergetism in the city under Augustus and throughout the first century CE: see *IRT2021* 273, 319, 321–23, 341; *IPT* 17, 24a–b, 28; Amadasi Guzzo 1983.

23. Aurigemma 1940, 44–49, figs 25–28; Rose 1997, 184–85, pls. 218–19; Boschung 2002, 8, nos. 1.1–2, pl. 2; Livadiotti and Rocco 2005, 231–32, fig. 2.63.
24. To these one should add a later group comprising seated statues of the deified Augustus and Claudius (Rose 1997, 185, pls. 235–36; Boschung 2002, 9, nos. 1.11–12, pl. 8), but their position on the temple is far from secure: see Musso 2008, 179–81. A series of inscribed bases, all datable to 45–46 CE (*IRT2021* 326–27, 333, 337, 340), were found in the vicinity of the temple and were meant to support statues of the deified Augustus and Livia, Tiberius, Messalina, and Claudius; it seems more likely, however, that they were placed on the other two temples on the north-west side or elsewhere in the forum: Bullo 2002, 183–84; Mugnai 2021, 107, with references.
25. On the Ionic-Italic style, see Batino 2006. The early chronology of the Sicilian examples, however, is based on old data and interpretations; most of these, in particular the capitals from Monte Iato, do not predate the second century BCE.
26. The façades of Temples A and B were renovated around the mid-second century CE with marble Corinthian columns, in line with the new architectural trends of the period at Lepcis Magna: Masturzo 2005, 123–28, fig. 1.123; Livadiotti and Rocco 2005, 245–52, figs 2.68–76. In contrast, it is possible that the original limestone peristasis of Temple C was left in place unaltered: see Mugnai 2021, 109–10, 113, with references.
27. *RT2021* 348; Cordovana 2007, 81–84, figs 1–4; Dolciotti *et al.* 2012; Mugnai 2021, 100–2, figs 31–33.
28. The next steps of this process were represented by the limestone Corinthian order of the Arch of Trajan, 109–10 CE (Mazzilli 2016, 91–99, figs 88–92) and, eventually, the large-scale use of marble architectural decoration of Asiatic style from Hadrian's reign onwards: see Pensabene 2001; Bianchi 2009; Mugnai 2021, 96–97.
29. The restoration of this text on the enclosure's front wall might be problematic in terms of visibility: see Mugnai 2020, 840; 2021, 100. However, a date for the curia in the Flavian era is not to be called into question, and fragments of other Flavian inscriptions (*IRT2021* 344a–b, 814) were recycled in the building during later phases.
30. Stucchi 1965; 1967; Bacchielli 1981; Ermeti 1981; Stucchi and Bacchielli 1983; Purcaro 2001.
31. See also the comparative analysis of the agorai of Athens, Cyrene, and Ephesus under Augustus in Walker 1997.
32. On the reshaping of architecture at Cyrene during Hadrian's reign and the Panhellenion, see especially Spawforth and Walker 1986, 96–101; Walker 2002.
33. The pastiche statue composed of a reworked female body matched with a head of Marcus Aurelius was also recovered inside the Augusteum, while a cuirassed torso was found in a pit outside it: Stucchi 1967, 129–38, figs 121–41.
34. On the evidence from Asia Minor, see in particular Rumscheid 1994, 118, 299, nos. 213.1, 235.1, pls. 126–27, 135; Ismaelli 2009, 184–91, 385, figs 212–14. The so-called 'Temple of Hercules' at Cori, c. late second century BCE, is a good example of such mixtures in the Italian Peninsula: Rocco 1994, 103–8, figs 63–65.
35. In the area of the agora, Doric-Ionic columns were set up during the refurbishment of the Temple of Apollo Archegetes and the Temple of Zeus in the second century CE: Stucchi 1975, 235–37, 242–43, figs 217–18, 231–32; Bonacasa and Ensoli 2000, 81, 89; Purcaro 2001, 93–96, fig. 53.
36. Fragmentary honorary bases and the respective foundations were discovered in the North Stoa: Stucchi 1965, 227–28, figs 140–42. Alongside these, a cuirassed bust of Antoninus Pius and a head of Faustina Minor were also found in this building: Rosenbaum 1960, 57, 59, nos. 47, 52, pls. 34.3–4, 36.1–2.
37. For instance: a stele with decrees of honours attributed to A. Pompeius M[---], Augustan period (*IRCyr2020* C.134); a base with dedication of a statue of Augustus to Hermes and Herakles, 8 BCE (*IRCyr2020* C.125); a fragmentary altar, perhaps set up in honour of Caius Caesar, which might be associated with a statue of the prince, before 4 CE (*IRCyr2020* C.120; Rosenbaum 1960, 42–43, no. 14, pl. 14.1–2); a stele with ephebic lists, 3–4 CE and 23–39 CE (*IRCyr2020* C.145); a circular base with dedication to the goddess Libya by M. Messius Atticus for the safety of the proconsul M. Pomponius Secundus, first century CE (*IRCyr2020* C.126).
38. It has been recently argued that the statue above the ship prow, rather than being a Nike, might be identified with Isis *Euploia/ Pelagia*: Ensoli 2016, 48–50. This remains speculative, but if true, one should not see a conflict in this connection of Augustus with Isis (often regarded as a deity too close to Antony), because Augustan religious policies did not seek to prohibit the worship of Isis but simply to regulate it: see Mazzuca 2015, with references.
39. It is believed that the gymnasium was named Ptolemaion (Luni 1987, 41; 1990, 93–93), but this assumption has been called into question recently (see *IRCyr2020* C.1, with commentary and references).
40. Luni 1987; Bonacasa and Ensoli 2000, 91–96; Kenrick 2013, 153–56; Trifogli 2014.
41. A second fragmented text was found during excavation of the building, but it was reburied afterwards; it would bear the word [*bas*]*ilic*[*am*] and might also belong to the pre-Hadrianic phase (Gasperini 1971, 15, fig. 18). Another inscription was recycled on the stylobate of the basilica during its reconstruction: it contains part of a dedication to the proconsul Bruttidius Sabinus in name of the Cyreneans and Roman citizens who did business there (*IRCyr2020* C.22).

References

Amadasi Guzzo, M.G. 1983. Una grande famiglia di Lepcis in rapporto con la ristrutturazione urbanistica della città (I sec. a.C. – I sec. d.C.). In *Architecture et société de l'archaïsme grec à la fin de la république romaine. Actes du colloque de Rome (2–4 décembre 1980)*. Rome: École française de Rome, 377–85.

Aounallah, S. 2010. *Pagus, castellum et civitas. Études d'épigraphie et d'histoire sur le village et la cité en Afrique romaine.* Bordeaux: Ausonius Éditions.

Aounallah, S. and Golvin, J.-C. (eds) 2016. *Dougga: Études d'architecture religieuse, 2. Les sanctuaires du forum, du centre de l'agglomération et de la Grande rue courbe.* Bordeaux: Ausonius Éditions.

Ardeleanu, S. 2021. *Numidia Romana? Die Auswirkungen der römischen Präsenz in Numidien (2. Jh. v. Chr. – 1. Jh. n. Chr.).* Wiesbaden: Reichert Verlag.

Aurigemma, S. 1940. Sculture del foro vecchio di Leptis Magna raffiguranti la dea Roma e principi della casa dei giulio-claudi (pubblicazione provvisoria). *Africa Italiana* 8: 1–94.

Bacchielli, L. 1981. *L'agorà di Cirene, II.1. L'area settentrionale del lato ovest della platea inferiore*. Rome: 'L'Erma' di Bretschneider.

Balty, J.C. 1991. *Curia ordinis. Recherches d'architecture et d'urbanisme antiques sur les curies provinciales du monde romain*. Brussels: Académie Royale de Belgique.

Baratte, F., Bejaoui, F., de Chaisemartin, N. and Naït-Yghil, F. (eds) 2022. *Les sculptures romaines du Musée National du Bardo. 1: Les portraits*. Bordeaux: Ausonius Éditions.

Batino, S. 2006. *Genus Ionicum. Forme, storia e modelli del capitello ionico-italico*. Oxford: British Archaeological Reports.

Beschaouch, A. 2011. Recherches récentes sur l'histoire municipale de Thugga, ville à double communauté civique, en Numidie proconsulaire (Dougga en Tunisie). *Comptes rendus des séances de l'Académie des Inscriptions et Belles-Lettres* 155.4: 1803–18.

Bianchi, F. 2005. La decorazione architettonica in pietra locale a Leptis Magna tra il I e il II sec. d.C. Maestranze e modelli nell'architettura pubblica. *Archeologia Classica* 56: 189–223.

Bianchi, F. 2009. Su alcuni aspetti della decorazione architettonica in marmo a Leptis Magna in età imperiale. *Marmora* 5: 45–70.

Bigi, F. 2006. I capitelli di Leptis Magna fra modelli italici e influenze alessandrine. In Akerraz, A., Ruggeri, P., Siraj, A. and Vismara, C. (eds), *L'Africa Romana. Mobilità delle persone e dei popoli, dinamiche migratorie, emigrazioni ed immigrazioni nelle province occidentali dell'impero romano. Atti del XVI convegno di studio (Rabat, 15–19 dicembre 2004)*. Rome: Carocci, 2351–76.

Birley, A.R. 1988. Names at Lepcis Magna. *Libyan Studies* 19: 1–19.

Bonacasa, N. and Ensoli, S. 2000. *Cirene*. Milan: Electa.

Boschung, D. 2002. *Gens Augusta. Untersuchungen zu Aufstellung, Wirkung und Bedeutung der Statuengruppen des julisch-claudischen Kaiserhauses*. Mainz: Philipp von Zabern.

Bullo, S. 2002. *Provincia Africa. Le città e il territorio dalla caduta di Cartagine a Nerone*. Rome: 'L'Erma' di Bretschneider.

Callot, J.-J. 1999. *Recherches sur les cultes en Cyrénaïque durant le Haut-Empire romain*. Paris: De Boccard.

Caputo, G. 1966–67. Spigolature architettoniche leptitane, II: tradizione ellenistica ed innovazione architettonica romana. *Libya Antiqua* 3–4: 29–39.

Christol, M. 1991. Remarques sur une inscription de Thugga: le pagus dans la colonie de Carthage au Ier siècle ap. J.-C. In *Epigrafia. Actes du colloque international d'épigraphie latine en mémoire de Attilio Degrassi pour le centenaire de sa naissance (Rome, 27–28 mai 1988)*. Rome: École française de Rome, 607–28.

Coarelli, F. and Thébert, Y. 1988. Architecture funéraire et pouvoir: réflexions sur l'hellénisme numide. *Mélanges de l'École française de Rome. Antiquité* 100: 761–818.

Cordovana, O.D. 2007. I Flavi e Leptis Magna. In Catani, E. and Di Vita, A. (eds), *Archeologia italiana in Libia: esperienze a confronto. Atti dell'incontro di studio (Macerata-Fermo, 28–30 marzo 2003)*. Macerata: EUM, 69–87.

De Miro, E. and Polito, A. 2005. *Leptis Magna. Dieci anni di scavi archeologici nell'area del Foro Vecchio. I livelli fenici, punici e romani (Missione dell'Università di Messina)*. Rome: 'L'Erma' di Bretschneider.

De Ruyt, C. 1983. *Macellum: Marché alimentaire des romains*. Louvain-la-Neuve: Institut Supérieur d'Archéologie et d'Histoire de l'Art.

Di Filippo Balestrazzi, E. 1996. La colonna acantina dell'agorà di Cirene e l'agyieus di Apollo. In Bacchielli, L. and Bonanno Aravantinos, M. (eds), *Scritti di antichità in memoria di Sandro Stucchi. Volume I: La Cirenaica – La Grecia e l'Oriente mediterraneo*. Rome: 'L'Erma' di Bretschneider, 61–72.

Di Vita, A. 1968. Shadrapa e Milk'ashtart dèi patri di Leptis ed i templi del lato nord-ovest del foro vecchio leptitano. *Orientalia* 37: 201–11.

Di Vita, A. 1982. Entgegnung. In *150-Jahr-Feier Deutsches Archäologisches Institut Rom. Ansprachen und Vorträge (Rom, 4.–7. Dezember 1979)*. Mainz: Philipp von Zabern, 46–49.

Di Vita, A. 2005. Liber Pater o Capitolium? Una nota. In Di Vita, A. and Livadiotti, M. (eds), *I tre templi del lato nord-ovest del foro vecchio di Leptis Magna*. Rome: 'L'Erma' di Bretschneider, 14–21.

Di Vita-Evrard, G. 1984. Municipium Flavium Lepcis Magna. *Bulletin Archéologique du Comité des Travaux Historiques et Scientifiques* 17: 197–210.

Di Vita-Evrard, G. 1990. IRT 520, le proconsulat de Cn. Calpurnius Piso et l'insertion de Lepcis Magna dans la provincia Africa. In *L'Afrique dans l'Occident romain (Ier siècle av. J.-C. – IVe siècle ap. J.-C.). Actes du colloque (Rome, 3–5 décembre 1987)*. Rome: École française de Rome, 315–31.

Dolciotti, A.M., Fiandra, E. and Mighetto, P. 2012. Il complesso templare della Gens Flavia a Leptis Magna (Libia) tra scenografia, funzionalità e colorismo. In Capogrossi Colognesi, L. and Tassi Scandone, E. (eds), *Vespasiano e l'impero dei Flavi. Atti del convegno (Roma, 18–20 novembre 2009)*. Rome: 'L'Erma' di Bretschneider, 263–72.

Ensoli, S. 2016. Alessandria e Cartagine: interazioni artistiche e culturali tra Egitto ellenistico e Maghreb latinizzato. In Vaccaro, L. (ed.), *Africa/Ifrīqiya. Il Maghreb nella storia religiosa di Cristianesimo e Islam*. Vatican City: Libreria Editrice Vaticana, 45–75.

Ermeti, A.L. 1981. *L'agorà di Cirene, III.1. Il monumento navale*. Rome: 'L'Erma' di Bretschneider.

Fentress, E. 2021. Coercive urbanism: the Roman impact on North African towns. In Belvedere, O. and Bergmann, J. (eds), *Imperium Romanum: Romanization between Colonization and Globalization (Villa Vigoni, centro italo-tedesco per il dialogo europeo, 4–8 novembre 2019)*. Palermo: Palermo University Press, 165–78.

Ferchiou, N. 1989. *L'évolution du décor architectonique en Afrique proconsulaire des derniers temps de Carthage aux Antonins. L'hellénisme africain, son déclin, ses mutations et le triomphe de l'art romano-africain*. Gap: Imprimerie Louis-Jean.

Ferchiou, N. 1991. Le Kbor Klib (Tunisie). *Quaderni di Archeologia della Libya* 14: 45–97.

Fishwick, D. 2002. *The Imperial Cult in the Latin West. Studies in the Ruler Cult of the Western Provinces of the Roman Empire. Volume III: Provincial Cult. Part 1: Institution and Evolution*. Boston-Leiden: Brill.

Gasperini, L. 1971. Le iscrizioni del cesareo e della basilica di Cirene. *Quaderni di Archeologia della Libya* 6: 3–22.

Ghaki, M. 1997. Épigraphie libyque et punique à Dougga (TBGG). In Khanoussi, M. and Maurin, L. (eds), *Dougga (Thugga): Études épigraphiques*. Paris: De Boccard, 27–45.

Golvin, J.-C. and Khanoussi, M. (eds) 2005. *Dougga: Études d'architecture religieuse. Les sanctuaires des Victoires de Caracalla, de 'Pluton' et de Caelestis*. Bordeaux: Ausonius Éditions.

Hiesel, G. and Strocka, V.M. 2002. Vorbericht über die Grabungen 1996–2000. In Khanoussi, M. and Strocka, V.M. (eds), *Thugga, I. Grundlagen und Berichte*. Mainz: Philipp von Zabern, 69–86.

Howard Carter, T. 1965. Western Phoenicians at Lepcis Magna. *American Journal of Archaeology* 69.2: 123–32.

Ismaelli, T. 2009. *Hierapolis di Frigia, III. Architettura dorica a Hierapolis di Frigia*. Istanbul: Ege Yayınları.

Jouffroy, H. 1986. *La construction publique en Italie et dans l'Afrique romaine*. Strasbourg: AECR.

Kenrick, P. 2009. *Libya Archaeological Guides: Tripolitania*. London: Silphium Press.

Kenrick, P. 2013. *Libya Archaeological Guides: Cyrenaica*. London: Silphium Press.

Khanoussi, M. 1994. Thugga (Dougga) sous le Haut-empire: une ville double? In Mastino, A. and Ruggeri, P. (eds), *L'Africa Romana. Atti del X convegno di studio (Oristano, 11–13 dicembre 1992)*. Sassari: Editrice Archivio Fotografico Sardo, 597–602.

Khanoussi, M. 1997. Thugga: épigraphie et constructions publiques. In Khanoussi, M. and Maurin, L. (eds), *Dougga (Thugga): Études épigraphiques*. Paris: De Boccard, 117–25.

Khanoussi, M. 2003. L'évolution urbaine de Thugga (Dougga) en Afrique proconsulaire: de l'agglomération numide à la ville africo-romaine. *Comptes rendus des séances de l'Académie des Inscriptions et Belles-Lettres* 147.1: 131–55.

Kleinwächter, C. 2001. *Platzanlagen nordafrikanischer Städte. Untersuchungen zum sogenannten Polyzentrismus in der Urbanistik der römischen Kaiserzeit*. Mainz: Philipp von Zabern.

Kreikenbom, D. 2011. *Lepcis Magna unter den ersten Kaisern*. Wiesbaden: Harrassowitz Verlag.

Kreikenbom, D. and Mahler, K.-U. 2010. Archäologische Projekte der Johannes Gutenberg – Universität Mainz in Lepcis Magna, 2002–2007. *Libya Antiqua* n.s. 5: 37–47.

Livadiotti, M. and Rocco, G. 2005. Il tempio di Roma e Augusto. In Di Vita, A. and Livadiotti, M. (eds), *I tre templi del lato nord-ovest del foro vecchio di Leptis Magna*. Rome: 'L'Erma' di Bretschneider, 165–308.

Livadiotti, M. and Rocco, G. 2018. *Exornata aedes. La curia del foro vecchio di Leptis Magna*. Rome: 'L'Erma' di Bretschneider.

Luni, M. 1976. Documenti per la storia della istituzione ginnasiale e dell'attività atletica in Cirenaica, in rapporto a quelle della Grecia. *Quaderni di Archeologia della Libya* 8: 223–84.

Luni, M. 1987. Il ginnasio-cesareo nel quartiere monumentale dell'agorà. In Stucchi, S. (ed.), *Da Batto Aristotele a Ibn El-'As. Introduzione alla mostra*. Rome: 'L'Erma' di Bretschneider, 41–46.

Luni, M. 1990. Il ginnasio-Caesareum di Cirene nel contesto del rinnovamento urbanistico della media età ellenistica e della prima età imperiale. In *Giornata lincea sulla archeologia cirenaica (Roma, 3 novembre 1987)*. Rome: Accademia Nazionale dei Lincei, 87–120.

Luni, M. 1992. Strutture monumentali e documenti epigrafici nel foro di Cirene. In Mastino, A. (ed.), *L'Africa Romana. Atti del IX convegno di studio (Nuoro, 13–15 dicembre 1991)*. Sassari: Gallizzi, 123–46.

Luni, M. 2002. Lo Xystos-Portico delle Erme nel quartiere dell'agorà di Cirene. *Quaderni di Archeologia della Libya* 16: 109–44.

Luni, M. 2007. La basilica nel foro di Cirene. In Gasperini, L. and Marengo, S.M. (eds), *Cirene e la Cirenaica nell'antichità. Atti del convegno internazionale di studi (Roma – Frascati, 18–21 dicembre 1996)*. Tivoli: Tored, 377–400.

Luni, M. and Cellini, G.A. 1999. L'abside della basilica nel foro di Cirene ed i due gruppi di sculture. *Karthago* 24: 27–73.

Mahler, K.-U. 2006. *Die Architekturdekoration der frühen Kaiserzeit in Lepcis Magna*. Worms: Wernesche Verlaggesellschaft.

Mahler, K.-U. 2012. The church in the Old Forum of Leptis Magna. A preliminary report. In Ensoli, S. (ed.), *For the Preservation of the Cultural Heritage in Libya: A Dialogue among Institutions. Proceedings of Conference (Caserta, 1–2 July 2011)*. Pisa-Rome: Fabrizio Serra, 49–53.

Marmouri, K. 2017. Temple de Liber Pater ou Capitole? L'apport des inscriptions à l'identification d'un lieu de culte de Lepcis Magna. *Antiquités Africaines* 53: 5–21.

Masturzo, N. 2003. Le città della Tripolitania fra continuità ed innovazione. I fori di Leptis Magna e Sabratha. *Mélanges de l'École française de Rome. Antiquité* 115: 705–53.

Masturzo, N. 2005. Il tempio occidentale – tempio di Liber Pater. In Di Vita, A. and Livadiotti, M. (eds), *I tre templi del lato nord-ovest del foro vecchio di Leptis Magna*. Rome: 'L'Erma' di Bretschneider, 35–163.

Masturzo, N. 2016. Da Šadrafa e Milk'Aštart a Roma e Augusto. Santuario poliade e assetto imperiale a Leptis Magna. In Russo Tagliente, A. and Guarneri, F. (eds), *Santuari mediterranei tra oriente e occidente. Interazioni e contatti culturali. Atti del convegno internazionale (Civitavecchia-Roma 2014)*. Rome: Scienze e Lettere, 557–69.

Mazzilli, G. 2016. *L'arco di Traiano a Leptis Magna*. Rome: 'L'Erma' di Bretschneider.

Mazzuca, V. 2015. Religione e politica: Iside e Augusto. In Baglioni, I. (ed.), *Saeculum Aureum. Tradizione e innovazione nella religione romana in epoca augustea. Volume II: La vita religiosa a Roma all'epoca di Augusto*. Rome: Quasar, 177–88.

Montali, G. 2016a. Nuove ricerche sul tempio della Magna Mater a Leptis Magna. In Rizzo, M.A. (ed.), *Macerata e l'archeologia in Libia: 45 anni di ricerche dell'ateneo maceratese. Atti del convegno (Macerata, 18 marzo 2014)*. Rome: 'L'Erma' di Bretschneider, 85–94.

Montali, G. 2016b. Il tempio della Magna Mater a Leptis Magna. Ipotesi ricostruttiva del podio. In Bonacasa, N., Buscemi, F. and La Rosa, V. (eds), *Architetture del Mediterraneo. Scritti in onore di Francesco Tomasello*. Rome: Quasar, 301–17.

Mugnai, N. 2020. Reconstructing the history and architecture of the Curia in the Forum Vetus at Lepcis Magna. *Journal of Roman Archaeology* 33: 795–805.

Mugnai, N. 2021. A promenade at Lepcis Magna: experiencing buildings from the Augustan to the Antonine era. *Libyan Studies* 52: 87–118.

Mugnai, N. 2022. Architecture and art. In Hitchner, R.B. (ed.), *A Companion to North Africa in Antiquity*. Hoboken, NJ: Wiley-Blackwell, 247–84.

Musso, L. 2008. La romanizzazione di Leptis Magna nel primo periodo imperiale: Augusto e Roma nel Foro Vecchio. In Kreikenbom, D., Mahler, K.-U., Schollmeyer, P. and Weber, T.M. (eds), *Augustus – Der Blick von außen. Die Wahrnehmung des Kaisers in den Provinzen des Reiches und in den Nachbarstaaten. Akten der internationalen Tagung an der Johannes Gutenberg-Universität Mainz vom 12. bis 14. Oktober 2006*. Wiesbaden: Harrassowitz Verlag, 161–96.

Pensabene, P. 1986. La decorazione architettonica, l'impiego del marmo e l'importazione di manufatti orientali a Roma, in Italia e in Africa (II–VI d.C.). In Giardina, A. (ed.), *Società romana e impero tardoantico, 3. Le merci, gli insediamenti*. Rome-Bari: Laterza, 285–429.

Pensabene, P. 2001. Pentelico e proconnesio in Tripolitania: coordinamento o concorrenza nella distribuzione? *Archeologia Classica* 52: 63–127.

Pensabene, P. 2016. Ripresa e continuità di tradizioni ellenistiche nell'architettura e nella decorazione architettonica tardoantica in Africa e altre province dell'impero romano. In Mugnai, N., Nikolaus, J. and Ray, N. (eds), *De Africa Romaque: Merging Cultures across North Africa. Proceedings of the International Conference Held at the University of Leicester (26–27 October 2013)*. London: Society for Libyan Studies, 231–48.

Pensabene, P. and Gasparini, E. 2017. Tra dorico e corinzio in Cirenaica: spunti per una riflessione sul linguaggio architettonico nell'edilizia privata. In Pensabene, P., Milella, M. and Caprioli, F. (eds), *Decor: decorazione e architettura nel mondo romano. Atti del convegno internazionale (Roma, 21–24 maggio 2014)*. Rome: Quasar, 655–82.

Poinssot, L. 1919. Les fouilles de Dougga en 1919 et le quartier du forum. *Nouvelles Archives des Missions Scientifiques et Littéraires* 22: 133–98.

Poinssot, C. 1983. *Les ruines de Dougga (deuxième édition)*. Tunis: Institut National d'Archéologie et d'Arts.

Purcaro, V. 2001. *L'agorà di Cirene, II.3. L'area meridionale del lato ovest dell'agorà*. Rome: 'L'Erma' di Bretschneider.

Quinn, J.C. 2010. The reinvention of Lepcis. *Bollettino di Archeologia Online* 1: 52–69.

Quinn, J.C. 2013. Monumental power: 'Numidian royal architecture' in context. In Quinn, J.C. and Prag, J.R.W. (eds), *The Hellenistic West. Rethinking the Ancient Mediterranean*. Cambridge: Cambridge University Press, 179–215.

Quinn, J.C. and Wilson, A.I. 2013. Capitolia. *Journal of Roman Studies* 103: 117–73.

Rakob, F. 1979. Numidische Königsarchitektur in Nordafrika. In Günter Horn, H. and Rüger, C.B. (eds), *Die Numider. Reiter und Könige nördlich der Sahara*. Bonn: Rudolf Habelt Verlag, 119–71.

Rakob, F. 1994. Der Tempelberg und seine Heiligtümer. In Rakob, F. (ed.), *Simitthus, II. Der Tempelberg und das römische Lager*. Mainz: Philipp von Zabern, 1–38.

Ricciardi, M. 2005. Il tempio di Milk'Ashtart Ercole. In Di Vita, A. and Livadiotti, M. (eds), *I tre templi del lato nord-ovest del foro vecchio di Leptis Magna*. Rome: 'L'Erma' di Bretschneider, 309–93.

Rives, J.B. 1995. *Religion and Authority in Roman Carthage from Augustus to Constantine*. Oxford: Clarendon Press.

Rocco, G. 1994. *Guida alla lettura degli ordini architettonici antichi, I. Il dorico*. Naples: Liguori.

Rocco, G. 2010. Tradizione locale e influssi esterni nei tre templi giulio-claudi del Foro Vecchio di Leptis Magna. *Bollettino di Archeologia Online* 1: 22–36.

Rocco, G. 2016. Ricerche del Politecnico di Bari nel Foro Vecchio di Leptis Magna: il tempio di Roma e Augusto. In Rizzo, M.A. (ed.), *Macerata e l'archeologia in Libia: 45 anni di ricerche dell'ateneo maceratese. Atti del convegno (Macerata, 18 marzo 2014)*. Rome: 'L'Erma' di Bretschneider, 61–76.

Rose, C.B. 1997. *Dynastic Commemoration and Imperial Portraiture in the Julio-Claudian Period*. Cambridge: Cambridge University Press.

Rosenbaum, E. 1960. *A Catalogue of Cyrenaican Portrait Sculpture*. London: British Academy.

Rumscheid, F. 1994. *Untersuchungen zur kleinasiatischen Bauornamentik des Hellenismus*. Mainz: Philipp von Zabern.

Saint-Amans, S. 2004. *Topographie religieuse de Thugga (Dougga), ville romaine d'Afrique proconsulaire (Tunisie)*. Bordeaux: Ausonius Éditions.

Scheding, P. 2019. *Urbaner Ballungsraum im römischen Nordafrika. Zum Einfluss von mikroregionalen Wirtschafts- und Sozialstrukturen auf den Städtebau in der Africa Proconsularis*. Wiesbaden: Reichert Verlag.

Scott, M. 2013. *Space and Society in the Greek and Roman Worlds*. Cambridge: Cambridge University Press.

Spawforth, A.J.S. and Walker, S. 1986. The world of the Panhellenion, II. Three Dorian cities. *Journal of Roman Studies* 76: 88–105.

Stucchi, S. 1965. *L'agorà di Cirene, I. I lati nord ed est della platea inferiore*. Rome: 'L'Erma' di Bretschneider.

Stucchi, S. 1967. *Cirene, 1957–1966. Un decennio di attività della missione archeologica italiana a Cirene*. Tripoli: Quaderni dell'Istituto Italiano di Cultura di Tripoli.

Stucchi, S. 1975. *Architettura cirenaica*. Rome: 'L'Erma' di Bretschneider.

Stucchi, S. and Bacchielli, L. 1983. *L'agorà di Cirene, II.4. Il lato sud della platea inferiore e il lato nord della terrazza superiore*. Rome: 'L'Erma' di Bretschneider.

Trifogli, A. 2014. Dal ginnasio ellenistico al forum di Cirene. In Luni, M. (ed.), *Cirene 'Atene d'Africa', VII. Cirene greca e romana*. Rome: 'L'Erma' di Bretschneider, 183–97.

Trillmich, W. 2014. Die Inschrift-Basis des Quadriga-Monuments für Germanicus und Drusus vor dem Augustus-Roma-Tempel in Lepcis Magna. *Jahrbuch des Deutschen Archäologischen Instituts* 129: 211–67.

Walker, S. 1994. The imperial family as seen in Cyrene. *Libyan Studies* 25: 167–84.

Walker, S. 1997. Athens under Augustus. In Hoff, M.C. and Rotroff, S.I. (eds), *The Romanization of Athens. Proceedings of an International Conference Held at Lincoln, Nebraska (April 1996)*. Oxford: Oxbow Books, 67–80.

Walker, S. 2002. Hadrian and the renewal of Cyrene. *Libyan Studies* 33: 45–56.

Ward-Perkins, J.B. 1949. Leptis Magna (no. 4021). *Fasti Archeologici* 4: 401–2.

Ward-Perkins, J.B. 1968. Pre-Roman elements in the architecture of Roman Tripolitania. In Gadallah, F.F. (ed.), *Libya in History. Historical Conference (16–23 March 1968)*. Benghazi: University of Libya, 101–19.

Ward-Perkins, J.B. 1970. From Republic to Empire: reflections on the early provincial architecture of the Roman west. *Journal of Roman Studies* 60: 1–19.

Ward-Perkins, J.B. 1982. Town planning in North Africa during the first two centuries of the Empire, with special reference to Lepcis and Sabratha: character and sources. In *150-Jahr-Feier Deutsches Archäologisches Institut Rom. Ansprachen und Vorträge (Rom, 4.–7. Dezember 1979)*. Mainz: Philipp von Zabern, 29–46.

Ward-Perkins, J.B., Balance, M.H. and Reynolds, J.M. 1958. The Caesareum at Cyrene and the basilica at Cremna. *Papers of the British School at Rome* 26: 137–94.

Wilson, A.I. 2012. Neo-Punic and Latin inscriptions in North Africa: function and display. In Mullen, A. and James, P. (eds), *Multilingualism in the Graeco-Roman Worlds*. Cambridge: Cambridge University Press, 265–316.

Żelazowski, J. 2014–15. La politica di Augusto in Cirenaica. *Palamedes* 9–10: 237–56.

11

Responding to 'Classical' architecture in Roman-era Athens: Spolia, emulation, agency, and audiences

Christopher Siwicki

Introduction

This chapter examines how buildings in Roman-era Athens were perceived by contemporaries – the reception of new interventions in the layered and historically charged cityscape by its inhabitants.[1] Specifically, it focuses on a selection of constructions from between the first century BCE to second century CE which appeared either to utilize or to look to historical precedents in their architecture. The question this chapter aims to answer is whether the ancients themselves understood the buildings in these terms? Did they conceive the inclusion of older architectural material and designs as deliberately historicizing, and was this part of wider 'Classicizing' trends (the conscious emulation of fifth- and fourth-century BCE Greek culture) discernible in other media at the time?

The study begins by outlining the key details of the structures under discussion. It moves on to consider why we would expect there to be a 'Classicizing' movement in architecture, how authors of the imperial period engaged with Classical-era buildings, and attempts to tease out the perception of what constituted 'Greek' architecture at the time. An examination of how columns are commented on in Greek and Latin literature adds to the picture by helping to establish the impression of architecture as a niche interest subject among ancient audiences. The question of agency – who was responsible for architectural decision making – becomes central to the discussion in the final section, where the reasons for emulation and reuse are examined.

This subject brings up important issues, not all of which can be fully resolved here, but which are relevant to understand ancient attitudes to architecture beyond the case of imperial-era Athens. Not least, what constituted 'Roman' or 'Greek', specifically 'Classical', architecture in this context and period? The research questions some commonly propagated assumptions about the ancient audiences and creators of monuments and how buildings conveyed meaning, including the extent to which historical associations were invested in architecture.[2] In answering this it is necessary, where possible, to go beyond assessing what those involved in the making of the structures might have understood (the masons, architects, patrons) and to try to get at how designs and features were comprehended among broader audiences. In places the paper at times strays into the territory of asking more questions than providing answers; parts of the discussion are what might be termed 'theoretical', but as it is without reference to theory, then 'exploratory' is perhaps more appropriate.

The buildings

In the second half of the first century BCE, a Pentelic-marble, Doric-order, peripteral temple of the mid-fifth century BCE was dismantled and moved from the Attic countryside to the Athenian Agora, where it was dedicated to the god Ares (Fig. 11.1). Reassembled in its new location, the superstructure was supplemented (or restored) with architectural elements from other buildings, specifically, the marble sima of the roof of the temple of Poseidon at Sounion (Figs 11.2a; 11.3–4).[3] The associated altar was also constructed of reused material, but from a different location. This is one of several known examples where between the first century BCE and second century CE parts of Classical-era buildings were re-employed in new contexts in Athens, variously called by scholars 'itinerant', 'wandering', or 'floating' temples. Four Doric columns belonging to a fifth-century BCE temple at Thorikos were brought to the Agora and likely used for the façade of the 'Southwest' Temple (Figs 11.2b; 11.5). Likewise, the hexastyle 'Southeast' Temple in the Agora is thought to have been built with Ionic columns from the temple of Athena at Sounion (Figs 11.2c; 11.6). Two further sets of Ionic columns discovered in the Agora are identified as analogous examples of peripatetic architectural reuse, although the new context to which they belonged is unknown.[4] To the north of the Agora, another small temple argued to be that of Aphrodite Ourania was also constructed at some point in the late first century BCE. The temple is tetrastyle, with a shallow cella and a frontal stair and porch (Fig. 11.2d). Noticeably, the design of the Ionic columns of the temple derives from those of the east porch of the fifth-century BCE Erechtheion, three quarters size of the original but with the same distinctive anthemion of the capital and profile of the base (Shear 1997, 496–507). Similarly, the columns of a small monopteros constructed on the Acropolis and dedicated to Roma and Augustus in the last decades of the first century BCE also reproduces the column design of the neighbouring Erechtheion (Fig. 11.7).[5]

These instances of reuse and emulation are often spoken about by modern scholars in terms of 'Classicizing', 'historicism', and 'antiquarianism'.[6] The choice to recycle or replicate elements of older buildings is interpreted as an attempt to promote an apparent and meaningful link with

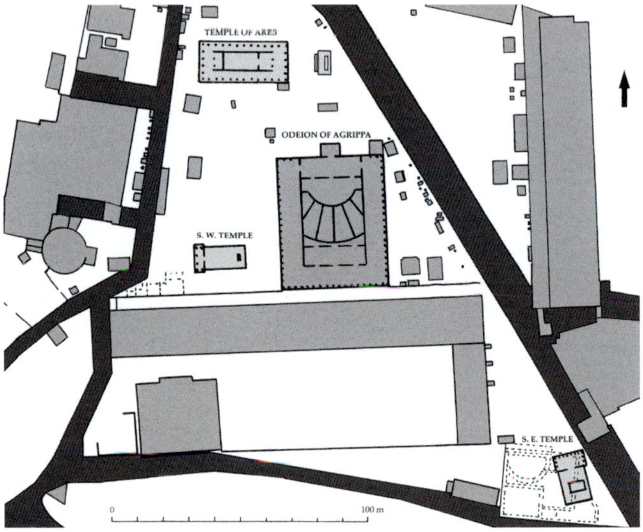

Fig. 11.1. Plan of the Athenian Agora in the early imperial period (image C. Siwicki, after Dinsmoor 1982, fig. 1).

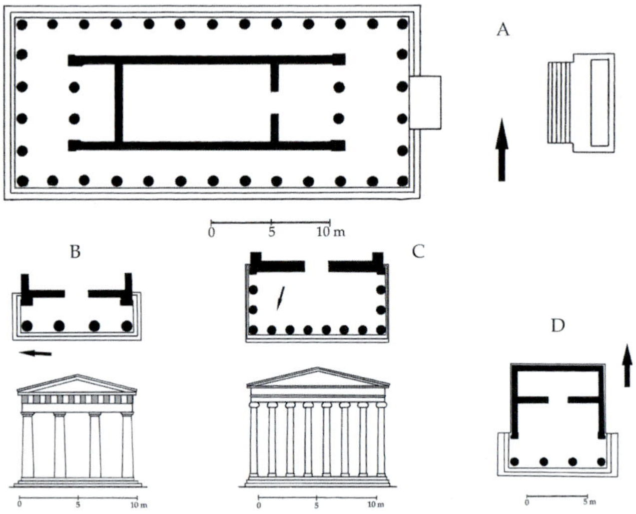

Fig. 11.2. Plans and restored elevations of temples. A: Temple of Ares (image C. Siwicki); B: 'Southwest' Temple (image C. Siwicki, after Dinsmoor 1982, fig. 12); C: 'Southeast' Temple (image C. Siwicki, after Dinsmoor 1982, fig. 14); D: Temple of Aphrodite (image C. Siwicki, after Shear 1997, fig. 3).

Fig. 11.3. Athenian Agora: Site of the Temple of Ares (photo C. Siwicki).

Fig. 11.4. Athenian Agora: Doric capital of the Temple of Ares (photo C. Siwicki).

Fig. 11.5. Athenian Agora: Doric capital associated with the 'Southwest' Temple (photo C. Siwicki).

Fig. 11.6. Athenian Agora: Architectural elements associated with the 'Southeast' Temple (photo C. Siwicki).

Fig. 11.7. Acropolis: Ionic capital of the Monopteros of Roma and Augustus (photo C. Siwicki).

Athens and/or Greece's Classical past (broadly understood here as the long fifth century BCE). The idea of the Agora as some form of an architectural 'museum' has even been proposed.[7] Ancient audiences are presumed to have recognized this conscious engagement with material heritage and to have responded to the new constructions accordingly, seeing in the architecture attendant cultural and political ideologies. In this way, the former pre-eminence of Hellas was called to mind through the built environment. It is a seductive picture because it accords with expectations that we have both about the cultural climate of Roman-era Greece and how meaning is invested in architecture. But was this how ancient audiences viewed these buildings? In his essay 'How Do Buildings Mean', William Whyte (2006, 154, 165) articulates some of the challenges that we face in answering such questions:

> Architecture is widely perceived to possess meaning: to be more than mere structure. As Umberto Eco has noted, 'we commonly do experience architecture as communication, even while recognizing its functionality'. Yet how that meaning is inscribed, how that communication works, and how it can be interpreted by historians remains unclear [...] How can historians be sure that they are accurately interpreting their subject? How can they avoid falling into the trap identified by Gombrich: approaching a medieval building with the 'a priori conviction that the Gothic style is a necessary result of feudalism or of scholasticism', projecting meaning onto architecture rather than seeking to encompass its true meaning?

Regarding the buildings of Athens, why assume there was a 'Classical' to recreate and why think that any such meaning would be embedded in the specifics of design?

Engaging with Classical Greek buildings in the Roman era

On the face of it there are good reasons to anticipate that people in Roman-era Greece would engage with the Classical past in the built environment. Greek and Latin literature of the early and high imperial period reveals an intense interest with the history and culture of fifth- and fourth-century BCE Greece, which is surely indicative of a broader societal curiosity in the achievements of that period. The 'movement' most closely associated with this trend is the so-called 'Second Sophistic'. An overly problematized term that in origin refers to the limited number of thinkers included in Philostratus' *Vitae sophistarum*, scholars have also applied the 'Second Sophistic' label to encompass a wider range of activity from approximately 50 to 250 CE.[8] Although the exact bounds of the phenomenon remain contested, it can be broadly understood as people engaging with, and deliberately looking to, adapting and emulating the cultural outputs of Greece's Classical past, in part as a way of creating their own Greek identity in a Roman world. Even if the literary, rhetorical, and philosophical components of the movement continue to dominate scholarly discussion, there is increasing evidence for how the trend was present in material culture too.[9]

Following from this, we might anticipate meaningful references to the Classical past in Greece's Roman-era buildings. We see 'Classicizing' trends in both the collecting and production of art, so why not in architecture? Buildings were a popular subject among Greek authors of the period. Structures, real or imagined, were the object of ekphrastic exercise, such as in Lucian's *De domo* and *Hippias* (on these texts, see Thomas 2007, 221–35). The built environment of mainland Greece is at the core of Pausanias' *Hellados Periegesis* and scholars have noted his preference for describing Classical-era buildings at the expense of more contemporary structures.[10] A sense of civic pride and admiration permeates the comments that Greek and Latin authors make about the monuments of Classical Athens, which are also the subject of two Athenian coins of the second century CE (Fig. 11.8).[11]

The relevance of particular monuments from Greece's Classical past is further revealed incidentally in a speech by Dio Chrysostom (*Or.* 40.8). Delivered in the first decade of the second century CE to the civic assembly of his home city of Prusa in Bithynia, the speech is part of his defence against having demolished a number of structures in the city centre in order to build a new stoa (Siwicki 2021, 1–18). Dio is relentless in his scathing put-downs of what he deems to be valueless structures and the hyperbolic reaction to their removal:

> One might have supposed that the Propylaea at Athens were being tampered with, or the Parthenon, or that we were wrecking the Heraeum of the Samians, or the Didymeium of the Milesians, or the temple of Artemis at Ephesus, instead of disgraceful, ridiculous ruins, much more lowly than the sheds under which the flocks take shelter. (translation H.L. Crosby)

Unlike the edifices he removed, the buildings which Dio holds up as examples of what would constitute the greatest act of vandalism were they to be destroyed, and are thereby presumably to be considered the most important, are all sixth- and fifth-century BCE structures in origin. That any such outrage would be on cultural-historical grounds rather than simply a sacrilegious act is shown by his inclusion of the Propylaea and not just temples. Dio's speech is of local importance, but its publication is for a wider audience and his examples are potentially illustrative of a more global idea of what constituted Greek built heritage by this date.

The centrality of the monuments of the past as illustrative examples of Greece's former glory is expressed by Dio elsewhere in his works. In the Rhodian oration (*Or.* 31.160), in contrast to certain Greeks of the present day he exclaims that:

> It is rather the stones which reveal the grandeur and the greatness of Hellas, and the ruins of her buildings; her inhabitants themselves and those who conduct her governments would not be called descendants of even the Mysians. (translation H.L. Crosby)

This idea that it is its buildings, specifically those of the Classical era, that best reflect the achievements of the Greek world is also articulated by Dio's contemporary Plutarch. In his *Pericles* (12.1), Plutarch prefaces his extended description of the Periclean building programme in Athens by stating:

> But that which brought most delightful adornment to Athens, and the greatest amazement to the rest of mankind; that which alone now testifies for Hellas that her ancient power and splendour, of which so much is told, was no idle fiction, – I mean his construction of sacred edifices, – this, more than all public measures of Pericles, his enemies maligned and slandered. (translation B. Perrin)

In this passage Plutarch is possibly responding to the well-known and prescient prediction of Thucydides (1.10) that future generations would erroneously judge the respective strength of Sparta and Athens on the basis of their monuments (see Pelling 2022, 105–21). But what is important for our purpose is that Plutarch considers buildings *the* foremost achievement of, and evidence for, the greatness of Greece in his own day. Indeed, he views them as part of a more global Hellenic legacy and not

Fig. 11.8. Two imperial-era Athenian coins showing the buildings of the Acropolis (Bröndsted 1826, 131; Stuart and Revett 1789, 85).

just an Athenian one. It is therefore apparent that Classical-era buildings had a role in the conception of 'Greekness' in the imperial period and it is a further reason to expect this to be reflected in new architectural projects.

Such a proposition is even more appealing when we consider that noted 'philhellenes', and even some of those who were at the very centre of the Second Sophistic movement, were avid builders. In his *Vitae sophistarum*, Philostratus notes that at Smyrna Nicetes by means of a stoa 'connected the city with the gate that looks to Ephesus' (511), while Heracleides the Lycian constructed a fountain for olive oil with a golden roof (569). Antiochus restored the dilapidated buildings of Cilicia (569) and Polemon persuaded the emperor Hadrian to grant 10 million drachmae to Smyrna with which a market, gymnasium, and temple were built (531); just as Aristides later inspired Marcus Aurelius to rebuild the city after a devastating earthquake (582–83). At Ephesus, Philostratus (605) reports that Damianus personally:[12]

> restored any public buildings that were in need of repair [and] connected the temple with Ephesus by making an approach to it along the road that runs through the Magnesian gate. This work is a portico a stade in length, all of marble, and the idea of this structure is that the worshippers need not stay away from the temple in case of rain. When this work was completed at great expense, he inscribed it with a dedication to his wife, but the banqueting hall in the temple he dedicated in his own name, and in size he built it to surpass all that exist elsewhere put together. He decorated it with an elegance beyond words, for it is adorned with Phrygian marble such as had never before been quarried. (translation W.C. Wright)

Most famously, Herodes Atticus engaged in widespread public and personal building projects, including the construction of a theatre and stadium in Athens, reconstructing another theatre at Corinth and the stadium at Delphi, building a bath at Thermopolyae and a water supply for Canusium in Italy (548; 550–51).

Such individuals and their peers dressed their words and themselves in Classical styles of Greek language and clothing as markers of identity, so we might anticipate that their buildings would also be dressed accordingly.[13] The construction of public and private edifices was one of the most conspicuous undertakings by members of the elite. Buildings were a means through which values, ideologies, and identities could be expressed to different audiences. Therefore, as asserting the idea of 'Greekness' through overt reference to the Classical past was an important and prevailing practice, evident in other cultural media, and as some of the individuals who subscribed to this outlook also engaged in public building works, then we might reasonably expect to find evidence of 'Classicizing' architecture in the buildings of the period. However, I am not certain that this is what we see, or at least on the scale comparable with the trend perceptible in other cultural forms. For example, there is nothing overly fifth century about the nymphaeum of Herodes at Olympia, and his Odeion in Athens is frequently labelled by modern scholars as 'Roman' in its design (Fig. 11.9). Herodes' stadium in Athens admittedly follows the traditional form of this type of building, but rather than it being a purposefully Classicizing act of design, it is unclear how or why he would have changed the shape of the stadium given that its function remained the same.

Alternatively, we might consider that perhaps it was the very act of engaging with Classical-era monuments by restoring them that such individuals expressed their 'Classical' values – by rebuilding the stadiums of Athens and Delphi, Herodes was engaging with that past, irrespective of the appearance of the finished design. Likewise, it is noticeable that many of the

Fig. 11.9. Athens, Odeion of Herodes Atticus (photo B. Werner, Wikimedia, CC BY-SA 3.0).

monuments of the Greek world that Roman emperors restored or completed are in origin also of the long Classical period: Hadrian finished the temple of Olympian Zeus in Athens; Caligula planned to do likewise to the temple of Apollo at Didyma, as well as to repair the palace of Polycrates at Samos (Suet. *Calig.* 21); Domitian restored the temple of Apollo at Delphi, as commemorated in a monumental Latin inscription at the site;[14] and Nero was honoured by an inscription on the Parthenon during its renovation (although this was likely on local rather than imperial initiative).[15] It is in the undertaking rather than the specifics that the message is made.

We should likewise consider the importance of naming structures in defining how they were meant to be understood. When Cicero talks of discussing philosophy in the parts of his villa at Tusculum labelled *Lyceum* and *Academia* – after Aristotle and Plato's schools – we need not assume that these replicated the appearance of their prototypes in Athens.[16] Rather, it was the name and the activity that took place there which conveyed the meaning of his Greek learning. Brutus drew links to Classical Sparta and Athens by having a Persian Stoa and a Parthenon constructed at his own retreats,[17] but we do not need to imagine these were architectural replicas, something akin to that the Parthenon now in Nashville, USA.

The ancients could engage with Classical culture through buildings at the macro levels of action and semantics, rather than structures actually having to replicate the architecture of the earlier period in order for a meaningful and apparent connection to be created. This is where our own understanding of how meaning is embedded in architecture possibly misleads our interpretation of the decisions behind ancient buildings. As observed by Nikolaus Pevsner (1968, 352), the idea that 'a building is clothed in the garb of a special style, because of the meditations which that style will rouse' belongs to eighteenth-century theorists. We are used to looking for meaning in the details, but to some extent this is a modern understanding of how buildings mean. It is not to deny that the ancients also invested meaning in specific details, but it is also possible that they placed meanings within buildings that were not tied to the architectural form and particulars of the structure. A consequence of the modern approach in regard to the subject currently under discussion is that we see what to us are recognizably 'Classical' details, make the association that they are 'Classical', and then give this perceived link primacy in interpreting why such details were used and what the 'message' being conveyed by the structure was. It is not evident that the ancients thought in the same way and with the same points of reference, and we now turn to what they did consider 'Greek' architecture to be.

Perceptions of 'Greek' architecture in Roman-era Greece

The apparent distinctions between what is 'Greek' and 'Roman', 'Classical' and 'Imperial' architecture – as neatly set out on the pages of architectural handbooks and general histories of world architecture for some two centuries – has been robustly and justly challenged in recent scholarship.[18] That particular forms and details are today so readily recognized as being either 'Hellenic' or 'Italic' is a construct of the eighteenth and nineteenth centuries, when advances in antiquarian learning and the scientific study of ancient buildings were co-opted to express national and cultural ideologies. Greco-Roman buildings were emulated, in part or in full, as a means of displaying values associated with their respective civilizations: architecturally, the United States initially looked to Republican Rome for inspiration; the Parisian monuments of Napoleonic France aspired to those of imperial Rome; the Parthenon at various moments was held as a fitting model to German, British, and Greek nationalism and independently served as a war memorial, a symbol of democracy, and a representation of enlightenment thinking.[19]

The consequences of this are threefold: one, this period taught us to see historicism as an architectural phenomenon; two, it established the canons of what constitutes particular historical styles – how we 'know' whether a building looks 'Greek' or 'Roman'; three, it cemented the idea that cultural and national meaning is embedded in the specifics of the design and details of buildings. This is a modern way of thinking. That said, the ancients did express related ideas through the construction of buildings, just not in the same way. Forgoing the inherent anachronisms of the terms 'national' and 'cultural identity' when applied to antiquity, Greco-Roman writers did distinguish certain structures along corresponding lines. This is most obvious in Vitruvius' *De architectura*, where in a series of well-known dichotomies he sets out what makes a Roman forum (5.1.1), theatre (5.7), and house (6.7), as opposed to their Greek counterparts (5.5.1):[20]

> The Greeks make their forum square, with a spacious and double portico, ornamenting it with columns placed at narrow intervals, and stone or marble epistylia, and forming walks above on the timber framed work. In the cities of Italy, however, this practice is not followed, because the antient custom prevails of exhibiting the shows of gladiators in the forum. (translation F. Granger)

Vitruvius has specific motives for elucidating such distinctions (see discussion in Wallace-Hadrill 2008, 144–210), but an awareness of certain Greek/Roman divides are also found in other authors. For example, Pausanias (2.27.5) comments that:

> The Epidaurians have a theatre within the sanctuary, in my opinion very well worth seeing. For while the Roman theatres are far superior to those anywhere else in their splendour, and the Arcadian theatre at Megalopolis is unequalled for size, what architect could seriously rival Polycleitus in symmetry and beauty? For it was Polycleitus who built both this theatre and the circular building. Within the grove are a temple of Artemis, an image of Epione, a sanctuary of

Aphrodite and Themis, a race-course consisting, like most Greek race-courses, of a bank of earth, and a fountain worth seeing for its roof and general splendour. (translation W.H.S. Jones and H.A. Ormerod)

The Greek/Roman distinctions are at the macro level: for Vitruvius the differences are in the plans of the buildings and are due to the way in which they function; for Pausanias it is in their opulence and method of construction. Indeed, based on Vitruvius' definitions, the monument erected in Athens during the early imperial period which looked most obviously 'Greek' is the so-called 'Roman Agora' on account of its approximately square plan, as he states in the passage above (on the modern label 'Roman Agora' see Dickenson 2017, 246 ff., with further bibliography).

Also telling is the instance where a building project is seemingly criticized for being un-Greek-like in its conception. This is the story of the cynic philosopher Peregrinus' remarks about Herodes Atticus constructing an aqueduct and fountain at Olympia.[21] As told by Lucian (*De mort. Peregr.* 19), Peregrinus maintained that spectators at Olympia ought to endure thirst and that Herodes, by way of his and his Roman wife Regilla's benefaction, was making the Greeks 'effeminate'. The alleged hostile reaction of the crowd at Olympia to Peregrinus' attack, Lucian's scornful assessment of the criticism, as well as the philosopher's recantation of his position at the subsequent games four years later, all suggest that this was a minority, extreme view. Yet before discounting the story entirely, it is noticeable that the criticism of the structure being un-Greek-like is not based on its appearance or architecture, but on its function.[22] This had precedent in the Roman world too; specifically, authors of the imperial period give credence to the reason a second-century BCE law was passed forbidding theatres in Rome to have seating was because to watch a play sitting down was a Grecian pleasure that would weaken the virility of the Roman people.[23] Moreover, that aqueducts were considered by some to be categorically 'Roman' structures is suggested by Pliny the Elder and Frontinus, the latter placing them in opposition to 'the idle Pyramids or the useless, though famous, works of the Greeks'.[24]

The dichotomies above are on the grounds of functionality and morality. Likewise, Cassius Dio (53.27.1–2) maintains that Agrippa gave the name 'Laconian' to his baths in the Campus Martius, not on account of the design, but because of how they were used 'as the Lacedaemonians had a greater reputation at that time than anybody else for stripping and exercising after anointing themselves with oil'. What is not present in any text I have come across is an indication that particular architectural details, which since the eighteenth century might be associated more readily with being distinctly Greek or Roman (for example, the order or arrangement of temple columns), were thought of as such in antiquity. There is no suggestion that to go Doric is to go Greek.

Who cared about columns?

Staying with the subject of column orders, it is worth contemplating further the potential reception that the use of specific orders in imperial-era Athens might have engendered. Since the fifteenth century, column orders (or *species*, 'orders' being an early modern term) have stood at the centre of discussions about Classical architecture; therefore it is perhaps surprising (at least to this author) to note how little interest ancient writers displayed in commenting on them.[25] The following results are based on searching the texts of the Loeb Classical Library, which while not comprising a full account of surviving Greco-Latin literature, nevertheless provides a large representative sample.

Among Latin authors only Vitruvius and Pliny the Elder mention column *species*. In Vitruvius' *De architectura* there is an extended discussion of the origin and dimensions of the Doric, Ionic, Corinthian, and Tuscan, as well as a comment on the mixing of these elements (3.5; 4.1–7). In his *Naturalis Historia*, Pliny briefly details the proportions of Doric, Ionic, Corinthian, and Tuscan, as well as noting that Attic is a quadrangular and equilateral type of column, although he refrains from describing the appearance of the respective capitals (35.178–79). The only incidental reference to the column order of a particular building in Latin literature that I am aware of is Pliny's remark (*HN* 34.13) that Gnaeus Octavius' *Porticus Octavia* was also known as 'Corinthian' on account of its columns, although this might instead be a reference to the capitals being made of bronze (*aes Corinthiacum*).

There are noticeably more incidental references to column orders among Greek writers (eight authors in total), but still relatively few given the ubiquity of the architectural feature in the ancient world. Heron of Alexandria details the geometry of an Ionic column base (*Pneum. LCL* pp. 476–79); Diodorus Siculus notes the presence of Ionic columns and describes Corinthian ones on Alexander the Great's funerary carriage (18.26–27); Strabo compares the fruit of a fig tree in Celtica to the appearance of a Corinthian capital (4.6); Philo moralizingly questions people's need to adorn capitals, 'vying with each other in enthusiasm over Doric and Ionic and Corinthian carvings and other embellishments devised by those who scorn to keep to the established styles' (*De somniis* 2.55); Josephus remarks that the 162 columns in the court of Herod's temple in Jerusalem were Corinthian (*AJ* 15.11.5; cf. *AJ* 8.5.2; on Herod's architecture see also Peleg-Barkat, this volume); according to Appian 'two Ionic columns stood in front of each ship shed' at the old harbour of Carthage (*Pun.* 8.96); Pausanias observes that the temples of Zeus, Hera and the Metroum at Olympia are Doric (5.10.2; 5.16.1; 5.20.9), as are two porticoes near the market place (6.24.2; 6.24.5), that the treasury of the Sicyonians had both Doric- and Ionic-style chambers (6.19.2), and that the temple of Athena Alea at Tegea is considered by him to be 'far superior to all other temples in the Peloponnese on many grounds, especially for its size. Its first row of columns is Doric, and next to it Corinthian; also, outside of the temple, stand columns of the Ionic order' (8.45.5); lastly, Athenaeus records that four of the columns in the pavilion of Ptolemy II 'were made to resemble palm trees and those in the middle were decorated like Dionysiac staffs' (5.196), while the largest cabin of the luxurious barge of Ptolemy II had capitals of Corinthian workmanship and a dining room that was:[26]

> decorated in the Egyptian style; for the columns built at this point bulged as they ascended, and the drums differed, one being black and another white, placed alternately. Some of their capitals are circular in shape; the entire figure described by them resembles rose-blossoms slightly opened. But around the part which is called the 'basket' there are no volutes or rough leaves laid on, as on Greek capitals, but calyxes of water-lilies and the fruit of freshly-budded date-palms; in some instances several other kinds of flowers are sculptured thereon. The part below the root of the cap, which, of course, rests upon the drum adjoining it, had a motif that was similar; it was composed of flowers and leaves of Egyptian beans, as it were, intertwined. This is the way in which Egyptians construct their columns. (translation S.D. Olson)

Allowing for the limitations posed by the size of this sample of authors, some observations can be made. One, the early modern/modern obsession with the column orders/*species* is not reflected in surviving ancient literature. The small number of references to the orders is even more apparent when placed in the context of there being hundreds of mentions of columns in general – the architectural element is referred to with regularity, just not its defining characteristic. This is in no way to suggest that the orders did not matter – it is evident from their near omnipresence in buildings across the Roman Empire that they did (cf. contributions by Mugnai, Stinson, and Gasparini in this volume) – only that outside of architectural circles they do not appear to have stimulated much comment, which might make us question the extent to which different audiences would be expected to understand specific meanings from their use.

In respect of this, the second observation is that there is no overt connection in the passages cited above between the use of the different column orders and historical periods. Although Vitruvius' discussion provides a chronological framework of progression from Doric to Ionic and then the later invention of Corinthian, nowhere is this presented as a particular order being identified predominantly with a particular time.

Three, beyond Athenaeus' description of Egyptian columns and the aetiological stories about the origins of the Doric, Ionic, and Corinthian as retold by Vitruvius, as well as the actual names of the orders, authors do not appear to connect types to geography, at least by the period under discussion.[27] Therefore, taken on these grounds alone there is nothing overtly 'Classicizing' about the use of the Doric and Ionic columns of the 'itinerant' temples in early imperial Athens, as conveyed in surviving literature. Moreover, it is relevant to note that the orders never went out of use in the city in the intervening centuries between the Classical and Roman period, making it less apparent that their subsequent employment was a 're-emergence' and, therefore, unmistakably backward looking.[28]

To reiterate, none of this is to deny that column orders and the specific and varying designs of capitals were invested with significance. The design of these architectural elements were choices, and these might reflect local and foreign, innovative and traditional influences. If the appearance of the columns did not matter or was random, then nuanced alterations would not have happened and no patterns in their development would be observable. A possible objection to the assertion at the end of the last paragraph about the continued use of the orders in Athens is that profiles and detailing of fifth-century BCE Doric and Ionic columns were discernibly different to those of the first century BCE; true, but here we must ask 'discernible to who?'; which viewers of the monuments would notice these features and recognize in them an agreed meaning in their significance? I would posit that the vast majority of people do not pay attention to such details, although two groups who do are ancient professional builders and modern scholars. Column orders have huge significance and meaning, but knowledge of it is largely confined to specialists.

The paucity of interest in column orders among Greco-Roman authors reflects a wider ignorance and apathy among the populaces of ancient cities in understanding certain architectural specifics – even if this view seems belied by a material record that shows an extremely complex, nuanced, and passionate engagement with architecture by the interested professionals who knew and cared about such things.[29] Buildings were evidently highly valued across Greco-Roman society, but one can find a work of architecture beautiful without knowing which components make it so; one can appreciate the majesty of a structure without comprehending how it was built; and one can find meaning in a building without interpreting all the intricacies of its ornament. The most common criteria of evaluation for buildings used by ancient authors were not architecturally specific, but concern sensation, as well as general ideas and generic terms and superlatives regarding scale, utility, beauty, and appropriateness.[30] On architectural awareness in twentieth-century Britain, Edwin Lutyens (quoted in Williams-Ellis and Williams-Ellis 1924, 17) commented that 'the public don't know and don't really care a dog's leg about architecture', while Osbert Lancaster (1938, ix) judged that 'the ordinary intelligent member of the public, when confronted with architecture, whether good, bad or indifferent, remains resolutely dumb – in both the original and transatlantic senses of the word'. That different people understand buildings differently based on their differing knowledge is obvious enough, but the implications and the reasons for this are not always fully acknowledged in studies of antiquity.[31]

Emulation and agency

Let us consider again the reproduction of the elaborate and distinctive design of the Ionic columns of the Erechtheion in the Temple of Aphrodite Ourania and the Monopteros of Roma and Augustus. In both instances they are slightly different; in the assessment of Leslie Shear (1997, 506), the capitals of the Monopteros of Roma and Augustus attempt to closely mimic their model, while those of the Temple of Aphrodite are slightly freer in their adaptation. But who made the decisions to copy the columns of the Erechtheion – the masons, the architects, the patrons? Manolis Korres (1997, 198) has noted that the capitals of the Monopteros of Roma and Augustus resemble the first-century BCE repairs to the Erechtheion and are likely by the same sculptors, but I do not know if this gets us any closer to determining who made the decision to include this feature in the new building.[32]

Moreover, would people other than those who worked on the buildings have noticed the similarities? The proximity of the new buildings to the prototype, particularly the Monopteros of Roma and Augustus, increases the likelihood that a comparison would be made. However, importantly, this does not mean that the message behind the decisions to include such a feature in the new buildings was deliberately to recall or connect to the specifically fifth-century history of the Erechtheion or the city. It is conceivable that whoever chose to follow this design in the two separate instances of the Monopteros and the Temple of Aphrodite did so for other reasons. For example, studies have tended to focus on the significance of these instances of emulation in the context of imperial agency and have therefore conceived the allusion as communicating to a broad, if undefined, public audience. But, as mentioned above, there is no immediate reason to assume that it was the patron who was responsible for such details. Instead, if the decision to include these features lay with the architects or masons, then it is interesting to consider the possibility that they were addressing their peers and referring to the tradition of their discipline. In the same way, subtle intertextual allusions in poetry can be primarily for other poets rather than the patron or general audience, even if the work as a whole is meant to be consumed by all. That members of the building profession engaged in dialogue on such matters with each other is certainly the impression given by Vitruvius (*De arch.* 4.3.1) when discussing the suitability of the use of the Doric order; here, it is architects talking to architects.

Predominantly, although with notable exceptions, modern ancient historians tend to seek political and ideological explanations for architectural details in public buildings. Most of the previous discussions of the examples included in this paper consider the design of the temples in respect of issues such as Augustan ideological or local Athenian politics – a valid and fruitful approach, but one I am here proposing an alternative to. For this comes at the expense of recognizing that the designers and builders of monuments can also be artists, and that certain features might be included for artistic reasons, not simply the politics of the patron. The decision to construct a particular building might be a political act, but it does not immediately follow that all of its executed features were directed to this message.

It is in a similar vein that many studies of ancient architecture (including at times probably this one) talk about the buildings themselves as speaking or communicating. It is a linguistic generalization which runs the risk of overshadowing the fact, and its attendant implications, that it is individuals or groups of individuals with their own ideas, motivations, and experiences who design buildings. The notion that an ill-defined collective force – i.e. the 'Augustan' – designed buildings for an indistinct collective audience of 'Athenians', 'Romans', etc. – who are also assumed to all possess a collective memory – seems an unnuanced simplification. Thinking about individual builders and targeted audiences can instead allow for the expectation of there being more layers of interpretation in the design of a structure.

That either the Temple of Aphrodite Ourania and the Monopteros of Roma and Augustus were not intended to make a big, overt statement about 'Classicism' seems increasingly likely when the designs of the temples are taken as a whole. The monopteros form of Roma and Augustus does not appear to be referencing any known fifth-century BCE building in the city, while the Temple of Aphrodite, with its deep, prostyle porch and frontal stair which extends beyond the width of the colonnade, is more akin to Italic temples. The extent to which this type of prostyle temple was explicitly associated with 'Roman' or 'Italic' architecture in first-century BCE Greece is an important and relevant question, although beyond the scope of this chapter; for now, it is enough to note that by adopting this design the temple is not conforming to fifth-century native prototypes (see Thomas 2013, 161). It is also worth observing that the two itinerant 'Southeast' and 'Southwest' temples have similar prostyle layouts, which might also make us question the extent to which the aim of the builders was to recreate an unambiguously 'Classical' aesthetic here too, despite using architectural elements from that period.

Conversely, the Temple of Ares has a peripteral plan which – anachronistically or not – *we* much more readily associate as being 'Greek', and perhaps we should consider the reconstruction of this building in the Agora as a separate phenomenon to the other wandering temples (Borg 2011, 226–27). It was brought to Athens and reconstructed, more or less, in its entirety – an act that was potentially more noteworthy and apparent than isolated elements of older structures being included in totally new constructions, as with the other floating temples. Moreover, the close similarity of its design to the nearby fifth-century BCE Hephaisteion meant that viewers could draw an immediate visual link between the two buildings and assess the new addition to the Agora in relation to this existing temple (something made even more apparent by the erection of radically different buildings, such as the Odeion of Agrippa). That said, there is still an assumption that the connection that was being drawn or recognized relates to its Classical-era association specifically; a conjecture we might question. As we are examining the ways in which new buildings in Athens looked like, or in certain ways recalled, older ones, it is also relevant to consider how these older ones were viewed by contemporaries in the first two centuries CE. Sources are scarce, but potentially illuminating are Plutarch's reflections on the Classical-era buildings of the Acropolis (*Vit. Per.* 13.3):

> For this reason are the works of Pericles all the more to be wondered at; they were created in a short time for all time. Each one of them, in its beauty, was even then and at once antique; but in the freshness of its vigour it is, even to the present day, recent and newly made. Such is the bloom of perpetual newness, as it were, upon these works of his, which makes them ever to look untouched by time, as though the unfaltering breath of an ageless spirit has been infused into them. (translation B. Perrin)

Plutarch is obviously aware of the historical context of these monuments; however, his insistence that they look newly made implies that their architecture – that of the fifth century – was not necessarily perceived as old-fashioned, historic, or anachronistic. This reading allows for the possibility that buildings constructed in the Roman era and which either emulated or literally borrowed architectural elements from buildings of this earlier period might also have been considered 'contemporary' in their appearance, rather than 'historicizing'. Aspects of the appearance of the buildings might well have been familiar to Athenian audiences based on comparison with existing structures in the city, and that might well have been the intention of the builders, but the intended and realized association was that the architecture looked local and appropriate to the city.

Spolia

The most obvious reason for thinking that any of the wandering temples were perceived by contemporary audiences as consciously historicizing, or specifically Classicizing, is the fact that some of the architectural elements actually come from fifth-century BCE buildings. However, this conclusion rests upon the necessary assumption that audiences would have been aware of the fact. The builders – the patrons, architects, and masons – would likely know the origin of the material, as well as other informed parties (elsewhere, for example, Cicero was aware that Aemilius Paullus was rebuilding his eponymous basilica in the Roman forum using a combination of old and new columns: *Att.* 4.16). But there is no indication that this information was then conveyed to wider Athenian audiences or that the selection of the original structures for spoliation was connected to their historical significance, as opposed to their convenience or quality.

Regarding the level of architectural knowledge among general audiences in antiquity, as can be deduced from surviving literature, I would err on the side of caution. Indeed, one of the recurrent issues that Pausanias reportedly encounters when enquiring about different buildings on his travels around Greece is the ignorance of locals and the difficulty in obtaining accurate information (for example: 5.18.6; 6.24.9; 8.32.12–13; 10.5.9–13; cf. 9.36.5). Regarding the Temple of Ares, Pausanias mentions that there is a sanctuary of the god in the Agora but does not refer to the shrine itself (1.8.4). Sarah Rous (2019, 76) has suggested that were people still aware of the fact that this temple had been moved from the countryside by the time Pausanias was writing, a century and a half after the event, then he would likely have commented on it as a curious detail. Pausanias' silence is taken as indicating that the story of the relocation of the temple became less significant over time, but maybe it was never actually significant?[33]

Beyond 'meaning', the other obvious reason for recycling elements of earlier structures is practical and financial pragmatism. Why go to the effort and expense of quarrying and carving new material when existing high-quality architectural elements are available? Such practice occurs throughout antiquity and not only at times of perceived crisis (although the damage inflicted upon Athens and Greece throughout the wars of the first century BCE potentially made the reuse of building material for new projects even more expedient, both for reasons of economy and availability).[34] There is, however, a risk of frustration and circularity at the inconclusiveness of setting out the competing arguments for the potential motivating factors behind instances of reuse. It is too easy to be sceptical that there is no explicit evidence for meaning in the use of older architectural elements in a new context, but it is also too tempting to assign meaning to what could actually have been a mundane and largely invisible practice. Recycling parts of monuments in Athens during this period was more widespread than the 'itinerant' temples: an unwanted geison block from the Erechtheion was found in the foundations of the Monopteros of Roma and Augustus, presumably having been removed during the first-century BCE restoration of the temple (Dörpfeld 1903, 466); numerous statue bases, freestanding and monumental, were also repurposed and rededicated (see Moser 2017, 169–81; Rous 2019, 121–75).

Although lacking a definitive answer as to what was occurring in Athens, in approaching the issue it is perhaps useful to observe the occasional variations in how analogous processes are differently labelled by scholars in the same field but who work on other periods of time or geographical areas of the Classical world. 'Spolia' is the term most readily employed in scholarship on architectural reuse in the city of Rome. This early modern term has come to be broadly applied to the practice of reusing earlier material (typically, but not exclusively, architectural and sculptural) in new contexts in the built environment.[35] 'Spolia' comes with a lot of baggage, not least the persistent perception of it as a Late Antique phenomenon connected (explicitly and implicitly) to 'decline', despite plenty of evidence for it occurring in various contexts throughout the imperial period. In contrast, 'spolia' is rarely used to describe the repurposing of the architectural elements in Athens discussed above. Avoidance of this term with its legacy of negativity perhaps allows such instances to be more readily construed as creative and positive (in particular, see use of the term 'upcycling' in Rous 2019). This is a completely legitimate approach to the material, but it engenders the need to search for political and ideological meaning at the expense of accepting base economic factors. It is telling that studies on the wandering temples tend to doubt the financial expediency of recycling architectural elements over creating a building *ex novo*, but offer little analysis to support this position.[36]

The situation in fourth-century CE Rome perhaps offers a useful comparison for thinking about first-century BCE Athens, not because it is a parallel – the contexts are markedly different – but because of the proliferation of spolia for different purposes. As in Athens, Rome saw magnificent new constructions such as the basilica of Maxentius, the Lateran and St Peter's Basilicas (cf. the Odeion of Agrippa and the Roman Agora in Athens), as well as extensive recycling of architectural elements. In Rome, different instances of constructing new buildings with spolia clearly had different ends: the employment of sculptural reliefs from monuments of Trajan, Hadrian, and Marcus Aurelius on the Arch of Constantine was intended to convey meaning (although not specifically referencing those particular periods and emperors, whose identities were erased through their heads being recarved); the mixture of Augustan, Flavian, and Severan-era columns, capitals, and entablatures in the so-called 'Temple of Romulus' in the Roman forum helped to create an exciting and original piece of architecture, but without any apparent reference to the earlier contexts that these pieces came from; blocks of Proconnesian marble from the Temple of Venus and Roma were recut and employed for purely practical purposes on the Arch of Janus. Even if a certain conservatism lay behind the construction of some of these monuments, the architecture is not typically spoken of by modern scholars as 'historicizing'. Nor are the reasons that they all reuse material considered part of the same phenomenon, except regarding the practical factors of economics and availability.

Reflecting on this, should we group the separate 'itinerant' temples of Athens together as part of the same historicizing or Classicizing movement? They were not constructed at a single moment but over the course of at least a century in different political and cultural contexts, and they had different builders with presumably different motivations.[37] We might also think about other instances of contemporary 'itinerant' temples that are excluded from such discussions because of where the material ends up. Between the late 30s and early 20s BCE, the Temple of Apollo Medicus Sosianus in Rome was rebuilt in marble. Within the pediment of the new building was placed a sculptural group depicting Greeks fighting Amazons, which had been taken from a fifth-century BCE temple in mainland Greece (La Rocca 1985). This example is not considered in discussions of the spoliation and reuse of temple architecture in Roman-era Athens, but it is analogous in action and temporality, just not geography. Likewise, scholars tend not to see the Temple of Apollo as overtly 'Classicizing' in its design, despite the fact that it employs fifth-century sculptures as its central and most conspicuous ornamentation.

This situation is perhaps due to the vagaries of scholarship as well as the very real differences in contexts – the sculptures being taken to Rome potentially belongs to the long, separate tradition of plundering of Greek art – and I am not suggesting they should definitely be considered part of the same process or movement as the wandering temples. Nevertheless, raising this point exposes how we study and label such activity. Would our interpretation of such monuments change if we knew that the patron of the Temple of Ares was Roman or the architect of the Temple of Apollo was Greek?[38] Staying with labelling and the city of Rome, the fact that the design of the Temple of Apollo included actual fifth-century sculpture but is not spoken of by scholars as 'Classicizing', yet the roughly contemporary Temple of Mars Ultor in the Forum of Augustus (dedicated in 2 BCE) copies relatively minor ornamental details of the Erechtheion and these features are labelled as 'Classicizing' and are interpreted as marking conscious and conspicuous links to fifth-century BCE Athens, further illuminates the difficulties in addressing this subject.[39]

Conclusion

The conclusion embraces the warning of the introduction that at times this paper offers more questions than provides answers. Understanding the meaning of buildings in antiquity is complicated, especially when examining the issue of what was considered historical architecture, as attempted in the preceding discussion. Partly, this is because it involves trying to ascertain what the ancients knew about their own past. On matters of architectural history, we are both better informed and more ignorant than people living in first-century BCE Athens. For example, decades of scholarly work means we likely know more about the chronological development of architectural forms across the Mediterranean than any one person did in antiquity; however, we have access to so little of the information available to ancient authorities regarding the people who built the various monuments. An abundance and a lack of knowledge both carry pitfalls for interpreting what the designs of buildings meant. Moreover, although buildings are the sum of their parts, they are comprised of different elements. Scholars rightly seek significance in the materiality, form, and ornament of buildings. But when should the various features be treated separately, and what does this mean for understanding the building as a whole? How best to do this when there are apparent contradictions – should the plan or the ornament be prioritized in interpreting whether the building was recalling a particular idea when these two distinct elements derive from different traditions? Are such contradictions deliberate or do they only seem so to our mind – in first-century BCE Athens, was the combination of 'Greek' Doric columns with a prostyle 'Roman' plan a mixing of elements or is that how we see it, with our knowledge of chronological and geographical architectural developments?

The important distinction between what might be labelled intent and consequence adds a further complication. The former refers to what the builder wished to convey through the building's structure, the latter to how the audience understood it – we cannot assume that they always corresponded. But this is also a simplification. Buildings are not the product of a single person but of many hands and minds. Knowing who was responsible for specific elements is rarely straightforward, yet it can have significant consequences for understanding why they were included – it matters whether it was the patron, the architect, or the mason who chose to use the capitals of the Erechtheion as a model. Similarly, there is not one audience. How a building was perceived at the time of its construction is different to how it is received by later generations and, ultimately, by us today, influenced on each occasion by different degrees of knowledge. Indeed, this last factor should also underscore the probability that even at the time of construction there were multiple potential audiences, and it is conceivable that different elements of a building were intended to be recognized by different groups.

The questions and issues above arise when examining the reception and perception of the reuse of earlier building material and the emulation of older architectural details in Roman-era Athens. Were the builders actively engaged in Classicizing? The circumstances certainly existed for this to be the case. We have seen how there was a deep vein of contemporary interest promoting ideas of Greek identity through reference to the Classical (fifth/fourth century) past. This was manifest in other cultural media, including sculpture. There was discernible interest in architecture and that buildings were singled out as symbols of the Greek Classical past. While the ideas associated with the 'Second Sophistic' were a cultural and intellectual movement, several prominent individuals associated with it were themselves builders. At a macro level – the act of restoring older structures and in the naming of new ones – I think we do see patrons engaging with Greece's Classical built heritage. But I am less convinced that this is always evident in the architecture of the buildings, which raises the question of the extent to which such meanings were invested in these elements.

With regard to the buildings discussed in this paper, it is not evident that particular details were considered exclusively 'Greek' to audiences in Roman-era Athens, let alone unambiguously 'Classical'. That the ancient builders took material and designs from fifth- and fourth-century buildings is undeniable, but whether these acts were intended to reference that specific past is not. It might be the newness of the building as a whole, not the reuse of particular elements that was important. The repeated use of particular styles and forms could be seen as continuity rather than recalling a particular moment in the past. The buildings might be considered appropriate in their design, emphasizing traditionalism or localism and not historicizing.

Further lines of inquiry could help to develop the picture. A longer study should include the Roman-era buildings at Eleusis, the architecture of which Margaret Miles has explicitly linked to 'Second Sophistic' ideas.[40] Building inscriptions are a further source for helping to understand the messages that structures were designed to convey. Language was central to ideas of identity in the period and a way of engaging with Hellenic culture and its past. A central feature of the educational training associated with 'Second Sophistic' culture, in its broad sense, was to produce written and spoken works in archaic Attic Greek (Kim 2017, 41–66). It is interesting that the inscription of the Monopteros of Roma and Augustus (*IG* II^2, 3173) was carved in Greek archaizing lettering.[41] Conversely, the dedicatory inscription of Appius Claudius Plucher's 'lesser' propylaea at Eleusis (*CIL* I^2, 775), erected in the 50s BCE, was in Latin. There are interesting implications of these further examples for understanding matters of identity and history in built environment of Roman-era Athens, but they go beyond the scope of the present study.

Notes

1. I am very grateful to Niccolò Mugnai for inviting me to give a paper at the workshop on which this chapter is based. I am also appreciative of the insightful and helpful comments on my paper given by the participants at the workshop, as well as for the remarks and suggestions from readers.
2. To an extent this study builds upon previous research on attitudes towards restoration and the notion of historic buildings in first-century CE Rome (Siwicki 2019).
3. The temple is generally agreed by scholars to be that of Ares mentioned by Pausanias (1.8.4). On the building, see Dinsmoor 1940, 1–52; 1974, 233–37; McAllister 1959, 1–64;

Baldassarri 1998, 153–72. Once thought to have been located at Acharnai, Korres (1998, 83–104) argued that the temple was originally that of Athena Pallenis in the Athenian deme of Pallene; cf. Shear (2016, 250–62) on the site at Pallene. Rous (2019, 67–68) supports a redating of the placement of the Temple of Ares after the construction of the Odeion of Agrippa, but this interpretation and the dating of the project remain contested. On the sculptural decoration associated with the temple, see Stewart 2016, 577–625; 2022, 197–216.

4. On these different elements, many of which were found reused in a post-Herulian wall of 276–82 CE, see Dinsmoor Jr. 1982, 410–52; Camp 1986, 184–47; 2001, 189–93; Borg 2011, 220–27; Rous 2019, 61 ff.; an alternative interpretation is that the Ionic columns belong to the 'Southwest' Temple and the Doric columns to the 'Southeast' Temple: Thompson and Wycherely 1972, 160–68; Osanna 1995, 103–18. An example outside of Athens is the apparent movement of a sixth-century BCE, Ionic-order temple into the centre of Thessaloniki in the Roman era: Allamani-Souri 2003, 103–6.
5. Hoff 1996, 188–89; Hurwit 1999, 179–80; Fouquet 2012, 35–83; Iliou 2014, 33–39; Morales 2017, 141–61.
6. In addition to studies cited above, see remarks in Shear 1981, 362; Bowersock 2002, 6 ff.; Spawforth 2012, 65–70, 128–29; Thomas 2013, 170; Evangelidis 2014, 346; Miles 2014a, 137–38; Dickenson 2017, 276–83. On this question in regard to Roman-era Corinth, see König 2001, 146–52; Thomas 2010, 114–44. One of the strongest cases for a Classicizing building in Attica during the Roman period and related to the Second Sophistic is made by Margaret Miles (2012, 114–51; 2014b, 9–11) with regard to the greater propylaea at Eleusis. Likewise, see also Edmund Thomas' (2013, 166–68) discussion of the architecture of Appius Claudius Pulcher's 'lesser' propylaea.
7. Shear 1981, 362; Alcock 1993, 191–96 (but revised in Alcock 2002, 51–58); Walker 1997, 72; McHugh 2017, 254; Morales 2017, 153; Rogers 2021a, 425–26; cf. discussion in Dickenson 2017, 279.
8. For example, Swain 1996; Goldhill 2001; Whitmarsh 2005; essays in Richter and Johnson 2017.
9. Smith 1998, 56–93; D'Ambra 2005, 201–16; essays in Borg 2008; Nasrallah 2010; Platt 2011; Newby 2020, 493–508; essays in Kouremenos 2022. *Contra* this position, Gleason (2006, 228–29) claims that 'since material culture was not a determining component of Greek identity, Greeks felt not less Greek when they adorned their cities with Roman amenities and integrated the emperor's effigy into the ceremonies of their civic life'; cf. Woolf (1994, 126–30) and Swain (1996, 417–21).
10. On Pausanias and the past, see Elsner 1992, 3–29; Arafat 1996; Bowie 1996, 207–30; Hutton 2017, 360–61. On the importance of Classical monuments in Plutarch, see McInerney 2004, 43–55; Stadter 2022, 50–54; Athanassaki 2022, 96; Geiger 2022, 76.
11. On praise of Athens and its Classical-era buildings: Dio Chrys. *Or.* 2.35–36; 6.4; 31.121; 40.8; 48.12; 64.16; Plut. *Vit. Per.* 12–13; *Vit. Cim.* 13; *Vit. Nic.* 3; *De glor. Ath.* 7 (349 D–E); Paus. 1.22.4; Aristid. *Panathenaic Or.* 191; 352–54; 364; 403; Epictetus *Diatribai* 3.73–74; Liv. 31.30; 45.27–28; Strabo 9.16; Cic. *Rep.* 3.32; *Off.* 2.17.
12. This subject is discussed by Thomas 2017, esp. 188–95. On physical spaces and buildings used by sophists and rhetoricians, also see Caruso 2018, 303–15.
13. On Greek and Roman clothing in statuary and its possible meaning on Herodes' nymphaeum, see Gleason 2021, 130–33.
14. *ILS* 8905. On Hadrianic restoration of temples, see Boatwright 2000; Horster 2017, 599–601.
15. *IG* II^2, 3277; see discussion in Williams 2013, 80–87.
16. Cic. *Div.* 1.5; 2.3; *Tusc.* 2.3; *Att.* 1.4; 6; 8; 9; 10; 11; Plin. *HN* 31.6.
17. Cic. *Att.* 15.9; 13.40. On this trend for naming, see also *Hist. Aug. Hadr.* 26.5; Varro *Rust.* 2.1.23; Cic. *Leg.* 2.1.2; Wallace-Hadrill 2008, 70–73; Hartswick 2017, 80–82.
18. Although not as robustly as scholarship on ancient sculpture, see discussions in Vout 2010, 55–78; Hallett 2015, 11–33; Smith 2015, 473–95; cf. discussions in Versluys 2017. On Classicism in Roman art, see Zanker 1988, 239–63; Galinsky 1999, 180–205; Hölscher 2004; Elsner 2006, 270–97. On the creation of Roman, in opposition to Greek, identity in late-Republican/Augustan-era material culture and architecture, see Wallace-Hadrill 2008, esp. 144–210. On the idea of 'Greekness' more broadly, see Hall 2002; Konstan and Saïd 2006; cf. Dench 2010, 266–80. The subject of 'copying'/'emulation' has likewise received more attention in regard to sculpture than architecture: see Gazda 2002; Perry 2005; Trimble and Elsner 2006; Kousser 2008; Marvin 2008; Di Napoli 2016, 307–25.
19. On Neo-Classical architecture and historicism in the eighteenth and nineteenth centuries, in particular Greek Revivalism, see Pevsner 1968, 350–403; Wiebenson 1969; Watkin 1992, 312–404; Bergdoll 2000, 9–41.
20. On different Greek building methods, also see Vitr. *De arch.* 2.8.5; 7.
21. Bol 1984; Walker 1987, 60–62; Strazdins 2022, 166–72.
22. There was also moralizing criticism of gladiatorial matches and forms of bathing in imperial-era Greece, but it is questionable as to the extent this was then conceptualized along Greek/Roman lines; see König 2001, 151–52. For the cynic Demetrius' attack on Greek bathing as effeminate at the opening of the gymnasium of Nero, see Philostr. *VA* 4.42; Thomas 2017, 190.
23. App. *B Civ.* 1.28; Val. Max. 2.4.2; cf. Tac. *Ann.* 14.20–21; Wallace-Hadrill 2008, 160–69.
24. Plin. *HN* 36.75; Frontin. *Aq.* 1.16–17; Siwicki 2020, 265–66.
25. The literature on the orders of columns in antiquity and beyond is vast; see in particular Onians 1988; Wilson Jones 1991, 89–150; 2000; Rykwert 1996.
26. Ath. 5.205–6. On a distinct Egyptian modular system, see Diod. 1.98.5.
27. On ancient criticism of Doric, Vitr. *De arch.* 4.3.1, but see discussion in Tomlinson 1963, 133–45.
28. On the continued use of Doric in Hellenistic-era Greece, see Thomlinson 1963, 133–45; on the use of Doric in Roman-era Asia Minor and its gradual replacement in the imperial period, see Waelkens 1989, 79–81; Fochetti 2020. The use of Doric at Cyrene during the reign of the emperor Hadrian is seen as archaizing by Spawforth and Walker 1986, 101; cf. Boatwright 2000, 160; on Cyrene's Doric and Corinthian architectures, see also contributions by Mugnai and by Gasparini in this volume.

29. On the limited nature of architectural descriptions in Latin authors, see Siwicki 2020.
30. See comments in DeLaine 2002, 205–30; Thomas 2007, esp. 207–20; 2014, 37–88; 2015, 274–90; Siwicki 2020.
31. In *De domo* Lucian comments on the non-discerning viewer and the discerning viewer, the latter possessing *paideia*; see Goldhill 2001, 160–61; Thomas 2007, 230.
32. On restoration of monuments in Athens at this time, also see Cully 1975, 207–23; Schmalz 2007–08, 9–46; on the topic more broadly see also essays in Broeck-Parant and Ismaelli 2021.
33. Conversely, Athanassaki (2022, 95) thinks it plausible that Plutarch was aware the building was part of a 'Periclean building programme'.
34. On Athens' financial difficulties in the first century BCE as a factor for architectural recycling, see Borg 2011, 215–18, 222–23. However, the state of the city after the Sullan sack and the speed of its recovery is contested: Hoff 2013, 567–74; Rogers 2021b, 288–318; *contra* Parigi 2019.
35. On the term 'spolia', see discussion in Kinney 1997, 117–48; cf. essays in Ng and Swetnam-Burland 2018.
36. Alcock 2002, 55; Spawforth 2012, 222; McHugh 2017, 253–54; Rous 2019, 69.
37. Stylistic architectural trends such as Gothic revivalism or Neo-Classicism do span similar stretches of time, but are also much more widespread and visibly pronounced, and take place in a world of very different attitudes to how historical and national identity might be expressed through architecture.
38. This question matters, but it is currently indeterminable – Romans funded buildings in Athens, as did locals, and Greek architects operated in Rome, as did Italians. On the argument for the Temple of Ares being a Greek rather than Roman initiative, see Dickenson 2017, 282 and Rous 2019, 68–69; cf. discussion in Borg 2011, 213–34 and Heijnen 2018, 18–110.
39. On elements of the Temple of Mars Ultor borrowing from the Erechtheion, see Wesenberg 1984, 161–85.
40. Miles 2012, 114–51; 2014b; cf. Thomas 2013, 166–68.
41. Bowersock 2002, 8–9. The use of archaizing lettering in inscriptions can be found in Roman-era Athens, such as on the Augustan boundary stones associated with the cult of Athena Polias (Schmalz 2007–08, 45). For other archaizing/Classicizing inscriptions of Roman-era Athens, see Aleshire 1999, 153–61.

References

Alcock, S.E. 1993. *Graecia capta. The Landscapes of Roman Greece*. Cambridge: Cambridge University Press.

Alcock, S.E. 2002. *Archaeologies of the Greek Past: Landscape, Monuments, and Memories*. Cambridge: Cambridge University Press.

Aleshire, S. 1999. The identification of archaizing inscriptions from Roman Attica. In *Atti dell'XI Congresso Internazionale di Epigrafia Greca e Latina (Roma, 18–24 settembre 1997)*. Rome: Quasar, 153–61.

Allamani-Souri, V. 2003. The imperial cult. In Grammenos, D.V. and Adam-Veleni, P. (eds), *Roman Thessaloniki (Thessaloniki 2003)*. Thessaloniki: Thessaloniki Archaeological Museum, 98–120.

Arafat, K.W. 1996. *Pausanias' Greece: Ancient Artists and Roman Rulers*. Cambridge: Cambridge University Press.

Athanassaki, L. 2022. Athenian monumental architecture, iconography, and topography in Plutarch's De Gloria Atheniensium. In Athanassaki, L. and Titchner, F. (eds), *Plutarch's Cities*. Oxford: Oxford University Press, 81–101.

Baldassarri, P. 1998. *ΣΕΒΑΣΤΩΙ ΣΩΤΗΡΙ. Edilizia monumentale ad Atene durante il Saeculum Augustum*. Rome: Giorgio Bretschneider Editore.

Bergdoll, B. 2000. *European Architecture 1750–1890*. Oxford: Oxford University Press.

Boatwright, M.T. 2000. *Hadrian and the Cities of the Roman Empire*. Princeton: Princeton University Press.

Bol, R. 1984. *Das Statuenprogramm des Herdoes-Atticus-Nymphäums*. Berlin: De Gruyter.

Borg, B. 2008. *Paideia: The World of the Second Sophistic*. Berlin: De Gruyter.

Borg, B. 2011. Who cared about Greek identity? Athens in the first century BCE. In Wiater, N. and Schmitz, T. (eds), *The Struggle for Identity. Greeks and their Past in the First Century BCE*. Stuttgart: Franz Steiner Verlag, 213–34.

Bowersock, G. 2002. The new Hellenism of Augustan Athens. *Annali della Scuola Normale Superiore di Pisa* 4.7.1: 1–16.

Bowie, E.L. 1996. Past and present in Pausanias. In Bingen, J. (ed.), *Pausanias Historien*. Geneva: Fondation Hardt, 207–30.

Broeck-Parant, J. and Ismaelli, T. (eds) 2021. *Ancient Architectural Restoration in the Greek World*. Rome: Quasar.

Bröndsted, P. 1826. *Reisen und Untersuchungen in Griechenland*. Paris: Firmin Didot.

Camp, J.M. 1986. *The Athenian Agora: Excavations in the Heart of Classical Athens*. London: Thames & Hudson.

Camp, J.M. 2001. *The Archaeology of Athens*. New Haven-London: Yale University Press.

Caruso, E. 2018. Lecturing in Athens. Investigation on the 'topography' of the Second Sophistic. In Di Napoli, V., Camia, F., Evangelidis, V., Grigoropoulos, D., Rogers, D. and Vlizos, S. (eds), *What's New in Roman Greece? Recent Work on the Greek Mainland and the Islands in the Roman Period: Proceedings of a Conference Held in Athens, 8–10 October 2015*. Athens: National Hellenic Research Foundation, 303–15.

Cully, G.R. 1975. The restoration of sanctuaries in Attica: I.G., II^2, 1035. *Hesperia* 44.2: 207–23.

D'Ambra, E. 2005. Kosmetai, the Second Sophistic, and portraiture in the second century. In Barringer, J.M., Hurwit, J.M. and Pollitt, J.J. (eds), *Periklean Athens and its Legacy: Problems and Perspectives*. Austin: University of Texas Press, 201–16.

DeLaine, J. 2002. The Temple of Hadrian at Cyzicus and Roman attitudes to exceptional construction. *Papers of the British School at Rome* 70: 205–30.

Dench, E. 2010. Roman identity. In Barchiesi, A. and Scheidel, W. (eds), *The Oxford Handbook of Roman Studies*. Oxford: Oxford University Press, 266–80.

Di Napoli, V. 2016. Looking at the classical past: tradition, identity, and copies of nobilia opera in Roman Greece. In Alcock, S.E., Egri, M. and Frakes, J.F.D. (eds), *Beyond Boundaries. Connecting Visual Cultures in the Provinces of Ancient Rome*. Los Angeles: Getty Publications, 307–25.

Dickenson, C.P. 2017. *On the Agora: The Evolution of a Public Space in Hellenistic and Roman Greece (c. 323 BC – 267 AD)*. Boston-Leiden: Brill.

Dinsmoor, W.B. 1940. The Temple of Ares at Athens. *Hesperia* 9.1: 1–52.

Dinsmoor, W.B. Jr 1974. The Temple of Poseidon: a missing sima and other matters. *American Journal of Archaeology* 78.3: 211–38.

Dinsmoor, W.B. Jr 1982. Anchoring two floating temples. *Hesperia* 51.4: 410–52.

Dörpfeld, W. 1903. Zum Erechtheion. *Mitteilungen des Deutschen Archäologischen Instituts, Athenische Abteilung* 28: 465–69.

Elsner, J. 1992. Pausanias: a Greek pilgrim in the Roman world. *Past and Present* 135: 3–29.

Elsner, J. 2006. Classicism in Roman art. In Porter, J.I. (ed.), *Classical Pasts: The Classical Tradition in Greece and Rome*. Princeton: Princeton University Press, 270–97.

Evangelidis, V. 2014. Agoras and fora: developments in the central public space of the cities of Greece during the Roman period. *Annual of the British School at Athens* 109: 335–56.

Fochetti, B. 2020. Aspects of continuity and change in the Doric order in the province of Asia during the imperial period. In Lohner-Urban, U. and Quatember, U. (eds), *Zwischen Bruch und Kontinuität – Continuity and Change: Architektur in Kleinasien am Übergang vom Hellenismus zur römischen Kaiserzeit – Architecture in Asia Minor during the Transitional Period from Hellenism to the Roman Empire*. Istanbul: Ege Yayınları, 119–32.

Fouquet, J. 2012. Der Roma-Augustus-Monopteros auf der Athener Akropolis: Herrscherkult und Memoria 'ad Palladis templi vestibulum'? *Thetis* 19: 25–83.

Galinsky, K. 1999. Augustan classicism: the Greco-Roman synthesis. In Titchener, F.B. and Moorton, R.F. Jr (eds), *The Eye Expanded: Life and the Arts in Greco-Roman Antiquity*. Berkeley, LA: University of California Press, 180–205.

Gazda, E.K. 2002. *The Ancient Art of Emulation: Studies in the Artistic Originality and Tradition from the Present to Classical Antiquity*. Ann Arbor, MI: University of Michigan Press.

Geiger, J. 2022. City and sanctuary in Plutarch. In Athanassaki, L. and Titchner, F. (eds), *Plutarch's Cities*. Oxford: Oxford University Press, 73–80.

Gleason, M.W. 2006. Greek cities under Roman rule. In Potter, D.S. (ed.), *A Companion to the Roman Empire*. Oxford: Wiley-Blackwell, 228–49.

Gleason, M.W. 2021. Making space for bicultural identity: Herdoes Atticus commemorates Regilla. In Whitmarsh, T. (ed.), *Local Knowledge and Microidentities in the Imperial Greek World*. Cambridge: Cambridge University Press, 125–62.

Goldhill, S. 2001. *Being Greek under Rome: Cultural Identity, the Second Sophistic and the Development of Empire*. Cambridge: Cambridge University Press.

Hall, J.M. 2002. *Hellenicity: Between Ethnicity and Culture*. Chicago: University of Chicago Press.

Hallett, C.H. 2015. Defining Roman art. In Borg, B. (ed.), *A Companion to Roman Art*. Chichester: Wiley-Blackwell, 11–33.

Hartswick, K.J. 2017. The Roman villa garden. In Jashemski, W.F., Gleason, K.L., Hartswick, K.J. and Malek, A.-A. (eds), *Gardens of the Roman Empire*. Cambridge: Cambridge University Press, 72–86.

Heijnen, S. 2018. Athens and the anchoring of Roman rule in the first century BCE (67–17). *Journal of Ancient History* 6.1: 80–110.

Hoff, M.C. 1996. The politics and architecture of the Athenian imperial cult. In Small, A. (ed.), *Subject and Ruler: The Cult of the Ruling Power in Classical Antiquity*. Ann Arbor, MI: Journal of Roman Archaeology Supplementary Series, 185–200.

Hoff, M.C. 2013. Greece and the Roman Republic: Athens and Corinth from the late third century to the Augustan era. In De Rose Evans, J. (ed.), *A Companion to the Archaeology of the Roman Republic*. Chichester: Wiley-Blackwell, 559–77.

Hölscher, T. 2004. *The Language of Images in Roman Art*. Cambridge: Cambridge University Press.

Horster, M. 2017. Cult. In Richter, D.S. and Johnson, W.A. (eds), *The Oxford Handbook to the Second Sophistic*. Oxford: Oxford University Press, 597–612.

Hurwit, J.M. 1999. *The Athenian Acropolis: History, Mythology and Archaeology from the Neolithic era to the Present*. Cambridge: Cambridge University Press.

Hutton, W. 2017. Pausanias. In Richter, D.S. and Johnson, W.A. (eds), *The Oxford Handbook to the Second Sophistic*. Oxford: Oxford University Press, 357–70.

Iliou, N.P. 2014. The Temple of Roma and Augustus on the Athenian Acropolis: a symbol of Roman power? *The Post Hole* 40: 33–37.

Kim, L. 2017. Atticism and Asianism. In Richter, D.S. and Johnson, W.A. (eds), *The Oxford Handbook to the Second Sophistic*. Oxford: Oxford University Press, 41–66.

Kinney, D. 1997. Spolia. Damnatio and renovatio memoriae. *Memoirs of the American Academy in Rome* 42: 117–48.

König, J.P. 2001. Favourinus' Corinthian Oration in its Corinthian context. *Proceedings of the Cambridge Philological Society* 47: 141–71.

Konstan, D. and Saïd, D. 2006. *Greeks on Greekness: Viewing the Greek Past under the Roman Empire*. Cambridge: Cambridge Philological Society.

Korres, M. 1997. Restoration and reconstruction work on monuments in antiquity. In Segarra Lagunes, M.M. (eds), *La reintegrazione nel restauro dell'antico. Atti del seminario di studi (Paestum, 11–12 aprile 1997)*. Rome: Gangemi Editore, 197–208.

Korres, M. 1998. Από τον Σταυρό στην αρχαία αγορά. *Horos* 10–12: 83–104.

Kouremenos, A. (ed.) 2022. *The Province of Achaea in the Second Century CE: The Past Present*. Abingdon: Routledge.

Kousser, R.M. 2008. *Hellenistic and Roman Ideal Sculpture: The Allure of the Classical*. Cambridge: Cambridge University Press.

La Rocca, E. 1985. *Amazzonomachia. Le sculture frontonali del Tempio di Apollo Sosiano*. Rome: De Luca Editore.

Lancaster, O. 1938. *Pillar to Post*. London: John Murray.

Marvin, M. 2008. *The Language of the Muses: The Dialogue between Roman and Greek Sculpture*. Los Angeles: J. Paul Getty Museum.

McAllister, M.H. 1959. The Temple of Ares at Athens: a review of the evidence. *Hesperia* 28.1: 1–64.

McHugh, S. 2017. *Renewing Athens: The Ideology of the Past in Roman Greece*. DPhil Thesis, University of Oxford.

McInerney, J. 2004. 'Do you see what I see?': Plutarch and Pausanias at Delphi. In de Blois, L., Bons, J., Kessels, T. and

Schenkeveld, D. (eds), *The Statesman in Plutarch's Works, Volume I. Plutarch's Statesman and his Aftermath: Political, Philosophical, and Literary Aspects*. Boston-Leiden: Brill, 43–55.

Miles, M.M. 2012. Entering Demeter's gateway: the Roman propylon in the city Eleusinion. In Wescoat, B.D. and Ousterhout, R.G. (eds), *Architecture of the Sacred: Space, Ritual, and Experience from Classical Greece to Byzantium*. Cambridge: Cambridge University Press, 114–51.

Miles, M.M. 2014a. Burnt temples in the landscape of the past. In Ker, J. and Pieper, C. (eds), *Valuing the Past in the Greco-Roman World. Proceedings from the Penn-Leiden Colloquia on Ancient Values, VII*. Boston-Leiden: Brill, 111–45.

Miles, M.M. 2014b. Roman architecture for Greek Eleusis: the Second Sophistic in marble. In Álvarez, J.M., Nogales, T. and Rodà, I. (eds), *Actas del XVIII Congreso Internacional Arqueología Clásica – Proceedings XVIIIth International Congress of Classical Archaeology. Centro y periferia en el mundo clásico – Centre and Periphery in the Ancient World*. Merida: Edit, 803–5.

Morales, F.A. 2017. The Monument of Roma and Augustus on the Athenian Acropolis. Imperial identities and local traditions. In Vanacker, W. and Zuiderhoek, A. (eds), *Imperial Identities in the Roman World*. Abingdon: Routledge, 141–61.

Moser, M. 2017. Reused statues for Roman friends: the past as a political resource in Roman art. In Dijkstra, T.M., Kuin, I.N.I., Moser, M. and Weidgennant, D. (eds), *Strategies of Remembering in Greece under Rome (100 BC – 100 AD)*. Leiden: Sidestone Press, 169–81.

Nasrallah, L.S. 2010. *Christian Responses to Roman Art and Architecture. The Second Century Church amid the Spaces of Empire*. Cambridge: Cambridge University Press.

Newby, Z. 2020. Depicted lives: the role of the visual arts in Sophistic self-representation. In de Temmerman, K. (ed.), *The Oxford Handbook of Ancient Biography*. Oxford: Oxford University Press, 493–508.

Ng, D.Y. and Swetnam-Burland, M. (eds) 2018. *Reuse and Renovation in Roman Material Culture: Functions, Aesthetics, Interpretations*. Cambridge: Cambridge University Press.

Onians, J. 1988. *Bearers of Meaning. The Classical Orders in Antiquity, the Middle Ages and the Renaissance*. Princeton: Princeton University Press.

Osanna, M. 1995. Thesmophorion ed Eleusinion ad Atene: problemi topografici e culturali. *Ostraka* 4.1: 103–18.

Parigi, C. 2019. *Atene e il sacco di Silla. Evidenze archeologiche e topografiche fra l'86 e il 27 a.C.* Wiesbaden: Reichert Verlag.

Pelling, C. 2022. Stereotyping Sparta, stereotyping Athens: Herodotus, Thucydides, and Plutarch. In Athanassaki, L. and Titchner, F. (eds), *Plutarch's Cities*. Oxford: Oxford University Press, 105–21.

Perry, E. 2005. *The Aesthetics of Emulation in the Visual Arts of Ancient Rome*. Cambridge: Cambridge University Press.

Pevsner, N. 1968. *An Outline of European Architecture*. London: Penguin.

Platt, V.J. 2011. *Facing the Gods: Epiphany and Representation in Greco-Roman Art, Literature and Religion*. Cambridge: Cambridge University Press.

Richter, D.S. and Johnson, W.A. (eds) 2017. *The Oxford Handbook to the Second Sophistic*. Oxford: Oxford University Press.

Rogers, D.K. 2021a. Roman Athens. In Neils, J. and Rogers, D.K. (eds), *The Cambridge Companion to Ancient Athens*. Cambridge: Cambridge University Press, 421–36.

Rogers, D. 2021b. Sulla and the siege of Athens: reconsidering crisis, survival, and recovery in the first century B.C. In Fachard, S. and Harris, E.M. (eds), *The Destruction of Cities in the Ancient Greek World. Integrating the Archaeological and Literary Evidence*. Cambridge: Cambridge University Press, 288–318.

Rous, S.A. 2019. *Reset in Stone: Memory and Reuse in Ancient Athens*. Madison, WI: University of Wisconsin Press.

Rykwert, J. 1996. *The Dancing Column: On Order in Architecture*. Cambridge, MA: The MIT Press.

Schmalz, G.C.R. 2007–08. Inscribing a ritualized past: the Attic restoration decree IG II² 1035 and cultural memory in Augustan Athens. *Eulimene* 8–9: 9–46.

Shear, T.L. 1981. Athens: from city-state to provincial town. *Hesperia* 50.4: 356–77.

Shear, T.L. 1997. The Athenian Agora: excavations of 1989–1993. *Hesperia* 66.4: 495–548.

Shear, T.L. 2016. *Trophies of Victory: Public Building in Periklean Athens*. Princeton: Princeton University Press.

Siwicki, C. 2019. *Architectural Restoration and Heritage in Imperial Rome*. Oxford: Oxford University Press.

Siwicki, C. 2020. Architectural criticism in the Roman world and the limits of literary interaction. In König, A., Langlands, R. and Uden, J. (eds), *Literature and Culture in the Roman Empire, 96–235. Cross-Cultural Interactions*. Cambridge: Cambridge University Press, 247–68.

Siwicki, C. 2021. An ancient debate on urban renewal and built heritage: Dio Chrysostom and the city of Prusa. *Urban History* 50.1: 4–21.

Smith, R.R.R. 1998. Cultural choice and political identity in honorific portrait statues in the Greek East in the second century A.D. *Journal of Roman Studies* 88: 56–93.

Smith, R.R.R. 2015. Greek art under Rome. In Borg, B. (ed.), *A Companion to Roman Art*. Chichester: Wiley-Blackwell, 473–95.

Spawforth, A.J.S. 2012. *Greece and the Augustan Cultural Revolution*. Cambridge: Cambridge University Press.

Spawforth, A.J.S. and Walker, S. 1986. The world of the Panhellenion, II. Three Dorian cities. *Journal of Roman Studies* 76: 88–105.

Stadter, P. 2022. Plutarch and Delphi. In Athanassaki, L. and Titchner, F. (eds), *Plutarch's Cities*. Oxford: Oxford University Press, 47–58.

Stewart, A. 2016. The Borghese Ares revisited: new evidence from the Agora and a reconstruction of the Augustan cult group in the Temple of Ares. *Hesperia* 85.3: 577–625.

Stewart, A. 2022. The sculptures of the Temple of Ares in the Agora: discoveries old and new. In Neils, J. and Palagia, O. (eds), *From Kallias to Kritias: Art in Athens in the Second Half of the Fifth Century B.C.* Berlin: De Gruyter, 197–216.

Strazdins, E. 2022. Herodes Atticus and the sanctuaries of Achaea. In Kouremenos, A. (ed.), *The Province of Achaea in the Second Century CE: The Past Present*. Abingdon: Routledge, 166–90.

Stuart, J. and Revett, N. 1789. *The Antiquities of Athens, Measured and Delineated*. London: J. Haberkorn.

Swain, S. 1996. *Hellenism and Empire. Language, Classicism, and Power in the Greek World, AD 50–250*. Oxford: Clarendon Press.

Thomas, C. 2010. Greek heritage in Roman Corinth and Ephesus: hybrid identities and strategies of display in the material record of traditional Mediterranean religions. In Friesen, S., Schowalter, D. and Walters, J. (eds), *Corinth in Context: Comparative Studies on Religion and Society*. Boston-Leiden: Brill, 114–44.

Thomas, E.V. 2007. *Monumentality and the Roman Empire: Architecture in the Antonine Age*. Oxford: Oxford University Press.

Thomas, E.V. 2013. Translating Roman architecture into Greek regional identities. In Schubert, P., Ducrey, P. and Derron, P. (eds), *Les Grecs héritiers des Romains: Huit exposés suivis de discussions*. Geneva: Fondation Hardt, 147–91.

Thomas, E.V. 2014. On the sublime in architecture. In Elsner, J. and Meyer, M. (eds), *Art and Rhetoric in Roman Culture*. Cambridge: Cambridge University Press, 37–88.

Thomas, E.V. 2015. The beauties of architecture. In Destrée, P. and Murray, P. (eds), *A Companion to Ancient Aesthetics*. Chichester: Wiley-Blackwell, 274–90.

Thomas, E.V. 2017. Performance space. In Richter, D.S. and Johnson, W.A. (eds), *The Oxford Handbook of the Second Sophistic*. Oxford: Oxford University Press, 181–201.

Thompson, H. and Wycherley, R.E. 1972. *The Athenian Agora XIV. The Agora of Athens: The History, Shape and Uses of an Ancient City Center*. Princeton: Princeton University Press.

Tomlinson, R.A. 1963. The Doric order: Hellenistic critics and criticism. *Journal of Hellenic Studies* 83: 133–45.

Trimble, J. and Elsner, J. 2006. Introduction: 'if you need an ancient statue…'. *Art History* 29.2: 201–12.

Versluys, J.M. 2017. *Visual Style and Constructing Identity in the Hellenistic World. Nemrud Dağ and Commagene under Antiochos I*. Cambridge: Cambridge University Press.

Vout, C. 2010. Hadrian, Hellenism, and the social history of art. *Arion* 3.18.1: 55–78.

Waelkens, M. 1989. Hellenistic and Roman influence in the imperial architecture of Asia Minor. In Walker, S. and Cameron, A. (eds), *The Greek Renaissance in the Roman Empire. Papers from the Tenth British Museum Classical Colloquium*. London: Institute of Classical Studies, 77–88.

Walker, S. 1987. Roman nymphaea in the Greek world. In Macready, S. and Thompson, F.H. (eds), *Roman Architecture in the Greek World*. London: Society of Antiquaries of London, 60–71.

Walker, S. 1997. Athens under Augustus. In Hoff, M.C. and Rotroff, S.I. (eds), *The Romanization of Athens. Proceedings of an International Conference Held at Lincoln, Nebraska (April 1996)*. Oxford: Oxbow Books, 67–80.

Wallace-Hadrill, A. 2008. *Rome's Cultural Revolution*. Cambridge: Cambridge University Press.

Watkin, D. 1992. *A History of Western Architecture*. London: Laurence King Publishing.

Wesenberg, B. 1984. Augustusforum und Akropolis. *Jahrbuch des Deutschen Archäologischen Instituts* 99: 161–85.

Whitmarsh, T. 2005. *The Second Sophistic*. Oxford: Oxford University Press.

Whyte, W. 2006. How do buildings mean? Some issues of interpretation in the history of architecture. *History and Theory* 45.2: 153–77.

Wiebenson, D. 1969. *Sources of Greek Revival Architecture*. Philadelphia: Pennsylvania State University Press.

Williams, D. 2013. *The East Pediment of the Parthenon: From Perikles to Nero*. London: Institute of Classical Studies, School of Advanced Study.

Williams-Ellis, C. and Williams-Ellis, A. 1924. *The Pleasures of Architecture*. London: Jonathan Cape.

Wilson Jones, M. 1991. Designing the Roman Corinthian capital. *Papers of the British School at Rome* 59: 89–150.

Wilson Jones, M. 2000. *Principles of Roman Architecture*. New Haven-London: Yale University Press.

Woolf, G. 1994. Becoming Roman, staying Greek: culture, identity and the civilizing process in the Roman East. *Proceedings of the Cambridge Philological Society* 40: 116–43.

Zanker, P. 1988. *The Power of Images in the Age of Augustus*. Ann Arbor, MI: University of Michigan Press.

12

A matter of perspective: The reception of early imperial composite column capitals in Asia Minor

Philip T. Stinson

So-called composite capitals in Roman architecture by definition and in simplest terms combine an Ionic capital with a Corinthian capital.[1] This chapter reconsiders the evidence for the first wave of composite capitals implemented in the eastern and western provinces of the Roman world during the Augustan and Julio-Claudian periods. I argue that a difference in perspective resulted in the main regional differences in the composite capitals from Asia Minor in comparison to those from Rome and the western provinces.[2] My methodology examines how composite capitals were used with respect to nearby Ionic or Corinthian architectures, a critical source of information for attempting to figure out what ancient architects thought about them. Highlights of this study include previously unpublished material from Aphrodisias in Caria,[3] and the reconsideration of an old problem in Roman architecture studies and numismatics about what kinds of capitals – Ionic or composite? – are shown for the Temple of Divus Augustus in Rome on Caligulan sestertii. My experience with the reception of the Roman basilica in Asia Minor interpreted from local and regional perspectives and my archaeological fieldwork at Aphrodisias and Sardis inform the study's approach, presentation style, and conclusions.

Early composite capitals from Asia Minor in context

Early composite capitals dating to the Augustan and Julio-Claudian periods from Asia Minor, including Samos, share a number of common regional characteristics. Three well-preserved contexts are considered here: the Temple of Augustus and Roma at Mylasa (12–2 BCE), the temple known as Prostylos I on Samos (Julio-Claudian), and the Sebasteion of Aphrodisias (Julio-Claudian). We will begin with a previously unpublished context from Aphrodisias.

Aphrodisias: Julio-Claudian Sebasteion

The imperial cult temple complex known as the Sebasteion was excavated under the directorship of K. Erim from 1979 to 1987.[4] Construction on the complex began during the early reign of the emperor Tiberius in c. 20 CE, only to be completed after delays from earthquake damage under Claudius and Nero (on the dating of the complex, see Smith 2013). The Sebasteion consists of a hexastyle Corinthian temple dedicated to Aphrodite Prometor, emperor Tiberius, and Livia, which was raised on a high podium and fronted by a staircase in Roman fashion, and three other buildings arranged along a processional avenue: the Propylon, and the North and South Buildings, three-storied façades decorated with c. 200 sculpted relief panels.[5]

A composite pier capital was excavated in 1980 from an architectural collapse layer at the east end of the Sebasteion's processional avenue (Fig. 12.1a). Based on the excavated findspot and configuration, the capital can be reconstructed confidently to the east corner pier of the North Building's second Ionic storey (Fig. 12.1b–c) (Aphrodisias excavation notebook 196, 17). The capital, 52 × 52 cm square at the base and 38 cm in height, is well preserved apart from missing two of the original three diagonal volutes. Three sides of the capital were ornamented; the rear side was originally attached to the marble wall at the corner of the North Building.

The height of the capital's echinus and the profile of its 'thin' abacus match the Ionic capitals from either North or South Building of the complex. The spirals of each diagonal volute are joined by a channel or canalis running horizontally along the top of each echinus (Fig. 12.1a, c). These are important characteristics that will be discussed further below. Due to the capital's squat proportions, each side of the echinus has seven eggs instead of the usual five.

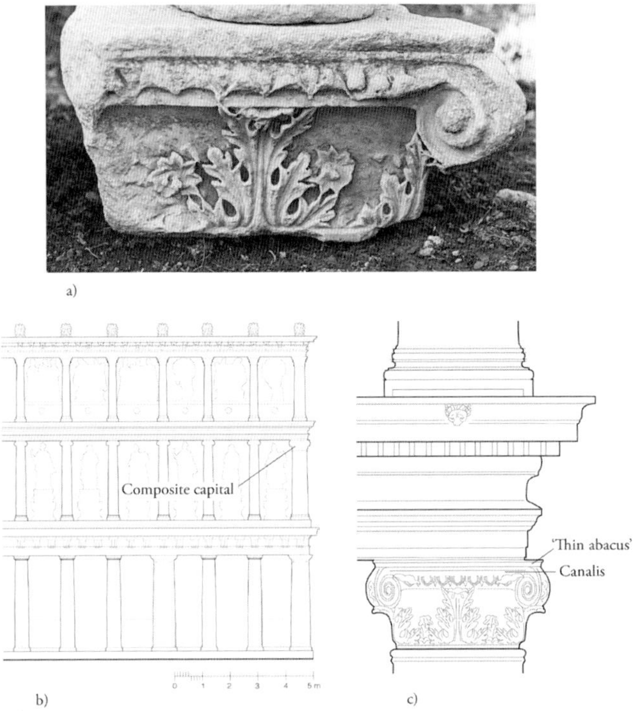

Fig. 12.1. Julio-Claudian Sebasteion, Aphrodisias: Composite capital. a: Archival excavation photo from 1983 (photo courtesy of New York University Aphrodisias Excavations); b–c: North Building, reconstructed east end and corner showing original location of composite capital on the second Ionic storey, and detail (image P. Stinson).

The eggs are triangular with sharp points at the bottom, while the intermediate leaves grow independently and have small dart heads. The diagonal volute from the right back corner of the capital flares out slightly at the bottom, a characteristic typical of diagonal volutes on two-, three-, or four-sided Ionic capitals, such as those from the Sebasteion's Propylon (three-sided), or of composite Ionic-Corinthian capitals in general. The spine of the volute preserves traces of a linear acanthus tendril motif, which is also found on the volutes of the three-sided Ionic capitals from the Propylon, and commonly on other composite capitals from Asia Minor. Traces of corner-palmettes survive at the connections between the echinus and the volutes.

The lower half of the capital, the kalathos, has a single row of widely proportioned acanthus leaves, one to each face, and one to each corner. The main leaves have modelled ribs, ovoid as well as heart-shaped eyelets, no signs of deep drilling, and bridging between adjacent leaflets – all features consistent with early and late Julio-Claudian dating.[6] Smaller pairs of acanthus leaves and floral motifs define the background plane of the kalathos between the main leaves. With eight-pointed petals and projecting stamens, the pendant flowers on the original right side of the capital, shown in Fig. 12.1a, resemble the pendant flowers commonly found on the kalathoi of metropolitan Roman or western provincial

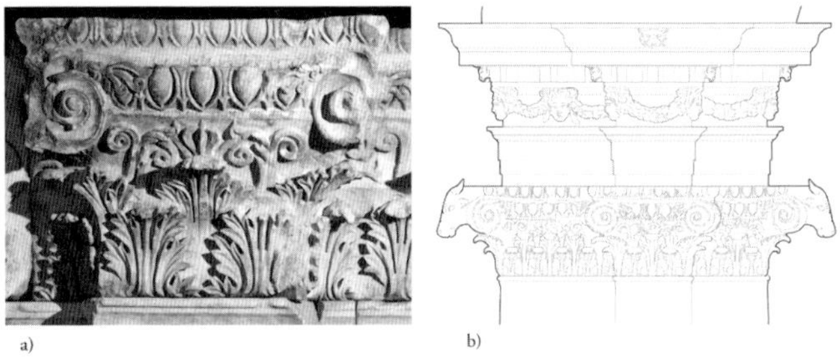

Fig. 12.2. Aphrodisias, Civil Basilica: Composite pilaster capital from the south hall. a: Front, central unit; b: Restored drawing showing Ionic entablature (photo and image P. Stinson, with permission of New York University Aphrodisias Excavations).

composite capitals.[7] The entablature of the North Building's second Ionic storey consisted of an architrave-frieze course and a cornice with dentils (Fig. 12.1b–c).

The North Building's composite capital assisted in differentiating the architectures of the North and South Buildings, which were built by two unrelated pairs of brothers and their families. The North Building was financed by brother Eusebes and Menandros together with the wife of Eusebes, Apphias; the South Building by brothers Attalos and Diogenes, together with the wife of Attalos, Attalis, and a son of Diogenes, Tiberius Claudius Diogenes.[8] The two teams may have employed different architects and different workers. Viewers of the North Building (at least those who could appreciate these decorative particulars) would have found a number of subtle distinctive details including but not limited to the composite capital, such as the refinement of upward curvature in its front façade, the tiny creatures (including frogs, scorpions, and lizards) sculpted beneath the abaci of its Doric capitals, or the frieze of sacrificial bulls' heads and military shields running along the top of its Corinthian entablature (Smith 2013, 31, pl. 4b).

The composite capital from the Sebasteion is the earliest known example from Aphrodisias. Later composite capitals of the Flavian period come from the south hall of the Civil Basilica, which like the composite capital from the Sebasteion also have a canalis between the echinus and the abacus (Fig. 12.2a–b) (Stinson 2016, 52, pls. 99–101). Composite capitals reused in Basilica A / Gaudin's Gymnasium date to the mid-late second century CE and come from an unknown original context.[9] In doing away with the canalis and having a more visually prominent abacus, they are consistent with composite capitals from Asia Minor of the high imperial period. We will return to these points later.

Mylasa: Temple of Augustus and Roma

Engravings and drawings of the Temple of Augustus and Roma of Mylasa in Caria have captivated scholars of Roman architecture for many years because of the composite capitals shown on the temple's façade and other distinctive

Fig. 12.3. Mylasa, Temple of Augustus and Roma. a: View of the temple from the south-west as it stood in the mid-eighteenth century; b: Details of the temple's front left corner. Recordings by architect G.B. Borra of the Robert Wood Expedition (after Zoller 1996, figs 18.15–16).

design details (Fig. 12.3). The temple is dated in the range of 12–2 BCE during the reign of Augustus from a dedicatory inscription recorded by early travellers.[10] The structure stood well into the eighteenth century and was drawn on several occasions by travelling expeditions. F. Rumscheid (2004) compiled and compared the various graphic recordings by early travellers such as Cyriacus of Ancona (1446), Jacob Spon and George Wheler (1675–76), Richard Pococke (1740), and Robert Wood/Giovanni Battista Borra (1750), among others. Two of Borra's recordings are shown in Fig. 12.3. Rumscheid confirmed the original existence of composite capitals on the temple's façade, arguing that Borra's drawings in particular should be trusted because of the level of care taken in making them, and due to the fact that the draftsman's recordings of other ancient monuments in Asia Minor have proven to be generally accurate when compared against surviving physical remains, as the present author can attest with respect to Borra's renditions of Sardis.[11]

The hexastyle podium temple had a nearly square cella with a 6 × 7 configuration of peristasis columns. Early travellers' recordings show composite capitals on the six front columns and Ionic capitals on the six columns to each side (Fig. 12.3a). The six front column shafts also have additional ornaments, garlands and rosettes at the top, and acanthus leaves at the bottom. The entablature, designed in the Ionic style, was also elaborate and consisted of an architrave with three *fasciae*, a frieze decorated with bucrania and other symbols of cult and sacrifice, and an Ionic dentilated cornice. The composite capitals have specific characteristics held in common with other early composite capitals from Asia Minor – most importantly, the echinus has a canalis (Fig. 12.3b).[12] This supersedes earlier thinking that composite capitals from Asia Minor did not have a canalis (Rumscheid 2004, 161–64; compare with Strong 1960, 127). The abacus is also thin and Ionicizing, like that of the later composite capital from Aphrodisias discussed above.

The temple's composite capitals were employed in the exalted position of the temple's façade relative to the normal Ionic capitals to the sides and rear. The 'basket' of acanthus leaves at the base of each façade column additionally served as a pendant to each composite capital's 'basket' of acanthus, drawing more attention to each capital and to their sextet. Similarly, the composite capital from the Sebasteion at Aphrodisias enjoyed a visually conspicuous location on a corner, serving either at the head of a series of 50 Ionic capitals, or conversely as an exclamation point of sorts at the end of the same series.[13] Such hierarchical, 'academic' employments of different kinds of capitals on the same monument, or among monuments belonging to the same complex, had been a major tenet of Hellenistic architecture. For instance, the architect of the great Temple of Apollo at Didyma reserved pride of place for columns with Corinthian capitals within a forest of Ionic ones, placed inside an antechamber atop the temple's vast interior court. The Bouleuterion or Council House of Miletus provides another nearby precedent but from a civic context.[14]

Samos: Temple known as Prostylos I

A third early context in the region of Asia Minor is the tetrastyle temple known as Prostylos I in the Sanctuary of Hera on Samos (Fig. 12.4). R. Posamentir recently proposed that Prostylos I was dedicated to Livia on the basis of a fragmentary bronze-lettered inscription from the temple's façade, a dating that aligns with a previous assessment by T. Schulz based mainly on the composite capitals' stylistic features.[15] Of the temple's original set of approximately 10 composite capitals, two survive in good condition,

Fig. 12.4. Samos, Sanctuary of Hera, temple known as Prostylos I. a: Restored front elevation (after Schulz 2002, fig. 10); b: Composite capital from an anta (after Schulz 2002, pl. 11.1); c: Restored drawing of same composite capital (after Schulz 2002, fig. 25).

one normal capital and one anta capital (Fig. 12.4b–c). The capitals have a four-sided echinus (the anta capital is three-sided based on a four-sided concept) with a canalis and a kalathos with two rows of acanthus leaves. Schulz compared the acanthus of the capitals with similar examples from Ephesus noting the common vertical composition of the leaf type, softly modelled ribs, pointed leaflets with minimal bridging between leaflets, and heart-shaped eyelets (Schulz 2002, 72–84). The Samian temple may have employed composite capitals solely, yet it is consistent with Aphrodisias and Mylasa in using a surrounding Ionic architectural framework in association with its composite capitals. Primary Ionic features of Prostylos I include the surrounding stepped platform or crepis and an entablature with a dentilated cornice (Fig. 12.4a).

Summary

The composite capitals from these contexts share formal characteristics and contextual architecture. A canalis and thin abacus, akin to typical Ionic capitals, are present in each case. Later composite capitals from high imperial contexts in Asia Minor do not have a canalis, and they have a heavier abacus akin to typical Corinthian capitals.[16] Therefore, we may conclude that the composite capital 'kit' in Asia Minor during the Augustan and Julio-Claudian periods included the canalis and thin abacus. A recently published composite capital from Ephesus dated stylistically to the Augustan period but from an unknown context also supports this conclusion (Büyükkolanci and Söğüt 2012). The close association with the regional Ionic order is another shared feature; as mentioned the canalis and thin abacus were common features of Hellenistic and contemporary Ionic capitals.

The wider setting for hybridizing Ionic-Corinthian architectures in Asia Minor

The appearance of the conventional Ionic-Corinthian composite capital in Asia Minor was part of a wider phenomenon of interactions between Ionic and Corinthian architectures in the region during the period ranging from the early Augustan to Julio-Claudian eras.

The acanthus-bolster Ionic capital

Another significant novelty interpreted the idea of combining an Ionic capital with a Corinthian capital differently. It placed acanthus leaves on the bolsters or pulvini of normal Ionic capitals, to be referred to here as the 'acanthus-bolster' Ionic capital (Fig. 12.5). The acanthus leaves are necessarily applied horizontally but can also be upright, and rinceau patterns are also sometimes found. A typical example of the acanthus-bolster Ionic capital incorporates four or six horizontal acanthus leaves per bolster, sometimes in combination with reed leaves. A central bun or balteus divides the composition and serves as the mirror-point for the arrangement of the acanthus leaves to the sides. W. Alzinger first documented the frequent presence of acanthus-bolster Ionic capitals on Augustan and early Julio-Claudian monuments at Ephesus, including in particular the west gate to the Tetragonos Agora, and the stoa-basilica of the upper agora or Staatsmarkt (Fig. 12.5a–b).[17] Ephesus however was not an isolated testing ground. A subsequent survey by O. Bingöl demonstrated that the new form of Ionic capital would become the norm in Asia Minor by the Julio-Claudian period.[18]

Building projects at Aphrodisias, for example, fully embraced acanthus-bolster Ionic capitals during the Augustan and early Julio-Claudian periods. The surviving capitals from the colonnades of the agora (Fig. 12.5d), begun perhaps in the 30s BCE by Zoilos, a freedman of the household of Octavian, show acanthus on the bolster.[19] The immense enterprise, which was not completed until the early first century CE, employed in total c. 200 such Ionic capitals and more than 100 Corinthian capitals. In addition, many of the surviving Ionic capitals from the peristasis columns of the Temple of Aphrodite at Aphrodisias also show acanthus on the bolster (Fig. 12.5c). The leaves display a variety of forms, which was likely stimulated by the involvement of several donors and workshops (Theodorescu 1990;

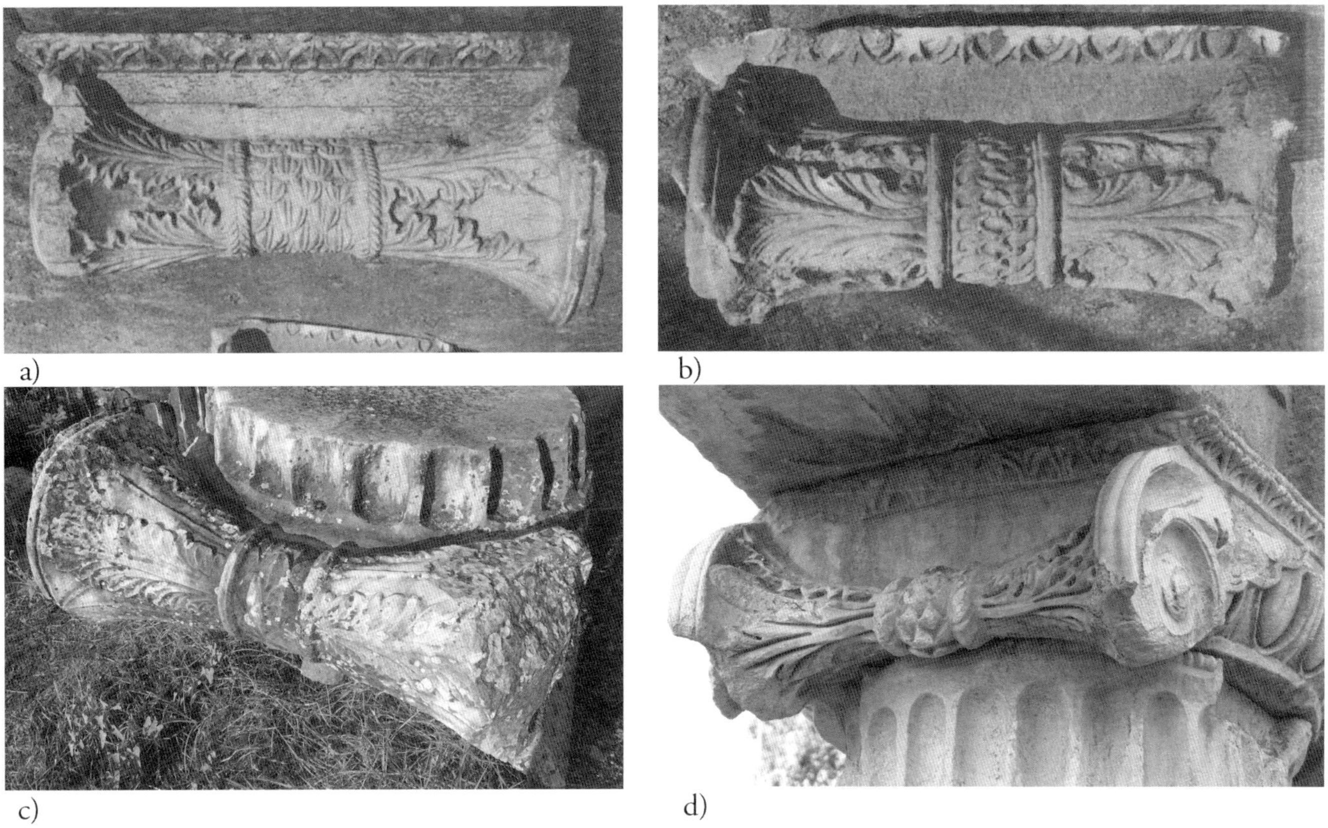

Fig. 12.5. Examples of Ionic capitals from Asia Minor with acanthus ornamentation on the bolster. Ephesus, west gate (a) and Stoa-Basilica (b) (after Alzinger 1974, 40, fig. 75; 58, fig. 96a); Aphrodisias, Temple of Aphrodite (c) and Agora (d) (photos courtesy of New York University Aphrodisias Excavations).

Ratté 2001, 11). The high consumption of acanthus-bolster Ionic capitals at Aphrodisias continued at least into the Flavian period, for example, with the production of over 70 more such capitals for the interior colonnades of the Civil Basilica (Stinson 2016, 29, fig. 18; 30, fig. 20; 35, fig. 21; pls. 32, 50).

In Asia Minor, acanthus had been used on the bolsters of Ionic capitals in limited ways since the early second century BCE. The first known instances come from Pergamon,[20] or from sites and monuments within the influential sphere of the Attalid kingdom, such as the Temple of Apollo Smintheus in the Troad, or the Stoa of Attalus in Athens (Rumscheid 1994, 127, 192, pl. 17). Examples from Italy, which offer an underappreciated category of evidence for interactions between Greek and Roman architects and work teams in the late Republican period, include but may not be limited to the Ionic capitals from the apsidal hall at Palestrina, the Temple of Portunus in the Forum Boarium in Rome, and a fragment from the Temple of Jupiter Stator in the Campus Martius.[21]

The Panayırdağ Monument at Ephesus

A comparison is provided by the strange and imaginative Panayırdağ Monument at Ephesus (Fig. 12.6). Consisting of a two-storey tholos-like structure, it stood on the hillside above the city centre on Pion Hill, now Panayırdağ. The monument was most likely both honorific and funerary in nature with a dating in the range of the mid-late first century BCE.[22] The superimposed Ionic and Doric orders would not appear so strikingly unusual if not for their details, which caused the excavators to characterize the architecture overall as nonconformist.[23] The Ionic capital design is an impressive performance. Apparently without precedent, the front side of the capital shows two large 'volutes' separated by an upright acanthus leaf where the echinus would normally be, while pendant vegetal leaves fill the faces of the volutes in substitution for the typical spirals (Fig. 12.6b). In addition, the upper fluting of the column stops short, creating a 'necking' for the capital, which is decorated with simple linear scrolls. As noted by the excavators, the Ionic capital design engenders the spirit of the conventional composite capital in creating a new form of Ionic capital with a more leafy and vegetal appearance like a Corinthian capital. And although the precise dating of the Panayırdağ Monument remains unclear, it makes sense to think of its capitals as a parallel exercise in having some of the same goals as the composite capital but interpreting the charge differently, ultimately not finding as much success in being repeated (Niemann and Heberdey 1906, 161).

Fig. 12.6. Ephesus, Panayırdağ Monument. a: Reconstructed view; b: Ionic capital, front and side; c: Elevation of Ionic capital with entablature; d: Section through Ionic entablature; e: Inside or rear face of Ionic capital (after Niemann and Heberdey 1906, figs 86–87, 99–100).

Acanthus leaves also appeared in other atypical locations on the Ionic storey, such as on the Ionic capital's bolster in upright form, making a connection to acanthus-bolster capitals, and on the entablature. Individual acanthus leaves are also arranged in rows on the frieze course, alternating with upright console brackets, and along the top moulding of the cornice (Fig. 12.6c–d) (Alzinger 1974, 88–91, figs 144–46, 170; Plattner 2009a, 108, fig. 3). The main entablature frieze of the so-called 'Octagon Monument' at Ephesus similarly uses acanthus leaves alternating with palmette leaves and protomes,[24] and the cornice also has Corinthian modillions with acanthus leaves, the earliest known example from Asia Minor.[25] When viewed from a distance, the acanthus leaves on the entablature of the Panayırdağ Monument also would have resembled Corinthian modillions. Although a more precise dating for the monument is unavailable, the entire Ionic storey of the building, not only its capitals, was clearly in active dialogue with the 'Corinthianizing' trends of the time.

In summary, Asia Minor's version of the Ionic-Corinthian composite capital is inseparable from a wider regional process, which was also responsible for the acanthus-bolster Ionic capital and the hybrid Ionic-Corinthian capitals of the Panayırdağ Monument.

Early contexts from the western provinces and Rome

For comparison, the evidence for early composite capitals from the western provinces can be revisited. The body of evidence has grown substantially since D. Strong's pioneering article of 1960. The early evidence from Rome consists regrettably as it always has of stray finds or reuse contexts, the most important of these being a set of composite capitals in the church of Santa Costanza (Fig. 12.7). Strong dated them on style to the period of the Second Triumvirate or early Augustan period.[26] Distinctive characteristics such as the pendant rosettes at the top of the kalathos, the compressed, 'hanging' Ionic echinus, the horizontal channel or canalis above the echinus, and the tall strongly pronounced abacus are often quoted as defining features of the 'orthodox' composite capital in Roman architecture. As we have seen, early composite capitals from Asia Minor also have a canalis, which is a correction from previous thinking, although they typically do not have a tall pronounced abacus or pendant rosettes on the upper kalathos. These are important points of distinction. An exception could be the composite capital from the Sebasteion at Aphrodisias, whose pendant floral motifs on the kalathos resemble the western type (Fig. 12.1a).

Fig. 12.7. Rome, composite capital reused in the Church of Santa Costanza (photo DAI Rome 41.2416).

Strong assumed that significant sites for composite capitals must have existed in the city of Rome before the Flavian period, but that they are missing from the archaeological record. In indirect support of that thesis, multiple contexts dating to the Augustan and Julio-Claudian periods are now known from Italy and the western provinces. They include the so-called 'Temple of Diana' at Nîmes (Fig. 12.8), the Arch of Germanicus at Saintes (Fig. 12.9), and the gate known as Porta Leoni at Verona (Fig. 12.10).[27] I chose these contexts because good preservation permits analysis of their entablatures and composite capitals together.[28] A hypothetical example from Rome is also considered, the

Fig. 12.8. Nîmes, so-called 'Temple of Diana'. a: General view of the hall (photo Wikipedia Commons, Public Domain); b: Detail of rear left corner showing pilaster with composite capital at right, Corinthian capital at left (photo Wikipedia Commons, Public Domain); c: Detail of same composite capital (photo DAI Rome 1110855).

Fig. 12.9. Saintes, Arch of Germanicus (photo Wikipedia Commons, CC-BY-SA-2.5).

Temple of Divus Augustus, whose appearance can be gauged only on the basis of numismatic evidence.

Nîmes

The so-called 'Temple of Diana' at Nîmes consists of an elaborate ashlar-masonry vaulted hall generally thought today to date to the Augustan period but whose function remains debated.[29] The side walls of the chamber preserve a series of five niches to each side with alternating triangular and curved or segmental pediments (Fig. 12.8a). The niches are separated by engaged columns with composite capitals, which survive in varying states of preservation (Fig. 12.8c). These 12 columns with composite capitals served as the space's primary architectural order, while additional Corinthian capitals adorned piers and engaged columns at the chamber's front entrance and to the sides of a large alcove centred on the back wall. The room's main entablature is Ionic in style. Consisting of an architrave with three *fasciae*, a plain frieze, and a cornice with dentils and projecting corona, it served both the composite as well as Corinthian columns (Fig. 12.8a–b).

Saintes

The ornamentation of the façade of the Arch of Germanicus at Saintes (18–19 CE), perhaps one or two decades later in dating, consists of two superimposed storeys using composite capitals on the upper storey and Corinthian capitals on the lower storey (Fig. 12.9). The composite capitals themselves are poorly preserved.[30] On the lower level 12 pilasters with Corinthian capitals frame two archways. The arch's lower and upper entablatures are both Corinthian using cornices with modillions.

Verona

The multi-storey gate in Verona, known as Porta Leoni, dates to the first half of the first century CE and preserves one of

a) b)

Fig. 12.10. Verona, Porta Leoni. a: General view from north-west. b: Composite impost capital from archway (photos courtesy of J. Lenaghan).

two original archways facing the east exterior (Fig. 12.10a). Composite capitals on two pairs of pilasters and engaged columns frame the surviving archway (Fig. 12.10b). Traces of the pedimental entablature above the arch indicate the use of Corinthian cornices with modillions. On the upper level, Corinthian columns frame a central apsidal statue niche (the main publication of the gate remains Kähler 1935).

Rome: Temple of Divus Augustus

Among the possibilities for early contexts for composite capitals in the city of Rome, the Temple of Divus Augustus as depicted on Caligulan sestertii provides the most tantalizing prospect. Remains of the temple's original phase are virtually unknown; the site can be located on the basis of literary sources in the Velabrum, the valley between the Palatine and Capitoline hills south of the Roman forum and Basilica Julia. Begun by emperor Tiberius, the temple was only finally dedicated by Gaius in August of 37 CE. After the fires of 64 and 80 CE, the temple was rebuilt by Domitian and then restored once again by Antoninus Pius. The edge of a substantial foundation identified through excavation behind the Basilica Julia could belong to the Domitianic phase.[31]

Discussions of what the temple looked like have necessarily relied on a series of Caligulan sestertii (Fig. 12.11). The large detailed image, 3 to 3.5 cm in diameter, shows emperor Gaius making a sacrifice in front of a garlanded hexastyle temple with pedimental sculpture and a quadriga on top, and with the inscription DIVO AVG to the sides and SC below. Numismatists have interpreted the temple's capitals depicted on these coins either as Ionic or composite.[32] Ionic volutes can be read on the basis of two large widely separated 'dots' at the top of each capital (Fig. 12.11b–d).[33] The dots are larger and more widely set apart than similar dots commonly used in depictions on coins of Corinthian capital volutes. The chance for composite capitals arises because of a gap between the Ionic volutes and the top of the column shaft where the fluting begins, and although the coins vary in their depictions of the capitals, in several instances a crown-like feature fills that space. The crown-like feature recalls depictions of Corinthian capitals on other coins of different temples. Consisting of two ribs at each side and one rib in the middle, is it the acanthus necking of a composite capital? The coins of Antoninus Pius show Corinthian capitals, but the temple is also octastyle, which would all make sense if it had been completely redesigned and rebuilt.[34] The assumption that Julio-Claudian temples to the deified Augustus theoretically could have shared architectural and ornamental associations supports a proposal

a) Reverse of ANS 1944.100.39338.

b) Detail of the reverse of ANS 1944.100.39338.

c) Detail of the reverse of ANS 1957.172.1526.

d) Detail of reverse of IMP-5878, Bibliothèque nationale de France.

Fig. 12.11. Bronze sestertii of emperor Gaius/Caligula, Rome, 37–38 CE.

by P. Pensabene (2020, 199) that a large early composite capital residing in the archaeological museum of Nola (Fig. 12.12) might come from a temple dedicated to Augustus, built after the death of the emperor at the site in 14 CE (Tac. *Ann.* 4.57).

Summary

These case studies from early contexts in the western provinces stand in contrast to those from Asia Minor, since their composite capitals are more closely associated with Corinthian capitals than Ionic capitals. Composite capitals are placed adjacent to Corinthian capitals (Temple of Diana at Nîmes), or above or below them (Arch of Germanicus at Saintes, Porta Leoni at Verona). And apart from the earliest example from Nîmes, where an Ionic entablature serves both composite and Corinthian capitals, in the other cases Corinthian entablatures consistently occur.

Conclusions: A difference in perspective

Early composite capitals from Asia Minor are consistently employed within an Ionic architectural framework. They are accompanied by an Ionic dentilated cornice, and they also often appear in close proximity to Ionic capitals. This trend continues in the region into the Flavian period. In multiple documented cases of ornamental façades featuring superimposed rows of columns, the columns with composite capitals

Fig. 12.12. Composite capital in the Archaeological Museum of Nola (photo courtesy of P. Pensabene).

are positioned beneath columns with Corinthian capitals, and their associated entablatures use an Ionic cornice with dentils, without modillions (Figs 12.2; 12.13). Furthermore, Corinthian entablatures with modillions are reserved for use with Corinthian capitals.[35] This leads to the summing-up that in Asia Minor architects thought of the composite capital as a variant of the Ionic capital, not a variant of the Corinthian capital. Conversely, because of their frequent association with Corinthian capitals and Corinthian entablatures complete with modillions, early composite capitals in the western provinces and Rome were thought of as a variation on, or a specialized version of, the Corinthian capital.[36]

The regional characteristics of composite capitals themselves betray this polar difference in perspective. In the western examples, beginning with the earliest known composite capitals from Santa Costanza in Rome (Fig. 12.7), the abacus of the capital has tall and heavy proportions resembling typical Augustan Corinthian capitals.[37] By contrast, early composite capitals from Asia Minor have a thin abacus like contemporary Ionic capitals from the same region (compare Figs 12.1, 12.3, 12.4 with Fig. 12.5). One exception to this pattern that comes from a well-understood context is the South Basilica at Corinth, a building of the Julio-Claudian period closely associated with Roman colonization, which used composite capitals of the metropolitan Roman variety at its entrance (Fig. 12.14) (Weinberg 1960, 70–71, pls. 41–43, plan 6). Tell-tale features include the capital's pendant floral motifs on the kalathos and the prominent abacus. In addition, the carving style of the lower two rows of acanthus leaves is consistent with western Roman workmanship, like the building's normal Corinthian capitals. But even in this case, interplay existed since the entablature associated with the composite capitals was Ionic through and through (Fig. 12.14b).[38]

Subsequent changes experienced by composite capitals of the western variety took them further from the Ionic tradition. As in the case of the Arch of Titus (Fig. 12.15),

a) b) c)

Fig. 12.13. Composite capitals associated with Ionic entablatures. a–b: Ephesus, Fountain of Trajan (photos courtesy of U. Quatember); c: Miletus, Market Gate (photo courtesy of G. Plattner).

by the Flavian period the volutes of composite capitals are consistently curved or arched at the top and have become leafier in appearance, altering the canalis, and 'blending' the Ionic capital top with the Corinthian lower half of the capital, actions that may have been intended to create a more unified 'Corinthianized' statement (for more examples, see Freyberger 1990, esp. 33–36). The seeds had been sown for some of these developments earlier (Figs 12.10; 12.12). As if in resistance to those developments, Ionic attributes of composite capitals in Asia Minor stay prevalent much longer. A canalis running along the top of the echinus remains a standard feature of composite capitals until the Flavian period, as demonstrated by capitals from the Civil Basilica at Aphrodisias (Fig. 12.2), the Temple of Zeus-Domitian at Aizanoi, or the Fountain of Bassus at Ephesus.[39] However, by the Trajanic period composite capitals in Asia Minor no longer have a canalis, and the thinner abacus has been replaced by a more pronounced abacus resembling western composite capitals or Corinthian capitals in general (Figs 12.2–3).[40] In a rare and interesting case, a single composite capital from the Fountain of Trajan at Ephesus with arching volutes like contemporary examples in Rome appears alongside a host of other contemporary composite capitals that do not (Fig. 12.13b).[41] Probably not a capital carver's 'mistake,' the arching volutes indicate knowledge of the western type, although under what circumstances the apparent transfer of knowledge occurred is unknown.[42]

In conclusion, the regional characteristics of Roman composite capitals were matters of perspective and cultural

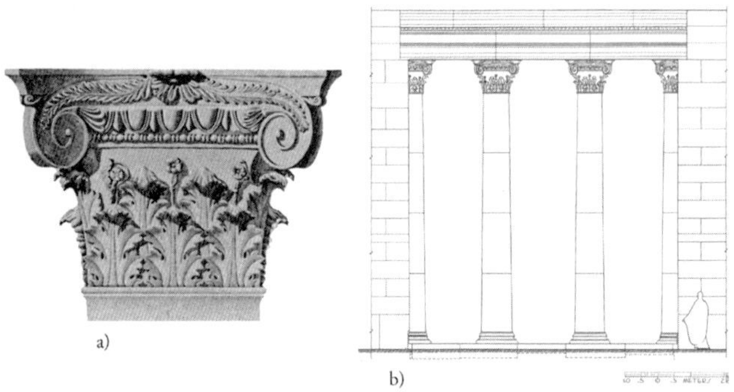

a) b)

Fig. 12.14. Corinth. a: Restored drawing of a composite capital from the entrance to the South Basilica (after Weinberg 1960, plan 9.1); b: Elevation showing the capital with its Ionic entablature (after Weinberg 1960, plan 6).

a) b)

Fig. 12.15. Rome, Arch of Titus. a: East side, detail of composite capital and entablature (photo P. Stinson); b: Detail of composite capital (photo courtesy of G. Plattner).

choice. What ultimately drove any local decision-making is up for debate, but again it might be helpful to attempt to consider the perspectives of architects. The parallel rise of composite capitals and acanthus-bolster capitals would be consistent if the 'idea' was to keep the strong regional tradition of the Ionic order viable and marketable to building patrons through the introduction of new hybridized Ionic-Corinthian forms. Choices were made. The regional features of Asiatic composite capitals did not result from Greek architects somehow misunderstanding or simplifying an imported Roman innovation, a notion suggested by Strong (1960, 127) and never refuted in subsequent scholarship to this author's knowledge. Assumptions of a passive role for the Ionic order or for that matter for architects of Greek origin regarding the 'invention' of the composite capital also should be rejected. Furthermore, it is scarcely credible that Asia Minor's particular brand of composite capital could have acted independently of older regional narratives for the mixing and hybridization of the so-called orders. A trend for mixing and hybridizing column types as well as building morphologies had been pervasive in Hellenistic architecture, so much so as to impact the entire repertoire of the monumental built environment, civic or religious (temples, theatres, gymnasia, other assembly buildings, as well as façades of gates, palaces, and regal tombs). The region of Asia Minor had also played a vital role in supporting the spread of the Doric-Ionic composite capital, the older of the two main types of composite capitals (Winter 2006, 219–34; Ismaelli 2009; Fochetti 2020). The fact that the major monuments of Hellenistic cityscapes mostly stood and remained visible and functional well into the period of the *pax romana* could have empowered a further loosening up of architectural definitions and boundaries in the mid-late first century BCE, when the 'orthodox' composite Ionic-Corinthian capital became set in stone.[43]

As a coda, one must acknowledge how vibrant the Ionic order was in Rome during the period of the Second Triumvirate and first half of the Augustan period. A full assessment extends beyond the scope of this chapter, but Ionic capitals and entablatures, for instance, featured prominently on the façade of the Theatre of Marcellus, inside the new basilicas of the forum, on the Palatine Hill in association with the Temple of Apollo (the 'Portico of the Danaids'), on a shrine of Vesta on the Palatine near the residence of Augustus, and likely on the Temple of Vesta in the Roman forum. The same period was rich with experimentation and hybridization with respect to architectural ornamentation as the Temple of Apollo Medicus Sosianus, started around 34 BCE and completed in the 20s BCE, shows us (Viscogliosi 1996). In this context the comments of Vitruvius (*De arch.* 4.1.12) concerning the existence of several variations of column capitals, perhaps alluding to the new composite capital, also ring truer than ever.[44] The Corinthian capital was obviously still 'unfixed' in the architect's mind, as he describes it as a third *genus* developed from Doric and Ionic and also accepts the Hellenistic tradition of mixing Corinthian capitals with Doric or Ionic entablatures (*De arch.* 1.2.6; 4.1.2–3; 4.1.12).

A final point considers messaging. Several of the known and hypothetical early contexts for composite capitals come from temples associated with the cult of the emperor or imperial family. Despite the regional differences in the formal characteristics and architectural associations for composite capitals, this pattern suggests they may have had other shared associations. The question of what columns, capitals, or the ornamental details of buildings meant in classical antiquity was perhaps a more vexing question for ancient architects than for their patrons (on this point see also Siwicki, this volume).

Notes

1. Kähler 1935, 194; Ziino 1941; Crema 1959, 272–73; Strong 1960; Heilmeyer 1970, 41, 139–40; Pensabene 1973, 106–11, 210–11; Pfanner 1983, 36–37; Onians 1988, 19–28; Wilson Jones 2000, 110, 144–46; Gros 2001, 499–502.
2. For recent scholarship on composite capitals from Asia Minor, see Thür 1989, 90–101; Köster 2004, 160; Quatember 2011, 56–58; Strocka 2012, 232–34; Stinson 2016, 52.
3. I thank Aphrodisias excavations director R.R.R. Smith for permission to publish material from the Sebasteion, and P. Pensabene, G. Plattner, T. Schulz, and U. Quatember for permission to publish photographs and for their advice and generous assistance in preparing this chapter.
4. For the history of Sebasteion excavations, see Erim 1986, 106–83; Smith 2013, 49–53.
5. For an overview of the Sebasteion's architecture, see Smith 2013, 24–41. See also Erim 1986, 106–23; Hueber 1987; Outschar 1987; Gros 1996, 108–9; Ratté 2001, 17–19; Stinson 2019.
6. Heart-shaped eyelets: Alzinger 1974, 72–76, pls. 112–21 (monuments at Ephesus, Augustan and Julio-Claudian); Rumscheid 1994, 267 (Hellenistic precursors); Vandeput 1997, 58, n. 101 (Sagalassos case study with comparanda); Görkay 2002, 221–23, n. 18 (early imperial temple, Alexandria Troas); Verlinde 2015, 181, fig. 91 (early imperial temple, Pessinus). Bridging between adjacent leaflets is also commonly found on capitals from the third storey of the Sebasteion's South Building (unpublished), and on capitals from the Civil Basilica of the Flavian period: Stinson 2016, pls. 18 (north façade), 58 (long hall), 88 (south hall).
7. For example, see Strong 1960, pls. 14–15; Heilmeyer 1970, pls. 49–50; Freyberger 1990, pls. 9, 16, 29, 38–39.
8. On the donors, see Smith 2013, 13–23. On the architectures of the North and South Buildings and their main comparative differences, see Hueber 1987; Outschar 1987; Smith 2013, 30–38.
9. Heilmeyer 1970, 98, pl. 32, nos. 1–2 (capital reused in late Roman or early Byzantine Basilica A / Gaudin's Gymnasium).
10. *CIG* 2696; *IMylasa* no. 31; *PHI – Packard Humanities Institute* 261084 (Mylasa 145); cf. Rumscheid 2004, 131, n. 1.
11. For Borra's recordings of ancient monuments at Sardis, see Greenewalt Jr *et al.* 2003, 20–21, cat. 1a–b (theatre); 30–31,

cat. 3 (city plan); 32–33, cat. 4 (Temple of Artemis). See also Yegül 2020, 15–17. For Borra's career, see Zoller 1996.

12. For additional Borra drawings of the temple, see Rumscheid 2004, 143, fig. 13; 175, fig. 28.
13. A second composite capital in theory could have appeared at the west end of the North Building where it met the Propylon at an interior corner.
14. Didyma, Corinthian capitals: Winter 2006, 11, 223–24, pl. 7, figs 25–28. Miletus, Council House, use of all three orders: Onians 1988, 23–28; Winter 2006, 82, 146–47, 164, 223. For mixed architectural orders in Hellenistic architecture in general, see Lauter 1986, 257–65; Onians 1988, 19–28; Liljenstople 1999; Winter 2006, 219–34.
15. Schulz 2002; Posamentir 2018. Cf. Rumscheid 2004, 162, who agrees with Schulz's dating.
16. Heilmeyer 1970, pls. 25, 27–28, 32–33 (examples from Ephesus, Pergamon, and Aphrodisias); Köster 2004, pls. 102–3, 121–22, 125 (examples from Miletus).
17. Alzinger 1974, 36 (emphasizing that no two acanthus designs on bolsters are alike), 47–48, figs 73–83, 94–105.
18. Bingöl 1980, 87–128. Some of the dates have subsequently been revised, but the main survey results remain correct.
19. Waelkens 1987. On the dating of the agora, see also Ratté 2001, 12; Ratté and Smith 2008, 723.
20. Rumscheid 1994, 36–39, pls. 121–22 (Great Altar); 36, pl. 133 (exedra of Diodorus Pasporus).
21. Palestrina: Gatti 2017, 100 ff., figs 33–35; Temple of Portunus, Forum Boarium: Adam 1994, 92–93 (noting poor preservation and later restorations), figs 26, 29, 48, 54 (drawing by A. Palladio in 1570); Temple of Jupiter Stator, Campus Martius: Bianchi 2010, figs 1, 3.
22. Niemann and Heberdey 1906, 143–80; Alzinger 1974, 16, fig. 26; 37–40, fig. 72; Rumscheid 1994, 165–69; Scherrer 2000, 98–99; Berns 2003, 199. On the dating and questions of function, see most recently Quatember and Scheibelreiter-Gail 2017, 300–1.
23. Niemann and Heberdey 1906, 157: 'Kaum ein einziges Bauglied fügt sich ganz den Regeln der classischen Baukunst'. See also similar comments by Alzinger 1974, 38; Rumscheid 1994, 165.
24. For the frieze, see Alzinger 1974, 91, fig. 146; Plattner 2009a, 108, fig. 3 (arguing for an early Augustan dating citing connections to the Arch of Augustus at Rimini); Quatember and Scheibelreiter-Gail 2017, 301, with bibliography, n. 467. Similar acanthus leaves (syntax as well as iconography) appear on the friezes of the skene building at Aphrodisias, dated to c. 28 BCE on epigraphic grounds: de Chaisemartin and Theordorescu 2017, pls. 43, 55b, 56a.
25. On the Corinthian modillion, see von Hesberg 1980; Wilson Jones 2000, 141–42; Gros 2001, 492–94. For early imperial examples of Corinthian modillions in Asia Minor, roughly in chronological order, see de Chaisemartin and Theodorescu 2017, 98, fig. 55; 107, pls. 50, 58 (skene building, Aphrodisias, c. 28 BCE); Plattner 2009a, 104 (Octagon Monument, Ephesus, early Augustan); Verlinde 2015, 199–203 (temple, Pessinus, early Julio-Claudian); Ismaelli 2017, 105–10 (Temple A, Hierapolis, Julio-Claudian).
26. Strong 1960, 123, pl. 14; Pensabene 2015, 946–47, cat. 840–51; 1073, fig. 817. To this author's knowledge, a full documentation of these capitals has never been published.
27. Composite capitals have also been identified from the Augustan phase of the theatre at Ostia: Pensabene 1973, 106–7, cat. 385–88.
28. The sanctuary at Tarraco, identified as a Julio-Claudian temple dedicated to Augustus, also employed composite as well as Corinthian capitals. However, the latest assessments of the fragmentary evidence by R. Mar and P. Pensabene suggest that the composite capitals, assigned to the porticoes of the complex and possibly to a propylon, are Flavian in date and belong to a second phase. Fragments of Corinthian capitals have been reconstructed to the façade of the temple itself: see Mar 1993, 137–44; Pensabene 1993; Pensabene and Mar 2010; Fishwick 2017.
29. Gans 1990; Gros 1996, 370–72, with bibliography; Yegül and Favro 2019, 476–78; Pensabene 2020, 201–2.
30. On the arch and its decoration, see Tardy 1989, 83–86; 2005, 68–69; Gros 1996, 69–70; Tranoy 2007, 231–34; Pensabene 2020, 201.
31. Fishwick 1992; Torelli 1993; Carandini 2012, vol. 1, 173–75; vol. 2, tab. 40–41; Elkins 2015, 71.
32. Fuchs 1969, 112 ('korinthischen oder der kompositen Ordnung'); Fishwick 1992, 233 ('composite?'); Torelli 1993, 145 ('tempio ionico'); Elkins 2015, 71 ('Ionic').
33. For example, ANS 1957.172.1526; 1984.176.5; 1944.100.39338; 1995.11.1543.
34. Torelli 1993, 404, fig. 79; Elkins 2015, 93–94; the plans of the Velabrum shown in Carandini 2012, vol. 2, tab. 40–41 propose a reorientation and enlargement of the temple in the Domitianic period.
35. Examples from Ephesus include the Fountain of Bassus, 80–81 CE (Jung 2006); Fountain of Trajan (Quatember 2011); so-called 'Street Fountain', Trajanic (Quatember 2008); Library of Celsus, Trajanic (Strocka 1988). From Miletus: Nymphaeum, Flavian (Köster 2004, 65–67); Market Gate, Flavian-Trajanic (Köster 2004, 123–32).
36. Freyberger 1990, 33–36 estimated that composite and Corinthian capitals in Rome during the Domitianic and Trajanic periods were made by the same workshop.
37. For examples from the Temple of Mars Ultor: Heilmeyer 1970, pl. 2; Gros 1996, 145, fig. 160; Wilson Jones 2000, 140–41, figs 7.13–14.
38. Readers of this study might be curious about the evidence for composite capitals of Asiatic type from Rome. Published examples date to the high imperial period: Pensabene 1986, 319–33, figs 7–8; 2015, 955–59, 1080–81, figs 891–914; Freyberger 1990, pl. 44c. Herrmann 2017 discusses examples of the western form of composite capital from modern Algeria, while Mugnai 2017 analyses those from the sites of Sala, Banasa, and Volubilis in Mauretania Tingitana.
39. Aizanoi: Naumann 1979, pl. 52 b–c; Jes *et al.* 2006, 67, fig. 63. Ephesus, Fountain of Bassus: Jung 2006, and personal communication with G. Plattner.
40. For additional examples, see Heilmeyer 1970, 25, 27–28, 32–33; Köster 2004, pls. 102–3, 121–22, 125 (examples from Miletus); Rohmann 1998, pls. 42–44 (examples from Pergamon).
41. For additional photographs of this capital, see Köster 2004, pl. 112.2; Quatember 2011, pls. 34.1–2.

42. For an early composite capital of western type from Pergamon, unknown context, see Plattner 2009b, 399, fig. 8.
43. For the notion of the Augustan period as 'catalyst' for globalized forms, see Plattner 2017.
44. Gros 1992, 89–90. On the dating of the writings of Vitruvius, see Rowland and Howe 1999, 2–7.

References

Adam, J.P. 1994. *Le temple de Portunus au Forum Boarium*. Rome: École française de Rome.

Alzinger, W. 1974. *Augusteische Architektur in Ephesos*. Vienna: Österreichisches Archäologisches Institut.

Berns, C. 2003. *Untersuchungen zu den Grabbauten der frühen Kaiserzeit in Kleinasien*. Bonn: Rudolf Habelt.

Bianchi, F. 2010. Il Tempio di Giove Statore e la scena del Teatro di Marcello. Maestranze e modelli decorativi tra epoca tardorepubblicana e media età imperiale. *Rendiconti Lincei. Scienze Morali, Storiche e Filologiche* 21: 285–322.

Bingöl, O. 1980. *Das ionische Normalkapitell in hellenistischer und römischer Zeit in Kleinasien*. Tübingen: Wasmuth.

Büyükkolanci, M. and Söğüt, B. 2012. Ephesos-Ayasuluk Kompozit Başliği. In Söğüt, B. (ed.), *Stratonikeia'dan Lagina'ya. From Stratonikeia to Lagina. Ahmet Adil Tırpan Armağanı. Festschrift in Honour of Ahmet Adil Tırpan*. Istanbul: Ege Yayınları, 115–25.

Carandini, A. (ed.) 2012. *The Atlas of Ancient Rome. Biography and Portraits of the City*. Princeton: Princeton University Press.

Crema, L. 1959. *L'architettura romana*. Turin: Società editrice internazionale.

de Chaisemartin, N. and Theodorescu, D. 2017. *Aphrodisias VIII. Le théâtre d'Aphrodisias: Les structures scéniques*. Wiesbaden: Reichert Verlag.

Elkins, N. 2015. *Monuments in Miniature: Architecture on Roman Coinage*. New York: American Numismatics Society.

Erim, K. 1986. *Aphrodisias. City of Venus Aphrodite*. New York: Muller.

Fishwick, D. 1992. On the temple of Divus Augustus. *Phoenix* 46.3: 232–55.

Fishwick, D. 2017. *Precinct, Temple and Altar in Roman Spain: Studies on the Imperial Monuments at Mérida and Tarragona*. Farnham: Ashgate.

Fochetti, B. 2020. Aspects of continuity and change in the Doric order in the province of Asia during the imperial period. In Lohner-Urban, U. and Quatember, U. (eds), *Zwischen Bruch und Kontinuität – Continuity and Change: Architektur in Kleinasien am Übergang vom Hellenismus zur römischen Kaiserzeit – Architecture in Asia Minor during the Transitional Period from Hellenism to the Roman Empire*. Istanbul: Ege Yayınları, 119–32.

Freyberger, K. 1990. *Stadtrömische Kapitelle aus der Zeit von Domitian bis Alexander Severus. Zur Arbeitsweise und Organisation stadtrömischer Werkstätten der Kaiserzeit*. Mainz: Philipp von Zabern.

Fuchs, G. 1969. *Architekturdarstellungen auf römischen Münzen*. Berlin: De Gruyter.

Gans, U.-W. 1990. Der Quellbezirk von Nîmes. Zur Datierung und zum Stil seiner Bauten. *Mitteilungen des Deutschen Archäologischen Instituts, Römische Abteilung* 97: 94–125.

Gatti, S. 2017. Tradizione ellenistica e sperimentazione italica: l'aula absidata nel foro di Praeneste. *Archeologia Classica* 68: 53–196.

Görkay, K. 2002. An early imperial podium temple at Alexandria Troas. In Berns, C., von Hesberg, H., Vandeput, L. and Waelkens, M. (eds), *Patris und Imperium. Kulturelle und politische identität in den städten der römischen Provinzen Kleinasiens in der frühen Kaiserzeit (Kolloquium Köln, November 1998)*. Leuven: Peeters, 217–32.

Greenewalt, C.H. Jr, Cahill, N.D., Stinson, P. and Yegül, F.K. 2003. *The Ancient City of Sardis: Approaches in Graphic Recording (Exhibition Catalogue)*. Cambridge, MA: Harvard University Press.

Gros, P. 1992. *Vitruve, de l'architecture: Livre IV*. Paris: Les Belles Lettres.

Gros, P. 1996. *L'architecture romaine du début du IIIe siècle av. J.-C. à la fin du Haut-Empire, 1: Les monuments publics*. Paris: Picard.

Gros, P. 2001. *L'architecture romaine du début du IIIe siècle av. J.-C. à la fin du Haut-Empire, 2: Maisons, palais, villas et tombeaux*. Paris: Picard.

Heilmeyer, W.D. 1970. *Korinthische Normalkapitelle. Studien zur Geschichte der römischen Architekturdekoration*. Heidelberg: F.H. Kerle.

Herrmann, J. 2017. Composite capitals in Algeria: a Roman implant, eccentric from its beginnings. In Pensabene, P., Milella, M. and Caprioli, F. (eds), *Decor: decorazione e architettura nel mondo romano. Atti del convegno internazionale (Roma, 21–24 maggio 2014)*. Rome: Quasar, 351–62.

Hueber, F. 1987. Der Baukomplex einer julisch-claudischen Kaiserkultanlage in Aphrodisias. (Ein Zwischenbericht zur theoretischen Rekonstruktion des Baubestandes). In de la Genière, J. and Erim, K. (eds), *Aphrodisias de Carie. Colloque du Centre de recherches archéologiques de l'Université de Lille III (13 novembre 1985)*. Paris: Éditions Recherche sur les Civilisations, 101–6.

Ismaelli, T. 2009. *Hierapolis di Frigia, III. Architettura dorica a Hierapolis di Frigia*. Istanbul: Ege Yayınları.

Ismaelli, T. 2017. *Hierapolis di Frigia, X. Il tempio A nel santuario di Apollo: architettura, decorazione e contesto*. Istanbul: Ege Yayınları.

Jes, K., Posamentir, R. and Wörrle, M. 2006. Der Zeustempel von Aizanoi, ein Grossbau flavischer Zeit. *Istanbuler Mitteilungen* 56: 227–46.

Jung, K. 2006. Das Hydrekdocheion des Gaius Laecanius Bassus in Ephesos. In Wiplinger, G. (ed.), *Cura Aquarum in Ephesus. Proceedings of the Twelfth International Congress on the History of Water Management and Hydraulic Engineering in the Mediterranean Region (Ephesus/Selçuk, Turkey, October 2–10, 2004)*. Dudley, MA: Peeters, 79–86.

Kähler, H. 1935. Die römischen Stadttore von Verona. *Jahrbuch des Deutschen Archäologischen Instituts* 50: 138–97.

Köster, R. 2004. *Die Bauornamentik von Milet, Teil 1: die Bauornamentik der frühen und mittleren Kaiserzeit*. Berlin: De Gruyter.

Lauter, H. 1986. *Die Architektur des Hellenismus*. Darmstadt: Wissenschaftliche Buchgesellschaft.

Liljenstople, P. 1999. Superimposed orders. The use of the architectural orders in multi-storeyed structures of the Roman period. *Opuscula Romana* 24: 117–54.

Mar, R. 1993. El recinto de culto imperial de Tárraco y la arquitectura Flavia. In Mar, R. (ed.), *Els monuments provincials de Tàrraco. Noves aportacions al seu coneixement*. Tarragona: Universitat Rovira i Virgili, 107–56.

Mugnai, N. 2017. At the edge of the Roman world: the Corinthian and composite capitals from Sala, Banasa and Volubilis (Mauretania Tingitana). In Pensabene, P., Milella, M. and Caprioli, F. (eds), *Decor: decorazione e architettura nel mondo romano. Atti del convegno internazionale (Roma, 21–24 maggio 2014)*. Rome: Quasar, 363–78.

Naumann, R. 1979. *Der Zeustempel zu Aizanoi*. Berlin: De Gruyter.

Niemann, G. and Heberdey, R. 1906. Der Rundbau auf dem Panajirdagh. In *Forschungen in Ephesos. Veröffentlicht vom Österreichischen Archaeologischen Institute, Band 1*. Vienna: A. Hölder, 143–80.

Onians, J. 1988. *Bearers of Meaning. The Classical Orders in Antiquity, the Middle Ages and the Renaissance*. Princeton: Princeton University Press.

Outschar, U. 1987. Betrachtungen zur kunstgeschichtlichen Stellung des Sebasteions in Aphrodisias. In de la Genière, J. and Erim, K. (eds), *Aphrodisias de Carie. Colloque du Centre de recherches archéologiques de l'Université de Lille III (13 novembre 1985)*. Paris: Éditions Recherche sur les Civilisations, 107–22.

Pensabene, P. 1973. *Scavi di Ostia, VII. I capitelli*. Rome: Istituto Poligrafico dello Stato.

Pensabene, P. 1986. La decorazione architettonica, l'impiego del marmo e l'importazione di manufatti orientali a Roma, in Italia e in Africa (II–VI d.C.). In Giardina, A. (ed.), *Società romana e impero tardoantico, 3. Le merci, gli insediamenti*. Rome-Bari: Laterza, 285–429.

Pensabene, P. 1993. La decorazione architettonica dei monumenti provinciali di Tarraco. In Mar, R. (ed.), *Els monuments provincials de Tàrraco. Noves aportacions al seu coneixement*. Tarragona: Universitat Rovira i Virgili, 33–106.

Pensabene, P. 2015. *Roma su Roma: reimpiego architettonico, recupero dell'antico e trasformazioni urbane tra il III e il XIII secolo*. Vatican City: Pontificio Istituto di Archeologia Cristiana.

Pensabene, P. 2020. Province ispaniche e galliche: la decorazione architettonica nelle pietre locali tra il I secolo a.C. e la fine del II secolo d.C. *Anas* 33: 189–233.

Pensabene, P. and Mar, R. 2010. Il tempio di Augusto a Tarraco. Gigantismo e marmo lunense nei luoghi di culto imperiale in Hispania e Gallia. *Archeologia Classica* 61: 243–307.

Pfanner, M. 1983. *Der Titusbogen. Beiträge zur Erschliessung hellenistischer und kaiserzeitlicher Skulptur und Architektur*. Mainz: Philipp von Zabern.

Plattner, G. 2009a. Zur Bauornamentik des Oktogons von Ephesos. In Ladstätter, S. (ed.), *Neue Forschungen zur Kuretenstrasse von Ephesos. Akten des Symposiums für Hilke Thür vom 13. Dezember 2006 an der Österreichischen Akademie der Wissenschaften*. Vienna: Verlag der Österreichischen Akademie der Wissenschaften, 101–10.

Plattner, G. 2009b. Zum Baubetrieb Kleinasiens in der römischen Kaiserzeit. In Bachmann, M. (ed.), *Bautechnik im antiken und vorantiken Kleinasien*. Istanbul: Ege Yayınları, 393–408.

Plattner, G. 2017. Die augusteische Globalisierung als 'Katalysator' kleinasiatischer Architektur? Traditionen und Innovationen eines Epochenwandels. In Cavalier, L., Ferriès, M.-C. and Delrieux, F. (eds), *Auguste et l'Asie Mineure*. Bordeaux: Ausonius Éditions, 291–308.

Posamentir, R. 2018. Die neue Hera: ein Tempel für Livia auf Samos. *Mitteilungen des Deutschen Archäologischen Instituts, Athenische Abteilung* 133: 239–92.

Quatember, U. 2008. Der Brunnen an der Straße zum Magnesischen Tor in Ephesos. *Jahreshefte des Österreichischen archäologischen Instituts in Wien* 77: 265–334.

Quatember, U. 2011. *Das Nymphaeum Traiani in Ephesos*. Vienna: Verlag der Österreichischen Akademie der Wissenschaften.

Quatember, U. and Scheibelreiter-Gail, V.T. 2017. Flavius Damianus und der Grabbau seiner Familie. *Jahreshefte des Österreichischen archäologischen Instituts in Wien* 86: 221–354.

Ratté, C. 2001. The urban development of Aphrodisias in the late Hellenistic and early imperial periods. In Berns, C., von Hesberg, H., Vandeput, L. and Waelkens, M. (eds), *Patris und Imperium. Kulturelle und politische identität in den städten der römischen Provinzen Kleinasiens in der frühen Kaiserzeit (Kolloquium Köln, November 1998)*. Leuven: Peeters, 5–32.

Ratté, C. and Smith, R.R.R. 2008. Archaeological research at Aphrodisias in Caria, 2002–2005. *American Journal of Archaeology* 112.4: 713–51.

Rohmann, J. 1998. *Die Kapitellproduktion der römischen Kaiserzeit in Pergamon*. Berlin: De Gruyter.

Rowland, I.D. and Howe, T.N. 1999. *Vitruvius: Ten Books on Architecture*. Cambridge: Cambridge University Press.

Rumscheid, F. 1994. *Untersuchungen zur kleinasiatischen Bauornamentik des Hellenismus*. Mainz: Philipp von Zabern.

Rumscheid, F. 2004. Der Tempel des Augustus und der Roma in Mylasa. Eine kreative Mischung östlicher und westlicher Architektur. *Jahrbuch des Deutschen Archäologischen Instituts* 119: 131–78.

Scherrer, P. (ed.) 2000. *Ephesus, the New Guide*. Istanbul: Ege Yayınları.

Schulz, T. 2002. *Die römischen Tempel im Heraion von Samos, I. Die Prostyloi*. Wiesbaden: Reichert Verlag.

Smith, R.R.R. 2013. *Aphrodisias VI. The Marble Reliefs from the Julio-Claudian Sebasteion*. Mainz: Philipp von Zabern.

Stinson, P. 2016. *Aphrodisias VII. The Civil Basilica*. Wiesbaden: Reichert Verlag.

Stinson, P. 2019. The multifaceted architectural refinements in the Julio-Claudian Sebasteion of Aphrodisias. *Journal of Roman Archaeology* 32: 39–65.

Strocka, V.M. 1988. Wechselwirkungen der stadrömischen und kleinasiatischen Architektur unter Trajan und Hadrian. *Istanbuler Mitteilungen* 38: 291–307.

Strocka, V.M. 2012. Bauphasen des kaiserzeitlichen Asklepieions von Pergamon. *Istanbuler Mitteilungen* 62: 199–287.

Strong, D. 1960. Some early examples of the composite capital. *Journal of Roman Studies* 50: 119–28.

Tardy, D. 1989. *Le décor architectonique de Saintes antiques. Les châpiteaux et bases*. Paris: Éditions du CNRS.

Tardy, D. 2005. *Le décor architectonique de Vesunna: Périgueux antique*. Pessac: Fédération Aquitania.

Theodorescu, D. 1990. La restitution de l'Aphrodision: certitudes et perplexités. In Roueché, C. and Erim, K.T. (eds), *Aphrodisias Papers. Recent Work on Architecture and Sculpture*. Ann Arbor, MI: Journal of Roman Archaeology Supplementary Series, 49–65.

Thür, H. 1989. *Das Hadrianstor in Ephesos*. Vienna: Verlag der Österreichischen Akademie der Wissenschaften.

Torelli, M. 1993. Augustus, divus, templum (novum); aedes. In Steinby, E.M. (ed.), *Lexicon Topographicum Urbis Romae, 1*. Rome: Quasar, 145–46.

Tranoy, L. 2007. Mediolanum Santonum, Saintes: de la fondation jusqu'à l'époque julio-claudienne. In *Simulacra Romae: Roma y las capitales provinciales del occidente europeo: estudios arqueológicos*. Alicante: Biblioteca Virtual Miguel de Cervantes, 223–38.

Vandeput, L. 1997. *The Architectural Decoration in Roman Asia Minor. Sagalassos: A Case Study*. Leuven: Peeters.

Verlinde, A. 2015. *The Roman Sanctuary Site at Pessinus from Phrygian to Byzantine Times*. Leuven: Peeters.

Viscogliosi, A. 1996. *Il tempio di Apollo in circo e la formazione del linguaggio architettonico augusteo*. Rome: 'L'Erma' di Bretschneider.

von Hesberg, H. 1980. *Konsolengeisa des Hellenismus und der frühen Kaiserzeit*. Mainz: Philipp von Zabern.

Waelkens, M. 1987. Notes d'architecture sur l'agora et le portique de Tibère à Aphrodisias de Carie. In de la Genière, J. and Erim, K. (eds), *Aphrodisias de Carie. Colloque du Centre de recherches archéologiques de l'Université de Lille III (13 novembre 1985)*. Paris: Éditions Recherche sur les Civilisations, 123–35.

Weinberg, S. 1960. *Corinth V.1. The Southeast Building, the Twin Basilicas, the Mosaic House*. Princeton: American School of Classical Studies.

Wilson Jones, M. 2000. *Principles of Roman Architecture*. New Haven-London: Yale University Press.

Winter, F. 2006. *Studies in Hellenistic Architecture*. Toronto: University of Toronto Press.

Yegül, F.K. 2020. *The Temple of Artemis at Sardis*. Cambridge, MA: Harvard University Press.

Yegül, F.K. and Favro, D.E. 2019. *Roman Architecture and Urbanism from the Origins to Late Antiquity*. Cambridge: Cambridge University Press.

Ziino, V. 1941. Introduzione al capitello composito. *Palladio* 5: 97–111.

Zoller, O. 1996. *Der Architekt und der Ingenieur Giovanni Battista Borra (1713–1770)*. Bamberg: Wissenschaftlicher Verlag.

13

Where do we live? Local stonescapes and globalized architecture in Cyrenaica and Cyprus

Eleonora Gasparini

Introduction

Where do we live? The answer to this question was obvious to those who had acquired honour and wealth administering the towns of the eastern Mediterranean already before the Roman Empire. Architecture was a feature of those cityscapes and a manifestation of the elites' power, and this is also true of provincial territories such as Cyprus and Cyrenaica (Fig. 13.1). The historical developments that affected both regions resulted in parallel architectural trends. For instance, elements typical of Alexandrian architecture have allowed to emphasize the connection between these lands and Egypt. Not only has this been pointed out for architectural elements of the Hellenistic age, but also for those of later centuries: after all, the cultural legacy of the Ptolemies endured under Roman rule. If, on the one hand, the study of the Cypriot and Cyrenaican cities has enriched our knowledge of Alexandria itself, on the other, much ink has been spilt over the possible existence of a direct connection between the two regions.[1] Though different in many respects, Cyrenaican and Cypriot architectures were conditioned by similar local attitudes towards Rome.

In order to investigate such attitudes, one ought to start from the assumption that the 'Roman world' included multiple features (not just architecture) that arose from a complex historical-cultural landscape. The phrase 'globalizing attitudes' recognizes a system of connections within the Roman world, which derive from the political, economic, social, and cultural hegemonic role of Rome.[2] In recent scholarship, traditional distinctions between 'provincial art' and 'art of Rome in the provinces' have been overcome also thanks to anthropological methodologies, which have shifted the focus on the individual.[3] The emphasis is on the concept of hybridization of space and culture, while space and society are seen as entities formed by multi-levelled aggregations (Alston 2022, 445). Even research on ancient construction has been affected by such approaches and, particularly, by the social and moral conditions in relation to the purely economic principles that affected the architecture of the Roman world (Maschek 2022, 13–17, 21–22). Along the same line of thought, scholars such as Domingo (2022, 111–30) have approached the economics of construction from a global perspective, taking into account social, political, historical, technical and ideological factors.

In this chapter, I explore some architectural characteristics of Cyrene, Ptolemais, Nea Paphos, Kourion, and Salamis, focusing on their impact, reception and perception. The aim is to investigate the elites who commissioned the construction projects. The urban centres under analysis provide a partial, yet significant, picture of the respective provinces. These were sophisticated societies with advanced technology and culture that had been already unified under the Ptolemies. When Cyrenaica and Cyprus were annexed to the Roman world in the first century BCE, the complex socio-cultural character of these societies, with their historical legacy, must have shaped the new cultural stimuli introduced by Rome's rule. As one can observe for Greece and Asia Minor, the Romans did not want – or were not able – to compete with local traditions. To succeed, the support of local civic institutions and the use of local traditions remained crucial.[4] Although differences continued to exist, urban life in the eastern provinces was undeniably affected by global tendencies. In this sense, being Roman meant being part of a larger community. Tangible mediation, blending, and adaptation between global and local architectural trends can be seen in the areas under consideration here: in recent years, archaeologists have often defined this phenomenon as 'glocalization'.[5]

Fig. 13.1. Location of main areas under discussion (image E. Gasparini, based on Google Earth).

The mid-imperial period represented a crucial moment, when political changes consolidated and the architectural language, based on the use of marble, displayed universally recognizable cultural, social, and economic meanings. Therefore, I focus on the architectural choices of the main public and private buildings from the second century CE onwards. Such choices should provide answers to questions such as: 'who are we?'; 'what distinguishes us from/unites us with the other inhabitants of the Empire?'; and, last but not least, 'where do we live?'. During the mid-imperial period, the Cyrenaican and Cypriot cityscapes can be described as dynamic entities under transformation. The use of marble in public building projects testifies to the economic power of local euergetes and their probable involvement in economic ventures under imperial control.[6] Marble, in particular, was used on specific types of monuments, such as public plazas, colonnaded streets, entertainment buildings, bath complexes, and sometimes also sacred areas. One can notice tendencies on part of the urban elites to conform to the fashions of the Empire: this is especially seen in the adoption of standardized marble products that dominated the Mediterranean market, with a clear prevalence of the Corinthian order.[7]

These styles and typologies also became a model for the workshops that employed local stones, further determining transformations in local styles. The new products satisfied the local and regional taste. In many newly built or renovated buildings of the mid-imperial era in Cyrenaica and Cyprus, marble was meant to foster a sense of increased socio-cultural prominence. Its actual use, however, was limited given the elevated costs and difficulty of supply, and local stone was therefore widely employed in both private and public architecture. These projects relied on local sources and local patterns of supply/distribution. In Cyrenaica and Cyprus, local materials are represented by calcareous stones (limestone and calcarenite). The continuity of activity of local workshops resulted in the survival and transmission of specific methods to carve, shape and sculpt stone. These methods define vernacular architecture, in which the inventiveness and skills of those involved in the project (patrons, builders, craftsmen) were combined.[8] For both regions, studies on the provenance of building materials, carried out with multidisciplinary analytical (geological, chemical or petrographic) methodologies, are still underdeveloped, especially in contrast with studies on marble provenance across the Mediterranean.[9] Yet, to shed light on this aspect, one can look at geological maps, the physical characteristics of materials, as well as knowledge of material supply.

This chapter focuses mainly on stylistic issues in relation to the Corinthian order and highlights the role of local materials and decorative schemes/choices in preserving the unique characters of cityscapes, alongside globalizing tendencies. Furthermore, the chapter postulates that the materiality of the stone, more specifically the colour, was also taken in consideration in building projects. Determining to what extent these aspects were decisive in shaping specific urban environments is controversial. This depends, first of all, on the variable use of stucco or plaster that was applied to the stone surface. However, if one refers at least to the walls of buildings, one can suppose that bare structures existed and that the surface and colour of the stone remained visible. These, in turn, would have contributed to the characterization of the local cityscapes, defined here as 'stonescapes'.

Cyrenaica

The development of the architectural decoration in Cyrenaica was influenced by the economic factors associated

Fig. 13.2. Shahat (Cyrenaica, Libya), modern quarry (photo E. Gasparini).

with material supply, particularly in relation to the absence of marble quarries in the region.[10] As a consequence, colonnades and architectural façades were predominantly built in limestone. At Cyrene, comparative studies carried out on samples from monuments and geological outcrops around the city (Fig. 13.2) have identified a stone that can be attributed to the Al Faidyah Formation (uppermost Oligocene to lower Miocene).[11] It consists of a fine-grained, yellow-greyish limestone, with pink and brown oxidation patinas on the most exposed areas of the surface. It is characterized by a scarce, but significant, presence of dolomite and, sometimes, potassium feldspar. The dolomitic component occasionally makes the rock friable, presenting an irregular stratification and exfoliation of its surface. The material does not react well to polishing. The state of preservation is negatively affected by the abundant presence of fossils (foraminifera and calcareous nannofossils), by the poor cementation, and by the clastic structure of the stone.

At Cyrene and Ptolemais, one can explain the more numerous attestations of marble on walls and floors rather than on architectural elements (such as columns and entablatures) by considering issues of transport vis-à-vis cost. Small blocks of coloured marble, from which slabs and tiles were carved, could have been supplied more easily than monolithic columns.[12] As for the choice of architectural orders, some differences emerge between the two cities. During the early imperial age, the Corinthian order was hardly ever used at Cyrene in favour of the Doric and Ionic counterparts, which featured heavily in both civic and religious public spaces (see Żelazowski 2014–15 and Mugnai, this volume). However, it should be pointed out that at Ptolemais, a tradition was established that made large use of the Alexandrian-Corinthian capital with free volutes: this decorative element features prominently in the renovation of the Colonnaded Palace between the first century BCE and the first century CE[13] (Fig. 13.3). Therefore, the Alexandrian architectural language

Fig. 13.3. Ptolemais, Archaeological Museum: Alexandrian-Corinthian capital of an engaged pillar from the northern façade opening onto the Great Peristyle of the Colonnaded Palace (photo E. Gasparini).

Fig. 13.4. Ptolemais, Archaeological Museum: Figured Corinthian capital from the entrance to room 7 of the Colonnaded Palace (photo E. Gasparini).

became part and parcel of the cityscape not only in relation to late Hellenistic influences, but also as part of the architectural transformations that took place in the early imperial age. One should also mention the occurrence of broken pediments and cornices with *travicello* modillions. At the same time, a specific type of acanthus began to appear on the local Corinthian order; though directly comparable to Alexandrian models, this autonomous form of acanthus remained in use over the centuries (Fig. 13.4). It is thus possible to identify a specific Cyrenaican trajectory in the stylistic development of the Corinthian capital (Pensabene and Gasparini 2017, 663–70).

Fig. 13.5. Cyrene, central quarter: Front of the Porticoed Building with Corinthian columns in Proconnesian marble (photo E. Gasparini).

Fig. 13.6. Cyrene, Temple of Zeus: Detail of marble moulding framing the socle of the platform where the cult statue was placed (photo E. Gasparini).

At both cities, *romanitas* can be glimpsed more from the introduction of certain types of buildings (such as the civic basilica in the Gymnasium-Caesareum of Cyrene and the baths in the Colonnaded Palace at Ptolemais) than from decorative schemes. However, in the wider province, public and private architecture underwent important changes from the Hadrianic period onwards, when marble played a crucial role in urban refurbishment.[14] After the Jewish Revolt, Hadrian encouraged the reconstruction of damaged buildings at Cyrene; he sent settlers to revive civic life and urged the population to take on the financial burdens of these reconstructions. From the late Antonine age, population and architecture flourished, giving life to a surprising amalgamation of local and imported trends. Coloured marble column shafts, especially in Carystian green (cipollino) marble and Aswan pink granite, as well as column bases and Corinthian capitals in Proconnesian white marble are connected to the (re)construction of large public buildings, such as the Great Baths on the Myrtousa, the various theatres, and the civic and sacred areas in the city's central quarter (Fig. 13.5).

The restoration of the cella in the Temple of Zeus, dated to the mid-second century CE, is particularly relevant since it was decorated with marble architectural elements: more specifically, column shafts in cipollino and entablatures, mouldings, Corinthian capitals, and bases of Proconnesian marble (Stucchi 1975, 253, pls. 245–46; Walker and Matthews 1996, 307–15; Pensabene 2006, 233) (Fig. 13.6). In contrast, architectural elements in other sacred buildings at Cyrene were prevalently carved out of local stone, even if their shape was inspired by the imported marble decoration. The Temple of Apollo in the Sanctuary on the Myrtousa was rebuilt after the Jewish Revolt reusing materials from the previous phases. Yet, it was adapted to the new architectural taste. This is evident in the shape of Doric columns with plain shafts. Inscriptions attest to the dedication of these columns at the priests' expense (*IRCyr2020* C.255). One should also mention the later reconstruction of the cella walls, with inscriptions celebrating the works that took place under Commodus and the priest Aristoteles (*IRCyr2020* C.306), and the presence of a triple-arched access to the *adyton* showing a Syrian influence (Stucchi 1975, 239).

If we shift our attention to the area of the agora, the restorations after the Jewish Revolt saw the introduction of new Ionic colonnades (Stucchi 1965, 241–47, 278–90; Bacchielli 1981, 168–79; Kenrick 2013, 153–85). They display square capitals with a thin echinus, an arched canalis, and large volutes following a model that recalls the *quadriporticus* of the Sanctuary of Asklepios at Balagrae (Stucchi 1975, 263–66; Kenrick 2013, 116–18). In the same part of the city, numerous Corinthian capitals in local stone were inspired by marble capitals imported to Cyrene from the eastern Mediterranean. They are attested in several buildings on the southern side of the agora, dated between the mid-second century and the early third century CE, such as the Tetrastyle Temple (Stucchi 1967, 47–83; Stucchi and Bacchielli 1983, 75–94), the Temple of the Octagonal Bases (Stucchi 1965, 255–77; 1967, 47–83), the propylon (Stucchi and Bacchielli 1983, 95–107), the Temple of the Muses (Luni and Mei 2007, 37–77), and the front porch of the prytaneum on the opposite side of the *skyrota* (Stucchi 1975, 281–82; Bonacasa and Ensoli 2000, 86). Particular attention should be devoted to the Temple of the Octagonal Bases (Temple E6), which was tetrastyle, *in antis*, and in local stone. It displayed Attic bases on an octagonal plinth and Corinthian capitals with prickly acanthus (Fig. 13.7). Decorative exuberance is particularly visible on the door lintel, on the pilasters at the corners of the cella, on the antae and, above all, on the mouldings of the cornices, suggesting a late second century CE date. The Temple of the Muses is also significant. It was tetrastyle and stood on a high podium, with a façade decorated with unfluted column shafts and Corinthian capitals; at the centre, given

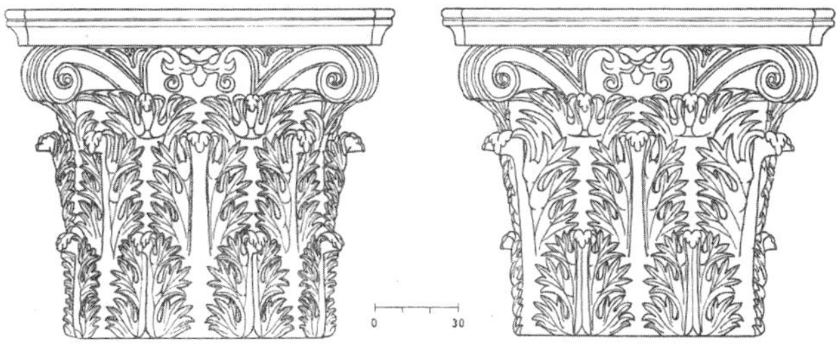

Fig. 13.7. Cyrene, Corinthian capitals from the Temple of the Octagonal Bases (image E. Gasparini, after Stucchi 1965, 261, fig. 169).

the much wider intercolumniation, a Syrian arch has been reconstructed. In the Temple of Zeus Aegiochus, the columns of the façade were reworked with fluted shafts and in the Doric order similarly to other buildings of the agora (Stucchi 1975, 235; Ensoli 2003, 62–91). The Temple of Athena was rebuilt on the site of a previous building and is well-known for the mosaic in the cella decorated with a *gorgoneion* (Venturini 2013, 56). The façade consisted of half-columns set against pillars at the end of the colonnaded front (the so-called 'Cyrenean façade': Bacchielli 1981; Mei 2016, 311–12; 2017, 370–71, 375, 378–79; 2020, 79–80).

Less evident are the transformations carried out after the Jewish Revolt in the porticoes of the Gymnasium-Caesareum.[15] Though the Doric colonnades were kept in place, novel interventions are attested by the presence of monumental inscriptions in Greek and Latin (Gasperini 1971, 10–12). As for the basilica, even if it had already been built in the first century CE in the Doric order,[16] it was renovated under Hadrian. Only the temple, located at the centre of the square and possibly dedicated to Bacchus, presented the Corinthian order, though this was adapted to a Cyrenean façade, characterized by two columns at the centre and two heart-shaped pillars at the corners. However, one should note

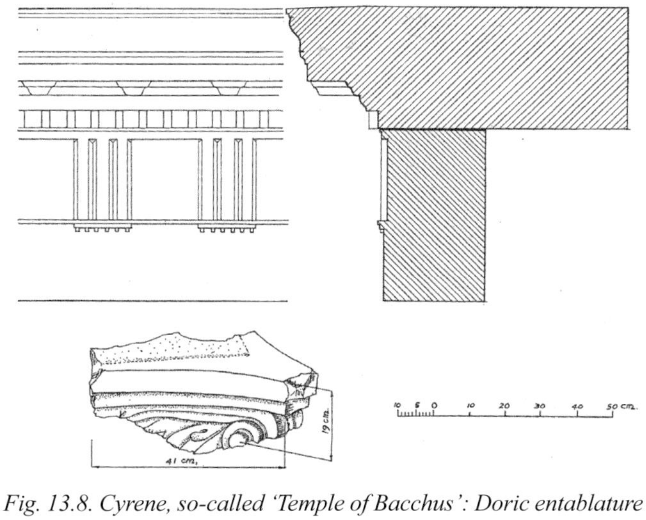

Fig. 13.8. Cyrene, so-called 'Temple of Bacchus': Doric entablature and a fragmentary Corinthian capital (image E. Gasparini, after Ward-Perkins et al. *1958, 158, fig. 10).*

that Corinthian was not the only style; the entablature, in fact, was Doric (Fig. 13.8).

Marble architecture was not associated with new productions of Ionic capitals in local stone, which are instead attested in the residences of the early imperial age, such as the Roman Villa, House G, House T at Ptolemais, and the Casa del Propileo at Cyrene (Kraeling 1962, 119–39, 222; Ward-Perkins *et al.* 1986, 109–53; Pensabene and Gasparini 2017, 674–76). From the second third of the second century CE, the Corinthian order acquired special significance for the self-representation of the urban elites. Types that were introduced through the importation of marble architectural elements were copied by local artisans on local materials. On capitals, this is particularly evident in the shape of the leaves with elongated and prickly leaflets. This Cyrenaican acanthus is more lively and 'graceful', in strident contrast with the monotonous shape of the imported marble capitals.[17] This is apparent when comparing some marble capitals (for instance, from the Eastern Basilica at Apollonia or the Porticoed Building at Cyrene) with capitals of the late Antonine and early Severan age, carved out of local stone (see the Temple of the Octagonal Bases at Cyrene and the temple by the Square of the Cisterns at Ptolemais) (Fig. 13.9). These peculiarities attest to an autonomy of style that would last for centuries in Cyrenaica. By looking at Corinthian capitals from public buildings, these features can be summarized as follows:

- Conic ribbed cauliculi with corolla hem; lack of calyces; thin helices and volutes (cf. propylon of the agora, second century CE);
- Thin and elegant stems of the helices, shaped as ribbons with grooves along the edges (cf. Tetrastyle Temple, mid-second century CE);
- Further decorative details introduced into the vegetal elements, such as a small calyx in the V space between the helices and volutes (cf. prytaneum and House of Jason Magnus, late second/early third century CE);
- Remarkable height, disregarding canonical proportions, of the two crowns of acanthus leaves and reduced height of the upper section of the kalathos (cf. Temple of the Octagonal Bases, late second/early third century CE);
- Underlining of the lower curve of the leaves' shadow zones with an engraved bow (cf. Temple of the Muses, late second/early third century CE).

The capitals of the temple by the Square of the Cisterns at Ptolemais are also representative of the provincial decorative landscape during the late Antonine and early Severan periods: by mixing forms inherited from the Hellenistic period, they reflected the Cyrenaican environment. This is also visible on a Corinthian capital in the Colonnaded Palace, dated to the first century CE, and currently located in the museum of Ptolemais (Pensabene and Gasparini 2017,

Fig. 13.9. Ptolemais, temple to the north-east of the Square of the Cisterns: Corinthian capitals of Hellenistic tradition with Asiatic influence (photo E. Gasparini).

668, fig. 19). The adherence to the Hellenistic tradition can be perceived in the reduced calyces and the V-shaped stems of the helices and volutes, with small leaves or rosettes placed between them. Instead, the ornamentation inspired by marble capitals consists of prickly acanthus leaves, with lobes separated by narrow and curved shadow zones. These capitals also feature a contrast between the rather organic development of the two crowns of leaves and the atrophied upper section of the kalathos. The leaves are slender and are articulated in five lobes; small calyces are inserted between the leaves of the second crown, whence the stems of the helices and volutes originate.

Unique in the city of Cyrene and in the entire province are the Corinthian capitals (in local stone) from a monumental complex on the Valley Street, which complemented the marble colonnades running along its northern and southern sides (Stucchi 1975, 275). This complex featured a building of uncertain function, known as the Building with the Windswept Capitals,[18] and a Severan-period propylon that gave access to the stepped street towards the agora (Stucchi 1975, 271–73; Ward-Perkins and Gibson 1976–77, 342–43; Kenrick 2013, 192–93). The capitals were decorated with half-figures of *victoriae* and windswept acanthus leaves, while the columns underneath featured spirally fluted shafts. Their details are heavily influenced by those of the imported capitals, in particular the sharply geometric shape of the leaves. The capitals of the propylon support an entablature with an inscribed architrave and a sculptured frieze. This is the only example of a Roman historical relief known from Cyrene commemorating a victory of Septimius Severus, whose manufacture has been attributed to eastern workshops (Stucchi 1988, 511–12). It is significant that, despite showcasing a clear message of imperial propaganda, this building did not involve the use of marble. The missing elements in the inscription do not allow identification of the patrons, but the use of local stone indicates that it was probably a local project, rather than an imperial-sponsored one.

If we turn to domestic architecture, Greek-Hellenistic decorative traditions throughout the imperial age contributed to the complexity of the Cyrenaican picture. J.A. Lloyd (1989, 77–90) noted that the major issues regarding private architecture in Cyrenaica concern the origins and chronology of the upper-class peristyle houses, since, from the early imperial age through to Late Antiquity, their plans show a continuity, while the architectural decoration displays new fashions. The private building that better shows the integration of the 'marble style' into a 'Cyrenaican style' is the House of Jason Magnus at Cyrene. It belonged to an eminent Cyrenean family, whose members were gymnasiarchs and priests of Apollo. Its status is reflected in the choice and disposition of the architectural orders during the mid-imperial age, when pre-existing houses were merged, forming a single residence.[19] Special attention was given to the public section of the house, which featured a large Rhodian peristyle. The main side of the peristyle was decorated with columns with figured Corinthian capitals with theatre masks (Fig. 13.10). Stucchi proposed that among these masks there were portraits of Cyrene's kings, interpreting the head of an old man flanked by silphium as a portrait of King Battus. This iconography would be based on a scheme that is also found on coins.[20] The building's decorative programme was complemented by marble statue portraits of members of the Antonine dynasty.[21] The Corinthian order, which became the preferred style of Cyrenean public architecture during the Antonine age, was also linked to the imperial cult. Rather than marble, the colonnades and entablatures of the house are made in limestone. Marble, instead, stands out on the wall and floor veneer, and its use is especially notable on the *opus sectile* floors (Gasparini 2010; Gasparini and Gallocchio 2015).

The House of Leukaktios at Ptolemais offers another example of a complex building history. It developed in four main phases, ranging from the Hellenistic age to the end of the fourth century CE and beyond (Rekowska 2012, 180–81). The restoration of mosaics and paintings

Fig. 13.10. Cyrene, House of Jason Magnus: Corinthian capitals on the southern side of the peristyle (photo E. Gasparini).

and the discovery of inscribed blocks reused in the walls attest to the house's long continuity of use. In these restorations, marble was limited to some of the thresholds and few architectural elements that might have been recycled from other buildings.[22] As observed for the House of Jason Magnus, even in the House of Leukaktios the Corinthian order was meant to highlight the prominence of specific spaces. Corinthian capitals enhanced the entrance to a room or the annex of a room; this space had a tripartite entrance composed of an arcuated lintel (Syrian arch) supported by Corinthian columns and pillars. These elements recall the Asiatic Corinthian (*corinzio asiatico*) style with prickly acanthus leaves and the absence of cauliculi, pointing to a date in the Severan age (Rekowska 2012, 171–76; 2013, 604–5). All the components of this Syrian arch show the presence of red, green, and white plaster (Fig. 13.11). Even if evidence for the application of coating to architectural elements at Cyrene is not particularly abundant, this practice is attested both there and at Ptolemais. Plaster would have strengthened the surface of the decorative elements and would have allowed the application of paint on them. The ornamentation of the Syrian arch from the House of Leukaktios demonstrates this decorative scheme was still used when the Asiatic Corinthian capital was adopted.

At this point, we must make some observations on the entablatures and, particularly, the cornices of Cyrenaican buildings featuring the Corinthian order. During the imperial period, entablatures at Cyrene and Ptolemais were only marginally influenced by imperial marble architecture. Instead, there was a preference for local traditions, which allowed the survival of forms that had been introduced in Hellenistic-Alexandrian architecture. Notwithstanding the transformations of individual details, cornices with *travicello* modillions exemplify this tradition (Pensabene and Gasparini 2019, 177–78, 188–89). An exception is an arched cornice from the House of Jason Magnus, which must have been part of a Syrian arch: the modillions are flat, rectangular, wide, and decorated with acanthus leaves, following the style of the modillions attested in mid-imperial Asiatic and Syrian architecture, in association with a strongly emphasized lower cornice with dentils, Ionic kymation, and astragal.[23]

A significant contribution to the study of local stone architecture in Cyrenaica comes from Late Antiquity. Most cases consist of residential buildings that spanned the late Hellenistic or early imperial age through to the Islamic period. They can shed light on the social value assigned to local architectural traditions by the cities' inhabitants, who in many cases opted to keep in place or reuse earlier stone elements. Therefore, during the late imperial and Byzantine periods, local stone continued to be used for architectural orders of the Greek-Cyrenaican or, more generally, Greek-Hellenistic tradition, together with other decorative elements. Even if patrons invested quite significantly on Christian public architecture, with the use of newly carved or reused Corinthian marble capitals (Ward-Perkins and Goodchild 2003), it is in domestic architecture that the local stone played a fundamental role.

As for Cyrene, the House of Hesychius displayed a rich array of *opera sectilia*, which were made at a stage when three sides of the Rhodian peristyle were closed off, while the local-stone Doric colonnade was kept in place on the fourth side (Gasparini 2012; Pensabene and Gasparini 2014, 233–35) (Fig. 13.12). This choice can perhaps be explained in relation to the semantic value of the Doric order, which, ultimately, reflected Cyrene's history (Walker 1985, 98–103;

Fig. 13.11. Ptolemais, House of Leukaktios: Painted lintel and capital from a Syrian arch (photos M. Rekowska).

Fig. 13.12. Cyrene, House of Hesychius: Doric capital from the main side of the peristyle (photo E. Gasparini).

Fig. 13.13. Cyrene, Casa della Kline Semicircolare: Corinthian capital reused in the restoration of the peristyle in the mid-imperial age (photo E. Gasparini).

Fig. 13.14. Ptolemais, House of Paulus: Two capitals and a base in Proconnesian marble (photo E. Gasparini).

Wright 1992, 56–58). Its coexistence with the Corinthian order must be approached by taking into account the importance of architectural language for the definition of spaces and functions. Even if Late Antique Doric columns employed reused materials, they still conveyed traditional messages of *decor*. They were not a simple means to create colonnaded spaces cheaply. Still at Cyrene, another example of a luxury house with *opus sectile* floors dated to the mid- and late imperial age is represented by the Casa della Kline Semicircolare (Pensabene and Gasparini 2017, 656): the large peristyle, with fluted columns and mixed Doric and Corinthian orders, features architectural elements from previous phases (Fig. 13.13). Therefore, even if in the Late Antique phase a *stibadium* was added to the southern side of the peristyle, with rooms paved in marble (Venturini 2013, 83–84, nos. 99–100), Corinthian capitals from earlier phases still decorated this side of the courtyard. They find comparisons with elements from Alexandria (Pensabene 1993, 182, 190, 353, 355), and at Cyrene they find a comparable example, at least for the acanthus, in the Corinthian capital of the Tempio Gemino within the insula of Jason Magnus.[24]

The archaeological evidence from domestic architecture shows that only at Ptolemais coloured marble was used for column shafts, matched with bases and capitals in the Corinthian order of Proconnesian white marble (House T, House of Paulus) (Fig. 13.14). This occurred when the city held the role of provincial capital from the late third century to the second half of the fifth century CE or slightly later. However, during the Byzantine period, local stone was the most attested decorative material, as seen in the Palace of the Dux at Apollonia (Gasparini 2021) (Fig. 13.15). This contrasts with the rich marble architecture – whether

Fig. 13.15. Apollonia, Palace of the Dux, eastern sector: Corinthian capital made of limestone (photo E. Gasparini).

carved from new blocks or reused elements – of the city's Christian monuments, even if Christian symbols appear in key points of the reception area of the palace, and a chapel was included in its public sector. In this building, beside the selected stone, the activity of local workshops was also influenced by the adoption of Corinthian capitals that followed the models of Constantinopolitan imperial architecture. The patron can probably be identified as someone at the top of the social hierarchy, but who did not have access to marble supply.

Cyprus

In Cyprus, the stone that was used extensively for construction and decorative architectural elements was quarried from local outcrops. Calcarenite, reef limestone, and chalk were the most exploited materials; calcarenite from the geological formation of Pachna, located in the south-western sector of the island, was used prominently (Fig. 13.16).[25] The style of architectural decoration of the island was strongly linked to Alexandrian Hellenism, as seen in the use of mixed orders with cornices with *travicello* modillions and Corinthian capitals with free volutes.[26] Some examples, such as two capitals in the museum at Kouklia and two from the 'Hellenistic' House at Nea Paphos, are dated to the late second century BCE (Tkaczow 2020, 211; Pensabene and Gasparini 2020, 154–56; 2021, 331) (Fig. 13.17). Though they represent the first local attempts to rework Alexandrian models locally, the workshops should still be placed within an Alexandrian cultural milieu, possibly inspired by Greco-Alexandrian elite culture. Such choices might have been influenced by the governor's presence at Nea Paphos during Ptolemaic rule of the island, as well as by the city's thriving elite of traders. As for the Doric capitals, the traditional model had been modified as early as the first century CE, following Mediterranean trends, yet with specific Cypriot characteristics. The three *anuli* under the echinus were replaced with *fasciae* to facilitate carving. Examples are found with one, two or three small *fasciae* often overlapping the echinus, thus making it bipartite or tripartite (Fig. 13.18). Two capitals from the House of Orpheus at Nea Paphos (Rekowska *et al.* 2019; 2021a–b) display the typical forms of Doric capitals attested in houses in Cyprus (Wright 1992, fig. 301.4, from Amathus).[27]

A development in the architectural decoration of Cyprus is attested by the adoption of a particular form of 'stylized capital' (also known as 'Nabataean', simplified, geometrized, unfinished, or blocked-out).[28] While it is absent in Cyrenaica, this form is attested in Cyprus between the late first and early second century CE. Stylized Corinthian capitals began to spread in sanctuaries (Sanctuaries of Apollo Hylates at Kourion and Aphrodite at Amathus) that had been rebuilt after the earthquakes of 76–77 CE or in the early second century CE.[29] In these reconstructions, Cypriot workshops abandoned the Alexandrian-Corinthian model, even in its local form. A type of stylized Corinthian capital with free helices and volutes started to circulate, as shown by the half-finished examples found at the quarries (Karageorghis 1969, 498–99, figs 135–36). Two rings in relief in the lower part of the capital stand for the two crowns of acanthus leaves; had they been finished, the protuberances would have served to carve the tips of the leaves. In the upper part, the four outer volutes still follow the Alexandrian model, being characterized by large plain leaves with the tip folded under the corners of the abacus. The lower and upper parts were commonly worked in two separate blocks, therefore determining a certain inhomogeneity (Fig. 13.19). These stylized forms have led to the hypothesis that the application of coating and stucco would had modified the surface of the capitals, and this would have had a prominent role in determining the final appearance.[30] However, these forms were not really adopted because of economic/financial reasons (i.e., to save time), or due to particular stylistic choices.[31] Rather, it appears they resulted from a lack of artisans trained in Alexandrian-style carving in Cyprus in the late first/early second century CE, which marked a breaking point with the Hellenistic architectural heritage on the island. Therefore, these capitals can be interpreted as the manifestation of an architectural culture that, for various reasons, adopted stylized forms because of the loss of specific Alexandrian-style, stone carving skills. A subsequent development consisted in the widespread adoption of these new stylized forms, which ultimately gave birth to an independent decorative tradition.

This type of capital was frequently adopted in private buildings that evoked the most prestigious sacred architecture of the island. The so-called 'Early Christian' House at Kourion is a relevant case in point, as it testifies to the use of such capitals in a colonnaded hall that can be dated to the early imperial period (Pensabene and Gasparini 2021). In the last phase of the 'Hellenistic' House at Nea Paphos (datable after the earthquake that affected the city in the Flavian period), the north side of the peristyle, or pseudo-peristyle, was made up of half-columns with stylized Corinthian capitals (Brzozowska-Jawornicka 2019; 2020; 2021). Still at Nea Paphos, a significant series of capitals can be found at Ktiston. In the early Severan age, the House of Dionysos, a residence with lavish mosaic floors, occupied the eastern part of the site and partly overlaid previous structures dated before the mid-second century CE, whose function remains unclear (Nicolaou 1967). Stylized Corinthian capitals have been found in the western sector: in the case of a heart-shaped pillar, the capital still preserves part of its stucco coating. Many capitals of this type are also present in the eastern sector. They were part of a courtyard attributed to the early imperial building, which was later incorporated in the mid-imperial residence. In the House of Orpheus, stylized capitals are attested through poorly preserved fragments from the early imperial phase of the building. One could suggest they were later restored as a 'vintage note' in the eclectic architectural ensembles of this residence.

Alongside the aforementioned elements and the more sporadic use of the Ionic order (Wright 1992; Brzozowska

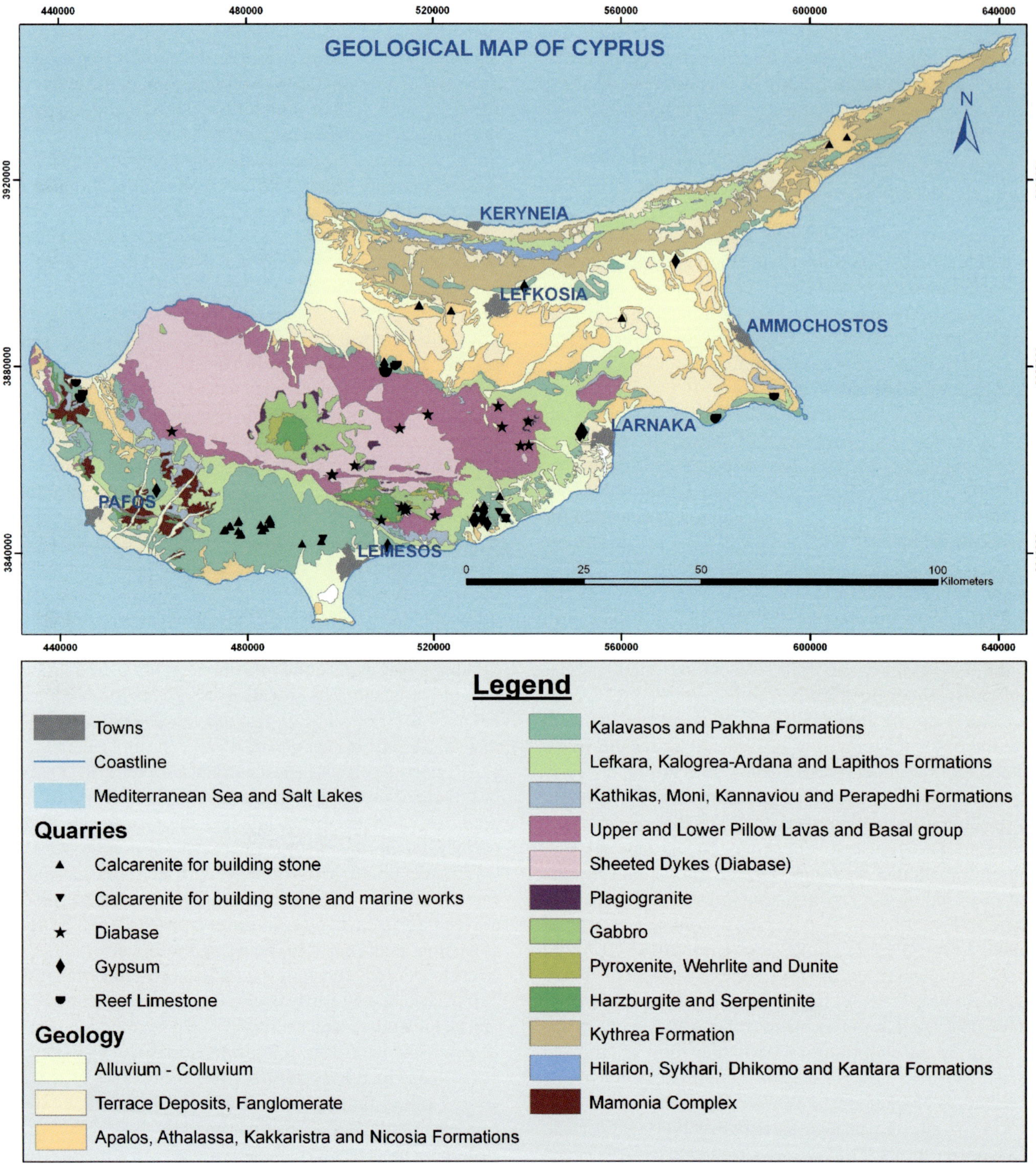

Fig. 13.16. Geological map of Cyprus (Ministry of Agriculture, Rural Development and Environment, Geological Survey Department of Cyprus).

Fig. 13.17. Corinthian capitals from the Museum of Kouklia (left) and from the 'Hellenistic' House at Nea Paphos (right) (photos P. Pensabene and E. Gasparini).

Fig. 13.18. Kourion, 'Early Christian' House: Doric capital from the heart-shaped pillar at the north-west corner of the colonnaded hall (photo E. Gasparini).

2019; 2020; 2021; Pensabene and Gasparini 2021), Corinthian capitals with a complete vegetal apparatus also occurred. These are found in monuments of the Paphos agora and in the Temple of Zeus at Salamis with its narrow front square (the so-called 'agora') (Argout *et al.* 1975, 122–41; Callot 2019, 502–9; Yon 2019, 37–50). The workers employed in these construction sites were able to refer to older models, and at the same time, they were also inspired by contemporary trends that had become fashionable in

Fig. 13.19. Salamis, Gymnasium: Stylized Corinthian capitals (photos E. Gasparini).

Fig. 13.20. Salamis, Corinthian capital from the front square of the Temple of Zeus (photo E. Gasparini).

Fig. 13.21. Kourion, Corinthian capital from an engaged pillar of the so-called 'Market Building' (photo E. Gasparini).

public architecture. In these examples, the acanthus is characterized by small 'eyes' with circular and triangular shadow zones, well-known in western artefacts from Rome at the time of the Second Triumvirate (Pensabene 2022, 608–12 with references) (Fig. 13.20). In the second century CE, local calcarenite was the material used for the Corinthian capitals with free volutes in the Temple of Zeus at Salamis. These derived from Alexandrian types, with water leaf volutes rising directly from behind the leaves of the lower crown, without the use of cauliculi and calyces. However, the different shape of the acanthus shows that the carving process followed the new taste for marble artefacts typical of public architecture. In Cyprus, the use of marble on public buildings can be generally dated from the Antonine age onwards.[32] In the main cities of the island, outstanding examples can be seen on the marble colonnades of public squares and along the main streets, in the reconstruction of the theatres' stage buildings, in the construction of public baths, and in the refurbishment of sanctuaries (Sinos *et al.* 1990; Kiessel 2013, 241–60; Grawehr 2019, 33–45).

The changes that took place in public architecture determined the reappearance of fully carved Corinthian capitals in local stone. However, the acanthus is characterized by prickly leaves, apparently deriving from the new models of marble imported capitals. Therefore, Cypriot Corinthian capitals in local stone dated to the mid-imperial period bear witness to a decorative creativity that can be compared to the stylistic landscape of Cyrenaica, even though the end results were different. In Cyprus, too, we find types of capitals that can be defined as novel creations. The transition might be identified in the so-called 'Market Building' of Kourion, where the façade was marked by corner pillars with engaged pilasters. These were provided with engaged half-columns, according to a Hellenistic tradition well-consolidated in Cyprus (Soren and James 1988). Upon the heart-shaped pillars, there were Corinthian capitals with prickly acanthus leaves derived from eastern marble capitals, though they were adapted to fit the particular shape of the pillars. On the basis of the capitals' decorative motifs, these pillars can be dated to the Antonine age (Fig. 13.21).

In the southern sector of the House of Orpheus at Nea Paphos, Corinthian capitals dated to the main restoration of the building (late second/early third century CE) reflect globalizing trends on Cypriot architecture in local stone. Corinthian capitals from the Hellenistic period are not preserved in this house, perhaps because of its several reconstructions. The imperial-period examples belong to the Corinthian type with free volutes, with water leaf volutes that rise directly from behind the leaves of the lower crown, without cauliculi and calyces. The spirals of the helices rest on a central vine leaf, while two rosettes occupy the space between the helices and volutes. The acanthus is flat with deeply drilled channels and lobes subdivided in irregular, sharp-tipped leaflets separated by peculiar 'eagle's beak' shadow zones (Fig. 13.22). These elements were inspired by the Alexandrian-Corinthian capital, but with a marked transformation of the shape of the acanthus. This appeared also in the later capitals of the Temple of Zeus at Salamis and in one example found by the odeion, where the fusion of the ogival and triangular shadow zones in a single large area of irregularly elliptical or arched shape can be recognized. As observed on Cyrenaican Corinthian capitals derived from marble models, the presence of coating on the surface is also evident on these capitals.

Subsequent architectural trends, from the period between the late third to the fifth century CE, should also be

Fig. 13.22. Nea Paphos, House of Orpheus: Corinthian capitals from the southern sector (ADHO Project, 3D scanning and processing by M. Gładki).

Fig. 13.23. Salamis, Corinthian capitals from the Basilica of Saint Epiphanius (photo E. Gasparini).

mentioned. A continuity in stone craftsmanship is attested, as well as influences from the capitals of the eastern Mediterranean, where marble was used for the most prestigious public monuments and in Christian basilicas. In the House of Aion at Nea Paphos, whose decoration dates to the early fourth century CE (Lichocka and Meyza 2001, with further references), we see smooth Corinthian capitals with four leaves, with a wide central rib and a strongly curved tip. They point either to an Egyptian-Corinthian model or to the so-called 'Kapitelle mit vollen Blättern' (Mikocki 1992, 148). Our understanding of Late Antique architectural decoration in stone from Cyprus is also informed by the Basilica of Saint Epiphanios at Salamis, which was built between the late fourth and early fifth century CE (Foulias 2019, 719–29). The Basilica was commissioned by the bishop Epiphanios and represents one of the oldest Christian monumental buildings on the island. Despite the lack of marble elements, the high status of patronage is evident. Therefore, for his church, Epiphanios must have hired the best Cypriot workshops of stonecutters available at the time. Various elements of the colonnade in the central nave are preserved, including numerous Corinthian limestone capitals (Fig. 13.23). These pieces show the final form of the Asiatic Corinthian capital attested from the late third and throughout the fourth century CE. Though the capitals are heavily eroded in their upper section, it is possible to draw some observations on the acanthus crowns of the lower section. The lateral ribs of the leaves are strongly arched, with the tips of the leaflets touching each other, so as to delineate intermediate spaces of regular geometric shapes. The details on the upper section also testify to the capital's atrophied form, with short V-shaped cauliculi represented by two oblique and flat incisions, and schematic helices in the form of ribbons.

The Cypriot picture can be completed with some data on the cornices, which can be compared to the Cyrenaican counterparts. Limestone elements were much more widespread than marble decoration imported for large-scale

Fig. 13.24. Kourion, cornice of Proconnesian marble from the theatre (photo E. Gasparini).

Fig. 13.25. Cornices with travicello *modillions from Cyprus. Upper row: Nea Paphos, House of Dionysos; lower row, left: Paphos District Museum; middle: Nea Paphos, House of Orpheus; right: Kourion, so-called 'Market Building' (photos E. Gasparini).*

public projects, such as the mid-imperial renovation of the theatre at Kourion (Stillwell 1961, 37–78) (Fig. 13.24). Local stone was used not only in the early imperial period, but also in Late Antiquity. A conservative tendency reproduced, albeit with different results, the Hellenistic form of the cornice with *travicello* modillions. This shape remained part of the know-how of the Cypriot workshops even though some variations gave life to different products. In the mid-imperial phase, these objects can be described as follows: on the upper cornice, we find an oblique *taenia*, a *cyma recta*, a low *corona*, and a soffit with *travicello* modillions with an ovolo frame[33] (Fig. 13.25). Modillions and hollow squares are joint and form a meander-like motif with deep grooves that are joint with a perpendicular, continuous groove on the back of the soffit. The lower cornice shows a double fillet instead of the *cyma* one would expect here, but the square flat ovolo mouldings could have been originally modelled with stucco as a *cyma*. Therefore, flattened modillions prevail and the shape that characterizes the Hellenistic elements of Alexandria or Cyrene is lost.[34] These choices were certainly due to a desire for simplification. The Cypriot taste for a specific type of entablature therefore was expressed with original results. In this context, chrono-typological classifications on stylistic grounds are probably not so effective, especially since these elements were mostly meant to be observed from afar and within a richly articulated architectural context. Viewers would have recognized them, even subconsciously, as cornices with *travicello* modillions and deemed their presence in that specific position as appropriate, but without being able to grasp any further particulars.

Concluding remarks

This analysis has focused on some architectural features in the provinces of Cyrenaica and Cyprus from the imperial age to Late Antiquity. Case studies from the most important cities show how the apparently opposing forces of 'tradition' and 'innovation' resulted in a synthesis which, ultimately, gave rise to original and distinct results in each province. The use of local stone for architectural decoration, in particular for Corinthian capitals, is a key element to understand the reasons and developments of this synthesis, in contrast to marble architecture, which has been identified as a marked innovation for the local workshops. The desire to conform to the fashion of the Empire and the resulting socio-cultural prestige were a clear prerequisite for innovation. However, the imperial-style message was counterbalanced by regional cultural heritage: in these provinces, such an element was widely valued, also in relation to the continuity promoted by imperial policies and attested in the local institutions, economy, and religion. The strength of tradition, however, was also determined by factors of a practical nature: the availability of local products as opposed to marble objects, which could not be sourced in Cyrenaica or Cyprus.

When dealing with local products, the tendency towards conservatism that characterizes craft traditions in the ancient world should also be considered. This can be particularly seen in the continuity of shapes and sometimes styles. The attachment to tradition was expressed not only in specific features of the newly carved products, but also in the decorative elements of buildings, or the reuse of older elements in the context of renovation projects. In the regions under consideration here, and, more broadly, in the eastern Mediterranean, these traditions allowed for the Hellenistic decorative/architectural language to survive and thrive. Its most recognizable motifs can be found on Corinthian capital with free volutes, namely the insertion of rosettes between the helices and volutes, and on cornices with *travicello* modillions.

In Cyrenaica, in particular in early imperial Cyrene, restorations or new constructions allowed the continuity of use of traditional materials and styles (such as the Doric order). Instead, at Ptolemais, the Colonnaded Palace is a clear example of the flowering of Alexandrian-style Corinthian architecture between the first century BCE and the first century CE. Only from the second decade of the second century CE was a clear Roman taste impressed on urban centres. This mostly consisted of imported marble artefacts. But other types of globalizing expressions ought to be considered: existence of local stone products that absorbed and reworked elements of marble architecture attest to a favourable reception, a strong impact, and a positive perception of these elements. In public monuments where marble decoration was not available, the use of local-stone Corinthian capitals with prickly acanthus found frequent application. Concurrently, the normal Corinthian capital replaced the Corinthian type with free helices and volutes. This also occurred in residential architecture, alongside the occurrence of architectural elements that were recycled or kept in place.[35] Such processes led to the construction of buildings that were often eclectic in form and style. Notwithstanding the standardization of the architectural language, the results varied from site to site. The urban landscape was, therefore, conditioned by innovation, which nevertheless engaged in a dialogue with tradition, firstly due to the continuity of building materials. Several factors must be considered when attempting to assign chronologies, which cannot be limited to stylistic considerations. As for Cyrene, one should mention the marked presence and continuity of the Doric order, while the friability of the local stone also determined the need for frequent reconstructions and restorations.[36]

The same considerations apply to Cyprus, where the global phenomenon of marble architecture as well as the consequent rise of a local response can be recognized. In this sense, the two provinces are comparable, although not for the end results. Since the Hellenistic period, Cyprus bore witness to a local tradition of carving Corinthian capitals that was heavily influenced by Alexandrian workshops. This tradition gave rise to particularly refined products. When the island became part of the Roman Empire, the Doric order, as well as the cornices with *travicello* modillions, were kept in use though with significant differences in form. Conversely, I have stressed the almost complete disappearance of the production of Corinthian capitals. Their survival, through multiple restorations, is in fact well identified only in the case of the Temple of Zeus at Salamis. In almost all urban monuments, the Corinthian capital with free volutes survived in a totally new form. This involved the stylization of its main components, which were sculpted on two distinct blocks and assembled only at the end of the work. These forms were so successful on the island to become the starting point for new productions. This happened from the mid-second century CE with the arrival of large quantities of Corinthian capitals from Asia Minor. On the other hand, the acanthus of the leaves in the lower section of the capitals acquired new forms. It has also been observed that, in some cases, the adoption of the normal Corinthian capital took place. However, this type was applied to Corinthian capitals crowning heart-shaped pillars, therefore giving continuity to a Hellenistic tradition. In Cyprus, as in Cyrenaica, the houses of the elites represent significant examples of these transformations. Their owners expressed the desire to mediate between old and new fashions to build an image of prestige for themselves and their family.[37]

Notwithstanding the relationships with other centres, or with Rome itself, the reference systems were undoubtedly the local cityscapes: architectural choices were motivated by comparing new and old civic buildings, thus further establishing a competition among members of the local ruling class. In this sense, the concepts of reception, impact and perception must be considered not only in relation to marble public architecture, but also and more broadly to the entire cities, which were characterized by use of specific local building materials and architectural forms. These artistic paradigms were based on typological and stylistic comparisons. Yet, one should also wonder whether they were partly based on the colour and quality of the various stones, bearing in mind the common practice of covering and painting architectural decoration. The presence of coating, which has been recorded on capitals, may not have been applied to column shafts or wall surfaces. This ultimately depended on the hardness of the stone that was employed. Moreover, one must take into consideration that the visibility of building materials was a constant feature of ancient cityscapes due to the abundance of ongoing construction sites.[38]

In many of the case studies, the lack of knowledge of the identification, characterization, and the supply dynamics of local materials does not allow us to draw broader conclusions. At Cyrene, as well as in the south-western area of Cyprus, where the cities of Nea Paphos and Kourion are located, some recent studies have focused on the provenance of local building stones by examining the geology of the territory. This type of approach, which looks in parallel at the territory and the stone artefacts that were produced there, is still to be developed for Ptolemais and Salamis. However, the present discussion has stressed that certain stonescapes represented a strong cultural feature within the urban societies of Cyrenaica and Cyprus in the imperial era. Ideological messages were conveyed by the uniformity of the buildings' layout within a multi-layered urban environment, in order to emphasize the history of a specific place. Therefore, these cityscapes were informed to some extent by the aesthetic taste of ancient audiences and the respective local culture.

Notes

1. See Pensabene and Gasparini 2017, 655–56, 659–60, 676–77; 2019, 175–76 (Cyrenaica); 2020, 164–65; 2021, 330–31 (Cyprus); Wright 2007, 769–802; Rekowska 2020, 195–208; Rekowska *et al.* forthcoming; Gasparini forthcoming (Cyprus and Cyrenaica). As for Cyprus, the data and interpretations have developed as part of the project 'Residence as a self-presentation of urban élites. Architecture and decoration of the Orpheus House in Nea Paphos, the ancient capital of Cyprus' (ADHO) financed by the Polish National Science Centre, project no. 2017/27/B/HS3/01131, under the direction of Monika Rekowska. This project investigates the architecture of the House of Orpheus between Ptolemaic and Roman rule, up to Late Antiquity. Preliminary results can be found in Rekowska *et al.* 2019; 2021a–b.
2. On 'globalization' and the relationship between Greece and Rome, see, among others, Hales 2003; Hingley 2005; Gardner 2013; Pitts and Versluys 2015, 3–31; Hodos 2017. In Papaioannou 2016, 31–45, the use of the term 'synoecism' is proposed. On the relationship between Roman and provincial society in Egyptian domestic architecture, as well as 'global' and 'local' attitudes, see Alston 2002, 44–127; Boozer 2015, 93–116. For an update on the general topic of 'provincial architecture', see Yegül and Favro 2019, 1–3; Mazzilli 2020, 6–8, and the various contributions in Belvedere and Bergemann 2021.
3. For anthropological investigations applied to the Roman world, see the summary and relevant references in Dardenay and Laubry 2020, 7–20. Recently, Alston (2022, 459) offered an overview of scholarship on the relationship between society and forms of living, putting individual desires at the centre of social production. Particularly relevant is Lefebvre's view whereby spatial practice determined the individual's behaviour; consequently, social change could not be achieved without spatial change. Moreover, Alston (2022, 447–49 and 451) emphasized Lefebvre's concept of 'representational space', which coincides with the space as understood, even unconsciously, by those who inhabit it.
4. At Cyrene, a good case in point is the role played by the priests of Apollo and gymnasiarchs until the late imperial period. On the history and epigraphy of Roman Cyrenaica, see Romanelli 1943; *IRCyr2020*. On Roman Cyprus, see Mitford 1980; Cayla 2018.
5. A theoretical framework on glocalization has been traced by Roudometof (2016a–b). The author defines glocality as 'experiencing the global locally or through local lenses' (Roudometof 2016b, 399). See also Van Alten 2017, 2–4.
6. On the administration of Cyrenaica during the mid-imperial period, and particularly on the *procuratores* of the Severan age, see Struffolino 2014, 350–55.
7. As observed by S. Walker (1985, 101): 'the Corinthian order began to appear. The innately conservative architects of Cyrene were finally unable to resist its arrival'.
8. For the Republican period, see Maschek 2021, 151–52. On the adaptation of materials and construction techniques in the Roman provinces, see the remarks on the architectural details of the Doric façades on the Via di Frontino at Hierapolis (Ismaelli 2010, 380–84). On the continuity of traditional building techniques and the relationship between techniques, materials and clients, see also the example of Cilicia in Spanu 2010, 399–403. On the relationship between the manufacturing process and style, and on the role played by workshops in the transformation of the original models, see Plattner 2014, 53–68. For an analysis of architectural decoration taking into account the manufacturing process and its perception, see the observations on Baalbek in Wienholz 2014, 117–18, 123–27.
9. On this subject, see the proceedings of the ASMOSIA conferences (http://asmosia.willamette.edu/).
10. Luni *et al.* 2003, 453–59; Lazzarini and Turi 2004, 189–204; Attanasio *et al.* 2009, 343–56; Kane *et al.* 2010, 101–4; Luni and Lazzarini 2010, 185–222.
11. The analyses were carried out on the Temple of Zeus and the rocky outcrops facing it. This was recognized as a quarry where the circus was later built (Busdraghi and Gessaroli 2006, 171–80; Busdraghi *et al.* 2010, 317–26).
12. Barresi 2002, 69–81; Wilson 2009, 213–49. For a comparison between marble and local stone costs in the colonnaded streets of Syria and Cilicia, see Borgia 2010, 296–99. On construction costs and required manpower, see also Barker and Russell 2012, 83–94; Domingo 2012, 75–91; 2022, 111–30; Russell 2013; Barker *et al.* 2022, 59–110.
13. Pesce 1950; Lauter 1971, 149–78; Bonacasa 2009, 85–109; Pensabene and Gasparini 2019, 175–76.
14. Walker 1985, 97–104; 2002, 45–56; Lloyd 1990, 41–53; Walker and Matthews 1996, 307–16; Pensabene 2006, 231–43; 2007, 551–90; Cariddi 2020, 23–25.
15. Ward-Perkins *et al.* 1958; Luni 1988, 276–77; 1990, 116–20; 1992, 127–30; Kenrick 2013, 153–56.
16. The first building phase of the basilica is generally attributed to the Flavian age (Luni 1990, 101–20; 2007, 388; Luni and Cellini 1999, 30), but see Mugnai in this volume for further discussion.
17. A question of stylistic controversy was raised at the workshop in relation to capitals with prickly acanthus leaves, wondering whether they could be reliably defined as 'Asiatic' and suggesting instead the possibility of a Greek origin. Their provenance from Proconnesus, which was my initial assumption, would require a more in-depth study that goes beyond the present discussion and remains destined to future work.
18. The Corinthian capitals from this building were considered contemporary to the ones of the Severan propylon, while the building was already in existence. Two phases preceding the Severan period were speculatively put forward, one in the Augustan or Julio-Claudian period and the other in the early second century CE (Ward-Perkins and Gibson 1976–77, 354). Conversely, Stucchi, following von Mercklin, believed

that the Corinthian façade was to be dated to the first half of the fourth century CE, representing a later copy of the form and style of the Severan propylon (von Mercklin 1962, 184, no. 445, fig. 863; Stucchi 1975, 345–46).

19. Mingazzini 1966; Stucchi 1975, 144–47, 297–99, 309–11, 319, 323–25; Gasparini 2010; Pensabene and Gasparini 2014, 216–25; 2019, 185–86.
20. Stucchi 1967, 112–14. For the main numismatic repertoires of Greek Cyrenaica, see Asolati 2006, 181–86. For the Roman period, see Asolati and Crisafulli 2018. However, Stucchi's interpretation remains speculative: in previous studies, von Mercklin (1962, 40, no. 764, fig. 1403) generically referred to a 'bärtigem Kopf', while Mingazzini (1966, 57) described it as a 'tragic mask of an old man (perhaps Oedipus)'.
21. Rosenbaum 1960, nos. 46, 48–49, 54, 68, 71, 76, 100, 140, 168; Huskinson 1975, nos. 70, 73, 77, 79, 81, 111, 122, 144, 150.
22. A reworked Ionic capital from a filling layer can be identified: Rekowska 2012, 158, no. 6, pl. 10.1.
23. Mingazzini 1966, 83, 96–98; Stucchi 1975, 285, 321–22; Rekowska 2013, 605; Pensabene and Gasparini 2017, 661.
24. Mingazzini 1966, 91, pl. 34.3–4 (h. cm 91); Pensabene and Gasparini 2014, 212–13; 2017, 656. An analogous capital comes from the Arch of Marcus Aurelius, but the chronological discrepancies between the monument and the typological and stylistic features of the capital have led to the conclusion that it does not originally belong there. The capital was repositioned on the arch during the 1959 restorations, when architectural elements found scattered along the *decumanus maximus* were used for the reconstruction of this monument (Pensabene and Gasparini 2017, 665).
25. This stone is currently known as 'Petra ton Kyvidon' when it is quarried from the region of Kyvides and Anogyra, and as 'Petra tis Tohnis' when quarried from the region of Tohni and Ayios Theodoros villages (source: Geological map of Cyprus, Ministry of Agriculture, Rural Development and Environment, Geological Survey Department of Cyprus: http://www.moa.gov.cy/moa/gsd/gsd.nsf/All/CA0FAA6590E26D58C22583940035042C/$file/domikosLithos_EN_2015.pdf?OpenElement.
26. Delbrück 1907; von Hesberg 1980; Wright 1992; Pensabene 1993; McKenzie 2007; Tkaczow 2010; Pensabene and Gasparini 2020; Shmid and Hermary 2021, 274–76.
27. I would like to express my gratitude to Monika Rekowska for allowing me to use data and graphs from the ADHO Project in this chapter.
28. In this chapter I adopt the term 'stylized' as suggested by Niccolò Mugnai. This term can explain the shape of these capitals in relation to their carving process; this does not involve a revised interpretation, and previous definitions of these elements as 'simplified' remain valid (cf. Pensabene and Gasparini 2020; 2021).
29. Sinos *et al.* 1990; Wright 1992; Brzozowska 2016; Brzozowska-Jawornicka 2020; Hermary and Schmid 2021; for further references on these capitals outside Cyprus, see Grawehr 2017; 2019; Pensabene and Gasparini 2020; 2021.
30. Although traces of plaster to smoothen the surface of the capitals have been frequently found, the analysis of the materials from Paphos and Kourion has not revealed the use of this material to add further decorative details.
31. I do not agree with the suggestion that stucco coating was applied to these capitals to imitate Roman marble architecture and architectural ornament. The use of stucco was a decorative praxis born in the frame of local stone architecture, as a technical requirement to give a more refined appearance to limestone and other stones that could not be polished. Conversely, see Grawehr 2019, 33–45.
32. That is the reason why the spread of stylized capitals cannot be interpreted as a consequence of the introduction of marble architecture in provinces such as Cyprus, but also in Egypt, where it acquired great relevance only from the time of Trajan or Hadrian, with a substantial increase during the Antonine and Severan periods. Conversely, Grawehr 2019, 33–45.
33. The main references for this description are the House of Orpheus, the House of Dionysos, and some elements in the storeroom of the archaeological museum at Nea Paphos; and the so-called 'Market Building' at Kourion.
34. On this respect, canonical examples are represented by elements from Alexandria (Pensabene 1993, nos. 875, 887) and Cyrene (Mingazzini 1966, 3–18).
35. In Rekowska 2012, 180–81 the occurrence of Hellenistic motifs in the jambs and architraves of the House of Leukaktios is explained by suggesting these were recycled elements. This hypothesis is based on the presence of inscribed blocks reused in the walls as well as other architectural spolia adapted to new functions.
36. Busdraghi and Gessaroli 2006, 171–80. For a micropaleontological analysis of calcareous stones used at Cyrene in antiquity, see Busdraghi *et al.* 2010, 317–26.
37. I refer here to R. Alston's (2022, 453) remarks, who considered the domestic environment as the primary location of acculturation in the Roman provinces. This term is used to indicate the house owner's desire to adopt international housing parameters.
38. I am grateful to Ben Russell for this observation.

References

Alston, R. 2002. *The City in Roman and Byzantine Egypt*, London-New York: Routledge.

Alston, R. 2022. Spaces of desire: houses, households and social reproduction in the Roman world. In Baird, J.A. and Pudsey, A. (eds), *Housing in the Ancient Mediterranean World: Material and Textual Approaches*. Cambridge: Cambridge University Press, 442–69.

Argout, G., Callot, O., Helly, B. and Larribeau, A.M. 1975. Le Temple de Zeus à Salamine. *Reports of the Department of Antiquities, Cyprus*: 122–41.

Asolati, M. 2006. La documentazione numismatica a Cirene. In Luni, M. (ed.), *Cirene 'Atene d'Africa', I*. Rome: 'L'Erma' di Bretschneider, 181–86.

Asolati, M. and Crisafulli, C. 2018. *Cirene e la Cirenaica in età greca e romana. Le monete, I. I ripostigli*. Rome: 'L'Erma' di Bretschneider.

Attanasio, D., Kane, S. and Herz, N. 2009. New isotopic and EPR data for 22 sculptures from the extramural sanctuary of Demeter and Persephone at Cyrene. In Maniatis, Y. (ed.), *ASMOSIA VII. Proceedings of the 7th International Conference of Association for the Study of Marble and Other Stones in Antiquity (Thassos, 15–20 September 2003)*. Athens: École française d'Athènes, 343–56.

Bacchielli, L. 1981. *L'agorà di Cirene, II.1. L'area settentrionale del lato ovest della platea inferiore*. Rome: 'L'Erma' di Bretschneider.

Barker, S.J. and Russell, B. 2012. Labour figures for Roman stone-working: pitfalls and potential. In Camporeale, S., Dessales, H. and Pizzo, A. (eds), *Arqueología de la construcción III. Los procesos constructivos en el mundo romano: la economía de las obras (École normale supérieure, Paris, 10–11 de diciembre de 2009)*. Madrid: Consejo Superior de Investigaciones Científicas, 83–94.

Barker, S.J., Snyder, J.R. and Ward, C.A. 2022. Reflections on energetics studies and Roman architecture. In Maschek, D. and Trümper, M. (eds), *Architecture and the Ancient Economy. Proceedings of a Conference Held at Berlin (26–28 September 2019)*. Rome: Quasar, 59–110.

Barresi, P. 2002. Il ruolo delle colonne nel costo degli edifici pubblici. In De Nuccio, M. and Ungaro, L. (eds), *I marmi colorati della Roma imperiale*. Venice: Marsilio, 69–81.

Belvedere, O. and Bergmann, J. (eds) 2021. *Imperium Romanum: Romanization between Colonization and Globalization (Villa Vigoni, centro italo-tedesco per il dialogo europeo, 4–8 novembre 2019)*. Palermo: Palermo University Press.

Bonacasa, N. 2009. Ancora su Tolemaide e Alessandria: riflessioni sul 'Palazzo delle Colonne'. In Jastrzębowska, E. and Niewójt, M. (eds), *Archeologia a Tolemaide. Giornate di studio in occasione del primo anniversario della morte di Tomasz Mikocki (Roma, 27–28 maggio 2008)*. Rome: Accademia Polacca delle Scienze, 85–109.

Bonacasa, N. and Ensoli, S. 2000. *Cirene*. Milan: Electa.

Boozer, A.L. 2015. Globalizing Mediterranean identities: the overlapping spheres of Egyptian, Greek and Roman worlds at Trimithis. *Journal of Mediterranean Archaeology* 25.2: 93–116.

Borgia, E. 2010. I cantieri delle vie colonnate nell'oriente romano. In Camporeale, S., Dessales, H. and Pizzo, A. (eds), *Arqueología de la construcción II. Los procesos constructivos en el mundo romano: Italia y provincias orientales (Certosa di Pontignano, Siena, 13–15 de noviembre de 2008)*. Madrid: Consejo Superior de Investigaciones Científicas, 281–99.

Brzozowska, A. 2016. A pseudo-Ionic blocked-out capital at Nea Paphos. *Études et Travaux* 29: 43–65.

Brzozowska-Jawornicka, A. 2019. Architecture of the official spaces of selected residences in Nea Paphos, Cyprus. *Światowit* 58: 87–105.

Brzozowska-Jawornicka, A. 2020. Blocked-out capitals from Nea Paphos: preliminary remarks. In Meyza, H. (ed.), *Decoration of Hellenistic and Roman Buildings in Cyprus*. Warsaw-Wiesbaden: Institute of Mediterranean and Oriental Cultures, Polish Academy of Sciences – Harrassowitz Verlag, 49–59.

Brzozowska-Jawornicka, A. 2021. 'Hellenistic' house in Nea Paphos, Cyprus – a first summary of its architecture. *Études et Travaux* 34: 93–121.

Busdraghi, P. and Gessaroli, O. 2006. Cave di pietra e monumenti a Cirene. In Luni, M. (ed.), *Cirene 'Atene d'Africa', I*. Rome: 'L'Erma' di Bretschneider, 171–80.

Busdgraghi, P., Catanzariti, R., Coccioni, R. and Gessaroli, O. 2010. Stratigraphy and micropaleontology of the Oligocene Cyrene-Apollonia highway section (Cyrenaica, NE Libya): archaeological implications. In Luni, M. (ed.), *Cirene 'Atene d'Africa', II. Cirene nell'antichità*. Rome: 'L'Erma' di Bretschneider, 317–26.

Callot, O. 2019. Le temple de Zeus à Salamine de Chypre. In Rogge, S., Ioannou, C. and Mavrojannis, T. (eds), *Salamis of Cyprus. History and Archaeology from the Earliest Times to the Late Antiquity (Conference in Nicosia, 21–23 May 2015)*. Munich: Waxmann Verlag GmbH, 502–9.

Cariddi, L. 2020. *Cirene e l'acqua. Ricerche e documenti sulla gestione delle risorse idriche in città e nella chora*. Rome: 'L'Erma' di Bretschneider.

Cayla, J.-B. 2018. *Les inscriptions de Paphos: La cité chypriote sous la domination lagide et à l'époque impériale*. Lyon: MOM Éditions.

Courault, C. and Márquez, C. (eds) 2020. *Quantitative Studies and Production Cost of Roman Public Construction*. Cordoba: Editorial Universidad de Córdoba.

Dardenay, A. and Laubry, N. (eds) 2020. *Anthropology of Roman Housing*. Turnhout: Brepols.

Delbrück, R. 1907. *Hellenistische Bauten in Latium, I. Baubeschreibungen*. Strasbourg: Karl J. Trubner.

Domingo, J.Á. 2012. El coste del mármol. Problemas e incertidumbres de una metodología de cálculo. *Marmora* 8: 75–91.

Domingo, J.Á. 2022. El cálculo del coste económico de la arquitectura, una aproximación necesariamente global al proceso constructivo. In Maschek, D. and Trümper, M. (eds), *Architecture and the Ancient Economy. Proceedings of a Conference Held at Berlin (26–28 September 2019)*. Rome: Quasar, 111–30.

Ensoli, S. 2003. La terrazza superiore dell'Agorà di Cirene. Il Tempio di Zeus e l'arco occidentale della Skyrotà. *Quaderni di archeologia della Libya* 18: 47–91.

Foulias, A. 2019. The Basilica of Saint Epiphanios: architecture and chronology. In Rogge, S., Ioannou, C. and Mavrojannis, T. (eds), *Salamis of Cyprus. History and Archaeology from the Earliest Times to the Late Antiquity (Conference in Nicosia, 21–23 May 2015)*. Munich: Waxmann, 719–29.

Gardner, A. 2013. Thinking about Roman imperialism: postcolonialism, globalization and beyond? *Britannia* 44: 1–25.

Gasparini, E. 2010. Sectilia pavimenta della Casa di Giasone Magno a Cirene. In Luni, M. (ed.), *Cirene 'Atene d'Africa', II. Cirene nell'antichità*. Rome: 'L'Erma' di Bretschneider, 247–62.

Gasparini, E. 2012. Protagonisti e simboli del potere nella Cirenaica tardo antica: la Casa di Esichio a Cirene, tra tradizione e innovazione. In Cocco, M.B., Gavini, A. and Ibba, A. (eds), *L'Africa Romana. Trasformazione dei paesaggi del potere nell'Africa settentrionale fino alla fine del mondo antico. Atti del XIX convegno di studio (Sassari, 16–19 dicembre 2010)*. Rome: Carocci, 2837–54.

Gasparini, E. 2021. Ancient and new models in Byzantine Cyrenaica: the case of the Palace of the Dux at Apollonia. In Ruppiene, V. (ed.), *Stone and Splendor: Interior Decorations in Late-Antique Palaces and Villas. Proceedings of a Workshop (Trier, 25–26 April 2019)*. Wiesbaden: Harrassowitz Verlag, 205–19.

Gasparini, E. forthcoming. Roman housing on two shores of the Mediterranean: the evidence from Nea Paphos (Cyprus) and Berenice (Cyrenaica). In Kassianidou, L. (ed.), *Convivium. Proceedings of the International Conference in Honour of Prof. Emeritus Demetrios Michaelides on the Occasion of his 75th Birthday (Nicosia, 26–28 October 2021)*. Oxford: Archaeopress.

Gasparini, E. and Gallocchio, E. 2015. Marble pavements from the House of Jason Magnus in Cyrene. In Pensabene, P. and Gasparini, E. (eds), *Interdisciplinary Studies on Ancient Stone, ASMOSIA X. Proceedings of the Tenth International Conference of ASMOSIA (Rome, 21–26 May 2012)*. Rome: 'L'Erma' di Bretschneider, 545–54.

Gasperini, L. 1971. Le iscrizioni del cesareo e della basilica di Cirene. *Quaderni di Archeologia della Libya* 6: 3–22.

Grawehr, M. 2017. Bossenstil und Baumaterial. In Kurapkat, D. and Wulf-Rheidt, U. (eds), *Werkspuren. Materialverarbeitung und handwerkliches Wissen im Antiken Bauwesen*. Regensburg: Schnell & Steiner, 103–18.

Grawehr, M. 2019. A process of glocalisation? Roman marble imports and the rise of blocked-out capitals in local stone. *Światowit* 58: 33–45.

Hales, S. 2003. *The Roman House and Social Identity*. Cambridge: Cambridge University Press.

Hingley, R. 2005. *Globalizing Roman Culture: Unity, Diversity and Empire*. London-New York: Routledge.

Hodos, T. (ed.) 2017. *The Routledge Handbook of Archaeology and Globalization*. London-New York: Routledge.

Huskinson, J. 1975. *A Catalogue of Roman Sculpture from Cyrenaica in the British Museum*. London: British Museum Publications.

Ismaelli, T. 2010. La via di Frontino a Hierapolis di Frigia. Aspetti tecnici, organizzazione e committenza di un grande cantiere pubblico della prima età imperiale. In Camporeale, S., Dessales, H. and Pizzo, A. (eds), *Arqueología de la construcción II. Los procesos constructivos en el mundo romano: Italia y provincias orientales (Certosa di Pontignano, Siena, 13–15 de noviembre de 2008)*. Madrid: Consejo Superior de Investigaciones Científicas, 375–96.

Kane, S., Attanasio, D. and Carrier, S. 2010. The use of Parian and Pentelic marble in the Greco-Roman city of Cyrene. In Luni, M. (ed.), *Cirene 'Atene d'Africa', III. Cirene e la Cirenaica nell'antichità*. Rome: 'L'Erma' di Bretschneider, 101–4.

Karageorghis, V. 1969. Chronique des fouilles et découvertes archéologiques à Chypre en 1968. *Bulletin de Correspondence Hellénique* 93.2: 431–569.

Kenrick, P. 2013. *Libya Archaeological Guides: Cyrenaica*. London: Silphium Press.

Kiessel, M. 2013. Spätantike Kapitellausstattungen in Zypern. Das Thermen-Gymnasium von Salamis/Constantia und der Forumbereich von Kourion. *Adalya* 16: 241–60.

Kraeling, C.H. 1962. *Ptolemais: City of the Libyan Pentapolis*. Chicago: Chicago University Press.

Lauter, H. 1971. Ptolemais in Libyen. Ein Beitrag zur Baukunst Alexandrias. *Jahrbuch des Deutschen Archäologischen Instituts* 86: 149–78.

Lazzarini, L. and Turi, B. 2004. Studio archeometrico dei marmi usati nella scultura e architettura di età arcaica a Cirene. *Rendiconti Lincei: Scienze Fisiche e Naturali* s. 9, 15: 189–204.

Lichocka, B. and Meyza, H. 2001. Seismic events and the evidence of coins and pottery. The case of destruction of the House of Aion in Paphos. *Études et Travaux* 19: 146–208.

Lloyd, J.A. 1989. Urban archaeology in Cyrenaica 1969–1989: the Hellenistic, Roman and Byzantine periods. *Libyan Studies* 20: 77–90.

Lloyd, J.A. 1990. The cities of Cyrenaica in the third century AD. In *Giornata lincea sulla archeologia cirenaica (Roma, 3 novembre 1987)*. Rome: Accademia Nazionale dei Lincei, 41–53.

Luni, M. 1988. Il Foro di Cirene tra secondo e terzo secolo. In Mastino, A. (ed.), *L'Africa Romana. Atti del V convegno di studio (Cagliari/Sassari, 11–13 dicembre 1987)*. Sassari: Gallizzi, 271–77.

Luni, M. 1990. Il Ginnasio-Caesareum di Cirene nel contesto del rinnovamento urbanistico della media età ellenistica e della prima età imperiale. In *Giornata lincea sulla archeologia cirenaica (Roma, 3 novembre 1987)*. Rome: Accademia Nazionale dei Lincei, 87–120.

Luni, M. 1992. Strutture monumentali e documenti epigrafici nel foro di Cirene. In Mastino, A. (ed.), *L'Africa Romana. Atti del IX convegno di studio (Nuoro, 13–15 dicembre 1991)*. Sassari: Gallizzi, 123–46.

Luni, M. 2007. La basilica nel foro di Cirene. In Gasperini, L. and Marengo, S.M. (eds), *Cirene e la Cirenaica nell'antichità. Atti del convegno internazionale di studi (Roma – Frascati, 18–21 dicembre 1996)*. Tivoli: Tored, 377–400.

Luni, M. and Cellini, G.A. 1999. L'abside della basilica nel foro di Cirene ed i due gruppi di sculture. *Karthago* 24: 27–73.

Luni, M. and Lazzarini, L. 2010. La scultura in marmo a Cirene in età greca. In Adornato, G. (ed.), *Scolpire il marmo. Importazioni, artisti itineranti, scuole artistiche nel Mediterraneo antico. Atti del convegno tenuto a Pisa, Scuola Normale Superiore, 9–11 novembre 2009*. Milan: LED, 185–222.

Luni, M. and Mei, O. 2007. Tempio con arco siriaco 'delle Muse' presso l'Agorà di Cirene. *Karthago* 27: 31–77.

Luni, M., Fabbricotti, E., Lazzarini, L. and Turi, B. 2003. Le statue greche in marmo di età arcaica a Cirene. *Rendiconti Accademia dei Lincei* s. 9, 14.3: 453–59.

Maschek, D. 2021. The meaning of building materials in late Republican architecture: moving from semantics to pragmatics. In Haug, A., Hielscher, A. and Taylor Lauritsen, M. (eds), *Materiality as Decor: Aesthetics, Semantics and Function*. Berlin: De Gruyter, 151–62.

Maschek, D. 2022. Homo structor – homo oeconomicus: why we need an 'architectural turn' in studying the ancient economy. In Maschek, D. and Trümper, M. (eds), *Architecture and the Ancient Economy. Proceedings of a Conference Held at Berlin (26–28 September 2019)*. Rome: Quasar, 13–34.

Mazzilli, G. 2020. L'architettura 'in prouinciali solo' (Gai. Inst. II, 7): per un contributo alla definizione delle forme della Baupolitik provinciale in età imperiale. In Mazzilli, G. (ed.), *In solo provinciali. Sull'architettura delle province, da Augusto ai Severi, tra inerzie locali e romanizzazione*. Rome: Quasar, 3–18.

McKenzie, J.S. 2007. *The Architecture of Alexandria and Egypt, c. 300 BC to AD 700*. New Haven-London: Yale University Press.

Mei, O. 2016. Recenti rinvenimenti monetali nel Quartiere dell'Agorà di Cirene: contesti e problemi archeologici. In Asolati, M. (ed.), *Le monete di Cirene e della Cirenaica nel Mediterraneo. Problemi e prospettive. Atti del V Congresso*

Internazionale di Numismatica e di Storia Monetaria (Padova, 17–19 marzo 2016). Padua: Esedra Editore, 305–24.

Mei, O. 2017. Architettura pubblica a Cirene nel III secolo a.C. In Caliò, L.M. and des Courtils, J. (eds), *L'architettura greca in Occidente nel III secolo a.C.* Rome: Quasar, 369–83.

Mei, O. 2020. Una placchetta plumbea dal tempietto 'di Cibele' di Cirene e ipotesi sulle divinità titolari dell'edificio. In Stortoni, E. (ed.), *Munera amicitiae. Miscellanea di studi archeologici per Enzo Catani*. Macerata: EUM, 79–92.

Mikocki, T. 1992. Essai de reconstruction du mur Ouest de la salle I dans la 'Maison d'Aion' à Nea Paphos. *Études et Travaux* 16: 135–50.

Mingazzini, P. 1966. *L'insula di Giasone Magno a Cirene*. Rome: 'L'Erma' di Bretschneider.

Mitford, T.B. 1980. Roman Cyprus. In Temporini, H. and Haase, W. (eds), *Aufstieg und Niedergang der römischen Welt, II. Principat, 7.2*. Berlin: De Gruyter, 1285–384.

Nicolaou, K. 1967. Excavations at Nea Paphos. The House of Dionysus. Outline of the campaigns 1964–1965. *Reports of the Department of Antiquities, Cyprus*: 126–67.

Papaioannou, M. 2016. A synoecism of cultures in Roman Greece. In Alcock, S.E., Egri, M. and Frakes, J.F.D. (eds), *Beyond Boundaries. Connecting Visual Cultures in the Provinces of Ancient Rome*. Los Angeles: Getty Publications, 31–45.

Pensabene, P. 1993. *Elementi architettonici di Alessandria e di altri siti egiziani*. Rome: 'L'Erma' di Bretschneider.

Pensabene, P. 2006. Marmi e pietre colorate nell'architettura della Cirenaica in età imperiale. In Fabbricotti, E. and Menozzi, O. (eds), *Cirenaica: studi, scavi e scoperte. Atti del X Convegno di Archeologia Cirenaica (Chieti, 24–26 novembre 2003)*. Oxford: British Archaeological Reports, 231–43.

Pensabene, P. 2007. Marmi e committenza nelle grandi terme di Cirene. In Gasperini, L. and Marengo, S.M. (eds), *Cirene e la Cirenaica nell'antichità. Atti del convegno internazionale di studi (Roma – Frascati, 18–21 dicembre 1996)*. Tivoli: Tored, 551–90.

Pensabene, P. 2022. L'acanto nei capitelli corinzi a Roma tra la seconda metà del II sec. a.C. e il periodo del II Triunvirato. *Archeologia Classica* 73: 599–613.

Pensabene, P. and Gasparini, E. 2014. Materiali per lo studio delle case di Cirene. In Luni, M. (ed.), *Cirene 'Atene d'Africa', VII. Cirene greca e romana*. Rome: 'L'Erma' di Bretschneider, 211–40.

Pensabene, P. and Gasparini, E. 2017. Tra dorico e corinzio in Cirenaica: spunti per una riflessione sul linguaggio architettonico nell'edilizia privata. In Pensabene, P., Milella, M. and Caprioli, F. (eds), *Decor: decorazione e architettura nel mondo romano. Atti del convegno internazionale (Roma, 21–24 maggio 2014)*. Rome: Quasar, 655–82.

Pensabene, P. and Gasparini, E. 2019. Houses, opera sectilia and architectural orders: some reflections on the society of Cyrenaica and Egypt during the imperial period. In Bąkowska-Czerner, G. and Czerner, R. (eds), *Greco-Roman Cities at the Crossroads of Cultures. The 20th Anniversary of Polish-Egyptian Conservation Mission Marina El-Alamein. International Interdisciplinary Conference (Wrocław, Poland, 17–18 September 2015)*. Oxford: Archaeopress: 174–93.

Pensabene, P. and Gasparini, E. 2020. The spreading of Alexandrian architectural types in the Eastern Mediterranean: the case of Cyprus. In Meyza, H. (ed.), *Decoration of Hellenistic and Roman Buildings in Cyprus*. Warsaw-Wiesbaden: Institute of Mediterranean and Oriental Cultures, Polish Academy of Sciences – Harrassowitz Verlag, 151–65.

Pensabene, P. and Gasparini, E. 2021. Colonnaded Hall in Kourion. How the Oecus Corinthius was interpreted in the Roman houses of Cyprus. *Études et Travaux* 34: 307–40.

Pesce, G. 1950. *Il 'Palazzo delle Colonne' in Tolemaide di Cirenaica*. Rome: 'L'Erma' di Bretschneider.

Pitts, M. and Versluys, M.J. 2015. Globalisation and the Roman world: perspectives and opportunities. In Pitts, M. and Versluys, M.J. (eds), *Globalisation and the Roman World: World History, Connectivity and Material Culture*. Cambridge: Cambridge University Press, 3–31.

Plattner, G.A. 2014. Werkstatt und Muster. Zur Methode der Scheidung von Arbeitsprozessen und Stilelementen. In Lipps, J. and Maschek, D. (eds), *Antike Bauornamentik. Grenzen und Möglichkeiten ihrer Erforschung*. Wiesbaden: Reichert Verlag, 53–68.

Rekowska, M. 2012. Architectural decoration of the House of Leukaktios: preliminary remarks. In Żelazowski, J. (ed.), *Ptolemais in Cyrenaica. Studies in Memory of Tomasz Mikocki*. Warsaw: University of Warsaw, Institute of Archaeology, 157–81.

Rekowska, M. 2013. Greek tradition and Roman invention. The arcuated lintel in the domestic architecture in Cyrenaica: a case study. In Bombardieri, L., D'Agostino, A., Orsi, V., Guarducci, G. and Valentini, S. (eds), *SOMA 2012. Identity and Connectivity: Proceedings of the 16th Symposium on Mediterranean Archaeology (Florence, Italy, 1–3 March, 2012)*. Oxford: Archaeopress, 603–11.

Rekowska, M. 2020. Decoration of houses in Cyprus and Cyrenaica, an architectural koiné? Toward research objectives and methodological approaches. In Meyza, H. (ed.), *Decoration of Hellenistic and Roman Buildings in Cyprus*. Warsaw-Wiesbaden: Institute of Mediterranean and Oriental Cultures, Polish Academy of Sciences – Harrassowitz Verlag, 195–208.

Rekowska, M., Michaelides, D., Pensabene, P. and Gasparini, E. 2019. A new project in progress: residence as self-presentation of urban elites. Architecture and decoration of the House of Orpheus in Nea Paphos, the ancient capital of Cyprus. Potential and prospects. *Światowit* 58: 197–218.

Rekowska, M., Michaelides, D., Pensabene, P. and Gasparini, E. 2021a. The House of Orpheus at Nea Paphos, Cyprus: the evolution of domestic space in a diachronic perspective. In Baldini, I. and Sfameni, C. (eds), *Abitare nel Mediterraneo tardoantico. Atti del III Convegno Internazionale del Centro Interuniversitario di Studi sull'edilizia abitativa tardoantica nel Mediterraneo (CISEM) (Bologna, 28–31 ottobre 2019)*. Bari: Edipuglia, 37–52.

Rekowska, M., Michaelides, D., Christodoulou, S. and Kaniszewski, J. 2021b. Adopting Roman habits – the baths in the House of Orpheus in Nea Paphos as a 'troublesome' case study? *Études et Travaux* 34: 341–62.

Rekowska, M., Michaelides, D., Pensabene, P. and Gasparini, E. forthcoming. The House of Orpheus in Nea Paphos and other residences in Cyprus and Cyrenaica: a local phenomenon in a global Empire. In Mazzini, L., Mazzilli, F. and Montoya, R. (eds), *From Globalization to Glocalization: Exploring Provincial Identities under Rome's Globalising Empire. Proceedings*

of the RAC/TRAC Conference, Session 12 (Split, 6–9 April 2022). London: Bloomsbury.
Romanelli, P. 1943. *La Cirenaica romana (96 a.C. – 642 d.C.).* Verbania: A. Airoldi Editore.
Rosenbaum, E. 1960. *A Catalogue of Cyrenaican Portrait Sculpture.* London: British Academy.
Roudometof, V. 2016a. *Glocalization: A Critical Introduction.* London-New York: Routledge.
Roudometof, V. 2016b. Theorizing glocalization: three interpretations. *European Journal of Social Theory* 19: 391–408.
Russell, B. 2013. *The Economics of the Roman Stone Trade.* Oxford: Oxford University Press.
Schmid, M. and Hermary, A. 2021. *Amathonte VII: Le temple de l'Aphrodite chypriote.* Athens: École française d'Athènes.
Sinos, S., Wenzel, F., Kalliri, E. and Ieronymidou, M. 1990. *The Temple of Apollo Hylates at Kourion and the Restoration of its South-West Corner.* Athens: A.G. Leventis Foundation.
Soren, D. and James, J. 1988. *Kourion. In Search of a Lost Roman City.* New York: Anchor Press – Doubleday.
Spanu, M. 2010. Tecniche costruttive nella Cilicia di età imperiale. In Camporeale, S., Dessales, H. and Pizzo, A. (eds), *Arqueología de la construcción II. Los procesos constructivos en el mundo romano: Italia y provincias orientales (Certosa di Pontignano, Siena, 13–15 de noviembre de 2008).* Madrid: Consejo Superior de Investigaciones Científicas, 397–409.
Stillwell, R. 1961. Kourion: the theater. *Proceedings of the American Philosophical Society* 105.1: 37–78.
Struffolino, S. 2014. Proprietà imperiali in Cirenaica. Alcune considerazioni. *Studi Classici e Orientali* 60: 349–80.
Stucchi, S. 1965. *L'agorà di Cirene, I. I lati nord ed est della platea inferiore.* Rome: 'L'Erma' di Bretschneider.
Stucchi, S. 1967. *Cirene, 1957–1966. Un decennio di attività della missione archeologica italiana a Cirene.* Tripoli: Quaderni dell'Istituto Italiano di Cultura di Tripoli.
Stucchi, S. 1975. *Architettura cirenaica.* Rome: 'L'Erma' di Bretschneider.
Stucchi, S. and Bacchielli, L. 1983. *L'agorà di Cirene, II.4. Il lato sud della platea inferiore e il lato nord della terrazza superiore.* Rome: 'L'Erma' di Bretschneider.
Stucchi, S. 1988. Il fregio del propileo severiano di Cirene e la presa di Seleucia nel 198 d.C. *Scienze dell'Antichità* 2: 497–512.
Tkaczow, B. 2010. *Alexandrie VIII: Architectural Styles of Ancient Alexandria. Elements of Architectural Decoration from Polish Excavations at Kom el-Dikka (1960–1993).* Warsaw: Polish Academy of Sciences.
Tkaczow, B. 2020. Two unusual Corinthian capitals from Nea Paphos. In Meyza, H. (ed.), *Decoration of Hellenistic and Roman Buildings in Cyprus.* Warsaw-Wiesbaden: Institute of Mediterranean and Oriental Cultures, Polish Academy of Sciences – Harrassowitz Verlag, 209–12.
Van Alten, D.C.D. 2017. Glocalization and religious communication in the Roman Empire: two case studies to reconsider the local and the global in religious material culture. *Religions* 8.140: 1–20.
Venturini, F. 2013. *I mosaici di Cirene di età ellenistica e romana.* Rome: 'L'Erma' di Bretschneider.
von Hesberg, H. 1980. *Konsolengeisa des Hellenismus und der frühen Kaiserzeit.* Mainz: Philipp von Zabern.
von Mercklin, E. 1962. *Antike Figuralkapitelle.* Berlin: De Gruyter.
Walker, S. 1985. The architecture of Cyrene and the Panhellenion. In Barker, G., Lloyd, J. and Reynolds, J.M. (eds), *Cyrenaica in Antiquity. Papers Presented at the Colloquium on Society and Economy in Cyrenaica Held at Newnham College, Cambridge, in March/April 1983.* Oxford: British Archaeological Reports, 97–104.
Walker, S. 2002. Hadrian and the renewal of Cyrene. *Libyan Studies* 33: 45–56.
Walker, S. and Matthews, K. 1996. Marbles from the Temple of Zeus and the Baths of Trajan at Cyrene. In Bacchielli, L. and Bonanno Aravantinos, M. (eds), *Scritti di antichità in memoria di Sandro Stucchi. Volume I: La Cirenaica – La Grecia e l'Oriente mediterraneo.* Rome: 'L'Erma' di Bretschneider, 307–16.
Ward-Perkins, J.B. and Gibson, S. 1976–77. The Market-Theatre at Cyrene. *Libya Antiqua* 13–14: 331–75.
Ward-Perkins, J.B. and Goodchild, R.G. 2003. *Christian Monuments of Cyrenaica.* London: Society for Libyan Studies.
Ward-Perkins, J.B., Ballance, M.H. and Reynolds, J.M. 1958. The Caesareum at Cyrene and the basilica at Cremna. *Papers of the British School at Rome* 26: 137–94.
Ward-Perkins, J.B., Little, J.H. and Mattingly, D.J. 1986. Town houses at Ptolemais. *Libyan Studies* 17: 109–53.
Wienholz, H. 2014. Baalbek und die Freiheit der Ausführung. In Lipps, J. and Maschek, D. (eds), *Antike Bauornamentik. Grenzen und Möglichkeiten ihrer Erforschung.* Wiesbaden: Reichert Verlag, 117–28.
Wilson, A.I. 2009. Approaches to quantifying Roman trade. In Bowman, A.K. and Wilson, A.I. (eds), *Quantifying the Roman Economy: Methods and Problems.* Oxford: Oxford University Press, 213–49.
Wright, G.R.H. 1992. *Ancient Building in Cyprus, Vol. 1.* Boston-Leiden: Brill.
Wright, G.R.H. 2007. Contrasted building in the Roman provinces of Cyrenaica and Cyprus. In Gasperini, L. and Marengo, S.M. (eds), *Cirene e la Cirenaica nell'antichità. Atti del convegno internazionale di studi (Roma – Frascati, 18–21 dicembre 1996).* Tivoli: Tored, 769–802.
Yegül, F.K. and Favro, D.G. 2019. *Roman Architecture and Urbanism from the Origins to Late Antiquity.* Cambridge: Cambridge University Press.
Yon, M. 2019. Un cinquantenaire. La mission de l'université de Lyon à Salamine. In Rogge, S., Ioannou, C. and Mavrojannis, T. (eds), *Salamis of Cyprus. History and Archaeology from the Earliest Times to the Late Antiquity. Conference in Nicosia, 21–23 May 2015.* Munich: Waxmann, 37–50.
Żelazowski, J. 2014–15. La politica di Augusto in Cirenaica. *Palamedes* 9–10: 237–56.

14

Architectures of the Roman World: Some conclusions

Janet DeLaine

This impressive collection of papers, which arose from a workshop held at Wolfson College, Oxford, in November 2022, does full justice both to the original aims, as outlined in Niccolò Mugnai's introduction, and to the lively, engaged and stimulating discussions which were such an important facet of it. Unsurprisingly, we were often left with more questions than answers, some of which have been addressed in the revised essays while many remain open for future research. At the same time, it has been possible in retrospect to identify some threads which link different essays independent of the original focus of the workshop on models, agency and reception and the current structure of the volume. It is these that I would like to draw out in my concluding remarks.

My first observation is that the most interesting things happen at interfaces and intersections. This is something I noted previously in the context of the first international conference on the archaeology of construction – '*Arqueología de la construcción*' – (DeLaine 2008, 327), where I highlighted the importance of the intersection of local resources, traditions and expertise with imported designs, materials and workmen. We can certainly see this here again in relation to construction techniques and practices, from earthen building techniques in the Roman West (Russell *et al.*), to the development of new terracotta tiles for the vaulting of Roman baths (Lancaster), the introduction of lime mortar in Greece (Vitti), or the use of brick in the baths of Nora (Previato). Given the economic value of using local building materials which limit the transport costs that are a major element in the overall price of bulk building materials, it is inevitable that any new techniques or new construction requirements would involve some level of adaptation or elicit new solutions driven by what was readily available, as for example Maschek also shows for Xanten and Carnuntum. Economic and possibly skills limitations are arguably also major factors in the selective use of new materials and techniques alongside established ones, which is clear both for bulk building materials as in Greece and Sardinia, and for decorative stones as Gasparini details for Cyrenaica.

In several of the chapters in this volume, interfaces and intersections at a cultural and often religious level are argued to have produced both meaningful visual juxtapositions and/or hybrid forms. This can be seen at the literal interface between the Ionic and Corinthian orders in Stinson's paper on the evolution of composite capitals, where the differences in detail and use between eastern and western examples argue for the importance of local pre-existing modes and uses of the orders in the diverse ways in which the composite develops. Mugnai and Gasparini develop these ideas on an urban scale in relation to cities in North Africa, Cyrenaica and Cyprus. Both see a dialogue between influence from Rome and pre-existing local modes of design and decoration in public buildings – the local elements in many cases being the result of earlier (or even continuing) interaction with another great city of the Mediterranean, Alexandria. In a very different situation, Peleg-Barkat observes the same combination of tension and dialogue between traditional modes and the new styles and architectural forms which came with increased Roman influence, in the Royal Portico of the Temple Mount in Jerusalem. This is but one, albeit extreme, example of a wider phenomenon also seen in the Levant with Semitic temples, and in Egypt, where the very different ritual requirements and practices of traditional Egyptian cults imposed quite stringent controls on the forms of actual temples, while increasingly allowing for the adoption of imported Hellenistic-Roman forms for subsidiary buildings (McKenzie 2007, 136–46; Minas-Nerpel 2012, 363–74).

In order to understand such innovations and adaptations we need to recognize the driving forces behind them. In several of the examples cited above it is possible to identify specific new conditions or imperatives which may have acted as catalysts for innovation. The introduction of imperial cults was one important new stimulus: the early examples of the composite in Asia Minor discussed by Stinson are all from imperial cult temples or related structures, while Mugnai argues that the Temple of Roma and Augustus at Lepcis Magna, by blending local and external influences, became part of the city's architectural language. Imperial cult is also the context of the Caesareum at Cyrene, where the westernmost example of the stoa-basilica, possibly of Alexandrian origin but which we usually associate with Roman Asia Minor where the greatest number of examples have been found, has been identified. In general, the Corinthian order at Cyrene was also linked to the imperial cult (Gasparini).

One particular cultural context, however, stands out: the spread of Roman bathing habits. In the form in which they appear in the Roman Empire at large, baths are unarguably the most Roman and widespread of functional building types, presenting a high level of specific technological demands, as well as, by and large, one of the easiest to recognize in the archaeological record. Unsurprisingly, the spread of Roman baths and bathing practices became, as Lancaster succinctly puts it, 'a nexus of technology transfer in the Roman world' (2015, 193 and quoted by Thomas in this volume). In the cases of the baths at Carnuntum and Xanten, Maschek emphasizes the specific choices made in construction techniques especially in the foundations to ensure the stability of these large structures, while Previato for Sardinia and Vitti for Olympia show the probable impact of imported workforces and/or specialists in constructing the baths. Bath construction was also subject to quite radical innovations, such as the armchair and hollow voussoirs discussed by Lancaster, or to less dramatic but still significant modifications, as Thomas points out in relation to the distinctly local variations used in the heating systems of baths in Asia Minor.

In several cases presented here, the army can be identified as the route by which new techniques were introduced and hence the catalyst for local adaptation and innovation, as Maschek shows for the walls of Carnuntum. It is also likely that retired army veterans, settled in colonies, contributed to the introduction of new construction techniques and their adaptation, like the stone/brick reticulate of Patras in Greece (Vitti). This does not however mean that the techniques adopted were necessarily those of Rome, as with turf construction which the ancient sources agree was a technique specifically associated with the military. Yet even within this technique, Russell *et al.* identify differences in practice and even possibly equipment which seem to relate to different units of different origins within the army. A similar pattern emerges with the introduction of armchair voussoirs to Britain, where they are associated largely with military sites, but where the influence is likely to have been via units originally from Spain or Gaul, not Rome (Lancaster). The personal and institutional mobility of the Roman army and its members have long been assumed to be important direct vectors of 'Romanization', but the examples discussed here present a far more nuanced picture of regional variations in techniques within the army itself. But the army was not the only possible pathway for change; the interests of the Empire-wide and mobile Roman elites, with their shared private culture and individual demands for novelty, also had a part to play. As Lancaster points out, a different form of terracotta vaulting – the hollow voussoirs – appears to have developed precisely to fulfil specific individual requirements for the baths of elite villas in southern Britain, at around the same time that the use of armchair voussoirs spread from urban contexts to rural villas in Gaul and Spain.

A further thread is the importance of recycling in architecture and construction, something that in Rome is commonly thought of as very much just a Late Antique phenomenon (see Dumser 2018 for a critical overview). This has recently become a 'hot topic' in ancient studies (see, for instance, Ng and Swetnam-Burland 2018; Duckworth and Wilson 2020), covering recycling in its broadest sense, from repurposing of objects as a variant of reuse (Duckworth *et al.* 2020) through to the recycling of materials, although much less has been done in relation to architecture than to objects. This is another important thread in this volume, where recycling forms a key part of Thomas' discussion of sustainability while other chapters provide a broad range of examples. The most extreme case is the complete Doric temple relocated to the Athenian Agora (Siwicki), an example of repurposing which Mugnai also notes at Cyrene, where the well on the north side of the agora and the *quadriporticus* of the gymnasium were converted into imperial cult monuments. More within what we generally think of as recycling are the visible re-employment of groups of Classical-period columns from various buildings in new Roman contexts (Siwicki) and the rebuilding of the Temple of Apollo at Cyrene using materials from the previous phase (Gasparini) in a form of direct recycling, not uncommon with temples. This kind of cannibalization of a previous structure of the same basic type on the same site also appears in the case of the third theatre of Augusta Raurica (Hufschmid), where the otherwise unusable waste from demolition of the previous phase was employed in levelling the site, while all the valuable building stone was set aside for reuse. Old material was not necessarily recycled on site; in the city walls of Carnuntum, worked blocks most likely from funerary monuments were deployed together with new material (Maschek), just as at Nikopolis ashlars from buildings in nearby abandoned sites were used in the Augustan theatre and recycled materials in the South Baths at Olympia (Vitti). The latter examples in particular support the arguments for the process of recycling in its broadest sense having a key role in the Roman building economy (Duckworth *et al.* 2020), especially if we move beyond simple ideas of direct cost-saving and include aspects such as waste disposal (even now a constant problem in relation to demolition) and speed of construction.

The repurposing of older buildings and the reuse of architectural elements raise important issues that are not easy to answer about visibility and audience perception, brought into focus by Siwicki and evident in other chapters that address questions of architectural ornament and decoration (Mugnai, Stinson, Gasparini). It is all very well for us to base ideas of chronology, transmission of ideas, hybridization of forms, the recognition of local traditions versus imported forms, etc., on close observation of fine difference in style and execution, but Siwicki's paper raises the questions not only of who in antiquity really noticed the details but also of what they might have understood by them. Two factors are important here, visibility and vocabulary. Much of the most telling detail of the orders happens at the top of columns and in the entablatures, but how much of this could be seen from the ground by different members of the viewing public, especially for monumental buildings? How far would the addition of colour, as identified by Gasparini at Cyrene, help? These are questions for future research where 3D computer reconstructions might provide valuable information.

Visibility is one problem, recognizability – or visual literacy – is another (for the idea of visual literacy in relation to Late Antique Rome, see Dumser 2018). How much of a city's population could recognize and name the different orders, let alone the details of them? In many ways this is a similar problem to the legibility of building inscriptions – how much of the population could actually read them? The problem of lack of vocabulary as an important element in recognition has come to the fore recently in studies of what has been called 'plant blindness': the widespread inability to recognize, name and recall individual plants or differentiate between types of vegetation (Wandersee and Schussler 2001; Balas and Momsen 2014). Modern humans, it is argued, are hard-wired to recognize other forms with what they read as faces and above all things with eyes and vertebrae, and much less so (apparently) immobile plant life. Human and animal forms also have the ability to carry narrative in a way that vegetation alone does not, which might be one reason for the success of figured capitals, such as that of the honorific column at Cyrene and the sphinx capitals from Thugga (Mugnai), or the windswept acanthus and Victoria capitals of Cyrene which go with a sculptured frieze, as discussed by Gasparini, or indeed the Hercules capitals of the Baths of Caracalla in Rome which echo the colossal statues of Hercules nearby (DeLaine 1997, 80–81); all are arguably made more visible and memorable through the introduction of anthropomorphic or zoomorphic forms.

Many decades of teaching Roman architecture to students and talking about architecture generally with friends and colleagues has made me realize that the same thing applies to architectural details. Who in Thugga, or Lepcis Magna, or Cyrene, or in the cities of Asia Minor, would have been aware of all the subtle differences in ornament which to us are so important? How many would distinguish between Corinthian, Corinthianizing, and composite capitals of various types, or different types of mouldings on entablatures? Siwicki suggests perhaps just architects and masons, or at most the educated elite who had read their Vitruvius, or were deciding between available options for buildings they had commissioned, or who were interested enough to notice. The same applies to the use of marble; to what extent would it be easily distinguishable from any substitutes, usually local hard stones sometimes enhanced with stucco and painting? From what distance and by whom? At the same time, we need some explanation for the choices being made, as in the continued use of the Doric order at Cyrene discussed by Gasparini. Ultimately, such choices were either made or at least approved by those who commissioned the buildings, arguably often at the suggestion of the architects or builders, and all the variations, large or small, presumably played on the desires of the commissioners for a unique creation, achievable within a specific budget, but – at least for temples and major public buildings – one that was appropriate to the local context, that is which fitted within the constraints of *decor*.

One level on which such choices might be generally noticeable by the local populace is in the arrival of something different on a sufficiently macro level to stand out easily from the local norms, for example the first Corinthian temple where the local vernacular was Doric or Ionic. All this may depend most on the timing. Change has most impact when we can actually see it happening, and I have long argued that the significance of the building process as an event is too often overlooked. It is in this context that the impact of re-erecting a Classical Doric temple in the Athenian Agora in the first century BCE discussed by Siwicki makes most sense. Unlike a text which can be endlessly revisited, once a building is finished it quickly becomes an accepted part of the cityscape, at least for the general population, its novelty quite rapidly diminishing especially in a world before the possibility of a precise visual record. At the most, we are talking about the length of living memory, and even then perhaps mainly about remembering only a general impression of size and shape together with the name and particular function, rather than any fine detail. As Mugnai points out, however, the use of monumental building inscriptions had the potential to act as reminders of the original context of the building within the socio-political history of the community, at least for those who could read, although whether this would aid the visual memory of what had gone before is a moot point. Certainly the Roman senator Cassius Dio, writing in the early years of the third century CE, did not seem to realize that the Pantheon he knew, with its concrete dome, was not the building he discusses as the work of Agrippa (Cass. Dio 53.27).

This takes me to my final thread, which is to do with time. One of the strengths of several of the chapters in this volume is their careful attention to detailed chronologies, in terms of both building programmes and construction process. On the whole, given the often limited dating evidence for any particular building, it has rarely been possible to give more than a specific single date based on written or epigraphic sources, or a general period based on archaeological evidence or stylistic grounds. Except in exceptional circumstances such as happened at Rome and Ostia in the first half of the second century CE because of closely datable brickstamps (see DeLaine 2002), the tendency has been to compress the creation of individual buildings and building programmes into a short timeframe creating a single, apparently coherent, narrative but one which makes it difficult to understand the evolution of architectural forms and construction techniques over real time. The possibility of new more detailed chronologies can have a major impact on traditional narratives, as has happened at the Augustan colony of Augusta Emerita (Mérida) (see Mateos Cruz and Pizzo 2011), where the 'Augustan' amphitheatre is now seen to be Flavian, and the forum with its supposed direct imitation of the Forum of Augustus also belongs to a second phase (Durán Cabello 2004; Ayerbe *et al.* 2009). Similar long-time developments are the focus of Mugnai's paper, especially for the fora of Thugga and Lepcis Magna, and are also indicated in the case of Xanten's forum by Maschek. On the other hand, identifying short timescales can be equally instructive, especially for the construction process. Dendrochronology has given a precise date for felling the timber for the pile foundations of Xanten's city walls, while close examination of the construction techniques has shown that sections of the walls were most likely built simultaneously by different teams (Maschek). The use of micromorphology at the construction site for the third theatre at Augusta Raurica, on the other hand, has produced evidence for a hiatus in the construction process which would otherwise have been undetectable (Hufschmid). While neither are techniques that can be replicated at every site, they show the advantages of using the broadest range of analytical tools for extracting information which no written sources are likely to provide, as is also the case with Russell *et al.*'s work on earthen construction. Understanding the timescale of a building project or broader urban development in something closer to real time helps to illuminate changes and indeed continuity in construction techniques and styles of architectural ornament, as well as bringing the reasons behind them into closer focus.

Refining chronologies also allows us to see more clearly the trajectories of innovations and adaptations. The building boom of the Augustan and early Julio-Claudian periods, under the new political dynamic of Empire and the concomitant release from the constraints and uncertainties of civil war, provided ideal conditions for experimentation and the introduction of new materials, techniques, styles of ornament and architectural forms. We can see this most directly in Augustus' new provincial capital of Nikopolis and at the new colony of Patras (Vitti), in the independent but allied city of Lepcis Magna (Mugnai), and even in Jerusalem, the sacred city of the Jews (Peleg-Barkat). As already noted above, many of the responses to the new imperatives of the imperial cult, such as the development of composite capitals (Stinson), also cluster in this period of heightened building activity. Later initiatives, such as the Trajanic colony at Xanten (Maschek) and the whole urbanization of Britain following the Claudian conquest, similarly brought new materials, techniques and building forms. Likewise the Severan period brought considerable change to building techniques at Nora in Sardinia (Previato) with the introduction of Roman-style construction techniques including the large-scale use of brick in the baths and other structures, even if the specific impetus is now impossible to determine. What these chapters do show, however, is how variable responses were in the longer term. Very few examples show wholesale and immediate adoption of new techniques and styles. In some cases they were more or less gradually adapted to suit local conditions, both physical and cultural, until – sometimes with further refinements – they became the new normal, while in others they coexisted with earlier styles and techniques. Each of the case studies presented here has its own story to tell of the very different architectural developments within specific local cultures and physical settings, in other words about their own specific Roman architectures which are the focus of this stimulating volume.

A word in conclusion. The chapters in this volume, while focusing on the often very different conditions in marginal areas of the Empire outside of Rome and Italy, can also serve to present us with fresh perspectives on the centre itself. Many of our interpretations of architecture, construction and ornament in Rome and central Italy are hampered by a retrospective sense of inevitability derived from long years of research into a relatively narrow range and small number of buildings and conditioned by the existence of written sources. Take construction: it has always been too easy to think of the development and use of Roman 'concrete' (i.e., mortared rubble) as somehow inevitable and natural, rather than the exception it is – the result of the intersection of unusual local conditions in terms of the quantity, quality and availability of suitable volcanic building materials, and the socio-political impetus of waves of veritable building booms which started in the second century BCE. The same applies to use of brick facing for mortared rubble; far from being a 'normal' form of construction easily applicable to the Roman Empire, it was a distinctive and exceptional technique increasingly promoted by members of the Roman elite exploiting the natural resources of their lands near Rome for profit, in order to provide a reliable supply of first-class facing material for high-status imperial building projects. On the other hand, the heating systems in the baths of Italy outside of Rome, Ostia and the few other large cities (Medri and Pizzo 2019) show the kind of variations in heating systems which can be paralleled not only at Nora (Previato) but elsewhere in the Empire, reminding us that much of the Italian Peninsula was just as 'provincial', and is still as little studied, as other marginal parts of the Roman world. Let us hope that the impact of this innovative volume encourages rethinking as much at the centre as on the peripheries of the Roman Empire.

References

Ayerbe, R., Barrientos, T. and Palma, F. (eds) 2009. *El foro de Augusta Emerita. Génesis y evolución de sus recintos monumentales*. Mérida: Consejo Superior de Investigaciones Científicas.

Balas, B. and Momsen, J.L. 2014. Attention 'blinks' differently for plants and animals. *CBE – Life Sciences Education* 13: 437–43.

DeLaine, J. 1997. *The Baths of Caracalla: A Study in the Design, Construction, and Economics of Large-Scale Building Projects in Imperial Rome*. Portsmouth, RI: Journal of Roman Archaeology Supplementary Series.

DeLaine, J. 2002. Building activity in Ostia in the second century AD. In Bruun, C. and Gallina Zevi, A. (eds), *Ostia e Portus nelle loro relazioni con Roma*. Rome: Institutum Romanum Finlandiae, 41–101.

DeLaine, J. 2008. Conclusions. In Camporeale, S., Dessales, H. and Pizzo, A. (eds), *Arqueología de la construcción I. Los procesos constructivos en el mundo romano: Italia y provincias occidentales (Mérida, Instituto de Arqueología, 25–26 de Octubre de 2007)*. Mérida: Consejo Superior de Investigaciones Científicas, 321–28.

Duckworth, C.N. and Wilson, A.I. (eds) 2020. *Recycling and Reuse in the Roman Economy*. Oxford: Oxford University Press.

Duckworth, C.N., Wilson, A.I, Van Oyen, A., Alexander, C., Evans, J., Green, C. and Mattingly, D.J. 2020. When the statue is both marble and lime. In Duckworth, C.N. and Wilson, A.I. (eds), *Recycling and Reuse in the Roman Economy*. Oxford: Oxford University Press, 449–60.

Dumser, E.A. 2018. Visual literacy and reuse in the architecture of late imperial Rome. In Ng, D.Y. and Swetnam-Burland, M. (eds), *Reuse and Renovation in Roman Material Culture: Functions, Aesthetics, Interpretations*. Cambridge: Cambridge University Press, 140–59.

Durán Cabello, R.-M. 2004. *El teatro y el anfiteatro de Augusta Emerita: contribución al conocimiento histórico de la capital de Lusitania*. Oxford: British Archaeological Reports.

Lancaster, L.C. 2015. *Innovative Vaulted Construction in the Architecture of the Roman Empire: 1st to 4th Centuries CE*. Cambridge: Cambridge University Press.

Mateos Cruz, P. and Pizzo, A. 2011. L'architecture monumentale d'Augusta Emerita. De nouvelles perspectives. *Mélanges de l'École française de Rome. Antiquité* 123: 581–95.

McKenzie, J.S. 2007. *The Architecture of Alexandria and Egypt, c. 300 BC to AD 700*. New Haven-London: Yale University Press.

Medri, M. and Pizzo, A. (eds) 2019. *Le terme pubbliche nell'Italia romana (II secolo a.C. – fine IV d.C.). Architettura, tecnologia e società. Seminario internazionale di studio (Roma, 4–5 ottobre 2018)*. Rome: Roma Tre Press.

Minas-Nerpel, M. 2012. Egyptian temples. In Riggs, C. (ed.), *The Oxford Handbook of Roman Egypt*. Oxford: Oxford University Press, 362–82.

Ng, D.Y. and Swetnam-Burland, M. (eds) 2018. *Reuse and Renovation in Roman Material Culture: Functions, Aesthetics, Interpretations*. Cambridge: Cambridge University Press.

Wandersee, J.H. and Schussler, E.E. 2001. Toward a theory of plant blindness. *Plant Science Bulletin* 47: 2–8.